Criminal Evidence For Police

SECOND EDITION

CRIMINAL JUSTICE TEXT SERIES
FORMERLY POLICE TEXT SERIES

By

JOHN C. KLOTTER, B.A., J.D.
DEAN, SCHOOL OF POLICE ADMINISTRATION,
UNIVERSITY OF LOUISVILLE

DIRECTOR, SOUTHERN POLICE INSTITUTE

AND

CARL L. MEIER, J.D.
OF THE CINCINNATI BAR

LECTURER ON EVIDENCE,
SALMON P. CHASE COLLEGE SCHOOL OF LAW

 anderson publishing co./cincinnati

Copyright © 1975

by

Anderson Publishing Co.

Fourth Printing—February, 1977

Library of Congress Catalog Card Number: 75-20721

ISBN: 0-87084-499-7

CRIMINAL JUSTICE NATIONAL ADVISORY BOARD

JOHN C. KLOTTER, CHAIRMAN
DEAN, SCHOOL OF POLICE ADMINISTRATION
DIRECTOR, SPI
UNIVERSITY OF LOUISVILLE

WILLIAM P. BROWN
PROFESSOR, SCHOOL OF CRIMINAL JUSTICE
STATE UNIVERSITY OF NEW YORK, ALBANY

E. WILSON PURDY
PUBLIC SAFETY DIRECTOR
METROPOLITAN DADE COUNTY
MIAMI, FLORIDA

STANLEY R. SCHROTEL
CINCINNATI CHIEF OF POLICE, RET.
DIRECTOR OF RISK MANAGEMENT, THE KROGER CO.

FREDERICK WARD, JR.
EXECUTIVE VICE PRESIDENT
NATIONAL COUNCIL ON CRIME AND DELINQUENCY

OTHER CRIMINAL JUSTICE PUBLICATIONS

Administrative Behavior and Police Organization
Jim L. Munro, Ph.D.

Changing Adolescent Attitudes Toward Police
Robert G. Portune, Ed.D.

Classes, Conflict, and Control
Jim L. Munro, Ph.D.

Constitutional Law for Police
John C. Klotter, J.D.
Jacqueline R. Kanovitz, J.D.

Constitutional Rights of Prisoners
John W. Palmer, J.D.

Correctional Classification and Treatment
American Correctional Association

Criminal Investigation and Interrogation
Samuel R. Gerber, M.D., LL.B.
Oliver Schroeder, Jr., LL.B.

Criminal Justice Procedure for Police
Ronald L. Carlson, J.D., LL.M.

Critical Issues in Law Enforcement
Harry W. More, Ph.D.

Guide to Modern Police Thinking
Raymond E. Clift, J.D.

Juvenile Offender and the Law
Paul H. Hahn, M.Ed.

Modern Photography for Police and Firemen
Sam J. Sansone, B.A.

Narcotics and Drug Abuse
Samuel M. Levine, LL.B.

Police in the Community
Charles P. McDowell, Ph.D.

Protection Management and Crime Prevention
Richard B. Cole, B.S.

We Are the Living Proof
David Fogel, D.Crim.

Published by
ANDERSON PUBLISHING CO
646 MAIN STREET
CINCINNATI, OHIO 45201

PREFACE

Although evidence rules are most often directed to the courts and concern the admissibility of evidence at the trial, they are of tremendous importance to all who are involved in the criminal justice process. Often evidence, whether it is testimonial, documentary, or real, is sought, located, evaluated, processed, and prepared for court before the prosecutor is aware of the existence of the evidence. The police officer who is not familiar with the laws concerning evidence can so contaminate the evidence that no amount of decontamination can cleanse it for trial. On the other hand, the officer who is familiar with the rules of evidence, as well as the reasons for these rules, and follows these rules during the initial stages of the investigation, can so collect, protect, and present the evidence that its admissibility will be assured.

In some instances the prosecutor enters into investigation of the case at an early stage and plays a major role in obtaining the evidence. In many instances, however, the prosecutor must use the evidence that is made available to him by the police investigator. Often he does not find out until too late that the evidence does not meet all of the admissibility tests.

Certainly the judge must make the determination that the evidence is or is not admissible. In making this determination he must apply all of the many and varied evidence rules. However, unlike the police officer, he has available many statutes, codes, and court cases to refer to in making these decisions. Also, in some instances he has the advantage of hearing arguments from counsel concerning the admissibility rules.

Even though probation and parole officers, as well as other corrections officials, are not as directly concerned with evidence rules, they obviously must know the rules of evidence if they are to understand the Anglo-Saxon criminal justice process.

This book is prepared primarily for use as a textbook by students enrolled in law enforcement or criminal justice courses in colleges and universities. However, it will answer many of the questions that are frequently raised by federal, state, and local enforcement officials who have the awesome responsibility of protecting society from the criminal who refuses to obey the laws established by his peers. But apprehension is only the first step. If the purpose of the criminal justice system is not only to apprehend but to convict and finally retrain the offender, everyone in the criminal justice process must be capable of carrying out his particular assignment effectively and efficiently.

A study of criminal justice necessarily involves legal principles discussed in such subjects as criminal law and constitutional law. For example, the requirements for proving the elements of murder discussed in criminal law are related to evidence, and the self-incrimination requirements discussed in constitutional law are often directly related to evidentiary requirements. To keep this book within reasonable limits only the traditional rules of evidence are discussed in detail. The related issues are discussed in other books in the Anderson Company Criminal Justice Series.

The cases discussed in the book are primarily criminal cases. However, in some instances civil or quasi-criminal cases are included in order to have complete coverage of the subject matter or to explain the difference in criminal and civil law.

In Part One of the book the rules of evidence are discussed in detail, especially as they concern criminal justice personnel and agencies. In Part Two leading decisions handed down by the courts are included to give the reader an understanding not only of the rules established by the courts but of the processes used by the courts in reaching these conclusions. These decisions should be studied carefully by the student or reader in order to develop a more thorough understanding of the policies and reasons underlying the rules which the courts have established.

In the Appendix of the book the rules of evidence as prepared by the United States Supreme Court and submitted to Congress are included in the total. As indicated, some of these were not approved by Congress but they remain in the Appendix, if for no other reason than the members of the Supreme Court recommended them as rules that should be followed in federal cases.

When the book is used as a text, it is recommended that the student be required to brief the cases in Part Two as well as additional cases which the instructor feels are of current importance. To make it possible for the reader to study cases relating to specific principles and rules, and to substantiate the conclusions reached, footnotes are used throughout the book. The cases referred to in the footnotes and other references should be utilized by the reader who desires a more thorough understanding of the reasoning of the courts as well as the resulting rules.

Although many of the rules of evidence have been unchanged for many years, these rules were developed through an evolutionary process and will continue to be changed either by the courts or by legislative action.

Also, new developments, such as the voice print, will require interpretation by the courts. It is therefore necessary that criminal justice personnel be made aware of the changes as they occur.

JOHN C. KLOTTER
CARL L. MEIER

January, 1975

CONTENTS

PART I:

CHAPTER 1: HISTORY AND DEVELOPMENT OF RULES OF EVIDENCE

Section
- 1.1 Introduction
- 1.2 Early attempts to determine guilt or innocence
- 1.3 Development of the jury system in England
- 1.4 Development of the rules of evidence in the United States
- 1.5 Future development of the rules of evidence
- 1.6 Summary

CHAPTER 2: APPROACH TO THE STUDY OF CRIMINAL EVIDENCE

Section
- 2.1 Definitions
- 2.2 Reasons for the rules of evidence
- 2.3 Reasons for excluding evidence
- 2.4 Criminal evidence distinguished from civil evidence
- 2.4a Pretrial flow of evidence
- 2.5 Function of the judge, jury, and witness in relation to evidence
- 2.6 Order of presenting evidence at the trial
- 2.7 Procedure for offering and challenging evidence
- 2.8 General approach to admissibility tests
- 2.9 Summary

CHAPTER 3: RELEVANCY AND MATERIALITY

Section
- 3.1 Introduction
- 3.2 Definitions and tests
- 3.3 Admissibility in general
- 3.4 Identification of persons
- 3.5 Identity of things
- 3.6 Circumstances preceding the crime
- 3.7 Subsequent incriminating or exculpatory circumstances
- 3.8 Defenses
- 3.9 Evidence concerning character, reputation and other crimes
- 3.10 Experimental and scientific evidence
- 3.11 Summary

CHAPTER 4: COMPETENCY

Section
- 4.1 Introduction
- 4.2 Definitions and scope
- 4.3 Competency of evidence—tests and experiments
- 4.4 Competency of evidence—conduct of trained dogs
- 4.5 Competency of evidence—telephone conversations
- 4.6 Negative evidence as competent evidence
- 4.6a Evidence competent for some purposes but not others
- 4.7 —Determination of witness' competency
- 4.8 —Mental incapacity
- 4.9 —Children
- 4.10 —Husband and wife
- 4.11 —Conviction of crime
- 4.12 —Religious belief
- 4.13 Summary

CHAPTER 5: BURDEN OF PROOF

Section
- 5.1 Introduction
- 5.2 Definitions and distinctions
- 5.3 —Preponderance of the evidence
- 5.4 —Clear and convincing evidence
- 5.5 —Reasonable doubt
- 5.6 Burden on prosecution
- 5.7 —Every element of crime
- 5.8 Burden on accused
- 5.9 —Matters of defense
- 5.10 —Alibi
- 5.11 —Insanity
- 5.12 Sufficiency of evidence
- 5.13 Summary

CHAPTER 6: DIRECT AND CIRCUMSTANTIAL EVIDENCE

Section
- 6.1 Introduction
- 6.2 Direct and circumstantial evidence distinguished
- 6.3 Sufficiency of circumstantial evidence
- 6.4 Character evidence in criminal cases
- 6.5 Proof of defendant's reputation
- 6.6 Reputation of victim of crime
- 6.7 Habit or custom of person
- 6.8 Similar or related acts or circumstances

- 6.9 Other offenses of defendant
- 6.10 Intent, mtive, or knowledge
- 6.11 Identity
- 6.12 Remoteness of other offenses
- 6.13 Probative value
- 6.14 Summary

CHAPTER 7: SUBSTITUTES FOR EVIDENCE
JUDICIAL NOTICE

Section
- 7.1 Introduction
- 7.2 Judicial notice defined
- 7.3 Judicial notice of facts
- 7.4 —Matters of common knowledge
- 7.5 —Historical facts
- 7.6 —Geographical facts
- 7.7 —Scientific facts
- 7.8 —Words and phrases
- 7.9 Judicial notice of laws
- 7.10 —Federal law
- 7.11 —Law of sister states
- 7.12 —Law of foreign countries
- 7.13 —Municipal ordinances
- 7.14 —Administrative regulations
- 7.15 —Jurisdiction of courts
- 7.16 —Court records
- 7.17 Summary

PRESUMPTIONS, INFERENCES, AND STIPULATIONS

Section
- 7.18 Introduction
- 7.19 Presumptions and inferences defined and distinguished
- 7.20 —Innocence
- 7.21 —Sanity
- 7.22 —Suicide
- 7.23 —Death after unexplained absence
- 7.24 —Regularity of official acts
- 7.25 —Receipt of mail
- 7.26 —Possession of fruits of crime
- 7.27 —Flight or concealment
- 7.28 Statutory presumptions
- 7.29 —Tests for constitutionality
- 7.30 —Effect of presumptions
- 7.31 Stipulations
- 7.32 —Polygraph tests
- 7.33 Summary

CHAPTER 8: EXAMINATION OF WITNESSES

Section

- 8.1 Introduction
- 8.2 Essential qualities of a witness
- 8.3 Judicial control of testimony
- 8.4 Separation of witnesses
- 8.5 Oath or affirmation
- 8.5a First hand knowledge
- 8.6 Interpreters
- 8.7 Leading questions
- 8.8 Refreshing memory—present memory revived
- 8.9 —Past recollection recorded
- 8.10 Cross-examination
- 8.11 —Scope and extent
- 8.12 —Witness' name and address
- 8.13 —Character witnesses
- 8.14 —Redirect and recross-examination
- 8.15 Impeachment
- 8.16 —Impeachment of surprise witness (own witness)
- 8.17 —Bias or prejudice
- 8.18 —Conviction of crime
- 8.19 —Prior inconsistent statements
- 8.19a Defects of recollections and perception
- 8.20 —Rehabilitation of witness
- 8.21 Summary

CHAPTER 9: TESTIMONIAL PRIVILEGES

Section

- 9.1 Introduction
- 9.2 Nature of testimonial privilege
- 9.3 Self-incrimination privilege
- 9.4 —Application of the privilege
- 9.5 —When privilege not violated
- 9.6 —Waiver of privilege
- 9.7 —Immunity
- 9.8 Attorney—client privilege
- 9.9 —Identity of client
- 9.10 —Advice in furtherance of crime
- 9.11 —Assertion and waiver of privilege
- 9.12 Physician-patient privilege
- 9.13 —Exclusions from privilege
- 9.14 —Persons within privilege
- 9.15 —Assertion and waiver of privilege
- 9.16 —Rationale of the privilege
- 9.17 Husband-wife privilege

9.18	—Exceptions to the privilege
9.19	—Duration of the privilege
9.20	Communications to clergymen
9.21	The confidential informant privilege
9.22	Governmental secrets privilege
9.23	Newsman-informant privilege
9.24	Summary

CHAPTER 10: OPINION TESTIMONY

Section

10.1	Introduction
10.1a	Definitions and distinctions
10.2	Admissibility of non-expert opinions
10.3	Subjects of non-expert opinion
10.4	Opinions of experts
10.5	Requirement of probability
10.6	Qualifications of an expert
10.7	Examination of expert witness
10.8	Cross-examination of expert
10.9	Subjects of expert testimony
10.9a	Experts from crime laboratories
10.10	Summary

CHAPTER 11: HEARSAY RULE AND EXCEPTIONS

Section

11.1	Introduction
11.2	Definition of hearsay evidence and the hearsay rule
11.3	History and development of the hearsay rule
11.4	Exceptions to the hearsay rule—general
11.4a	—Former testimony
11.5	—Declarations against interest
11.5a	—Confessions and admissions
11.6	—Dying declarations
11.7	—Physical or mental condition of declarant
11.8	—Spontaneous and excited utterances
11.9	—Business and public records
11.10	—Public surveys
11.11	—Family history and records (pedigree)
11.11a	Non-testimonial utterances
11.12	Summary

CHAPTER 12: DOCUMENTARY EVIDENCE

Section

12.1	Introduction
12.2	Authentication

12.3	Ancient documents
12.4	Newspapers
12.5	Official records and public documents
12.6	Death certificates and autopsy reports
12.7	Private writings
12.8	Best evidence rule
12.9	Secondary evidence
12.10	Summaries (voluminous writings)
12.11	Learned treatises
12.12	Summary

CHAPTER 13: REAL EVIDENCE

GENERAL

Section

13.1	Introduction
13.2	Exhibition of person
13.3	Articles connected with the crime
13.4	View of the scene
13.5	Photographs
13.6	Motion pictures
13.7	X-rays
13.8	Sound recordings
13.9	Diagram, maps and models
13.10	Experiments
13.11	Summary and practical suggestions

RESULTS OF EXAMINATIONS AND TESTS

Section

13.11a	Introduction
13.11b	Examination of the person
13.12	Intoxication tests
13.13	Blood grouping tests
13.14	Polygraph examination
13.15	"Truth serum" results
13.16	Fingerprint comparisons
13.17	Ballistic experiments
13.18	Speed detection readings
13.19	Spectogram voice identification
13.19a	Neutron activation analysis
13.20	Summary and practical suggestions

CHAPTER 14: EVIDENCE UNCONSTITUTIONALLY OBTAINED

Section

14.1	Introduction

14.2 Development of the exclusionary rules
14.3 Search and seizure exclusions
14.4 Exclusion of evidence obtained by illegal wiretapping or eavesdropping
14.5 Exclusion of confessions obtained in violation of constitutional provisions
14.6 Self-incrimination and related protections
14.6a Due process exclusions
14.7 Right to counsel as it relates to the exclusion of evidence
14.8 Summary

CHAPTER 15: PRACTICAL CONSIDERATIONS IN COLLECTING AND PRESENTING EVIDENCE

Section
15.1 Introduction
15.2 Developing the "evidence sense"
15.3 Steps in evaluating evidence
15.4 Preparing real evidence for trial
15.5 Preparing for the use of testimonial evidence
15.6 Coordinating efforts in preparing for trial
15.7 Convincing the jury beyond a reasonable doubt
15.8 Sources of evidence
15.9 Summary

PART II:

JUDICIAL DECISIONS RELATNG TO PART I, page 303

Table of cases relating to Part II, page 305

APPENDIX, page 537

Federal Rules of Evidence for United States Courts and Magistrates

INDEX, page 561

Chapter 1

HISTORY AND DEVELOPMENT OF RULES OF EVIDENCE

> The fundamental basis upon which all rules of evidence must rest—if they are to rest upon reason—is their adaptation to the successful development of the truth.
> *Funk v. United States*, 290 U.S. 371 (1933).

Section
1.1 Introduction
1.2 Early attempts to determine guilt or innocence
1.3 Development of the jury system in England
1.4 Development of the rules of evidence in the United States
1.5 Future development of the rules of evidence
1.6 Summary

§ 1.1 Introduction

The observer of the trial in a criminal case is often confused by the procedures he witnesses. Logically assuming that the purpose of the trial is to seek the truth, the lay observer is especially bewildered by the objections to the introduction of apparently relevant evidence. Some evidence which would have a direct bearing on the case is in fact excluded at the trial in a criminal case. To understand why certain evidence is admitted and other evidence is rejected, it is necessary to study the long history of the rules of evidence.

§ 1.2 Early attempts to determine guilt or innocence

Down through the ages man has sought fair methods of reaching the truth in criminal cases. Each culture arrived at a method which was congenial to that culture. Some of these systems of determining guilt or innocence were ridiculous and often barbarous. However, a study of history has helped succeeding generations to develop systems that are more workable.

This study leads to the conclusion that every tribe and every people devised a system for protecting the life and property of the citizens. According to the authorities, however, there were only a few who developed a well-defined, organized, continuous body of legal ideas and methods which can be referred to as a legal system. According to Mr. Wigmore,[1] sixteen legal systems developed to a stage where they could be recognized as such. These sixteen legal systems are as follows: Egyptian, Mesopotamian, Chinese, Hindu, Hebrew, Greek, Maritime, Roman, Keltic, Germanic, Church, Japanese, Mohammedan, Slavic, Romanesque, and Anglican. Although all of these systems had some effect on modern evidence rules only a few of the older systems have been selected for discussion as these represent systems that were adopted in part by other cultures and finally led to our judge-jury system, which in turn was responsible for our rules of evidence. Some of the procedures developed under these systems are gone; some remain.

To demonstrate that our system of evidence was adopted only after empirical investigation over many centuries, some of the methods followed in determining guilt or innocence will be described briefly.

In the Egyptian system (the oldest of these systems) the thirty judges who were chosen from the states that made up the country of Egypt constituted the court. The defendant was advised in writing of the charges against him and he was authorized to answer in writing each point by asserting either that he did not do it or that if he did it, it was not wrongful or if it was, it bears a lesser penalty than advocated by his accusers. It is interesting to note that at this time (starting about 4000 B.C.) all formal proceedings of the court were without speeches from advocates. It was believed that speeches of advocates would cloud the legal issues and that such speeches, the cleverness of the speakers, the spell of their delivery, and the tears of the accused would influence many persons to ignore the strict rules of law and the standards of truth.

The Greek historian Diodorus describes the procedure developed by the Egyptians as follows:[2]

---

[1] For a complete, interesting, and informative study of the world's legal systems, see Wigmore, A PANORAMA OF THE WORLD'S LEGAL SYSTEMS, 3 Volumes (1928).

[2] Kocourek & Wigmore, SOURCES OF ANCIENT AND PRIMITIVE LAW, Evolution of Law Series, vol. 1, Boston, 1915, Little, Brown and Co.

After the parties had thus twice presented their case in writing, then it was the task of the thirty judges to discuss among themselves their judgment and of the chief justice to hand the image of truth to one or the other of the parties.

Under the early Mesopotamian system the king was the fountain of justice receiving the law from divine guidance. But under King Hammurabi, about 2100 B.C., the administration of justice passed from the hands of the royal priests to a body of royal secular judges sitting at the great gate and market place of the city. A record of the trials of this period indicates that the judges called upon the accusers to "produce witnesses or instruments to show guilt." The judges then examined the facts and reached a conclusion as to guilt or innocence. This perhaps was the origin of the modern use of testimony and real evidence.

Under the Hebrew legal system the Rabbi developed the law in the early periods. However, the law was tied closely with religion and the judges were considered to act with divine authority. Even after the Jewish people came under the control of the Persian, Greek, and the Roman rulers, they continued to have their own court system. Decisions were made by individual jurists. There appears to be no record of the use of a jury or of counsel to represent the defendant.

One of the earliest recorded legal systems in the world is the Chinese legal system, beginning before 2500 B.C. It is unique in that it is the only one that survived for approximately 4,000 years. It survived until the country was taken over by the communists during this century. Under the ancient Chinese system there was little difference between civil law and criminal law since the Chinese believed in the existence of the natural order of things, or law of nature, and considered the written law good only if it was a correct translation of the law of nature. The decision as to guilt or innocence was made by one man from emperor down to magistrate. Under the Chinese system there was little distinction between morality and law and in determining guilt or innocence there were no lawyers as we know them. There were notaries or brokers but no licensed professional class. Decisions were made by judges only and these decisions could be reviewed by higher courts.

Unlike the systems previously discussed, the method of trial used under the early Greek legal system provided a jury. According to the records, in about 500 B.C., at Athens a jury list of about 6,000 or more names was made up. Ordinarily a panel of 201 names was drawn by lot, but for special cases a panel might consist of as many as 1,000 or 1,500 people. In the Socrates trial in about 400 B.C., 501 jurors voted and he was found guilty by a majority of only 60.[3] In one period in Greek history the decision of guilt or innocence was entirely in the hands of nonprofessionals. The presiding magistrate was selected by lot and the jurors were drafted from the whole citizen body. Under this system the defendant conducted his own defense and presented his own evidence. There was no presiding judge to declare the law and there was no appeal.

Thus we have examples of ancient systems where guilt or innocence was determined by professional judges without the assistance of a jury and other examples where the determination was made entirely by lay persons who were not instructed in the law. Not only have the experiences of other cultures affected our evidence rules, they have served as guides for other modern systems and surely will be considered when future changes are contemplated.

According to Mr. Wigmore, two legal systems which have developed through the ages are dominant in modern times.[4] One is the Romanesque system which began to develop in the 1200's and which today dominates Continental Europe and Latin America. Under this system a bench of judges was established and there were few rules of evidence as we know them.

When this system was first developed, the judges established the rules for the gathering and admissibility of evidence and were the deciders of the facts as well as the law. At first there were few rules of evidence but inevitably a complex set of rules for obtaining and weighing evidence evolved. And according to Mr. Wigmore these rules began to be merely cramping rules; not guides but self-sufficient formulas.

These restrictive rules of evidence became so overdeveloped that by the end of the 1700's the system was abolished in France and soon after that other countries followed. To replace this system the

---

[3] Wigmore, A PANORAMA OF THE WORLD'S LEGAL SYSTEMS, vol. 1, p. 291 (1928).

[4] Wigmore on EVIDENCE, ch. 1, (1935).

continental nations of France, Germany, and Italy adopted a system that allowed the judge to hear and weigh any evidence, without legal limitations. Although certain rules have been developed in recent times to limit the type and amount of evidence to be considered in this judge directed system, there are no elaborate controlling rules such as have been developed in the Anglo-American system.

The other system, the English system and the one that has become the inheritance of our country, has its judge and lay jury and an elaborate network of rules. It is these rules which will be discussed in future chapters.

§ 1.3 Development of the jury system in England

The English system, and later the system in this country, differs from the judge directed system chiefly because of the use of the jury. Also, the system differs in that under it there has developed a controversial spirit of "fair play" or "sportsmanship" in legal procedure generally.

The early methods of determining guilt or innocence in England were often difficult to understand. For example, a mode of trial known as trial by battle was brought to the English Isles by William the Conqueror in 1066. Instead of a formal trial before a judge the accused was required to fight his victim or the victim's representative. The case which finally brought this to the attention of Parliament involved a man who was accused of murdering his sweetheart. He claimed the right of trial by battle. The judges, after considering the matter, agreed that this type of trial which once existed as part of the English law had never been abolished. They therefore allowed the accused to select this type of trial. The brother of the deceased refused to fight the accused and the accused went free. Thereupon Parliament passed an act abolishing this method of trial.[5]

Following the Norman Conquest, the Norman judges organized the jury to assist them in their investigations. However, the jurors were not selected as unbiased triers of the fact as is the practice to-

---

[5] Tracy, HANDBOOK OF THE LAW OF EVIDENCE, (1952).

day, but were selected because they had special knowledge of the case. An ordinance of Henry II in the twelfth century provided that a certain number of jurors should be selected in criminal cases and specified that they be knights.[6] In contrast to modern procedure, the prospective juror was excused if he were ignorant of the facts of the case. The jurors were first left to their own discretion in the use of evidence and were allowed to go among the people in the community asking for information outside of court. During this period the jurors were forbidden to call in outside witnesses. However, starting about 1500, witnesses were used more frequently and gradually the requirement that the triers of the facts possess knowledge of the crime came to be less important. And by the end of the 1600's the jury was deemed to have no information except that which was offered in court. Thus in a period of three or four hundred years there was a complete reversal of the juror's role.

With the development of the jury system as it now exists and the English tradition of protecting the rights of the individual, the need for guidance was obvious. Both the judges and the laymen who participated in the trial recognized that the jurors must have guidance to prevent them from being misguided by evidence that was not relevant to the issue or by false testimony. Accordingly, in the 1600's and 1700's there gradually developed numerous exclusionary rules which kept certain kinds of evidence from the jurors unless it met the various tests as determined by the judge. These rules of admissibility are based upon long judicial experience with parties, witnesses, and jurors. Their purpose is to allow the jury to consider only evidence that is as free as feasible from the known risks of irrelevancy, confusion, and fraud.[7]

§ 1.4 Development of the rules of evidence in the United States

During the past two centuries a system of rules for the presentation of evidence has been established in the United States. In some instances the rules are the result of centuries of deep thought and experience. In other instances the rules have been established in a haphazard manner and often without much thought. Although this

---

[6] Ibid.   [7] Wigmore on EVIDENCE, p. 5, (1935).

country adopted the English system the rules concerning admissibility of evidence are not the same in the two countries. Due to court decisions, some of which interpret constitutional provisions, and legislation, the rules for obtaining and weighing evidence are now more restrictive in this country than in England.

Certainly the rules are not perfect and are always subject to change either by the courts or by statute. As stated in the case of *Funk v. U.S.*,[8]

> The fundamental basis upon which all rules of evidence must rest—if they are to rest upon reason—is their adaptation to the successful development of the truth. And, since experience is of all teachers the most dependable, and since experience also is a continuous process, it follows that a rule of evidence at one time thought necessary to the ascertainment of the truth should yield to the experience of a succeeding generation whenever that experience has clearly demonstrated the fallacy or unwisdom of the old rule.

Not only are the rules of evidence changed by court decisions but by congressional or legislative enactments. For example, in 1878 Congress made the defendant in a criminal case a competent witness when he so requested.[9] And in Illinois the legislature provided under the Sexually Dangerous Persons Act that it shall be competent to introduce evidence of the commission by the respondent of any number of crimes together with whatever punishment, if any, was inflicted.[10] More recently Congress has enacted specific legislation relating to the admissibility of confessions, wiretap evidence, and eyewitness testimony.[11]

In an effort to obtain more uniformity in court procedures the Supreme Court of the United States in 1972 adopted the Rules of Evidence for United States Courts and Magistrates.[11a] A study of the development and application of this set of rules demonstrates how rules of evidence can and do change. The Supreme Court

---

[8] 290 U.S. 371, 54 S.Ct. 212 (1933).
[9] 28 U.S.C., § 632.
[10] Ch. 38, § 105-5.
[11] Omnibus Crime Control and Safe Streets Act of 1968.
[11a] Federal rules of evidence prescribed pursuant to Sections 3402, 3771, and 3772, Title 18, United States Code, and Sections 2072 and 2075, Title 18, United States Code, November 20, 1972. These rules are included in the book as Appendix A and are referred to in various sections.

Order of November 20, 1972 directed the Federal Courts of Appeals, Federal District Courts, and U.S. Magistrates to follow these rules after July 1, 1973. However, in accordance with the Federal laws the proposed rules were required to be transmitted to Congress for approval. The House Judiciary Committee wrestled with the provisions for nearly a year and finally in early 1974 approved a modified version by a vote of 377 to 130.

Before approving the Supreme Court draft of the Rules of Evidence, the House Judiciary Committee changed provisions concerning privileged communications. The Rules were finally approved by the Senate and became effective July 1, 1975. It is interesting to note that Justice Douglas did not agree with the other members of the Court concerning the proposed Rules of Evidence arguing that the Supreme Court did not have authority to promulgate such rules and that the rules should be:

". . . channeled through the Judicial Conference whose members are more qualified than we to appraise their merits when applied in actual practice."

Today then the evidence rules in the United States are a product of a combination of court decisions, decided on a case by case basis; legislative acts; and court-ordered mandates. Some rules such as those considered above apply only to Federal Courts while some which are based on constitutional requirements are binding in all courts.

§ 1.5 Future development of the rules of evidence

In studying rules of criminal evidence, then, it must be recognized that our rules were developed by a progressive growth and adaptation to the new circumstances. Some rules have been preserved; some have been wisely dropped. The rules of evidence will continue to change and in fact probably will change more rapidly in the next decade as judicial officials and members of the legislature attempt to fashion a more effective system to meet the modern needs of society. To meet some attractive current theory some changes will be made and later rejected and some will be made in the future which will be based on good reasoning and will have lasting effect.

The application of the rules of evidence in the administration of the law is and should be within the sound discretion of the judges.

However, contrary to statements made in some cases, recent decisions of reviewing courts appear to require more strict application of the rules of evidence and lower courts are left with less discretion concerning the administration of the business of the court and the admissibility of evidence.

In 1967 the President's Commission on Law Enforcement and the Administration of Justice, after seeking to describe the criminal justice system in the United States, pointed out some of the shortcomings. The report states that court proceedings are the subject of continual, careful study by lawyers and are now receiving intensive scrutiny from other groups.[12] Certainly there is sufficient justification to warrant such a study. As stated in the Commission Report, "An inquiry into the performance of America's Criminal Courts, therefore, must of necessity examine both their effectiveness and their fairness, and proposals for improving their operations must aim at maintaining or redressing the essential equilibrium between these two qualities."

Have the restrictive rules of evidence become overdeveloped? Perhaps we have reached the point where the exclusionary rules no longer rest on reason. However, it would be unwise to abolish our system entirely as was done in France in the 1700's. Appropriate changes should be made by the courts and legislatures after careful study and with regard to the objectives to be achieved. Not only is it necessary therefore that all who are involved in the criminal justice system be aware of the rules of evidence as they exist today, they must be familiar with the history of the rules, keep up with changes as they occur, and take an active part in recommending improvements when experience has demonstrated that the old rules are no longer workable.

§ 1.6 Summary

In each culture efforts have been made to determine the guilt or innocence of persons charged with violation of the rules of that society. Some of the legal systems were built on sound foundations and continued for many centuries. Others disappeared when the governments were overthrown or the systems were replaced by other more workable systems. Fortunately history has preserved for

---

[12] The President's Commission on Law Enforcement and the Administration of Justice, TASK FORCE REPORT: THE COURTS, p. 1 (1967).

consideration by future generations a description of some of these methods with the faults as well as the desirable features.

After centuries of empirical investigation a system was developed in England utilizing parts of earlier methods of determining guilt or innocence. With the development of the jury system, a complex set of rules for determining the admissibility of evidence gradually developed. Although the jury system patterned after that of England was adopted by the United States, the rules for admitting the evidence have been changed by the courts and legislative bodies of this country. And today the rules of exclusion are more strict in the United States than in England.

Not only have the rules for determining the admissibility of evidence changed but they are now in the process of further change. Changes will continue as society seeks better methods for determining guilt and protecting society while at the same time protecting the rights of the individual.

Chapter 2

APPROACH TO THE STUDY OF CRIMINAL EVIDENCE

> The law, in its tender solicitude for the life and liberty of the citizen, seeks to equalize the inequalities between the state and the accused, by conjuring up a staunch ally of the accused, one who accompanies him from the moment of apprehension to the moment of conviction, one who is doubly armed with those mighty bulwarks of the criminal law—*presumption of innocence and reasonable doubt*. Rice, THE GENERAL PRINCIPLES OF THE LAW OF EVIDENCE, Chapter 1 (1893).

Section
2.1 Definitions
2.2 Reasons for the rules of evidence
2.3 Reasons for excluding evidence
2.4 Criminal evidence distinguished from civil evidence
2.4a Pretrial flow of evidence
2.5 Function of the judge, jury, and witness in relation to evidence
2.6 Order of presenting evidence at the trial
2.7 Procedure for offering and challenging evidence
2.8 General approach to admissibility tests
2.9 Summary

§ 2.1 Definitions

In order to fully comprehend the discussion of the rules of evidence it is necessary to define some of the words and phrases used. Other words or phrases are defined in future chapters as they are discussed.

a. Evidence

Evidence has been defined as the means employed for the purpose of proving an unknown or disputed fact, and is either judicial or extrajudicial. Every determination of the judgment, whatever may be its subject, is the result of evidence.[1] Evidence is any information upon which a person can make a decision. For example, before a

---

[1] Rice, LAW OF EVIDENCE, The Lawyers' Cooperative Publishing Co. (1893).

used car is purchased, the car dealer is questioned as to the condition of the car or perhaps the former owner is called and in some instances, the car is taken to another garage for an inspection. All of this information or evidence then is considered before a decision is reached as to whether the purchase will be made.

b. Legal evidence

Legal evidence is defined in Black's Law Dictionary as, "Any species of proof, or probative matter, legally presented at the trial of an issue, by the act of the parties and through the medium of witnesses, records, documents, concrete objects, etc., for the purpose of inducing belief in the minds of the court or jury as to their contention."[2] Legal evidence is that which is used or is intended to be used at the trial or at inquiries before courts, judges, commissioners, referees, etc. To state this more succinctly, evidence as used in law means, "That which demonstrates or makes clear or ascertains the truth of the very fact or point in issue, either on the one side or the other."[3]

c. Direct evidence

Direct evidence is that means of proof which tends to show the existence of a fact in question, without the intervention of the proof of any other fact.[4] Direct evidence has also been defined as that which immediately points to a question at issue. For example, a witness testifies that he saw the acts which constituted the precise fact to be proved. If in a homicide case the witness testifies that he saw the accused stab the victim, this would be direct evidence.

d. Circumstantial evidence

Circumstantial evidence, sometimes called indirect evidence, is so called because the truth is arrived at through entrances of probabilities arising from an association of facts. Circumstantial evidence means that the existence of a principal fact is only inferred from the circumstances.[5] One judge stated that the only difference between direct and circumstantial evidence is that the direct evidence

---

[2] Black, LAW DICTIONARY, West Publishing Co. (1951).
[3] Leonard v. State, 127 N.E. 464 (1919).
[4] Black, LAW DICTIONARY, West Publishing Co. (1951).
[5] Twin City Fire Ins. Co. v. Lonas, 75 S.W.(2d) 348 (1934).

is more immediate and has fewer links in the chain of connection between the premise and the conclusion. An example of circumstantial evidence is testimony of a witness in an adultery case that he saw the accused and a woman who was not his wife together in a hotel room and that both were undressed. It should be noted that circumstantial evidence is not necessarily of less value than direct evidence.

e. Testimony

Testimony is evidence which comes to the court through witnesses speaking under oath or affirmation. In some instances the word "testimony" is used synonymously with the word "evidence." It is obvious when considering the two words, however, that testimony is limited to that which is oral while the word "evidence" includes writing and other forms. The word "evidence" is the broader term and includes "testimony" which is only one type of evidence.[6]

f. Documentary evidence

Documentary evidence includes all kinds of documents, records, and writings which are not objectionable under some of the various exclusionary rules of evidence. It is such evidence as is furnished by written instruments, inscriptions and documents of all kinds.[7] An extortion note in a kidnapping case is an example of documentary evidence.

g. Real evidence

Real evidence or "physical" evidence has been defined as meaning a fact, the existence of which is perceptible to the senses. A clearer definition is as follows: "Evidence furnished by things themselves, on view or inspection, as distinguished from the description of them by the mouth of the witness; e.g., the physical appearance of the person when exhibited to the jury (marks, scars, wounds, fingerprints, etc.)"[8] Real evidence also includes weapons or implements used in the commission of a crime and evidence of the physical appearance of a place as obtained by a jury when they are taken to view it.

---

[6] Corpus Juris Secundum, vol. 31, p. 818.
[7] Black, Law Dictionary.
[8] Black, Law Dictionary.

h. Prima facie evidence

Prima facie evidence is evidence which, if unexplained or uncontradicted, is sufficient to carry a case to the jury and to sustain a verdict in favor of the issue which it supports but which may be contradicted by other evidence. The word prima facie means "at first sight" or "on the first appearance" or "on the face of it." It is evidence which suffices for the proof of a particular fact until contradicted and overcome by other evidence.[9] An example is the certificate of a recording officer where a document is part of the record. It may be afterward rejected upon proof that there is no such record.

i. Proof

Proof is the effect of evidence; that is, it is the establishment of fact by evidence. Even though proof and evidence sometimes are used as synonymous, they are different. Properly speaking, evidence is only the medium of proof; proof is the effect of evidence. Proof is defined as "the conviction or persuasion of the mind of a judge or a jury, by the exhibition of evidence, of the reality of a fact alleged."[10]

j. Cumulative evidence

Cumulative evidence is that which goes to prove what has already been established by other evidence. In legal phrase it means evidence from the same or a new witness simply repeating, in substance and effect, or adding to what has been before testified.

k. Corroborating evidence

Corroborating evidence is evidence supplementary to that already given, and tending to strengthen or confirm it. It is additional evidence of a different character but to the same point. For example, a conviction cannot stand on a confession without corroborating evidence. Such corroborating evidence might be the testimony of a witness who saw the accused at the scene of the crime.

---

[9] Dotson v. Watson, 220 S.W. 771 (1920).

[10] Ellis v. Wolfe-Shoemaker Motor Co., 55 S.W.(2d) 309 (1932).

l. Relevant evidence

Relevant evidence is evidence having any tendency to make the existence of any fact that is of consequence to the determination of the action more probable or less probable than it would be without the evidence.[10a]

m. Hearsay evidence

Hearsay is a statement, other than one made by the declarant while testifying at the trial or hearing, offered to prove the truth of the matter asserted.[10b]

§ 2.2 Reasons for the rules of evidence

As was indicated in Chapter 1, by the 17th century the evolution of the jury function was about complete and the jury depended on the testimony of witnesses for facts on which to base a verdict. As the members of the juries were generally ordinary lay people unacquainted with the laws and impressionable, it was recognized that specific rules for sifting the evidence were necessary. To protect the accused, rules were gradually developed to help assure that evidence was dependable, credible, and trustworthy before it could be considered. Evidentiary rules, then, were developed in part to keep out evidence that was not trustworthy or was unduly prejudicial to the accused. Also, it was obviously necessary for the court to establish rules to carry on the proceedings in an orderly and efficient manner. To achieve these and other lesser objectives our evidentiary rules have been formulated by the courts and by legislative action.

Efforts have been made to state in more specific terms the reasons for the rules of evidence and to account for the many varied rules which must be interpreted by the courts. As these rules have been developed by gradual evolution and in fact are still developing, it is difficult to categorize them and explain why each rule exists. However, some progress has been made toward this goal. Although it appears that in some instances there is an effort to rationalize or

---

[10a] Federal Rules of Evidence, Rule 401. For further discussion concerning relevant evidence, see Chapter 3.

[10b] Federal Rules of Evidence, Rule 801(c). For further definitions of hearsay and terms related to hearsay evidence, see Chapter 11.

§ 2.3   CRIMINAL EVIDENCE FOR POLICE

justify an outmoded or outdated rule, there is some logic to the explanation given for most of the specific rules of evidence.

§ 2.3 Reasons for excluding evidence

Much evidence is excluded even though it would help the jury or the court in determining the true facts concerning the matters at issue. The reasons for excluding this evidence have been numerous and phrased in many ways. An effort has been made here to categorize these reasons in order to make them more meaningful and comprehensible. These general reasons for excluding otherwise pertinent evidence are listed in the following paragraphs of this section.

a. Protect interests and relationships

Certain evidence, even though pertinent to the issue before the court, is excluded solely because the courts, in weighing the value of having all of the facts before the court against the protection of certain interests and relationships, have decided that testimony should not be admitted. Such interests and relationships, rightly or wrongly, are regarded as of sufficient social importance to justify some incidental sacrifice of sources of facts needed in the administration of justice.[11] Examples of evidence excluded on the basis of this public policy[12] or protection of relationship are:

1. Evidence protected by the husband and wife privilege.

2. Evidence protected by the attorney-client privilege.

3. Evidence protected by the penitent-confessor privilege.

b. Avoid undue prejudice to the accused

Some evidence which would be relevant to the issue is not admitted because it may be unduly prejudicial to the accused. For example, the criminal record of the accused generally may not be admitted except to impeach the testimony of the accused because to admit this would unduly prejudice the accused in the minds of the jurors. And certain photographs are not admitted into evidence,

---

[11] McCormick, EVIDENCE, § 72.
[12] These testimonial privileges will be discussed in ch. 9.

even though relevant, because to do so would unduly prejudice the accused.

c. Prohibit consideration of unreliable evidence

Other evidence is not permitted even though it might have a bearing on the case, if it is considered unreliable. In this category are hearsay evidence and opinion evidence.[13] To illustrate, the testimony of a police officer that a bystander told him the accused was driving the car involved in an accident is not admissible. Such evidence is relevant but not reliable enough for use in court.

d. Reduce violations of constitutional safeguards

A more recently developed reason for the exclusion of evidence is that which provides that certain evidence which has been obtained in violation of the Constitution will not be admitted into evidence. Until after the beginning of the present century it was almost universally accepted that evidence would be admissible even though illegally obtained. However, the courts now reason that such evidence as that secured by illegal search, in violation of the self-incrimination provisions, or in violation of the right to counsel provisions, is not admissible even though pertinent to the issue and in fact often the only basis for a conviction.[14] The rationale for excluding such evidence has not been consistent but generally it has been justified on the ground that by rejecting such evidence public officials will be less likely to violate these constitutional rights.

There have been arguments that some of the historical reasons for excluding relevant evidence have long since disappeared, leaving the technical rules without a logical basis. And in some instances so many exceptions have developed that the rules are no longer meaningful. However, most of the justification for the rules still exists and should be carefully considered as the reasons behind the rules help to understand their application.

§ 2.4 Criminal evidence distinguished from civil evidence

An early English case stated that there is no distinction as re-

---

[13] These rules are discussed in chs. 10 and 11.

[14] Discussed more thoroughly in ch. 14.

§ 2.4

gards the rules of evidence between criminal and civil cases. The case continued with the comment that,[15]

> What may be received in the one case, may be received in the other; and what is rejected in the one ought to be rejected in the other. A fact must be established by the same evidence, whether it is to be followed by a criminal or civil consequence.

This is still true to a great extent. There are, however, some differences in current rules.

In civil cases the two parties approach the contention indicated by the pleadings upon terms of approximate equality, with no legal presumption favoring the plaintiff or defendant. In criminal cases the law seeks to protect the person accused of crime and a presumption accompanies him from the time of apprehension to the moment of conviction. This is the presumption that he is innocent until proved guilty. Throughout the trial the burden of proof is on the state and the state must prove the accused guilty beyond a reasonable doubt rather than by the preponderance of the evidence. Because of this presumption of innocence special rules for overcoming the presumption have been developed. One writer spells out the difference in these terms.[16]

> The chief distinction which prevails will be found to originate in that caution which is always observed when life or liberty is in question, and in those benign presumptions with which the law meets every accusation involving moral turpitude.

In addition to requiring the state to have a higher or greater degree of proof in a criminal prosecution, rules differ in a few other instances. For example, the rule concerning admission of a dying declaration is different in criminal cases than in civil cases.[17]

Obviously the degree of proof must be stronger in a criminal case since, with few exceptions,[17a] the accused must be found guilty by all twelve members of the jury, while in a civil case a unanimous de-

---

[15] Rice, EVIDENCE, p. 8.
[16] Ibid.
[17] AMERICAN JURISPRUDENCE, vol. 20, p. 7.
[17a] See Johnson v. Louisiana, 406 U.S. 356, 92 S.Ct. 1620 (1972) which upholds a conviction in a criminal case where the state statute provides that 9 of 12 jurors may find the defendant guilty.

cision is not required. Therefore, it is much easier to obtain a money judgment against a person in a civil case than it is to find him guilty under the penal laws. A good example is assault and battery. In many instances a money judgment is obtained even after an attempt to convict has failed.

Although the distinction between criminal evidence and civil evidence may be slight when defining the rules, from a practical standpoint there is a great deal of difference. While a jury might accept weak evidence in determining the rights of parties in a civil case, the members of the jury will be more hesitant to accept such evidence when life or liberty is in issue. To the police and prosecutor this means that evidence must be presented which will be given great weight by the jury and sufficient evidence must be presented in court to overcome any "reasonable doubt" on the part of the jury or judge.[18]

§ 2.4a Pretrial flow of evidence

Although much valuable evidence is made available in court by lay persons who are not connected with the criminal justice process, in most instances the police officer is responsible for discovering, evaluating, protecting, analyzing, and presenting evidence. If he does not present the evidence himself, he is still primarily responsible to guide the flow of evidence, at least until the indictment or information stage.

He must develop and preserve the evidence in such a way so as to maximize its usefulness in subsequent proceedings. For example, if at this point names and addresses of witnesses to a crime are not recorded by the officer, this information would be forever lost. The technical techniques of sound criminal investigation are outside the scope of this work, but it bears repeating that the failure to gather the available evidence in a workmanlike manner will affect all subsequent proceedings.

The Federal Rules of Criminal Procedure and the rules of criminal procedure of all states require an officer making an arrest to take the arrestee before the nearest available magistrate without

---

[18] State v. Perkins, 45 S.E.(2d) 17 (1947). Parts of this case are included in Part II of this book.

unnecessary delay. The officer at this first appearance is not required to present the evidence to convict; nevertheless, he must produce at the preliminary hearing sufficient evidence for the magistrate to determine whether there is probable cause to believe an offense has been committed and if the accused committed the offense.[8a]

If the magistrate determines there is probable cause to "bind" the defendant over to the grand jury in a felony case, the officer must make available all of the evidence he has collected, together with the names and pertinent information to the prosecutor. Although the prosecutor may and should enter into the case at an earlier time, this is usually the step where the prosecutor takes charge, at least temporarily.

The next step in the procedure is the indictment or information. The prosecution must have sufficient evidence available for the indictment or information. One might argue—and with justification —that the process is redundant. Evidence that a crime has been committed and evidence that the accused committed the crime has already been presented to a magistrate and will be presented at the trial. But in most states evidence must be presented again to the grand jury before an indictment is returned.

The grand jury proceeding is usually guided by the prosecutor but here too he must in almost every case call on the officer-investigator to give evidence before the grand jury. As a rule the formal evidence rules are not followed when presenting evidence to the grand jury, but certainly sufficient admissible evidence must be presented to convince this jury (usually twelve persons) that an offense against the state has been committed by the person accused.

In some states process by way of the information is substituted for the grand jury hearing. Here the prosecutor, still using the evidence presented by officers and other witnesses, makes the decisions and prepares the information which notifies the accused of the specific charge.

Is the case now ready for trial? Not quite. Following the return of the indictment or the preparation of the information, the defendant appears personally before the judge. Here he is arraigned

---

[8a] See Chapter 13 for a discussion of evidence needed to determine probable cause for the issuance of a search warrant.

(informed of the charges against him) and enters his plea. Evidence is not presented at the arraignment but often a date is set to hear pretrial motions.

At the pretrial hearing some evidence is often required, especially if a motion to suppress is made by the defense attorney. Evidence of the facts surrounding the seizure or taking of evidence by the officer is presented in order for the judge to determine the legality of the procedure. Often the outcome of the suppression hearing determines the fate of the accused. If, for example, the judge determines that a confession was obtained in violation of the protective rules or a piece of evidence was obtained illegally, the prosecutor may decide to drop the charge. Conversely, if the judge rules against the defendant at the suppression hearing, the defendant's attorney may advise the defendant to enter a guilty plea.

Now if there are no more delaying motions, the case is ready for trial.

§ 2.5 Function of the judge, jury, and witness in relation to evidence

In addition to the parties on each side, the court is made up of the judge, the jury, and the witnesses. The functions of these persons or groups have changed over the years. As indicated in a prior section, in early English proceedings the jurors were only witnesses and were called upon by the judge to give information concerning the case because they had knowledge of the facts. However, as civilization progressed, it became the province of the judge to interpret the law, and the jury, under the guidance of the judge, to determine the facts.

The judge instructs the jury concerning the law applicable to the case, and determines, sometimes with the later approval of the jury, if the evidence is relevant, material, and competent. He is also responsible for insuring that the trial is administered in an orderly way and that it progresses efficiently and smoothly. This is often a real challenge to the judge. The judge also has the duty to instruct the jury as to what findings it might return and in some cases the limits as to punishment.[8b]

[8b] *See* Rule 105, Federal Rules of Evidence, for comments concerning the authority of the judge to sum up the evidence in a federal case.

In a jury trial the function of the jury is to evaluate the testimony and other evidence presented in the case and to determine the facts from the evidence presented at the trial. In almost every case contradictory evidence is presented by the prosecution and the defendant and the jury has the almost impossible task of determining what actually happened. The ultimate goal of the jury is to determine whether the defendant is guilty of the crime as defined in the indictment, but in making the determination the jury must determine the truth or falsity of testimony presented in court and relate those truths to the ultimate issue.

The witnesses, too, play a most important part. The jury is instructed by the judge to determine the facts only from the evidence presented in court. In other words, the witnesses are the eyes and ears of the court. The police officer usually appears in the capacity of a witness and plays a most important role. In many instances police officers are the only witnesses for the prosecution and without their testimony there could be no prosecution. Even real evidence or documentary evidence is of little value if the witness does not properly explain these pieces of evidence.

In a trial without a jury, the judge not only acts as a decider of the law but he evaluates the evidence and also decides the facts. In other words, he acts as both the judge and jury.

§ 2.6 Order of presenting evidence at the trial[18c]

The judge has much discretion in establishing court procedures but generally follows the procedures which have been developed over a period of years and which have become generally standard. The usual order of proceeding in presenting the case is as follows:[19]

1. State's (prosecution) evidence in chief.
2. Defendant's evidence in chief.
3. Prosecution's evidence in rebuttal.
4. Defense's evidence in rejoinder.

[18c] For a more comprehensive explanation of the criminal procedures from arrest to final release, see Carlson, CRIMINAL JUSTICE PROCEDURES FOR POLICE, W. H. Anderson Company, 1970 (Criminal Justice Text Series).

[19] McCormick, EVIDENCE, p. 7.

Each of these steps will be discussed to point out their scope and limitations.

a. State's evidence in chief

As the prosecutor has the burden of proof, he first introduces evidence on behalf of the state. He may call as many witnesses as he feels necessary and may introduce exhibits, photographs, documents, or other types of evidence which may help the jury in determining the guilt or innocence of the accused, provided these meet the admissibility tests. During this phase of the procedure, the prosecutor is carrying the ball and calling the plays. He selects the witnesses for the prosecution and guides the flow of evidence. Each prosecution witness is questioned by the prosecutor first.[20] Although the defense has an opportunity to cross-examine the prosecution witnesses, the defense at this stage can not introduce its own witnesses and according to the majority view must limit cross-examination to matters testified to on direct examination.

When the prosecution has introduced his evidence in chief or what he feels is sufficient evidence to make a case against the defendant, he signifies the completion of his case in chief by announcing, "The prosecution rests."

b. Defendant's evidence in chief

After the prosecution rests, the defendant has the opportunity to present his evidence in chief. The defendant may present evidence in denial of the prosecution's claim; he may attempt to establish an alibi; or attempt to establish one of the other affirmative defenses. The defendant does not have to take the stand in his own behalf but he may do so. If he does, the defendant is usually the first witness to take the stand at this stage of the procedure.[20a] As in the case of the prosecution, each defense witness is questioned first by defense counsel and then may be cross-examined by the prosecution. When the defendant has completed the presentation of his

---

[20] The procedure to be followed in the examination of witnesses will be discussed in ch. 8.

[20a] In 1972 the United States Supreme Court held that a rule which requires the defendant to testify before other defense witnesses violates the self-incrimination provisions of the Court. Brooks v. Tenn., 406 U.S. 605, 92 S.Ct. 1891 (1972).

evidence the defendant's attorney announces that "The defense rests."

c. Prosecution's rebuttal

The prosecution now has the opportunity to rebut the evidence presented by the defense. The prosecution at this stage may not present witnesses who merely support the allegations of the indictment. This should have been done when the prosecution presented its evidence in chief. <u>At this point the prosecution is limited to the introduction of testimony or other evidence which is directed to refuting the evidence of the defendant</u>. New witnesses may be called at this time but only if they can rebut the evidence presented by the defendant. For example, if the defense raises the question of insanity, the prosecution may offer evidence to show that the defendant was not insane as defined by law. In this stage as in other stages the witness may not only be examined on direct but may be cross-examined by opposing counsel.

d. Defense rejoinder

The defense also has the opportunity to introduce evidence contrary to that introduced by the prosecution during the rebuttal. This is called the rejoinder. Again the evidence here is limited to refuting the evidence presented by the prosecution on rebuttal.

There are instances when the case may continue with the prosecution and the defense having the opportunity to refute the evidence presented by the other. However, it is obvious that this becomes more and more limited and, in the usual case, both parties will have presented all the evidence they intend to present by the end of the defendant's rejoinder.

When both parties have announced that they have rested their cases, the hearing on the facts comes to an end and the trial proceeds with the arguments of counsel and the court's instructions to the jury.

§ 2.7 Procedure for offering and challenging evidence

It is obvious that not all evidence is admitted into court. The courts follow a complex set of rules in determining what evidence should be admitted and what evidence should be excluded. Much of the rest of the book will be devoted to the rules which have been developed for the judge in determining the admissibility of evidence. It is safe to say that most of the rules are rules of exclusion.

The normal way of offering and eliciting oral testimony is to place the witness on the stand and ask him a question or series of questions. If either the prosecution or the defense challenges the question, then objection is made and the court decides if the answer should be allowed. If an objection is made, the party who elicited the information may be required to state the purpose of the proof offered and the objector may be required to state the specific grounds for his request that answers be excluded.

In the case of real evidence such as bullets, guns, articles of clothing, or the like, the party offering the evidence, after having it identified or authenticated by a witness, submits it to the opposing counsel for inspection. When this has been done, he presents it to the judge and, depending upon the type of evidence, shows it to each juror individually or to the jury as a whole.

The rules of evidence for U.S. Courts contain specific requirements concerning the effect of the judge's rulings on the admissibility of evidence. Rule 103 of this document states:

"(a) *Effect of erroneous ruling.*—Error may not be predicated upon a ruling which admits or excludes evidence unless a substantial right of the party is affected, and

(1) *Objection.*—In case the ruling is one admitting evidence a timely objection or motion to strike appears of record, stating the specific ground of objection, if the specific ground was not apparent from the context; or

(2) *Offer of proof.*—In case the ruling is one excluding evidence, the substance of the evidence was made known to the judge by offer or was apparent from the context within which questions were asked."

In some states it is still necessary to "except." That is, after the judge's adverse ruling excluding the evidence or overruling the objection, the counsel comments, "We except." That is in effect a protest against the correctness of the ruling of the judge and saves the matter for review. To avoid the waste of time the rules in many states provide that the formal exception procedure is not necessary.

If there is no objection or if the objection is overruled, the witness is allowed to answer the question or to identify or authenticate the real or documentary evidence.

§ 2.8 General approach to admissibility tests

As the rules of evidence are for all practical purposes rules of exclusion, all evidence offered is admissible unless, upon objection, it is subject to exclusion under some of the rules. When one party asks a question of the witness and his adversary has an objection to it, it will be found that the objection is either objectionable as to the form that the question was asked or as to the substance of the answer solicited. One way to approach the rules of evidence is to keep these simple tests of form and substance in mind as each rule is discussed.

a. Objections as to form

In order to avoid confusing the witness, the court will require that a question be clear and intelligent. Questions which are confusing, improperly phrased, misleading or argumentative, will not be allowed if objected to by opposing counsel. In fact, often the judge himself will ask that such questions be rephrased. The question which is so phrased that there can be no definite answer will, of course, mislead the witness as well as the jury. An example which is often cited is the one where the witness is asked the question, "Are you still having an affair with your secretary? Give a yes or no answer." Obviously, this is a confusing and misleading question and is not properly stated.

Also, a question which has two parts is sometimes objectionable as to form as it is impossible to answer both parts with one answer. Other questions which are sometimes objectionable as to form are classified as leading questions.[21]

b. Objections as to substance

If there is no objection as to form or such objection is settled, the test of substance is applied. One way to comprehend the test of substance easily is to consider three hurdles as having been erected between the evidence and the court. Before the evidence can be

---

[21] Leading questions will be discussed in ch. 8.

admitted into court each of these hurdles must be cleared. These hurdles are: relevancy, materiality, and competency.[22] Briefly, the relevancy test is, does the information have a tendency to prove or disprove one or more of the facts and issues of the case? To be relevant the information must have a tendency to establish or disprove the matter in issue in the case being tried. Materiality concerns the importance of evidence. Evidence is material only when it affects a fact or issue of the case in a significant way.

The definition of competency is more elusive. Competent evidence is that which is legally adequate and sufficient. The competency test is a catch-all for the exclusionary rules. For example, evidence obtained by illegal search in violation of the Constitution is inadmissible not because it is immaterial or irrelevant but because of its legal inadequacy or incompetency.

If the proposed evidence meets the tests of form and substance, it is admitted into court. The weight or the importance of the evidence depends on many other factors.

§ 2.9 Summary

The objective at the criminal trial is to determine the truth and ultimately to determine the guilt or innocence of an accused. However, after long empirical investigation, the courts have determined that certain evidence will be excluded even though it would help in determining the true facts of the case. These rules for excluding relevant evidence are generally justified on the grounds that they protect certain interests and relationships, avoid undue prejudice to the accused, protect the jury from the consideration of unreliable evidence, and enforce the Constitutional safeguards.

Generally, there is little distinction as regards the rules of criminal evidence and civil evidence. However, because the prosecution must prove the accused guilty beyond a reasonable doubt and because the jury verdict usually must be unanimous, a stronger degree of evidence is required in a criminal case.

Over a period of years the functions of the various persons and groups involved in the criminal trial have become fairly stan-

---

[22] Relevancy and materiality will be discussed more completely in ch. 3. The general rules concerning competency will be discussed in ch. 4.

dard. As a general rule in a jury trial the judge is responsible for the administration of the trial and for determining the law applicable to the case; the jury has the responsibility of evaluating the evidence and determining the facts from the evidence presented; and witnesses act as the eyes and ears of the court, presenting evidence from which a jury may determine the facts.

In presenting evidence, the usual procedure is for the state to present its evidence in chief, followed by the defendant's evidence in chief. The state or prosecution then has the opportunity to rebut the evidence presented by the defendant and the defense has an opportunity in the rejoinder to refute the evidence presented by the prosecution in rebuttal. The witnesses, too, follow a certain routine as far as questions are concerned.[23]

The usual way of objecting to the admissibility of evidence is for the opposing counsel to state that he objects. When this is done, the judge either sustains the objection, in which case the evidence or question is not allowed in its present form, or overrules the objection and authorizes the witness to answer the question or authorizes the admissibility of the evidence.

Generally, evidence is objected to because of the form, such as an improperly phrased question or because of the substance. If the answer solicited is not relevant, material, and competent, it will not be authorized.

Although the rules of evidence which have developed over a period of years are many, varied, and sometimes confusing, in most instances they do have a purpose and can be learned and understood without too much difficulty.

---

[23] Further discussion concerning the examination of witnesses will be discussed in ch. 8.

Chapter 3
RELEVANCY AND MATERIALITY

> There is a principle—not so much a rule of evidence as a presupposition involved in the very conception of a rational system, as contrasted with the old formal and mechanical systems—which forbids receiving anything irrelevant, not logically probative....
>
> The two leading principles should be brought into conspicuous relief, (1) that nothing is to be received which is not logically probative of some matter requiring to be proved; and (2) that everything which is thus probative should come in, unless a clear ground of policy or law excludes it.
>
> Thayer, EVIDENCE (1898).

Section
3.1 Introduction
3.2 Definitions and tests
3.3 Admissibility in general
3.4 Identification of persons
3.5 Identity of things
3.6 Circumstances preceding the crime
3.7 Subsequent incriminating or exculpatory circumstances
3.8 Defenses
3.9 Evidence concerning character, reputation and other crimes
3.10 Experimental and scientific evidence
3.11 Summary

§ 3.1 Introduction

As was pointed out in previous chapters, the primary objective in criminal trials is to determine the truth as to the issues presented. Therefore, all evidence offered is admissible unless upon objection it is subject to exclusion under some of the established rules. When evidence is offered for admission into court, the opposing counsel may object on the grounds that the evidence is not relevant. In other words, one of the first hurdles that the evidence must overcome is the relevancy hurdle. If the court, based upon prior decisions, codes or statutes, determines that the evidence is not relevant, it will not be admissible. The same, of course, is true if the evidence does not meet the materiality test.

The usual procedure followed in challenging the evidence is an objection by the opposing counsel. However, a general objection that the requested evidence is "irrelevant, immaterial, and incompetent" will usually not suffice. Unless the reason for the objection is obvious, the judge may require a more detailed explanation concerning the challenge.

For the police officer, the investigator, and the prosecutor, it is essential that the rules concerning relevancy and materiality be understood thoroughly. In many instances evidence has been laboriously obtained and prepared for introduction only to be excluded because it does not meet the relevancy and materiality tests.

§ 3.2 Definitions and tests

Lawyers and judges frequently use the terms "relevant" and "material" and particularly their opposites, "irrelevant" and "immaterial," as interchangeable and synonymous. Although relevant is a broader term and is often used in the double sense of relevant and material, the distinction between the two concepts is substantial. Some of the definitions as found in law dictionaries and cases are as follows:

a. Relevant evidence

BLACK'S LAW DICTIONARY defines relevant evidence as "such evidence as relates to, or bears directly upon, the point or fact in issue, and proves or has a tendency to prove the proposition alleged."

One author describes relevant evidence as "evidence that in some degree advances the inquiry, and thus has probative value and is prima facie admissible."[1]

In CORPUS JURIS SECUNDUM logical relevancy is defined as "the existence of such a relationship in logic between the fact of which evidence is offered and a fact in issue that the existence of the former renders probable or improbable the existence of the latter."[2]

A more simple definition from a Georgia case is, "Relevancy is

---

[1] McCormick, LAW OF EVIDENCE, p. 319.

[2] CORPUS JURIS SECUNDUM, vol. 31A, § 158.

a logical relationship between evidence and a fact in issue or to be established."³

And more recently in the Federal Rules of Evidence the United States Supreme Court Rule 401 states:

> "Relevant evidence" means evidence having any tendency to make the existence of any fact that is of consequence to the determination of the action more probable or less probable than it would be without the evidence.

b. Material evidence

BLACK's LAW DICTIONARY defines material evidence as that which goes to the *substantial* matters in dispute or has a legitimate and effective influence or bearing on the decision of the case.

Materiality concerns the importance of evidence. Evidence is material only when it affects the matter or issue in a case significantly. It boils down to this: Would the evidence offer a *substantially* material fact in this particular case to prove or disprove a charge against the defendant?

c. Materiality and relevancy distinguished

In one case the court distinguished between materiality and relevancy by stating, "As used with respect to evidence, 'material' has wholly different meaning from 'relevant.' To be relevant means to relate to the issue. To be material means to have probative weight, that is, reasonably likely to influence the tribunal in making the determination required to be made."⁴

Although evidence may be relevant, it is not necessarily material. Whether facts are material to any inquiry depends upon the particular facts and circumstances involved. Thus, although evidence may be relevant in that it relates to or has some bearing on the case, it might have such slight relevancy as to be immaterial.

After making these fine distinctions between relevancy and materiality, the discussion would not be complete if it were not pointed out that in actual practice the distinction is blurry at best

---

³ Continental Trust Co. v. Bank of Harrison, 36 Ga.App. 149, 136 S.E. 319 (1926).

⁴ Weinstock v. United States, 231 F. (2d) 699 (D.C. Cir. 1956).

and in most cases whether it is characterized as irrelevant or immaterial makes little practical difference in effect.[5]

d. Matters in which relevancy and materiality are in issue

In determining whether evidence is relevant, the court must decide whether the evidence has a tendency to prove or disprove a pertinent fact in issue. Obviously, the evidence which tends to prove the elements of the offense charged, the identity of the accused, the defense put forth by the accused, motives for the crime, etc., are relevant and admissible unless excluded for some other accepted reason. In the following paragraphs general principles concerning relevancy and materiality will be discussed. In addition some of the specific issues where the relevancy and materiality rules have been applied will be explored further.

§ 3.3 Admissibility in general

The general rule that all relevant evidence is admissible is subject to several exceptions. The judge, in his discretion, may exclude evidence if he finds that its probative value is substantially outweighed by the risk that its admission will necessitate undue consumption of time, create substantial danger of undue prejudice, confuse the issues, mislead the jury, or unfairly and harmfully surprise a party who has not had reasonable opportunity to anticipate that such evidence would be offered.[6]

The Federal Rules state very simply that:[6a]

> All revelant evidence is admissible, except as otherwise provided by the Constitution of the United States, by Act of Congress, by these rules, or by other rules adopted by the Supreme Court. Evidence which is not relevant is not admissible.

And as to the exclusion of otherwise relevant evidence the rules include the directions that:

> Although relevant, evidence may be excluded if its probative value is substantially outweighed by the danger of unfair prejudice, confusion of the issues, or misleading the jury, or

---

[5] Holmes v. State, 112 S.(2d) 511 (Ala. App. 1959). See case in Part II of book.

[6] UNIFORM RULES OF EVIDENCE, p. 45. Also see Rule 303, American Institute Model Code of Evidence.

[6a] See Rules 402 and 403, Federal Rules of Evidence.

by considerations of undue delay, waste of time, or needless presentation of cumulative evidence.

A trial judge is constantly faced with questions on evidence in their special relation to the issue to be tried. He must deal with such questions in the light of the purposes of the ultimate inquiry and does so in the exercise of what is known as judicial discretion. He should see that nothing relevant is excluded, so long as its admission will not unduly distract the attention of the jury from the main inquiry. He must determine in the first instance whether evidence which, though logically relevant on the ultimate issue, may nevertheless be excluded because its general effect on the trial will be to confuse the issue by distracting the attention of the jury from primary to collateral issues, or by unduly prolonging the trial, or perhaps by unfairly surprising the other side.[7]

Generally, evidence which tends to prove that a defendant committed a crime other than the one for which he is on trial is not admissible, but this rule is subject to exceptions to the end that all relevant facts and circumstances tending to establish any of the constituent elements of the crime charged may be made to appear. In a manslaughter prosecution, evidence that defendant had stolen the automobile he was driving at the time of the fatal collision was material because it indicated defendant's purpose in attempting to escape from police officers who were in pursuit of the defendant at the time of the accident, and the fact that it also tended to show another offense did not render it inadmissible.[8]

The trial court has great latitude in passing on the admissibility of evidence and its determination of legal relevancy must be considered an act of discretion not to be disturbed absent a clear showing of abuse. Thus, guns seized in a search of automobiles of defendants charged with conspiracy to break and enter a post office were relevant to prove conspiracy and were properly admitted into evidence even though there was no direct evidence that the guns were actually used by defendants.[9] And in a prosecution for entering a bank with intent to commit larceny, where it was shown that a

---

[7] Holmes v. State, 112 S.(2d) 511 (Ala.App. 1959) See case in Part II of this book.

[8] Cantrell v. United States, 323 F.(2d) 613 (D.C. Cir. 1963).

[9] Wangrow v. United States, 399 F.(2d) 106 (8th Cir. 1968).

revolver appeared in plain view lying on the front seat of the truck at a place where it had previously been concealed by the defendant's body, and that one shot had been fired from such revolver, its seizure and admission into evidence were permissible and relevant to the offense charged.[10]

On the other hand, in the trial on a charge of armed robbery of a bank, there was discussion before the jury of guns which police officers took from defendant's dresser at the time of his arrest, but the guns were not admitted into evidence. The trial court instructed the jury that there was no testimony that the guns had been used in the robbery, that they were not relevant to the issues in the case, and that the jury was not to consider the testimony about the guns in any way whatsoever.[11]

Testimony irrelevant and inadmissible on one issue may be relevant and admissible on another; and in such an instance the rule favors admission, limiting applicability by judicial instruction to the issue where relevance is established.[12]

§ 3.4 Identification of persons

Generally, evidence which tends to establish the identity of persons involved is admissible as being relevant and material. For example, in a criminal prosecution the testimony of a witness that he saw the accused commit or participate in the commission of the crime for which the accused is being tried is admissible in evidence.[13] Identification witnesses frequently know from extensive newspaper and television publicity that the accused has been arrested, and they may be shown photographs of the accused after he has been arrested; nevertheless, their testimony identifying the accused in court may be considered by the jury where it has an independent origin arising from their observation of the accused at the time of commission of the crime.[14]

Improper employment of photographs by police may sometimes cause witnesses to err in identifying criminals. A witness may have

---

[10] McClard v. United States, 386 F.(2d) 495 (8th Cir. 1967).
[11] United States v. Peacock, 400 F.(2d) 992 (6th Cir. 1968).
[12] Segal v. Cook, 329 F.(2d) 278 (6th Cir. 1964).
[13] Crime Control Act, 18 U.S. Code § 3502 (1968 Supp.)
[14] United States v. Zeiler, 296 F.Supp. 224 (W.D.Pa. 1969).

obtained only a brief glimpse of a criminal, or may have seen him under poor conditions. Even if the police subsequently follow the most correct photographic identification procedures and show him the pictures of a number of individuals without indicating whom they suspect, there is some danger that the witness may make an incorrect identification. This danger will be increased if the police display to the witness only the picture of a single individual who generally resembles the person he saw, or if they show him the pictures of several persons among which the photograph of a single such individual recurs or is in some way emphasized. The chance of misidentification is also heightened if the police indicate to the witness that they have other evidence that one of the persons pictured committed the crime. Regardless of how the initial misidentification comes about, the witness thereafter is apt to retain in his memory the image of the photograph rather than of the person actually seen, reducing the trustworthiness of subsequent lineup or courtroom identification.

Despite the hazards of initial identification by photograph, this procedure has been used widely and effectively in law enforcement for the purpose of apprehending offenders and of sparing innocent suspects the ignominy of arrest by allowing eyewitnesses to exonerate them through scrutiny of photographs. The danger that use of the technique may result in convictions based on misidentification may be substantially lessened by a course of cross-examination at trial which exposes to the jury the method's potential for error.

The Supreme Court of the United States is unwilling to prohibit its employment, either in the exercise of its supervisory power or, still less, as a matter of constitutional requirement. Instead, the Court holds that each case must be considered on its own facts, and that convictions based on eyewitness identification at trial following a pretrial identification by photograph will be set aside on that ground only if the photographic identification procedure was so impermissibly suggestive as to give rise to a very substantial likelihood of irreparable misidentification.[15]

As an example of the use of photographs in an armed robbery

---

[15] Simmons v. United States, 390 U.S. 377, 19 L.Ed.(2d) 1247, 88 S.Ct. 967 (1968).

prosecution, the admission of photographs showing federal agents in the relative positions of the defendant and savings and loan employees at the time of the robbery of the association, and showing the height of the person standing in the position allegedly occupied by the defendant, was proper in view of the positive identification of the defendant in the courtroom by one employee of the association. The court held that photographs are admissible as long as what they purport to depict is relevant to the issue, and substantial identity to relevant times and conditions is established by oral testimony.[16] On the other hand, evidence of a witness's identification of the defendant from photographic slides will not be admitted where it appears that officers attending the witness at the showing, in their overzealousness to secure strong identification of the person they felt to be the robber, had unwittingly communicated this to the witness. Because the officer spoke first when the defendant's picture appeared and later told the witness that another person had recently identified the defendant as the one who committed a similar offense, the evidence was contaminated.[17]

§ 3.5 Identity of things

Although there are some exceptions, evidence which concerns the identity of things connected with the crime is also considered relevant. For example, for the purpose of identifying the accused as the guilty party, evidence that the accused's tracks are identical to tracks found near the scene of the crime is admissible. This is similar to fingerprint evidence that is usually admissible for the purpose of identifying the accused as the offender and to connect him with the offense.[18] Where a merchandise tag of a certain clothing company found on the floor of a savings and loan association after the robbery led officers to the defendant who was identified by the victims as wearing a dark business suit, two dark suits of clothing identified by the defendant's wife as belonging to the defendant were relevant and material as evidence.[19] In another case, trousers belonging to the defendant and found abandoned in a dress-

---

[16] United States v. Daniels, 377 F.(2d) 255 (6th Cir. 1967). See § 13.5 of this text for the use of photographs in evidence.

[17] United States v. Trivette, 284 F.Supp. 720 (D.C. 1968).

[18] McClard v. United States, 386 F.(2d) 495 (8th Cir. 1967). See § 13.15 of this text as to fingerprints.

[19] United States v. Alloway, 397 F.(2d) 105 (6th Cir. 1968).

ing room at the scene of a robbery were admissible in evidence. Police officers were also permitted to testify that they found at the scene of the crime a paper identifying the defendant by name and address, and that such information led to his arrest.[20]

§ 3.6 Circumstances preceding the crime

It is obvious that evidence which relates to circumstances and events preceding the crime would reasonably be relevant to the issue. The best test of relevancy of testimony as to antecedent circumstances which might shed light upon the alleged crime is whether a particular fact tends to render probable a material proposition in issue.[21] Generally, evidence of conduct of the accused shortly before the offense, which is inconsistent with his innocence, is relevant and admissible. For example, the trial judge admitted in evidence testimony of a witness that he had discussed with the defendant the selling of lewd films and had been engaged by the defendant to go to another city to pick up films but that he changed his mind. Also this same witness was allowed to testify that he was told by the defendant that he was not needed any more, as defendant had obtained his sales list and was able to make the purchase contact. This evidence was relevant as related to the charges of interstate transportation of lewd, lascivious and filthy films for the purpose of sale and distribution, and of conspiracy to commit such act.[22]

Also, the testimony of a police informer, who set up and participated in an illegal narcotics transaction and was in a position to throw light on the defendant's contention that she was the unwitting agent of another, may be relevant and helpful to the defense or essential to a fair determination of the case and is therefore admissible.[23]

§ 3.7 Subsequent incriminating or exculpatory circumstances

Equally important and relevant is evidence of conduct subse-

---

[20] United States v. Dorman, 294 F.Supp. 1221 (D.C. 1967).

[21] State v. Hymore, 9 OhioSt.(2d) 122, 38 OhioOp.(2d) 298, 224 N.E.(2d) 126 (1967). United States v. Gipson, 385 F.(2d) 341 (7th Cir. 1967). See case in Part II of this book.

[22] Kirschbaum v. United States, 407 F.(2d) 562 (8th Cir. 1969). See case in Part II.

[23] United States v. Lloyd, 400 F.(2d) 414 (6th Cir. 1968).

quent to the act. For example, evidence of flight, resistance to arrest, concealment, assumption of a false name or criminal conduct during flight for the purpose of financing and accomplishing further flight is admissible in a criminal prosecution. And while such conduct does not raise a presumption of guilt, the jury may consider circumstances thereof, together with other facts in evidence, to determine whether there was a guilty connection with the crime charged.[24]

In a Texas case the court clearly stated the rule concerning the admissibility of a pistol taken from the defendant who was arrested within hours after the crime in possession of the weapon. The court not only found the weapon admissible under the general "flight" doctrine but that it makes no difference whether the weapon is the same as used in the crime for which defendant was arrested. The state court justices explained that the weight to be given to the evidence or the question of "identity" is to be resolved by the jury and does not affect its admissibility.[24a]

There are limitations on the weight of such evidence. The United States Supreme Court in *Hickory v. United States*[25] reversed a conviction because the trial judge had charged the jury that flight created a presumption of guilt. The Court concluded that flight and concealment "are mere circumstances to be considered and weighed in connection with other proof with that caution and circumspection which their inconclusiveness when standing alone require." The assumption that one who flees shortly after a criminal act is committed or when he is accused of committing it does so because he feels some guilt concerning that act has been subjected to considerable judicial criticism on the ground that, in fact, common experience does not support it. In *Miller v. United States*[26] a federal court decided that when evidence of flight has been introduced into a case, the trial court should explain to the jury that flight does not necessarily reflect feelings of guilt, and that feelings of guilt, which are present in many innocent people, do not necessarily reflect actual guilt. This explanation may help the jurors to

---

[24] State V. Ross, 92 OhioApp. 29, 49 OhioOp. 196, 108 N.E.(2d) 77 (1952).
[24a] Hicks v. State (and cases cited therein) 508 S.W.(2d) 400 (1974).
[25] 160 U.S. 408, 40 L.Ed. 474, 16 S.Ct. 327 (1896).
[26] 320 F.(2d) 767 (D.C. Cir. 1963).

understand and follow the instruction which should then be given, that they are not to presume guilt from flight; that they may, but need not, consider flight as one circumstance tending to show feelings of guilt; and that they may, but need not, consider feelings of guilt as evidence tending to show actual guilt.[27] Evidence of attempts or threats to commit suicide is admissible, on the same theory, as a form of flight.[28]

Since the law permits the jurors to infer that a person fleeing from crime does so out of a consciousness of guilt, they are likewise permitted to infer that a person refusing to flee from crime, though opportunity offers, does so because of no consciousness of guilt.[29]

§ 3.8 Defenses

In a criminal case evidence is not only relevant to show the guilt of the accused, but the accused must have the opportunity to introduce evidence in his defense. Such evidence is usually admissible if it meets the other admissibility tests. Some of these defenses are discussed here.

a. Defense of insanity

The test of sanity applicable in a criminal prosecution is directed toward mental responsibility at the very time of the alleged criminal act; and therefore, temporary insanity is recognized as a defense. Evidence as to an accused's mental condition, before or after the offense, if not unreasonably far removed in time, is usually admissible because it is relevant to the question of mental condition at the time of the offense.[30]

b. Involuntary intoxication as a defense

Intoxication and insanity are not unalike. Drunkenness is a voluntary insanity, and will not excuse from crime. It is so generally accepted as to be a truism that voluntary intoxication is neither an excuse for the commission of crime nor a defense to a prosecution for it. This general rule is the settled view of the common law and

---

[27] *Ibid*, at p. 773.
[28] People v. Duncan, 261 Ill. 339, 103 N.E. 1043 (1914).
[29] Wigmore, EVIDENCE (3d Ed.), § 276, p. 111. State v. Milam, 108 OhioApp. 254, 9 OhioOp. (2d) 252, 156 N.E. (2d) 840 (1959).
[30] Beardslee v. United States, 387 F.(2d) 280 (8th Cir. 1967).

is articulated in the statutes of some twenty states. It also is the rule by judicial decision in the federal courts.

It also is well settled that an exception to the general rule exists where one is accused of a crime, the definition of which involves some specific intent or the operation of some mental process such as deliberation or premeditation. Under the so-called "exculpatory" rule drunkenness may be taken into account to show that a particular state of mind, or "specific intent," regarded as a necessary ingredient of some crimes, was not present.

Where intoxication is established as a defense to a specific intent crime, the result may be not acquittal but conviction of a lower degree of the offense as to which no proof or specific intent is necessary. And evidence that the defendant at the crucial time was so drunk that he could not have committed the physical acts constituting the offense is relevant on the issue of guilt.[31]

c. Other defenses

Evidence can also be introduced as relevant to show other defenses claimed by the accused. However, these must meet the other tests of admissibility in addition to the relevancy and materiality tests.

§ 3.9 Evidence concerning character, reputation and other crimes

It would seem that the character of the accused would be relevant in any criminal case. If the state can prove that a person's character is not as sterling as it should be, this should have some probative value in determining whether he actually committed the offense. But evidence showing the bad character of the accused is often not admitted because of the possibility of overriding dangers. However, the rule excluding such evidence has quite a few exceptions.[32]

---

[31] Murphy v. Commonwealth, 279 S.W.(2d) 767 (Ky. 1955).

[32] Rule 404(a) of the Federal Rules of Evidence states that: Evidence of a person's character or a trait of his character is not admissible for the purpose of proving that he acted in conformity therewith on a particular occasion, except:

(1) *Character of accused.*—Evi-

The general rule is that in criminal cases evidence of other crimes or misconduct by the defendant is admitted to establish an element of the crime charged as opposed to showing that the defendant had a criminal propensity.[33] For example, evidence of prior crimes by the accused is admissible to prove the existence of a larger continuing plan, scheme, or conspiracy of which the present crime is a part. This is relevant to show motive and hence the doing of the criminal act or the identity of the actor and his intention where any of these is in dispute. Also, evidence is admissible to prove that other crimes were committed by the accused which were so nearly identical in method as to indicate that the defendant's modus operandi was the same. For this evidence to be admitted it must be shown that the devices or methods used were so unusual and distinctive as to be unique.[34]

Another example of the admissibility of evidence indicating past criminal acts is the exception which allows the prosecution to show that the act for which the defendant is on trial was not inadvertent, accidental, unintentional, or without guilt or knowledge. For example in the case of *People* v. *Williams*[35] the defendant who was charged with larceny of a coin purse claimed that he picked up the purse from the floor thinking it was lost. The court allowed evidence that detectives had seen the defendant take another purse from another woman's bag in the same manner.

Although evidence concerning character, reputation and other

---

dence of a pertinent trait of his character offered by an accused, or by the prosecution to rebut the same;

(2) *Character of victim.*—Evidence of a pertinent trait of character of the victim of the crime offered by an accused, or by the prosecution to rebut the same, or evidence of a character trait of peacefulness of the victim offered by the prosecution in a homicide case to rebut the evidence that the victim was the first aggressor.

See Chapter 6 for further discussion of the admissibility of character evidence.

[33] People v. Peete, 28 Cal. (2d) 306 (1946). People v. Zackowitz, 245 N.Y. 192, 172 N.E. 466 (1930). See case in Part II.

Rule 404(b) of the Federal Rules states this negatively as: Evidence of other crimes, wrongs, or acts is not admissible to prove the character of a person in order to show that he acted in conformity therewith. This subdivision does not exclude the evidence when offered for other purposes, such as proof of motive, opportunity, intent, preparation, plan, knowledge, identity, or absence of mistake or accident.

[34] Whiteman v. State, 119 OhioSt. 285, 164 N.E. 51 (1928).

[35] 58 Pac. (2d) 917 (Cal. 1936).

crimes is sometimes relevant, such evidence is often excluded for one of many other reasons.[36] For example, evidence of facts which are too remote in time or too far removed from the scene of a transaction may be relevant but, in the discretion of the court, not material.[36a] This rule which excludes facts which are remote or offer little to the jury in determining the facts is more strongly applied in criminal cases. The reason is that such evidence may draw the minds of the jurors away from the point in issue and thereby prejudice the defendant. It is essentially important in a criminal case that the facts laid before the jury relate exclusively to the transaction forming the subject of the indictment and matters closely connected thereto.[36b]

§ 3.10 Experimental and scientific evidence

Of great importance to police officers are the rules concerning the admissibility of scientific evidence. This will be discussed more thoroughly in the chapters that follow, especially the chapter concerning real proof. Here we will only discuss this type of evidence as the relevancy test is involved.

It would seem reasonable to assume that the introduction of evidence concerning the testing of firearms to show patterns of powder and shot made upon the object at different distances, tests of speed of motor vehicles, blood tests, etc. should be admissible as relevant in criminal cases. And such evidence does most often come within the relevancy and materiality scope. But the other rules of exclusion must not be overlooked. While weapons, bullets, etc. are generally admitted at the trial, the trial court can exclude the evidence even though relevant if it tends to shock or inflame the jury. Generally the admissibility of such evidence by the trial court is a matter of discretion. This is usually sustained by the reviewing courts unless there is a clear abuse of discretion.

Some examples of instances where the evidence has been admitted as being relevant and having probative value are as follows. In *State* v. *Criger*[37] the court upheld testimony concerning the test-

---

[36] The admissibility of character and reputation evidence and evidence relating to other crimes will be discussed in more detail in later chapters.

[36a] McGuire v. Caledonia, 167 N.W. 425 (1918).

[36b] Farris v. People, 21 N.E. 821 (1889).

[37] 151 Kan. 176 (1940).

ing of firearms to show patterns of powder and shot made upon an object at a certain distance. And in the case of *Crecelius v. Gamble-Skogmo, Inc.*[38] tests of how fast a vehicle can be stopped when the brakes are applied were upheld as being relevant to the case.

§ 3.11 Summary

At the criminal trial the primary objective is to determine the truth as to the issues presented in order that the court or jury may come to a conclusion as to the facts of the case. However, over the years the courts have developed rules of exclusion, including rules concerning relevancy and materiality. If the evidence does not meet the test of relevancy and materiality, it will not be admitted. Generally, evidence which has a tendency to prove or disprove a pertinent fact in issue is relevant. And that which goes to substantial matters in dispute and has an effective influence or bearing on the decision of the case is material.

The trial court has great latitude in passing on the admissibility of the evidence and in determining whether it has legal relevancy or materiality. The court's interpretation as to what evidence is relevant and material is usually given great weight and its determination will be final unless there is a clear abuse of discretion.

Both court decisions and statutes must be considered in determining what evidence meets the relevancy and materiality tests. The following general rules have been developed through this procedure.

- *1 Evidence which tends to establish the identity of persons involved is admissible as being relevant and material. This of course, is subject to the other rules of admissibility.*

- *2 Evidence which concerns the identity of things connected with the crime is considered relevant, although there are some exceptions.*

- *3 Generally evidence which relates to the circumstances and events which precede or follow the crime is admissible as relevant to the issues.*

---

[38] 144 Neb. 394 (1944).

- *4 Evidence relating to the defenses claimed by the defendant, such as mental disease, coercion, self defense, and alibi, is generally admissible if it meets the other admissibility tests in addition to the relevancy and materiality tests.*

- *5 Although evidence concerning the character and reputation of the accused as well as other evidence concerning the commission of other crimes is recognized as relevant and material, it is often excluded because of overriding dangers. For this reason only certain evidence of this type is admissible.*

- *6 Evidence concerning bullets, weapons and other experimental scientific evidence is also usually considered relevant, but it must pass other tests before it can be admitted into court.*

From the discussion it is obvious that even though the parties may object when evidence is not relevant and material, there is certainly no reciprocal assurance that evidence which is relevant and material will necessarily be admitted. In future chapters some of the other requirements will be discussed, and relevancy and materiality as they relate to specific types of evidence will be explored in more detail.

Chapter 4

COMPETENCY

> The terms "relevancy," "competency," and "materiality" are frequently used conjunctively in such manner as to suggest that they are synonymous, yet it is obvious upon second thought that a matter which may be relevant to an issue of the case may be rendered incompetent and inadmissible as to the established rules of evidence, such as the rule which excludes hearsay evidence or requires the production of the best evidence. . . . In other words evidence must be not only logically relevant, but of such a character as to be receivable in courts of justice. (20 Am.Jur. 253)

Section
4.1 Introduction
4.2 Definitions and scope
4.3 Competency of evidence—tests and experiments
4.4 Competency of evidence—conduct of trained dogs
4.5 Competency of evidence—telephone conversations
4.6 Negative evidence as competent evidence
4.6a Evidence competent for some purposes but not others
4.7 —Determination of witness' competency
4.8 —Mental incapacity
4.9 —Children
4.10 —Husband and wife
4.11 —Conviction of crime
4.12 —Religious belief
4.13 Summary

§ 4.1 Introduction

In the preceding chapters some of the rules concerning relevancy and materiality were discussed. The third hurdle which must be cleared before evidence is admissible is the competency hurdle. Evidence is inadmissible if it is incompetent but on the other hand evidence is admissible where it is competent provided it is also relevant and material.[1]

Simply stated, evidence which is competent, relevant, and material is admissible evidence. The application of this rule, how-

---

[1] Egger v. Egger, 123 S.W. 928 (1909).

ever, is not so simple. As a matter of fact, many writers and even some of the legal encyclopedias fail to explain adequately the competency restrictions. In some legal writings the authors seem to take it for granted that the definition and explanation of incompetency as it relates to evidence is known and they start discussing cases without a definition.

This chapter will consider the rules relating not only to the competency of the witnesses but also to the competency of evidence. The fact that a witness is competent to testify does not necessarily mean that the proof which may be offered by a witness is competent.

§ 4.2 Definitions and scope

In Black's Law Dictionary competent evidence is defined as that which the very nature of the thing to be proven requires; as, the production of the writing where its contents are the subject of inquiry. It goes on to define competent evidence as generally admissible, the opposite of "incompetent."

Perhaps a better understanding can be had of the definition of competent evidence if incompetent evidence is defined. In Black's Law Dictionary incompetent evidence is defined as evidence which is not admissible under the established rules; evidence which the law does not permit to be presented at all, or in relation to the particular matter, on account of lack of originality or of some defect in the witness, the document, or the nature of the evidence itself. One court defines incompetent evidence as that which is not proper to be received; inadmissible, as distinguished from that which the court should admit for the consideration of the jury, though they may not find it worthy of credence. If evidence is not found to be incompetent due to one of the many rules, it should be admitted if it meets the other tests.[2]

In seeking answers as to which evidence is held to be incompetent and therefore not admissible, many avenues are open and volumes of material are available. In fact much of the rest of this book will be devoted to determining what evidence is considered to be incompetent and therefore inadmissible in court.

---

[2] International Brotherhood of Electrical Workers v. Commission on Civil Rights, 102 A.2d 366 (1953).

If evidence is found to be incompetent it is usually because the courts have found that it is constitutionally incompetent, that to admit the evidence would violate a federal or state statute, or the courts in determining the rules of evidence have found that the evidence is inadmissible for one reason or another. Some examples are as follows:

Evidence Wrongfully Obtained

Evidence which has been obtained in violation of the Constitution such as that obtained by an illegal search will not be admitted because the courts have reasoned that to admit such evidence would encourage disregard of constitutional rights. This evidence is inadmissible not because it is not relevant and material but because it is incompetent as determined by the courts. Similarly, evidence obtained directly or indirectly as a result of an involuntary confession will likewise not be admitted because the process used in obtaining the evidence violates the due process clauses of the Constitution.

Statutory Incompetency

Some evidence is admissible as competent evidence because the statute says it is and similarly some evidence is not admissible because the state or federal statute prohibits the admissibility of this evidence. For example, Section 2515 of the Omnibus Crime Control and Safe Streets Act of 1968 provides that evidence obtained by wiretapping or eavesdropping in violation of the statute is not admissible. Again, this is not because the evidence is not relevant or material but because the statute specifically provides that it is not admissible or usable in court.

Evidence Excluded Because of the Court Established Rule

Although many of the rules of evidence have now become codified, most evidence is excluded because the courts over a period of years have established certain rules concerning the admissibility of evidence. Some excellent examples which will be discussed more thoroughly in forthcoming chapters are those rules which prohibit the use of certain opinion testimony, hearsay evidence, and privileged communications such as that between husband and wife.

Because much of the rest of the book is devoted to a discussion of evidence rules which determine the competency of evidence, these will not be considered here. However, some types of evidence which are especially important in the investigative process have been challenged as incompetent and deserve at least some mention before the rules concerning the competency of the witness are examined.

§ 4.3 Competency of evidence—tests and experiments

Evidence relating to tests and experiments made in or out of court is challenged for many reasons, among them the competency of such tests. Generally where it is necessary to show the condition or quality of a certain article or substance, that thing itself may be introduced in evidence as supplementing the testimony of the witness or as direct evidence when properly identified. Evidence showing the outcome of an experiment or test is admissible to aid in determining the issues in a case where it is shown that the condition under which the experiment or test was made is similar to the circumstances prevailing at the time of the occurrence.

Some examples of this type of evidence where courts have found the evidence to be competent and admissible are blood tests, ballistics tests, and evidence showing that a piece of cloth found at the scene of the crime was from a garment worn by a suspect.

§ 4.4 Competency of evidence—conduct of trained dogs

Evidence of the conduct of a dog in tracking a suspect (sometimes referred to as "bloodhound evidence") has been held to be competent and admissible in both civil and criminal cases provided the proper foundation has been laid.[3]

Evidence of the conduct of a dog in tracking the accused, as from the scene of the crime to the place where he is found, is competent and admissible merely as circumstantial or corroborative evidence against a person toward whom other circumstances point as being guilty of the commission of the crime charged. The

---
[3] Crosby v. Moriarity, 181 N.W. 199 (1921).

Kentucky Court of Appeals set forth the basic rule in 1898 when it decided *Pedigo* v. *Commonwealth*,[4] stating:

> In order to make such testimony competent, even when it is shown that the dog is of pure blood, and of a stock characterized by acuteness of scent and power of discrimination, it must also be established that the dog in question is possessed of these qualities, and has been trained or tested in their exercise in the tracking of human beings, and these facts must appear from the testimony of some person who has personal knowledge thereof. We think it must also appear that the dog so trained and tested was laid on the trail, whether visible or not, concerning which testimony has been admitted, at a point where the circumstances tend clearly to show that the guilty party had been, or upon a track which such circumstances indicated to have been made by him. When so indicated, testimony as to training by a bloodhound may be permitted to go to the jury for what it is worth as one of the circumstances which may tend to connect the defendant with the crime of which he is accused. When not so indicated, the trial court should exclude the entire testimony in that regard from the jury.

Before any evidence pertaining to the results of the dog's tracking is admitted, the handler of the dog must testify as to his own qualifications and experience and that of the dog, along with an account of the dog's skill and ability to track. Next, the circumstances pertaining to the training itself must be shown, for example, that the trail was fresh and had not been trampled, or that there was no interference with the dog while he was tracking. The dog must have been placed on the trail at such a point where it is known that the perpetrator of the crime had been. Some courts require that the dog's pedigree must be shown but the most recent cases have not stressed pedigree as a prerequisite for the admission of evidence. Once the proper foundation has been laid, the evidence may be used to identify the accused as the perpetrator, or for some other reason, as long as this evidence is corroborated.

Besides stating the majority rule, *Pedigo, supra*, set the groundwork for the minority by referring to the superstitious attitude towards the bloodhound. In 1903 the Nebraska Supreme Court in

---

[4] 103 Ky. 41, 44 S.W. 143, 42 L.R.A. 432 (1898).

Brott v. *State*,⁵ reversed a burglary conviction based on "bloodhound evidence." The evidence so adduced was not competent for, "It is unsafe evidence, and both reason and instinct condemn it." A close examination of the facts in *Brott* shows that there had been a time lapse before the dogs were used, during which time the trail had been walked on "a hundred times" by observers. Therefore, even under *Pedigo, supra*, the evidence would be excluded. Nineteen jurisdictions have followed the majority rule; six states⁶ have adopted the minority view.

In a more recent Maryland case the trial court properly admitted evidence that a German Shepherd dog had tracked the defendant, where the qualifications and experience of the dog and the trainer were shown, the scene of the robbery had been protected until the dog arrived, the dog had been placed on the apparent trail that the perpetrator of the crime had taken, there were no interruptions in tracking, the dog went to the automobile in which defendant was hiding, and the defendant was identified by the robbery victim.⁷

§ 4.5 Competency of evidence—telephone conversations

Evidence of a telephone conversation is generally competent and admissible as substantive evidence where the identity of the parties to the conversation is established, either by direct evidence or by facts and circumstances.

Before evidence of a telephone conversation may be admitted at trial, it is necessary to have the declarant's voice identified. This identification may be made on the basis of the witness' then existing familiarity with the declarant's voice, or on the basis of a subsequent conversation with the declarant and a retroactive recognition of the voice used in the antecedent conversation.⁸

The requirement of direct recognition of the voice is not an inexorable or mechanical rule. Circumstantial evidence may be sufficient to identify the speaker. In *Van Riper* v. *United States*,⁹

---

⁵ 70 Neb. 395, 97 N.E. 593, 63 L.R.A. 789 (1903).

⁶ Illinois, Indiana, Iowa, Montana, Nebraska, and New York.

⁷ Terrell v. State, 239 A.(2d) 128 (1968).

⁸ U.S. v. Lo Bue, 180 F.Supp. 955 (S.D.N.Y. 1960).

⁹ 13 F.2d 961 (2nd Cir. 1926), cert. denied sub. nom. Ackerson v. U.S., 273 U.S. 702, 71 L.Ed. 848, 47 S.Ct. 102.

Judge Learned Hand approved lower court decisions which held that when a witness obtains the correct telephone number of the person whose admissions are relevant, calls that number, and gets an answer from one professing to be the person called, it is prima facie proof of identity. However, the mere announcement of identity by a person who has placed a telephone call does not suffice to make it admissible against the person so identified.

In a prosecution for selling heroin, a telephone call was made by a third person to defendant in the hearing of a narcotics agent through a long distance telephone operator to whom the defendant's telephone number was verbally given by a third person. The agent shared the receiver with the third person for at least part of the time, and the agent testified that he was able to hear and identify the voice at the other end as that of the defendant, with whom the agent had spent three hours about a week before. The admission of the agent's testimony concerning the telephone conversation was proper, over an objection that the testimony of the telephone call constituted a conversation outside of defendant's presence.[10]

In another case, testimony of a federal agent concerning statements he had overheard over the phone was properly admitted when the agent had listened to telephone conversations between the witness and the defendant during which the witness had identified the other voice as that of the defendant.[11]

§ 4.6 Negative evidence as competent evidence

Negative evidence, that is, evidence that an act did not exist or that a thing was not done, is generally incompetent evidence. However, such evidence even though it might be weak is admissible if it tends to contradict positive evidence introduced by the other party. In such circumstances the testimony of the witness is not confined to what he saw or heard, but he may also state what he did not see or did not hear.[12]

In one case the court authorized the statement of a lay witness that he had never observed an abnormal act on the part of the

---

[10] U.S. v. Glass, 277 F.(2d) 566 (7th Cir. 1960).

[11] U.S. v. Cooper, 365 F.(2d) 246 (6th Cir. 1966).

[12] Weber v. Park Auto Transportation Company, 244 P. 718 (1926).

accused when the issue was one of insanity, and the witness had had a prolonged and intimate contact with the accused.[13] And as will be discussed in a later chapter, negative evidence is sometimes admissible to establish a good reputation when reputation has been put in issue.

§ 4.6a Evidence competent for some purposes but not others

The courts have decided that in the usual situation evidence which is competent for one purpose can not be excluded merely because it might be incompetent for some purposes even though there is a certain risk of confusion by the jury.[14] If, on the other hand, the risk is so great as to upset the balance of advantages of receiving it, it will not be admissible. Where the evidence is competent for one purpose but not competent for others, the court should limit its application by proper instruction.

Before moving to the discussion relative to the competency of witnesses and the rules relating thereto, a further reminder is in order. As previously mentioned, many of the rules of exclusion, as for example, the hearsay rule, the opinion rule, and the rule rejecting proof of bad character as evidence of crime, which in effect hold that such evidence is incompetent are not discussed here, not because they are not pertinent but because they will be discussed in detail in future chapters.

§ 4.7 —Determination of witness' competency

Again, to avoid any confusion a distinction should be made between the competency of the witness and the competency of evidence. For example, a witness may meet the tests of competency and yet not be authorized to testify concerning evidence which is *incompetent* such as certain hearsay evidence:

The test of the competency of a witness is his capacity to communicate relevant material and to understand that there is an obligation to do so truthfully. The determination of the competency of a witness is within the sound discretion of the trial judge. Thus, in a prosecution for transportation of a stolen motor vehicle in

---

[13] Carter v. U.S., 252 F.(2d) 608 (1956).

[14] City of Phoenix v. Boggs, 403 P.(2d) 305 (1971).

interstate commerce, where the only evidence relating to a witness' credibility was his previous brief addiction to narcotics, the trial judge properly decided that the witness was competent to testify.[15]

Every person is qualified to be a witness as to any material matter unless the judge finds that (a) the proposed witness is incapable of expressing himself concerning the matter so as to be understood by the judge and jury, or (b) the proposed witness is incapable of understanding the duty of a witness to tell the truth.[16]

In determining the competency of a witness an "understanding of the proceedings" is clearly not a prerequisite, as it would be in the case of a defendant. Such an argument was rejected in *Carter v. United States*,[17] where the difference in the standards to determine competency of witnesses and competency of a defendant to stand trial was clearly spelled out.

The tests in determining competency of a witness before the grand jury are basically, (1) the witness must have a sufficient understanding to comprehend the obligation of an oath, and to tell the truth before the grand jury; (2) the witness must be capable of giving a correct account, or at least a reasonably correct account, of the matters which he or she has seen or heard, and in reference to which the questions at issue are being asked; (3) these two issues must be determined by the court, not only upon the testimony of expert medical witnesses who may be called by the prosecution or by the witness' counsel, but also upon the court's own examination. This is a duty that the court cannot avoid merely by referring to or quoting from statements of the medical experts. The court must make its own determination and its own examination, so to speak, and (4) the court must be assured that the physical and mental health of the witness will not be damaged, impaired, or harmed in any significant way.[18]

In the sections immediately following the specific grounds advanced for challenging the competency of witnesses are discussed.

---

[15] Brown v. United States, 222 F.(2d) 293 (9th Cir. 1955); Gurleski v. United States, 405 F.(2d) 253 (5th Cir. 1968).

[16] Model Code of Evidence, Rule 101.

[17] 332 F.(2d) 728 (8th Cir. 1964).

[18] In re Loughran, 276 F.Supp. 393 (C.D.Cal. 1967).

§ 4.8 —Mental incapacity

The basic standard or rule applied when considering the mental capacity of the witness to testify is the one first announced by the United States Supreme Court in *District of Columbia* v. *Armes.*[19] There the court stated:

> The general rule is that a lunatic or a person affected with insanity is admissible as a witness if he has sufficient understanding to apprehend the obligation of an oath, and to be capable of giving a correct account of the matters which he has seen or heard in reference to the questions at issue; and whether he has that understanding is a question to be determined by the court, upon examination of the party himself, and any competent witnesses who can speak to the nature and extent of his insanity.

In *Armes*, the Court upheld the admissibility of the testimony of an acute melancholic who was confined to an asylum and had several times attempted suicide by sticking a fork into his neck. The Court stressed that "the existence of partial insanity does not unfit individuals so affected . . . from giving a perfectly accurate and lucid statement of what they have seen or heard."[20]

The standard of competency established in *Armes* was cited and relied upon by the Ninth Circuit Court of Appeals in *Shibley* v. *United States*,[21] holding a trial court did not err in admitting the testimony of a witness previously adjudicated insane. The fact that the witness was formerly committed for insanity is not conclusive, and a subsequent adjudication of insanity and confinement in a mental hospital does not render the prior testimony of the witness incompetent.

Even if a trial court accepts abstruse psychiatric concepts of mental ailment or illness as a basis for measuring criminal capacity and responsibility, it will not project such theoretical concepts into the field of competency of witnesses as a substitute for the test of capacity to communicate relevant material and to understand the obligation to do so truthfully. For example, the trial judge was not

---

[19] 107 U.S. 519, 522, 27 L.Ed. 618, 2 S.Ct. 840 (1882).

[20] See Juvilier, *Psychiatric Opinions As To The Credibility of Witnesses: A Suggested Approach*, 48 Calif. L. Rev. 648 (1960).

[21] 237 F.(2d) 327 (9th Cir. 1956), cert. denied 352 U.S. 873, 1 L.Ed.(2d) 77, 77 S.Ct. 94.

required to hold incompetent a witness who had been found by the warden and psychiatric staff of a medical center for federal prisoners to be competent to understand the proceedings against him and to consult with his attorney.[22]

§ 4.9 —Children

It is the duty of the trial judge to determine the competency of a child to testify. The determination rests largely within his discretion and his exercise of such discretion will not be disturbed unless the error is plain. The trial judge should consider the child's age, intelligence or lack of intelligence, and sense of moral and legal responsibility. A child is competent to testify if he possesses the capacity to observe the events, to recollect and communicate them, has the ability to understand questions and to make intelligent answers with an understanding of the duty to speak the truth. It is not necessary to show that the child witness has religious beliefs or detailed knowledge of the nature of the oath. All that is required is that the child understands that some punishment will follow if he does not tell the truth.

Although some state statutes provide that "children under ten years of age, who appear incapable of receiving just impressions of the facts respecting which they are examined, or of relating them truly" are incompetent as witnesses, there is no fixed age at which a child must have arrived in order to be a competent witness. In *Wheeler v. United States*[23] the United States Supreme Court said:

> That the boy was not by reason of his youth [five and one-half years], as a matter of law, absolutely disqualified as a witness is clear. While no one would think of calling as a witness an infant only two or three years old, there is no precise age which determines the question of competency. This depends on the capacity and intelligence of the child, his appreciation of the difference between truth and falsehood, as well as of his duty to tell the former. The decision of this question rests primarily with the trial judge, who sees the proposed witness, notices his manner, his apparent possession or lack of intelligence, and may resort to any examination which will tend to disclose his capacity and intelli-

---

[22] Carter v. United States, 332 F.(2d) 728 (8th Cir. 1964).

[23] 159 U.S. 523, 40 L.Ed. 244, 16 S.Ct. 93 (1895).

§ 4.10

gence as well as his understanding of the obligations of an oath. As many of these matters cannot be photographed into the record the decision of the trial judge will not be disturbed on review unless from that which is preserved it is clear that it was erroneous.

In numerous cases children of very tender years are accepted as witnesses. To cite an instance, a five-year-old rape victim and her seven-year-old sister have been permitted to testify in a rape case even though challenged as incompetent due to youth.[24]

The child's capability to receive just impressions of the facts relates to the time the events occurred, while his capacity to state them truly relates to the later time of trial. For example, where a proffered witness is over ten years of age when he is called to testify but was only four years old at the time he witnessed happenings about which he proposes to testify, the capability of such witness to receive just impressions of such happenings must necessarily be determined as of the time of those happenings.[25] On the other hand, the child's competency or incompetency to testify must be determined as of the date the child is offered as a witness and not at the time the incidents testified to occurred. In a Virginia case[26] the court held that the fact a child was held to be incompetent at the time of the first trial is not of itself an adjudication of his continued incompetency to testify concerning events that occurred prior to his becoming competent.

§ 4.10 —Husband and wife

The common-law rule was that husband and wife were incompetent as witnesses for or against each other. The rule rested mainly on a desire to foster peace in the family and on a general unwillingness to use testimony of witnesses tempted by strong self-interest to testify falsely. Since a defendant was barred as a witness in his own behalf because of interest, it was quite natural to bar his spouse in view of the prevailing legal fiction that husband and wife

---

[24] Pocatello v. United States, 394 F.(2d) 115 (9th Cir. 1968); (an eight-year-old witness) Webster v. Peyton, 294 F.Supp. 1359 (E.D.Va. 1968).

[25] Huprich v. Paul W. Varga & Sons, Inc., 3 OhioSt.(2d) 87, 32 OhioOp.(2d) 61, 209 N.E.(2d) 390 (1965).

[26] Cross v. Commonwealth, 195 Va. 62, 77 S.E.(2d) 447 (1953).

were one person.²⁷ This early rule, however, yielded to exceptions in certain types of cases. Thus, in *Stein v. Bowman*,²⁸ the U.S. Supreme Court noted that the rule did not apply where the husband committed an offense against the person of his wife.

In 1933 the United States Supreme Court rejected the phase of the common-law rule which excluded testimony by spouses *for* each other.²⁹ The Court recognized that the basic reason underlying this exclusion of evidence had been the practice of disqualifying witnesses with a personal interest in the outcome of a case. Widespread disqualifications because of interest, however, had long since been abolished both in this country and in England in accordance with the modern trend which permitted interested witnesses to testify and left it for the jury to assess their credibility. Certainly, since defendants were uniformly allowed to testify in their own behalf, there was no longer a good reason to prevent them from using their spouses as witnesses.

In a prosecution for conspiracy to defraud the United States by obtaining illegal entry into the country of three aliens as spouses of honorably discharged veterans, there was evidence from which the jury might reasonably have believed that the three aliens went through marriage ceremonies with the veterans, both aliens and veterans intending to exploit the marriages solely for the purpose of obtaining admission to the United States, and never intending to live in normal marriage relationships. The question confronting the court was whether the so-called wives were competent to testify against their purported husbands in this criminal prosecution. The court held that where it is made to appear that the relationship was entered into with no intention of the parties to live together as husband and wife but only for the purpose of using the marriage ceremony in a scheme to defraud, the ostensible spouses are competent to testify against each other.³⁰

In another case of antispousal testimony the Supreme Court decided that a man prosecuted for transporting in interstate com-

---

²⁷ 1 Coke, COMMENTARY UPON LITTLETON, p. 6b (19th ed. 1832).
See Chapter 9 for a discussion of the husband-wife testimonial privilege.

²⁸ 13 Pet. 209, 38 U.S. 209 10 L.Ed. 129 (1837).

²⁹ Funk v. United States, 290 U.S. 371, 78 L.Ed. 369, 54 S.Ct. 212 (1933).

³⁰ Lutwak v. United States, 344 U.S. 604, 97 L.Ed. 593, 73 S.Ct. 481 (1953).

merce for the purpose of prostitution a woman whom he thereafter married before trial was subject to having the compelled testimony of his wife introduced against him.[31] As to the husband's objection the Court invoked the common-law doctrine that in the case of certain kinds of offenses committed by the party against the spouse witness, the party may not bar the spouse's testimony. This exception is applicable in a Mann Act prosecution.

In 1887 Congress enabled either spouse to testify in prosecutions against the other for bigamy, polygamy or unlawful cohabitation. In 1917 and again in 1952 Congress made wives and husbands competent to testify against each other in prosecutions for importing aliens for immoral purposes.[32] Statutes in many states permit spouses to testify against each other in prosecutions for only certain types of crimes. Under the Ohio statute[33] relative to the competency of witnesses in criminal cases, a husband and wife are competent to testify in behalf of each other in all criminal prosecutions; but they are competent witnesses to testify against each other only in prosecutions for personal injury of either by the other; bigamy; failure to provide for, neglect of, or cruelty to their minor children; and neglect of wife.

In California neither husband nor wife is a competent witness for or against the other in a criminal action or proceeding to which one or both are parties, except with the consent of both.[34] Under the California statute the privilege[35] in a criminal case may be claimed by either the defendant spouse or the witness spouse, and the defendant spouse cannot require the other to testify. But if both consent, or neither makes a sufficient objection, the privilege is waived as in many other states. The privilege cannot be asserted in criminal prosecutions for crimes: (1) committed by one against the person or property of the other, whether before or after marriage; (2) involving violence upon one by the other; (3) relating to violence upon the child or children of one by the other; (4) committed against another person by a husband or wife engaged in committing a crime by one against the other; (5) of bigamy or adultery; and (6) charging nonsupport of child or wife.

---

[31] Wyatt v. United States, 362 U.S. 525, 4 L.Ed. (2d) 931, 80 S.Ct. 901 (1960).
[32] 8 U.S. Code § 1328.
[33] Ohio Revised Code § 2945.42.
[34] California Penal Code § 1322.
[35] See Chapter 9 for discussion of testimonial privilege.

Where a state statute makes a wife a competent witness against her husband, it is not optional with the wife to testify or not; if presented as a witness she may be compelled to testify. Thus, where an indictment is returned against a husband for an assault upon his wife with a dangerous weapon or instrument likely to produce death or great bodily harm, the wife is a competent witness against her husband and like any other witness can be compelled to testify. If she refuses she can be found in contempt and imprisoned until she agrees to testify.[36]

§ 4.11 —Conviction of crime

More than fifty years ago the United States Supreme Court decided that "the dead hand of the common-law rule" disqualifying a witness who had been convicted of crime should no longer be applied in criminal cases in the federal courts.[37] Most states have enacted statutes which expressly remove the disqualification of a witness convicted of crime to testify, but allow the conviction to be shown for the purpose of affecting the credibility of the witness.[38]

In a few states, however, the disqualification has been retained for conviction of perjury and subornation thereof.[39]

§ 4.12 —Religious belief

In most jurisdictions the state constitutions or statutes provide that no person shall be rendered incompetent to be a witness on account of his religious opinions or for want of any religious belief.[40] This, however, does not prohibit inquiry concerning religious opinions for purposes of impeachment.

§ 4.13 Summary

To be admissible in court at the trial in a criminal case, evidence must pass the competency hurdle. Even though the evidence has

---

[36] State v. Antill, 176 OhioSt. 61, 26 OhioOp. (2d) 366, 197 N.E.(2d) 548 (1964).

[37] Rosen v. United States, 245 U.S. 467, 62 L.Ed. 406, 38 S.Ct. 148 (1918).

[38] For impeachment of a witness, see § 8.16 et seq.

[39] See Alabama statute quoted in § 4.6, herein.

[40] Gillars v. United States 182 F.(2d) 962 (1950). *See* case in Part II.

passed the relevancy and materiality tests, it will be excluded if the court finds that it is not competent under one of the many subtests included in the competency test.

Care must be taken to avoid confusion concerning the rules regarding competency of the evidence and competency of the witness. A witness may be competent and yet the evidence incompetent.

Evidence may be competent or incompetent because a federal or state statute so designates it or it might be determined as incompetent by the courts which establish certain rules of evidence.

Both the courts and legislative bodies have established rules concerning the competency of persons to testify in court. Although the rules have been liberalized in recent years, still there are certain requirements which, if not met, may make a witness incompetent to testify in court.

Even though a person may not have normal mental capacity, he will, in the discretion of the court, be allowed to testify if he can understand the obligation of an oath and can give a correct account of the matters which he has seen or heard. A child is generally competent to testify if he possesses the capacity to observe the events, to recollect and communicate them, and has the ability to understand questions and to make intelligent answers with the understanding of the duty to speak the truth.

At common law neither the husband nor the wife could testify for or against the other. Most statutes have made the husband and wife competent to testify for the accused, but it is generally provided that the prosecution cannot force the spouse to testify against the accused. This rule is subject to the exception that the spouse can be required to testify if the crime is committed by one against the other.

The prevailing rule is that a person who has been convicted of a crime is not made incompetent to testify. However, certain convictions may be shown for the purpose of challenging the credibility of the witness.

As a practical matter the police investigator should be fully aware of the rules which may make testimony or other evidence inadmissible because of the competency rules. In some instances the case may hang on the one piece of real evidence or testimony which the defense attorney will attempt to have excluded. If there is any doubt as to the competency of the witness or evidence, the investigator should make this fact immediately known to the prosecutor.

Chapter 5

BURDEN OF PROOF

> The term "burden of proof" imports the duty of ultimately establishing any given proposition. This phrase marks the peculiar duty of him who has the risk of any given proposition on which the parties are at issue, who will lose the case if he does not make this proposition out, when all has been said and done.
> Thayer, PRELIMINARY TREATISE ON EVIDENCE AT THE COMMON LAW, Ch. 9, p. 353.

Section
5.1 Introduction
5.2 Definitions and distinctions
5.3 —Preponderance of the evidence
5.4 —Clear and convincing evidence
5.5 —Reasonable doubt
5.6 Burden on prosecution
5.7 —Every element of crime
5.8 Burden on accused
5.9 —Matters of defense
5.10 —Alibi
5.11 —Insanity
5.12 Sufficiency of evidence
5.13 Summary

§ 5.1 Introduction

Despite efforts to define "burden of proof" much confusion still exists in the minds of attorneys as well as police officers and administrators. As analyzed in Chapter 2, the term "proof" is not the same as the term "evidence." Properly speaking, evidence is only the medium of proof and proof is the effect of evidence.

It is especially important that the police investigator understand what is meant by the responsibility of the prosecution to prove the accused's guilt "beyond a reasonable doubt." In a criminal case the investigator must compile enough evidence to convince the jury or the judge not merely by the "preponderance of the evidence" but that the accused is guilty "beyond a reasonable doubt." That is, the prosecution has the burden of proving the existence of every element necessary to constitute the crime charged.

Recognizing this requirement the defense can be expected to deliver an attack against the weak links in the chain, knowing that if only one of the elements is not proved beyond a reasonable doubt, there can be no conviction on that charge.

In the following sections of this chapter the comparative relationship between the prosecution and the defense regarding the burden of proof will be discussed in detail.

§ 5.2 Definitions and distinctions

The phrase "burden of proof" denotes the duty of establishing the truth of a given proposition or issue. The term is often used in two senses: (1) the primary meaning of the burden of proving the issues; (2) the secondary meaning of the burden of going forward with the evidence. In the first and proper sense, the burden never shifts, but rests throughout the case on the party who has the affirmative of the issue. In the second sense, when one party offers a prima facie case, the burden of producing evidence shifts to the other party. Thus, when the state proves that the defendant killed another person with a deadly weapon, this, without more, makes out a prima facie case of murder; and the burden of going forward with the evidence, to show any matter of excuse, justification, or extenuation of the offense, rests with the accused. But the burden of proving defendant's guilt rests with the prosecution throughout the trial and does not shift.

The phrase as used in law denotes the duty of establishing the truth at trial by such a quantum of evidence as the law demands in a particular type of case: Generally in a civil case the party who has the duty of establishing the truth of a specific proposition must do so by the preponderance of the evidence. However, there are some issues even in a civil case which must be proved by a higher degree of proof; clear and convincing evidence. And in a criminal case the state has the burden of proving its proposition—the guilt of the accused—beyond a reasonable doubt.[1]

---

[1] Kohlsatt v. Parkersburg & Marlitte Sand Co. 266 F. 283 (1920).

These three degrees of proof are discussed and distinguished in the following sections.

§ 5.3 —Preponderance of the evidence

In a civil case the burden of proof rests on the plaintiff. That means that it must be established by a fair preponderance of the credible evidence that the claim plaintiff makes is true. A preponderance means the greater weight of such evidence. That does not mean the greater number of witnesses nor the greater length of time taken by either side. The phrase "preponderance of the evidence" refers to the quality of the evidence, that is, its convincing quality, the weight and the effect that it has on the jurors' minds. The law requires that, in order for the plaintiff to prevail, the evidence that supports his claim must appeal to the jurors as more nearly representing what took place than that opposed to his claim. If it does not, or if it weighs so evenly that the jurors are unable to say that there is a preponderance on either side, then the jury must resolve the question in favor of the defendant. It is only when the evidence favoring the plaintiff's claim outweighs the evidence opposed to it that the jury can find in favor of plaintiff.

§ 5.4 —Clear and convincing evidence

Ordinarily, in civil matters, the burden of proof is carried by a preponderance (greater weight) of the evidence. In some civil cases, however, the evidence must be clear and convincing. "Clear and convincing evidence" is that measure or degree of proof which will produce in the mind of the trier of facts a firm belief or conviction as to the facts sought to be established. Such evidence is intermediate, being more than a mere preponderance, but not to the extent of such certainty as is required beyond a reasonable doubt in criminal cases. It does not mean clear and unequivocal. For example, in order to maintain an action to rescind a contract on the ground that it was procured by fraudulent representations, it must be proved by clear and convincing evidence that (1) there were actual or implied false representations of material matters of fact, (2) such representations were false, (3) such representations were made by one party to the other with knowledge of their falsity, (4) they were made with intent to mislead a party to rely thereon, and (5) such party relied on such representations with a right to rely thereon.

Clear and convincing evidence is usually required in suits to correct a mistake in a deed or other writing, on oral contracts to make a will, to establish the terms of a lost will, and for the specific performance of an oral contract.

§ 5.5 —Reasonable doubt

In criminal cases the guilt of the defendant must be established "beyond reasonable doubt." In a number of states[2] the trial judge reads to the jury the statutory definition of reasonable doubt as follows: "It is not a mere possible doubt; because everything relating to human affairs, and depending on moral evidence, is open to some possible or imaginary doubt. It is that state of the case, which, after the entire comparison and consideration of all the evidence, leaves the minds of jurors in that condition that they cannot say they feel an abiding conviction, to a moral certainty, of the truth of the charge."[3]

While some courts have declared that the "reasonable doubt" is almost incapable of any definition which will add to what the words themselves imply,[4] others have held that failure to give a clear and full instruction as to what is meant by "reasonable doubt" is reversible error. One approved definition is that which describes "reasonable doubt" as an honest, substantial doubt of the defendant's guilt, reasonably arising from the evidence or want of evidence, as opposed to a captious or possible doubt.[5]

In 1970 the U. S. Supreme Court traced the history of the "beyond a reasonable doubt" requirement and concluded that this standard of proof is indispensable to command the respect and confidence of the community in applications of criminal law.[5a]

---

[2] California Penal Code § 1096; Ohio Revised Code § 2945.05.

[3] This statutory definition has been taken from the charge of Chief Justice Shaw in Commonwealth v. Webster, 5 Cush. (Mass.) 295 (1850).

[4] Bater v. Bater, 2 AllEng.L.Rep. 458 (1950); State v. Sauer, 38 Minn. 438, 38 N.W. 355 (1888) see case in Part II.

[5] Lane v. State, 222 A.(2d) 263 (1966).

[5a] In re Winship, 397 U.S. 358, 51 OhioOp.(2d) 323 (1970). See case in Part II for a discussion of the history of the rule.

In making this a constitutional requirement the majority emphasized:

> Lest there remain any doubt about the constitutional stature of the reasonable doubt standard, we explicitly hold that the Due Process Clause protects the accused against conviction except upon proof beyond a reasonable doubt of every fact necessary to constitute the crime with which he is charged.

§ 5.6 Burden on prosecution

Throughout the trial the prosecution has the burden of proof and the obligation to convince the jury of the accused's guilt beyond a reasonable doubt as to all facts and circumstances essential to the guilt of the accused, including the criminal intent where a specific intent is an element of the crime charged. The failure of the accused to substantiate his defense does not relieve the prosecution from the burden to prove guilt beyond a reasonable doubt.

In a criminal case in which the prosecution relies solely on circumstantial evidence to establish guilt the defendant may argue that the proven circumstances must be such as to exclude every reasonable hypothesis but that of guilt.[6] The exclusion of every reasonable hypothesis other than that of guilt is no longer valid.[7] As stated by the United States Supreme Court in *Holland v. United States*:[8]

> Circumstantial evidence in this respect is intrinsically no different from testimonial evidence. Admittedly, circumstantial evidence may in some cases point to a wholly incorrect result. Yet this is equally true of testimonial evidence. In both instances, a jury is asked to weigh the chances that the evidence correctly points to guilt against the possibility of inaccuracy or ambiguous inference. In both, the jury must use its experience with people and events in weighing the probabilities. If the jury is convinced beyond a reasonable doubt, we can require no more.

§ 5.7 —Every element of crime

No person may be convicted of an offense unless each element

---

[6] Williams v. United States, 361 F.(2d) 280 (5th Cir. 1966).
[7] United States v. Lodwick, 410 F.(2d) 1202 (8th Cir. 1969).
[8] 348 U.S. 121, 99 L.Ed. 150, 75 S.Ct. 127 (1954).

of such offense is proved beyond a reasonable doubt. The prosecution has the burden to establish each of the essential elements of its case against the defendant beyond a reasonable doubt, and such right of the defendant is appropriately protected by proper instructions on reasonable doubt. Thus, under an indictment for rioting, the averment of unlawful assemblage, where this is a constituent part of the offense of riot, as well as that of subsequent riotous acts must be proved beyond a reasonable doubt before the accused can be convicted of riot.[9]

While the burden of proof does not shift in a criminal case, when the prosecution establishes a prima facie case it is then defendant's duty to go forward with the evidence to overcome the inferences reasonably to be drawn from the proven facts.

§ 5.8 Burden on accused

The older decisions have placed upon the accused the burden of proof with respect to matters of justification or excuse, and in a number of states there are statutes to this effect. The California statute[10] requires: "Upon a trial for murder, the commission of the homicide being proved, the burden of proving circumstances of mitigation, or that justify or excuse it devolves upon" the accused. In *Leland v. Oregon*[11] the Supreme Court held that an Oregon statute which required an accused pleading insanity to establish that defense beyond a reasonable doubt was not unconstitutional as against the due process clause of the Fourteenth Amendment.

Where the pertinent information is much more readily available to the defendant than to the prosecution, the burden of going forward with the evidence may be shifted to him, provided this can be done without subjecting the accused to hardship or oppression.[12] In an early case a federal statute provided that government allegations in forfeiture proceedings were to be taken as proved if a claimant refused to produce documents which the government

---

[9] State v. Smith, 97 OhioApp. 86, 55 OhioOp. 314, 121 N.E.(2d) 199 (1954).
  Also see U.S. v. Carter, 486 F.(2d) 1027 (1973).
[10] Calif. Penal Code § 1105. Texas has a similar statute. Tex. Vernon's Ann. P.C. art. 46.
[11] 343 U.S. 790, 96 L.Ed. 1302, 72 S.Ct. 1002 (1952).
[12] Morrison v. California, 291 U.S. 82, 78 L.Ed. 664, 54 S.Ct. 281 (1934).

said would tend to prove its allegations.[13] The Supreme Court held that forcing a claimant to give up documents which might well be incriminating, in order to refute government allegations which would result in loss of his property, was unconstitutional because it put pressure on the claimant to waive his privilege not to testify against himself. In two later cases[14] the Supreme Court upheld placing on the defendant the burden of showing justification for failure to produce books and records of an organization, but it does not appear in either case that he would have subjected himself to the danger of self-incrimination in discharging his burden.

On the other hand, in *Heikkinen* v. *United States*[15] an alien had been convicted under the Immigration Act of willfully failing to depart the United States within six months after he was ordered deported. He could not depart unless another country would accept his application for admission. The government showed that the alien made no such application but did not show that any country would have admitted him. The Supreme Court reversed the conviction for lack of evidence, saying "there can be no willful failure to depart until the country willing to receive the alien is identified."

§ 5.9 —Matters of defense

Certain matters of justification or excuse, such as intoxication, insanity, duress, self-defense, or being within an exception or proviso in the statute defining the crime, are frequently referred to as "affirmative defenses."

In some instances the burden of proving affirmative defenses by the preponderance of the evidence is placed on the defendant. Some courts, however, refuse to require the accused to prove such defenses by the preponderance of the evidence. In any event the accused has the burden of going forward with the evidence in order that the matters of defense be raised and submitted to the jury. At the close of the evidence the jurors must be told that if they have a reasonable doubt due to the "affirmative defense" evidence, they must acquit.[16]

---

[13] Boyd v. United States 116 U.S. 616, 29 L.Ed. 746, 6 S.Ct. 524 (1886).

[14] United States v. Fleischman, 339 U.S. 349, 94 L.Ed. 906, 70 S.Ct. 739 (1950); McPhaul v. United States, 364 U.S. 372, 5 L.Ed.(2d) 136, 81 S.Ct. 138 (1960).

[15] 355 U.S. 273, 2 L.Ed.(2d) 264, 78 S.Ct. 299 (1958).

[16] McCormick, EVIDENCE, p. 684.

In the sections that follow some of the matters of justification or excuse, sometimes referred to as "affirmative defenses" are discussed.

§ 5.10 —Alibi

Although alibi is more correctly a denial of participation in the criminal act than an affirmative defense, in some jurisdictions courts have held that the issue of alibi is an affirmative defense. When asserted in these states the burden to prove alibi by a preponderance of the evidence rests upon the defendant.[17]

In at least one U. S. Circuit Court of Appeals case, however, the justices agreed with the defense that to require the accused to prove his alibi by the preponderance of evidence violated the Due Process Clause.[18] If alibi is looked upon as only a denial of any connection with the crime, it seems logical that the defendant must be acquitted if his proof raises a reasonable doubt of guilt.[18a]

In one of the more recent decisions a Federal District Court refused to approve an instruction charging the jury that "alibi as a defense must be established to the reasonable satisfaction of the jury and must be such as reasonably to exclude the possibility of the presence of the defendant at the scene. . . ."[18b] Notwithstanding the fact that there was no "preponderance of the evidence" requirement there was *some* burden on the defendant to prove alibi and the conviction was set aside. This court reasoned that:

> Evidence of alibi should come into a case like any other evidence and must be submitted to the jury for consideration of whether the evidence as a whole on the issue of presence proves the defendant's guilt beyond a reasonable doubt.

Although there is still some question as to the classification of the alibi defense, it is apparent that a greater burden rests on the prosecutor to prove that the defendant *was* at the scene and less burden on the defendant to prove that he *was not*.

---

[17] State v. Stump, 254 Iowa 1181, 119 N.W.(2d) 210 (1963). See case in Part II.

[18] Stump v. Bennett, 398 F.(2d) 111 (1968).

[18a] Halko v. State, 54 Del. 180, 175 A.(2d) 42 (1961).

[18b] Smith v. Smith, Warden, 454 F.(2d) 572 (1971). *See* case in Part II.

§ 5.11 —Insanity

There are two distinct and divergent rules respecting the degree of evidence necessary to rebut the presumption of sanity normally prevailing in a criminal case. Under the first rule the ultimate burden of proof of sanity is, like any other element of the offense, upon the prosecution and must be shown beyond a reasonable doubt. The matter of defendant's insanity must be put in issue before the duty of the prosecution to prove sanity beyond a reasonable doubt will arise. Some evidence of insanity will suffice to dissipate the presumption of sanity and put the prosecution on its proof. In order for the defendant to raise the issue of insanity at all, he has the burden of producing some evidence sufficient to raise a doubt that as a result of mental disease or defect he lacked a substantial capacity to appreciate the wrongfulness of his conduct or conform it to the requirements of law.[19]

When the defendant introduces substantial evidence of his insanity, the issue of his capacity to commit the offense becomes a question of proof and the prosecution's burden of going forward with the evidence requires it to introduce sufficient evidence on the issue of sanity to preclude a verdict of acquittal for the defendant.[20]

A considerable number of courts, however, hold that insanity is an affirmative defense which must be shown by defendant by a preponderance of the evidence.

§ 5.12 Sufficiency of evidence

In determining the sufficiency of the evidence to sustain a conviction the question is not whether evidence forecloses all possibility of doubt but whether the evidence, construed most favorably for the prosecution, is such that a jury might find the defendant guilty beyond a reasonable doubt.[21]

In criminal cases involving defendant's sanity, in order to remove a case from a jury's consideration, a judge must conclude that on the basis of the evidence reasonable men must necessarily possess a

---

[19] United States v. Currier, 405 F.(2d) 1039 (2d Cir. 1969).
[20] United States v. Westerhausen, 283 F.(2d) 844 (7th Cir. 1960).
[21] Wallace v. United States, 281 F.(2d) 656 (4th Cir. 1960).

reasonable doubt as to defendant's sanity and that reasonable men must conclude that the prosecution has failed to sustain its burden of proving beyond a reasonable doubt that the accused had a capacity to commit the crime. The quantum and nature of proof the prosecution must offer to take the case to the jury varies in different situations and to some degree depends upon the quantum and nature of the proof the defendant offers.[22]

§ 5.13 Summary

The burden of proving the accused guilty beyond a reasonable doubt is always on the prosecution and never shifts to the defense in a criminal case. This is one of the primary differences between the criminal and the civil case, as in a civil case the plaintiff has only the burden of proving his claim by a preponderance or by the greater weight of evidence.

There are many definitions for reasonable doubt but in effect the prosecution has the responsibility of presenting such strong evidence that the jury will honestly find to a moral certainty that the charges placed against the defendant are true. The burden is on the prosecution not only to prove guilt but to establish each of the essential elements of the charge against the defendant. This burden does not shift at any time. However, the defense does have the responsibility of going forward with the evidence if a defense is raised in order to submit the matter to the jury.

Recognizing this additional burden on the part of the prosecution, law enforcement investigators must obtain sufficient admissible evidence to convince the jury or the judge not only that the accused is probably guilty of the offense charged but that he is guilty beyond any reasonable doubt. This means that the investigator should do more than convince himself that the accused committed the crime charged; he must have such convincing admissible evidence that the jury, too, will be persuaded to the extent as required by law. This must be accomplished with the knowledge that the defense will make every effort to create that doubt which will be sufficient to cause the jury to find the accused not guilty.

---

[22] United States v. Westerhausen, n. 20, *supra.*

Chapter 6

DIRECT AND CIRCUMSTANTIAL EVIDENCE

> At the trial of a person charged with murder, the fact of death is provable by circumstantial evidence, notwithstanding that neither the body nor any trace of the body has been found and that the accused has made no confession of any participation in the crime. Before he can be convicted, the fact of death should be proved by such circumstances as render the commission of the crime morally certain and leave no ground for possible doubt; the circumstantial evidence should be so cogent and compelling as to convince a jury that upon no rational hypothesis other than murder can the facts be accounted for.
> *Rex v. Horry,* 1952 N.Z.L.R. 111.

Section

6.1 Introduction
6.2 Direct and circumstantial evidence distinguished
6.3 Sufficiency of circumstantial evidence
6.4 Character evidence in criminal cases
6.5 Proof of defendant's reputation
6.6 Reputation of victim of crime
6.7 Habit or custom of person
6.8 Similar or related acts or circumstances
6.9 — Other offenses of defendant
6.10 — Intent, motive, or knowledge
6.11 — Identity
6.12 — Remoteness of other offenses
6.13 — Probative value
6.14 Summary

§ 6.1 Introduction

The fact that evidence is characterized as direct or circumstantial does not mean, as some think, that circumstantial evidence is not reliable. Although it is true that all things being equal, direct evidence is generally better, circumstantial evidence has a definite place in the trial of criminal cases. History is replete with examples of convictions based exclusively on circumstantial evidence.

The value of circumstantial evidence is obvious when one considers that crimes are generally not committed in the open. Law enforcement officers would be pleased if every crime were witnessed by someone who could testify that he saw the acts which made up the crime. But in some cases, such as burglary cases, it would be impossible to convict without the use of circumstantial evidence.

There is often the mistaken belief that direct evidence always has more weight than circumstantial evidence. In some instances, circumstantial evidence can be more persuasive than direct evidence. For example, if an unbiased witness testifies that he saw the accused near the scene at the approximate time of the crime, such evidence would be considered circumstantial. But this would probably have more weight in the eyes of the jury than testimony of an obviously biased witness who stated that he saw the crime committed and the accused did not commit the crime.

In this chapter direct and circumstantial evidence are defined and cases which distinguish the types are discussed. In addition rules and related cases concerning "character" evidence, "habit" evidence, and evidence concerning similar or related acts are considered. Even though such evidence is circumstantial, it is admissible under certain well-defined limitations and certainly is pertinent in determining the guilt or innocence of the accused.

§ 6.2 Direct and circumstantial evidence distinguished

Direct evidence proves a fact without inference. Direct evidence is that which is applied to the fact to be proved, immediately and directly, and without the aid of any intervening fact or process: as where, on a trial for murder, a witness positively testifies he saw the accused inflict the mortal wound or administer the poison.

Circumstantial evidence is that which is applied to the principal fact, indirectly, or through the medium of other facts, from which the principal fact is inferred. Circumstantial evidence is testimony not based on actual personal knowledge or observation of the facts in controversy, but of other facts from which deductions are drawn, showing indirectly the facts sought to be proved. The characteristics of circumstantial evidence, as distinguished from that which is direct, are, first, the existence and presentation of one or more evi-

§ 6.2

dentiary facts; and, second, a process of inference, by which these facts are so connected with the fact sought as to tend to produce a persuasion of its truth.¹

After making this distinction between direct evidence and circumstantial evidence it must be quickly pointed out that all that is required of the jury is that it weigh all of the evidence, direct or circumstantial, against a standard of reasonable doubt.²

The *Holland* case (cited in the footnote) was referred to in a 1969 Circuit Court case where the court held:³⁻⁶

> Thus the trial court properly instructed the jury that "the law makes no distinction between direct and circumstantial evidence but simply requires that the jury be satisfied of the defendant's guilt beyond a reasonable doubt from all of the evidence in the case," including "such reasonable inferences as seem justified, in the light of your own experiences."

There is no doubt that under the existing decisions some circumstantial evidence may be equally or more reliable than direct evidence. And as the Circuit Court of Appeals in the above mentioned case stated it would be wholly irrational to impose an absolute bar upon the use of circumstantial evidence to prove any fact, including a fact from which another fact is to be inferred. Therefore, either direct evidence or circumstantial evidence may be used to prove the fact in issue and likewise either direct or circumstantial evidence may fail to prove the fact in issue.

The classification of circumstantial and direct evidence is not mutually exclusive, since testimony may be direct evidence of one fact, and circumstantial of another. As an example, a witness' testimony that the accused fled from the scene of a murder is direct evidence of his flight and at the same time circumstantial evidence of guilt.

---

¹ People v. Goldstein, 139 Cal.App. (2d) 146, 293 P.(2d) 495 (1956); State v. Famber, 358 Mo. 288, 214 S.W.(2d) 40 (1948).
People v. Christiansen, 118 Ill. App. (2d) 151, 254 N.E.(2d) 156 (1969).

² Holland v. U.S., 348 U.S. 121, 75 S.Ct. 127 (1954).

³⁻⁶ U.S. v. Nelson, 419 F.(2d) 1237 (1969). See case in Part II.

§ 6.3 Sufficiency of circumstantial evidence

Direct evidence is not necessary to sustain a conviction. The law recognizes that circumstantial evidence is of value equal to direct evidence. As was said by the court in *United States v. Burch*:[7]

> "Circumstantial evidence, if strong enough to convince the trier of the facts of a defendant's guilt beyond a reasonable doubt, is sufficient to sustain a finding of guilt."

But mere suspicion is not sufficient to sustain a conviction. Thus, evidence consisting of circumstantial evidence sufficient to establish a suspicion that the defendant, after the robbery, might have rendered some assistance to a party who admitted the robbery is insufficient to sustain conviction.[8] Likewise, the mere fact of previous acquaintance between an admitted bank robber and the defendant is not sufficient to sustain a conviction.[9]

In every criminal case the defendant is protected by the presumption of innocence, and consistently therewith, the jury must be informed of the effect of circumstantial evidence offered by the prosecution. The trial judge in most state courts gives an instruction in substance as follows: "Where circumstantial evidence is relied upon by the prosecution it must be irreconcilable with the theory of innocence in order to furnish a sound basis for conviction." In the famous Dr. Sam Sheppard case the trial judge gave the following charge to the jury:[10]

> It is for you to determine how much of circumstantial evidence adduced in this case is credible and what fair inferences are to be drawn from it. You are instructed that any inference drawn must in every instance be drawn from a proven or established fact. In other words, you are not to draw a second or further inference upon an inference but that is not to say that you are confined to drawing only one inference from one fact. There is no limit to the number of independent inferences that may be drawn from a fact. The rule is simply that every inference must be drawn from, and based on, a fact and that once having drawn an inference one may not draw a second inference from the first. It is necessary

---

[7] 313 F.(2d) 628 (6th Cir. 1963).
[8] United States v. Grimes, 332 F.(2d) 1014 (6th Cir. 1964).
[9] *Ibid.*
[10] State v. Sheppard, 165 OhioSt. 293, 59 OhioOp. 398, 135 N.E.(2d) 340 (1956).

that you keep in mind, and you are so instructed, that where circumstantial evidence is adduced it, together with all other evidence, must convince you on the issue involved beyond a reasonable doubt and that where circumstantial evidence alone is relied upon in the proof of any element essential to a finding of guilt such evidence, together with any and all other evidence in the case, and with all the facts and circumstances of the case as found by you must be such as to convince you beyond a reasonable doubt and be consistent only with the theory of guilt and inconsistent with any theory of innocence. If evidence is equally consistent with the theory of innocence as it is with the theory of guilt it is to be resolved in favor of the theory of innocence.

While some states hold otherwise, it is now well settled in the federal courts that circumstantial evidence need not be inconsistent with every reasonable conclusion except that of guilt, provided it does establish a case from which the jury can find the defendant guilty beyond a reasonable doubt.[11]

All doubts concerning the federal requirement were clarified in the case of *U.S. v. Nelson* which held that where the jury is properly instructed on the standards of reasonable doubt but in addition an instruction is given that if the evidence is circumstantial it must be such as to exclude every reasonable hypothesis other than that of guilt such instruction is confusing and incorrect. Citing a Supreme Court case the Nelson Court emphasized that the Supreme Court did more than reject the particular instruction; it clearly stated that no instruction is to be given distinguishing the manner in which direct and circumstantial evidence are to be weighed.[11a]

§ 6.4 Character evidence in criminal cases

In the chapter on relevancy and materiality the rules concerning the admissibility of evidence relating to character, reputation, and other crimes were discussed as they relate to the relevancy

---

[11] Holland v. United States, 348 U.S. 121, 99 L.Ed. 150, 75 S.Ct. 127 (1954); United States v. Olivo, 278 F.(2d) 415 (3d Cir. 1960); United States v. Luxenberg, 374 F.(2d) 241 (6th Cir. 1967); U.S. v. Taylor, 482 F.(2d) 1376 (1973). But see State v. Slaughter, 70 Wash.(2d) 606, 425 P.(2d) 876 (1967). See case in Part II.

[11a] U.S. v. Nelson, 419 F.(2d) 1237 (1969). See case in Part II.

question. It was pointed out there that although such evidence is often relevant, it is sometimes excluded for other reasons.

Over the years the courts have developed rules concerning character evidence which attempt to balance the desirability of having all relevant evidence admitted at the trial against the possible dangers of prejudice, distraction, and injustice. Because of the dangers involved, considerable latitude is allowed in the reception of this type of circumstantial evidence.

In the following sections some of the rules relating to character and reputation evidence will be discussed and specific examples examined.

Although the words "character" and "reputation" are frequently used interchangeably, they are not synonymous. "Character" may be defined as consisting of the qualities which make up an individual, while "reputation" implies the sum of the opinions concerning him. In brief, character is what a person is; reputation is what people believe he is.

In criminal cases the evil character of the defendant cannot in the first instance be used by the prosecution to establish the probability of his guilt, and the whole matter of the defendant's character, disposition, and reputation is closed to the prosecution and can be put in issue only by the defendant. If the defendant testifies as a witness in his own behalf, his general reputation, like that of any other witness, for truth and veracity in the community where he resides, among his friends, neighbors and acquaintances, and the people with whom he transacts business, may be shown.[12]

Under the Federal Rules of Evidence, evidence of a person's character or a trait of his character is not admissible for the purpose of proving that he acted in conformity therewith on a particular occasion. However, there are some exceptions to this rule. One exception is that evidence of a pertinent trait of his character may be offered by the accused or by the prosecution to rebut the same.[12a]

When the defendant calls character witnesses who testify to his

---

[12] United States v. Harris, 331 F. (2d) 185 (4th Cir. 1964).

[12a] Rule 404 Fed. Rules of Evidence.

good character in general, the prosecution can meet this evidence by the introduction of witnesses who contradict such testimony; but, in the absence of character witnesses introduced by the defendant, the prosecution is not entitled to introduce testimony concerning the defendant's bad character. The purpose of proving the good reputation of an accused in a criminal case is to establish a general character which is inconsistent with guilt. It is not proof of innocence, but it may be such as to raise a reasonable doubt as to guilt.[13] It is well settled that when a defendant in a criminal case offers evidence of his good character, it is prejudicial error for the trial judge to refuse to instruct the jury that such evidence, when considered with other evidence, may in itself be sufficient to create a reasonable doubt.[14]

In criminal cases the question also arises as to the admissibility of evidence relating to the character of the victim. Under the Federal Rules as adopted by the Supreme Court evidence of a pertinent trait of character of the victim of the crime offered by an accused, or by the prosecution to rebut the same, or evidence of a character trait of peacefulness of the victim offered by the prosecution in a homicide case to rebut evidence that the victim was the first aggressor also may be admitted. Before such evidence can be admitted, however, a foundation must be laid for its admission.[14a]

§ 6.5 Proof of defendant's reputation

When the defendant elects to initiate a character inquiry, not only is he permitted to call witnesses to testify from hearsay, but such witnesses are not allowed to base their testimony on anything but hearsay. Character witnesses are not permitted to testify to their own opinions as to whether a defendant is a person of good character, but only as to the defendant's reputation in the community in which the defendant lives for such qualities as peacefulness, sobriety, dependability, honesty, and good character generally.

A witness may not testify about a defendant's specific acts or

---

[13] Edgington v. United States, 164 U.S. 361, 41 L.Ed. 467, 17 S.Ct. 72 (1896).

[14] Bird City Equity Merchantile Exchange v. United States, 338 F.(2d) 790 (10th Cir. 1964).

United States v. Lewis, 482 F.(2d) 632 (1973).

[14a] Rule 404(a)(2) Fed. Rules of Evidence. Also see Chapter 8 for a discussion of the use of character evidence in impeachment situations.

courses of conduct or his possession of a particular disposition, or of benign mental and moral traits; nor can he testify that his own acquaintance, observation, and knowledge of a defendant leads to his own independent opinion that a defendant possesses a good general or specific character, inconsistent with commission of acts charged. Thus, in a prosecution for murder, proffered testimony by a defendant's employer as to the defendant's conduct as an employee and activities in his own home is not admissible as character evidence.[15] Although the general rule is that specific instances of conduct are not admissible, in cases in which character or a trait of character of a person is an essential element of the charge, claim, or defense, proof may be made of specific instances of his conduct.[16]

The community in which a man lives, for the purpose of determining admissibility of character evidence, is not necessarily a geographical unit, but is rather composed of those relationships with others which arise where a man works, worships, shops, relaxes, and lives. The reputation to be proved should be the defendant's reputation in the community in which he lives at the time of the alleged crime or shortly preceding that time.[17]

The character witness must qualify to testify as to defendant's reputation by showing such acquaintance with the defendant, the community in which he has lived, and the circles in which he has moved, as to speak with authority. To require affirmative knowledge of the reputation may seem inconsistent with the latitude given to a character witness when all he can say of the reputation is that he has "heard nothing against the defendant." This negative evidence is permitted upon the assumption that, if no ill is reported of one, his reputation must be good. But this type of testimony is accepted only from a witness whose knowledge of defendant's habitat and surroundings is intimate enough so that his failure to hear of any relevant ill repute is an assurance that no ugly rumors were about.

The character trait as to which evidence is admissible must be relevant to the trait of character which is in question, and bear

---

[15] United States v. White, 225 F. Supp. 514 (D.C. 1963).

[16] Rule 405(b) Fed. Rules of Evidence.

[17] Lomax v. United States, 37 App. D.C. 414 (1911).

Awkard v. United States, 352 F. (2d) 641 (1965).

analogy and reference to the nature of the charge. Numerous cases illustrating the rule that character evidence is confined to traits relevant to the crime in question involve chaste character to repel a charge of rape, and peaceable character against a charge of murder by violence. In a statutory rape case it is proper to exclude evidence of the reputation of accused for truth and veracity.[18] Likewise, where the defendant puts his good character in issue by introducing evidence to sustain the same, the prosecutor, in attacking the character of the accused, must be confined to his general reputation for the particular traits involved in the offense charged.[19]

§ 6.6 Reputation of victim of crime

In a homicide case the accused, after offering evidence that he acted in self-defense, may introduce evidence that the deceased was reputed to be a violent and dangerous person. If this reputation was known to the defendant, the knowledge is a factor to be considered in determining whether he reasonably apprehended bodily harm.[20] Regardless of whether the defendant knew of the victim's reputation, such evidence is admissible to show that the victim probably was the aggressor. The law recognizes the well-established fact in human experience that the known reputation of an assailant as to violence has a very material bearing on the degree and nature of the apprehension of danger on the part of a person assaulted.[21]

In a rape case, where the defense is that the prosecutrix voluntarily submitted to intercourse, the defendant may show the unchaste character of the prosecutrix to support the inference that consent was probable. Generally, evidence of specific acts is not admissible for this purpose; proof must be by reputation. In California, however, the courts have admitted the usual evidence of reputation for unchastity as well as evidence of specific acts.

When the defendant introduces evidence of the bad reputation of the victim of the crime, the prosecutor may in rebuttal offer evidence of the victim's good reputation.

---

[18] State v. Howland, 157 Kan. 11, 138 P.(2d) 424 (1943).
[19] State v. Williams, 337 Mo. 884, 87 S.W.(2d) 175 (1935).
[20] People v. Gibson, 385 Ill. 371, 52 N.E.(2d) 1008 (1944).
[21] People v. Brophy, 122 Cal.App. (2d) 638, 265 P.(2d) 593 (1954). See Rule 404(a)(2) Fed. Rules of Evidence.

§ 6.7 Habit or custom of person

As in the case of character evidence, certain evidence concerning human habit or custom is competent, even though circumstantial. Habit evidence refers to routine acts in particular situations and differs from character evidence in that character evidence refers to the quality of a person's conduct in general. As in the case of character evidence the judge is given great latitude in determining if such evidence is to be admitted.

In the following sections, the rules are discussed further and specific instances where such evidence has been considered proper are summarized.

Habit, in contrast with character, may be defined as a settled way of doing a particular thing. Evidence of a person's habit or custom is admissible to prove that his behavior on a specified occasion conformed to that habit or custom.[21a] Whether such evidence is admissible depends upon the invariable regularity of the habit or custom. To be admissible the habit or custom must have sufficient regularity to make it probable that it would be carried out in every instance or in most instances. For example, in an action for criminal conversation, the prosecutor called as a witness the hotel room clerk, who was on duty when the defendant registered with complainant's wife, to prove the presence of luggage. The clerk testified that the room was not paid for in advance and that it was the uniform practice of the hotel to require payment in advance for lodging when the registrant was without luggage.[22]

Habit or custom evidence as to a routine followed in a business is admissible as tending to prove that it was followed on the occasion in question. Thus, to prove that a store made no sale on a particular occasion, testimony was admitted to show that it was customary to give a sales slip with each purchase and that there were no register records of sales.[23] However, evidence of the existence of a routine standing alone is not sufficient to prove what was done on the particular occasion; some corroboration that the routine was then followed is usually necessary.

[21a] See Rule 406 Fed. Rules of Evidence.

[22] Baldridge v. Matthews, 378 Pa. 566, 106 A.(2d) 809 (1954).

[23] Commonwealth v. Torrealba, 316 Mass. 24, 54 N.E.(2d) 939 (1944).

§ 6.7   CRIMINAL EVIDENCE FOR POLICE   82

Negative evidence as to habit, custom and procedure may create a presumption that the ordinary course of business or procedure was followed on a given day. In a taxpayer's suit for refund of income taxes, evidence of the habit and customs of court officers and employees showing in detail that their methods of handling mail arriving at the Court of Claims, including testimony as to the placing of dates thereon, was not sufficient to overcome the presumption that the taxpayer's petition, properly mailed in time to arrive at the court before the expiration of the two-year statute of limitations but stamped one day after the expiration of such period, had arrived in due course of mails.[24]

Evidence with respect to customs and practice of a trade is admissible when offered by a competent witness. In a wrongful death action brought by the administrator of the estate of a decedent who died while accidentally locked in the body of his truck which had been remodeled for him by the defendant contractor, a witness who had been in the business of building truck bodies, some of them of insulated type, for thirty-five years, and who had studied literature concerning the construction of insulated bodies was competent to testify as to the custom and usage of the trade with respect to installation of safety releases on the inside of doors of insulated truck bodies.[25]

Generally, evidence of the habit of exercising or not exercising care is not admissible. For example in a manslaughter case where death occurred while hunting, the defendant was not permitted to prove by the testimony of his hunting companions that he was a careful hunter and that his reputation for care in hunting was good.[26]

Courts in some states will admit habit testimony when there are no eyewitnesses to an accident. In wrongful death actions evidence of the deceased's habits is admissible as a circumstance tending to prove his freedom from contributory negligence,[27] or to prove his

---

[24] Charlson Realty Co. v. United States, 384 F.(2d) 434 (U.S.C.C., 1967).

[25] Frankel v. Styer, 386 F.(2d) 151 (3d Cir. 1967). In Pressley v. Bloomington & N. Ry. etc. Co., 271 Ill. 622, 111 N.E. 511 (1916) the court admitted evidence of the customary and approved method of constructing high voltage lines.

[26] State v. Lewis, 37 Wash.(2d) 540, 225 P.(2d) 428 (1950).

[27] Hardware State Bank v. Cotner, 55 Ill. 240, 302 N.E.2d 257 (1973); contra: Tresise v. Ashdown, 118 Ohio St. 307, 160 N.E. 898 (1928), where the court rejected evidence of the care usually exercised by the deceased in operating his motorcycle.

negligence.[28]

§ 6.8 Similar or related acts or circumstances

In studying the rules relating to the admissibility of evidence concerning similar or related acts or circumstances it is preferable to state the general rule and then discuss the exceptions. The general rule is that evidence of other acts, even of a similar nature, is not competent to prove the commission of a particular act charged against the defendant. And the general rule has long been established that *res inter alios acta* are incompetent evidence. This is not to say, however, that all evidence of similar or related acts is inadmissible. There are definite and specific limitations upon the general rules. Some of these exceptions are discussed here.

Evidence of similar acts, including other crimes, is admissible when it is substantially relevant for a purpose other than merely to show defendant's criminal character or disposition[29] or to raise an inference that he was likely to commit a crime. Under the Federal Rules evidence of other crimes, wrongs or acts is not admissible to prove the character of a person in order to show he acted in conformity therewith. But this does not exclude evidence of other crimes, wrongs or acts when offered for other purposes such as proof of motive, opportunity, intent, preparation, plan, knowledge, identity or absence of mistake or accident.[30-34]

§ 6.9 — Other offenses of defendant

The well-established common-law rule is that in a criminal prosecution proof which shows or tends to show that the accused is guilty of the commission of other crimes is incompetent and inadmissible for the purpose of showing the commission of the crime charged. The exceptions to this rule are related in the following paragraphs.

A person charged with a particular crime generally has the right

---

[28] Boone v. Bank of America, 220 Cal. 93, 29 P.(2d) 409 (1934), in which the court admitted evidence of the deceased's habit of driving his motorcycle at excessive speed on the highway in the vicinity of the fatal accident.

[29] United States v. Cuadrado, 413 F.(2d) 633 (2d Cir. 1969).

[30-34] Rule 404(b), Fed. Rules of Evidence.

to require the prosecution to limit its evidence to that offense only, and he should not be required to defend against evidence of other unrelated criminal acts. However, evidence of other criminal acts may be admissible to prove the accused guilty of the crime charged, to connect him with the crime, or to prove some particular element or material fact of the crime. For example, evidence that the defendant, charged with interstate transportation of a stolen automobile, had used stolen credit cards for identification in renting automobiles approximately one month prior to committing the charged offense involving substantially the same methods, was admissible to show his intent and course of conduct.[35]

The majority of courts express their "other crimes" rule in an exclusory form, that is, evidence of other crimes is not admissible except for a host of purposes.[36] Because the exceptions are so numerous, it is difficult to determine whether the doctrine should be stated in reverse. A minority of courts has adopted the inclusory form of the rule, that is, that evidence of other crimes is admissible except when offered solely to prove criminal character.[37] Commentators have criticized the rule of general exclusion and have suggested a broader range of admissibility.[38] Whichever method is adopted, the trial judge is required, as with any potentially prejudicial evidence, to balance all of the relevant factors to determine whether the probative value of the evidence of other crimes is outweighed by its prejudicial character.

Where evidence of another offense is relevant and competent to prove and to establish a material fact for which the defendant is charged, and the other offense is inextricably a part of the guilty act itself, the court will allow testimony relating to the other offense. Thus, in a murder case the court did admit evidence that on the night of the murder defendant participated in the theft of a 1967 Thunderbird automobile with red bucket seats, where the prosecution contended that it was in this automobile that the victim was picked up by defendant and from which he was pushed and

---

[35] United States v. Coleman, 410 F.(2d) 1133 (10th Cir. 1969).

[36] See summary in Spencer v. State of Texas, 385 U.S. 554, 17 L.Ed.(2d) 606, 87 S.Ct. 648 (1967). See case in Part II.

[37] United States v. Deaton, 381 F.(2d) 114 (2d Cir. 1967).

[38] Spencer v. State of Texas, n. 36, *supra*.

shot. The theft of the car was a crime which was an inseparable part of the whole deed.[39]

§ 6.10 —Intent, motive, or knowledge

As the intent with which an act is done is rarely if ever susceptible of proof by direct evidence, it must be ascertained from outward manifestations—from words or acts of a party in accomplishing the act and from the facts and circumstances attendant upon the act. Where intent and guilty knowledge are essential elements of the offense charged, evidence of similar offenses closely connected with the offense charged and tending to show criminal intent or guilty knowledge is admissible. In one case[40] a federal court held that where a package of blank checks of a corporation had been stolen from an automobile of the corporation's employee, evidence that defendant had cashed three of such checks, other than the check on which the charge was based, was admissible since it tended to establish intent.

The general rule that evidence of another crime unconnected with the one on trial is inadmissible is subject to a number of exceptions, the first of which is that evidence of other offenses by the accused is admissible to show his criminal intent as to the offense charged, where the other offenses are similar to and not too remote from that charged, and where intent is in issue as an element of the offense charged. Another exception is where the evidence of a separate crime tends to explain, illustrate, or characterize the act charged when such act is capable of more than one construction. Another is to rebut a claim of mistake or inadvertence. An exception also applies where the crime charged is one of a series of swindles or other crimes involving a fraudulent intent, or where the crime charged is part of a plan or system of criminal action. As was said by Judge McGowan in *Drew v. United States*,[41]

> Evidence of other crimes is admissible when relevant to (1) motive, (2) intent, (3) the absence of mistake or accident, (4) a common scheme or plan embracing the commis-

---

[39] Ignacio v. People of Territory of Guam, 413 F.(2d) 513 (9th Cir. 1969).

[40] United States v. Spica, 413 F.(2d) 129 (8th Cir. 1969).

[41] 118 U.S. App. D.C. 11, 331 F.(2d) 85 (1964).

sion of two or more crimes so related to each other that proof of the one tends to establish the other, and (5) the identity of the person charged with the commission of the crime on trial. When the evidence is relevant and important to one of these five issues, it is generally conceded that the prejudicial effect may be outweighed by the probative value.

It is well settled that a prior offense of a like nature to that charged may be proved to show guilty intent. This is particularly true in White Slave Traffic Act cases.[42] In a Dyer Act prosecution evidence as to two previous trips across state lines with rented automobiles, one of which resulted in conviction and one of which did not, was admissible to show defendant's manner of operation, as such evidence would tend to shed light on presence or absence of criminal intent.[43] Some specific examples of cases where evidence of other crimes was admitted are stated in the paragraphs which follow.

Evidence of defendant's previous assault and battery upon his purported wife was relevant in a voluntary manslaughter prosecution arising out of his alleged stabbing of her to show his state of mind and probable intent and also to show motive, identity of the aggressor, and the absence of any mistake or accident.[44]

Evidence of numerous similar transactions, objected to by defendant charged with making false entries with intent to defraud a federally insured bank, which were attributable to her manipulations and falsifications of books and records of the bank, were admissible to show an intent on her part to injure or defraud the bank.[45] In a prosecution for the sale of illegal drugs, evidence of defendant's sale to federal agents of non-narcotic illegal drugs was admissible to show common scheme, plan or design, and state of mind and intent, although the other crimes established did not require the element of intent.[46]

Despite its prejudicial effect, evidence of other crimes is admissible to establish motive if it is of high relevance. For example,

---

[42] United States v. Jackson, 344 F.(2d) 922 (6th Cir. 1965).
[43] United States v. Welborn, 322 F.(2d) 910 (4th Cir. 1963).
[44] Wakaksan v. United States, 367 F.(2d) 639 (8th Cir. 1966).
[45] United States v. Kirkpatrick, 361 F.(2d) 866 (6th Cir. 1966).
[46] Robinson v. United States, 366 F.(2d) 575 (10th Cir. 1966).

evidence with regard to the armed robbery of a restaurant was prejudicial to the defendants charged with the federal felony offense of kidnapping, but was highly relevant and was introduced for the proper purpose of showing motive for two men to intrude upon a strange residence late in the nighttime, abduct three adults, lock them in the trunk of an automobile, and transport them across state boundaries.[47] One of the more frequently cited cases is *Suhay v. United States*,[48] which was an appeal from a conviction of murder in the first degree. The defendant and a companion were on parole from a sentence for armed robbery, and robbed a person of a car and then held up a bank. The officer who attempted to arrest the two was killed, and the trial was for this crime. The trial court permitted evidence to be introduced concerning the commission by defendant of the several crimes which preceded the murder. The defendant urged that this evidence was of separate crimes and that it was prejudicial. The court held that this evidence tended to show that the defendants killed the officer to avoid arrest and with premeditation. The trial court, when the evidence was admitted and as part of the instructions at the end of the trial, instructed the jury that it was to be considered only as bearing on the question of motive.

§ 6.11 —Identity

Proof of conduct similar to that charged, which is peculiar, unique, or bizarre, is admissible to tend to prove identity. In the trial of a defendant charged with armed robbery of national banks, including charges that he forced six different hostages to accompany him into banks to assist in the robberies, the prosecution called a witness who testified as to defendant's similar acts several months after those charged in the indictment. The court admitted such testimony to prove defendant's modus operandi and to aid in establishing his identity. Defendant's actions in relation to the witness were identical to those alleged in the indictment.[49]

When two crimes arise out of the same set of events, if the facts surrounding the two crimes on trial show that there is a reasonable probability that the same person committed both crimes due to

---

[47] Reed v. United States, 364 F.(2d) 630 (9th Cir. 1966).
[48] 95 F.(2d) 890 (10th Cir. 1938); certiorari denied, 304 U.S. 580, 82 L.Ed. 1543, 58 S.Ct. 1060.
[49] Parker v. United States, 400 F.(2d) 248 (9th Cir. 1968).

the concurrence of unusual and distinctive facts relating to the manner in which the crimes were committed, the evidence of one is admissible in the trial of the other to prove identity.[50]

§ 6.12 —Remoteness of other offenses

Prior or subsequent, the similar act should not be too remote in point of time from the offense charged. Evidence of other offenses by the accused is admissible to show his criminal intent as to the offense charged, where the other offenses are similar to and not too remote from that charged, and where intent is in issue as an element of the offense charged. A prior offense of forgery, although committed five years before the forgery offense charged, was held not too remote in time to be admitted on the issue of intent to defraud.[51] One court, however, has decided that evidence of a similar offense is admissible only if it occurred very shortly before or very shortly after the offense charged.[52]

§ 6.13 —Probative value

Evidence of crimes other than the one charged must have a real probative value and not just a possible worth on issues of intent, motive, absence of mistake or accident, or to establish a scheme or plan. The admissibility of this kind of evidence is a matter in which the trial judge should be allowed a wide range of discretion. The exercise of discretion must be addressed to a balancing of the probative value of the proffered evidence, on the one hand, against its prejudicial character, on the other. The probative value is measured by the extent to which the evidence of prior criminal activities, other than a conviction, closely related in time and subject matter, tends to establish that the accused committed the criminal act charged in the indictment knowingly or with criminal intent or tends to negate the claim that the acts were committed innocently or through mistake or misunderstanding.

It is generally recognized that there can be no complete assurance that the jury, even under the best of instructions, will strictly confine the use of this kind of evidence to the issue of

---

[50] Drew v. United States, 331 F.(2d) 272 (5th Cir. 1968).
F.(2d) 85 (D.C. Cir. 1964).
[51] Miller v. United States, 397 F.(2d) 416 (7th Cir. 1968).
[52] United States v. Cobb, 397

knowledge and intent and wholly put out of their minds the implication that the accused, having committed the prior similar criminal act, probably committed the one with which he is actually charged.[53]

§ 6.14 Summary

Direct evidence proves a fact without any inference while circumstantial evidence is that which is applied to the principal fact indirectly or through the medium of other facts.

Although it might be argued that direct evidence is generally more desirable, certainly direct evidence is not necessary to sustain a conviction. All that is required is that the circumstantial (and/or direct) evidence be strong enough to convince the trier of the facts of the defendant's guilt beyond a reasonable doubt.

One type of circumstantial evidence is that designated as "character" evidence. In a criminal case the character of the defendant cannot in the first instance be used by the prosecution to establish the probability of guilt. But when the defendant calls witnesses to testify as to his good character, the prosecution can introduce evidence to rebut such testimony.

Evidence of a person's habits or custom is generally admissible to prove that his behavior on a specified occasion conformed to that habit or custom, but only under strictly regulated conditions and at the discretion of the judge. And under like reasoning evidence of similar or related acts which have a relevant and material bearing upon a fact in issue is generally admissible.

In a special category is evidence of other offenses. Although the general rule is that such evidence is not admissible, exceptions authorize the use of evidence of other crimes to establish some element of the present crime charged, as opposed merely to showing that the defendant had a criminal propensity. Examples of evidence authorized under this exception include (1) evidence of a common scheme, (2) evidence of a state of mind, (3) evidence concerning identity of the accused and (4) evidence to show lack of mistake.

The law enforcement investigator will not always find direct

---

[53] United States v. Byrd, 352 F.(2d) 570 (2d Cir. 1965).

evidence to prove the defendant guilty of a crime and must of necessity rely on circumstantial evidence. His concern is not so much whether the evidence is circumstantial but whether there is sufficient admissible evidence of whatever classification to reasonably convince the trier of facts.

Concerning evidence of character and reputation, the knowledgeable investigator recognizes that he cannot rely on the bad reputation of defendant to obtain a conviction but that a careful background check is necessary in order to give the prosecutor sufficient information with which to rebut defendant's evidence of good character. He must also be able to rebut evidence relating to the bad reputation of the deceased victim in a homicide case.

Although the investigator cannot build his case on similar or related acts he certainly should investigate the other related acts. Some evidence of this type is admissible for specific purposes. This could be just the additional evidence required to convince the jury of the defendant's guilt.

Chapter 7

SUBSTITUTES FOR EVIDENCE

JUDICIAL NOTICE

Section

- 7.1 Introduction
- 7.2 Judicial notice defined
- 7.3 Judicial notice of facts
- 7.4 —Matters of common knowledge
- 7.5 —Historical facts
- 7.6 —Geographical facts
- 7.7 —Scientific facts
- 7.8 —Words and phrases
- 7.9 Judicial notice of laws
- 7.10 —Federal law
- 7.11 —Law of sister states
- 7.12 —Law of foreign countries
- 7.13 —Municipal ordinances
- 7.14 —Administrative regulations
- 7.15 —Jurisdiction of courts
- 7.16 —Court records
- 7.17 Summary

PRESUMPTIONS, INFERENCES, AND STIPULATIONS

Section

- 7.18 Introduction
- 7.19 Presumptions and inferences defined and distinguished
- 7.20 —Innocence
- 7.21 —Sanity
- 7.22 —Suicide
- 7.23 —Death after unexplained absence
- 7.24 —Regularity of official acts
- 7.25 —Receipt of mail
- 7.26 —Possession of fruits of crime
- 7.27 —Flight or concealment
- 7.28 Statutory presumptions
- 7.29 —Tests for constitutionality
- 7.30 —Effect of presumptions
- 7.31 Stipulations
- 7.32 —Polygraph tests
- 7.33 Summary

JUDICIAL NOTICE

Judicial Notice is the cognizance of certain facts which judges and jurors may properly take and act on without proof because they already know them. 31 C.J.S. Sec. 6.

§ 7.1 Introduction

At the close of the criminal trial the jury members are instructed that they are to determine guilt or innocence from the facts presented at the trial. Generally the prosecution and the defense have the burden of establishing facts by producing sworn witnesses, authenticated documents, or objective evidence. However, there are some necessary exceptions. Obviously, it would be unreasonable to require that the opposing parties introduce evidence for every fact considered by the jury or the judge. Criminal trials are drawn out enough under our present system and it would be ridiculous to require that the parties prove, for example, that the state of Kentucky is located in the United States or that the force of gravity causes an object to fall to the earth. As the rules of evidence are reasonable rules, the courts have over the years adopted a principle which is known as judicial notice and which authorizes the court to take notice of certain facts without the necessity of introducing evidence to show these facts.

To save the time of the court and for procedural convenience, other substitutes for evidence have found their way into the procedure. By court decision and statutory enactment certain facts are presumed, thereby relieving the parties from the burden of presenting evidence to prove these particular facts.

The third substitute for evidence is the stipulation. This exception is also designed to save the time of the court and allow the court to continue about its business without being bogged down with introducing evidence concerning each possible question. The stipulation renders proof unnecessary as to the matter stipulated.

Judicial notice is discussed in the following sections (§§ 7.2-7.17). The other procedural substitutes for evidence, those relating to presumptions, inferences and stipulations are discussed in the latter part of this chapter (§§ 7.18-7.32).

§ 7.2 Judicial notice defined

Judicial notice is the taking cognizance by the court of certain facts and laws without the necessity of proof. That a matter is judicially noticed means merely that it is taken as true without the offering of evidence by the party who ordinarily should do so. The court assumes that the matter is so well known that it will not be disputed. But the opponent is not prevented from disputing the matter by evidence, if he believes it disputable. Judicial notice is thus a substitute for formal proof.

In determining the propriety of taking judicial notice of a matter, the judge may consult and use any source of pertinent information, whether or not furnished by a party's counsel. The court may, for example, resort to appropriate books or documents for reference.

For convenience, the rules concerning judicial notice are often categorized as judicial notice of facts and judicial notice of laws.

§ 7.3 Judicial notice of facts

Under Rule 9 of the Uniform Rules of Evidence, adopted in some states, judicial notice *must* be taken, without request by a party, of such specific facts and propositions of generalized knowledge as are so universally known that they cannot reasonably be the subject of dispute; and judicial notice *may* be taken, without request by a party, of specific facts and propositions of generalized knowledge which are capable of immediate and accurate determination by resort to easily accessible sources of indisputable accuracy.

The general rule is that the trial court may take judicial notice without motion or counsel for a party may request the court to take judicial notice of specific facts. If counsel so requests, he must furnish the judge with sufficient information to enable him to comply with the request and give notice to counsel for the adverse party to enable him to prepare to meet the request. For example, in a suit by a state prisoner for relief under the Civil Rights Act for alleged discrimination, the Attorney General for the State of Illinois asked the federal court to take judicial notice of certain social studies which show that the Black Muslim Movement, despite its pretext of a religious facade, is an organization that, outside of prison walls, has for its object the overthrow of the white race, and inside prison walls, has an impressive history of inciting riots and violence. The court decided to take judicial notice of official or otherwise accredited social studies of the Black Muslim Movement.[1]

---

[1] Cooper v. Pate, 324 F.(2d) 165 (7th Cir. 1963).

Also see Stevens v. United States, 440 F.(2d) 144 (1971) where, based

Other examples of instances where the court took judicial notice of facts are indicated in these two well-known cases.

In the famous school desegregation case[2] the Supreme Court of the United States relied upon and took judicial notice of social studies, citing them at length and digesting them in footnotes. In an earlier case[3] in which the Supreme Court held constitutional state laws fixing a minimum wage for women, Chief Justice Hughes took judicial notice of, and accepted social economics studies on, the effect of a depressed wage level upon the health and lives of women workers.

Under Rule 201 of the Federal Rules of Evidence which governs judicial notice of adjudicative facts, limits are placed upon the kinds of facts which may be judicially noticed. This rule provides that a judicially noticed fact must be one not subject to reasonable dispute in that it is either (1) generally known within the territorial jurisdiction of the trial court or (2) capable of accurate and ready determination by resort to sources whose accuracy can not reasonably be questioned. Under this rule judicial notice may be taken at any time during the proceeding and the judge is required to instruct the jury to accept as established any facts judicially noticed.[3a]

Although the courts are not in complete agreement as to what facts *must* be judically noticed and what facts *may* be judicially noticed on request, some matters are traditionally considered as being proper for consideration. These are discussed in the sections that follow. They are not, however, meant to be exhaustive.

§ 7.4 —Matters of common knowledge

Matters of common knowledge are usually judicially noticed. Such facts judicially noticed may be of purely local knowledge. For example, the character of the location where an accident oc-

---

on a congressional report so finding, the court took judicial notice that firearms are used to highjack airplanes.

[2] Brown v. Board of Education, 347 U.S. 483, 98 L.Ed. 873, 74 S.Ct. 686 (1954).

[3] West Coast Hotel Co. v. Parrish, 300 U.S. 379, 81 L.Ed. 703, 57 S.Ct. 578 (1937).

[3a] See Rule 201, Fed. Rules of Evidence and the advisory committee's comments for a discussion concerning the authority of the federal judge to take judicial notice of facts.

curred, as a business area, may be a matter of common knowledge.[4] A federal court in South Carolina decided, in an action under the Federal Tort Claims Act, that it is common knowledge that livestock in general and mules in particular are easily frightened by sudden loud noises and by helicopters which are propelled directly at and over their heads.[5]

Facts generally known throughout the state or nation also may be judicially noticed. For instance, the vital role of Nike missile sites in national defense is an appropriate subject for judicial notice.[6] And a federal district court took judicial notice of the fact that a former major general who brought a libel action was generally well-known, that he was the subject of nationwide news reports while serving as major general and while a candidate for state governor, and that he had made announcements in matters of public concern.[7] However, a court could not take judicial notice of the wealth of defendant Charles Chaplin from so-called common knowledge derived from newspapers and magazines.[8]

It is common knowledge that there is an alarming increase in the number of serious crimes committed by boys under eighteen years of age. The economic facts of the constant increase in the cost of living and the decreased purchasing power of the dollar are frequently noticed judicially without the necessity of proof.

Where the standard of common knowledge is applied, the test is not whether everybody knows it, but whether it is knowledge which every intelligent and well-informed person has.

§ 7.5 —Historical facts

Courts will take judicial notice of events which make up the history of the state or country. The financial history of the United States, including events such as the 1929 stock market collapse and

---

[4] Varcoe v. Lee, 180 Cal. 338, 181 Pac. 223 (1919). Also see State v. Lawrence, 234 P.(2d) 600 (Utah 1951) case, included in Part II.

[5] Long v. United States, 241 F. Supp. 286 (W.D.S.C. 1965).

[6] United States v. National Surety Corp., 179 F.Supp. 598 (E.D.Pa. 1959).

[7] Walker v. Courier-Journal and Louisville Times Co., 246 F.Supp. 231 (W.D.Ky. 1965), (reversed on other grounds, 368 F.(2d) 189 (1966)).

[8] Berry v. Chaplin, 74 Cal.App. (2d) 669, 169 P.(2d) 453 (1946).

the depression of the early 30's, is a matter of common knowledge. The day of the week on which a particular date fell, the date on which war was declared or ended, the destructive character of a flood or other disaster, are all matters of judicial notice. The court, in an action to declare life insurance policies in force, judicially noticed the flight of Miami's Cuban refugees from Castro's Cuba and their acceptance, encouragement, and support by the United States.[9]

As is true where the judge takes judicial notice of other facts, the judge does not have to be personally aware of historical facts. He may refer to properly authenticated public official documents, to encyclopedias, history books, periodicals, or even newspaper articles. However, such judicial knowledge is generally limited to what a judge may properly know in his judicial capacity and he cannot take judicial notice of a historical fact of which only he is aware.

§ 7.6 —Geographical facts

Judicial notice will be taken of the location and navigability of large rivers and inland lakes; the location and boundaries of counties, cities, and villages; and the population of states and cities. The distance between two cities such as to permit the accused to be at the scene of both the crime and the alibi on the same day was a proper subject of judicial notice.[10]

§ 7.7 —Scientific facts

Scientific facts which have been well established by authoritative scientists and are generally accepted as irrefutable by living scientists will be judicially noticed. Courts frequently take judicial notice of the elementary principles of physics, such as the force of gravity, and other sciences.

The general reliability of the radar speed meter as a device for measuring the speed of a moving vehicle is now recognized, and it is no longer necessary to require expert testimony in each case as

---

[9] Blanco v. Pan-American Life Ins. Co., 221 F.Supp. 219 (S.D.Fla. 1963).

[10] People ex rel. Lejcar v. Meyering, 345 Ill. 449, 178 N.E. 80 (1931).

to the nature, function, or scientific principles underlying it.[11] Likewise, courts may take judicial notice of the scientific validity of blood-grouping tests resulting in exclusion of paternity.[12] The scientific foundation for blood alcohol tests for sobriety is not yet so well established that a court can take judicial notice as to their significance;[13] and the results of polygraph or "lie detector" tests are excluded by the court unless the parties stipulate that the results of such tests may be admitted.[14]

§ 7.8 —Words and phrases

A court will take judicial notice of definitions in standard dictionaries. A Utah statute[15] provides that courts take judicial notice of "the true signification of all English words and phrases and of all legal expressions"; and adds, "In all cases the court may resort for its aid to appropriate books or documents of reference."

Not only will the court take judicial notice of dictionary definitions but under certain circumstances will take judicial notice of the meaning of idioms which have acquired a special meaning. As for example, the term "democrat" connotes the Democratic Party, its members, and candidates. The court may even take judicial notice that "pig" has, in recent times, come to be used as a derisive name for the police.[15a]

§ 7.9 Judicial notice of laws

In addition to taking judicial notice of facts the courts take judicial notice of most laws. The normal method of finding the applicable law, common as well as statutory, is by informal investigation. Opposing counsel usually bring to the judge's attention

---

[11] State v. Dantonio, 18 N.J. 570, 115 A.(2d) 35 (1955); People v. Magri, 3 N.Y.(2d) 562, 147 N.E.(2d) 728 (1958); State v. Graham, 322 S.W.(2d) 188 (Mo. 1959); East Cleveland v. Ferell, 168 OhioSt. 298, 7 OhioOp.(2d) 6, 154 N.E.(2d) 630 (1958); People v. Abdallah, 226 N.E.(2d) 410 (1967).

[12] Jordan v. Mace, 144 Me. 351, 69 A.(2d) 670 (1949); Commissioner of Welfare of City of New York v. Costonie, 277 App.Div. 90, 97 N.Y. S.(2d) 804 (1950).

[13] Parton v. Weilnau, 169 OhioSt. 145, 8 OhioOp.(2d) 134, 158 N.E. (2d) 719 (1959).

[14] See Chapter 13 of this text.

[15] Utah Code Ann., tit. 78, § 78-25-1 (1953).

[15a] City of St. Petersburg v. Waller, 261 So.(2d) 151 (1972).

citations and references to decisions or statutes applicable to the case being tried. Occasionally the judge will make his own independent investigation of the law. State trial courts judicially notice federal law, and a federal court will judicially notice the law of every state. When, however, the United States Supreme Court reviews a decision of a state court, it will not take judicial notice of the law of another state unless the state court below could have done so.[16]

§ 7.10 —Federal law

All state courts, as well as the federal courts, will take judicial notice of the Constitution of the United States, federal statutes, and federal treaties.

§ 7.11 —Law of sister states

Many states have adopted the Uniform Judicial Notice of Foreign Law Act, which provides that every court in the state must take judicial notice of the common law and statutes of every state, territory and other jurisdiction of the United States. The court may inform itself of such laws in such manner as it may deem proper, and may call upon counsel to aid it in obtaining such information. To enable counsel for a party to ask that judicial notice be taken of the law in another jurisdiction, reasonable notice must be given to counsel for the adverse party in the pleadings or otherwise. The reasonable notice requirement is to assure fairness to the opponent when a party plans to rely on laws of other jurisdictions.

In addition to those public laws of general application clearly included within the term "statutes," that term also fairly includes other states' constitutions and rules of procedure having force of law throughout each such state, although such rules were adopted by the highest court of the state rather than its legislature. These materials are usually readily accessible through state codes, and, being of the general nature of public laws, should be judicially noticed.[17]

---

[16] Hanley v. Donoghue, 116 U.S. 1, 29 L.Ed. 535, 6 S.Ct. 242 (1885).
[17] Litzinger Sign Co. v. American Sign Co., 11 OhioSt.(2d) 1, 40 OhioOp.(2d) 30, 227 N.E.(2d) 609 (1967).

§ 7.12 —Law of foreign countries

The federal courts and most state courts will not take judicial notice of the law of a foreign country.[18] As a result the rules of law for a foreign country must be pleaded and proved as facts along with the other elements of a cause of action.

§ 7.13 —Municipal ordinances

Generally, judicial notice may be taken of municipal ordinances only when the case is being tried in a municipal court. In all other courts municipal ordinances must be pleaded and proved. Recent statutory amendments in a few states now allow every court to take judicial notice of ordinances.

A municipal court which has exclusive jurisdiction of cases involving the violation of traffic ordinances of the city situated within its territorial jurisdiction will take judicial notice of those ordinances.[19]

§ 7.14 —Administrative regulations

The Uniform Rules of Evidence provide that judicial notice may be taken of the published regulations of governmental subdivisions or agencies of the state. The federal administrative regulations published in the FEDERAL REGISTER must be judicially noticed by all federal courts, and many state courts also notice such regulations. A federal court will judicially notice a state administrative regulation.[20]

§ 7.15 —Jurisdiction of courts

A court will take judicial notice of the limits of its jurisdiction and the extent of the territory included therein. In a criminal case the state or municipality is required to prove that the offense was committed within the territorial jurisdiction of the court; however, a court may take judicial notice of the fact that a particular milepost or interchange of an interstate highway is within the court's

---

[18] Kearney v. Savannah Foods, 350 F.Supp. 85 (1972).

[19] People v. Cowles, 142 Cal.App.(2d)Supp. 865, 298 P.(2d) 732 (1956).

[20] Milwaukee Mechanics Ins. Co. v. Oliver, 139 F.(2d) 405 (5th Cir. 1943).

territorial jurisdiction.[21]

§ 7.16 —Court records

Both trial and appellate courts take notice of their own records in the same case; but matters of record in other cases and other courts are not noticed, and formal proof of such records is required. Records of a previous case will be judicially noticed if the two cases constitute related litigation. This was exemplified in a habeas corpus proceeding by a federal prisoner, when a district court took judicial notice of prior published reports and the files and records of cases in which the prisoner had figured.[22]

§ 7.17 Summary

Although the usual procedure is for the parties to introduce evidence to prove a fact in dispute, in some instances such evidence is not necessary as the court will take judicial notice of certain facts. This procedure is obviously necessary and reasonable in order to save the time of the court.

Judicial notice is merely the court taking cognizance of certain facts and laws without requiring the opposing parties to introduce proof. For convenience the rules concerning judicial notice are often categorized as judicial notice of facts and judicial notice of laws. Rule 201 of the Federal Rules of Evidence relates only to the taking of judicial notice of adjudicative facts.

The general rule is that the trial judge may take judicial notice without motion of counsel or he may take judicial notice of certain facts on the request of counsel. The judge, in fact, is given much discretion concerning judicial notice and he is not second-guessed by a higher court unless there is a clear abuse of discretion.

It is obvious that there are many facts and laws which are commonly known and need not be proved in court. Some of these are historical facts, geographical facts, scientific facts and other facts that are generally known to the ordinary person.

In addition to facts the judge may take judicial notice of certain laws such as the Constitution of the United States, laws of the

---

[21] State v. Scott, 3 OhioApp.(2d) 239, 32 OhioOp.(2d) 360, 210 N.E. (2d) 289 (1965).

[22] Smith v. Settle, 212 F.Supp. 622 (W.D.Mo. 1962).

various states and in some instances, municipal ordinances.

All of the persons involved in the criminal justice process must be aware of the fact that the judge may take notice of certain facts and certain laws but it is a grave mistake to assume that the judge may take judicial notice of all facts. If there is any doubt as to the character of the fact to be introduced or proved in court, evidence should be acquired and made ready for presentation in court. Also, the good investigator must recognize that even though the judge takes judicial notice of certain matters, evidence to dispute them may be presented, and failure to have information to enable the court to take judicial notice of certain facts could weaken the case.

PRESUMPTIONS, INFERENCES, AND STIPULATIONS

> The use of presumptions and inferences to prove an element of the crime is indeed treacherous, for it allows men to go to jail without any evidence on one essential ingredient of the offense. It thus implicates the integrity of the judicial system. Dissenting opinion—*Barnes v. United States*, 412 U.S. 837, 93 S.Ct. 2357 (1973).

§ 7.18 Introduction

As was pointed out in previous sections (7.01-7.17) the parties usually have the burden of introducing evidence to establish facts on which a decision is made. However, in some instances certain facts are presumed, thereby relieving the parties from the burden of presenting evidence to prove these particular facts. And under traditional common law principles some facts can be inferred from other facts presented in court. For centuries courts have instructed juries, for example, that an inference of guilty knowledge may be drawn from the fact of unexplained possession of stolen goods. As early as A.D. 688 the laws of England provided that, "if stolen property be attached with a chapman, and he has not brought it before good witnesses, let him prove . . . that he was neither privy (to the theft) nor thief."[23]

Notwithstanding the fact that presumptions and inferences are authorized as substitutes for evidence, the burden of proving guilt

---

[23] Barnes v. U.S., 412 U.S. 837, 93 S.Ct. 2357 (1973). See case in Part II.

beyond a reasonable doubt is on the prosecution and the jury is not bound to accept or believe the correctness of the inference or the presumption.

The final substitute for evidence which will be discussed in this chapter is the stipulation. The stipulation renders proof unnecessary as to the matter stipulated. This exception is also designed to save the time of the court and allow the court to continue about its business without being bogged down by requiring the parties to introduce evidence concerning every possible question.

§ 7.19 Presumptions and inferences defined and distinguished

The term "presumption" has been used by courts and legal writers to describe several different consequences which flow from the introduction of evidence in trials. A general definition is that a presumption is a rule of law that attaches definite probative value to specific facts or draws a particular inference as to the existence of one fact, not actually known, arising from its usual connection with other particular facts which are known or proved. It is a legal principle whereby the court accepts the existence of one fact from other facts already proved.

Presumptions are not "evidence" but substitutes for evidence. A presumption is an aid to legal reasoning applied to particular subjects.[24]

Presumptions are divided into presumptions of fact and presumptions of law. In Black's Law Dictionary a presumption of fact is defined as "an inference affirmative or disaffirmative of the truth or falsehood of any proposition or fact drawn by a process of probable reasoning in the absence of actual certainty of its truth or falsehood, or until such certainty can be ascertained." Presumptions of fact are not the subject of fixed rules, but are merely natural presumptions, such as appear from common experience, to arise from the particular circumstances of any case.

A presumption of law is described as a particular inference that must be drawn from ascertained facts. One court attempted to distinguish these two by stating that presumptions of law derive

---

[24] Siler v. Siler, 277 S.W. 886 (1925).

their force from the law of the jurisdiction, not from logic or probability; whereas a presumption of fact is not a presumption at all, but a mere inference.

Courts have attempted to distinguish between presumptions and inferences as to both their origin and effect. According to some courts an inference should be recorded as a permissible deduction from the evidence before the court which the jury may accept or reject. A presumption is a rule of law, fixed or relatively definite in scope and effect, which attaches to certain evidentiary facts and is productive of a specific procedural consequence. To state this more simply, in these courts a presumption is a mandatory deduction that the law expressly requires while an inference is no more than a permissible deduction which the trier of facts may adopt.

One court has stated that a presumption and an inference are not the same thing, a presumption being a deduction which the law requires triers to make; an inference being a deduction which the trier may or may not make according to his own conclusions. A presumption is mandatory; an inference permissible.[25] If all courts consistently used the terms presumptions and inferences as thus defined, there would be less confusion. However, as will be found on examination of the cases, many courts still refer to presumptions as presumptions of law and presumptions of fact while others make reference to presumptions and inferences.

A presumption of law is laid down by the courts or legislature for convenience and the public benefit. Some rules like the sanity and sobriety of witnesses are applied mainly to expedite the courts' caseloads.[26] Other presumptions, like the legitimacy of children, allow us all to live more secure, orderly lives. Other presumptions, as honest and proper conduct by public officials, allow the normal governmental activities to be accepted at face value.[27]

---

[25] Joyce v. Missouri and Kansas Telephone Company, 211 S.W. 900 (1918), Sewell v. U.S., 406 F.(2d) 1289 (1969).

[26] Practically all witnesses are sane and sober anyway, so presuming their competency accomplishes justice without the expense and delays of bringing in one or more psychiatrists and drunkometer technicians in every case.

[27] Without this presumption it would be very burdensome for all concerned to try to affirmatively prove each and every routine record material to the case. It would be virtually impossible where, for example, the clerk who made the entry has died, or due to the heavy caseload of a police court no one in the court or clerk's office can personally remem-

§ 7.19 CRIMINAL EVIDENCE FOR POLICE 104

Finally, rules such as the presumption of innocence and presumption against murder protect the accused by forcing the prosecution to affirmatively prove each element of the crime charged. In short, a presumption of law is a rule of law that (1) if one fact is proved then a second fact *must* also be concluded to be true, or (2) that certain facts are taken for granted at the beginning of every trial. The presumption of law takes the place of evidence to prove the second fact or to establish the assumed condition at the outset of the trial.

However, just because the law presumes a fact does not necessarily make it true. We all know that children can be bastards, that witnesses can be insane or intoxicated, that suspects can be guilty, that clerks can make mistakes, and that judges sometimes are bribed. Therefore the opposing party is usually free to present evidence that the presumed fact is not really so. If the opposing party presents enough credible evidence to refute the presumption, the presumption of law in some instances fails. It is then up to the original party to rebuild the fact by presenting evidence that it is really true. The jury then ignores the presumption and weighs the evidence on both sides to decide whether the fact is or is not true.

Speaking on a more abstract level, a presumption of law is a procedural device which takes the place of evidence in certain cases until the facts in lieu of which the presumption operates are shown. A particular fact *must* be presumed when the first fact is proved or when expediency so requires. Should nothing on the second fact or the assumed condition be presented by the opposing party, the presumption stands. It establishes a prima facie case on that point.[28]

The second classification of presumption, the presumption of fact, operates much like the first form of presumption of law which says that if Fact A is proved, then Fact B must be concluded. The main difference is the strength of the presumption. With a pre-

---

ber a thing about the case in question. Also, suppose that a judge decides a case and then dies. It would be absolutely impossible to prove affirmatively that the judge was not bribed any time during the several months preceding the case. There will always be periods of a few hours or minutes when the judge was out of sight of your witnesses and could have been bribed.

[28] Shepherd v. Midland Mut. Life Ins. Co., 152 OhioSt. 6, 39 OhioOp. 352, 87 N.E.(2d) 156 (1949).

sumption of law, the jury *must* find the second fact true. With a presumption of fact, the jury *may* find the second fact true, but is not required to say the second fact is true. For example, if a party fails to call a particular available witness to testify, the jury may conclude that the witness would have hurt the party's case. Another example is that when the accused is caught red-handed holding recently stolen property, and offers no believable explanation, the jury may conclude that such holding is guilty possession.[29] Also, if a party destroys some of the real evidence in a case, the jury may conclude that the evidence was unfavorable to him.

Presumptions of fact, or inferences, have developed by the process of logic and reason. They are based upon the human experience that when one fact occurs a second fact usually follows. Like presumptions of law, they cannot be based on speculation or on uncertain evidence. They can be rebutted just as some presumptions of law, except that ordinarily the presumption of fact is considered weaker, and can be rebutted with less or weaker evidence. As with presumptions of law, a presumption of fact (or inference) is, if believed by the jury and not rebutted by contrary evidence, sufficient to establish a prima facie case on that point.

Presumptions are further divided into "conclusive" or "rebuttable." Conclusive or irrebuttable presumptions (*presumption juris et de jure*) are those which the law will not suffer to be rebutted by counter evidence even though a conclusive presumption may be fictitious. As for example, a child born to a married woman is legitimate. It can not be rebutted, notwithstanding that evidence is offered to the contrary.

A rebuttable presumption (*presumption juris tantum*) is one which requires the trier of fact to consider the deduction as true until disproved by contrary evidence. An example of the rebuttable presumption, where counter evidence may be offered to overcome the presumption, is the presumption which states that an accused is presumed to be innocent.

The justification for presumption, like that of the judicial notice principle, is to economize the time of the court. It is a practical principle based on probability, and sometimes on public policy. The presumption conclusions may be predicated on consistent

---

[29] Sewell v. United States, 406 F. (2d) 1289 (8th Cir. 1969). Also see Barnes v. U.S., 412 U.S. 837, 93 S.Ct. 2357 (1973). See case in Part II.

judicial determinations or on legislation. And a legislative enactment may change the effect of a judicially instigated presumption.

Some of the areas where the presumption rules most often are considered are discussed in the following sections.

§ 7.20 —Innocence

The defendant in a criminal case is presumed to be innocent until he is proved guilty of the crime charged. This rebuttable presumption of innocence places upon the prosecution the burden of proving him guilty beyond a reasonable doubt.

The so-called presumption of innocence is not, strictly speaking, a presumption in the sense of a deduction from a given premise. It is more accurately an assumption which, as a procedural aid, compels the state to maintain the burden of proving guilt.[30]

A federal court has pointed out that the presumption of innocence:

> is not a mere belief at the beginning of the trial that the accused is probably innocent. It is not a will-o'-the-wisp, which appears and disappears as the trial progresses. It is a legal presumption which the jurors must consider along with the evidence and the inferences arising from the evidence, when they come finally to pass upon the case. In this sense, the presumption of innocence does accompany the accused through every stage of the trial.[31]

The accused is entitled to a definite instruction on the presumption of innocence, and it is reversible error for the trial court to refuse such an instruction when requested.[32] The theory that the presumption is simply the same thing as the requirement of proof beyond a reasonable doubt, so that the instruction on the latter adequately comprehends the former, is incorrect.

§ 7.21 —Sanity

Every person is presumed to be sane, in the absence of evidence to the contrary. Without evidence of insanity, therefore, it is not

---

[30] Carr v. State, 192 Miss. 152, 4 S.(2d) 887 (1941). Wells v. State, 288 S.(2d) 860 (1974).

[31] Dodson v. United States, 23 F.(2d) 401 (4th Cir. 1928). U.S. v. Thaxton, 483 F.(2d) 1071 (1973).

[32] Allen v. Commonwealth, 211 Va. 805, 180 S.E.(2d) 513 (1971). Whaley v. Com., 200 S.E.(2d) 556 (1973).

incumbent upon the prosecution to prove defendant's legal sanity. The presumption of sanity is a rule of law which stands in place of evidence; but when evidence of insanity is produced, from whatever source, the presumption of sanity disappears and mental capacity of the accused to commit the crime becomes an essential element to be proven by competent evidence beyond a reasonable doubt.[33]

The sufficiency of the evidence to dissipate the presumption of sanity and raise the issue of insanity is a question of law for the court to decide in the first instance, and if the evidence is legally sufficient to raise the issue of insanity and the prosecution offers no evidence of sanity, there is no factual issue for the jury and the defendant is entitled to a directed verdict of acquittal.[34] In one case a diagnosis of mental illness necessitating commitment to a mental institution a little more than a month after the commission of the crime, based on alcoholism with some hallucinations, was held legally sufficient to raise the issue of mental capacity to commit the offense and to dissipate the presumption of sanity.[35]

The nature and quantum of evidence which the prosecution must produce to meet the burden of proving sanity, so as to justify submission of the sanity issue to the jury, varies with the nature and quantum of evidence indicating mental illness. Lay testimony can be sufficient to satisfy the prosecution's burden of proving sanity, even though there is expert testimony to the contrary.[36] While expert testimony of insanity, particularly that of psychiatrists, may be adequately rebutted by personal opinions of laymen, the opinions of experts may not be arbitrarily ignored.[37]

A prior adjudication of mental incompetency gives rise to a rebuttable presumption of continued incompetency. Such rebuttable presumption is a rule of evidence which has the effect of overcoming the legal presumption of sanity and mental capacity to commit the crime charged. For example, in a mail fraud case,[38] the defense

---

[33] Davis v. United States, 160 U.S. 469, 40 L.Ed. 499, 16 S.Ct. 353 (1895); Hartford v. United States, 362 F.(2d) 63 (9th Cir. 1966); United States v. Bohle, 445 F.(2d) 54 (1971).

[34] Fitts v. United States, 284 F.(2d) 108 (10th Cir. 1960).

[35] Ibid.

[36] Mims v. U.S., 375 F.(2d) 135 (1967).

[37] Brock v. United States, 387 F.(2d) 254 (5th Cir. 1967).

[38] Hurt v. United States, 327 F.(2d) 978 (8th Cir. 1964).

offered an authenticated copy of a prior adjudication that defendant had been unable to distinguish right from wrong and unable properly to assist in his own defense to charges then pending against him. The prosecution did not undertake to introduce any evidence at the trial as to defendant's competency to commit the offense. The trial judge's determination that defendant was mentally competent to commit the crime for which he was then on trial was error.

§ 7.22 —Suicide

The presumption against suicide stems from and is raised by our common knowledge and experience that most sane men possess a natural love of life and an instinct for self-protection which effectively deter them from suicide or the self-infliction of serious bodily injury. It is commonly recognized that there is an affirmative presumption of death by accidental means which arises under appropriate circumstances from the negative presumption against suicide.[39]

Where it was shown that an insured under a double indemnity policy of life insurance met his death by external and violent means and there was no ground for an inference that his death was brought about through suicide, intentional self-infliction of injury, criminal assault by a third person or other nonaccidental means, there was a presumption that death was caused by accidental rather than nonaccidental means. This legal presumption arises and operates only where the means of causing death as distinguished from the cause of death are unknown. It is a procedural device which will, on the proof of basic facts which bring the presumption into operation, stand in lieu of any evidence of the accidental nature of the means causing death and thus make a prima facie case for the plaintiff. But the presumption cannot prevail against any substantial evidence of a nonaccidental nature of the means.[40]

The presumption against suicide and in favor of accidental or other means of causing death is not evidence and is not to be weighed as evidence. However, courts in several states follow the

---

[39] Hinds v. John Hancock Mut. Life Ins. Co., 155 Me. 349, 155 A.(2d) 721 (1959).

[40] Shepherd v. Midland Mut. Life Ins. Co., 152 OhioSt. 6, 39 OhioOp. 352, 87 N.E.(2d) 156 (1949).

minority view that the presumption is itself evidence or has evidentiary weight.[41] This presumption against suicide and in favor of accident or natural cause operates procedurally once the insurance company has set up the defense of suicide. The presumption serves to place the burden of coming forward with evidence of suicide upon the insurer.[42]

When the party against whom the presumption against suicide operates produces substantial credible evidence to the contrary as to the means of causing death, the presumption disappears as a rule of law, and the case must be disposed of as to the issue of means of causing death on the facts produced, independently, without reference to any presumption, and under the burden of proof and on the weight of the evidence as though no presumption had ever existed.[43]

§ 7.23 —Death after unexplained absence

At common law, where a person leaves his home or usual place of residence and goes to parts unknown and is not heard of or known to be living for a period of seven years, the legal presumption arises that he is dead. Some states have enacted Presumed Decedents Laws, under the provisions of which the presumption of death in the case of an unexplained absence for seven or more years arises as of the date of the court decree finding of a legal presumption of death.

The cases are not in agreement with respect to the presumed death of a fugitive from justice. In an action on a life insurance policy an Illinois court held that the fact that the absent person was a fugitive from justice did not preclude the application of the presumption.[44] A surety on a defendant's bail bond attempted to avoid forfeiture of bail and introduced evidence that defendant had disappeared, after leaving his car at an airport, and that an

---

[41] Under North Dakota law the presumption that death was accidental has the weight of affirmative evidence. Dick v. New York Life Ins. Co., 359 U.S. 437, 3 L.Ed(2d) 935, 79 S.Ct. 921 (1959).

[42] Hines v. Prudential Ins. Co., 235 F.Supp. 695 (E.D.Tenn. 1964).

[43] Carson v. Metropolitan Life Ins. Co., 165 OhioSt. 238, 59 OhioOp. 310, 135 N.E.(2d) 259 (1956); Kettlewell v. Prudential Ins. Co., 4 Ill.(2d) 383, 122 N.E.(2d) 817 (1954); Ziegler v. Equitable Life Assur. Soc., 284 F.(2d) 661 (7th Cir. 1960).

[44] Blodgett v. State Mutual Life Assur. Co., 32 Ill.App.(2d) 155, 177 N.E.(2d) 1 (1961).

intensive search failed to locate him. Other evidence indicated that defendant had been indicted, was a member of a group on whom a murderous assault had been made, and had good reason for flight. The court upheld the forfeiture on the ground that where a motive or doubt as to the reason exists, the presumption of continued life remains.[45]

The presumption of death is not conclusive and may be rebutted by proof of facts which tend to show the contrary, or which raise a conflicting presumption.

§ 7.24 —Regularity of official acts

A presumption of regularity supports the official acts of public officials and courts presume they have properly discharged their official duties.[46] The presumption that public officials will in good faith discharge their duties and observe the law is a very strong presumption, and will prevail until overcome by clear and convincing evidence to the contrary.

The proceedings of grand juries are covered by the presumption that official acts are regular. For example, in *Costello* v. *United States*, the United States Supreme Court refused to dismiss the indictment even though it was alleged that there were some irregularities.[47] In doing so the Court stated:

> "An indictment returned by a legally constituted and unbiased grand jury, like an information drawn by a prosecutor, if valid on its face, is enough to call for a trial of the charges on the merits."

§ 7.25 —Receipt of mail

Mail, properly addressed and placed in the mail with postage prepaid, is presumed to have been received by the addressee. In applying this rule in a prosecution for wilfully refusing to submit to induction, the court held that it will be presumed that a selective service form informing the registrant of his right to a personal appearance before a local board and to appeal his classification

---

[45] People v. Niccoli, 102 Cal.App. (2d) 814, 228 P.(2d) 827 (1951).
[46] United States v. Chemical Foundation, Inc., 272 U.S. 1, 71 L.Ed. 131, 47 S.Ct. 1 (1926).
[47] 350 U.S. 365, 76 S.Ct. 406 (1956).

arrived in the regular course of mail where the record showed that the form was properly addressed and mailed.[48]

§ 7.26 —Possession of fruits of crime

Where the evidence establishes that the accused possesses recently stolen property and there is no plausible explanation for such possession consistent with innocence, the jury may be instructed that inferences of guilty knowledge may be drawn from the fact of unexplained possession of the stolen goods.[49] In the *Barnes* case part of the instruction was as follows:

> "Possession of recently stolen property, if not satisfactorily explained, is ordinarily a circumstance from which you may reasonably draw the inference and find, in the light of the surrounding circumstances shown by the evidence in the case, that the person in possession knew the property had been stolen."

In this case the judge pointed out that the jury is not required to make the inference and has the exclusive province to determine whether the facts and circumstances shown by the evidence in the case warrant an inference which the law permits the jury to draw.

The strength of such presumption which the possession of stolen property raises depends upon the circumstances surrounding the case. And defendant's possession must be exclusive and have occurred within a relatively short time after the commission of the crime.

§ 7.27 —Flight or concealment

As some enforcement officers assume that flight or concealment raises a presumption of guilt, this evidence rule should be studied carefully. Although there are some cases in certain jurisdictions indicating that flight before arrest raises a presumption of guilt, the better and majority rule is that the flight of the accused or his concealment does not raise a legal presumption or inference of guilt although it may constitute evidence thereof.[50] Evidence may be admitted to show that the defendant after the commission

---

[48] United States v. Jones, 384 F. (2d) 781 (7th Cir. 1967).

[49] Barnes v. United States, 412 U.S. 837, 93 S.Ct. 2357 (1973).

Case in Part II.

[50] State v. Rodriguez, 167 Pac. 426 (1918).

of a crime fled from the vicinity as a circumstance tending to indicate guilt. When, however, the state introduces evidence to show flight or concealment the defendant is entitled to introduce evidence to explain why he fled or concealed himself.[51]

Instructions to the effect that flight raises a presumption of guilt have in some instances been declared erroneous and this is probably the majority view.[52] And certainly an instruction that flight raises a conclusive presumption of guilt would be erroneous.

§ 7.28 Statutory presumptions

The legislature has power to enact and prescribe that in criminal prosecutions certain facts, when duly established, shall be held to be presumptive or prima facie evidence of guilt. But this power is not without its limitations, one of which is that the legislature may not arbitrarily create a conclusive presumption of guilt against the accused, as to any element of the crime charged, by giving evidential force and effect to certain facts which otherwise would be wholly irrelevant and inconclusive. It has been said that presumptions of law are especially dangerous, in the administration of criminal justice, when used to control or impair the natural fundamental presumption of innocence; their effect being to give to evidence a technical probative force beyond that which it would naturally and ordinarily possess in producing conviction in the minds of the jury.[53]

§ 7.29 —Tests for constitutionality

The Fourteenth and Fifth Amendments set limits upon the legislature to make proof of one fact, or group of facts, proof of the ultimate fact upon which guilt is predicated.[54] Early decisions of the United States Supreme Court set forth a number of different standards to measure the validity of statutory presumptions. One test was whether there was a "rational connection" between the basic fact and the presumed fact. A second was whether the legislature might have made it a crime to do the thing

---

[51] Hines v. Com., 117 S.E. 843 (1923).
[52] Jenkins v. Com., 111 S.E. 101 (1922).
[53] Hammond v. State, 78 OhioSt. 15, 84 N.E. 416 (1908).
[54] United States ex rel. Schott v. Tehan, 37 OhioOp.(2d) 341, 365 F.(2d) 191 (6th Cir. 1966).

from which the presumption authorized an inference. A third was whether it would be more convenient for the defendant or for the prosecution to adduce evidence of the presumed fact.

However, in *Tot v. United States*,[55] the Court singled out one of these tests as controlling, and the *Tot* rule has been adhered to in the two subsequent cases in which the issue has been presented. The *Tot* Court had before it a federal statute which, as construed, made it a crime for one previously convicted of a crime of violence to receive any firearm or ammunition in an interstate transaction. The statute further provided that "the possession of a firearm or ammunition by any such person shall be presumptive evidence that such firearm or ammunition was shipped or transported or received, as the case may be, by such person in violation of this Act."

The Court held the presumption unconstitutional and decided that the controlling test for determining the validity of a statutory presumption was that there be a rational connection between the fact proved and the fact presumed. The Court stated:

> Under our decisions a statutory presumption cannot be sustained if there be no rational connection between the fact proved and the ultimate fact presumed, if the inference of the one from proof of the other is arbitrary because of lack of connection between the two in common experience. This is not to say that a valid presumption may not be created upon a view of relation broader than that a jury might take in a specific case. But where the inference is so strained as not to have a reasonable relation to the circumstances of life as we know them, it is not competent for the legislature to create it as a rule governing the procedure of courts.

Two subsequent cases in which the Supreme Court ruled upon the constitutionality of criminal statutory presumptions, *United States v. Gainey*,[56] and *United States v. Romano*,[57] involved companion sections of the Internal Revenue Code, dealing with illegal stills. The presumption in *Gainey* permitted but did not require that a jury to infer from a defendant's presence at an illegal still that he was "carrying on" the business of a distiller unless the defendant explained such presence to the satisfaction of the jury.

---

[55] 319 U.S. 463, 87 L.Ed. 1519, 63 S.Ct. 1241 (1943).
[56] 380 U.S. 63, 13 L.Ed.(2d) 658, 85 S.Ct. 754 (1965).
[57] 382 U.S. 136, 15 L.Ed.(2d) 210, 86 S.Ct. 279 (1965).

§ 7.29   CRIMINAL EVIDENCE FOR POLICE

The Court held that the *Gainey* presumption should be tested by the "rational connection" standard announced in the *Tot* case, and sustained the statutory presumption.

The presumption under attack in the *Romano* case was identical to that in *Gainey* except that it authorized the jury to infer from the defendant's presence at an illegal still that he had possession, custody, or control of the still. The Court held this presumption invalid, on the ground that "absent some showing of the defendant's function at the still, its connection with possession is too tenuous to permit a reasonable inference of guilt; the inference of the one from proof of the other is arbitrary."

A criminal statutory presumption must be regarded as "irrational" or "arbitrary" and hence unconstitutional unless it can at least be said with substantial assurance that the presumed fact is more likely than not to flow from the proved fact on which it is made to depend. This was spelled out by the Supreme Court when it held that in the absence of a showing that the majority of marijuana possessors either were cognizant of the high rate of importation or otherwise were aware that their marijuana was grown abroad, a federal statute authorizing the jury to infer from defendant's possession of marijuana that the defendant knew that the marijuana was illegally imported or brought into the United States was invalid under the due process clause.[58]

In the year following the *Leary* decision described above, the Supreme Court considered the constitutionality of instructing the jury that it may infer from the possession of heroin and cocaine that the defendant knew these drugs had been illegally imported.[59] The court held there that the inference with regard to heroin was valid judged by either of the two tests stated in the *Tot* decision.

When determining the constitutionality of statutory presumptions then the court must find a rational connection between the basic fact and the presumed fact and that there is a reasonable possibility in the ordinary course of events that the conclusion required by the presumption is in accord with human experiences.

The question of the constitutionality of a state statute making the fact that a defendant was armed with a pistol, for which he

---

[58] Leary v. United States, 395 U.S. 6, 23 L.Ed.(2d) 57, 89 S.Ct. 1532 (1969).

[59] Turner v. U.S., 396 U.S. 398, 90 S.Ct. 642 (1970).

had no license, prima facie evidence of his intent to commit a crime of violence, has been raised in a number of cases. A Washington court held such a statute constitutional since there was a rational connection between carrying pistols without a license and intending crimes of violence.[60] On the other hand, an Indiana court concluded that the fact that a person was armed with an unlicensed gun was completely irrelevant to the question of whether or not that person intended a crime of violence.[61]

A municipal ordinance imposing prima facie responsibility on the registered owner or owners of motor vehicles for the illegal parking of such vehicles on the public streets of the municipality, in those instances in which the identity of the drivers cannot be determined, constitutes a valid exercise of the police power.[62] The prosecution establishes a prima facie case against the defendant when it proves (1) the illegal parking and (2) the ownership of the illegally parked car in the defendant.

§ 7.30 —Effect of presumptions

It can be generally stated that a presumption operates to relieve a party of the duty of presenting evidence at least until his adversary has introduced proof to rebut the presumption. As stated in the Féderal Rules of Evidence:[63]

> In all cases not otherwise provided for by Act of Congress or by these rules a presumption imposes on the party against whom it is directed the burden of proving that the nonexistence of presumed fact is more probable than its existence.

According to the Federal Rules the judge is not authorized to direct the jury to find a presumed fact against the accused. When the presumed fact establishes guilt or is an element of the offense or negatives a defense, the judge may submit the question of guilt or of the existence of the presumed fact to the jury, if, but only if, a reasonable juror on the evidence as a whole, including the evidence of the basic facts, could find guilt or the presumed fact beyond a reasonable doubt. When the presumed fact has a lesser

---

[60] State v. Thomas, 58 Wash.(2d) 746, 364 P.(2d) 930 (1961).

[61] Everett v. State, 208 Ind. 145, 195 N.E. 77 (1935).

[62] Columbus v. Webster, 170 Ohio St. 327, 10 OhioOp.(2d) 419, 164 N.E.(2d) 734 (1960).

[63] See Article III, Fed. Rules of Evidence.

effect, its existence may be submitted to the jury if the basic facts are supported by substantial evidence, or are otherwise established, unless the evidence as a whole negatives the existence of the presumed fact.[64]

These Rules of Evidence provide that when the existence of a presumed fact against the accused is submitted to the jury the judge *must* instruct the jury that it may regard the basic facts as sufficient evidence of the presumed fact but that it is not required to do so. Moreover, if the presumed fact establishes guilt or is an element of the offense, or negatives a defense, the judge must instruct the jury that existence of the presumed fact must be proved beyond a reasonable doubt.[65]

Although limitations are placed upon their use by Supreme Court decisions and by legislation as well as rules established by the court, when properly used presumptions and inferences have a very important function. Without the presumption and inference it would be almost prohibitively burdensome for all concerned to try to prove affirmatively each and every routine matter material to the case.

§ 7.31 Stipulations

Another substitute for evidence is the stipulation. A stipulation is a concession by both parties to the existence or non-existence of a fact, to the contents of a document, or to the testimony of a witness. It may be written or oral and is generally encouraged in order to expedite the trial.

A stipulation as to a fact authorizes the court to find the existence of such a fact and to consider that fact without any further proof. The triers of fact are not, however, bound to accept the fact as true and may find to the contrary if persuaded by other evidence.

Stipulated testimony merely amounts to a mutual agreement by both parties that if a certain person were present, he would testify under oath to the facts stated. This, of course, does not concede to the truth of the indicated testimony nor does it add to its weight. It is subject to contradiction and otherwise subject to the

---

[64] Rule 303(b), Fed. Rules of Evidence.

[65] See Rule 303(c), Fed. Rules of Evidence.

other rules of evidence.

A stipulation is also used as a means of determining whether certain evidence will be admitted into court. In criminal cases where the parties have stipulated to the admissibility of certain evidence, that evidence is admissible to corroborate other evidence of the defendant's participation in the crime charged. In the absence of any claim that the stipulation was entered into by mistake, inadvertence, fraud, or misrepresentation, counsel may stipulate as to that evidence which may be received.

There are limitations upon the use of stipulations. It is clear that a stipulation that would amount to a complete concession by the defense of the prosecutor's case would be inconsistent with a plea of not guilty and should not be permitted. Stipulations which are clearly erroneous should not be accepted and their acceptance probably would be justification for reversal on constitutional grounds.

As a general rule a stipulation may be withdrawn and if so it ceases to be effective for any purpose. The withdrawal of a stipulation, however, would be a reasonable basis for a continuance in order for the opposing party to prepare evidence concerning matters formerly embraced by the stipulation.

§ 7.32 —Polygraph tests

Although it is generally held that polygraph tests are not judicially acceptable as scientifically infallible there is a distinction drawn when there is a stipulation; then the result of the test may be admitted. Courts from many jurisdictions have found a valid distinction between the admissibility of polygraph tests taken on stipulation, where the results will be admissible in evidence, and those where there is no stipulation.[66]

In a recent Washington State case the Supreme Court of that state held that the results of a polygraph test pursuant to a stipulation entered into by the defendant, his counsel, and the prosecuting attorney, providing for the defendant's submission to the test and

---

[66] State v. Chambers, 451 P.(2d) 27 (1969). State v. McNamara, 252 Iowa 19, 104 N.W.(2d) 568 (1960). Herman v. Eagle Star Insurance Company, 283 F.Supp. 33 (1966).

admission of graphs and examiner's opinion at the trial was not error.[67]

In the *Ross* case the defendant was charged with two counts of second-degree assault with a knife. Results of a polygraph test which was based upon a stipulation that the results, whether favorable or unfavorable, would be admissible into evidence were admitted. However, when at trial the examiner testified that Ross was not telling the complete truth in answering certain questions which were prejudicial to the defendant, the defendant's attorney complained. The court agreed that notwithstanding these stipulations the admissibility of results of polygraph tests is subject to the discretion of the trial judge. However, he found that all of the safeguards were followed and admitted the evidence over the objection of the defendant.

There are some cases to the contrary[68] but the trend is to allow the examiner's opinion after a polygraph examination is conducted where the parties stipulate to its admissibility. The courts, however, have laid down some conditions which must be met. If the polygraph and examiner's opinion are offered in evidence, the opposing party must have the right to cross-examine the examiner regarding (a) examiner's qualifications and training, (b) conditions under which the tests were administered, (c) possibilities for errors and technique of polygraph interrogation and (d) at the discretion of the trial judge other matters deemed pertinent to the inquiry.

Also, where such evidence is admitted the trial judge should instruct the jury that the examiner's testimony does not tend to prove or disprove any element of the crime but tends only to indicate that at the time of the examination the defendant was not telling the truth.

§ 7.33 Summary

To save the time of the court and to achieve the results which the courts or legislature have determined to be necessary in the administration of justice, presumptions and inferences are utilized. A presumption takes the place of evidence in certain instances, and

---

[67] See Chapter 15 this book and State v. Ross, 497 P.(2d) 1343 (1972) in Part II of book for a good example of the form of the stipulation.

[68] State v. McNamara, 252 Iowa 19, 104 N.W.(2d) 568 (1960).

until the facts in lieu of which a presumption operates are shown, the presumptive facts are accepted as true. For example, a person is presumed to be innocent until he is proved to be guilty. But these, as other rebuttable presumptions, may be overcome. Stated differently, a presumption places upon the opposing party the burden of proving a particular fact contrary to the presumed fact. Other examples of presumptions are the presumption against suicide, the presumption of death after long unexplained absence, and the presumption that public officials acted in good faith.

Presumptions are classified as rebuttable presumptions and conclusive presumptions. The former can be rebutted by other evidence while the latter cannot be rebutted.

The legislative body may provide that certain facts shall be presumptive of other facts, but there must be a rational connection between the fact proved and the fact presumed. Especially in recent years statutory presumptions have been subject to review on the grounds that they are not constitutional. Obviously a presumption that is arbitrary or irrational would be in violation of the due process clause of the Constitution.

Another means of relieving the parties of the necessity of introducing evidence is the use of a stipulation. The stipulation, which should be used more by the courts, indicates that the parties are willing to agree to the truth of certain allegations, leaving only the truly disputed facts to be determined by the jury or court.

It is a mistake to rely too heavily on presumptions. Countervailing evidence may be offered where the presumption is in favor of the prosecution and the prosecution must be prepared to reinforce the presumption. Also, the prosecution must be prepared to rebut presumptions in favor of the defense.

Although stipulations are excellent in saving the time of the court and concerned parties, their improper use can lead to acquittal of guilty persons. Many prosecutors have gone to trial unprepared because of a misinterpretation of a stipulation. To avoid this pitfall, the investigator and prosecutor should be prepared in the event the prosecution disputes the stipulation or claims mistake or fraud.

Chapter 8

EXAMINATION OF WITNESSES

> For two centuries past, the policy of the Anglo-American system of Evidence has been to regard the necessity of testing by cross-examination as a vital feature of the law. The belief that no safeguard for testing the value of human statements is comparable to that furnished by cross-examination, and the conviction that no statement (unless by special exception) should be used as testimony until it has been probed and sublimated by that test, has found increasing strength in lengthening experience.
> Wigmore, EVIDENCE, Vol. 5, § 1367 (3d ed. 1940).

Section

8.1 Introduction
8.2 Essential qualities of a witness
8.3 Judicial control of testimony
8.4 Separation of witnesses
8.5 Oath or affirmation
8.5a First hand knowledge
8.6 Interpreters
8.7 Leading questions
8.8 Refreshing memory—present memory revived
8.9 —Past recollection recorded
8.10 Cross-examination
8.11 —Scope and extent
8.12 —Witness' name and address
8.13 —Character witnesses
8.14 —Redirect and recross-examination
8.15 Impeachment
8.16 —Impeachment of surprise witness (own witness)
8.17 —Bias or prejudice
8.18 —Conviction of crime
8.19 —Prior inconsistent statements
8.19a Defects of recollections and perception
8.20 —Rehabilitation of witness
8.21 Summary

§ 8.1 Introduction

Without witnesses there could be no trial in a criminal case. The function of the witness is to present evidence from which the trier of facts can make a determination as to what happened. As the purpose of the trial in the criminal case is to determine if the accused is in fact guilty of the crime charged, it would seem logical to assume that all testimony of witnesses would be admissible. However, for various reasons as discussed in prior chapters, the witnesses are limited not only in what they may reveal but how they can reveal it.

In conducting the trial in a criminal case the normal procedure is for the prosecution to present its case first. In so doing the prosecution calls a witness to testify and then proceeds to ask questions of the witness. Asking questions by the prosecutor of his own witness is known as direct examination. There are definite restrictive rules which must be followed on direct and these rules will be discussed to some extent in the following sections.

Following the direct examination the witness may be cross-examined by the opposing party. Here too, specific and limiting rules have been developed. Following the cross-examination further questions referred to as redirect and recross-examination are usually authorized. In this chapter some of the evidence rules relating to the testimony of witnesses will be discussed and some examples given which demonstrate the application of these rules in criminal cases.

§ 8.2 Essential qualities of a witness

The witness presents testimony from which the triers of fact decide the issue. Generally to be eligible to testify, a witness must have a personal connection with the relevant occurrences, coupled with mental and physical facilities sufficient to observe the events at the time of their occurrence, and to recollect and relate them to the jury or court in a manner which renders his testimony relevant.[1] It is a well-known fact that what a person observes depends largely upon the keenness of his senses, the duration of the sensory impression, and the amount of attention directed to the event. Furthermore, there is considerable variation in the ability to remember.

---

[1] Rule 601 of the Federal Rules of Evidence, however, does not allow preclusion of testimony on grounds of mental incompetence; the matter instead being one of weight and credibility to be ascertained by the jury.

§ 8.3 CRIMINAL EVIDENCE FOR POLICE 122

Therefore, selection of qualified and dependable witnesses becomes an important consideration for both the prosecution and the defense.

§ 8.3 Judicial control of testimony

The ordinary method of introducing evidence in a trial is by answers of a witness in response to questions put by the attorney. Whether testimony shall be in the form of a free narrative or responses to specific questions is a matter to be decided by the trial judge under the particular circumstances. The judge must exercise reasonable control over the mode and order of interrogating witnesses and presenting evidence so as to make the interrogation and presentation effective for the ascertainment of the truth, to avoid needless consumption of time, and to protect witnesses from undue harassment or embarrassment.

The trial judge has wide discretion in ruling on forms of questions and the examination of witnesses; and he not only may rule upon objections to questions but also may instruct a witness to answer the questions as propounded. The Federal Rules of Evidence provide:[2]

> "The judge shall exercise reasonable control over the mode and order of interrogating witnesses and presenting evidence so as to (1) make the interrogation and presentation effective for the ascertainment of the truth, (2) avoid needless consumption of time, and (3) protect witnesses from harassment or undue embarrassment."

This rule recognizes the necessity of the trial court's having wide discretion in matters relating to the reception of evidence and examination of witnesses. The rule places ultimate responsibility for the orderly reception of evidence on the trial judge.

§ 8.4 Separation of witnesses

Statutes or rules of court in all jurisdictions authorize the judge to exclude witnesses from the courtroom except when testifying.

---

[2] Rule 611(a) Fed. Rules of Evidence.

The purpose is to prevent one witness from being influenced deliberately or subconsciously by hearing what another witness says in court. This procedure is variously called separation, exclusion, or sequestration of witnesses or "putting witnesses under the rule." A request for separation of witnesses is generally made before any evidence is introduced. Although the judge has discretion as to separation of witnesses, a motion for separation is seldom denied in a criminal case. Recognizing that the officer who prepared the case for trial is often more familiar with the case than the prosecutor, the judge usually allows the officer to remain in court even though he is a witness.

§ 8.5 Oath or affirmation

Before testifying every witness is required to declare that he will testify truthfully, by oath or affirmation administered in a form calculated to awaken his conscience and impress his mind with his duty to do so.[2a] This rule is designed to afford the flexibility required in dealing with religious cults, atheists, conscientious objectors, mental defectives, and children.

§ 8.5a First hand knowledge

It is basic to Anglo-American jurisprudence that witnesses testifying to past events base their testimony on their personal observations. The hearsay rule, for example, has as a purpose the making of testimony of witnesses more reliable by excluding the out-of-court statements of others. The Rules of Evidence for the United States Courts provide:[2b]

> "A witness may not testify to a matter unless evidence is introduced sufficient to support a finding that he has personal knowledge of the matter."

The party offering the testimony must prove that the witness had an opportunity to observe the incident about which he testifies. The witness himself may testify that he is testifying from first hand knowledge. Frequently in criminal cases witnesses are called upon to testify about events which they only casually observed, as

---

[2a] See Rule 603 Fed. Rules of Evidence.

[2b] Rule 602, Fed. Rules of Evidence.

when making an identification. It is permissible under the first hand knowledge requirement for a witness to testify that to the best of the witness's belief, the defendant committed the criminal act, while acknowledging he may be mistaken as to the identity of the defendant.

§ 8.6 Interpreters

Although the usual procedure is to require the witness to answer questions directed to him, interpreters are allowed where the witness cannot speak English, must use sign language, or in other unusual situations.

Upon the examination of witnesses who cannot understand or speak English, the interpreter will not be permitted to give his individual conclusions with respect to answers of the witnesses, but must give a literal interpretation of the language employed by the witness.[2c]

§ 8.7 Leading questions

The use of leading questions on direct or redirect is, with certain exceptions, forbidden and the adversary has the right to object to such questions.[2d]

The principal test of a leading question is: "Does it suggest the answer desired?" In order to elicit the facts, a trial lawyer may find it necessary to direct the attention of a witness to the specific matter concerning which his testimony is desired, and if the question does not suggest the answer, it is not leading. Even though the question may call for a yes or no answer, it is not leading for that reason, unless it is so worded that, by permitting the witness to answer yes or no, he would be testifying in the language of the interrogator rather than in his own.

The alternative form of question: "State whether or not . . . ," or "Did you or did you not . . . ," is free from this defect of form, because both affirmative and negative answers are presented for the witness' choice. Nevertheless, such a question may become leading, insofar as it rehearses lengthy details which the witness might not

---

[2c] Rule 604, Fed. Rules of Evidence.

[2d] See Rule 611(c) Fed. Rules of Evidence for detailed rule in federal courts.

otherwise have mentioned, and thus supplies him with full suggestions which he incorporates without any effort, by the simple answer, "I did," or "I did not." Such a question may or may not be improper, according to the amount of palpably suggestive detail which it embodies.[2e]

The extent to which the use of leading questions may be indulged or limited is a matter primarily for the discretion of the trial judge. Generally, abuse of discretion will not be found in permitting or limiting the use of leading questions in the absence of prejudice or clear injustice to the defendant.[3]

Although the general rule is that leading questions may not be used on direct examination, there are well-known exceptions to this rule. These exceptions are based upon necessity, and the right to lead is given only to the extent reasonably required to meet the necessity. The best-known exceptions are as follows:

a. Introductory matters

Questions relating to the name of the witness, his address, or other matters which are introductory only are authorized. These permissible introductory leading questions must always stop short of the disputed facts, however.

b. Hostile witnesses

Anyone who has watched the television court battles recognizes the rule that leading questions are authorized where the witness is hostile, even though he is the witness of the party presenting his case. Where the witness has manifested an intention to evade and an unwillingness to testify, the court may authorize the use of leading questions to the extent deemed necessary.

The rule permitting leading questions of hostile witnesses is of special significance in criminal matters where the state must often rely on reluctant or hostile witnesses to prove its case. The trial judge must rule that the witness is hostile or reluctant before leading questions may be asked.

[2e] State v. Scott, 20 Wash.(2d) 696, 149 P.(2d) 152 (1944).

[3] United States v. Durham, 319 F.(2d) 590 (4th Cir. 1963). Case included in Part II. People v. Fields, 49 Mich.App. 652, 212 N.W.(2d) 612 (1973).

c. Obviously erroneous statements

Where it appears that the witness has inadvertently answered a question incorrectly, or that he didn't comprehend the question, a leading question may be used on direct to afford the witness an opportunity to correct the mistake. For example, if a police witness in answer to a question inadvertently gave the date as 1964, the prosecutor would be authorized to say, "You mean, 1974, don't you?"

d. Child witnesses, mentally retarded witnesses, and witnesses with slight command of the English language

Because of necessity the court will allow restricted use of leading questions in order to obtain testimony from children or witnesses who have difficulty in expressing themselves. Included in this category are witnesses who are mentally retarded but not incompetent to testify. The rule is limited to the leading questions reasonably necessary to overcome the obstacle of securing testimony.

e. Cross-examination

Leading questions are allowed on cross-examination as a means of obtaining the truth. This will be discussed further in later sections.

f. The use of memoranda to refresh memory

The use of memoranda to refresh the memory of the witness or as a past recollection recorded necessarily requires the use of leading questions. These will be discussed in the next section.

§ 8.8 Refreshing memory—present memory revived

It is clear that witnesses do not remember all the facts, especially after a long period of time. It is also apparent that the latent memory of experience may be revived by referring to a written statement. In other words, by referring to statements or other past experience, the recollection of the witness may be refreshed. If the witness has absolutely no recollection regarding the matters being contested, he obviously is not competent to testify at all. However, if the witness remembers the transaction in general but not the essential details, or if he remembers that he recorded the transaction, some evidence concerning the transaction will be admissible. This process involves two concepts which have become known as "present memory revived" and "past memory recorded." These two concepts are different in theory and therefore the tests for admissibility differ. In the first instance the testimony of the witness and not the writing is the evidence, while in the second instance (past recollection recorded) the writing and not the testimony is the evidence.

In this section the first of these two concepts, that is present memory revived or refreshing memory or as it is sometimes called, refreshing recollection, will be discussed. In the next section the second concept, or past recollection recorded, will be discussed further.

In many instances the trial court will allow a witness to refer to records, accounting sheets or reports in testifying. Generally, doctors, engineers, accountants, and other lay witnesses testifying will be allowed continuously to refer to data on their reports. It is practically impossible for police officers, making daily investigations of alleged violations of law, to remember the names, dates, and what took place, without referring to notes made by them at the time or immediately thereafter. However, the court must exercise caution to assure that the memorandum is not a written summary made specifically for use in court.

When a witness has a lapse of memory while testifying, the court normally will allow the witness to refer to some form of memorandum to refresh or revive his recollection of the facts. After the witness' memory is revived and he presently recollects the facts and swears to them, his testimony, and not the writing, is the evidence. When a party uses an earlier statement of his own witness to refresh the witness' memory, the only evidence recognized as such is the testimony so refreshed.

Documents shown to a witness for the purpose of reviving his recollection may not be read or shown to the jury, since the documents themselves are not evidence and have no independent evidentiary value; and the fact that such material is sought to be introduced on cross-examination rather than on direct examination is not a difference of significance. The fact that a tape recording rather than a written document is involved does not affect the result.[4]

As an example of the use of memorandum to refresh the memory the reviewing court found that the trial court did not abuse its discretion in a prosecution for violation of the antiracketeering statute when it permitted a witness to refresh his recollection with a copy of the statement given by him to an agent of the F.B.I.;[5] moreover, the use of grand jury testimony for the purpose of refreshing the recollection of a witness was not abuse of the discretion of the trial judge.[6] But the deposition used in an attempt to refresh the witness' recollection was not itself admissible as evidence.[7]

The trial judge has a duty to prevent a witness from putting into the record the contents of an otherwise inadmissible writing under the guise of refreshing recollection; and counsel should not be permitted to give a witness a written statement, especially prepared for his use in testifying, to obviate the necessity of introducing original records, on the assumption that anything can be used to refresh recollection.[8]

Although the court may allow witnesses to refer to records or reports to refresh memory while testifying, it is preferable to testify without this "crutch." If the witness, and especially the officer witness, prepares adequately, he will need to refer to written statements only in rare instances. If the question concerns a situation where the jury would normally expect the witness to remember the facts without the aid of the writing, use of the "crutch" lessens the weight of the testimony.

---

[4] United States v. McKeever, 271 F.(2d) 669 (2d Cir. 1959). Also see United States v. Booz, 451 F.(2d) 719 (3rd Cir. 1971); People v. Parks, 485 P.(2d) 257 (1971).

[5] Esperti v. United States, 406 F.(2d) 148 (5th Cir. 1969).

[6] Collins v. United States, 383 F.(2d) 296 (10th Cir. 1967).

[7] United States v. Socony-Vacuum Oil Co., 310 U.S. 150, 84 L.Ed. 1129, 60 S.Ct. 811 (1940).

[8] Thompson v. United States, 342 F.(2d) 137 (5th Cir. 1965).

Also, in criminal cases, the defendant has the right to compel the production of any document used by a prosecution witness to refresh his memory. If the document is not produced, the judge may order the testimony stricken.

§ 8.9 —Past recollection recorded

When the witness has no present recollection of the events recorded in the writing, the writing becomes a substitute for his memory, and hence substantive proof of the facts it relates. However, before it is admitted a foundation must be laid.

A memorandum of past recollection recorded is admissible in evidence when the witness who made it or under whose direction it was made testifies that he at one time had personal knowledge of the facts, that the writing was, when made, an accurate record of the event, and that after seeing the writing, he has not sufficient present independent recollection of the facts to testify accurately in regard thereto.[9] To meet the accepted standards of admissibility, the trial judge must be satisfied that the writing was made at a time when the events were fresh in the writer's mind, and the witness must verify the writing's authenticity and truthfulness.

The doctrine of past recollection recorded has long been favored by the federal and practically all the state courts that have had occasion to decide the question.[10] But the application of this doctrine does not deprive the accused of the opportunity to cross-examine the witness as guaranteed by the Sixth Amendment.[11] As an example of the application of this concept the Supreme Court of Oregon has held that a checklist used by a police officer in the operation of a breath analysis machine was admissible in a prosecution for drunken driving, although the witness had a present recollection of the subject matter of which the checklist was a record. The witness had identified the checklist, recalled making it at the time of the event when his recollection was fresh, and had

---

[9] Kinsey v. State, 49 Ariz. 201, 65 P.(2d) 1141 (1937). Morgan v. Paine, 312 A.(2d) 178 (Me. 1973). Also see Rule 803(5) Fed. Rules of Evidence.

[10] United States v. Riccardi, 174 F.(2d) 883, (3d Cir. 1949); cert. denied, 337 U.S. 941, 93 L.Ed. 1746, 69 S.Ct. 1519.

[11] United States v. Kelly, 349 F.(2d) 720; People v. Banks, 50 Mich. App 622, 213 N.W.(2d) 817 (1974); People v. Hobson, 369 Mich. 189, 119 N.W.(2d) 581 (1963).

testified as to its accuracy.[12] The admission of portions of a witness' grand jury testimony as evidence of past recollection recorded was not improper, where the grand jury testimony failed to refresh the witness' memory.[13-14]

As the recorded report is admitted as evidence of the facts recited, and was made out of court, it is in a sense considered hearsay. However, it is admitted into court as an exception to the hearsay rule, discussed in a later chapter.

§ 8.10 Cross-examination

It was indicated earlier that the purpose of the direct examination is to have the witness relate to the court whatever relevant and competent information he may possess. It was there stated that leading questions ordinarily cannot be asked on direct. Leading questions are, however, allowed on cross-examination. Three reasons are given for authorizing leading questions when examining the opposing party's witnesses. These are: (1) to challenge the credibility of the direct examination; (2) to bring out additional facts relating to those elicited on direct in addition to the facts which were favorable to the opposing party; (3) to give the triers of fact an opportunity to observe the witness under stress.

The right of cross-examination is included in the right of an accused in a criminal case to confront the witnesses against him. No one experienced in the trial of lawsuits would deny the value of cross-examination in exposing falsehood and bringing out the truth in the trial of a criminal case. The fact that this right appears in the Sixth Amendment of our Constitution reflects the belief of the framers of those liberties and safeguards that confrontation was a fundamental right essential to a fair trial in a criminal prosecution. The decisions of courts throughout the years have constantly emphasized the necessity for cross-examination as a protection for defendants in criminal cases.[15]

A full cross-examination of a witness upon the subjects of his examination in chief is an absolute right, and not the mere privilege

---

[12] State v. Sutton, 450 P.(2d) 748 (Ore. 1969).

[13-14] United States v. Barrow, 363 F.(2d) 62 (3d Cir. 1966).

[15] Pointer v. Texas, 380 U.S. 400, 13 L.Ed.(2d) 923, 85 S.Ct. 1065 (1965) Chambers v. Miss., 410 U.S. 287, 93 S.Ct. 1038 (1973).

of the party against whom he is called. The denial of this right is reversible except in certain limited circumstances, as, for instance, when a witness, having given his direct testimony dies prior to cross-examination. Here, the judge often allows the direct examination to stand and gives precautionary instructions to the jury.

The police officer can play a vital role in assisting the prosecutor in cross-examining defense witnesses. The key to effective cross-examination is preparation. It is frequently said that a good cross-examiner never asks a question unless he knows in advance what the answer will be. The police officer can provide a wealth of valuable information on prospective defense witnesses and how they are likely to testify. The officer's familiarity with the case should enable him to anticipate defenses and lines of counter attack. However, unless such information is given to the prosecutor, it is useless.

Often the police officer too is the subject of cross-examination during a trial. An officer should not be frightened at being cross-examined. Perhaps the best way for the officer to prepare for cross-examination is to go over the case with the prosecutor. The prosecutor will be able to tell the officer the likely areas of cross-examination. The officer should make every effort to avoid being drawn into an argument with defense counsel. On cross-examination the officer should answer the questions asked and no more. If an officer is asked a question which he does not understand, he should refuse to answer it, saying he does not understand the question. However, the officer should be cooperative.

§ 8.11 —Scope and extent

The extent of cross-examination with respect to an appropriate subject of inquiry is within the sound discretion of the trial judge. He may exercise a reasonable judgment in determining when the subject is exhausted.

A long established and quite strictly enforced rule in federal courts has been that cross-examination of a witness is limited to the scope of direct examination. One exception to this rule is that cross-examination may be permitted for the purpose of testing the capacity of the witness to remember, to observe, to recount, and for the purpose of testing the sincerity and truthfulness of the

§ 8.11

witness. This may be done with respect to subjects not strictly relevant to the testimony given by the witness on direct examination. In the area of scope of cross-examination, the minority English rule is gaining increased acceptance in our state courts and, indeed, has been adopted as a part of the Federal Rules of Evidence.[15a] This rule allows a witness to be examined on anything relevant to an issue in the case regardless of the scope of direct examination.

Although under the traditional rules the prosecution usually cannot cross-examine on matters not brought out on direct, he can and should make the opposing witness the prosecution witness at the proper time and ask additional questions of the witness if necessary to get all the facts before the court. But the prosecution in a criminal proceeding may not seek to establish, either by cross-examination of the defendant himself or by the independent testimony of other witnesses, that it is likely that the accused is guilty of the offense with which he is presently charged because he has committed prior criminal acts.[16]

The extent to which cross-examination upon collateral matters will be permitted is a matter peculiarly within the discretion of the trial judge. His action will not be interfered with by a reviewing court unless there has been on his part a plain abuse of discretion. Although the shutting off of cross-examination is not a practice to be encouraged, a trial judge does not abuse his discretion when he shuts off a continuation of extended cross-examination into collateral and immaterial matters.[17]

The trial court may not preclude all inquiry into a subject appropriate for cross-examination, but it may and should exercise such control over the scope of the examination as is necessary to prevent the parties from unduly burdening the record with cumulative or irrelevant matter[17a] To enable the court to discharge this duty, when a question is objected to as irrelevant, counsel conducting the inquiry should advise the court of the question's purpose. If he fails to do so, and the question is not "inevitably and patently material"

[15a] Rule 611(b) Fed. Rules of Evidence.

[16] United States v. Hall, 342 F.(2d) 849 (4th Cir. 1965); Unbaugh v. Hutto, 486 F.(2d) 904 (8th Cir. 1973).

[17] United States v. Mills, 366 F.(2d) 512 (6th Cir. 1966).

[17a] Rule 611(b) Fed. Rules of Evidence.

the objection may be sustained without error.[18]

§ 8.12 —Witness' name and address

When the credibility of a witness is in issue, the very starting point in exposing falsehood and bringing out the truth through cross-examination must necessarily be to ask the witness who he is and where he lives. The witness' name and address open countless avenues of in-court examination and out-of-court investigation. To forbid this most rudimentary inquiry at the threshold is effectively to emasculate the right of cross-examination itself.

This principle was well stated in the case of *Alford* v. *United States*[19] where the Supreme Court reversed a federal conviction because the trial judge had sustained objections to questions by the defense seeking to elicit the "place of residence" of a prosecution witness over the insistence of defense counsel that "the jury was entitled to know who the witness is, where he lives and what his business is." The reviewing court said:

> The question, "Where do you live?" was not only an appropriate preliminary to the cross-examination of the witness, but on its face, without any such declaration of purpose as was made by counsel here, was an essential step in identifying the witness with his environment, to which cross-examination may always be directed.

Under almost all circumstances the true name of the witness must be disclosed. For example, defendant in a state narcotics case has the right guaranteed to him under the Sixth and Fourteenth Amendments to cross-examine the informer, who is the principal prosecution witness, as to the informer's actual name and address;[20] and if the witness is residing in a penal institution, this too must be disclosed. The purpose of the inquiry as to the witness' address and present employment is to make known to the jury the setting in which to judge the character, veracity or bias of the witness, and it is not necessary to show the possibility of the witness' being in custody in order to make such inquiry.

---

[18] Harris v. United States, 371 F. (2d) 365 (9th Cir. 1967).

[19] 282 U.S. 687, 75 L.Ed. 624, 51 S.Ct. 218 (1931).

[20] Smith v. Illinois, 390 U.S. 129, 19 L.Ed.(2d) 956, 88 S.Ct. 748 (1968).

As is true with many rules of evidence, this rule has an exception. Where there is a threat to the life of the witness, the right of the defendant to have the witness' true name, address, and place of employment is not absolute.[21] However, the threat to the witness must be actual and not the result of conjecture. When threat to the life of a witness is shown, the prosecution must disclose to the judge in chambers relevant information and the judge must then determine whether information as to the witness' true name, address, and place of employment must be disclosed in order not to deny effective cross-examination. If the trial judge concludes that the defendant does not have a right to the exact address of the witness and his place of employment, the defendant is entitled to ask any other relevant questions which may aid the jury in weighing the witness' credibility.[22]

§ 8.13 —Character witnesses

Generally the state may not introduce evidence of defendant's character, however, when a defendant places his reputation in issue by the introduction of what are loosely described as "character" witnesses, he opens the way for the prosecution to test the credibility of such witnesses by making inquiry on cross-examination as to whether the witness had knowledge of specific facts which, if known generally, would have a tendency to detract from the summary of reputation testified to by the character witnesses. The exercise of the right to test the credibility of character witnesses by such means is fraught with great danger. Unless circumscribed by rules of fairness and grounded in demonstrated good faith on the part of the prosecution, the result could be most prejudicial to the defendant and make for a miscarriage of justice.

When the prosecution attempts to attack the credibility of the defendant's character witnesses by questions beginning "Have you heard this" or "Have you heard that," there should be a prior showing, out of the hearing of the jury, establishing to the trial judge's satisfaction the truth of this basis for such inquiry and, further, cautionary and guiding instructions should be given, pre-

---

[21] United States v. Varelli, 407 F. (2d) 735 (7th Cir. 1969). United States v. Smaldone, 484 F.(2d) 311 (10th Cir. 1973).

[22] United States v. Palermo, 410 F.(2d) 468 (7th Cir. 1969).

ferably both at the time of the inquiry and in the closing charge to the jury.

In *Michelson v. United States*[23] the Supreme Court carefully considered the manner and extent of cross-examination of character witnesses in criminal cases. The court there stated:

> Wide discretion is accompanied by heavy responsibility on trial courts to protect the practice from any misuse. The trial judge was scrupulous to so guard it in the case before us. He took pains to ascertain, out of the presence of the jury, that the target of the question was an actual event, which would probably result in some comment among acquaintances if not injury to defendant's reputation. He satisfied himself that counsel was not merely taking a random shot at a reputation imprudently exposed or asking a groundless question to waft an unwarranted innuendo into the jury box.

Where the defendant's character witnesses have been cross-examined by inquiry as to whether the witness had knowledge of specific facts which, if known generally, would have a tendency to detract from the character testimony, the jury must be carefully cautioned to the effect that the testimony has reference solely to reputation and not to the truth of collateral facts.[24] The prosecution may explore the scope and basis of the witness' knowledge of the defendant's reputation by asking if he has heard various reports about the defendant, provided the questions have a basis, in the sense that arrests or accusations, for example, which neighbors normally discuss about one another, have been rumored and discussed. The danger lurking in this impeachment process is that in order to frame an intelligible question, the examiner's query often gives details of specific misconduct affecting general reputation which would not otherwise be admissible.[25]

The prosecutor can in some instances inquire on cross-examination whether a defendant's character witness "has heard" of defendant's prior arrests or convictions. Such cross-examination is not admitted to establish that such events took place, but only to test

---

[23] 335 U.S. 469, 93 L.Ed. 168, 69 S.Ct. 213 (1948). See case in Part II.

[24] Gross v. United States, 394 F.(2d) 216 (8th Cir. 1968). United States v. Lewis, 482 F.(2d) 632 (D.C. Cir. 1973).

[25] Shimon v. United States, 352 F.(2d) 449 (D.C. Cir. 1965).

§ 8.13

the foundations and reliability of the witness' testimony. It is, in general, inadmissible to establish defendant's bad character or his propensity to commit the crime charged. The often stated purpose for permitting such questions, even when they refer to a defendant's prior arrests, is that they better enable the jury to evaluate the character testimony which has been proffered. If a witness has heard of these damaging rumors and adheres to his statement that the defendant's reputation is good, some light will have been shed upon the standards which he has employed; alternatively, if he has not heard of these rumors, some doubt will have been cast upon his ability to speak on behalf of the community.

In one case in which the defendant's character witness was cross-examined, there was no prejudicial error in permitting questions as to whether the witness ever discussed the fact of defendant's association with a convicted felon and gambler.[26] On the other hand, where defendant was on trial for willfully making false entries in bank records, embezzlement and misapplication of bank funds, direct examination of his character witness was properly limited to areas involving the question of his honesty and fair dealing; and rumors of an illicit affair with a woman, even if true, were wholly immaterial to the character traits involved.[27]

Recognizing some of the problems relating to the use of character evidence the Supreme Court in framing the federal rules attempted to answer some of the questions. Under these rules the credibility of a witness may be attacked or supported by evidence in the form of reputation or opinion, but it is subject to several limitations. Under this rule (1) the evidence may refer only to character for truthfulness or untruthfulness, and (2) evidence of truthful character is admissible only after the character of the witness for truthfulness has been attacked by opinion or reputation evidence or otherwise. Specific instances of conduct of the witness may not be proved by extrinsic evidence unless there is conviction of a crime as provided in Rule 609 of the Federal Rules.[27a]

---

[26] United States v. Gosser, 339 F. (2d) 102 (6th Cir. 1964).
[27] Aaron v. United States, 397 F. (2d) 584 (5th Cir. 1968).
[27a] Rule 608, Fed. Rules of Evidence.

§ 8.14 —Redirect and recross-examination

After a witness has been cross-examined the party calling him may by redirect examination afford the witness opportunity to make full explanation of the matters made the subject of cross-examination, so as to rebut the discrediting effect of his testimony on cross-examination and correct any wrong impression which may have been created. On redirect examination a witness may give his reasons for his actions in order to refute unfavorable inferences from matters brought out on cross-examination. He may state the circumstances connected with the matter inquired about, although the facts brought out may be detrimental to the other party.

The scope and extent to which the redirect examination of a witness will be permitted is a matter largely within the discretion of the trial judge, and his ruling will not be disturbed unless an abuse of discretion is clearly shown.

Recross-examination generally is limited to new matters brought out on redirect examination. While a court should not by a rule prohibit recross-examination of a witness as to new matters brought out on redirect examination, where there is no new matter developed on the redirect examination of the witness recross-examination is properly denied.[28]

§ 8.15 Impeachment

Impeachment is defined as the process of attempting to diminish the credibility of a witness by convincing the jury or court that his testimony may not be truthful or is unreliable. Although conflicting testimony of one witness by the other is not considered to be impeachment, it may have a similar result. There are various methods of impeachment, some of which will be discussed in the following sections.

The prerogative of impeachment in a criminal case is subject to limitation by the trial judge in the exercise of his discretion. In determining whether the trial judge abused his discretion in limiting defendant's impeachment of the complaining witness, the question is whether the rejection of defendant's efforts to impeach the

---

[28] State v. McSloy, 127 Mont. 265, 261 P.(2d) 663 (1953). United States v. Morris, 485 F.(2d) 1385 (5th Cir. 1973).

credibility of the complaining witness withholds from the jury information necessary to a discriminating appraisal of his trustworthiness to the prejudice of defendant's substantial rights. Thus, denying impeachment of the complaining witness in a prosecution for robbery by reference to the complaining witness' prior convictions for assault and rape was not an abuse of discretion affecting substantial rights of the defendant. But impeachment of the witness with three convictions for the crimes of auto theft, robbery, and burglary, each crime having an element of dishonesty, was properly permitted.[29]

A witness may not be impeached by evidence that merely contradicts his testimony on a matter that is collateral and not material to any issue in the trial.[30] The rule precluding impeachment of a witness by otherwise inadmissible evidence directed to collateral issues serves policies such as the prevention of confusion and surprise. Those policies have peculiar force where the attempt is to discredit by means of purported misconduct short of a conviction.[31]

A criminal defendant who takes the stand to testify in his own behalf can be cross-examined and impeached as any other witness, unless under the particular circumstances of the case specific questions should be excluded because their probative value on the issue of the defendant's credibility is so negligible as to be far outweighed by their possible impermissible impact on the jury.[32]

§ 8.16 —Impeachment of surprise witness (own witness)

The traditional rule in evidence is that a party who calls a witness to the stand may not impeach his own witness. An exception to that rule is that the party may impeach his own witness if there is a showing of surprise. Where the Federal Rules of Evidence are followed, the credibility of the witness may be attacked even if the witness is the party's own witness.[32a]

When a party is taken by surprise by the evidence of his witness, the latter may be interrogated as to inconsistent statements pre-

---

[29] Davis v. United States, 409 F.(2d) 453 (D.C. Cir. 1969).

[30] Byomin v. Alvis, 169 OhioSt. 395, 8 OhioOp.(2d) 420, 159 N.E.(2d) 897 (1959). Kilpatrick v. State, 285 So.(2d) 516 (Ala. 1973).

[31] Lee v. United States, 368 F.(2d) 834 (D.C. Cir. 1966).

[32] Raffel v. United States, 271 U.S. 494, 70 L.Ed. 1054, 46 S.Ct. 566 (1926); Sharp v. United States, 410 F.(2d) 969 (5th Cir. 1969).

[32a] Rule 607, Fed. Rules of Evidence.

viously made by him for the purpose of refreshing his recollection and inducing him to correct his testimony; and the party so surprised may also show the facts to be otherwise than as stated, although this incidentally tends to discredit the witness.[33] In order for the party to claim surprise, the witness' testimony must be contrary to that which had been anticipated and the testimony must be actually injurious to the party's case.[34] Also, the jury must be given precautionary instructions concerning the limited purpose of the testimony.

If the judge is satisfied that the party producing a witness has been taken by surprise by the testimony of the witness, he may allow the party to prove, for the purpose only of affecting the credibility of the witness, that the witness has made to the party or to his attorney statements substantially variant from his sworn testimony about material facts in the case. Before such proof is given, the circumstances of the supposed statement sufficient to designate the particular occasion must be mentioned to the witness, and he must be asked whether or not he made the statements and if so, allowed to explain them.[35]

The orthodox view is that when a witness takes the offering side by surprise and alters his story, a prior inconsistent statement is admissible for impeachment purposes but not as substantive evidence of the facts stated. The contradictory statements can have no legal tendency to establish the truth of the subject matter.[36]

Where a prior inconsistent statement is used in the examination of the recalcitrant or hostile witness, with the witness finally affirming the truthfulness and correctness of the statement, rather than the initial oral court testimony, the statement is effectually embraced by the witness, becomes a part of his oath-supported, court-given testimony subject to cross-examination, and is therefore not hearsay. The prior statement is then no longer limited to use on the issue of credibility, but is admissible as substantive evidence for

---

[33] Hickory v. United States, 151 U.S. 303, 38 L.Ed. 170, 14 S.Ct. 334 (1894).

[34] United States v. Miles, 413 F.(2d) 34 (3d Cir. 1969).

[35] United States v. Scarbrough, 470 F.(2d) 166 (9th Cir. 1972). But compare Eubanks v. State, 516 P.(2d) 726 (Alaska 1973). Dist. of Colum. Code § 14-102 (1973 ed.) Also see Rule 613(b) Fed. Rules of Evidence.

[36] Eisenberg v. United States, 273 F.(2d) 127 (5th Cir. 1959); United States v. Wright, 489 F.(2d) 1181 (D.C. Cir. 1973).

all purposes.[37]

§ 8.17 —Bias or prejudice

Evidence to show bias of a witness is always relevant to impeach the witness. A party's right to undertake demonstration of the bias of his adversary's witness coexists on the same plane with the adversary's prerogative to use the witness. In criminal cases great latitude is generally permitted in cross-examination of a witness in order to test his credibility and to develop facts which may tend to show bias or prejudice or any other motive the witness may have for giving his testimony.

The range of evidence that may be elicited for the purpose of establishing bias of a witness is quite broad. A previous quarrel between the witness and the party testified against readily suggests the possibility of residual hostility, and the admissibility of extrinsic testimony to establish the event is unquestioned.[38] For example, it was error for the trial judge to exclude defendant's testimony, concerning an altercation with the prosecution witness over allegedly stolen whiskey, subsequent to the date of such witness' report to the police, which was offered to show that the prosecution witness was biased against the defendant.[39]

Even evidence of police brutality is admissible to establish bias of a witness. One case held that when the trial judge believes that admission of evidence of police brutality would inevitably disclose to the jury the event which prompted any brutality, before making his decision to exclude the police brutality evidence the judge should take testimony on the question outside the presence of the jury.[40] This is to avoid the introduction of evidence which would be unduly prejudicial.

Although cross-examination pertinent to the credibility of a witness and for the development of facts which may tend to show bias or prejudice should be given the largest possible scope, the

---

[37] Slade v. United States, 267 F. (2d) 834 (5th Cir. 1959).

[38] Carlyle v. State, 85 Ga.App. 223, 68 S.E.(2d) 605 (1952); State v. Rowe, 238 Iowa 237, 26 N.W.(2d) 422 (1947); State v. Pontery, 19 N.J. 457, 117 A.(2d) 473 (1955).

[39] Wynn v. United States, 397 F. (2d) 621 (D.C. Cir. 1967). And see Austin v. United States, 418 F.(2d) 456 (D.C. Cir. 1969) case included in Part II.

[40] Blair v. United States, 401 F. (2d) 387 (D.C. Cir. 1968).

trial judge has a duty to assure its proper conduct, and the limit of cross-examination is necessarily within the court's discretion As an example, the refusal to permit defendant to question a prosecution witness, a detective employed by the county sheriff's department, as to why the detective left employment with a city police department so as to establish that the detective had been requested to resign because of insubordination in that the detective was too zealous in his work, was not an abuse of discretion where the detective testified he had left the police department for a better job.[41]

§ 8.18 —Conviction of crime

As a general rule it would be unfair to introduce evidence concerning former crimes committed by a suspect in a criminal case. And the rule is that such evidence may not be admitted to show that the defendant committed the crime for which he is being tried. On the other hand, if the credibility of the ordinary witness is an issue, the traditional rule applicable in most states is that a witness may be asked, for purposes of impeachment, whether he has been convicted of a felony, infamous crime, or crime involving moral turpitude. The reason for exposing defendant's prior criminal record is to call into question his reliability for telling the truth.

Apparently the drafters of the recently adopted Federal Rules of Evidence looked with disfavor upon this method of impeachment. In the new rules the credibility of a witness may be attacked by introducing evidence that he has been convicted of a crime only if the crime (1) was punishable by death or imprisonment in excess of one year or (2) involved dishonesty or a false statement regardless of the punishment. This section goes on to state that even this evidence can not be admitted if the crime were committed more than ten years ago or if there has been a pardon, annulment, or certificate of rehabilitation.[41a]

The cross-examiner is bound by the defendant's answer regarding his prior conviction unless the record of conviction is

---

[41] Abeyta v. United States, 368 F. (2d) 544 (10th Cir. 1966).

[41a] Rule 609 Fed. Rules of Evidence. Also see Section 6.9 for a discussion of the admissibility of evidence of other crimes committed by the accused.

produced to refute the answer of the defendant.[42] On rebuttal the record of such conviction is admissible.

Traditionally a witness may be impeached by inquiry into prior misdemeanor as well as felony convictions if those crimes involve moral turpitude. Shoplifting, whether it be labeled a felony or misdemeanor, involves moral turpitude, and accordingly, a shoplifting conviction may be used as a basis for impeachment of a witness.[43] However, the disposition of a child in a juvenile court proceeding does not constitute "conviction of crime" within a statute providing that the fact of conviction may be given in evidence to affect credibility as a witness.[44]

Great liberality is indulged in the cross-examination of a character witness as to his knowledge of arrests of and charges made against defendant whose character is the subject of the inquiry; but the cross-examination of a defense character witness concerning his prior arrest not involving moral turpitude is reversible error.[45]

Questions asked on cross-examination for purposes of impeachment should be confined to acts or conduct which reflect upon the witness' integrity or truthfulness, or so pertain to his personal turpitude, such as to indicate such moral depravity or degeneracy on his part as would likely render him insensible to the obligations of an oath to speak the truth.[46] This principle was applied in a federal trial where the court stated that the question propounded to a witness as to whether he had "ever been convicted of a crime" was too broad and unspecific, since the term "crime" includes many misdemeanors not involving moral turpitude.[47]

The cross-examiner, in his inquiries about convictions, generally may not go beyond the name of the crime, the time and place of conviction, and the punishment; further details such as the name of the victim and the aggravating circumstances may not be inquired into. A substantial number of courts, while not opening the door to a retrial of the previous conviction, do permit the

---

[42] United States v. Yarbrough, 352 F.(2d) 491 (6th Cir. 1965). People v. Cole, 213 N.W.(2d) 814 (Mich. 1973).

[43] United States v. Lloyd, 400 F.(2d) 414 (6th Cir. 1968).

[44] Brown v. United States, 338 F.(2d) 543 (D.C. Cir. 1964).

[45] United States v. Benson, 369 F.(2d) 569 (6th Cir. 1966).

[46] Butler v. United States, 408 F.(2d) 1103 (10th Cir. 1969).

[47] Pinkney v. United States, 380 F.(2d) 882 (5th Cir. 1967).

witness himself to make a brief and general statement in explanation, mitigation or denial of guilt, or recognize a discretion in the trial judge to permit it.[48]

Proof of prior convictions for impeachment should be excluded if the trial judge, in the exercise of his discretion, concludes that it lacks sufficient probative value because of the remoteness in time of convictions.[49-50] A prior conviction, even one involving fraud or stealing, if it occurred long before and has been followed by a legally blameless life, should generally be excluded for impeachment purposes on the ground of remoteness.[51] As expressed by Circuit Judge Feinberg,[52] the decision whether ancient or even middle-aged convictions should be used to impeach calls for most careful consideration by the trial judge.

Within the rules relating to impeachment by introduction of evidence of conviction of former crimes, even the defendant's prior criminal record may be introduced for impeachment purposes, that is, to question his reliability for telling the truth. In this instance caution by the judge is necessary for such evidence may not only be used to impeach the testimony of the defendant but may result in casting such an atmosphere of aspersion and disrepute about the defendant as to convince the jury that he is a habitual law breaker who should be punished and confined for the good of the community. On the other hand, it would be unfair to allow evidence of prior convictions to impeach the prosecution witness and not allow such evidence to impeach the testimony of the defendant who takes the stand in his own behalf.

§ 8.19 —Prior inconsistent statements

The testimony of a witness, after a proper foundation has been laid, may be impeached by showing former declarations, statements, or testimony which are contradictory or inconsistent with the answers given at a trial. The purpose of the impeachment is to discredit the witness, not to establish the existence of the fact in dis-

---

[48] Wittenberg v. United States, 304 F.Supp. 744 (D. Minn. 1969); United States v. Bray, 445 F.(2d) 178 (5th Cir. 1971).

[49-50] United States v. Allison, 414 F.(2d) 407 (9th Cir. 1969). United States v. Walling, 486 F.(2d) 229 (9th Cir. 1973).

[51] Gordon v. United States, 383 F.(2d) 936 (D.C. Cir. 1967).

[52] United States v. Zubkoff, 416 F.(2d) 141 (2d Cir. 1969).

pute. The proper procedure for laying a foundation for impeachment by prior inconsistent statements made orally is to call the attention of the witness to the particular time and occasion when the witness purportedly made the statement. The witness should be informed what the statements were and the conditions and circumstances under which they were made.[53] The witness should given an opportunity to admit, deny, or explain them. Only those portions of the prior statements which tend to contradict the testimony given at the trial are admissible.[54]

A circuit court case decided in 1967 held that if the veracity of the accused testifying in his own behalf is to be attacked by a prior inconsistent or contradictory statement made while he was under in-custody interrogation, the prosecution must show that the statement was voluntarily made after the accused had been fully advised of all of his rights and had effectively waived them in accordance with the standards prescribed in the *Miranda* case.[55] However, in *Harris* v. *United States*, the U.S. Supreme Court held that the *Miranda* warnings are not required where the confession is voluntary and used only for impeachment purposes.[55a]

Former contradictory statements introduced for the purpose of impeachment are not admissible as substantive evidence. For example, in a trial on a counterfeiting charge statements allegedly made by defendants to a special agent of the Secret Service were admissible to impeach them, but were not admissible as substantive evidence where the defendants denied making the statements.[56] Such contradictory statements become substantive evidence when the witness recants his testimony given at the trial and admits that his prior statements correctly reflect the true facts. The effect of so doing is to make the statements a part of the witness' present testimony.[57]

§ 8.19a Defects of recollections and perception

Another method of impeaching a witness is by demonstrating

---

[53] Rule 613(a) Fed. Rules of Evidence abolishes this requirement.

[54] Brooks v. United States, 309 F.(2d) 580 (10th Cir. 1962).

[55] Wheeler v. United States, 382 F.(2d) 998 (10th Cir. 1967). But see Title II of the Omnibus Crime Control Act of 1968 for possible limitations on application of *Miranda* requirements.

[55a] Miranda v. Arizona, 401 U.S. 222, 91 S.Ct. 643 (1971).

[56] Tripp v. United States, 295 F.(2d) 418 (10th Cir. 1961).

[57] Ibid.

to the judge or jury a defective capacity of the witness to observe, remember, or recount matters testified about. For example, a witness whose hearing or eyesight is impaired may be impeached by calling this to the attention of the jury or judge or by demonstrating this in court. Also, the witness's testimony may be impeached by showing that he has poor memory and is unable to recall like events. Here, as in other matters involving impeachment of the witness, the trial judge has much discretion in determining whether to admit or exclude such evidence.[58]

In determining that the witness's ability to perceive what took place was impaired, evidence may be introduced to show that the witness was under the influence of drugs or alcohol at the time he perceived the events or when testifying. However, evidence to show that the witness is a chronic alcoholic, without more, is not admissible on the issue of the witness's credibility.[58a]

§ 8.20 —Rehabilitation of witness

It is not proper in direct examination to seek corroborative support of a witness by showing that after the event under inquiry and before trial he made statements consistent with his testimony at the trial.[59] A witness impeached on the basis of prior inconsistency may always endeavor to explain away the effect of supposed inconsistency by relating whatever circumstances would naturally remove it, and the fear of consequences of plain speaking is such a circumstance. Such reasoning was applied in a bank robbery case when the prosecution was properly allowed to rehabilitate its witnesses. The witnesses had been impeached on the basis of prior inconsistent statements given to the FBI and before the grand jury, but allowed to explain that their previous failure to mention defendant's involvement was due to fear for the safety of themselves and their families.[60]

Where, on cross-examination, a witness is impeached by a showing of prior statements made by him in a written instrument and apparently inconsistent with his statements on direct examination, an effort to rehabilitate such witness by reference to the same

---

[58] State v. Vigliano, 50 N.J. 51, 232 A.(2d) 129 (1966).

[58a] Wilson v. United States, 232 U.S. 563 (1914).

[59] Schoppel v. United States, 270 F.(2d) 413 (4th Cir. 1959).

[60] United States v. Franzese, 392 F.(2d) 954 (2d Cir. 1968).

document used to impeach him is proper. In such case the statements referred to and sought to be introduced in an effort to rehabilitate such witness are confined to an explanation of the apparent inconsistencies and do not serve to inject new issues into the case.[61]

Prior consistent statements are ordinarily not admissible on redirect examination for the purpose of rehabilitating the credibility of a witness. But where defendants had used portions of extrajudicial statements of a codefendant in cross-examining him, it was proper in one case to permit the government on redirect examination to use portions of such statements to round out and complete the quotations on which defendants had based their questions in cross-examination.[62]

Some examples will help to clarify the rules.

In a bribery prosecution, wherein defendant's counsel on cross-examination of a police officer used extracts of the police reports to impair and undermine the credibility of the police officer in the eyes of the jurors, it was within the sound discretion of the trial court to permit relevant portions of the remainder of police reports to go to the jury for the limited purpose of reestablishing the credibility of the police officer.[63] And testimony of a physician and a detective as to statements which were made to them by the prosecuting witness while in the hospital after an alleged attempted abortion and which were consistent with her trial testimony was relevant and proper to an evaluation of the credibility of the prosecuting witness' statements which had been attacked by defense counsel in cross-examination.[64]

§ 8.21 Summary

Although the testimony of witnesses is essential in a criminal case, not all witnesses who have information concerning the facts

---

[61] Shellock v. Klempay Brothers, 167 OhioSt. 279, 4 OhioOp.(2d) 318, 148 N.E.(2d) 57, 75 A.L.R.(2d) 900 (1958); United States v. Smith, 328 F.(2d) 848 (6th Cir. 1964).

[62] United States v. Lev, 276 F.(2d) 605 (2d Cir. 1060).

[63] Short v. United States, 271 F.(2d) 73 (9th Cir. 1959).

[64] Copes v. United States, 345 F.(2d) 723 (D.C. Cir. 1964).

of the case are allowed to testify and the witnesses who are authorized to testify are limited as to the manner and extent of the testimony given. The trial judge has the responsibility to apply the rules of evidence in determining whether a witness may testify at all and as to the extent of his testimony. Usually the trial judge has wide discretion in making this determination.

To prevent witnesses from being influenced by testimony of other witnesses the judge has the discretion of separating the witnesses during the trial so that they are in the court room only when called upon to testify.

As a general rule leading questions are not allowed on direct examination. However, there are certain exceptions to this rule. For example, introductory matters such as the address of the witness are allowed and hostile witnesses may be asked leading questions. Also, leading questions may be authorized upon direct examination in order to correct an obviously erroneous statement, and children and others with slight command of the English language may when necessary be asked leading questions on direct.

Although it would be preferable for witnesses to testify from memory in all situations, it is clear that witnesses do not always remember the facts after a substantial period of time has passed. Recognizing this human weakness, witnesses are allowed in some instances and under very controlled conditions to refresh their memories by referring to statements. This is known as refreshing memory or as some courts call it, "present memory revived."

When the witness has no present recollection of the events which took place at the time of writing a report but remembers that he did record the facts concerning the action, this writing or memorandum of past recollection is admitted when a proper foundation has been laid.

The right of cross-examination has for years been considered a constitutional right coexistent with the right of confrontation. The purpose of the cross-examination is to give the opposing party an opportunity to challenge the credibility of the statements of the witnesses given on direct. With some exceptions the cross-examination of the witness is limited to the scope of matters brought out on direct examination. One exception to the rule is that cross-examination may be permitted for the purpose of testing the capacity of the witness to remember, to observe, or to recount. For this purpose questions may be asked that are not strictly relevant to the testimony given by the witness on direct examination.

One method (often misused) to diminish the credibility of the witness is to cast doubt upon his truthfulness. This is known in law as impeachment. The general rule is that a prosecutor or the defense counsel cannot impeach his own witness. However, there is an exception to this rule if the party who presents the witness can show that the testimony of the witness is a surprise and substantially different from that given on previous occasions. Some of the methods of impeaching a witness are: showing bias or prejudice, exposing a previous criminal record of the witness, bringing out the fact that prior inconsistent statements were made, or by showing a defective capacity of the witness to observe, remember, or recount matters testified about.

An impeached witness may be rehabilitated. For example, a witness impeached on the basis of prior inconsistent statements may show that he made the prior statements because of fear.

The officer conducting the investigation is often confused and disappointed when testimony which he feels to be relevant and important is not admissible. If he, however, is familiar with the rules concerning the testimony of witnesses, he can prepare for some of the contingencies.

Chapter 9

TESTIMONIAL PRIVILEGES

> Since it results in the exclusion of evidence, the doctrine of privileged communications between attorney and client runs counter to the fundamental theory of our judicial system that the fullest disclosure of facts will best lead to the truth and ultimately to the triumph of justice. In adjusting this conflict in policy our courts have uniformly recognized that the privilege is not absolute, but rather an exception to a more fundamental policy. It is therefore to be strictly limited to the purposes for which it exists.
> *In re Selser,* 15 N.J. 393, 105 A.(2d) 395 (1954).

Section
9.1 Introduction
9.2 Nature of testimonial privilege
9.3 Self-incrimination privilege
9.4 —Application of the privilege
9.5 —When privilege not violated
9.6 —Waiver of privilege
9.7 —Immunity
9.8 Attorney-client privilege
9.9 —Identity of client
9.10 —Advice in furtherance of crime
9.11 —Assertion and waiver of privilege
9.12 Physician-patient privilege
9.13 —Exclusions from privilege
9.14 —Persons within privilege
9.15 —Assertion and waiver of privilege
9.16 —Rationale of the privilege
9.17 Husband-wife privilege
9.18 —Exceptions to the privilege
9.19 —Duration of the privilege
9.20 Communications to clergymen
9.21 The confidential informant privilege
9.22 Governmental secrets privilege
9.23 Newsman–informant privilege
9.24 Summary

§ 9.1 Introduction

The early courts and, more recently, legislative bodies, have determined that some testimony, even though relevant, should not be admitted at the trial. This reasoning reflects a public policy determination that the protection of a particular relationship, interest, or right is more important than making all relevant evidence available to the triers of fact. This right of certain defined persons to refrain from giving testimony has become known as testimonial privilege or privileged communication.

Often the student of the rules of evidence is confused in attempting to distinguish between the rules concerning privileged communications and rules of exclusion. However, the two groups of rules are readily distinguishable if the underlying reasons are considered. The rules concerning testimonial privileges, which will be discussed in this chapter, are justified solely because of the desirability to protect rights, interests, and relationships. The rules of exclusion (hearsay rule, opinion rule, etc.) are not designed to protect such relationships but to guard against the consideration of evidence which is unreliable or is calculated to prejudice or mislead.

Some authorities argue that the reasons for exclusion of valuable testimony, because of the testimonial privilege rules, are no longer valid and should be abandoned or at least modified. There is an apparent tendency by the courts to construe the rules narrowly, but little has been done to change the traditional rules, especially those which were recognized at common law.

Apparently the United States Supreme Court decided in 1972 that the rules relating to privilege should be clarified and codified. The draft of the Federal Rules of Evidence which was submitted to Congress that year included rules 501 through 513 relating to "privileges." Rules 503, 504, 505, and 506 defined terms and detailed requirements concerning the Lawyer-Client Privilege, the Psychotherapist-Patient Privilege, the Husband-Wife Privilege, and the Communications-to-Clergyman Privilege.

The House of Representatives, after debate and discussion, deleted the codifications and sent the rules to the Senate without the specific provisions concerning privileges. Instead the House version provided that the rules to be applied were, "the principles of the common law as they may be interpreted by the courts of the United States, except as modified by statute or the Constitution."

Notwithstanding the fact that the House of Representatives deleted this article relating to privileges, the definitions and requirements are well worth studying. Some of the definitions are used in this chapter and the proposed rules are included in the Appendix.

Although there are other privileges created by statute, only the rules relating to the following types will be discussed in this chapter: the self-incrimination privilege, the attorney-client privilege, the physician-patient privilege, the husband-wife privilege, communications made to the clergy, confidential informant privilege, government secrets privilege, and newsman's privilege.

§ 9.2 Nature of testimonial privilege

A testimonial privilege merely means that a witness will not be required to testify in court if the privilege is properly claimed. A privilege usually is personal in that it must be claimed by the person protected—the accused, the client, the patient, or the spouse. Only the holder of the privilege may claim error on a trial court's ruling disallowing a claim of privilege.

The rules of privilege have been designed to protect personal relationships or other rights and interests where the protection is considered more important than the need for the evidence. Very few privileges were recognized at common law, but a number of privileges have been created by statutory enactments.

Privileges created by federal statutes do not assume the form of broad principles; instead, they are the product of resolving particular problems in particular terms. By way of illustration, a federal statute prohibits official disclosure of census information and confers a privileged status on retained copies of census reports. Other statutes make inadmissible in evidence reports of railroad accidents, airplane accident investigation reports, and anything said or done during an Equal Employment Opportunity conciliation proceeding.

State statutes creating privileges cover such relationships as attorney and client, physician and patient, husband and wife, and communications to clergymen.

§ 9.3 Self-incrimination privilege

One testimonial privilege, the self-incrimination privilege, is predicated on a constitutional guarantee. The Fifth Amendment to the Federal Constitution provides that "No person . . . shall be compelled in any criminal case to be a witness against himself." Practically identical provisions are found in most state constitutions. This privilege protects an accused from being required to testify against himself, and protects a witness from being required to give testimony which might subject him to criminal liability.[1]

According to the U.S. Supreme Court, the privilege against self-incrimination reflects (1) unwillingness to subject those suspected of crime to the cruel trilemma of self-accusation, perjury, or contempt; (2) preference for an accusatorial rather than an inquisitorial system of criminal justice; (3) fear that self-incriminating statements will be elicited by inhumane treatment and abuses; (4) respect for the inviolability of the human personality; (5) distrust of self-deprecatory statements; and (6) realization that the privilege, while sometimes "a shelter to the guilty," is often a protection to the innocent.[1a]

In 1964 the Supreme Court decided that the privilege is applicable to state as well as federal proceedings,[2] and that the constitutional privilege protects a state witness against incrimination under federal as well as state law and a federal witness against incrimination under state as well as federal law.[3]

§ 9.4 —Application of the privilege

The privilege not only extends to answers that would in themselves support a conviction under a criminal statute but likewise embraces those which would furnish a link in the chain of evidence needed to prosecute the claimant for a crime. But this protection must be confined to instances where the witness has reasonable cause to apprehend danger from a direct answer. The witness is

---

[1] See Chapter 14 for a full discussion of the law relating to exclusion of confessions, and other evidence obtained in violation of the self-incrimination and other constitutional protections.

[1a] Murphy v. Waterfront Commission of N.Y., 378 U.S. 52, 12 L.Ed. (2d) 678, 84 S.Ct. 1594 (1964).

[2] Malloy v. Hogan, 378 U.S. 1, 12 L.Ed.(2d) 653, 84 S.Ct. 1489 (1964).

[3] Murphy v. Waterfront Commission of N.Y., n. 1 supra.

not exonerated from answering merely because he declares that in so doing he would incriminate himself—his say-so does not of itself establish the hazard of incrimination. It is for the court to say whether his silence is justified, and to require him to answer if it clearly appears to the court that he is mistaken.[4]

The privilege against self-incrimination may not be asserted in advance of questions actually propounded, and in no event may an ordinary witness refuse to be sworn.[5] The accused may, of course, refuse to take the stand and be sworn.

§ 9.5 —When privilege not violated

The privilege is not violated by requiring the accused to model articles of clothing,[6-8] to stand for identification in court,[9] to submit to a blood test to obtain evidence of the presence of alcohol,[10] to submit to routine fingerprinting,[11] or to submit to the taking of handwriting exemplars.[12] Nor is the privilege violated either by having the defendant sign a fingerprint card or by the failure to advise him of his right to counsel and his right to remain silent prior to signing the card.[13]

§ 9.6 —Waiver of privilege

Since the privilege against self-incrimination of a witness is personal to him, it cannot be claimed by another party for him.

Where the accused acts voluntarily he may waive his privilege protected by the self-incrimination provisions, either in court or outside of court. Although the accused may waive this right, the burden is on the prosecution to show that the defendant knowingly

---

[4] Hoffman v. United States, 341 U.S. 479, 95 L.Ed. 1118, 71 S.Ct. 814 (1951). U.S. v. Malnik, 489 F.(2d) 682 (5th Cir. 1974).

[5] United States v. Harmon, 339 F.(2d) 354 (6th Cir. 1964).

[6-8] Holt v. United States, 218 U.S. 245, 54 L.Ed. 1021, 31 S.Ct. 2 (1910).

[9] People v. Curran, 286 Ill. 302, 121 N.E. 637 (1918).

[10] Schmerber v. California, 384 U.S. 757, 16 L.Ed.(2d) 908, 86 S.Ct. 1826 (1966).

[11] Napolitano v. United States, 340 F.(2d) 313 (1st Cir. 1965). Ward v. United States, 486 F.(2d) 305 (5th Cir. 1974).

[12] Gilbert v. California, 388 U.S. 263, 18 L.Ed.(2d) 1178, 87 S.Ct. 1951 (1967). United States v. Ryan, 478 F.(2d) 1008 (5th Cir. 1973).

[13] Johnson v. Bennett, 291 F.Supp. 421 (S.D. Iowa 1968).

and intelligently waived the privilege.

At the trial itself, both the accused and the ordinary witness may waive the rights protected by the self-incrimination provisions. However, the procedure in waiving the right differs between the ordinary witness and the defendant.

   a. Waiver by the defendant
      The accused has the option under the criminal procedure provisions in this country to remain off the stand altogether or to testify. However, by volunteering to become a witness he waives his right as it concerns relevant inquiries about the charges against him.[14] With few exceptions the defendant cannot take the stand and testify in his own behalf and then refuse to answer relevant inquiries on cross-examination.[15] Even at the trial the accused must be made aware that he is waiving his rights and this waiver must be made intelligently and knowingly.
   b. Waiver by the ordinary witness
      Unlike the accused, the ordinary witness has no privilege to decline altogether to testify. On the other hand by taking the stand he waives nothing. He makes the choice as each question is asked. However, when the witness has testified to an incriminating fact, he is considered to have waived his privilege as to all further questions relevant to the same transaction. The decision of the witness not to answer questions on the grounds it may incriminate him is not conclusive, of course. Although the judge should give the claim careful consideration, he makes the final decision as to whether the witness will be required to answer the question.

In an out-of-court situation, if the witness or accused refuses to answer questions, neither the police nor the prosecutor can force him to do so. But if the statement is made after waiver and is made knowingly and intelligently, it may be used in court.

§ 9.7 —Immunity

Notwithstanding the self-incrimination privilege, answers may be required if immunity from criminal prosecution is properly

---

[14] Johnson v. United States, 318 U.S. 189, 87 L.Ed. 704, 63 S.Ct. 549 (1943).

[15] Carpenter v. United States, 264 F.(2d) 565 (4th Cir. 1959). State v. Foster, 284 N.C. 259 (1973).

granted. In order to secure testimony which because of the privilege would not otherwise be procured, federal and state legislative bodies have enacted legislation to grant immunity to witnesses.[16] These statutes merely provide that if a witness claims a protection as granted by the Fifth Amendment, and the government still seeks his answers, immunity can be granted by the proper authorities and the person will then be required to testify. The theory is that if immunity is granted, there is no longer any reason to claim the privilege.

These statutes have been challenged as violating the Constitution but if the statutes give complete immunity, the witness can be required to testify and this does not violate any constitutional provisions.

§ 9.8 Attorney-client privilege

It is a general rule that confidential communications between an attorney and his client, made because of the professional relationship and concerning the subject matter of the attorney's employment, are privileged from disclosure. Confidential communications between client and attorney were privileged under common law and the privilege is of ancient origin. The doctrine is subject to statutory regulation and limitation, but except as so modified the statutes are merely declaratory of the common-law rule. While it is the objective at the trial to ascertain the truth, there is the countervailing necessity of insuring the right of every person freely and fully to confer and to confide in one having knowledge of the law and skilled in its practice, in order that the former may have adequate advice and a proper defense. This assistance can be made safely and readily available only when the client is free from the consequences of apprehension of disclosure by reason of the subsequent statements of the skilled lawyer. Thus the public policy factor outweighs the desirability of placing all facts before the jury.

There cannot be an attorney-client privilege unless the party to whom the communication was made is an attorney or a repre-

---

[16] Counselman v. Hitchcock, 142 U.S. 547, 35 L.Ed. 1110, 12 S.Ct. 195 (1892).

sentative of the attorney. Each state determines, within constitutional limitations, who may or may not practice law within its courts. Because the requirements for licensing of attorneys are established by state law, and differ from state to state, the nature and extent of the privilege that exists between attorney and client varies.

The following definitions are included in the Federal Rules of Evidence as submitted to Congress in 1972:[17]

(1) A "client" is a person, public officer, or corporation, association, or other organization or entity, either public or private, who is rendered professional legal services by a lawyer, or who consults a lawyer with a view to obtaining professional legal services from him.

(2) A "lawyer" is a person authorized, or reasonably believed by the client to be authorized, to practice law in any state or nation.

(3) A "representative of the lawyer" is one employed to assist the lawyer in the rendition of professional legal services.

(4) A communication is "confidential" if not intended to be disclosed to third persons other than those to whom disclosure is in furtherance of the rendition of professional legal services to the client or those reasonably necessary for the transmission of the communication.

A frequently quoted test relating to the privilege is found in *United States v. United Shoe Mach. Corp.*[18] In that case the court commented:

> The privilege applies only if (1) the asserted holder of the privilege is or sought to become a client; (2) the person to whom the communication was made (a) is a member of the bar of a court, or his subordinate and (b) in connection with this communication is acting as a lawyer; (3) the communication relates to a fact of which the attorney was informed (a) by his client (b) without the presence of strangers (c) for the purpose of securing primarily either (i) an opinion on law or (ii) legal services or (iii) assistance in some legal proceeding, and not (d) for the purpose of committing

---

[17] Rule 503, Fed. Rules of Evidence as submitted to Congress.

[18] 89 F.Supp. 357 (D. Mass. 1950).

Also see United States v. Schmidt, 360 F.Supp. 339 (1973) for a discussion of the scope of the privilege.

a crime or tort; and (4) the privilege has been (a) claimed and (b) not waived by the client.

Although the attorney-client privilege is recognized in all courts, not all of the relationships are protected. Some of the situations where the protection is not applicable are discussed in the following sections.

§ 9.9 —Identity of client

Generally, the identity of the attorney's client is not considered privileged matter. The existence of the relation of attorney and client is not a privileged communication. The privilege pertains to the subject matter, and not to the fact of the employment as attorney, and since it presupposes the relationship of attorney and client, it does not attach to the creation of that relationship. The client or the attorney may be permitted or compelled to testify as to the fact of his employment as attorney, or as to the fact of his having advised his client as to a certain matter, or performed certain services for the client.[19]

Neither the fact of employment nor the amount of fee paid is a confidential communication within the basic philosophy of the privilege. Thus, in a proceeding to require two attorneys to respond to an administrative summons in connection with the investigation of tax returns of the attorneys' clients, information as to the amount of fees paid, dates of payment, and by or through whom payments were made was not privileged.[20]

Although the authorities are substantially uniform against any privilege as applied to the fact of retainer or identity of the client, there is an exception to the general rule, firmly bedded as the rule itself. That exception is that the privilege may be recognized when so much of the actual communication has already been disclosed that identification of the client amounts to disclosure of a confidential communication.[21]

---

[19] Morris v. State, 242 A.(2d) 559 (Md. 1968). See case in Part II.
[20] In re Wasserman, 198 F.Supp. 564 (D.C. 1961).
[21] In re Kaplan, 8 N.Y.(2d) 214, 168 N.E.(2d) 660 (1960); N.L.R.B. v. Harvey, 349 F.(2d) 900 (4th Cir. 1965).

§ 9.10 —Advice in furtherance of crime

The attorney-client relationship offers no shield to either client or attorney if the client has been engaged in a plan to commit a crime or fraud in the future.[22] The interests of public justice require that no shield such as the protection afforded to communications between attorney and client shall be interposed to protect a person who takes counsel on how he can safely commit a crime. This rule extends to one who, having committed a crime, seeks advice as to how he can escape arrest and punishment. As an example, communications relating to advice regarding the destruction or disposition of the murder weapon or of the body following a murder are not within the privilege.[23]

The announced intention of a client to commit a crime is not included within the confidences which the attorney is bound to respect. The attorney may properly make such disclosures as may be necessary to prevent the act or protect those against whom it is threatened.[24]

§ 9.11 —Assertion and waiver of privilege

The privilege against disclosure of information confidentially revealed to an attorney is personal to the client and may be asserted only by him. This privilege is not a right effective without claim or assertion. It is a mere privilege that has no practical existence or effect unless personally and timely claimed by its possessor. A claim of privilege must be timely raised or it will be deemed to have been waived.

Testimony by the client, or at his request by the attorney, revealing a portion of the communication is a waiver as to the remainder. The client waives the privilege when he discloses what he claims were communications between himself and his attorney, especially when his version reflects on the attorney and calls for an explanation.[25] If an attorney is accused by his client, the attorney

---

[22] Clark v. United States, 289 U.S. 1, 77 L.Ed. 993, 53 S.Ct. 465 (1933); United States v. Weinberg, 226 F.(2d) 161 (3d Cir. 1955). Cited with approval in United States v. Hoffa, 349 F.(2d) 20 (6th Cir. 1965).

[23] Clark v. State, 159 Tex.Cr.R. 187, 261 S.W.(2d) 339 (1953).

[24] American Bar Association, CANONS OF PROFESSIONAL ETHICS, No. 37.

[25] Cooper v. United States, 5 F.(2d) 824 (6th Cir. 1925).

is not precluded from disclosing the truth in respect to the accusation.[25a]

§ 9.12 Physician-patient privilege

At common law there was no privilege protecting the confidences reposed by sick or injured persons in their physicians. Today about two-thirds of the states have enacted statutes creating a testimonial privilege which prohibits a disclosure by the physician, when called to testify, of confidential communications made to, or information acquired by, him in the course of his professional attendance upon the patient. A majority of the courts declare that the primary purpose of such statute is to encourage the utmost confidence between the patient and his physician and to preserve it inviolate.

In the rules approved by the U.S. Supreme Court to govern procedure in Federal Courts the following definitions were included:[26]

(1) A "patient" is a person who consults or is examined or interviewed by a psychotherapist.

(2) A "psychotherapist" is (A) a person authorized to practice medicine in any state or nation, or reasonably believed by the patient so to be, while engaged in the diagnosis or treatment of a mental or emotional condition, including drug addiction, or (B) a person licensed or certified as a psychologist under the laws of any state or nation, while similarly engaged.

(3) A communication is "confidential" if not intended to be disclosed to third persons other than those present to further the interest of the patient in the consultation, examination, or interview, or persons reasonably necessary for the transmission of the communication, or persons who are participating in the diagnosis and treatment under the direction of the psychotherapist, including members of the patient's family.

Although this rule was omitted from the version passed on to the Senate by the House, the definitions should be considered. It should be noted that the definition of "psychotherapist" has a broad coverage and includes not only physicians but psychologists

---

[25a] State v. Simmons, 57 Wisc.(2d) 285, 203 N.W.(2d) 887 (1973).

[26] Rule 504 of draft of Fed. Rules of Evidence.

and those "reasonably believed" by the patient so to be. This broad definition is not applicable in most instances.

Two important prerequisites must be met before a communication can become privileged under the physician-**patient** doctrine. First, the communication must come in the course of the lawful medical treatment of a patient. Second, the subject information that is sought to be privileged must be gained in the course of direct observation of the patient or in direct communication with him as to treatment.

§ 9.13 —Exclusions from privilege

While many states have by statute created the privilege, the exceptions which have been found necessary in order to obtain information required by the public interest or to avoid fraud are so numerous as to leave little basis for the privilege. Among the exclusions from the statutory privilege, the following may be enumerated: communications not made for purposes of diagnosis and treatment; commitment and restoration proceedings; issues as to wills or otherwise between parties claiming by succession from the patient; actions on insurance policies; required reports (venereal diseases, gunshot wounds, child abuse); communications in furtherance of crime or fraud; mental or physical condition put in issue by patient (personal injury cases); malpractice actions; and some or all criminal prosecutions. California, for example, excepts cases in which the patient puts his condition in issue, all criminal proceedings, will and similar contests, malpractice cases, and disciplinary proceedings, as well as certain other situations, thus leaving virtually nothing covered by the privilege.

Where a physician is required by state law to report to a law-enforcement officer a gunshot wound or wound inflicted by a deadly weapon, the former may testify, without violating the physician-patient privilege, as to the description of the wounded person, as to his name and address, if known, and as to the description of the nature and location of such wound, obtained by examination, observation, and treatment of the victim.[27]

---

[27] State v. Antill, 176 OhioSt. 61, 26 OhioOp.(2d) 366, 197 N.E.(2d) 548 (1964). Marcus v. Superior Court of Los Angeles, 18 Cal.App.(3d) 22, 95 Cal.Rptr. 545 (1971).

In 1959 Illinois enacted a modern statute defining the physician-patient privilege. It provided that the physician or surgeon shall not be permitted to disclose any information he may have acquired in attending any patient in a professional character, necessary to enable him professionally to serve such patient. It, however, provided that exceptions would apply (1) in trials for homicide when the disclosure relates directly to the fact or immediate circumstances of the homicide, (2) in actions, civil or criminal, against the physician for malpractice, (3) with the expressed consent of the patient, or in case of his death or disability, of his personal representative or other person authorized to sue for personal injury or of the beneficiary of an insurance policy on his life, health, or physical condition, (4) in all civil suits brought by or against the patient, his personal representative, a beneficiary under a policy of insurance, or the executor or administrator of his estate wherein the patient's physical or mental condition is an issue, (5) upon an issue as to the validity of a document as a will of the patient, (6) in any criminal action where the charge is either murder by abortion, attempted abortion or abortion or (7) in actions, civil or criminal, arising from the filing of a report with respect to neglect or injury to children.[28] Of interest to enforcement personnel is the rule in most jurisdictions that the privilege extends only to civil actions.

§ 9.14 —Persons within privilege

Some jurisdictions have taken the view that statutes, making communications between physicians and patients privileged, include, by implication, the attendants who are assisting or acting under the direction of the physician in his treatment of a patient, and that such an attendant is precluded from disclosing any information concerning the patient which is acquired during such treatment. Some jurisdictions hold to the contrary. When an intern may properly be said to be the agent of the physician in taking part in the treatment of a patient, the privilege applies in the case of the intern as it would in the case of the physician on whose behalf he acts. Thus, where an intern was a "medical servant" at the time he obtained information from the patient who entered

---

[28] Ill. Rev. Stat. 1967, Ch. 51, § 5.1.

the hospital while suffering from brain lesion, the intern's duties under rules of the hospital included the taking of medical histories from patients who were to undergo medical treatment or surgery, and the intern was acting under the direction of the attending physician and also the hospital administrator, what the patient told the intern was a privileged communication.[29]

The courts are divided on the question of whether an attending nurse comes within the statutory privilege expressly applicable to physicians, but agree that the privilege pertains to matters germane to the physician's diagnosis and treatment of the patient. Therefore, when a statement is not made in confidence, and not intended to be so treated, and is not germane to the diagnosis or treatment of the patient, but is simply a deathbed statement apparently made to anyone who happened to be listening, it is not privileged and the testimony of the attending nurse is admissible.[30]

§ 9.15 —Assertion and waiver of privilege

The physician-patient privilege definitely belongs to the patient, and the physician may be compelled to testify if the patient has waived the privilege.

State statutes creating a physician-patient privilege usually provide that if the patient voluntarily testifies as to privileged matter, the physician may be compelled to testify on the same subject. The physician also may testify by express consent of his patient, or if the patient be deceased, by the express consent of the surviving spouse or the executor or administrator of the estate of the deceased patient.

The privilege is justified only when disclosures are made in confidence. Therefore where the communication is made in the presence of unnecessary third persons, the privilege is waived.

§ 9.16 —Rationale of the privilege

A statute which prevents a physician, when lawfully summoned as a witness, from testifying to facts within his personal knowledge and relevant and material to the issue on trial, can be justified only

---

[29] Franklin Life Ins. Co. v. Wm. J. Champion & Co., 353 F.(2d) 919 (6th Cir. 1965).

[30] Taylor v. Reo Motors, Inc., 275 F.(2d) 699 (10th Cir. 1960).

by clear proof that the claimed advantage and benefits which may result to the general public from the shielding of confidences arising from the physician-patient relationship, far outweigh the harm and injustice which necessarily results to litigants from the concealment or suppression of the truth in actions in which the public has little or no concern.[31]

§ 9.17 Husband-wife privilege

One of the most discussed but most misunderstood testimonial privileges is the husband-wife privilege. The modern rule is that testimony by either spouse against the other is prohibited. This rule probably has grown out of a fusion of two so-called common-law rules of evidence. One of the early rules prohibited either spouse from testifying for or against the other. The other rule prohibited either spouse from revealing confidential communications from the other during the marriage.[32] The modern courts have rejected the first common-law rule insofar as it prohibits either spouse from testifying *for* the other.

Today a spouse may testify for the other but not against the other in the criminal proceeding, if either spouse objects.[33] In most states today either spouse may claim the privilege and refuse to testify against the other party even though the other party consents.[34]

Attention should be called to the minority view taken by a few courts. These courts take the position the privilege belongs solely to the spouse who is to be called as a witness. They hold that a married person has a privilege not to be called as a witness to testify against his spouse; however, if the spouse wants to testify, the other party cannot prevent it.

---

[31] See DeWitt, Clinton, PRIVILEGED COMMUNICATIONS BETWEEN PHYSICIAN AND PATIENT. 10 W. Res. L. Rev. 488, 494 (Sept. 1959).

[32] Hawkins v. United States, 358 U.S. 74, 3 L.Ed.(2d) 125, 79 S.Ct. 136 (1958). See case in Part II.
Also see Funk v. United States, 290 U.S. 371, 54 S.Ct. 212 (1933). Parts included in Part II of this book.

[33] Wyatt v. United States, 362 U.S. 525, 4 L.Ed.(2d) 931, 80 S.Ct. 901 (1960).

[34] Orfield, Lester B., THE HUSBAND-WIFE PRIVILEGES IN FEDERAL CRIMINAL PROCEDURE. 24 OhioSt. L. J. 144 (1963).

§ 9.18 —Exceptions to the privilege

There are certain well-known exceptions to this husband-wife privilege. Some will be discussed in this section.[34a]

a. Situations where the communication is not in confidence

The privilege is generally limited to confidential communications. Therefore, if others are present when the statements are made, they no longer come within the scope of the privilege. This is true even if the persons present are members of the family, including children, if the children are not too young to understand the communication.

b. Prosecutions against one spouse for acts against the other

It would be obviously a miscarriage of justice and not within the scope of the reasons for the rule to prohibit one spouse from testifying against the other in situations where that spouse has been injured by the other. This same reasoning applies in prosecutions where crime is committed by one spouse against the children of either. This exception to the so-called common-law rule of evidence was held to apply in a prosecution for violation of the Mann Act.[35] This exception has also been applied in bigamy and adultery cases.

c. Communications overheard by third parties

Another exception which is related to the one first mentioned concerns the testimony of a third party who overheard the confidential communications. Where a third party has overheard conversations between the husband and wife he may testify as to the communications. The reasoning for this is that the justification for the rule does not exist, at least in whole, under the circumstances. Other reasoning to justify this exception is that by failing to take precautions to prevent others from hearing, the spouses are deemed to have waived the right to secrecy.[36]

[34a] Wyatt v. United States, 362 U.S. 525, 4 L.Ed.(2d) 931, 80 S.Ct. 901 (1960).
[35] Draft of Rule 505 of Fed. Rules of Evidence enumerates similar exceptions.
[36] People v. Melski, 10 N.Y.(2d) 78, 176 N.E.(2d) 81 (1961).

§ 9.19 —Duration of the privilege

Although the authorities on evidence question the advisability of the rule, the courts in this country have accepted the need for permanent protection and provide that the protection continues after divorce or death as to statements made during the marriage. The protection, however, does not extend after the divorce to acts or utterances made prior to or subsequent to the marriage.[37] A communication made during a purported marriage, later annulled because of fraud, was held to be within the privilege. The general rule is that the privilege exists when the parties are separated if there is in fact no legal divorce

§ 9.20 Communications to clergymen

Forty-four states have statutes making confidential communications to clergymen privileged.[38] Many of these statutes have substantially the same wording: A clergyman or priest shall not testify concerning a confession made to him in his professional character in the course of discipline enjoined by the church to which he belongs.[39] A communication made to a priest, to be deemed privileged under such a statute, must apply only to a confession made in the understood pursuance of church discipline which gives rise to the confessional relation and not to communications of other tenor.[40]

Other statutes confer a broader privilege and apply to information communicated to the clergyman or priest in a confidential manner, properly entrusted to him in his professional capacity, and necessary to enable him to discharge the functions of his office according to the usual course of his practice or discipline, wherein the person so communicating is seeking spiritual counsel and advice.[41]

The term "clergyman" as used in these statutes means a min-

---

[37] Pereira v. United States, 347 U.S. 1, 98 L.Ed. 435, 74 S.Ct. 358 (1954).

[38] Reese, Seward, CONFIDENTIAL COMMUNICATIONS TO THE CLERGY. 24 OhioSt.L.J. 55 (1963).

[39] Mullen v. United States, 263 F. (2d) 275 (D.C. Cir. 1958). See case in Part II. Also see Ariz. Rev. Stats Ann. § 12-2233 (1956); Ohio Rev. Code § 2317.02 (1953).

[40] In re Soeder, 7 OhioApp.(2d) 271, 36 OhioOp.(2d) 404, 220 N.E. (2d) 547 (1966).

[41] Fla. Stats. Ann. § 90.241 (1960).

ister, priest, rabbi, or other similar functionary of a religious organization. The communicating person is entitled to prevent disclosure not only by himself, but also by the clergyman. Although the privilege belongs to the communicating person, the clergyman may claim the privilege on behalf of the person.[41a]

§ 9.21 The confidential informant privilege

There has been some confusion concerning the confidential informant privilege. Some of this confusion can be avoided by approaching this from two angles. One approach is to consider the confidential informant who gives information from which the court can determine "probable cause" for the securing of a search warrant. This is different from the informer who was an integral part of the illegal transaction and whose identity is essential to the defense.

Recent Supreme Court decisions have made it clear that in most instances the state does not have to disclose the name of the informant who gave information upon which probable cause for the search warrant was based. In the case of *United States v. Ventresca*,[42] the Court stated:

> And, in *Aguilar*, we recognized that "an affidavit may be based upon hearsay information and need not reflect the direct personal observations of the affiant," so long as the magistrate is "informed of some of the underlying circumstances" supporting the affiant's conclusions and his belief that any informant involved "whose identity need not be disclosed . . . was 'credible' or his information 'reliable.' "

As a rule, therefore, the informant who only gives an officer information for a search warrant does not have to be disclosed if the officer can give information to the issuing official indicating

---

[41a] The definitions included in the draft of Rule 506 of the Federal Rules of Evidence prepared by the U.S. Supreme Court in 1972 are:
(1) A "clergyman" is a minister, priest, rabbi, or other similar functionary of a religious organization, or an individual reasonably believed so be to be by the person consulting him.
(2) A communication is "confidential" if made privately and not intended for further disclosure except to other persons present in furtherance of the purpose of the communication.

[42] 380 U.S. 102, 13 L.Ed.(2d) 684, 85 S.Ct. 741 (1965). Also see United States v. Harris, 91 S.Ct. 2075 (1971) where informer refused to appear because he feared for his life and safety.

that the informant has been reliable in the past. Generally, communications made by informants to public officers engaged in the discovery of crime are privileged. This privilege exists in order to conceal the identity of the informant and thereby allow him to continue as a source of future information as well as to protect him from reprisals for his actions in giving the information. The public policy encouraging others to assist in the prevention and detection of crime is deemed to outweigh the harm which is done to the defense by denying it the knowledge of the informant's identity. This rule, however, has exceptions. This was clearly stated in a recent case,[43] in which the court held:

> The State has the privilege to withhold from disclosure the identity of persons who furnish information to police officers concerning the commission of crimes. However, the privilege is not absolute. On the issue of guilt or innocence (not on Fourth Amendment issues) and only upon demand by the defendant, the trial court may, in the exercise of its judicial discretion compel such disclosure upon determination that it is necessary and relevant to a fair defense. Factors to be considered in ascertaining whether such disclosure is necessary and relevant to a fair defense include the nature of the crime charged; the importance of the informer's identity to determination of innocence, as for example, whether the informer was an integral part of the illegal transaction and the possible significance of his testimony; and the possible defenses. Whether the privilege must yield depends upon the facts and circumstances of the particular case. But if the informer testifies for the State the privilege may not be invoked by it.

Several examples might help to clarify this exception. In one case the prosecutor was not privileged to withhold the name of the informant where the informant played a direct and prominent part as the sole participant with the accused in the very offense for which the latter was being tried.[44] However, in another case the accused was not entitled to know the identity of the informer where the record revealed only that the informant contacted the police and informed them that a pickup of narcotics was to take

---

[43] Nutter v. State, 8 Md. App. 635, 262 A.(2d) 80 (1970).
[44] Roviaro v. United States, 353 U.S. 53, 1 L.Ed.(2d) 639, 77 S.Ct. 623 (1957).

place, but was otherwise silent as to participation by the informant in the transaction itself.⁴⁵

The privilege is that of the governmental authority, not the informant, and may be waived by the government.

§ 9.22 Governmental secrets privilege

Another type of privilege that should be mentioned concerns state secrets and confidential and secret communications. As a general rule state secrets and diplomatic correspondence and other official communications, the disclosure of which would be detrimental to the public interests in the opinion of the head of the executive or military department or other governmental agency concerned, are privileged. There is some conflict in the cases as to whether the judge must accept the statement of the government official that disclosure would be dangerous to the public interests or whether the judge can look into the matter. The better view seems to be that the judge should have some facts on which to base the decision unless there is clear evidence that the disclosure would be dangerous to the government concerned.

This privilege, as others, has some exceptions. In some instances where a refusal would seriously hamper the defense, the prosecution may be required to dismiss the charges or to request a dismissal of the charges, or make the confidential communications available.

§ 9.23 Newsman—informant privilege

Over the years efforts have been made to extend the privileged communication doctrine so as to protect communications made to accountants,⁴⁶ engineers, newsmen, and others. The argument is that information communicated in professional confidence should be privileged to protect professional relationships. The courts have been reluctant to extend this privilege, however.

In 1972 the Supreme Court held, in *Branzburg* v. *Hayes*⁴⁷ that there is no common law protection in the First Amendment against members of the press having to disclose their sources in court proceedings. The Court, however, pointed out that legislatures can constitutionally create such privilege by statute.

---

⁴⁵ Jimenez v. United States, 397 F. (2d) 271 (5th Cir. 1968).
⁴⁶ United States v. Schmidt, 360 F.Supp. 339 (1973).
⁴⁷ Branzburg v. Hayes, 408 U.S. 665 (1972).

To date, seventeen states have enacted newsman's privilege laws. Such laws are one of two types: 1) statutes that protect only the identity of the source of the information; 2) and those that protect the information itself as well as the source.

Moreover, there has been action in Congress to create a national privilege statute in this area.[48] If enacted into law, this statute would allow the newsman an *absolute privilege* to refuse disclosure of sources of information gathered in his capacity as a reporter when called before Congress or its committees, before any federal agency or before any federal grand jury. In civil and criminal proceedings before federal courts, disclosure would remain privileged unless the party seeking such privileged information "has established by clear and convincing evidence that such information or identity is relevant to a significant issue in the action and cannot be obtained by alternative means."

Although there are arguments for enlarging the confidential communications concept to include communications made to newsmen, there are also strong arguments that all relevant evidence should be made available in enforcing the laws. At the present time states providing for newsman's privilege are in the minority.

§ 9.24 Summary

It is desirable that all relevant evidence be made available to the triers of fact in a criminal case. However, it is also desirable that certain rights, interests, and relationships be protected. In balancing these two considerations, the courts, and in some instances legislators, have determined that certain communications and testimony will be privileged. In these situations the protection of the relationship or right is considered more important than the need for the evidence.

In a criminal case, one cannot be required to testify against himself. To require such testimony would violate the Fifth Amendment guarantee. This privilege must be claimed personally by the witness and may be waived by the witness. When an accused takes the stand he waives the privilege as to the matters related to the particular charge. And when an ordinary witness answers questions on the stand he is considered to have waived the privilege.

---

[48] H.R. 5928, 93rd Congress.

One of the traditional common-law privileges is the attorney-client privilege. This privilege applies only when the client is seeking advice of a legal nature and cannot be claimed when the communication concerns the commission of a crime some time in the future. <u>The privilege must be claimed by the client and can be waived by the client even if the attorney does not agree</u>.

Although at common law there was no physician-patient privilege, most states have enacted statutes creating this testimonial privilege. In most jurisdictions this privilege does not apply in criminal cases and even where it does apply, there are many exceptions. For example, it does not apply where a statute requires reports of gunshot wounds, or wounds inflicted by deadly weapons. The privilege applies only when the disclosures are made in confidence. It must be claimed by the patient and only he may waive the privilege.

Another privilege that has been developed over a period of many years is the husband-wife privilege. Unlike the others discussed this can be invoked by either spouse in most jurisdictions and can be waived only if both agree. There are some well-defined exceptions to the privilege. If statements are made in the presence of third parties they are not within the scope of the privilege. Also the privilege does not apply if the prosecution is against one spouse for the injury to the other spouse or the children. The privilege exists during the legal marriage and after divorce as to statements made during the marriage but <u>not to communications before or after the marriage.</u>

A lesser known privileged communication is that between the clergyman and the person communicating with the recognized clergyman or priest. This privilege has only limited application and can be claimed only by the communicator.

One of the privileges which is of more concern to the enforcement officer is that relating to the confidential informant. It can be said that as a general rule the name of the informant does not have to be disclosed, especially if his information relates only to facts on which probable cause can be based. However, if the informant played an integral part in the illegal transaction and his disclosure is necessary and relevant to a fair defense, his identity may be required. Much discretion in this regard is in the hands of the judge.

Although the United States Supreme Court has decided that there is no common law rule protecting communications made to newsmen, statutes in some states recognize the newsman-informant privilege.

Because of the above discussed privileges much relevant evidence is excluded at the trial. However, there are so many exceptions to the rules that much valuable evidence can be obtained if the investigator is familiar with the rules and the exceptions. For example, in one case testimony of the wife was allowed in a murder case after the prosecution introduced evidence to show that a teenage child was present when the statements were made to the wife.

There is some indication that the courts and legislatures are modifying some of the privilege rules in order to prevent abuse. These changes should be watched carefully. There is a need for courts to determine the truth in criminal cases and danger of injustice if the truth is suppressed by unjustified rules.

Chapter 10

OPINION TESTIMONY

> Opinion evidence, to be of any value, should be based either upon admitted facts or upon facts, within the knowledge of the witness, disclosed in the record. Opinion evidence that does not appear to be based upon disclosed facts is of little or no value.
> *Balaban & Katz Corp.* v. *Commissioner of Internal Revenue,* 30 F. (2d) 807 (7th Cir. 1929).

Section
- 10.1 Introduction
- 10.1a Definitions and distinctions
- 10.2 Admissibility of non-expert opinions
- 10.3 Subjects of non-expert opinion
- 10.4 Opinions of experts
- 10.5 Requirement of probability
- 10.6 Qualifications of an expert
- 10.7 Examination of expert witness
- 10.8 Cross-examination of expert
- 10.9 Subjects of expert testimony
- 10.9a Experts from crime laboratories
- 10.10 Summary

§ 10.1 Introduction

The general rule of evidence is that the testimony of witnesses must be confined to statements of concrete facts within their own observation, knowledge and recollection—that is, facts perceived by the use of their own senses, as distinguished from their opinions, inferences, impressions, and conclusions drawn from such facts. Whenever a question is to be determined by common experience or by inference from particular facts, the determination is to be made or the inference drawn by the jury or the judge, as the case may be, and not by the witnesses. It is an established and familiar principle that the opinion or conclusion of a witness is, in general, incompetent and inadmissible.

Necessity requires that there be exceptions to this rule. It is often impossible to testify to naked facts. Thus, witnesses are permitted to testify as to distance, time, speed, size, direction, and similar matters, all of which require the witness to state an opinion. Generally, however, the ordinary witness cannot be asked questions calling for opinions if the witness could give facts which are capable of being detailed sufficiently so that they can be fully placed before the jury or the court by the witness.

Although the principles relating to opinion testimony are fairly certain, the application of these principles sometimes becomes difficult. For example, in many cases it is almost impossible to determine what is a fact and what is an opinion. For example, when a witness states that he saw what took place at an incident, he is in fact stating his opinion as to what took place. So even statements of fact are based upon the powers of observation as well as the memory of the witness.

The rules relating to lay witnesses differ from those concerning the expert witness, therefore, the rules and the cases to exemplify the rules will be discussed under separate headings. However, it should be noted that both lay and expert witnesses may be authorized to give opinion testimony in certain instances and often the determination as to whether a witness is an expert or a lay witness is unnecessary.

§ 10.1a Definitions and distinctions

Before discussing the general rules and the exceptions relating to opinion testimony of expert and non-expert witnesses some definitions are necessary to assist in understanding these rules.

a. Opinion evidence

Opinion evidence is defined in Black's Law Dictionary as "evidence of what the witness thinks, believes, or infers in regard to facts in dispute, as distinguished from his personal knowledge of the facts themselves." The term refers to opinions declared from the witness stand, as distinguished from extrajudicial opinions.

b. Expert witness

An expert witness as used in law is a person who is particularly skilled, learned, or experienced in a particular art, science, trade, business, profession, or vocation; one who has gained a thorough knowledge of a subject which is not possessed by the average layman in regard to matters connected therewith. In Black's Law

§ 10.2 CRIMINAL EVIDENCE FOR POLICE 174

Dictionary an expert witness is defined as "men of science, educated in the arts, or persons possessing special or peculiar knowledge acquired from practical experience." In one case an expert witness was defined as one who has acquired ability to deduce correct inferences from hypothetically stated facts, or from facts involving scientific or technical knowledge.[1]

c. Non-expert witness

A non-expert or lay witness is one who is not particularly skilled, learned, or experienced in the particular area that is at issue in the court. One who is an expert in one field, for example, Psychology, is a lay witness when he is on the stand to testify in another area. The lay witness bases his conclusions on facts personally observed while the expert witness must qualify as such by establishing that he has some special skill, knowledge, or experience and may base his opinions on facts of his own observation or on evidence presented by other witnesses.

§ 10.2 Admissibility of non-expert opinions

The general rule that witnesses must state facts and not give their conclusions or opinions is subject to the exception that where the facts are of such a character as to be incapable of being meaningfully presented the witness will be allowed to add his opinion. A lay or non-expert witness may testify to a relevant opinion if (1) based on facts which he has observed, (2) the opinion is of a kind which normal persons form constantly and correctly, and (3) the witness cannot adequately or accurately describe the facts upon which his opinion is based.[1a] Lay witnesses are frequently permitted to use so-called "short hand" descriptions, in reality opinions, in testifying as to their impression of the general physical condition of a person; e.g., "mentally and physically ill," and "in a terrible shape."[2]

---

[1] City of Chicago v. Lehmann, 262 Ill. 468, 104 N.E. 829 (1914). "Expert witness" will be further defined in later sections of this chapter.

[1a] A recently drafted Rule 701 of the Federal Rules would apparently expand the use of non-expert testimony to "opinions or inferences which are helpful to a clear understanding of the testimony or the determination of a fact in issue."

[2] State v. Garver, 190 Ore. 291, 225 P.(2d) 771. See State v. Collins, 294 P. 957 (1950) in Part II of Book.

As an example a witness may describe a person as having gray hair, a wrinkled face, an unsteady gait, and other facts which indicate advanced years; yet the jury, from such testimony, cannot determine his exact age, beyond the conclusion that he was an old man. In such a situation, the witness who has detailed all the facts which he has observed will be permitted to give his opinion as to the age of the man.

§ 10.3 Subjects of non-expert opinion
a. Appearance

If the conditions mentioned in earlier sections are met, testimony concerning the appearance of another is admissible. For example, in a bank robbery case, testimony that the teller who handed over the money was "distraught and upset" was admissible.[3] And in a case involving the question of the competency of an elderly person, a witness testified to circumstances of irrational behavior, such as disgusting eating habits, irritability, and wild expressions. When asked: "What was the appearance of this man at that time with reference to his being rational or irrational?", his answer "irrational" was competent evidence. The court explains that to say that a man acts rationally or irrationally is merely to describe an outward manifestation drawn from observed facts. It is the ultimate fact, deduced from evidentiary facts coming under observation, but so transitory and evanescent as to be like drunkenness, easy of detection and difficult of explanation.[4]

b. Intoxication

Where it is proper to permit nonexpert opinion evidence, the witness may state his opinion without first detailing the facts on which he bases such opinion, where the matter testified about is not of a complex nature. Intoxication is such a matter.[5] Therefore a police officer who testified that during his years as an officer he had observed many persons under the influence of intoxicating liquor, was permitted to testify that he had observed the defendant

---

[3] Cole v. United States, 327 F.(2d) 360 (9th Cir. 1964). Also see United States v. Brown, 490 F.(2d) 748 (D.C. Cir. 1973).
[4] Holland v. Zollner, 102 Cal. 633, 36 Pac. 930 (1894).

[5] Gladden v. State, 36 Ala.App. 197, 54 S,(2d) 607 (1951). But compare State v. Steale, 211 N.W.(2d) 855 (N.D. 1973).

§ 10.3

on the day in question and had formed an opinion that the defendant "was drunk." Opinion evidence of intoxication is not restricted to expert testimony.[6] However, the lay witness must show that he had ample opportunity to observe the defendant.

c. Sanity or mental condition

A non-expert witness may never, in response to purely hypothetical questions stating the facts, be permitted to give an opinion on the question of sanity. But by the great weight of authority one who, in the opinion of the trial judge, shows adequate means of becoming acquainted with the person whose mental condition is in issue, and after detailing the facts and circumstances concerning his acquaintance and the acts, conduct, and conversation upon which his conclusion is based, may give his opinion on the question of sanity.[7] Before a non-expert witness is competent to testify to the sanity or insanity of another person, he must show an acquaintance of such intimacy and duration as to clearly indicate that his testimony will be of value in determining the issue. And in some states the conclusion must be based upon the witness' testimony as to specific instances of behavior or conduct.[8]

There is no requirement as to length of acquaintance. For example, the testimony of two police officers who were with the defendant for about ten and four hours respectively was not disqualified on the ground that the witnesses had insufficient opportunity of observing defendant. The fact that the officers had not known him for a longer period went to the weight of the testimony on the sanity question and not to admissibility.[9]

d. Identification

Often the only adequate way a person can be identified is by opinion. Therefore the identification of a person need not be made in positive terms. A witness may testify that an accused "resembles"

---

[6] People v. Ravey, 122 Cal.App. (2d) 699, 265 P.(2d) 154 (1954). State v. Huff, 202 S.E.(2d) 342 (N.C. 1974).

[7] Rupert v. People, 429 P.(2d) 276 (Colo. 1967).

[8] McKenzie v. United States, 266 F.(2d) 524 (10th Cir. 1959); United States v. Milne, 487 F.(2d) 1232 (5th Cir. 1973).

[9] Kaufman v. United States, 350 F. (2d) 408 (8th Cir. 1965).

or "looks like" the person who committed the crime. He may testify that in his opinion the accused is the person who perpetrated the crime. The sound of a voice also may be the basis of an opinion as to the identity of a person.

This rule also applies to identity of things. A person who has tasted alcoholic beverages before may testify as to the nature of a drink. In a prosecution for destroying property by means of dynamite, witnesses familiar with the odor were held properly permitted to testify to having smelled dynamite after the explosion.[10] The court, in permitting the testimony explained, "Most persons would probably find it difficult to describe the odor of a rose, whiskey, beer or limburger cheese, but this difficulty could scarcely be regarded as affecting the value of their testimony that they were familiar with and recognized the particular odor."

e. Handwriting

The opinion of a lay witness as to a person's handwriting, of which he has knowledge, is admissible. Since handwriting testimony involves a process of comparison, the lay witness will not be permitted to fortify his opinion by making a physical comparison in court of the contested writing with genuine standards, for the reason that he has no more skill for making the comparison than do the jurors.[11-12] The lay witness must show that he had an opportunity to become familiar with the handwriting. This can be accomplished by showing that he corresponded with the writer, handled documents written by him, or by other means.

f. Speed

Most courts admit the testimony of a non-expert witness relative to the speed of a motor vehicle, provided he has had sufficient opportunity to observe the vehicle in motion. In automobile negligence suits testimony of witnesses as to speed is admissible where the witnesses are experienced drivers and were in a position to observe under such circumstances and for a sufficient time to re-

---

[10] People v. Reed, 333 Ill. 397, 164 N.E. 847 (1929).

[11-12] Bowles v. Kennemore, 139 F.(2d) 541 (4th Cir. 1944).

move their conclusions from the realm of speculation.[13] If a witness is shown to be in a position to observe the speed of a train, and from such observation forms an opinion as to such speed, he should be permitted to give his opinion whether he is shown to be experienced or inexperienced in estimating the speed of trains.[14]

§ 10.4 Opinions of experts

Of particular importance in criminal cases are the opinions of experts. An observer is qualified to testify because he has firsthand knowledge which the jury does not have of the situation or transaction at issue. The expert has something different to contribute. This is a power to draw inferences from the facts which a jury would not be competent to draw. To warrant the use of expert testimony, then, two elements are required: (1) the subject of the inference must be so distinctively related to some science, profession, business, or occupation as to be beyond the knowledge of the average layman; and (2) the witness must have such skill, knowledge, or experience in that field or calling as to make it appear that his opinion or inference will probably aid the jury in its search for truth.[15]

By applying these qualifications it is evident that an expert need not necessarily be one who is well educated, such as a physician or scientist. He can just as easily be a plumber or a carpenter or a police officer if his technical expertise in his occupation might help the jury to understand the particular point in evidence.

Generally either the prosecutor or the defense attorney or both request that experts be qualified to testify in the case. However, in some jurisdictions and under the new Federal Rule 706, the judges may on their own motion appoint expert witnesses agreed upon by the parties, and may appoint witnesses of their own selection. Under the Federal Rules of Evidence a witness so appointed shall be informed of his duties by the judge in writing, a copy of which shall be filed with the clerk; or at a conference in which the parties shall have opportunity to participate. Such an

---

[13] Ohio Cas. Co. v. Landon, 1 OhioApp.(2d) 317, 30 OhioOp.(2d) 313, 204 N.E.(2d) 566 (1961).
Womack v. Pierson, 299 So.(2d) 279 (La. 1974).
[14] Central of Georgia R.R. v. Luther, 129 Ga.App. 178, 196 S.E.2d 149 (1973).
[15] Jenkins v. United States, 307 F (2d) 637 (D.C. Cir. 1962).
See Long v. State, 274 P.(2d) 553 in Part II of this book.

expert witness shall advise the parties of his findings, if any; his deposition may be taken by any party; and he may be called upon to testify by the judge or any party. Also, he shall be subject to cross-examination by each party. The judge in the exercise of his discretion may also authorize disclosure to the jury of the fact that the expert was appointed by the judge.

§ 10.5 Requirement of probability

The terms "probable" and "possible" occur frequently in expert testimony. In many fields, of which medicine, nuclear physics, and oftentimes unexplained accidents are examples, the utmost that the best of scientists can say is that such-and-such is "probable" or is "possible." But when it comes to translating that testimony into findings of fact, which is the duty of a judge or a jury, we have another problem. What is probable as a scientific fact may under some circumstances be a consideration in the finding of a fact. So the "probable" may be admissible and may be considered. What weight the merely probable should be given is a serious and delicate problem. Certainly such testimony is short of direct assertion. But what is merely possible is not a basis for finding a fact. A person perfectly well today may possibly be ill tomorrow or may possibly have been ill last month. Of course an opinion that a certain something is possible may be, and frequently is, useful and of probative value as a buttress to a flat assertion that the something is a fact. Such is frequently the case where the issue of fact lies in an area of doubt—for example, blood tests in a paternity case. And assertions that a thing or act is possible may be useful and admissible, as a response to an opponent's assertion that the thing or act is impossible. But mere possibility is not an affirmative basis for a finding of fact.

In the language of the law of evidence, that which is merely possible, standing alone and not offered as auxiliary or rebuttal testimony, is immaterial to the ascertainment of the fact and so is inadmissible as evidence of that fact. So, if an expert scientist can say only that such-and-such is possible, he has done the best he can do from the scientific point of view, but from the standpoint of the law such testimony does not permit the finder of fact to say that such-and-such is actually a fact.[16]

Where on the trial of a criminal case upon an indictment for rape, before the court and a jury, the state presents a witness, qualified as an expert, who has conducted what is known as a neutron activation analysis of pubic hairs taken from the victim of the rape and from the clothing of the accused, and where in answer to a question whether, as a result of the analysis, he has an opinion "based on reasonable scientific certainty as to the similarity or dissimilarity of these hair specimens," his response is "the samples are similar and are likely to be from the same source," such response falls short of the legal requirement of "reasonable certainty" or "probability." Therefore, the admission in evidence of such answer, over objection, constitutes error prejudicial to the accused, requiring reversal of the judgment of conviction.[17]

§ 10.6 Qualifications of an expert

An expert has been defined as one who has acquired special knowledge of the subject matter about which he is to testify, either by study of the recognized authorities or by practical experience and who can assist and guide the jury in solving a problem which the jury is not able to solve because its knowledge is inadequate. A witness who by education and experience has become expert in any art, science, profession, or calling may be permitted to state his opinion as to a matter in which he is versed and which is material to the case, and may also state the reasons for such opinion.

One who has the necessary training, experience, and skill and has familiarized himself retrospectively with the necessary data can form an expert opinion which is substantially superior to that of the average man and therefore useful to the jury. Any difference between the reliability of information currently received and that which is retrospectively obtained is a difference which goes merely to the weight of the evidence.[18] Absence of certificates, memberships,

---

[16] Martin v. United States, 284 F.(2d) 217 (D.C. Cir. 1960).

[17] State v. Holt, 17 OhioSt.(2d) 81, 46 OhioOp. (2d) 408, 246 N.E.(2d) 365 (1969).

[18] United States v. 60.14 Acres of Land, 362 F.(2d) 660 (3d Cir. 1966); Ziegler v. Crofront, 516 P.(2d) 954 (Kan. 1973).

and the like does not in and of itself detract from the competency of an expert witness which otherwise exists.[19]

When a witness is offered as an expert upon a matter in issue, his competency, with respect to special skill or experience, is to be determined by the court as a question preliminary to the admission of his testimony. There should be a finding by the court, in the absence of an admission or a waiver by the adverse party, that the witness is qualified; and since there is no presumption that a witness is competent to give an opinion, it is incumbent upon the party offering the witness to show that the latter possesses the necessary learning, knowledge, skill, or practical experience to enable him to give opinion testimony.

The weight and value of the testimony of an expert witness depends largely upon his qualifications as such expert, and these qualifications may be the subject of intensive inquiry by the opposing counsel.

§ 10.7 Examination of expert witness

There are two avenues through which expert opinion evidence may be presented to the jury: (1) through testimony of the witness based on his personal knowledge or observation; (2) through testimony of the witness based upon a hypothetical question addressed to him, in which the pertinent facts are assumed to be true, or rather assumed to be so found by the jury. An expert witness may base his opinion partly on facts of his own observation and partly on factual (as opposed to opinion) evidence of other witnesses, hypothetically presented.[20] A hypothetical question need not include all the facts in evidence, nor facts or theories advanced by opposing counsel.

A trial judge may properly accept expert testimony with respect to certain types of primary facts which have already been admitted in evidence as testimony by witnesses who themselves made relevant observations of primary facts. A common case in the trial courts is where a doctor is called to give his expert medical opinion as

---

[19] Tank v. Commissioner of Int. Rev., 270 F.(2d) 477 (6th Cir. 1959). See also Moran v. Ford Motor Co., 476 F.(2d) 289 (8th Cir. 1973).

[20] State v. David, 222 N.C. 242, 22 S.E.(2d) 633 (1942).

to whether the primary facts already in evidence support an inference of causation or support a particular diagnosis or prognosis. A more familiar use of expert opinion is where an expert real estate appraiser testifies in a valuation case as to his opinion of the value of property, the characteristics of which have been independently proved either by his or other persons' observations.[21]

§ 10.8 Cross-examination of expert

On cross-examination an expert witness may be interrogated concerning his knowledge of textbooks, treatises, articles, and other publications in his field, and he may be confronted with extracts from them and asked whether he is familiar with them and whether he agrees with them. An expert witness who bases an opinion to a significant degree upon his reading may be cross-examined as to that opinion by reference to other reputable works in his field. The rationale of the rule is that such cross-examination tests the expert witness' credibility and reliability by inquiring as to the extent of his familiarity with authorities in his speciality and by asking him whether he agrees with them. The extracts with which the witness is confronted on cross-examination do not, however, become affirmative evidence in the case.[22]

Where the cross-examiner directs the attention of the expert witness to the contents of treatises expressing an opinion at variance with the opinion of the witness, and does so, not to prove the contrary opinion but merely to call into question the weight to be attached by the jury to the opinion of the witness, the law allows such use of the treatise. This is so even if the writing is not relied upon by the witness in arriving at his opinion, provided the witness admits that the treatise is a recognized and standard authority on the subject.[23]

§ 10.9 Subjects of expert testimony

In previous sections in this chapter some of the general rules relating to the testimony of expert witnesses were discussed. It is

---

[21] United States v. Sisson, 294 F. Supp. 520 (D. Mass. 1968).
[22] Stottlemire v. Cawood, 215 F. Supp. 266 (D.C. 1963).
[23] Ruth v. Fenchel, 21 N.J. 171, 121 A.(2d) 373 (1956). But compare Seeley v. Eaton, 506 S.W.(2d) 719 (Tex. 1974).

apparent that there are numerous areas where the expert could meet the qualifications and in fact assist the triers of fact in reaching a logical conclusion. Although it would be impossible here to discuss all of the areas where expert testimony would be valuable especially in criminal cases, some of the most common areas or subjects of expert testimony will be discussed.

a. Automobile accidents

Expert testimony of a police officer, who arrived at the scene of the accident within one-half hour after its occurrence and who made close observations and measurements as to the point of collision of approaching vehicles, is properly admitted.[24] Under Oklahoma law a police officer who has had proper training and experience in the investigation of traffic accidents and has made studies of reports on the facts and causes of accidents may give expert testimony as to the point of impact when his opinion is based upon physical evidence observed at the scene of the collision.[25]

A patrolman who had fifteen years' experience as a highway patrolman, during which time he had investigated a considerable number of automobile accidents and who had kept abreast of the field of automobile investigations by attending various refresher courses at institutions, was qualified as an expert to testify as to the speed of automobiles involved in an accident.[26] Where, however, the police officer was not a witness to a nighttime collision, did not arrive at the scene until some time thereafter, and observed no skid marks, he was not sufficiently qualified as an expert to give an opinion as to the speed of the automobile.[27]

It is proper for an expert witness to reconstruct an accident by basing his opinion upon exhibits showing the physical facts as well as numerous photographs.[28] In an action arising out of the death of an automobile driver in a head-on collision to which there were no eyewitnesses, testimony of a safety engineer who saw one of

---

[24] Rhynard v. Filori, 315 F.(2d) 176 (8th Cir. 1963).

[25] Parris v. Harris, 351 F.(2d) 52 (10th Cir. 1965).
Also see Tipsword v. Melrose, 301 N.E.(2d) 614 (1973), where the court took the same position.

[26] Bonner v. Polacari, 350 F.(2d) 493 (10th Cir. 1965).

[27] Chesapeake & Ohio R. Co. v. Schlink, 276 F.(2d) 114 (6th Cir. 1960).

[28] Frank's Plastering Co. v. Koenig, 341 F.(2d) 257 (8th Cir. 1965); Edwards v. Rudowicz, 368 S.W.(2d) 503 (Mo. 1963).

the automobiles only after it had been brought to a salvage yard and altered was admissible where in his personal examination of the automobile in the salvage yard he considered pertinent to the subject of his investigation only those parts of the automobile that were shown by the photographs taken immediately after the collision to have been affected by it.[29]

b. Airplane crashes

Witnesses may qualify as experts in airplane accident cases. For example, one who had been assistant chief flight engineer for an airline for eleven years, who had investigated about thirty cases of airplane engine overspeed, who was familiar with hundreds of other cases through air force reports and similar sources, whose work was to initiate corrective action and procedures necessary to cope with overspeeds, who had participated in investigation of between thirty and forty airplane crashes, and who was the inventor of devices having to do with propeller vibration and featherability, was qualified to testify as an expert witness in an action arising out of the crash of an airplane which had an overspeeding propeller which could not be feathered.[30]

c. Physical and mental condition

A general practitioner may testify concerning matters within a medical specialty if his education or experiences, or both, involves demonstrable knowledge of the subject. Nor need a skilled witness on a medical subject be duly licensed to practice medicine. The general rule is that anyone who is shown to have special knowledge and skill in diagnosing and treating human ailments is qualified to testify as an expert, if his learning and training show that he is qualified to give an opinion on the particular question at issue.

It is not essential that the witness be a medical practitioner. Thus, non-medical witnesses who have had experience in electrical work may testify to the effects of electrical shock upon the human body. Optometrists, whose training includes instruction in the symptoms of certain eye diseases, may testify to the presence of cataract discovered in the course of fitting glasses. A toxicologist has been

---

[29] Leeper v. Thornton, 344 P.(2d) 1101 (Okla. 1959).

[30] Noel v. United Aircraft Corp., 342 F.(2d) 232 (3d Cir. 1964).

permitted to testify to the effect of oxalic acid, a poison, upon the human eye.[31]

In view of the long and extensive training and experience of a medical technician, his lack of certification or license was without significance and did not affect his competency to perform blood grouping tests.[32]

d. Summaries

Summaries prepared by an accountant of various complex transactions are admissible in evidence. An accountant who is qualified as an expert may testify that the summaries are based on matter in evidence.[33] The originals of the records thus summarized must be made available to the opposite party for examination in advance of trial.

e. Handwriting comparisons

Of special importance in the investigation of crime is evidence relating to handwriting. Testimony that an individual piece of writing was written by a certain person, in the absence of actual observation of the event is, in reality, an opinion, which a witness may testify to only if he has special qualifications to do so. To be qualified he must have expert training and experience in handwriting analysis in general or be familiar with the handwriting of the individual in question. A witness who has neither, who can merely express an untrained comparison of two writings which are in evidence, supplies nothing to aid the jury.[34] An expert handwriting witness is allowed in the course of his testimony, as well as before he takes the stand, to fortify his views by comparing the disputed document with genuine standards.

Especially since the Supreme Court has made it clear that submitting handwriting specimens for comparison purposes does not violate the Constitution, the use of this technique is important. In the case of *Gilbert v. California*,[35] the Supreme Court held that com-

---

[31] Jenkins v. United States, 307 F. (2d) 637 (D.C. Cir. 1962).
[32] Lew Moon Cheung v. Rogers, 272 F.(2d) 354 (9th Cir. 1959).
[33] United States v. Pollack, 417 F. (2d) 240 (5th Cir. 1969).
[34] Ryan v. United States, 384 F. (2d) 379 (1st Cir. 1967).
[35] 388 U.S. 263, 18 L.Ed.(2d) 1178, 87 S.Ct. 1951 (1967).

pelling the suspect to give handwriting specimens did not violate the Fifth Amendment protection against self-incrimination.

f. Typewriter comparisons

In earlier years the experts who could qualify to identify handwriting comparisons were more in demand than those who could give testimony regarding typewritten documents; however, as the typewriter has become more popular, expert testimony as to typewritten documents has become of great importance. In many criminal cases it becomes very necessary to show that a certain typewritten document was written on the specific machine which can be identified as belonging to the accused or one that is available to him. Not only can the expert testify as to the identity of the machine which was used when the document was written, in some instances evidence has been admitted as to the identity of the writer who used a particular machine.

Expert evidence is generally admissible to prove that a document was typed on a particular type of machine, such as an Underwood typewriter, even though the typewriter itself is not located. And expert evidence is generally admissible also to prove that a document was typed on a particular machine that was located by the police officer during the investigation.[36] In making comparisons the expert usually points out the particular mechanical characteristics and peculiarities of the machine which produced the written instrument. As in other instances the expert witness in order to give opinion testimony must show that he is qualified by training and experience to be an expert in his field. Experts are available from the FBI laboratory in Washington who can testify not only as to the fact that a certain document was typed on a specific machine but also can often testify as to the make of the machine even if no particular machine has been located by the investigator.

In some instances the court has allowed the opinion of an expert as to the identification of the operator of the typewriter. In so doing, the expert points out the individuality of the person typing the instrument. This identification is primarily predicated upon the manner of punctuation, the length of the lines, the depth

---

[36] People v. Storrs, 207 N.Y. 147, 100 N.E. 730.

of the indentation, and other indications that each person has a different touch.[37]

g. Polygraph examination results

As was discussed in Chapter 10 courts have not generally admitted the results of the lie detector or polygraph tests because such tests are not yet sufficiently reliable. However, such tests as explained will be admitted if all parties consent. Even if the defense consents to the admissibility of the polygraph results, he may cross-examine the expert who testifies concerning the results. In such instance the person who administered the examination can be questioned concerning his training at a recognized school, his experience, and his general education which would enable him to interpret the results of the machine.

h. Voice print identification

Although voice print analysis has not yet gained the degree of general acceptance necessary to make spectrogram results admissible for identification purposes in a criminal prosecution, there is evidence that some courts will accept this at least for limited purposes.[38] In the case of *U.S. v. Addison* the United States Court of Appeals for the D.C. District acknowledged the persuasiveness of the voice print technique but expressed the fear that a minimal reserve of experts did not exist who could critically examine the validity of a scientific determination in a particular case.[39] The Court in that case continued by stating:

> Since scientific proof may in some instances assume a posture of mystic infallibility in the eyes of a jury of laymen, the ability to produce rebuttal experts, equally conversant with the mechanics and methods of a particular technique, may prove to be essential.

i. Neutron activation analysis

Although some courts have authorized expert witnesses to testify concerning the results of neutron activation analysis, some of these

---

[37] Thomas v. State, 197 Okla. 450, 172 P.(2d) 973 (1946).
[38] U.S. v. Raymond, 337 F.Supp. 641 (D.C. Cir. 1972).
[39] U.S. v. Addison, 498 F.(2d) 741 (D.C. Cir. 1974).

courts have expressed some doubts concerning expert opinions. For example, in a Minnesota Supreme Court case, the neutron activation technique was used to show that the defendant who was accused of shooting a policeman had fired a pistol shortly before his arrest. After the suspect was taken into custody, but prior to the time he was booked in the county jail, his hands were swabbed with a nitric acid solution. These swabs were sent to the Treasury Department laboratory in Washington for neutron activation analysis, a testing procedure which can determine the presence and amount of certain chemical elements. Although admitting the testimony of a representative of the Treasury Department, the court expressed its concern about the sweeping and unqualified manner in which expert testimony was offered. The court said,

> An expert witness can be permitted to testify that in his opinion the chemicals present on the defendant's hand may have resulted from the firing of a gun. He should not have been permitted to state, as he did, that this defendant had definitely fired a gun. To allow this testimony to stand without a cautionary instruction to the jury was technical error.

Notwithstanding this caution the evidence was admissible and the court concluded by stating,

> We believe that neutron activation analysis is a useful law enforcement technique and that the increasing use of technology in criminal investigations should not be inhibited but encouraged where consistent with the rights of the accused.[40]

j. Fingerprint identification

The average officer can testify that he obtained latent prints at the scene of the crime, but to show that these fingerprints are the prints of a known suspect usually requires an expert. As in other situations the expert must show that by study, training, and experience he is qualified as such. Such experts are available in the F.B.I. laboratory as well as in many of the large law enforcement agencies.

To give more weight to his testimony, the fingerprint expert

---

[40] State v. Spencer, 216 N.W.(2d) 131 (1974).

will in almost all cases use blown-up photographs or other means to show the points of similarity upon which he based his conclusion.

§ 10.9a Experts from crime laboratories

Because of the limitations placed on the use of confessions, more reliance is being placed upon the use of real evidence and other evidence obtained by laboratory technicians. With the addition of crime laboratories in all parts of the country, experts from these laboratories will become more and more available. These experts must qualify as any other experts through experience, training, or knowledge before they can give opinions concerning the significance of laboratory tests and other scientific evidence. Expert testimony of this type is especially important in the field of ballistics; that is, comparing bullets found at the scene with those fired from a known weapon. No attempt will be made here to list all of the other areas in which the crime laboratory expert can testify, but these include tool mark comparisons, and testimony concerning glass and glass fractures, clothing, hairs and fibers.

§ 10.10 Summary

The general rule is that the witness cannot testify as to his opinions but must confine his testimony to facts perceived. This rule is based on the principle that the witnesses are to furnish the facts and the jury has the responsibility of reaching conclusions based on these facts.

There are, however, necessary exceptions to the general rule. These common sense exceptions have been developed so that the jury will have better information and because the courts have recognized that it is often impossible to give facts to describe all situations. For example, it is difficult to give facts to explain that a person was "nervous" or "irrational."

The rules relating to the exceptions to the "opinion" rule are discussed in two categories: those relating to non-expert opinions and those relating to expert opinions. If the ordinary lay witness cannot adequately or accurately describe the facts so as to enable the jurors to draw an intelligent conclusion, the witness is allowed to give his opinion. For example, a lay witness may in the usual case and with certain limitations give opinion testimony as to age, appearance, identifications, and speed of a vehicle.

The expert witness also may, when properly qualified, give his opinion. However, this exception is based on different reasoning and therefore the rules are different. This opinion testimony is allowed because the expert, due to training, experience or knowledge, can give information on a specific subject substantially superior to the ability of the average person. The opinion of the expert witness does not have to be, and usually is not, based on direct observations of incidents which brought about the trial. His opinions may be based on hypothetical questions and on facts already presented by other witnesses.

Examples of testimony of expert witnesses are (1) speed of automobile from tire marks, (2) cause of death, and (3) handwriting comparisons.

Although the investigator will not present the case in court, it is important that he understand the "opinion" rule and just as important, the exceptions to the rule. With this knowledge he is not as likely to overlook opinion testimony that *is* admissible.

Chapter 11

HEARSAY RULE AND EXCEPTIONS

> The determination that a statement is hearsay does not end the inquiry into admissibility; there must still be a further examination of the need for the statement at trial and the circumstantial guaranty of trustworthiness surrounding the making of the statement.
> *Zippo Mfg. Co. v. Rogers Imports, Inc.*, 216 F. Supp. 670 (S.D.N.Y. 1963).

Section
- 11.1 Introduction
- 11.2 Definition of hearsay evidence and the hearsay rule
- 11.3 History and development of the hearsay rule
- 11.4 Exceptions to the hearsay rule—general
- 11.4a —Former testimony
- 11.5 —Declarations against interest
- 11.5a —Confessions and admissions
- 11.6 —Dying declarations
- 11.7 —Physical or mental condition of declarant
- 11.8 —Spontaneous and excited utterances
- 11.9 —Business and public records
- 11.10 —Public surveys
- 11.11 —Family history and records (pedigree)
- 11.11a Non-testimonial utterances
- 11.12 Summary

§ 11.1 Introduction

One of the most commonly known rules of evidence is the hearsay rule. Many of those who have heard about the rule itself, however, are not familiar with the fact that the rule has many exceptions. In fact, one could argue that the rule has so many exceptions that more hearsay evidence is admitted than excluded. If the hearsay rule were applied without exceptions it would be very difficult in many criminal cases to present sufficient facts to prove guilt and certainly much valuable evidence would be excluded from consideration.

The general rule excluding hearsay statements is justified on several grounds. It is important to understand the historical reasons for the rule in order to understand the exceptions. If the reasons

§ 11.1

for the rule do not exist in a particular situation, then the evidence should be admitted to assist in determining the facts of the case. Some of the reasons for the hearsay rule are discussed in the following paragraphs.[1]

(1) The declarant was not under oath to speak the truth. Although the person who has repeated what someone else has said is under oath, the person who actually made the statement is not under oath as are the witnesses who testify in court. Therefore, it is reasoned the statement lacks trustworthiness.

(2) The demeanor or conduct of the person who actually makes the statement cannot be observed by the judge and jury. Because the declarant is not present the triers of fact cannot observe the demeanor of the declarant which might shed some light on his credibility.

(3) There is a danger that the in-court witness who is reporting what was said by an out-of-court person may repeat the statement inaccurately.

(4) The declarant cannot be cross-examined. As pointed out earlier, one of the purposes of cross-examination is to solicit the truth. In a hearsay situation the person who actually made the statement cannot be cross-examined, hence, the adverse party is deprived of the opportunity to challenge his memory or sincerity.

Obviously, some hearsay is more reliable than others and the courts in seeking to allow as much evidence into court as possible while sifting out unreliable evidence, have developed many exceptions to the hearsay rule. For each exception however, there exists some justification to assure trustworthiness of the hearsay evidence.

Some evidence which might be challenged as hearsay has been discussed in other chapters of the book. For example, an out-of-court confession when repeated by another in court is technically hearsay. However, this is admitted under one of the exceptions as discussed in Chapter 14.

---

[1] Gaines v. Thomas, 241 S.C. 412, 128 S.E.(2d) 692 (1962); Donnelly v. United States, 228 U.S. 243, 57 L.Ed. 820, 33 S.Ct. 449 (1913). Case in Part II.

In Chapter 8 "past recollections recorded" is discussed. "Official records," "ancient documents," and "learned treatises" are discussed in Chapter 12. In this chapter the hearsay rule is discussed and defined and some of the other exceptions to the hearsay rule are discussed. These include declarations against interest, dying declarations, spontaneous and excited utterances, family history, etc.

§ 11.2 Definition of hearsay evidence and the hearsay rule

The United States Supreme Court in writing the Federal Rules of Evidence for the Federal District Courts and the District Courts of Appeals defined hearsay as "a statement, other than one made by the declarant while testifying at the trial or a hearing, offered in evidence to prove the truth of the matter asserted."[2] In law hearsay evidence is evidence which derives its value, not from the credit to be given to the witness upon the stand, but at least in part from the veracity and competency of some other person who is not testifying. As an example, in one case the witness, a bus company employee, testified that he had been advised by another person that the defendant stole two suitcases and was apprehended for the theft. The bus company employee's testimony was offered to prove that the defendant committed the theft. However, since the witness did not have personal knowledge of the event, his testimony was hearsay and inadmissible.[3]

The hearsay rule is merely that hearsay evidence is not admissible. To state this differently, the rule is that courts will not receive testimony of the witness if that witness is repeating what he heard another state outside of court when such statement is offered as an assertion to show the truth of the matters asserted therein.

It must be pointed out quickly that the rule has so many exceptions that much hearsay evidence is admissible. Also, testimony is not "hearsay" when it is introduced to prove only that a statement was made and not as to the truth of the statement.

---

[2] Rule 801, Fed. Rules of Evidence.

[3] For another example see State v. Gibson, 502 S.W.(2d) 310 (Mo. 1973).

§ 11.3

§ 11.3 History and development of the hearsay rule

In 1813 Chief Justice Marshall in explaining the justification for the hearsay rule stated, "Our lives, our liberty, and our property, are all concerned in the support of these rules, which have been matured by the wisdom of ages, and are now revered from their antiquity and the good sense in which they are founded.[4] One of these rules is, that 'hearsay' evidence is in its own nature inadmissible." Justice Marshall goes on to say that "Its intrinsic weakness, its incompetency to satisfy the mind of the existence of the fact, and the frauds which might be practiced under its cover, combine to support the rule that hearsay evidence is totally inadmissible."

The hearsay rule had its origin as we know it in England in the Sixteenth Century. Prior to the 1500's juries were permitted to obtain evidence by consulting persons who were not called as witnesses. During this period the jurors were not bound to decide the case on the basis of testimony given in open court, but were in fact chosen because they had some knowledge of the case.

As the pendulum began to swing to the other side, that is, as jurors began to be chosen only if they had no knowledge of the case that would influence their decision, the hearsay rule began its development. By 1700 the rule prohibiting the admission of hearsay statements was formulated in criminal cases. Over the centuries exceptions to the hearsay rule have developed because of the harshness of the rule.

§ 11.4 Exceptions to the hearsay rule—general

In 1813 when Chief Justice Marshall discussed the intrinsic weaknesses of hearsay evidence he concluded; "This court is not inclined to extend the exceptions further than they have already been carried." However, there are many exceptions to the hearsay rule—some of which are historical; some, as for example, those relating to market reports and commercial publications—have developed more recently. Rule 803 of the Federal Rules of Evidence lists 23 specific exceptions and concludes that an exception will be

---

[4] Mima Queen and Child v. Hepburn, 7 Cranch 290 (1813). See Donnelly v. United States, 288 U.S. 243, 33 S.Ct. 449 (1913) for a discussion of the History of the Rules.

recognized if it is "a statement not specifically covered by any of the foregoing exceptions but having comparable circumstantial guarantees of trustworthiness."[5]

As indicated in the first part of this chapter there are four general reasons for the hearsay rule. In brief, these are: 1) the declarant is not under oath to speak the truth, 2) the demeanor of the person who actually makes the statement can not be observed by the judge and jury, 3) there is danger that the statement may be repeated inaccurately and 4) the declarant can not be cross-examined. In general it can be argued then that if these obstacles (or most of them) are not present, the evidence should be admissible even if it is hearsay. In the sections that follow some of the specific exceptions to the hearsay rule are discussed as well as the justification for allowing this type of hearsay as an exception to the rule.

§ 11.4a —Former testimony

Some authorities assert that former testimony is actually not hearsay, since it was under oath and subject to cross-examination. Others, however, recognize reported testimony as hearsay but recognize that it is admissible under an exception to the hearsay rule. Under either approach, when a witness for the prosecution or defendant is unavailable and cannot be produced at the present trial, the testimony of such witness at a former criminal proceeding relating substantially to the same subject matter and between the same parties will usually be admitted.

Under various state statutes the term "unavailable as a witness" means that the witness is unable to be present or to testify at the hearing because of death or then existing physical or mental illness, or is absent beyond the jurisdiction of the court to compel his appearance by its process, or is absent and his whereabouts cannot be ascertained by due diligence.[6]

In criminal prosecutions the mere temporary illness or disability of a witness is not sufficient to justify the reception of his former

---

[5] See Rule 803, Fed. Rules of Evidence in the Appendix for a list of the exceptions.

[6] See Rule 804, Fed. Rules of Evidence for definition of unavailability.

testimony; it must appear that the witness is in such a state, either mentally or physically, that in reasonable probability he will never be able to attend the trial. Therefore, testimony given at the former trial by a witness unable to attend the subsequent trial because of pregnancy was inadmissible on any issue at the subsequent trial, where she was neither dead, beyond the reach of process nor permanently incapacitated, and a continuance might have been requested to the time when the witness could probably be present.[7]

§ 11.5 —Declarations against interest

One of the exceptions to the hearsay rule, which has been found to be based on trustworthiness or a probability of truthfulness and veracity, and which has arisen due to necessity, is the exception admitting declaration when it is against the interest of the declarant. The courts have reasoned that a person does not make statements against his own pecuniary interest unless they are true and have thus considered such statements trustworthy, even though there is no opportunity to confront the witness or to cross-examine him.

A declaration against interest by one not a party or in privity with a party to an action is admissible in evidence where (1) the person making such declaration is either dead or unavailable as a witness due to sickness, insanity or absence from the jurisdiction, (2) the declarant had peculiar means of knowing the facts which he stated, (3) the declaration was against his pecuniary or proprietary interest and (4) he had no probable motive to falsify the facts stated.[8] Thus, in a civil action by an insured against his fidelity insurer to recover for defalcations by employees of the former, where such employees are unavailable as witnesses, they having been summoned and not found in the jurisdiction by the sheriff, written and signed confessions of such employees were admissible in evidence as declarations against interest as to both the fact and the amount of the loss.[9]

---

[7] Peterson v. United States, 344 F.(2d) 419 (5th Cir. 1965).

But compare State v. Julian, 509 P.(2d) 1123 (Kan. 1973), which applies less strict requirements.

[8] Gichner v. Antonio Troiano Tile Co., 410 F.(2d) 238 (D.C. Cir. 1969).

[9] G. M. McKelvey Co. v. General Cas. Co., 166 OhioSt. 401, 2 OhioOp.(2d) 345, 142 N.E.(2d) 854 (1957).

A hearsay statement is against a declarant's pecuniary and proprietary interest and, therefore, susceptible to being admitted as a declaration against interest when it threatens loss of employment, or reduces chances for future employment, or entails possible civil liability. Thus, a hearsay statement made by the lessee's employee to a fire investigator that he and others were smoking on the leased premises a few hours before the fire started was against the employee's pecuniary and proprietary interest, and since the statement also concerned a subject of which the employee was personally cognizant and there was no conceivable motive to falsify, the statement was admitted as a declaration against interest. The court agreed, however, that the statement would not be admitted unless the employee was unavailable to testify at the trial.[10]

In the Federal Rules of Evidence the statement against interest exception includes statements which are against penal interests as well as pecuniary and proprietary interests.[11] Under this definition a statement by a witness who repeated the statement of a third party which would tend to subject him to criminal liability would be admissible. This rule, however, provides "A statement tending to expose the declarant to criminal liability and offered to exculpate the accused is not admissible unless corroborated." Although some states such as the state of California have by judicial decision and legislative enactment provided that statements against penal interests are valid exceptions to the hearsay rule,[12] this is still a minority view.

In those jurisdictions which recognize the declaration against penal interests as an exception to the hearsay rule, such testimony will be admitted only in the event of the declarant's death or unavailability.[13]

§ 11.5a —Confessions and admissions

Closely related to the exception discussed in the preceding paragraph is the exception concerning admissions and confessions. A confession as it is used in criminal law is an admission, declara-

---

[10] Gichner v. Antonio Troiano Tile Co., n. 8, *supra*.

[11] See Rule 804(b)(4). Federal Rules of Evidence.

[12] See Jones v. U.S., 400 F.(2d) 134 (9th Cir. 1968).

[13] United States v. Miller, 277 F. Supp. 200 (D. Conn. 1967). Bunge Corp. v. Manufacturers Hanover Trust Co., 318 N.Y.S.(2d) 819 (1971).

tion, or acknowledgment made by one who has committed a crime, that he committed the act, or participated in its commission. The confession is the admission of the criminal act itself, not an admission of a fact or circumstances from which guilt may be inferred. An admission, as distinguished from a confession, is not an admission of the criminal act itself but an admission of incriminating acts or conduct which may tend to establish guilt.

When a police officer takes the stand and states what has been told to him by the accused, such testimony is hearsay and as one court said, "since confessions are hearsay testimony, they are to be received with great caution."[13a]

When confessions are brought to the attention of the court by other than those on trial, the evidence is hearsay. Such evidence is nevertheless admissible as an exception to the hearsay rule when certain conditions are met.[13b] The reason for admitting the confession as an exception to the hearsay rule is that such statements are against the interest of the person making them and that a rational being will not make admissions prejudicial to his interest and safety unless urged thereto by the promptings of conscience to tell the truth.

§ 11.6 —Dying declarations

A dying declaration is a statement by the victim concerning the cause and circumstances of a homicide, made under a fixed belief that death is impending. Dying declarations in homicide cases have from ancient times been admitted in evidence either (1) because of solemnity—the solemnity of the occasion and the fear of punishment in the hereafter if one tells a lie just before death, or (2) because of necessity—since the victim of the homicide cannot testify, it is necessary to protect the public against homicidal criminals and prevent a miscarriage of justice.

Generally the dying declaration has the same effect as if made under oath. However, a number of authorities point out that while it is a substitute for an oath and its credibility and weight is for the jury, it is merely hearsay and is not the equivalent of nor does

---

[13a] Damas v. People, 62 Cal. 418, 163 P. 289 (1917).
[13b] See Chapter 14 for a discussion of the constitutional issues concerning confessions and admissions.

it have the same value or weight as the testimony of a witness given under oath in open court which is subject to cross-examination.[14]

The dying declaration is admissible only insofar as it relates to the circumstances immediately surrounding or leading up to the conduct which caused death. A dying declaration may be made in answer to a leading question or urgent solicitation. It is not necessary to prove expressions indicating apprehension of death, if it is clear that the victim does not expect to survive the injury. This expectation may be shown by the circumstances of his condition or by his acts, such as sending for a priest of his church before making the declaration.

This exception to the hearsay rule is restricted to statements made by the victim of a homicide and obviously the victim must die. In one case the court admitted evidence of the dying declaration of a woman who died as a result of an abortion where the court regarded death as an element of the offense.[15] Ohio has added to its statute defining the crime of illegal abortion: "On such trial the dying declaration of a woman who dies in consequence of the miscarriage or attempt to produce a miscarriage under investigation, as to the cause and circumstances of such miscarriage or attempt, shall be admissible."[16]

A dying declaration may be either written or oral and must relate to the killing of the declarant and not to the killing of a third party. As in many instances the dying statements are made to officers, the officer should be aware that he will be cross-examined concerning what he heard. He should, therefore, make notes so that he can testify as to the exact words he heard the declarant state.

§ 11.7 —Physical or mental condition of declarant

Another exception to the rule against hearsay admits declarations indicative of the declarant's intention, feeling, or other mental state, including his bodily feelings. Where the bodily or mental feelings of a person are to be proved, the usual and natural expressions and exclamations of such person which are the spontaneous manifesta-

---

[14] Commonwealth v. Brown, 388 Pa. 613, 131 A.(2d) 367 (1957). See case in Part II.

[15] People v. Murawski, 2 Ill.(2d) 143, 117 N.E.(2d) 88 (1954).

[16] Ohio Rev. Code § 2901.17.

tions of pain, are competent and original evidence, which may be testified to by any party in whose presence they are uttered.

A person's state of mind or feeling can be manifested to others only by countenance, attitude or gesture, or by sounds or words, spoken or written. Whenever intention is of itself a distinct and material fact in a chain of circumstances, it may be proved by contemporaneous oral or written declarations of the person.[17] For example, in an action to recover double indemnity benefits under life policies, the testimony of the deceased insured's last statement before pulling the trigger of a gun pointed at his head was admissible for the purpose of proving the insured's state of mind.[18]

Proof of the state of mind of the victim is relevant, indeed essential, to a prosecution for extortion, and this may be evidenced by the victim's own testimony at the trial, or, pursuant to this exception to the hearsay rule, by statements made by him to others.[19]

§ 11.8 —Spontaneous and excited utterances

Hearsay testimony as to a statement or declaration may be admissible under an exception to the hearsay rule for spontaneous exclamations if the requirements are met. In order for such statements to be admissible the judge must find that: (a) there was some occurrence startling enough to produce a nervous excitement in the declarant, which was sufficient to still his reflective faculties and thereby make his statements and declarations the unreflective and sincere expression of his actual impressions and beliefs; (b) the statement or declaration, even if not strictly contemporaneous with its exciting cause, was made before there had been time for such nervous excitement to lose a domination over declarant's reflective faculties; (c) the statement or declaration related to such startling occurrence or the circumstances of such startling occurrence; and (d) the declarant had an opportunity to observe personally the

---

[17] Mutual Life Ins. Co. v. Hillmon, 145 U.S. 285, 36 L.Ed. 706, 12 S.Ct. 909 (1892).

[18] New York Life Ins. Co. v. Harrington, 299 F.(2d) 803 (9th Cir. 1962).

[19] United States v. Kennedy, 291 F.(2d) 457 (2d Cir. 1961). According to Rule 803(8) Fed. Rules of Evidence, this exception applies even though the declarant is available as a witness.

matters asserted in his statement or declaration.[20]

To illustrate, in an action to recover for the wrongful death of a pedestrian, the testimony of a police officer as to what a streetcar operator said to him within fifteen to twenty minutes after the streetcar struck a pedestrian and while the operator seemed to be upset, was admissible as an excited utterance exception to the hearsay rule.[21] But where defendant's automobile, immediately after proceeding through an intersection governed by a traffic light, struck the plaintiff who was crossing the street and rendered her unconscious, plaintiff's testimony that, on regaining consciousness and shortly before she again lapsed into unconsciousness, she heard an unidentified man standing near her state, "God, he rushed the light," did not come within the spontaneous exclamations exception to the hearsay rule because there had been a substantial lapse of time between the accident and the statement.[22]

In rape cases, the fact that the prosecuting witness made complaint of the offense without unexplained delay is admissible to corroborate her testimony. The complaint must have been spontaneous and not made as a result of a series of questions to which answers were given. Most courts will admit into evidence only the fact of the complaint, not the details thereof;[23] however, more recent decisions show a trend toward allowing more details of the offense and the identity of the offender as part of the spontaneous declaration heard by a witness.[24] In a prosecution for housebreaking with intent to commit rape, the victim's statement to her father as to what had happened was properly admitted, under the spontaneous declaration exception to the hearsay rule, in the light of the extremely brief lapse of time between the exciting event and the utterance.[25]

---

[20] Potter v. Baker, 162 OhioSt. 488, 55 OhioOp. 389, 124 N.E.(2d) 140 (1955); People v. Washington, 81 Cal.Rptr. 5, 459 P.(2d) 259 (1969)—parts of case in Part II of this book; Forssen v. Rieke, 295 N.E.(2d) 84 (Ill. 1973).

[21] Wabisky v. D. C. Transit System, Inc., 309 F.(2d) 317 (D.C. Cir. 1962).

[22] Potter v. Baker, n. 20, *supra*.

[23] People v. Damen, 28 Ill.(2d) 464, 193 N.E.(2d) 25 (1963).

[24] People v. Burton, 55 Cal.(2d) 328, 359 P.(2d) 433 (1961).

[25] Baber v. United States, 324 F.(2d) 390 (D.C. Cir. 1963); People v. Alexander, 298 N.E.(2d) 355 (Ill. 1973).

§ 11.9 —Business and public records

Many states have adopted the uniform business records act. This law provides that a record of an act, condition or event, insofar as relevant, shall be competent evidence if the custodian or other qualified witness testifies to its identity and the modes of its preparation, and if it was made in the regular course of business, at or near the time of the act, condition or event, and if, in the opinion of the court, the sources of information, method and time of preparation were such as to justify its admission.

The purpose of such statute is to provide, as an exception to the hearsay rule, an acceptable substitute for the specific authentication of records kept in the ordinary course of business. The underlying rationale permitting this exception is that business records have the "earmark of reliability" or "probability of truthworthiness," since they reflect the day to day operations of the enterprise and are relied upon in the conduct of business.

Under the Federal Rules of Evidence which are applicable in federal courts, the uniform law concerning records has been greatly expanded. According to these rules, various business and public records may be the source of evidence as exceptions to the hearsay rule. Some of these are records of regularly conducted activity, public records and reports, records of vital statistics, records of religious organizations, records of marriage, baptism and similar certificates, family records, etc. Not only is information from the records admissible but evidence may be introduced to prove the absence of public records or entries or the absence of an entry in records of regularly conducted activities.[26] All such records are admissible under this rule subject to exclusion if the sources of the information or other circumstances indicate lack of trustworthiness.

Originally shopbooks were admissible to prove an account where preliminary proof could be made that there were regular dealings between the shopkeeper and the customer, that the former kept honest books, that some of the articles charged had been delivered, and that the shopkeeper had no clerk. The purpose in enacting business records laws was to permit a writing or record,

---

[26] See Rule 803, Fed. Rules of Evidence

made in the regular course of business, to be received in evidence without the necessity of calling as witnesses all of the persons who had any part in making it, provided the record was made as a part of the duty of the person making it, or on information imparted by persons who were under a duty to impart such information.

Although police reports containing statements concerning the cause of or responsibility for an accident are in a sense business or public records, they are generally excluded for the reason that the person making the report is relying on what someone else told him, not affirming what he observed with his own senses. Such information is pure hearsay. If, however, the information in a police report of an accident is within the personal knowledge of the investigating officer (e.g., that the skidmarks at the scene of the accident were more than one hundred feet in length), such an item is admissible in evidence under the rule that written records of a public nature which public officers are required to keep, made either by the officers themselves or under their supervision, are admissible as proof of the facts recorded therein.

For example, a police report indicating that a vehicle was reported stolen, and records of the insurer indicating that it had paid the owner for the loss of the vehicle, though made in the ordinary course of business, constituted hearsay and were not admissible by virtue of the federal business records act, or any other recognized exception to the hearsay rule, to show that the vehicle had been stolen.[27] Although a police report reflecting that a car was reported stolen cannot be admitted to establish that the car was in fact stolen, it would be admissible as proof that the car to which it referred had been *reported* stolen.[28]

A hospital record, so far as it pertains to the cause of an accident resulting in injuries to a person causing his resort to a hospital, and not to the medical or surgical treatment of the patient in the hospital, is inadmissible in evidence as a business record. The admissibility of hospital records in acccident cases depends upon whether they relate to acts, transactions, occurrences, or events

---

[27] United States v. Shiver, 414 F. (2d) 461 (5th Cir. 1969).

[28] United States v. Graham, 391 F. (2d) 439 (6th Cir. 1968).

incident to the hospital treatment.²⁹

A time card and time sheet of defendant's place of employment, although hearsay, were admissible in evidence as a record made in the regular course of business.³⁰ Evidence as to long distance telephone tickets, railway ticket records or hospital records is not the same as evidence concerning a book account. The elements necessary for admission of a telephone ticket are identification by one or more telephone employees who either make or have supervision and charge of the records, and who know the ticket to be a genuine part of the records of the company, and who can testify it was made at or about the time shown thereon.³¹ Likewise, in a prosecution for transporting a minor in interstate commerce for purposes of prostitution, wherein the evidence showed that defendant had induced the minor to accompany him from Montana to Florida by commercial airlines, the airline tickets used by the defendant and the minor were admissible under the business records law.³²

Records stored on magnetic tape by data processing machines are unavailable and useless except by means of the print-out sheets. In admitting the print-out sheets reflecting the record stored on the tape, the court is actually following the best evidence rule. This is not departing from the shopbook rule, but only extending its application to electronic record keeping. Print-out sheets of business records stored on electronic computing equipment are admissible in evidence if relevant and material, without the necessity of identifying, locating, and producing as witnesses the individuals who made the entries in the regular course of business. Before such sheets are admitted it must be shown that the electronic computing equipment is recognized as standard equipment, the entries are made in the regular course of business at or reasonably near the time of the happening of the event recorded, and the foundation testimony satisfies the court that the source of information, method and time of preparation were such as to indicate its truthworthiness and justify its admission.³³

---

²⁹ Melton v. St. Louis Public Service Co., 363 Mo. 474, 251 S.W.(2d) 663 (1952). See State v. Griffin, 497 S.W.(2d) 133 (Mo. 1973), indicating a trend to admit certain hospital records.

³¹ Olesen v. Henningsen, 247 Iowa 883, 77 N.W.(2d) 40 (1956).

³² Rotolo v. United States, 404 F.(2d) 316 (5th Cir. 1968).

³³ King v. State ex rel. Murdock Accept. Corp., 222 S.(2d) 393 (Miss. 1969).

§ 11.10 —Public surveys

The weight of case authority, the consensus of legal writers, and reasoned policy considerations all indicate that the hearsay rule should not bar the admission of properly conducted public surveys. Although courts were at first reluctant to accept survey evidence or to give it weight, the more recent trend is clearly contrary. Surveys are now admitted over the hearsay objection on two technically distinct bases. Some cases hold that surveys are not hearsay at all; other cases hold that surveys are hearsay but are admissible because they are within the recognized exception to the hearsay rule for statements of present state of mind, attitude, or belief. Still other cases admit surveys without stating the ground on which they are admitted.[34]

Objections that a survey sought to be admitted was taken by untrained people and that it was irrelevant go only to its weight, rather than to its admissibility.[35]

§ 11.11 —Family history and records (pedigree)

Evidence relating to pedigree, genealogy, and family history, usually consists of hearsay and presents an exception to the general rule on that subject. The family history exception to the hearsay rule is based in part on the inherent trustworthiness of a declaration by a family member regarding matters of family history and usual unavailability of other evidence on these matters. As an example, testimony of a son that his mother told him that he was born in a certain place in the United States is admissible under the pedigree exception to the hearsay rule.[36] Such evidence is admissible if the declarant is related by blood or marriage to the other person, or has been so intimately associated with the other person's family as to be likely to have accurate information concerning the birth, marriage, divorce, death, ancestry, or relationship.

Not only are declarations by a family member regarding matters of family history admissible as an exception to the hearsay rule, such records as the family Bible are admissible where a proper

---

[34] Zippo Mfg. Co. v. Rogers Imports, Inc., 216 F.Supp. 670 (S.D.N.Y. 1963).

[35] General Motors Corp. v. Cadillac Marine & Boat Co., 226 F.Supp. 716 (W.D.Mich. 1964).

[36] Liacakos v. Kennedy, 195 F. Supp. 630 (D. C. 1961).

showing is made as to the authority or authenticity of entries of the family record and where better evidence is not available. Such matters as births, deaths, and marriages are competent in evidence. In some states entries in the family Bible or hearsay evidence concerning the family history are not admitted where the person making it is alive or capable of being examined as a witness.[37] In some instances, however, the absence of the person who made the statements or made the entries from the jurisdiction, insanity or illness hindering his presence at the trial is enough to make the evidence admissible. In some jurisdictions entries in family Bibles are declared admissible by statute. As an example, the Federal Rules of Evidence provide, "Statement of fact concerning personal or family history contained in family Bibles, geneologies, charts, engravings on rings, inscriptions on family portraits, engraving on urns, crypts, or tombstones or the like," are admissible as exceptions to the hearsay rule even though the declarant is available as a witness.[38]

§ 11.11a Non-testimonial utterances

In the previous sections the hearsay rule was defined and some of the exceptions to the hearsay rule discussed. There is a category of evidence which is similar to hearsay but is not described as hearsay evidence. In some instances a witness on the stand can repeat what was said by another outside of court if the evidence is introduced not for the facts asserted but only to indicate that a statement was made. In some courts this is distinguished as original evidence rather than pure hearsay. This evidence is not admitted as an exception to the hearsay rule but rather on the reasoning that it does not amount to testimonial hearsay as included in a definition of the hearsay rule. In this category of evidence is that relating to the state of mind of a person.

Where the sanity of a person accused of crime is an issue, the statements made at the time of the offense or immediately preceding or following the offense are admissible to prove his mental condition. Here the evidence is admitted not for its assertive or testimonial use but to show the state of mind of the person making

---

[37] State v. Adkins, 146 S.E. 732 (Ga. 1929).

[38] Rule 803(13), Fed. Rules of Evidence.

the statements.[39]

On like reasoning it has been held that the hearsay rule will not exclude a statement if the utterance of the statement tends to prove an operative fact. For example, in *Braswell* v. *United States* the police officers were permitted to testify that they heard the use of words which were commonly used by narcotics addicts coming from a motel room they were about to enter.[40] The evidence was admitted not for the message the words contained but as circumstantial evidence that narcotics were in the room.

Under what is sometimes referred to as the verbal act doctrine, a statement which accompanies conduct is admissible to give legal significance to the act. Here the evidence is offered only to show that words were spoken, not as proof of the truth of what was said. As an example, in a prosecution for intimidating the witness, the witness' testimony as to the substance of what his wife had reported to him as having been said to her by the defendant was admissible but only as evidence of a "verbal act." The evidence was introduced for the purpose of proving the fact that statements which the wife testified she made to her husband were in fact made.[41]

§ 11.12 Summary

The general rule is that "hearsay evidence" is not admissible in court. Hearsay evidence is testimony or written evidence presented in court from a statement made out of court, such statement being offered to prove the truth of matters asserted therein, and thus resting for its value upon the credibility of the out-of-court asserter. Although this general rule is universally applied and is based on sound reasoning, there are many exceptions to this rule. If the testimony comes within the definition of the exception, it is admissible even though it is hearsay.

Examples of exceptions to the hearsay rule are "declarations against interest," "dying declarations," "spontaneous utterances," certain "business and public records," statements concerning "family history," evidence from "learned treatises," and "ancient documents." Hearsay evidence is not admissible as an exception, how-

---

[39] Bridges v. State, 247 Wisc. 350, 19 N.W.(2d) 529 (1945).
[40] 200 F.(2d) 597 (5th Cir. 1952).
[41] Overton v. United States, 403 F.(2d) 444 (5th Cir. 1968). Parts of case in Part II of this book.

ever, unless it meets the specific qualification established for that particular exception.

The hearsay rule is not applicable where out-of-court statements are offered solely to explain an act or conduct. And out-of-court statements may be repeated by another in court, not for the content of that statement but to indicate the person's physical or mental condition.

It is obvious that some hearsay evidence is not admissible in court but it is just as obvious that if the investigator does not know that there are exceptions to the hearsay rule, he cannot adequately perform his duties. To be assured that all competent evidence, including hearsay evidence, will be used effectively and to the best advantage, every law enforcement agent should be fully familiar with the hearsay rule and the exceptions.

Chapter 12

DOCUMENTARY EVIDENCE

> Before any writing will be admitted in evidence, it must be authenticated in some manner—i.e., its genuineness or execution must be proved. Even a competent public record or document must be properly identified, verified or authenticated by some recognized method before it may be introduced in evidence.
> *City of Randleman v. Hinshaw*, 2 N.C. App. 381, 163 S. E. (2d) 95 (1968).

Section

12.1 Introduction
12.2 Authentication
12.3 Ancient documents
12.4 Newspapers
12.5 Official records and public documents
12.6 Death certificates and autopsy reports
12.7 Private writings
12.8 Best evidence rule
12.9 Secondary evidence
12.10 Summaries (voluminous writings)
12.11 Learned treatises
12.12 Summary

§ 12.1 Introduction

Evidence is categorized in many ways. From the point of view of the type of evidence introduced in court, it can be divided into three categories: (1) oral testimony, (2) documentary evidence, and (3) real evidence. Many of the rules relating to oral testimony have already been discussed. The rules relating to real evidence will be discussed in the following chapter. In this chapter some of the more important rules concerning documentary evidence will be discussed.

A document may be defined as any matter expressed or described upon any substance by means of letters, figures, or marks, or by more than one of such means and intended to be used for the purpose of recording that matter.[1] It includes all kinds of documents, records and writings of whatever nature.

Obviously, to be admissible documentary evidence must meet the same requirements as to relevancy, competency, or materiality as oral testimony. It would not make good law to allow, for example, hearsay evidence when it is written and not to allow it as a form of oral testimony. However, as there are exceptions to some of the rules which relate to oral testimony, there are exceptions to these rules as they relate to written documents.

The hearsay rule as discussed in previous chapters is one of the rules which applies to documentary evidence. There are specific exceptions—some by statutes and some by court decision—which are peculiar to documentary evidence. These and other evidentiary rules relating to the documentary evidence will be discussed in the following sections.

§ 12.2 Authentication

Documentary evidence is not admissible until it has been authenticated. As a general rule, authentication can be accomplished by any competent evidence to show that the writing is genuine, that is, it is what it purports to be.[1a] Authentication is usually accomplished by sworn testimony of a witness as to the source and genuineness of the writing. However, in some instances, such specific testimony is not required. For example, official records may be authenticated by an attesting certificate, which is a signed statement of the custodian of the records that the paper in question is the original or true copy thereof. In such case, of course, then the attesting certificate must itself be authenticated by competent evidence. In some cases the required formal authenticity requirement may be dispensed with if the parties agree to the genuineness of the writing.

Some records do not have to be formally authenticated because they "prove themselves." By statutes in some states some instruments such as deeds which have been acknowledged by the signers before

---

[1] 29 Am.Jur.(2d) 834.
[1a] Rule 901(a), Fed. Rules of Evidence.

a notary public are considered self-identifying. In an effort to save the time of the court, statutes have been designed to do away with the formal authentication requirements where such requirements obviously serve little purpose. Courts are beginning to recognize the practical aspects of authentication and are authorizing the use of certain documents without the formal requirements.

The Supreme Court in drafting the rules of evidence for federal courts listed ten types of writings that are now to be considered as self-authenticating.[1b] In Rule 902 of the Rules of Evidence the Supreme Court explained that extrinsic evidence of authenticity as a condition precedent to admissibility is not required with respect to the following: 1) domestic public documents under seal; 2) domestic public documents not under seal but certified by the appropriate public officer in charge of them; 3) foreign public documents accompanied by certification as to genuineness of signature and official position of executing or attesting person; 4) copies of public or official records certified by the custodian of the original record; 5) official publications issued by public authority; 6) newspapers and periodicals; 7) trade inscriptions and labels; 8) documents acknowledged by a notary public or other officer authorized by law to take acknowledgments; 9) commercial paper and related documents; and 10) documents declared by Congress to be presumptively authentic.

Case law and studies have developed a substantial amount of law indicating that authenticity is taken as sufficiently established for purposes of admissibility without extrinsic evidence to that effect. However, it must be emphasized that the opposing party is not foreclosed from disputing authenticity and even where statutes are codified rules make these documents self-authenticating, there is no guarantee that it will be admissible.

In the sections that follow specific types of documents and the rules relating to the admissibility of this type of documentary evidence will be discussed in more detail.

§ 12.3 Ancient documents

Under the ancient document rule a writing may be authenticated by using circumstantial evidence. This rule is that writing

---

[1b] See Rules 902 and 903 in the appendix.

purporting to be thirty years or more old, if relevant to the inquiry, when produced from proper custody, and on its face free from suspicion, is admissible in evidence, without the ordinary requirements as to proof of execution or handwriting.[1c] The rationale behind the ancient documents exception is that after a long lapse of time, ordinary evidence regarding signatures or handwriting is virtually unavailable, and it is therefore permissible to resort to circumstantial evidence.

The fact that a written instrument is an ancient document does not affect its admissibility in evidence further than to dispense with proof of its genuineness. The presumption of authenticity is therefore rebuttable.

§ 12.4 Newspapers

Printed books or publications are generally not received as evidence of any fact stated in them because the statements made therein are not made under oath and no opportunity for cross-examination of their author is afforded. Under this rule newspapers ordinarily are not admissible However, historical writings are admissible in cases which delve into relatively ancient and obscure origins. On the basis that newspaper accounts are among the source materials of history, a federal court held that newspaper accounts describing the use of the Missouri River during the 19th century were admissible in evidence.[2]

In other cases an Ohio court admitted as ancient documents newspapers eighty years old containing notices of advertisements for bids relating to the town hall;[3] and in a suit by a county against its fire insurers for damage sustained to the courthouse in the collapse of its clock tower allegedly due to lightning, a federal court admitted in evidence a fifty-eight-year-old newspaper account of a fire in the tower. The court did not characterize the newspaper as a "business record," nor as an "ancient document," nor as any other

---

[1c] Although most states hold that an ancient document must be thirty years old, Federal Rule 901(b)(8) drops the requirement to twenty years for cases tried in federal courts.

[2] Montana Power Co. v. Federal Power Comm., 87 U.S.App.D.C. 316, 185 F.(2d) 491 (D.C. Cir. 1950).

[3] Trustees of German Twp. v. Farmers & Citizens Sav. Bank, 51 OhioOp. 346, 113 N.E.(2d) 409 (1953).

identifiable species of hearsay exception; but decided that the contemporary newspaper account was admissible because it was necessary and trustworthy, relevant and material.[4]

§ 12.5 Official records and public documents

Another well-established hearsay exception makes admissible the record of a public official which he was under a duty to make, and as to which he had personal knowledge. Where public officers are under a duty to keep a record of transactions which occur in the course of their public service, the official records and writings so made by such officers, or under their supervision, are of a public nature and are ordinarily admissible in evidence as proof of their contents, even though not proved by the person who actually made the entries.[4a] The extraordinary degree of confidence reposed in such documents is founded principally upon the circumstance that they have been made by authorized and accredited officers and deputies appointed for the purpose.

Many states have enacted statutes which provide that official reports made by officers of the state, or certified copies of the same, on a matter within the scope of their duty as defined by statute, shall, insofar as relevant, be admitted as evidence of the matters stated therein. Under the provisions of a federal statute[5] properly authenticated copies or transcripts of any books, records, papers, or documents of any department or agency of the United States shall be admitted in evidence equally with the originals thereof.

Rule 1005 of the Federal Rules of Evidence provides that an official record or an entry therein, when admissible for any purpose, may be evidenced by an official publication thereof or by a copy attested by the officer having the legal custody of the record, or by his deputy, and accompanied with a certificate that such officer has the custody. The certificate may be made by a judge of a court of record of the district or political subdivision in which the record is kept, authenticated by the seal of the

---

[4] Dallas County v. Commercial Union Assur. Co., 286 F.(2d) 388 (5th Cir. 1961).

[4a] Fed. Rule 902(4), however, requires certification of records required to be filled out by the custodian of the record. See also Rules 902(1), 902(2), and 902(3).

[5] 28 U.S.C. 1733.

court; or may be made by any public officer having a seal of office and having official duties in the district or political subdivision in which the record is kept, authenticated by the seal of his office. Under this rule a photostatic copy of the record of the judgment and sentence of a court showing that the defendant was sentenced to two years imprisonment, and a copy of the return of the marshal showing delivery of defendant pursuant to the sentence to a federal prison, authenticated by the clerk of the court with the seal of the court affixed, were admitted in evidence.[6]

An out-of-state certificate of title for a motor vehicle is a public act and record of the state where issued, and as such is entitled to full faith and credit in the courts of another state. Likewise, a foreign notarial seal is sufficient prima facie authentication of a document executed elsewhere for use locally.

§ 12.6 Death certificates and autopsy reports

In legislation governing death certificates it is usually provided that a certified copy of an original death certificate shall be prima facie evidence of the facts therein stated. In addition, the records of the coroner, made by himself or by anyone acting under his direction or supervision are considered public records, and such records or transcripts thereof, or photostatic copies thereof, certified by the coroner, are received as evidence in any criminal case. Public documents of this type are not conclusive of the facts therein stated, but are subject to contradiction.

The statement in a death certificate or a coroner's record that a decedent committed suicide, where there was no witness to the infliction of the wound from which the decedent died, is a mere opinion and is not admissible in evidence in the trial of a case in which the question of whether the decedent was a suicide is involved.[7] On the other hand, the admission into evidence of statements in a death certificate or a coroner's report that the decedent was beaten by an unknown assailant or that there was extensive beat-

---

[6] Mullican v. United States, 252 F. (2d) 398 (5th Cir. 1958); United States v. McCray, 486 F.(2d) 446 (10th Cir. 1972).

[7] Carson v. Metropolitan Life Ins. Co., 156 OhioSt. 104, 45 OhioOp. 103, 100 N.E.(2d) 197 (1951).

Also see In re Weils Estate, 21 Ariz.App. 278, 518 P.(2d) 995 (1974). But see Bickford v. Metropolitan Life Ins. Co., 317 A.(2d) 573 (1974).

ing involving the entire body does not constitute prejudicial error, where there is testimony as to the condition of decedent's body at the time of death and as to the cause of death, and where such statements in the documents do not connect the defendant with the death of the decedent.[8]

In an insurance company's action against the beneficiary under life policies for a judgment declaring its liability, brought on the theory that the insured had committed suicide, both the original death certificate executed by the medical examiner and indicating that death was due to suicide and an amended certificate indicating that death was due to an accident were admissible. They were, however, admitted only as prima facie evidence and were subject to full explanation and contradiction, and the trial court's action in admitting only the original certificate and refusing to admit the amended certificate and tendered testimony of the medical examiner with respect to the making of it, was prejudicial error.[9]

§ 12.7 Private writings

All private writings must be proved to be genuine before they are admissible in evidence. The genuineness may be proved by the testimony of anyone who saw the writing executed or by indirect or circumstantial evidence the same as many other facts; but the circumstantial evidence must be of such force and character that the person's authorship of the writing can be legitimately deduced from it.

Both expert and lay witnesses may testify to their opinions respecting authorship or genuineness of writings, provided they are properly qualified to do so. A lay witness must be reasonably familiar with the handwriting of the person whose authorship of the contested document is at issue.[9a] The necessary familiarity ordinarily is obtained by observing the person write or by receiving from him letters or other written material. For example a bank teller frequently has the requisite familiarity with the signature

---

[8] State v. Woodards, 6 OhioSt.(2d) 14, 35 OhioOp.(2d) 8, 215 N.E.(2d) 568 (1966).

[9] Marker v. Prudential Ins. Co., 273 F.(2d) 258 (5th Cir. 1959).

[9a] Rule 901(b)(2) of the Fed. Rules of Evidence specifies that the familiarity not be acquired for purposes of the litigation.

of a depositor.

§ 12.8 Best evidence rule

It has often been stated as a universal rule of evidence that the best evidence that is obtainable in the circumstances of the case must be adduced to prove any disputed fact. This rule is especially applicable when documentary evidence is used. Although the rule apparently enjoyed a broader application at one time it is now generally recognized that the "best evidence" phrase denotes only the rule of evidence which requires that the contents of an available written document be proved by introduction of the document itself.[9b] Where proof is to be made of some fact which is recorded in a writing, the best evidence of the contents of the writing consists in the actual production of the document itself. Any proof of a lower degree is secondary evidence which will be received as proof only where nonproduction of the writing is properly accounted for.

The real purpose of, and reasons for, the best evidence rule are well stated by Dean Wigmore:[10]

> (1) As between a supposed literal copy and the original, the copy is always liable to errors on the part of the copyist, whether by wilfulness or by inadvertence; this contingency wholly disappears when the original is produced. Moreover, the original may contain, and the copy will lack, such features of handwriting, paper, and the like, as may afford the opponent valuable means of learning legitimate objections to the significance of the document. (2) As between oral testimony, based on recollection, and the original, the added risk, almost the certainty, exists, of errors of recollection due to the difficulty of carrying in the memory literally the tenor of the document.

The best evidence rule is aimed only at excluding evidence which concerns the contents of a writing; testimony as to other facts about a writing, such as its existence or identity, may be admissible. Thus, in a case in which the defendant was convicted of the unlawful possession of intoxicating liquor, police officers

---

[9b] Rule 1002, Fed. Rules of Evidence.

[10] IV Wigmore, EVIDENCE, § 1179 (3d ed. 1940).

testified that they had seen a federal liquor license bearing the name of the defendant on the wall of a filling station where the intoxicants were found. Subsequently, a certified copy of the license was admitted in evidence. The court, after pointing out that officers could testify to the fact that they had seen a liquor license, stated "but we have not permitted them to testify concerning the contents of the license as the license itself would be the best evidence of what it contained." Here the court determined that the admission of testimony concerning the contents of the license was error, but held that the error had been rendered harmless by the subsequent production of a certified copy.[11]

In a prosecution for possession of a particular treasury check which had allegedly been stolen from an authorized mail depository, the receipt into evidence of a copy of the check rather than the check itself constituted a violation of the best evidence rule where the terms of the check were vitally material to the government's case and where no reason was advanced why the check itself could not have been produced.[12]

All the decisions rejecting copies of writings in the absence of demand for originals when in the hands of an adversary, or of a proper accounting for their loss or destruction, were based upon the rule requiring the "best evidence" to be introduced. But with reference to letters written in duplicate or greater number by the use of carbon paper, all are written by the same mechanical act. If the duplicate original made from the carbon paper by the striking of the type should be mailed and that made from the ribbon be retained, the one mailed would certainly be a letter, as much so as the other, if sent, would be. The carbon impressions are not copies but duplicate originals.[13]

A retained carbon copy of a letter was not subject to exclusion under the best evidence rule, where the carbon copy was signed, as was the other copy of it, by the person who prepared it, and this retained copy, as well as the copy sent, was a counterpart or

---

[11] Chambless v. State, 94 Okla.Cr. 140, 231 P.(2d) 711 (1951).

[12] United States v. Alexander, 326 F.(2d) 736 (4th Cir. 1964). Parts of case included in Part II.

[13] Davis v. Williams Bros. Constr. Co., 207 Ky. 404, 269 S.W. 289 (1925); Hartstock v. Strong, 318 A.(2d) 237 (Md. 1974).

duplicate.[14]

§ 12.9 Secondary evidence

When the original writing has been lost or destroyed secondary evidence of its contents is admissible. Reasonable search should be made for the lost writing in the place where it was last known to have been, and inquiry made of persons most likely to have its custody, or who may have some knowledge of its whereabouts. Before secondary evidence may be offered there must be proof that the writing was destroyed without fraudulent intent on the part of the proponent, or intentionally destroyed for wholly innocent reasons.[15]

As indicated if the original document or the primary evidence is not available, secondary evidence may be admitted. Rule 1004 of the Federal Rules of Evidence provides that the original is not required and secondary evidence of the contents of a writing (also recording or photograph) is admissible if, 1) originals are lost or destroyed (not in bad faith), 2) the original is not obtainable, 3) the original is in the possession of an opponent, or 4) the writing, recording, or photograph is not related to the controlling issue. Before secondary evidence is admitted the party requesting that it be admitted must lay a foundation. The party must show to the satisfaction of the court that the primary evidence or the original is unavailable through no fault of his own or because of one of the reasons as indicated.

As noted in a previous section, carbon copies of documents made on the same typewriter are generally considered as duplicate originals and may be introduced in evidence without accounting for the non-production of the original. Some cases hold to the contrary on the reasoning that the parties did not intend that the carbon be considered an original. Even if the carbon is not considered as the best evidence, it is certainly considered one of the best types of secondary evidence and may be introduced as such if the proper foundation has been laid.

Unlike carbon copies, copies of documents made by a photographic or photostatic process or other similar processes are not considered in any case the same as the original. This type of copy

---

[14] Bruce v. United States, 351 F. (2d) 318 (5th Cir. 1965).

[15] United States v. England, 480 F. (2d) 1266 (5th Cir. 1973).

is inadmissible if the original can be produced in court and are admissible only as secondary evidence after the proper foundation has been laid. Notwithstanding this general rule making photographic copies inadmissible except as secondary evidence, some states have adopted by statute legislation making photostatic copies regularly kept admissible without accounting for the original document.

Often a question arises as to what type of secondary evidence is preferable. There is a category of evidence which might be considered as secondary to secondary evidence. This is a copy of a copy. Obviously, if a copy of the original is available, the copy of the copy would not be admissible under the best evidence rule. However, where both the original and the copy have been destroyed or are not available, even the copy of the copy is admissible.

The extensive use of the computer and the print-out has introduced another question into the law of evidence. In at least one case data and records stored on computer cards and magnetic tape have been held to fall within the bounds of "best evidence." The print-outs are the best evidence because of the impossibility in practice of reading the original which is a piece of tape or punch card.[16]

The rules relating to best and secondary evidence generally apply to recordings or photographs as well as documents. For example, where an original tape recording was available and would normally be the best evidence, the trial court nevertheless permitted introduction of a copy, conceded to be accurate. The court reasoned that where a copy is proven accurate and serves to prove the substance of the original in a more easily understood form, the spirit of the rule permits the admission of the copy.[17]

§ 12.10 Summaries (voluminous writings)

The general rule is that the use of a summary is a matter that rests within the sound discretion of the trial court. Certain criteria have evolved to guide a court in exercising its discretion. So, a

---

[16] Rule 1004, Fed. Rules of Evidence.

[17] Johns v. U.S., 323 Fed.(2d) 421 (5th Cir. 1963). Also, People v. Marcus, 107 Cal.Rptr. 264 (1973).

proper foundation must be laid with reference to the admissibility of the originals. More importantly, it must be shown that the summation accurately summarizes the materials involved by not referring to information not contained in the original. Usually the records or materials summarized must first be made accessible to the opposing party for inspection and for use in cross-examination.[17a] A summary of the reconstructed inventory was properly admitted in a mail fraud case, where the records which were the basis of the summary were available and the prosecution offered to produce the records in court.[18]

The preparation and submission to the jury of summaries prepared by an expert is well nigh indispensable to the understanding of a long and complicated set of facts. But when summaries are used and given to the jury, the court must ascertain with certainty that they are based upon and fairly represent competent evidence already before the jury. Such summaries, if given to the jury, must be accompanied by appropriate instructions concerning their nature and use. The jury should be advised that the summaries do not, of themselves, constitute evidence in the case but only purport to summarize the documentary and detailed evidence already admitted; that it should examine the basis upon which the summaries rest and be satisfied they accurately reflect other evidence in the case; and that, if not so satisfied, the summaries should be disregarded. In addition, broad cross-examination should be permitted upon the summaries to afford a thorough test of their accuracy. It was not error in a prosecution for willfully subscribing to and filing of a false income tax return to permit the use of summaries of the evidence prepared by the revenue agent and given to the jury under proper instructions pertaining to summaries.[19]

§ 12.11 Learned treatises

Medical books or treatises, even though properly identified and authenticated and shown to be recognized as standard authorities on the subjects to which they relate, are not admissible in evidence to prove the truth of the statements therein contained.

[17a] Rule 1006, Fed. Rules of Evidence, requires that summaries or charts be made available to other parties at a reasonable time and place.

[18] Bruce v. United States, n. 14, *supra*.

[19] Conford v. United States, 336 F. (2d) 285 (10th Cir. 1964).

The decided weight of authority is to the effect that medical and other scientific treatises representing inductive reasoning are inadmissible as independent evidence of the theories and opinions therein expressed. The bases for exclusion are lack of certainty as to the validity of the opinions and conclusions set forth, the technical character of the language employed which is not understandable to the average person, the absence of an oath to substantiate the assertions made, the lack of opportunity to cross-examine the author, and the hearsay aspect of such matter.

A few states have adopted the rule that a published treatise, periodical, or pamphlet on a subject of history, science, or art may be admitted in evidence to prove the truth of a matter stated therein if the judge takes judicial notice, or a witness expert in the subject testifies, that the treatise, periodical, or pamphlet is a reliable authority on the subject. Under a Massachusetts statute,[20] as a prerequisite to the admission of a medical treatise in evidence in a malpractice action, the party offering such evidence must satisfy the trial judge that the author was recognized in his profession or calling as an expert on the subject.[21]

§ 12.12 Summary

In addition to oral testimony, documentary evidence may be used in court to assist the jury or judge in determining the ultimate facts. Documentary evidence includes all kinds of documents, records, and writings. To be admissible documentary evidence must meet the same requirements as to relevancy, competency, and materiality as oral evidence and in addition meet other requirements.

One of the requirements concerning documentary evidence is that it must be authenticated. That is, competent evidence must be generally introduced to show that it is what it purports to be. To save time of the court, simplified methods of authentication have been recognized in specific instances. For example, ancient documents are generally admissible into evidence without the ordinary requirement as to proof of execution simply because evidence to show authenticity by the usual method is not available.

---

[20] Mass. Gen. Laws Ann. ch. 233, § 79C.

[21] Ramsland v. Shaw, 166 N.E.(2d) 894.(Mass. 1960).

§ 12.12

As a general rule official records are admissible into evidence as an exception to the hearsay rule and without the same degree of authenticity as required for other records. These are allowed because of the extraordinary degree of confidence reposed in such documents because they are drafted by authorized and accredited officers. This same degree of confidence is not placed in private writings and such writings must be proved to be genuine before they are admissible in evidence.

The generally accepted principle of law is that the best evidence that can be obtained in the circumstances of the case must be introduced to prove a disputed fact. It follows that secondary evidence is admissible only if the primary evidence is unavailable. The historical basis for this rule is that a copy is more likely to have errors and that the copy will lack such features as handwriting and paper which provide the opponent a means of finding legitimate objections to the admissibility. Because of modern means of reproduction of documents some of the reasons for requiring the original are no longer valid.

Although the courts have in some instances made common sense exceptions the general rule is still that secondary evidence can be admissible only when it is shown that the primary evidence is unavailable. The courts have allowed secondary evidence where the original has been lost or destroyed, where it is beyond the jurisdiction of the court, or where it is in the hands of one who refuses to produce it.

In many criminal cases it is necessary that documentary evidence be used in order to supply the jury or judge with facts from which to make a sound determination. Obviously, if the investigator fails to follow the rules concerning documentary evidence, some evidence will be excluded with the result that the judge or jury will not have these facts.

The officer cannot wait until the trial to determine if the evidence will be properly authenticated or to determine if the evidence is the best evidence under the circumstances. He must be familiar with these rules at the time the investigation is being conducted and obtain the necessary evidence or witnesses to assure that the documents will be admitted into court and given the weight to which they are entitled. To avoid the possibility of having such documentary evidence excluded, it is necessary that the investigator work with the prosecutor concerning the requirements for admission.

Chapter 13

REAL EVIDENCE

> Stains of blood, found upon the person or clothing of the party accused, have always been recognized among the ordinary indicia of homicide. The practice of identifying them by circumstantial evidence and by the inspection of witnesses and jurors has the sanction of immemorial usage in all criminal tribunals . . . the degree of force to which it is entitled may depend upon a variety of circumstances to be considered and weighed by the jury in each particular case; but its competency is too well settled to be questioned in a court of law.
> *People* v. *Gonzalez,* 35 N.Y. 49 (1866).

GENERAL

Section

- 13.1 Introduction
- 13.2 Exhibition of person
- 13.3 Articles connected with the crime
- 13.4 View of the scene
- 13.5 Photographs
- 13.6 Motion pictures
- 13.7 X-rays
- 13.8 Sound recordings
- 13.9 Diagram, maps and models
- 13.10 Experiments
- 13.11 Summary and practical suggestions

RESULTS OF EXAMINATIONS AND TESTS

Section

- 13.11a Introduction
- 13.11b Examination of the person
- 13.12 Intoxication tests
- 13.13 Blood grouping tests
- 13.14 Polygraph examination
- 13.15 "Truth serum" results
- 13.16 Fingerprint comparisons
- 13.17 Ballistic experiments
- 13.18 Speed detection readings
- 13.19 Spectogram voice identification
- 13.19a Neutron activation analysis
- 13.20 Summary and practical suggestions

GENERAL

§ 13.1 Introduction

Recent United States court decisions have emphasized the necessity of developing more sophisticated methods of obtaining and utilizing real evidence in criminal cases. Although these decisions have limited the use of confessions, the opinions of the majority have encouraged the use of real or physical evidence. In *Schmerber* v. *United States*[1] the United States Supreme Court limited the application of the Fifth Amendment self incrimination protection to evidence of a testimonial or communicative nature stating,

> On the other hand, both federal and state courts have usually held that it offers no protection against compulsion to submit to fingerprinting, photographing, or measurements, to write or speak for identification, to appear in court, to stand, to assume a stance, to walk, or to make a particular gesture.

The court went on to say, "Compulsion which makes a suspect or accused the source of 'real or physical evidence' does not violate it."

Although the United States Supreme Court has held that as a general rule real evidence does not violate the self-incrimination protection of the Constitution, there are many tests and rules which have been established by courts and legislative bodies which must be recognized. To be admissible real evidence must generally meet the requirements as to relevancy, competency, and materiality as is the case with documentary evidence and oral testimony.

The material on the admissibility of real evidence has been divided into two categories. The first deals with the *general* rules concerning admissibility. In the latter part of this chapter (§§ 13.11a et seq.) rules relating to *specific* types of evidence will be discussed.

In Black's Law Dictionary real evidence is defined as evidence furnished by things themselves, on view or inspection, as distinguished from a description of them by the mouth of a witness.

---

[1] 384 U.S. 757, 16 L.Ed.(2d) 908, 86 S.Ct. 1826 (1966). See case in Part II.

One example of real evidence is the physical appearance of the person when exhibited to the jury. Other examples are weapons or implements used in the commission of a crime, other inanimate objects, and evidence of the physical appearance of the place of the commission of a crime.

Real proof is evidence acquired directly by the jurors or the judge through the medium of their own senses by an inspection of the subject matter itself. Real proof can appeal to the sense of sight, hearing, touch, smell, or taste.

Whenever an object, cognizable by the senses, has such a relation to the fact in dispute as to afford a reasonable grounds of belief respecting it, such object may be exhibited to the jury.[2]

§ 13.2 Exhibition of person

Where in a criminal case the prosecution of the defendant is based on physical harm to the victim, it would seem the best evidence of such harm when possible is the exhibition of the person of the victim to the jury. Such witness would be more valuable in determining what happened than oral testimony, photographs, or even x-rays in some instances. Courts as a rule will allow the display of the injury to the jury—often in spite of the fact that it might be gruesome.

The trial judge has much discretion in determining whether the physical display of the injury is so inflammatory as to unduly influence the jury in the decision. His discretionary decision is seldom over-ruled unless there is a clear abuse of the discretion. However, if in the opinion of the judge the display of the person and the injury is determined to be so inflammatory as to prejudice the jury, the judge may require that the injury be described rather than allowing the exhibition of the person and the display of the injury.

The person of the witness may be exhibited at the trial in a criminal case to assist the jury or judge in determining the nature and extent of the injury. For example, it is permissible for the prosecution to exhibit the child to the jury to prove the commission of the crime of statutory rape. And in a paternity proceeding the court

---

[2] California Code of Civil Procedure § 1954.

may generally require the alleged father to stand close to the illegitimate child to enable the jury to compare their physical features.

§ 13.3 Articles connected with the crime

Generally devices and instruments used in the commission of a crime as well as articles connected therewith are admitted into evidence. To be admissible the prosecution must show that there was or is a connection between the article and the accused.

Some examples of types of articles which have been acquired by investigators and submitted for consideration are discussed in the paragraphs which follow.

a. Weapons

In a bank robbery prosecution in which the defendant was charged with the violation of a federal statute making it a crime to take money from a bank by intimidation, the trial court admitted into evidence the component parts of a non-explosive simulated bomb consisting of a brown paper bag, a small box, a short length of wire, and an ordinary alarm clock. Although counsel for the defendant argued that these exhibits were irrelevant to the proof of any element of the crime, the appellate court upheld the use of the real evidence on the theory that the introduction of such evidence helped to demonstrate the method by which the crime had been committed.[3]

In the case of *People v. Riser*,[4] the court stated that if the specific type of weapon used to commit a homicide is not known, any weapons found in the defendant's possession after the crime and which could have been used in committing a homicide, are admissible; but that if the prosecution relies on the specific weapon or type it is error to admit evidence that other weapons were found in defendant's possession. It was explained that to allow the intro-

---

[3] Caldwell v. United States, 338 F.(2d) 385 (8th Cir. 1964). In Evans v. United States, 122 F.(2d) 461 (10th Cir. 1941), the court admitted a string and broom used in the commission of a homicide. In State v. Fulcher, 20 N.C. App. 259, a hammer found at the scene of a murder was admitted into evidence in view of bruise marks on the victim's body, even though there was no evidence particularly identifying it as the murder weapon.

[4] 47 Cal.(2d) 566, 305 P.(2d) 1 (1956).

duction of other types of weapons would tend to show not that he committed the particular crime but only that he was the sort of person who would carry deadly weapons.

b. Instruments used in the crime

In a prosecution for burglary of a tavern where there was evidence that the front door had been forced open and the tavern proprietor testified that one of the burglars was trying to pry open the side door with a screwdriver and that one of the burglars wore gloves, the court authorized the introduction into evidence of a screwdriver and gloves found in a field where the defendant had admitted running, holding that such items were sufficiently connected with the crime and the defendant to render them admissible.[5] And where there was direct positive evidence that tools found on the street had been used in the burglary, evidence tending to show that these tools had been in the possession of the defendants and thrown from their fleeing car was properly admitted.[6]

But where in the case of *People* v. *McCall*[7] the defendant testified that he struck the deceased in the deceased's car in self-defense and that the deceased fractured his skull when he fell to the pavement. The reviewing court held that the introduction into evidence of an auto crank, wrench, hammer handle, and tire iron, all found in the car, was reversible error since there were no fingerprints or blood stains on the implements to connect them with the accused.

c. Clothing

Clothing which had been identified by a witness as that worn by the accused at the time of the crime is properly submitted to the jury for inspection. For example, a coat and hat which were admittedly owned by the defendant and found in an abandoned automobile used by a bank robber, and which were identified as similar to those worn by the robber, were admissible as connecting

---

[5] People v. Allen, 17 Ill.(2d) 55, 160 N.E.(2d) 818 (Ill. 1959).
[6] McNeely v. United States, 353 F.(2d) 913 (8th Cir. 1965). See case in Part II. Also see Buck v. State, 503 S.W.(2d) 558 (Tex. 1974).
[7] 10 Cal.App.(2d) 503, 52 P.(2d) 500 (1935).

the defendant with the bank robbery.[8] And a cap, jacket and trousers found in a washing machine a few minutes after the robber had allegedly entered the house wearing similar clothing were properly admitted. The court held that such evidence was relevant and that the obtaining of the evidence did not violate the Fifth Amendment.[9]

d. Bloodstains

Stains of blood found upon the person or clothing of the party accused have been recognized among the ordinary indicia of homicide. The practice of identifying them by circumstantial evidence and by the inspection of witnesses and jurors has had the sanction of immemorial usage in all criminal tribunals.[10]

e. Other types of evidence

Other articles connected with the crime are also admissible if they meet the general tests. For example, paint chips and dust found on the clothing of the defendant which matched samples gathered from the scene of the burglary and the debris found on some of the burglary tools were properly admitted into evidence.[11]

When an object, article, tool, weapon or similar concrete thing is to be used in evidence to prove a fact with which it is related as of a previous time or event, it is not competent evidence unless it is first identified as the same object and shown to be substantially in the same condition as of the time or event to which it is claimed to be related.[12] The requirement of identification is designed not only to prevent the introduction of an object other than the one about which there has been testimony, but to insure that significant changes in the condition of the object have not occurred.[13]

Articles are sometimes admitted into evidence even though a slight alteration or change has occurred; e.g., a knife blade which

---

[8] Caldwell v. United States, 338 F.(2d) 385 (8th Cir. 1964). Also see State v. Brierly, 509 P.(2d) 203 (Ariz. 1973).
[9] Warden, Maryland Penitentiary v. Hayden, 387 U.S. 294, 18 L.Ed.(2d) 782, 87 S.Ct. 1642 (1967).
[10] People v. Gonzales, 35 N.Y. 49 (1866).
[11] McNeely v. United States, 353 F.(2d) 913 (8th Cir. 1965).
[12] Gutman v. Industrial Comm., 71 OhioApp. 383, 26 OhioOp. 302, 50 N.E.(2d) 187 (1942).
[13] McElfresh v. Commonwealth, 243 S.W.(2d) 497 (Ky. 1951).

was scraped for the purpose of obtaining a chemical analysis of the substance by which the blade was discolored;[14] clothing worn by the deceased which was washed by his widow after having been returned by the police;[15] a murder weapon dusted by the police for fingerprints and then wiped clean;[16] a shell which was marked for identification by the sheriff who scratched his initials into it;[17] and counterfeit plates from which lacquer had been removed.[18]

In order to dispel any inference of substitution or change in the contents of an exhibit, the prosecuting attorney frequently will call a witness to testify as to the chain or continuity of custody of an article from the time it is first obtained until produced in court.[19] The prosecution need not exclude all possibilities of tampering before evidence is admissible in a criminal case. The trial court need only be satisfied that in reasonable probability the article has not been changed in important respects. In *West v. United States*,[20] the trial court did not abuse its discretion in admitting in evidence packets containing marijuana on the ground that there was sufficient foundation to establish the chain of custody from the accused to the time of analysis, in view of the testimony of an undercover officer who had purchased the packets, concerning the care with which the packets had been kept by him and forwarded in sealed and initialed envelopes.

§ 13.4 View of the scene

Except in Texas where jury views are prohibited, the trial judge has power in both civil and criminal cases to order the jurors to be conducted to a place where a material fact occurred or an offense was committed. The judge has considerable discretion in granting

---

[14] Fabian v. State, 97 OhioSt. 184, 119 N.E. 410 (1918).

[15] Davidson v. State, 208 Ga. 834, 69 S.E.(2d) 757 (1952).

[16] State v. Cooper, 10 N.J. 532, 92 A.(2d) 786 (1952).

[17] Duke v. State, 257 Ala. 339, 58 So.(2d) 764 (1952).

[18] State v. Stewart, 1 OhioApp.(2d) 260, 30 OhioOp.(2d) 274, 204 N.E.(2d) 397 (1963).

[19] United States v. Burris, 393 F.(2d) 81 (7th Cir. 1968), holding that the evidence established the chain of custody so that narcotics received from defendant and placed in a sealed envelop and later tested by a government chemist were admissible in evidence.

[20] State v. Frates, 503 P.(2d) 47, (Mont. 1972); 359 F.(2d) 50 (8th Cir. 1966).

or refusing a request for a view by the jury. Under a statute providing that "when it is proper for the jurors to have a view of the place at which a material fact occurred, the trial court may order them to be conducted in a body to such place," the word "may" implies discretion.[21] And the trial court may, over objection by the defendant, in the exercise of sound discretion after it has been fully informed of the nature of the evidence to be offered and proper safeguards are taken to protect the rights of the defendant, permit the jurors to view premises where the acts are alleged to have been committed by the defendant.[22] Among the factors which the judge will consider are the degree of importance to the issue of the information to be gained by a view, the extent to which this could be adequately secured from photographs, maps, or diagrams, and the extent to which the premises or object have changed in appearance or condition since the occurrence.[23]

The procedure for viewing premises varies from state to state and the manner of viewing the scene is often regulated by either statute or rule of court. Usually the jury is conducted to the place by an officer of the court, who directs the jurors' attention to features of the scene which will be or have been referred to in the testimony given in court. Ordinarily the parties and their counsel are allowed to be present; however, they are not permitted to discuss the case with members of the jury. In criminal cases some states permit the accused to be present; others hold that allowing the accused to be present is within the discretion of the judge. In one case refusal to grant the defendant's request to be present, where his counsel was present, and there was no showing of resulting injustice, was not a denial of due process under the Fourteenth Amendment.[24] However in California the trial judge must accompany the jury when taken to view the scene.[25]

The purpose of the view is to enable the jury to observe places

---

[21] Commonwealth v. Chance, 174 Mass. 245, 54 N.E. 551 (1899).
[22] Commonwealth v. Gedzium, 259 Mass. 453, 156 N.E. 890 (1927); State v. Pigott, 1 OhioApp.(2d) 22, 30 OhioOp.(2d) 56, 197 N.E.(2d) 911 (1964); People v. Crossan, 87 Cal.App. 5, 261 Pac. 531 (1927). But see Peyton v. Strickland, 203 S.E.(2d) 388 (S.C. 1974).
[23] McCormick, EVIDENCE, § 183.
[24] Snyder v. Massachusetts, 291 U.S. 97, 78 L.Ed. 674, 54 S.Ct. 330 (1934).
[25] Rau v. Redwood City W. Club, 111 Cal.App.(2d) 546, 245 P.(2d) 12 (1952).

or objects which are pointed out to them, and thus provide them with a mental picture of the locality. There is a conflict in the decisions as to whether a view constitutes independent evidence. Some courts take a position that it does; while other courts hold that a view does not supply evidence, but merely enables the jury to better understand and apply the evidence offered upon trial. Inevitably what the jurors see on a view will be utilized in reaching a verdict, and in that sense that which is disclosed on a view is evidence.

§ 13.5 Photographs

As was pointed out in previous sections often it is possible to exhibit the person to the jury or judge, to introduce articles connected with the crime, or for the jury to view the scene of the crime. In other instances it is impracticable to bring all of the tangible evidence before the court. On the other hand, it is often impossible to define this type of evidence by words alone and photographs, if properly taken and explained, bring this evidence into court in a more convenient fashion. Photographs frequently convey information to the court and jury more accurately than words. Photos, although merely graphic representations of the oral testimony of witnesses, are in fact often worth more than a thousand words.

Photographs are generally inadmissible as original or substantive evidence. They must be sponsored by a witness whose testimony they serve to explain or illustrate. To be admissible the photograph must first be made a part of some qualified person's testimony. Someone, often the police officer, must stand forth as its testimonal sponsor; in other words, it must be verified. A photograph cannot be received anonymously; it must be verified by some witness.[26]

Before a trial court will admit a photograph in evidence a foundation must be laid. A competent witness who has personal knowledge must testify that the picture is an accurate representation of the objects or persons depicted. For example, where a bank teller has examined photographs and testifies that they are fair and accurate representations of the event, photographs taken by an automatic camera of a bank robbery are properly admitted into evidence.[27]

---

[26] 3 Wigmore, EVIDENCE, § 794 (3d ed.).

[27] United States v. Hobbs, 403 F. (2d) 977 (6th Cir. 1968).

The correctness of such representation may be established by any witness who is familiar with the scene, object, or person portrayed, or is competent to speak from personal observation. It is not necessary to prove this fact by the photographer who took the photograph. A witness qualifying a photograph does not have to be the photographer or see the picture taken; it is only necessary that the witness recognize and identify the object depicted and testify that the photograph fairly and correctly represents it.[28] Whether there is sufficient evidence of the correctness of a photograph to render it competent to be used by a witness for the purpose of illustrating or explaining his testimony is a preliminary question of fact for the trial judge.[29]

a. Posed photographs

There is a decided conflict of authority as to whether or not photographs of an attempted reproduction of the scene of a crime showing posed persons, dummies, or other objects are admissible to illustrate the contention of the party offering them as to the relative positions of the movable objects so represented at the time and place of the crime involved in the prosecution under consideration. In most jurisdictions where this question of admissibility has arisen, the courts have held such photographs admissible, when a proper foundation therefor has been laid by preliminary testimony showing that the objects and situations portrayed are faithfully represented as to position. An Oklahoma court held that posed photographs are admissible if properly identified, and if they purport to represent conditions as they actually existed at some crucial time and place, but not if they are intended only to illustrate hypothetical situations and to explain certain theories of the parties.[30]

---

[28] Kleveland v. United States, 345 F.(2d) 134 (2d Cir. 1965).

[29] State v. Gardner, 228 N.C. 567, 46 S.E.(2d) 824 (1948). In this case the trial judge, when he admitted a photograph, instructed the jury: "You will not consider this photograph as substantive evidence—it is not competent for that purpose. It is only competent, and the court limits the evidence in the way of a photograph to illustrating the testimony of the witness, and it is a question for you as to whether or not it does illustrate his testimony, and you will receive it and consider the photograph in no other way than as tending to illustrate the testimony of the witness, and not as substantive evidence."

[30] Roberts v. State, 166 P.(2d) 111 (1946).

b. Gruesome photographs

Although a photograph may be rendered inadmissible by its inflammatory nature, the mere fact that it is gruesome or horrendous is not sufficient to render it inadmissible if the trial court, in the exercise of its discretion, feels that it would prove useful to the jury. The real question is whether the probative value of such photograph is outweighed by the danger of prejudice to the defendant.[31] For example in the trial of a defendant charged with murder in the first degree, the admission or exclusion of photographs of the murder victim taken at the scene of the murder was properly within the sound discretion of the court.[32] And a police photographer's gruesome pictures of a burned woman in her hospital bed on the day after the defendant allegedly set her afire were properly admitted in evidence.[33] Also the admission of a photograph showing the decedent lying in a pool of blood was not an abuse of discretion, where it tended to assist the jury in understanding testimony of an autopsy surgeon concerning the injuries the decedent suffered and the testimony of a criminologist regarding articles found in the vicinity of the body.[34] The trial judge did not abuse his discretion in admitting photographs of the decedent's body, taken in a tavern where the shooting occurred, to corroborate testimony about the absence of powder burns on the flesh and on the deceased's shirt and undershirt.[35]

c. Time of taking

In some instances the correctness of the photograph depends upon the time it was taken. If the time between the incident and the taking of the photograph is so great as to make it unlikely that the photograph actually portrays the situation as it existed

---

[31] State v. Woodards, 6 OhioSt. (2d) 14, 35 OhioOp.(2d) 8, 215 N.E. (2d) 568; (1966); Maxwell v. United States, 368 F. (2d) 735 (9th Cir. 1966). See case in Part II. State v. Curry, 292 So.(2d) 212 (La. 1974).

[32] State v. Hill, 12 OhioSt.(2d) 88, 41 OhioOp.(2d) 369, 232 N.E.(2d) 394 (1967), in which the reviewing court found no abuse of discretion and held that "inspection of the photographs taken of decedent soon after his murder shows that they are not so gory or gruesome as to produce an inflammatory reaction by the jury against the defendant, and they were introduced in connection with the testimony of the state's witnesses to explain and clarify certain aspects of that testimony."

[33] State v. McClain, 256 Iowa 175, 125 N.W.(2d) 764 (1964).

[34] People v. Arguello, 37 Cal.Rptr. 601, 390 P.(2d) 377 (1964).

[35] State v. O'Conner, 42 N.J. 502, 201 A.(2d) 705 (1964).

at the time, such a photograph will not be admissible. It is obvious that the nature of the thing photographed has great weight in determining the importance of the time element. Some examples will emphasize this point.

As a rule photographs taken by an officer at the time of an accident will be admitted in evidence. However, in the case of *Hopper v. Reed* the court excluded photographs taken fourteen months after the accident in which a fourteen-year-old boy was struck while crossing the highway because the photographs did not show the traffic as it existed at the time of the accident.[36] But a photograph of a section of a highway where a head-on collision of a truck and pickup truck occurred was admitted in evidence even though taken some days after the accident, where the state trooper testified that the photograph correctly portrayed the same conditions as existed at the scene immediately after the collision.[37] And in a prosecution for the illegal possession and sale of narcotics it was not error to admit in evidence photographs that showed police surveillance of the defendant while dealing with an informer where the photographs were taken between the dates of the several indictments.[38]

Changes in conditions portrayed between the time of the event under investigation and the taking of a photograph do not render the photograph inadmissible where the changes can be explained by a witness, and the changes are not of such a character as to render the photograph deceptive.[39] In an action for injuries sustained in an automobile accident, a photograph taken six years previously and showing plaintiff in military uniform, accompanied by evidence to prove that the photograph accurately depicted plaintiff's appearance two months before the accident, was admissible.[40]

---

[36] 320 F.(2d) 433 (6th Cir. 1963).

[37] Jenkins v. Associated Transport, Inc., 330 F.(2d) 706 (6th Cir. 1964). In a prosecution for burglary of a tavern, where the tavern door was open at the time of the burglary, it was proper to introduce in evidence the photograph of the open door. People v. Allen, 17 Ill.(2d) 55, 160 N.E.(2d) 818 (1959).

[38] State v. Good, 110 OhioApp. 415, 11 OhioOp.(2d) 459, 165 N.E.(2d) 28 (1960).

[39] McKee v. Chase, 73 Idaho 491, 253 P.(2d) 787 (1953).

[40] Highshew v. Kushto, 126 Ind. App. 584, 131 N.E.(2d) 652 (1956). See also Burnett v. Cabo, 7 Ill.App.(2d) 266, 285 N.E.(2d) 619 (1972).

d. Colored photographs

Color photographs and color slides are admissible in evidence subject to the same limitations and restrictions placed on black and white photographs. Even though the color photographs are often more life-like and consequently more gruesome and revolting, this in itself does not constitute grounds for exclusion.[41] Because color photographs are subject to color distortion, however, it is more difficult to take photographs that show the actual colors as they existed at the scene and the offerer is often subject to a strong cross-examination on the subject of distortion.

Some examples of cases where color slides were admissible are as follows. In a murder trial color slides of a nude body of the deceased showing the location of his wounds were admissible.[42] The admission of color slides taken during the course of the autopsy performed on the alleged first-degree murder victim was not an abuse of discretion.[43] Color photographs of the deceased's body taken during the autopsy were admitted to give the jury a clear understanding of the cause of death.[44] And color photographs of injuries were admitted where the attending doctors identified the photographs as a fair representation of the plaintiff's condition as of the time they were taken.[45]

Apparently, colored photography is used more in criminal cases than in civil cases and the courts have recognized their probative value outweighs their probable adverse effect.[46] On the other hand, the officer must be cautioned that the colored photographs can be over-used. At the trial in a Pennsylvania case the evidence showed that the trial lasted 4½ days during which gruesome colored slides were used during a period of 1½ days. Although the court did not reverse the conviction on this ground the court stated:

> Since the case will be remanded, we are constrained to suggest that the pictures should not if used be put before the jury for so long a time and although they were subjected

---

[41] State v. Fulcher, 20 N.C. App. 259.

[42] State v. Farley, 112 Ohio App. 448, 16 Ohio Op.(2d) 343, 196 N.E.(2d) 232 (1960).

[43] State v. Swafford, 520 P.(2d) 1151 (Ariz. 1942). State v. Woodards, 6 Ohio St.(2d) 14, 35 Ohio Op. (2d) 8, 215 N.E.(2d) 568 (1966).

[44] State v. McClellan, 6 Ohio App. (2d) 155, 35 Ohio Op.(2d) 315, 217 N.E.(2d) 230 (1966).

[45] Jenkins v. Associated Transport, Inc., 330 F.(2d) 706 (6th Cir. 1964).

[46] People v. Love, 53 Cal.(2d) 843, 350 P.(2d) 705 (Cal. 1960).

to medical explanation we regard the duration of their view as excessive. Such pictures may be used as a fine point of demonstration but not as a bludgeon for winning the case.[47]

e. Enlargements and aerial photographs

The mere fact that a photograph sought to be introduced in evidence is an enlarged one, while often made a ground of objection thereto, has not been considered a bar to its admission in either civil or criminal cases when it has been properly authenticated and is material to an issue in the case.[48] Enlarged photographs are frequently used in cases involving the comparison of handwritings, or to show the place of an accident or scene of a crime.

There seems to be no distinction between aerial and other types of photographs insofar as their admissibility is concerned. Aerial photographs have been admitted into evidence for the purpose of giving the jury an accurate picture of some relevant fact in issue; but they may be excluded from evidence, in the discretion of the court, where other evidence gives the jury a sufficiently accurate picture of the subject matter involved.[49]

§ 13.6 Motion pictures

Motion pictures are admissible in evidence, within the sound discretion of the court, where such pictures are relevant to the issues, are accurate reproductions of persons and objects testified to in oral examination before the jury, and the conditions under which such pictures were taken conformed substantially to the facts related in open court.[50] However, a California court has warned that

> motion pictures should be received as evidence with caution, because the modern art of photography and the devices of an ingenious director frequently produce results which may be

---

[47] Commonwealth v. Johnson, 402 Pa. 479, 167 A.(2d) 511 (1961). For an interesting discussion of the use of color photography, see the article by Edward C. Conrad which appears in the Fingerprint and Identification Magazine, April 1961 issue.
[48] Annotation, 72 A.L.R.(2d) 308.
[49] Annotation, 57 A.L.R.(2d) 1351.

[50] Streit v. Kestel, 108 OhioApp. 241, 9 OhioOp.(2d) 245, 161 N.E.(2d) 409 (1959). In this case the photographed experiment was one showing pictures of an automobile making turns at an intersection where the collision occurred. State v. Johnson, 18 N.C. App. 606, 197 S.E.(2d) 592 (1973).

§ 13.6

quite deceiving. Telescopic lenses, ingenious settings of the stage, the elimination of unfavorable portions of a film, an angle from which a picture is taken, the ability to speed up the reproduction of the picture and the genius of a director may tend to create misleading impressions.[51]

Before motion pictures are admissible in evidence their relevancy, authenticity and accuracy of portrayal must be established by the laying of an adequate foundation. Basically, the admissibility of moving pictures depends upon testimony by the operator of the camera that the film accurately portrays what he observed at the time and place. But complete and formal laying of the foundation for admissibility would require:

1. Evidence as to the circumstances surrounding the taking of the pictures, which should include evidence as to the competency of the operator of the camera, the type of camera and operational methods, the type of lens and lens adjustment, sensitivity of the film, lighting, visibility and speed of the camera;

2. The manner and circumstances in regard to the development of the film;

3. Evidence in regard to the projection of the films, including speed at which the projector is run and its distance from the screen; and

4. Testimony of one present when the pictures were taken that they accurately portray the subject matter filmed.[52]

In a Mississippi case[53] the court held that a proper foundation had been laid for the introduction of films showing the injured party walking and running where the testimony established the identity and relevancy of the subject matter; the prevailing weather conditions; how the films would be projected; that the photographer was trained in the proper use of the camera and the making of films; that the camera was a standard make and in good working condition; that the camera was set and the pictures taken at a particular speed; and that the films accurately reproduced the scenes portrayed.

---

[51] Harmon v. San Joaquin L. & P. Corp., 37 Cal.App.(2d) 169, 98 P.(2d) 1064 (1940).

[52] Richardson, MODERN SCIENTIFIC EVIDENCE, § 16.22.

[53] Barham v. Nowell, 243 Miss. 441, 138 So.(2d) 493 (1962).

So long as sound motion pictures are properly authenticated and portray the situations as they actually occurred, there is no serious question as to their admissibility, both as to the visual evidence provided and the audio evidence.[54] A sound motion picture of the defendant making a confession to police officers will be admitted in evidence provided a double foundation is laid, showing that the picture is an accurate reproduction and that the confession is voluntary.[55] Likewise, the court will admit into evidence a sound motion picture showing the defendants re-enacting the crime and admitting that they had committed the crime in the manner depicted.[56]

§ 13.7 X-rays

Since an x-ray picture portrays only shadows of an internal part of the body which cannot be seen by the eye, it cannot be verified in the same manner as an ordinary photograph, that is, by testimony that it is a correct representation of the object it purports to picture. The earlier decisions required that correctness be shown by comparison with what the witness saw through a fluoroscope or by proving skill in x-ray techniques, proper working conditions and accuracy of equipment, manner of taking the picture, and correctness of result based on experience.[57]

In more recent decisions the courts have held that an x-ray is sufficiently authenticated if the evidence shows that it was taken by a qualified expert who is familiar with x-ray technique and procedure, and that it is a true representation of what it purports to represent. There is no problem as to laying the foundation for x-ray pictures where the physician or roentgenologist under whose super-

---

[54] Miles Laboratories, Inc. v. Frolich, 195 F.Supp. 256 (S.D. Cal. 1961). Properly authenticated sound motion pictures of reaction test interviews of consumers to determine whether they would confuse an alleged infringing brand name with a registered trade-mark were admissible. State v. Johnson, supra note 50.

[55] People v. Hayes, 21 Cal.App. (2d) 320, 71 P.(2d) 321 (1937).

[56] People v. Dabb, 32 Cal.(2d) 491, 197 P.(2d) 1 (1948). A rehearsal was first held, then the scene was shot, and the resulting film with sound was exhibited to the jury after a foundation was laid by testimony of defendants' consent and of the authenticity of the film.

[57] Stevens v. Illinois Cent. R. Co., 306 Ill. 370, 137 N.E. 859 (1923); Sim v. Weeks, 7 Cal.App.(2d) 28, 45 P.(2d) 350 (1935).

vision and control the picture was taken interprets it in court for the jury.

Professional medical witnesses may illustrate x-rays through a view screen or illuminator in the court room.[58] Colored drawings prepared by a medical artist from x-rays were admitted in evidence where a doctor testified that the drawings were accurate reproductions of the x-rays also admitted in evidence.[59]

§ 13.8 Sound recordings

Although the fantastic advances in the field of electronic communication constitute a great danger to the privacy of the individual, and the indiscriminate use of recording devices in law enforcement raises grave constitutional questions, sound recordings are frequently admitted into evidence. Before a sound recording is admitted into evidence a foundation must be established by showing that (1) the recording device was capable of taking the testimony or conversation offered in evidence; (2) the operator of the device was competent to operate it; (3) the recording is authentic and correct; (4) changes, additions, or deletions have not been made in the recording; (5) the recording has been preserved in a manner that is shown to the court; (6) the speakers are identified; and (7) the conversation elicited was made voluntarily and in good faith, without any kind of duress.[60]

When a portable transmitting and receiving set or other device is used to overhear conversations, the initial qualification for admission of evidence so obtained involves two sets of interrelated problems: first, whether the device used is an effective means of communicating sound, and second, the identification of the alleged speaker.[61] Electronic recordings of conversations had with one who is equipped with a wire recording device and also with a portable transmitting device are not secured in violation of the Fourth Amendment and are admissible in evidence.[62]

---

[58] Crocker v. Lee, 261 Ala. 439, 74 So.(2d) 429 (1954).

[59] Slow Development Co. v. Coulter, 88 Ariz. 122, 353 P.(2d) 890 (1960).

[60] United States v. McKeever, 169 F.Supp. 426 (S.D.N.Y. 1958).

[61] United States v. Sansone, 231 F.(2d) 887 (2d Cir. 1956).

[62] Carbo v. United States, 314 F.(2d) 718 (9th Cir. 1963). United States v. White, 401 U.S. 745 (1971).

Before the jury is permitted to hear any part of a recording, there must be a preliminary hearing outside the jury's presence in order to determine the admissibility of the recording. The trial judge should first have the recording played before him, and afford counsel an opportunity to raise objections. If the recording includes incompetent, irrelevant, or immaterial matter, or is inaudible, its admissibility will be questioned. When the recording contains incompetent matter it will be rejected unless such matter can be erased from the tape, or the jury prevented from hearing the incompetent portion by stopping and starting the recording instrument. The deletion of inaudible, irrelevant and repetitive portions of a tape recording does not necessarily render the tape inadmissible at the trial.[63]

Whether a tape recording is treated as independent or merely corroborative evidence, the test of its admissibility is basically the same, and where it is clear that the inaudible portions of the recording are not substantial and do not render the audible parts unintelligible, the recording is admissible for either purpose.[64] Unless the unintelligible portions are so substantial as to render the recording as a whole untrustworthy, the recording is admissible, and the decision should be left to the sound discretion of the trial judge. In a federal prosecution the court held that a tape recording with approximately one half of the tape defective so that the speech or conversation recorded therein was not understandable was nevertheless admissible in evidence, since there was ample basis for the trial court's finding that the part that was reproduced was an accurate reproduction of the conversation it purported to reproduce.[65] The admission of tape recordings which are inaudible in part but not to such extent as to make the remainder more misleading than helpful is not an abuse of discretion.[66]

The use of devices whereby one may overhear conversations beyond the area in which they might normally be heard does

---

[63] United States v. Maxwell, 383 F.(2d) 437 (2d Cir. 1967), holding that although a taped conversation between the defendant and another was erased by the government, admitting into evidence a typewritten transcript previously made from the tape was not improper, where the tapes were not erased to prevent their production for trial. United States v. Young, 488 F.(2d) 1211 (8th Cir. 1973).

[64] Cape v. United States, 283 F.(2d) 430 (9th Cir. 1960).

[65] Addison v. United States, 317 F.(2d) 808 (5th Cir. 1963).

[66] Gorin v. United States, 313 F.(2d) 641 (1st Cir. 1963).

not in itself render the evidence thus obtained inadmissible.⁶⁷ The Omnibus Crime Control Act of 1968 (18 U.S.C. 2518) states in detail the procedures which must be followed in the use of electronic surveillance devices to overhear and record conversations. Under this Act and the cases which have been decided before and after the Act, the admission of the recording of a telephone conversation or conversation between two persons, including the defendant, is not unconstitutional if made with the consent of one party to the conversation.⁶⁸

If one party does not agree to the recording of a conversation, the procedures specified in the Omnibus Crime Control Act of 1968 must be followed to the letter if the recording is to be free from challenge on constitutional grounds.⁶⁹ Even if the recordings meet constitutional standards, the evidence standards must also be met. Therefore, a taped confession was not admissible where a police captain admitted that the recorder on which the defendant's confession was originally recorded, was not under his exclusive control and that some of the defendant's statements had not been recorded.⁷⁰

The fact that the prosecution allowed a witness to retain custody of the original tape recording of a conversation between the witness, her attorney and the defendant charged with endeavoring to influence the witness when she was under subpoena to appear before the grand jury did not prevent the admission of a re-recording of the conversation on the ground that the prosecution should be held responsible for the loss of the original recording where the original tape belonged to the witness and she insisted on keeping it.⁷¹

§ 13.9 Diagram, maps and models

The propriety of permitting a witness to explain his testimony by visual illustration is now firmly established; but unless the illustration is essential to an understanding of the testimony, it is largely

---

⁶⁷ On Lee v. United States, 343 U.S. 747, 96 L.Ed. 1270, 72 S.Ct. 967 (1952); United States v. Vittoria, 284 F.(2d) 451 (7th Cir. 1960).

⁶⁸ Harris v. United States, 400 F.(2d) 264 (5th Cir. 1968); United States v. White, 401 U.S. 745 (1971).

⁶⁹ 18 U.S. Code 2511 and cases.

⁷⁰ Monts v. State, 214 Tenn. 171, 379 S.W.(2d) 34 (1964).

⁷¹ United States v. Knohl, 379 F.(2d) 427 (2d Cir. 1967). See case in Part II.

cumulative in effect, and the admission or exclusion rests within the discretion of the trial judge. The use of a map, drawing, or plat for purposes of illustration must be distinguished from its admission in evidence. In the latter case the map or plat possesses within itself evidential characteristics tending to establish a particular fact; while in the former case the testimony of the witness is the evidence and the map or diagram is merely an aid to its understanding.[72]

There also is a distinction between a diagram or chart which is in evidence or used for evidentiary purposes, and one used only in counsel's argument, in that the former may be exhibited throughout the trial or a portion thereof to which it is relevant, while the latter should be withdrawn from the jury's observation at the conclusion of the argument in which it is employed. The chart used by counsel in his argument should refer only to matters which are in evidence or to inferences which properly may be drawn from the evidence.[73]

The use of a blackboard for the purpose of illustrating testimony or in aid of counsel's argument has been held to be within the sound discretion of the trial judge. Although it is proper to use a blackboard, it is improper according to one decision to photograph it in the presence of the jury for purposes of the record on appeal, since this would unduly impress the jury with the importance of the material on the blackboard.[74] A witness should not be asked to indicate the place of impact or the location of skid marks by pointing to a place on the blackboard or map and saying merely "here" and "there"; instead he should indicate the particular point by means of a distinctive mark which is either numbered or identified by colored chalk or pencil. An advantage of a drawing on paper is that it can be identified and introduced in evidence when the testimony has been completed, and in jurisdictions where jurors are permitted to take exhibits with them, may be carried to the jury room during deliberations.

---

[72] Crocker v. Lee, 261 Ala. 439, 74 So.(2d) 429 (1954).
[73] Ratner v. Arrington, 111 So. (2d) 82 (Fla. 1959).
[74] Affett v. Milwaukee & Sub. Transport Corp., 11 Wis.(2d) 604, 106 N.W.(2d) 274 (1960).

A map, diagram, or drawing is admissible in evidence when a witness testifies that it is a correct portrayal of the existing facts; moreover, it is not essential that such witness be the one who made the map or diagram. When a map is used by a witness to illustrate the scene of an accident, it must be representative of the area at the time of the accident. Where the map has been prepared long after the accident, it must be shown that the condition of the area has not changed materially from the date of the accident to the date when the map was prepared.

Models, when properly identified and authenticated, are admissible as a type of real evidence. An exact model is not required if the original is substantially represented and there are no distortions which will mislead the jury. A federal court held that the trial judge did not abuse his discretion in refusing to permit defendant to introduce in evidence a replica of a homemade periscope used by a treasury agent while hiding in the trunk of a car fitted with a periscope through which he observed the sale of nontaxpaid whiskey. The replica, although similar to the government periscope, was not a complete and accurate reproduction.[75]

Plastic models of human skeletons, the heart, brain, kidney, or other organs, where injury to one of them is involved, are frequently used to illustrate the testimony of a medical expert.

§ 13.10 Experiments

Although in some earlier cases the courts were often reluctant to admit evidence of experiments, the courts now very generally permit experiments to be performed in court in the presence of the jury or evidence to be given of experiments performed out of court. It would seem logical that experiments should be admitted, as they put the jury in possession of knowledge to assist them in determining the issues which they could not as readily or as accurately obtain from the testimony of witnesses only. As the purpose of the trial is to determine the truth, evidence obtained from experiments made in or out of court should certainly be admitted.

When experiments are performed out of court, for example in the police laboratory, the prosecution must introduce evidence to

---

[75] Longmire v. United States, 404 F.(2d) 326 (5th Cir. 1968).

show that they were made under similar conditions and like circumstances to those existing at the time of the crime. Some examples of experiments made outside of the court are: testing firearms to show the patterns of powder and shot made upon the object at different distances;[76] tests concerning the speed of motor vehicles and the effectiveness of their brakes and headlights;[77] tests concerning the ability of the witness to see at certain distances;[78] tests to show the direction and path of bullets;[79] chemical tests for intoxication, and many others. It is obvious that these many types of experiments which are conducted outside of the court successfully accomplish the purpose, that is, to show to the court and to the jury what took place. Certainly police officers and prosecutors should be aware of the experiments that can be made outside of the court and should take advantage of every opportunity to use this very persuasive type of evidence. Although many of the tests do not require scientific knowledge, some of the tests should be performed by qualified experts.

§ 13.11 Summary and practical suggestions

In addition to the use of oral testimony and documentary evidence, real evidence may be introduced to help the jury or other fact-finders in determining what happened in a particular case. The use of real evidence to assist the court and jury in determining the guilt or innocence of the accused in criminal cases has had the sanction of immemorial usage. In many instances the real evidence is more persuasive and aids the jury more in reaching a decision than the testimony of the witness. The courts in recognizing the desirability of obtaining all the facts have in fact encouraged the use of real evidence.

Notwithstanding this fact, certain rules have been established and must be followed if such evidence is to be admitted into court. For example, the prosecution must show that there is a connection between the instrument or article introduced and the accused; that the article is relevant to the particular case; and

---

[76] State v. Criger, 151 Kan. 176, 98 P.(2d) 133 (1940).
[77] People v. Crawford, 41 Cal.App.(2d) 198, 106 P.(2d) 219 (1940).
[78] Carpenter v. Kurn, 348 Mo. 1132, 157 S.W.(2d) 213 (1941).
[79] Shanks v. State, 185 Md. 437, 45 A.(2d) 85 (1943). See case in Part II.

that the object is substantially in the same condition as when used in connection with the crime or the change, if any, is explained. Also, the prosecution must show a chain or continuity of custody concerning the article to be introduced.

There are various types of real evidence which have been held admissible in courts but for each type certain conditions must be met. In some instances the exhibition of the person of the witness may be the best way to explain an injury. In this event, the judge in his discretion may allow such exhibition even though it might be somewhat gruesome.

Articles connected with the crime, such as weapons or clothing, may be introduced as real evidence if the prosecution can show that there was or is a connection between the article and the accused. Also, the judge may allow the jury to visit and view the scene of the incident if in his discretion this will help the jury in determining the facts of the case.

If it is not practicable to let the witnesses view the scene or bring all of the evidence into court, photographs are admissible as a form of real evidence. Before a photograph may be introduced, a foundation must be laid, i.e., a competent witness who has personal knowledge of the area or thing photographed must testify that the picture is an accurate representation of the objects or persons depicted. In addition to photographs, motion pictures, x-rays, and sound recordings may be introduced. As in the case of photographs a foundation must be laid before such evidence is admitted into court.

Often it is possible for the witness to more effectively explain what took place by using diagrams, maps, charts, and models. When such a diagram, map, or model is to be admitted into evidence, a witness must testify that it is a correct portrayal of the situation or thing represented.

As the purpose of the trial is to determine the truth, evidence obtained from experiments made in or out of court is often admitted. When experiments are performed out of court, the prosecution must introduce evidence to show that they were made under similar conditions and like circumstances as those existing at the time of the crime or explain why the evidence is authentic even though not made under such circumstances.

The law concerning the use of real evidence is especially important to the police administrator and the police investigator. In many instances the investigator himself may testify concerning the real evidence and use of such evidence to help the prosecutor in proving the case. In other instances the police officer will not be the witness who describes or discusses the real evidence but in most cases the officer will have had something to do with the collection and protection of the evidence. If the officer is not familiar with the rules concerning real evidence, it could become so contaminated that the judge will have no alternative but to exclude the evidence.

RESULTS OF EXAMINATIONS AND TESTS

> It is now well established that a witness who qualifies as an expert in the science of ballistics, may identify a gun from which a particular bullet was fired by comparing the markings on that bullet with those on a test bullet fired by the witness through the suspect gun.
> Roberts v. Florida, 164 So. 2d 817 (1964).

§ 13.11a Introduction

In the previous sections some of the general rules concerning the collection, protection, and introduction of real evidence were considered. Evidence is characterized as real evidence if it is the result of experiments and tests either in or out of court even though in many cases the evidence is of little value unless it is accompanied by oral testimony.

Although a comparatively small part of the evidence produced at the trial in the usual criminal case is of the real evidence variety, such evidence is often very convincing and certainly important in helping the fact finders in determining what actually occurred.

Because this book is prepared primarily for police officers and others involved in the criminal justice process and because in most instances the tests or examinations are conducted not by the prosecutor but by enforcement personnel, emphasis in this chapter is placed upon the common tests and examinations.

§ 13.11b   Examination of the person

Examination of the body of the defendant in a criminal case in a reasonable manner is not considered violative of his constitutional right of privacy or his privilege against self-incrimination. Both federal and state courts have usually held that the privilege against self-incrimination as protected by the Fifth Amendment to the United States Constitution offers no protection against compulsion to submit to fingerprinting, photographing, or measurements, to write or speak for identification, to appear in court, to stand, to assume a stance, to walk, or to make a particular gesture.[80] The courts have recognized procedures which involve minor interferences, for purposes of identification, with the person of individuals charged with crimes. Numerous cases uphold reasonable identification procedures against claims of violation of the Fifth Amendment; for example, requiring the prisoner to try on a blouse that fitted him;[81] requiring the accused to submit to lineup;[82] requiring the accused to speak for voice identification;[83] examination of defendant's body for traces of blood;[84] examination of body for marks and bruises;[85] requiring defendant to remove items of clothing or assume poses;[86] taking penis scrapings and saliva samples from defendant.[87]

In both homicide and wrongful death cases an examination of the body of the deceased by a trained pathologist is sometimes made, and his testimony may be given on issues relating to the cause of death. The medical examiner's report is admissible as

---

[80] Schmerber v. California, 384 U.S. 757, 16 L.Ed.(2d) 908, 86 S.Ct. 1826 (1966).

[81] Holt v. United States, 218 U.S. 245, 54 L.Ed. 1021, 31 S.Ct. 2 (1910); State v. Lerner, 308 A.(2d) 324 (R.I. 1973).

[82] Rigney v. Hendrick, 355 F. (2d) 710 (3d Cir. 1965); Bonaparte v. Smith, 362 F.Supp. 1315 (S.D. Ga. 1973).

[83] Kennedy v. United States, 353 F.(2d) 462 (D.C. Cir. 1965).

[84] McFarland v. United States, 150 F.(2d) 593 (D.C. Cir. 1945); Brattain v. Herron, 309 N.E.(2d) 150 (Ind. 1974).

[85] Leeper v. Texas, 139 U.S. 462 (1891).

[86] Gilbert v. United States, 366 F.(2d) 923 (9th Cir. 1966).

[87] Brent v. White, 276 F.Supp. 386 (E.D.La. 1967).

to his anatomical findings, anatomical diagnosis, and cause of death; but matters of history, such as "the deceased was struck by an automobile while crossing the street," will be excluded.

§ 13.12 Intoxication tests

Intoxication may be scientifically determined by testing the subject's blood, breath, urine or saliva.

a. Blood tests

Statutes in numerous states have adopted the Uniform Vehicle Code which incorporates recommendations of the National Safety Council and the American Medical Association with respect to chemical tests for alcohol. These statutes usually provide that:

> 1. Where there is less than 0.05 percent alcohol in the blood, or equivalent amounts in other body fluids or breath, the subject shall be presumed to be not under the influence of alcohol so far as the operation of a motor vehicle is concerned.
> 2. Where there is 0.15 (some 0.10) per cent or more alcohol in the blood, or equivalent amounts in other body fluids or breath, the subject is presumed to be under the influence of alcohol, as far as the operation of a motor vehicle is concerned.
> 3. Where there is between 0.05 per cent and 0.15 (some 0.10) per cent alcohol in the blood, or equivalent amounts in other body fluids or breath, the results of such tests may be received along with other tests or observations for consideration by the court or jury as bearing upon the question of alcohol influence.[87a]

Neither the National Safety Council nor the American Medical Association ever suggested that a strict line of demarcation could be drawn at which the blood alcohol concentration could be used as a sole criterion by which to judge whether or not an individual was intoxicated or unfit to drive an automobile. On the contrary, all of the recommendations of these committees emphasized the desirability of introducing all available evidence of abnormal reactions or conditions. There was never any intimation that the re-

---

[87a] These percentage figures refer to alcohol in the blood. When breath or urine tests are used the readings are converted into equivalent blood concentrations.

sults of the chemical tests should be the only evidence or that the report of chemical tests should dominate other evidence in importance.[88]

If a witness is to give testimony on the relationship between blood alcohol concentrate, or other body fluid, and intoxication, he must be a medical doctor, chemist, or medical technician with experience in this field. The trial court will decide whether or not the witness is an expert qualified to give an opinion on a blood analysis to determine intoxication.

A number of cases involving blood tests to determine intoxication have reached the Supreme Court of the United States. In *Breithaupt v. Abram*,[89] police officers caused blood to be withdrawn from the driver of an automobile involved in an accident, and there was ample justification for the officer's conclusion that the driver was under the influence of alcohol. The extraction was made by a physician in a medically acceptable manner in a hospital environment, although the driver was unconscious at the time the blood was withdrawn and hence had no opportunity to object to the procedure. The Supreme Court affirmed the conviction resulting from the use of the test in evidence, holding that under the circumstances the withdrawal did not offend its sense of justice.

In *Schmerber v. California*[90] the Supreme Court held that the extraction of blood samples from the accused while he was in the hospital after being arrested for driving while under the influence of intoxicating liquor was a reasonable test to measure the accused's blood-alcohol level and did not violate his right under the Fourth Amendment to be free of unreasonable searches and seizures. The Court also decided that the physician's withdrawal, at the direction of a police officer, of a blood sample and the admission of the blood analysis in evidence did not deny the accused due process of law. Neither was the evidence inadmissible on the theory that it violated the Fifth Amendment privilege of any person not to be compelled in a criminal case to be a witness against himself.

---

[88]Gerber, Dr. S. R., Practical Use of Results of Biochemical Tests for Alcohol. 47 A.B.A.J. 477 (May 1961).

[89] 352 U.S. 432, 1 L.Ed.(2d) 448, 77 S.Ct. 408 (1957).

[90] 384 U.S. 757, 16 L.Ed.(2d) 908, 86 S.Ct. 1826 (1966).

b. Breath tests

As indicated in the previous sub-section, a doctor, chemist, or medical technician with the proper equipment can determine the percent of alcohol in the blood from a sample of blood from the body of the person. Because the obtaining of the blood sample and the inconvenience in analyzing the sample are often present, other means have been invented to determine blood alcohol content without actually taking the blood. For example, the use of breath samples to determine alcohol content is quite common and certainly has the advantage of being more convenient and less painful.[90a] This method is also preferable because a trained officer may usually administer it while generally a physician or nurse is needed where actual blood is to be withdrawn.

In the use of devices such as "breathalizers," "drunkometers" and "alcometers" the blood alcohol content is determined by a formula applied to a test of the breath of the subject, who is required to blow into a balloon. The breath, thus captured, is allowed to expel itself through a tube containing a mixture of potassium permanganate and sulphuric acid until a certain shade or color is reached. By a measure of the water displaced by the breath which has passed through this tube, it is determined how much air was required to create the color above described. This amount is determined from a reading of a calibrated scale. The number read from the calibrated scale must then be calculated and translated into a percentage of alcohol in the blood.[91]

Before evidence as to the results of breath tests is admissible there must be proof (1) that the chemicals were compounded to the proper percentage for use in the machine; (2) that the operator and the machine were under periodic supervision of one who has an understanding of the scientific theory of the machine; and (3) by a witness who is qualified to calculate and translate the reading of the machine into the percentage of alcohol in the blood.[92] An expert, testifying as to the results of a test may testify that the

---

[90a] Klebs v. State, 305 N.E.(2d) 781 (Ind. 1974). Case in Part II.

[91] Richardson, MODERN SCIENTIFIC EVIDENCE, § 13.5.

[92] Hill v. State, 158 Tex. Crim. 313, 256 S.W.(2d) 93 (Texas Cr. R. 1953); State v. Baker, 56 Wash. (2d) 846, 355 P.(2d) 806 (1960); Klebs v. State, 305 N.E.(2d) 781 (Ind. 1974). Case in part II of book. Owens v. Commonwealth, 487 S.W. (2d) 877 (Ky. 1972).

§ 13.12

result indicates intoxication, but not that the subject was in fact intoxicated.[93]

There is no deprivation of constitutional rights where a person charged with the offense of operating a motor vehicle while under the influence of intoxicating liquor voluntarily submits to a drunkometer test, during a brief investigation at police headquarters, in the absence of any coercion and after being informed that the test is voluntary and that he is not required to answer any questions.[94] However, a complaint alleging that the arresting police officers beat the plaintiff with the intent of punishing him for his refusal to incriminate himself by taking a drunkometer test states a cause of action against the officers under the Civil Rights Act.[95]

c. Urine tests

Although the use of urine to determine alcohol content of blood has some advantages, it also has disadvantages. One is that the concentration of alcohol in the urine lags behind the blood alcohol concentration. The test results are rendered further unreliable by the fact that dilution is greater or lesser according to the amount of urine in the bladder, and this information is not known to the person making the test. In a case where a sample of a suspect's urine was shown to have been taken at a time reasonably soon after the incident complained of occurred, and to have been subjected to a test having general scientific recognition, with the results correlated to the probable blood concentration at the time of the violation charged, the court held that the evidence as to the results is properly admissible in a prosecution for drunkenness on the question of intoxication.[96]

Objections to the admission of urine test evidence, in a prosecution for driving while intoxicated, on the grounds that proof of the purity of the chemicals used was lacking, that the defendant was not apprised of his right to have the test administered by a physician or registered nurse, and that proper procedures were

---

[93] Toms v. State, 239 P.(2d) 812 (Okla. 1952).

[94] Toledo v. Dietz, 3 OhioSt.(2d) 30, 32 OhioOp.(2d) 16, 209 N.E. (2d) 127 (1965).

[95] Hardwick v. Hurley, 289 F.(2d) 529 (7th Cir. 1961).

[96] People v. Miller, 357 Mich. 400, 98 N.W.(2d) 524 (1960).

not used in producing the specimen, go to the weight and credibility of the evidence and not to its admissibility.[97]

d. Implied consent statutes

Many states have enacted statutes providing that a driver, whether licensed locally, unlicensed, or licensed in another state, is deemed to have given his consent, in return for the privilege of driving, to submit to an alcohol test if there are reasonable grounds to believe that he is driving while intoxicated; and if he refuses to take the test, his license may be suspended. In upholding the constitutionality of such law, the Supreme Court of Nebraska said:

> The validity of a sample of blood or urine under the implied consent law is not impaired by a request for legal counsel, or the failure of defendant's counsel to appear before the sample is taken. . . . A defendant loses no rights subject to protection by legal counsel when he is requested and furnishes a sample of blood or urine for chemical analysis to be used as evidence against him under the implied consent law.[98]

§ 13.13 Blood grouping tests

Blood grouping tests, conducted for the purpose of determining non-paternity, are based upon the scientific principle that the type of blood of a child is inherited from a combination of blood groups in the blood of its parents. If the blood groups of the child in question do not correspond to the parental combinations of blood groups, the accused man cannot possibly be the father of that child. Thus, if a factor is present in the blood of the child and is absent in the blood of the mother, that factor should be found in the blood of the man who is the child's true father. However, if the blood of the accused man charged with being the father lacks that factor, that lack excludes him as the true father.

Whenever it is relevant to the defense in a paternity proceeding, the trial court, at the request of the defendant, may make an order requiring the mother, her child, and the defendant to submit to one or more blood grouping tests to determine whether the defendant

---

[97] State v. Schwade, 177 Neb. 844, 131 N.W.(2d) 421 (1964).

[98] State v. Oleson, 180 Neb. 546, 143 N.W.(2d) 917 (1966).

can be determined not to be the father of the child. The tests must be made by a qualified physician or specialist in the field of blood tests. The parties involved must be properly identified, by signature and fingerprint, to avoid the possibility of substitution. An infant may be identified by footprint or handprint, or both. A specimen of blood is taken from each of the participants and labeled. The report contains a summary of the blood group of each of the persons, together with an interpretation of the result that exclusion of paternity is demonstrated, or that the defendant cannot be excluded as the father of the child.

Where it is shown that the person who made the tests is qualified, that proper safeguards were drawn around the testing procedure, and that no discrepancies were found in the testing methods, a court is warranted in taking judicial notice of the correctness of such tests.[99] The results of blood grouping tests are admissible in evidence only where they establish non-paternity; their admission where a mere possibility of parentage is disclosed is prejudicial.[1] Most courts take the position that blood test evidence to show paternity should be excluded as dangerously prejudicial.

Under the provisions of the Uniform Act on Blood Tests to Determine Paternity, adopted by California, Illinois, New Hampshire, Oklahoma, Oregon, Pennsylvania and Utah, if the court finds that the conclusions of all the experts, as disclosed by the evidence based upon their tests, are that the alleged father is not the father of the child, the finding of exclusion is conclusive. In other states the courts have held that the findings and result of blood grouping tests admitted in evidence are not conclusive of non-paternity, but may be considered for whatever weight they may have in proving that fact.[2] The better view would seem to be that blood grouping tests which establish non-paternity are conclusive on the issue of non-paternity except where the evidence is such as to support a jury finding that because of a defect in testing methods employed in a particular case, or because of a failure to show that the tests were accurately conducted, the results of the test could not be

---

[99] Cortese v. Cortese, 10 N.J.Super. 152, 72 A.(2d) 117 (1950).

[1] State ex rel. Freeman v. Morris, 156 OhioSt. 333, 46 OhioOp. 188, 102 N.E.(2d) 450 (1951); Hansom v. Hansom, 75 Misc.(2d) 3, 346 N.Y. Supp. 996 (1974).

[2] State ex rel. Walker v. Clark, 144 OhioSt. 305, 29 OhioOp. 450, 58 N.E.(2d) 773 (1944).

accepted as accurately reflecting the operation of the immutable laws of genetics.[3] Blood grouping tests often serve a useful purpose of identification in criminal prosecutions for rape,[4] assault and battery,[5] or non-support.

§ 13.14 Polygraph examination[5a]

The polygraph, better known as the lie detector, is an electronic device that, on being applied to the human body, graphically records changes in blood pressure, pulse and respiration. These basic features may be supplemented with a unit for recording what is known as the galvanic skin reflex, based on changes in the activity of the sweat pores in a subject's hands, and another unit for recording muscular movements and pressures. A galvanometer, used alone, is totally inadequate for lie detector testing.

As an investigative technique the use of the lie detector is based on the assumptions that lying leads to conflict; that conflict causes fear and anxiety; that this mental state is the direct cause of measurable physical changes that can be accurately recorded; and that the polygraph operator by a study of these reactions can tell whether the subject is being deceptive or truthful. None of these assumptions is wholly true.[6]

The examiner should receive his training in the lie-detector technique under the guidance of an experienced examiner with a sufficient volume of actual cases to permit the trainee to make frequent observations of lie-detector tests and to conduct tests himself under the instructor's personal supervision. In addition, the trainee should read and take courses in the pertinent phases of psychology and physiology, and examine and interpret a considerable number of lie-detector test records in verified cases.[7] Some states now require licensing of polygraph operators. Under the Illinois

---

[3] Annotation, 46 A.L.R.(2d) 1000, at 1028; Clark v. Rysedorph, 281 App.Div. 121, 118 N.Y.S.(2d) 103 (1952); State ex rel. Steiger v. Gray, 3 OhioOp.(2d) 394, 145 N.E.(2d) 162 (Juv. Ct. 1957).

[4] Shanks v. State, 185 Md. 437, 45 A.(2d) 85 (1945).

[5] Commonwealth v. Statti, 16 Pa. Super. 577, 73 A.(2d) 688 (1950).

[5a] See Chapter 7 for discussion of admissibility of polygraph results on stipulation.

[6] Burkey, Lee M., THE CASE AGAINST THE POLYGRAPH. 51 A.B.A.J. 855 (Sept. 1965).

[7] Inbau, Fred E., John E. Reid, THE LIE-DETECTOR TECHNIQUE: A RELIABLE AND VALUABLE INVESTIGATIVE AID. 50 A.B.A.J. 470 (May, 1964).

§ 13.14 CRIMINAL EVIDENCE FOR POLICE 256

statute an operator must have an academic degree at least at the baccalaureate level and have completed satisfactorily not less than six months of internship.

Lie-detector testing consists essentially of asking a number of relevant and irrelevant questions, along with the control questions. A control question is one which is unrelated to the matter under investigation but of a similar, though less serious nature, and one to which the subject will, in all probability, lie. For instance, in a burglary case the control question might be: "Have you ever stolen anything?" All of the questions usually will not total more than ten, and the time involved generally will not exceed approximately three minutes.[8]

Several state legislatures have been induced by labor unions to enact laws prohibiting or severely curtailing the use of polygraph examinations of applicants for employment or existing employees in private industry. **The testing of policemen or applicants for** police positions is specifically exempted from the California statute.

The results of a lie-detector test consistently have been held to be inadmissible in evidence unless both parties stipulate to its admissibility.[9] Emotional unresponsiveness, ability to beat the machine, physiological abnormalities, mental abnormalities, nervousness or extreme emotional tension, and the conflict and disagreement among the examiners and authorities are some of the variables which vitiate the alleged effectiveness of the tests and thus militate against their admissibility in evidence.[10] The use of a lie detector in the process of interrogation, however, does not render a subsequent confession involuntary or inadmissible.[11] In *Tyler v. United States*,[12-14] a policeman was permitted to testify that the defendant was told that the lie detector indicated that he was lying. This testimony was admitted to prove that defendant's

---

[8] *Ibid.*
[9] State v. Ross, 497 P.(2d) 1343 (1972). See case in Part II of book.
[10] Commonwealth v. Fatalo, 346 Mass. 266, 191 N.E.(2d) 479 (1963).
[11] United States v. McDevitt, 328 F.(2d) 282 (6th Cir. 1964). See also United States ex rel. Sanney v. Mantanye, 364 F.Supp. 905 (W.D. N.Y. 1973).
[12-14] 90 App.D.C. 2, 193 F.(2d) 24 (1951); cert. denied, 343 U.S. 908, 96 L.Ed. 1326, 72 S.Ct. 639.

subsequent confession was voluntary.

Evidence of the refusal or willingness of a defendant to take a lie-detector test is not admissible.[15] The state is not permitted to inquire whether the defendant has offered to take a lie-detector test;[16] and since lie-detector tests generally have not been proved scientifically reliable, it is improper to admit evidence that an accused has been willing or unwilling to take such test, or to comment thereon.[17]

The defendant in a criminal prosecution does not have a constitutional right to have a lie-detector test administered to him.[18]

§ 13.15 "Truth serum" results

The term "truth serum" has no precise medical or scientific meaning.[19] To refer to sodium amytal and sodium pentothal as "truth serums" is definitely a misnomer, since they have no propensity or chemical effect to cause a person to "speak the truth." These drugs do not induce a state of mind in which a person tells the truth, but instead cause him to speak more freely than he otherwise might. The use of sodium amytal can produce any one of four results: truth, falsehood, fantasy, or response to suggestion.[20]

It is generally recognized that the administration of sufficient doses of scopolamine will break down the will. The early literature

---

[15] State v. Kolander, 236 Minn. 209, 52 N.W.(2d) 458 (1952). State v. McDavitt, 62 N.J. 36, 297 A.(2d) 849 (1972).

[16] State v. Smith, 43 N.J. 67, 202 A.(2d) 669 (1964).

[17] Barber v. Commonwealth, 206 Va. 241, 142 S.E.(2d) 484 (1965).

[18] State v. Freeland, 125 N.W.(2d) 825 (Iowa, 1964); Hayden v. Warden of Maryland Penitentiary, 202 A.(2d) 382 (Md. 1964); State ex rel. Sheppard v. Koblenz, 174 OhioSt. 120, 21 OhioOp.(2d) 384, 187 N.E.(2d) 40 (1962).

[19] See dissenting opinion of Mr. Justice Stewart in Townsend v. Sain, 372 U.S. 293, 9 L.Ed.(2d) 770, 83 S.Ct. 745, 768 (1963).

[20] Freeman v. New York Central R. Co., 15 OhioOp.(2d) 187, 174 N.E.(2d) 550 (App. 1960), a civil action in which plaintiff told his psychiatrist that he was unable to recall the events leading up to his accident, and requested the doctor to try to restore his memory. The doctor administered a treatment of sodium amytal which placed plaintiff in a hypnotic or semiconscious state during which the doctor conversed with plaintiff and made a record of the questions and answers. At the trial plaintiff's testimony was based upon his medically refreshed memory. The court did not expressly decide on the propriety of this method of refreshing one's memory.

on the subject designated scopolamine as a "truth serum" and it was thought to produce true confessions by criminal suspects.[21] More recent commentators, however, state that scopolamine's use is not likely to produce true confessions, and that persons under the influence of drugs are very suggestible and may confess to crimes which they have not committed. False or misleading answers may be given, especially when questions are improperly phrased. For example, if the police officer asserts in a confident tone "You did steal the money, didn't you?" a suggestible suspect might easily give a false affirmative answer.[22]

A confession induced by the administration of drugs is constitutionally inadmissible.[23] In a prosecution for murder, the trial court properly refused to admit testimony of a psychiatrist that the defendant had been given a narcoanalysis test, and that the test revealed that the defendant was telling the truth when he said the shooting was an accident.[24] Courts generally agree that the results of a sodium-amytal test or sodium-pentothal test are not admissible for or against the defendant in a criminal case because of the lack of scientific certainty about the results.[25]

§ 13.16 Fingerprint comparisons

The science of fingerprint comparison for identification purposes is as old as civilization itself. The courts take judicial notice of the well-recognized fact that fingerprint identification is one of the surest methods of identification known. The primary purpose of fingerprinting is the positive identification of an accused. Another purpose of fingerprinting is an evidentiary purpose; e.g., to compare the fingerprints of the defendant with fingerprints left at the scene of the crime. The evidentiary purpose may or may not be present in a given case.

The Fifth Amendment offers no protection against compulsion to submit to fingerprinting. Furthermore, fingerprinting of persons validly arrested or formally charged with a crime does not con-

---

[21] WHY TRUTH SERUM SHOULD BE MADE LEGAL, 42 Medico-LegalJ. 138 (1925).
[22] MacDonald, TRUTH SERUM, 46 J.Crim.L. 259 (1955).
[23] Townsend v. Sain, n 19, *supra*.
[24] Dugan v. Commonwealth, 333 S.W.(2d) 755 (Ky. 1960).
[25] State v. Heminger, 210 Kan. 587, 502 P.(2d) 791 (1972).

stitute a search and seizure within the meaning of the Fourth Amendment.[26]

In a criminal case an official police department fingerprint record may be authenticated for admission in evidence by the person who, having the duty to compile and file such records, is the lawful custodian thereof.[27] A fingerprint expert, to qualify as such, should have formal training in the science of fingerprinting, and be skilled in the photographic procedure of enlarging and developing photographs of fingerprints.[28] Thus, an officer who has been in the identification section of the county sheriff's office for two years, has received direct training in fingerprint work and has received instructions in fingerprinting under an expert in the department, is qualified to testify as an expert on fingerprints.[29] Whether a witness possesses the requisite qualifications of a fingerprint expert is a question within the discretion of the trial court.

In a bank robbery case five police fingerprint cards containing defendant's genuine signature were offered in evidence for the limited purpose of establishing the fact that defendant bought travelers checks at the bank in question four days prior to the crime, and to prove the authenticity of his signature at the time of purchase. Nowhere on the cards was it expressly revealed that defendant had been arrested, or that he had been charged with or convicted of a crime. The court carefully instructed the jury to disregard the cards except for the limited purpose for which they were offered.[30] Palmprints, left at the scene of a crime, have been held to be just as reliable and accurate as fingerprints.[31] Likewise, a bare footprint may be photographed and compared with that of the defendant.[32]

§ 13.17 Ballistic experiments

The science of forensic ballistics is a well recognized subject of

---

[26] United States v. Laub Baking Co., 283 F.Supp. 217, 44 OhioOp. (2d) 39 (1968); Schmerber v. California, 384 U.S. 757, 16 L.Ed.(2d) 908, 86 S.Ct. 1826 (1967).

[27] State v. Shank, 115 OhioApp. 291, 20 OhioOp.(2d) 371, 185 N.E. (2d) 63 (1962).

[28] McGarry v. State, 82 TexasCrim. R. 597, 200 S.W. 527 (1918).

[29] Todd v. State, 170 Tex. Crim. 552, 342 S.W.(2d) 575 (1961).

[30] Duncan v. United States, 357 F. (2d) 195 (5th Cir. 1966).

[31] People v. Les, 267 Mich. 648, 255 N.W. 407 (1934).

[32] State v. Rogers, 233 N.C. 360, 64 S.W.(2d) 572 (1951).

expert testimony. Courts will allow such expert testimony to show that the bullet which killed a person was fired from a weapon belonging to the defendant in the case. Before a witness may testify in regard to the identification of firearms and bullets, his qualifications to give such testimony must be clearly shown. If he testifies as to his specialized training and his experience as a member of the criminal laboratory of a police department the court will permit him to testify as an expert. On the subject of a witness' qualifications, it has been held proper to ask him if he has studied the techniques and methods of the Federal Bureau of Investigation at Washington, D. C., and of the Crime Laboratory at Northwestern University and compared them with the methods employed by him.[33]

A ballistics expert may testify that the firing-pin marking on cartridge shells found at the scene of a homicide correspond to the marking on a shell test fired from the defendant's revolver.[34] Likewise, a witness may testify that an empty shotgun shell, found at the scene of a homicide, had been fired from the defendant's shotgun, basing his opinion on breech-face markings revealed by a comparison microscope and photographs.[35]

Gunpowder-pattern test sheets of blotting paper which were identified, explained and testified to by a qualified ballistic expert who had made the tests were held to have been adequately authenticated and were properly admitted to illustrate his testimony.[36] In a prosecution for murder the trial court will exclude the testimony of an officer in regard to experiments as to distances at which powder burns might appear, where the experimental conditions are not shown to be similar to the actual event.[37] Where, however, a sheriff conducted experiments with respect to the distance at which a gun would powder burn cloth, and used a piece of cloth similar to that worn by the deceased, the court admitted his testimony as to powder burns.[38]

---

[33] State v. Dallao, 187 La. 392, 175 So. 4 (1937).

[34] Roberts v. State, 164 So.(2d) 817 (1964). Case in Part II.

[35] Ferrell v. Commonwealth, 177 Va. 861, 14 S.E.(2d) 293 (1941). Also see Holland v. State, 49 Ala. App. 104, 268 So.(2d) 883 (1972).

[36] Opie v. State, 389 P.(2d) 684 (Wyo. 1964).

[37] Rhea v. State, 49 Ala.App. 104, 268 So.(2d) 883. See Johnson v. State, 506 P.(2d) 963 (Okla. 1973); see also Wrenn v. State, 506 P.(2d) 418 (Nev. 1973).

[38] State v. Truster, 334 S.W.(2d) 104 (Mo. 1961).

§ 13.18 Speed detection readings

The principle of *R*Adio *D*etection *A*nd *R*anging is the use of exact laws of science and nature in the measurement of distance and speed. The radar speed-detecting devices commonly used in traffic control operate on what is known as the Doppler effect and utilize a continuous beam of microwaves sent out at a fixed frequency. The operation depends upon the physical law that when such waves are intercepted by a moving object the frequency changes in such a ratio to the speed of the intercepted object that, by measuring the change of frequency, the speed may be determined.[39]

In operation the radar device is set up along the side of a road or street, usually in or upon a parked police car, with the beam being played along the highway. When a moving vehicle crosses that beam, the speed of the vehicle is registered on a graph or calibrated dial on the meter device. The speed, if it is excessive, is then transmitted by radio by the officer reading the graph or dial, along with a description of the vehicle, to another officer stationed some distance farther on, and the vehicle is intercepted by this officer.

For many years the public has been aware of the widespread use of radio microwaves or other electronic devices in detecting the speed of motor vehicles or other moving objects; and while the intricacies of such devices may not be fully understood, their general accuracy and effectiveness are not seriously questioned.[40]

The readings of a radar speed meter are now accepted in evidence, just as the courts have accepted photographs, X-rays, electroencephalographs, speedometer readings, and the like, without the necessity of offering expert testimony as to the scientific principles underlying them. Within the past decade courts have recognized by judicial knowledge what those learned in electronics confirm—that a radar speed meter is a device which, within a reasonable engineering tolerance, and when properly functioning and properly operated, accurately measures speed in terms of miles per hour.[41]

---

[39] Kopper, Dr. John M., THE SCIENTIFIC RELIABILITY OF RADAR SPEEDMETERS. 33 N.C.L.Rev. 343 (1955).

[40] Dooley v. Commonwealth, 198 Va. 32, 92 S.E.(2d) 348 (1956).

[41] State v. Graham, 322 S.W.(2d) 188 (Mo. 1959).

§ 13.18   CRIMINAL EVIDENCE FOR POLICE   262

In a prosecution on a charge of speeding based on a reading taken by one police officer from a radar speed meter and radioed to another officer who thereupon arrested the offender, the court held that it was sufficient to show that the meter was properly set up and tested by a technician trained by experience to do so, and that at the time it was functioning properly. It was not essential to the admissibility of such evidence to show, by independent expert testimony, the nature and function of or the scientific principles underlying such speed meter.[42] In this case the prosecutor introduced evidence that the meter had been checked by the city electrician on the morning of the violation; that it had been calibrated by injecting into it known frequencies checked against those transmitted by the United States Bureau of Standards radio station; that it had been checked, after installation in the police car, in its actual operation by driving a police car through the beam and comparing the meter-registered speed with actual speedometer readings; that the meter was found to be working properly in all respects; and that the officer in charge of the radar car had five years' experience in reading the dial on the meter.

Where a reading taken from a radar speed meter is relied upon to establish a charge of speeding, it is necessary to prove the accuracy of the particular equipment used in testing the speed involved in the case being tried.[43] A test of radar equipment for accuracy by the speedometer of an automobile driven through the zone, which itself had not been tested, or if tested no proof thereof had been introduced in evidence, was no evidence of accuracy and such evidence, though admissible, would not be sufficient to sustain a conviction for speeding without additional evidence.[44]

To defendant's objection that the testimony of the officers in regard to run-through tests was hearsay, the court ruled that, since both officers had testified as to what their respective meters showed during the run-through tests, the fact that they communicated these results to each other via radiophone did not lessen the fact

---

[42] East Cleveland v. Ferell, 168 Ohio St. 298, 7 OhioOp.(2d) 6, 154 N.E.(2d) 630 (1958).

[43] Everight v. Little Rock, 230 Ark. 695, 326 S.W.(2d) 796 (1960).

[44] People v. Johnson, 196 N.Y.S. (2d) 227 (N.Y. 1960); People v. Fletcher, 216 N.Y.S.(2d) 34 (N.Y. 1961).

that when each testified in respect to his individual meter readings he related what he saw, and not what the other told him.[45]

Visual Average Speed Computer and Recorder has been accepted in more than half of the states. The first Vascar arrest was made in Indiana, in July, 1966. About the size of a cigar box, Vascar can be fitted into a police car and is limited in portability only to the extent of the patrol cruiser in which it is used. Only one officer is needed to operate it, instead of the two required for radar.

The operation of Vascar is very simple. A police officer feeds the distance covered and the time it takes to cover that distance into the unit. The speed of the vehicle being observed is then automatically computed by the unit in miles per hour. The unit is equipped with two toggle switches, one which controls the time measuring portion and one which controls the distance measuring mechanism. These switches are manually turned on and off by the operator of the machine to measure the distance between two fixed markers on the highway and the time taken by a vehicle to travel that same distance. The time may be placed into the unit before, during, or after the distance measurement is made.

Vascar computes the average speed for the amount of distance involved between the two location points used. The units are checked daily for accuracy. Since slight variations are caused by the difference in wear of the tires on each police car, the individual unit is checked with the patrol car in which it is to be used.

§ 13.19 Spectogram voice identification

A recently developed technique for identification by the voice print or spectogram has presented an evidentiary problem. Apparently such voice prints or speech spectograms were first developed in the United States in the 1930's at the Bell Telephone Laboratories. The speech spectogram, broadly speaking, is a picture showing the distribution of speech energy over the audio frequency spectrum plotted against time. According to those who favor the use of this technique, every person has a unique voice different from

---

[45] State v. Graham, n 41, *supra*.

§ 13.19

others so as to make it identifiable with the same accuracy of a fingerprint identification.

According to the Michigan State University Department Information Service publication dated August 9, 1973, a Michigan State University audiology and speech scientist, Dr. Oscar Tosi, declared that in 39 cases experts were authorized to testify in court for purposes of identification. In the paper Dr. Tosi explained that of 3,000 voice examinations made in cooperation with the Michigan State Police, 550 were positive identifications, 1,600 were probable identifications and positive eliminations, and 850 were no decisions. In criticizing a California judge's ruling which rejected the voice print, Dr. Tosi pointed out that the voice identification is effective, but only if strict guidelines are observed including:

1. The examination must include both aural and visual comparisons of the known voice with the unknown voice.
2. The examiner must be qualified, with at least two years of practical experience in an apprenticeship program.
3. In positively identifying the voice, the examiner can not have the slightest hint of a doubt.

Notwithstanding the arguments for the use of the voice identification, the technique is still certainly not uniformly accepted. The United States Court of Appeals for the District of Columbia Circuit held in 1974 that the voice print analysis has not yet gained the degree of general scientific acceptance necessary to make spectrogram results admissible as identification evidence in a criminal prosecution.[46] However, the Florida Court of Appeals, Third Circuit, held that the spectrograph evidence was admissible in a criminal prosecution and cited other cases to buttress this opinion.[47] In the Florida case the court pointed out that the identity of the perpetrator of the crime was not based solely upon the voice or the spectrograph but in addition there was proof that the voice was identified as that of the person making the threats by two witnesses who testified without the aid of the spectrographic voice print identification.

---

[46] U.S. v. Addison, 498 F(2d) 741, (D.C. Cir. 1974).

[47] Alea v. State, Florida Court of Appeals, Third District (1972).

§ 13.19a Neutron activation analysis

A neutron activation analysis is a relatively new process by which the chemical composition of materials can be determined. In the 1973 supplement of 15 Am. Jur., 96 cases are listed in which results of neutron activation analysis can accurately detect the presence and amount of certain chemical elements.

This process was approved in a federal case involving the sending of a package bomb through the mails and more recently in a Minnesota Supreme Court case involving the shooting of a policeman in the head at point blank range.[48]

In the case of *U.S. v. Stifel* the Court approved the explanation of the process which appeared in American Jurisprudence, stating:

> But we feel that the following description is the most understandable and succinct explanation which we have found available.

American Jurisprudence's "Proof of Facts" describes the process thus:

> One of the newest and most promising techniques of forensic science is neutron activation analysis. The ability of this nuclear method to detect traces of elements in minute samples enables it to solve many problems of identification that have heretofore been considered hopeless . . . the process is essentially one whereby the material to be analyzed is first made radioactive—i.e., it is "charged" so that it will give off or emit radiation in the form of gamma rays. This radioactive sample is then exposed to a scintillation crystal; and every time a gamma ray from the radioactive material interacts with the crystal, it emits a flash of light, which is converted into an electrical pulse whose voltage is proportional to the energy of the gamma rays. An electronic device called a multichannel differential analyzer then sorts the electrical impulses into different energy groups and adds up the pulses in each group. The result is a graph shown on an oscilloscope screen. The graph contains information related to the kind and amount of elements in the radioactive sample and can be transcribed immediately or stored on magnetic tape or punches paper tapes for future reference.

---

[48] U.S. v. Stifel, 433 F.(2d) 431 (6th Cir. 1970).

Virtually no sample of material is too small to be analyzed by activation analysis. A single hair, a shred of marijuana, or a fleck of automobile paint no longer than the period at the end of this sentence can be analyzed and correctly identified. Furthermore activation analysis's high sensitivity allows quantitative measurement of elements in the parts per million and parts per billion range. For instance if one thimbleful of arsenic poison were diluted in ten tankcars of water, the exact amount of arsenic present could be determined by activation analysis. In most cases the analysis is also nondestructive, so that material evidence may be preserved for presentation in court or saved for analysis by another method.

In the *Spencer* case the results of a neutron activation analysis were admitted to show that the suspect had fired a gun on the night of the shooting.[49] Here the neutron activation technique was used to determine if barium and antimony were on the hands of the accused. The court agreed that the neutron activation analysis can accurately detect the presence and amount of certain chemical elements and that the lower court did not err in admitting the test results. The Supreme Court of Minnesota, however, was concerned that the evidence may be given more weight than warranted and that the testimony of the expert witness was too conclusive. In approving the use of the neutron activation analysis, the court stated:

> We believe that neutron activation analysis is a useful law enforcement technique and that the increasing use of technology in criminal investigations should not be inhibited but encouraged where consistent with rights of the accused.

§ 13.20 Summary and practical suggestions

In recent years the trend has been for the courts to allow and encourage the use of real evidence when this is consistent with the rights of the accused. As the use of real evidence often is important and very persuasive, the police officer should certainly be aware of the types of evidence that are admissible and some of the specific rules that determine the admissibility of the various types of evidence.

---

[49] State v. Spencer, 216 N.W. (2d) 131 (1974).

In many instances the results of examinations and tests such as the results of intoxication tests, blood-grouping tests, fingerprint comparisons, ballistics tests, etc., will be admitted if a proper foundation is laid. Some evidence such as that relating to fingerprints is well recognized as reliable and therefore competent while others such as the neutron activation analysis is relatively new and all of the rules have probably not been formulated.

Courts have generally refused to admit certain types of evidence which is characterized as real evidence such as the polygraph unless both parties stipulate concerning its admissibility.

As each category of evidence has admissibility conditions that are peculiar to that type of evidence, the officer must be familiar with all of these requirements if he is to be sure that the evidence will be admissible and given the proper weight. The officer must also be aware that even though there is a tendency of jurors to give more weight to real evidence, he must be careful not to rely too heavily on the real evidence and neglect other evidence. With the assistance of the prosecutor, procedures should be established in each police department for the collection, preservation, preparation, protection, and introduction of real evidence.

Chapter 14

EVIDENCE UNCONSTITUTIONALLY OBTAINED

> Today we once again examine Wolf's constitutional documentation of the right of privacy free from unreasonable state intrusion, and, after its dozen years on our books, are led by it to close the only courtroom door remaining open to evidence secured by official lawlessness in flagrant abuse of that basic right, reserved to all persons as a specific guarantee against that very same unlawful conduct. We hold that all evidence obtained by searches and seizures in violation of the Constitution is, by that same authority, inadmissible in a state court.
> *Mapp v. Ohio*, 367 U.S. 643, 16 OhioOp.(2d) 384, 6 L.Ed(2d) 1081, 81 S.Ct. 1684 (1961).

Section
14.1 Introduction
14.2 Development of the exclusionary rules
14.3 Search and seizure exclusions
14.4 Exclusion of evidence obtained by illegal wiretapping or eavesdropping
14.5 Exclusion of confessions obtained in violation of constitutional provisions
14.6 Self-incrimination and related protections
14.6a Due process exclusions
14.7 Right to counsel as it relates to the exclusion of evidence
14.8 Summary

§ 14.1 Introduction

In the discussion of the reasons for the rules of evidence in Chapter 2, it was pointed out that relatively recently developed rules exclude evidence obtained in violation of one of the rights protected by the Constitution. This is not because the evidence is not relevant or is not material. In fact, in many instances the evidence obtained in violation of the constitutional provisions as interpreted by the courts is very relevant and very material. The courts have reasoned that even though the evidence is relevant and material and would shed some light as to the actual happenings, such evidence should not be admitted because authorizing use of illegally obtained evidence would encourage violation of the individual rights as enumerated in the Constitution.

Although the exclusionary rules relating to the various types of evidence have been extended greatly in recent years, much doubt remains as to what evidence will be excluded and what will be admissible. Under the recent Supreme Court decisions evidence is primarily excluded because the seizure or the obtaining of such evidence violated the rights protected by the Fourth, Fifth, or Sixth Amendments to the Constitution. The general rules concerning search and seizure, self incrimination, right to counsel, and other constitutional provisions cannot be discussed comprehensively due to space limitations. However, rules relating to the exclusion of the evidence so obtained will be discussed briefly.[1]

§ 14.2 Development of the exclusionary rules

Comparatively speaking, the search and seizure exclusionary rule is of recent origin. This rule provides very succinctly that evidence which has been illegally obtained or obtained in violation of the Constitution will be excluded from use in a judicial tribunal.

First, it should be pointed out that this exclusionary rule is certainly not universally applied. Today in England and in most of the other Anglo-Saxon countries evidence is admitted even if obtained illegally. The principle that evidence should not be excluded merely because the constable blundered in obtaining evidence was in fact followed in about half of the states even as late as 1961. This rule, commonly called the Common Law or English Rule, was justified by an English judge in one case, the judge explaining:[2]

> I think it would be a dangerous obstacle to the administration of justice if we were to hold that because evidence was obtained by illegal means, it could not be used against the party charged with an offense. It therefore seems to me that the interests of the state must excuse the seizure of documents, which seizure would otherwise be unlawful, if it appears in fact that such documents were evidence of a crime committed by anyone.

---

[1] For a more comprehensive discussion of the constitutional limitations, see Klotter and Kanovitz, CONSTITUTIONAL LAW FOR POLICE, The W. H. Anderson Co. (1971).

[2] Elias v. Pasmore, 2 K.B. 65 (1934).

Although the exclusionary rule as it relates to searches in violation of the Constitution was mentioned as far back as 1886 by the United States Supreme Court, it was not until 1914 that the Supreme Court in the case of *Weeks v. United States*³ made the exclusionary rule applicable in federal courts in this country. The Supreme Court held in that case that in a federal prosecution the Fourth Amendment barred the use of evidence secured through an illegal search and seizure.

The reason for adopting the exclusionary rule is that this (according to the court) is the only way to insure that police and prosecutors will not violate or encourage violation of the rights protected by the Constitution and the amendments. While the English courts argue that the remedy is action against the officer who violates these provisions, the courts in this country emphasize that only by excluding the evidence can these privileges be sufficiently protected.

Although the exclusionary rule as it relates to search and seizure has been applied in federal courts since 1914, it was not until 1961 that the Supreme Court made the exclusionary rule applicable in search and seizure cases in state courts.⁴

The courts in the early decisions decided that evidence obtained by eavesdropping and wiretapping did not come within the scope of the exclusionary rule but such evidence is now inadmissible in certain instances. Also, confessions and statements taken contrary to the rules established by the Supreme Court are excluded, even though relevant. And over the years the courts have established rules concerning the admissibility of evidence obtained in violation of the self-incrimination provisions of the Fifth Amendment. More recently the courts have applied the exclusionary reasoning and excluded some evidence obtained in violation of the right to counsel provisions.

The degree of application of these exclusionary rules will be discussed in the following paragraphs.

---

³ 232 U.S. 383, 58 L.Ed. 652, 34 S.Ct. 341 (1914).

⁴ Mapp v. Ohio, 367 U.S. 643, 16 OhioOp.(2d) 384, 6 L.Ed.(2d) 1081, 81 S.Ct. 1684 (1961). See case in Part II. There is some indication that the exclusionary rule will be modified by the Supreme Court. (See Justice Burger's dissenting opinion in Bivens v. Six Agents, 403 U.S. 398, 91 S.Ct. 1999 (1971)).

§ 14.3 Search and seizure exclusions

The Fourth Amendment to the Constitution provides:

> The right of the people to be secure in their persons, houses, papers and effects against unreasonable searches and seizures, shall not be violated, and no Warrant shall issue but upon probable cause supported by oath or affirmation, and particularly describing the place to be searched, and the persons or things to be seized.

This Amendment was added to the Constitution in 1791 at the insistence of some of the leaders of the day who complained that the Constitution itself which was ratified in 1789 did not include some of the protections which should be guaranteed to English-speaking people. At this point in history the Fourth Amendment did not apply to state officials but was added to prohibit the officials of a strong central government from abridging the rights of the citizens of the various states.

Although the provisions of the Fourth Amendment applied only to the federal government in the beginning, the Supreme Court of the United States using the Fourteenth Amendment as a vehicle stated clearly that the protections of the Fourth Amendment are to be applicable to the states. The court also established minimum standards which must be met by state officials. In other words, since 1961 if a state or federal officer makes an illegal search as defined by the Supreme Court of the United States, the evidence so obtained will not be admissible in state or federal criminal trials.

It must be pointed out that not all evidence obtained by a search is inadmissible. The courts have laid down specific rules which must be followed; if these rules are followed, the evidence obtained by the search will be admissible. Specifically, evidence is admissible if it is

1. obtained under a properly issued and executed search warrant;
2. obtained incidental to a lawful arrest following the rules as to the scope of the search;[5]

---

[5]Chimel v. California, 395 U.S. 752, 23 L.Ed.(2d) 685, 89 S.Ct. 2034 (1969). Also, see U.S. v. Robinson, 414 U.S. 218, 66 Ohio Op.(2d) 202, (1973) which held that the authority to search incidental to lawful arrest includes the right to search the person arrested for evidence not related to the crime. Parts of case included in Part II of book.

3. secured after a proper waiver of the constitutional rights;
4. obtained from a vehicle which is moving or about to be moved when proper conditions exist;[6] or
5. seized from an area not protected by the Constitution.[7]

Also, evidence is generally considered admissible if obtained by a private individual who has no connection with an enforcement official, as the constitutional provisions are interpreted to protect one against official action and not private action. And evidence is admissible even though the constitutional protection is violated if the person has no right to challenge the search. For example, if the home of another is searched in violation of the Constitution, the homeowner can complain but one who has no interest of any type in the home cannot complain.

To make the discussion concerning the admissibility of search and seizure evidence complete, mention must be made of the Stop and Frisk seizure. In 1968 the United States Supreme Court authorized the admission of evidence obtained by a police officer who articulated his reasons for "frisking" a person he suspected was "casing a job."[7a] The Court explained the limitations of such a seizure in this language:

> The sole justification of the search in the present situation is the protection of the police officer and others nearby, and it must, therefore, be confined in scope to an intrusion reasonably designed to discover guns, knives, clubs, or other hidden instruments for the assault of the police officer.

Not only is the evidence obtained by an illegal search or a search in violation of the Constitution inadmissible, any information obtained as a result of that illegal act is generally excluded. This is known as the "fruit of the poisonous tree" doctrine. For example, in the *Wong Sun* case[8] the United States Supreme Court held that the arrest was illegal and the resulting search therefore illegal. It decided in addition, however, that narcotics which were used in evidence and which were seized from another person but as a result of the illegal search were also not admissible even though

---

[6] Chambers v. Maroney, 399 U.S. 42, 90 S.Ct. 1975 (1970).

[7] Katz v. United States, 389 U.S. 347, 19 L.Ed.(2d) 576, 88 S.Ct. 507 (1967).

[7a] Terry v. Ohio, 392 U.S. 1, 44 Ohio Op.(2d) 383, 88 S.Ct. 1868.

[8] Wong Sun v. United States, 371 U.S. 471, 9 L.Ed.(2d) 441, 83 S.Ct. 407 (1962).

found in a different place and at a different time.

It can be seen from this discussion that the application of the exclusionary rule as it relates to search and seizure is difficult. It can generally be said that evidence is excluded if the search is illegal. However, in determining whether the search is illegal, the police officers, the prosecutors, and the courts must look to many statutes and court decisions.

§ 14.4 Exclusion of evidence obtained by illegal wiretapping or eavesdropping

The Supreme Court in the early cases refused to include wiretapping within the scope of the Fourth Amendment. Chief Justice Taft in the case of *Olmstead* v. *United States*,[9] after reviewing the historical context in which the Fourth Amendment was adopted, concluded that the proscription was limited to search and seizures of material things and not evidence procured by a sense of hearing. However, in a later decision, *Nardone* v. *United States*,[10] the Supreme Court held that although wiretapping did not violate the Constitution it did violate the Federal Communications Act of 1934 and that evidence obtained by officers who violated the provisions of this Act was inadmissible in federal court. This rule was not originally applied to the state courts but many of the states adopted the rule either by legislation or by court interpretation. In a landmark decision in 1967, *Katz* v. *United States*,[11] the Supreme Court rejected the contention that surveillance without trespass and without the seizure of material fell outside the purview of the Constitution. This and other decisions make it clear that wiretapping and eavesdropping are within the protection of the Fourth Amendment.

After several efforts, Congress finally in 1968 enacted a comprehensive scheme designed to regulate eavesdropping and wiretapping on a uniform nation-wide basis.[12] This law must be studied thoroughly in order to understand the requirements for wiretapping or eavesdropping. Broadly speaking, the interception of wire or

---

[9] 277 U.S. 438, 72 L.Ed. 944, 48 S.Ct. 564 (1928).
[10] 302 U.S. 379, 82 L.Ed. 314, 58 S.Ct. 275 (1937).
[11] 389 U.S. 347, 19 L.Ed.(2d) 576, 88 S.Ct. 507 (1967).
[12] See Chapter 119 of the Omnibus Crime Control Act of 1968.

oral communications is illegal unless conducted in conformity with statutory procedures. To be admissible, evidence obtained by wiretapping or eavesdropping must comply with the standards established by the Omnibus Crime Control Act. At the present time the law concerning wiretapping and eavesdropping is very confusing.

Although Title 3 of the Omnibus Crime Control Act authorizes wiretapping under certain conditions, this Act has no effect on eavesdropping and interception by state officials unless a state statute is passed to supplement the federal statute or one party to the conversation approves. Approximately twenty states have passed such statutes. But some states still have laws prohibiting wiretapping and some states have by court decision determined that evidence obtained by wiretapping will not be admissible. Until the state laws are changed by legislation or court decision wiretapping is still illegal in those states unless authorized by one party to the conversation, and evidence obtained will be inadmissible.

In conclusion, although the United States Supreme Court has held that wiretapping and eavesdropping are within the protection of the Fourth Amendment, the federal law legalizes electronic surveillance techniques only insofar as the states have in existence procedures for prior authorization of the electronic surveillance or one party consents. As a result, in some states wiretapping and eavesdropping evidence may be admissible while in other states such evidence is not admissible. Therefore, the investigator must look to the state statutes and decisions to determine if this type of evidence is admissible in that state. If the evidence is obtained in violation of federal or state laws, it usually cannot be admitted into court.

§ 14.5 Exclusion of confessions obtained in violation of constitutional provisions

Although a confession or an admission of guilt would seem to be the best kind of relevant evidence, in many instances evidence of a confession is not admitted because the officer obtaining the confession violated certain constitutional provisions. Over the years the courts (especially the United States Supreme Court) have developed rules concerning the admissibility of confessions and other statements. Not only have the rules changed over a period of time but the rationale justifying the rules has changed.

At early common law an admission or confession was admissible as evidence of guilt despite the fact that it was a product of force or duress. The rule allowing the admissibility of such evidence was abandoned because it was found by experience that often persons accused of a crime would admit to committing the crime in order to avoid torture. As a result the courts developed what came to be known as the "free and voluntary" rule.

The free and voluntary rule states that a confession of a person accused of crime is admissible against the accused only if freely and voluntarily made, without fear, duress or compulsion in its inducement and with full knowledge of the nature and consequences of the confession. This was first justified on the theory that only free and voluntary confessions are reliable. Later cases, however, stated that the free and voluntary rule was predicated on the portion of the Fifth Amendment commanding that no person shall be compelled in a criminal case to be a witness against himself.[13]

Regardless of which historical approach is most persuasive, at the present time a confession if obtained by force or duress or by promises of reward, whether the confession is a judicial confession or an extrajudicial confession, is not admissible. Judges in various courts have often disagreed as to the amount of evidence required to determine if a confession is voluntary. This was partially reconciled in the case of *Lego v. Tomey* in 1972.[13a] Here the judge in the lower court had adjudged the confession voluntary "beyond a reasonable doubt" and the defendant argued that this made the admission of the confession erroneous. The Supreme Court, however, disagreed. The majority explained that the defendant is presumed innocent and the burden falls on the prosecution to prove guilt beyond a reasonable doubt; but, the Court continued, "This is not the same burden that applies in determining the admissibility of confession." The Court agreed that the prosecution must prove the confession to be "free and voluntary" by a "preponderance" of the evidence but was not required to prove the

---

[13] Bram v. United States, 168 U.S. 532, 42 L.Ed. 568, 18 S.Ct. 183 (1897).

[13a] Lego v. Twomey, 404 U.S. 477, 92 S.Ct. 619 (1972).

§ 14.5   CRIMINAL EVIDENCE FOR POLICE   276

confession to be free and voluntary "beyond a reasonable doubt."

In addition to the free and voluntary rule which was historically applied, the United States Supreme Court has more recently applied what has become known as the "delay in arraignment" rule. This rule provides that if there has been a delay in bringing the accused person before a magistrate and that if a confession has been obtained during this unnecessary delay, the confession will not be admitted even though voluntarily made.[14] In the *Mallory* case the defendant was convicted of rape in a Washington, D.C. court and the jury returned a sentence of death. The defendant appealed on the grounds that the confession obtained was improperly admitted into court. The facts indicate that the petitioner was apprehended between 2:00 and 2:30 on the afternoon following the rape along with his older nephews who were also suspects. After questioning by police the three suspects were asked to submit to lie-detector tests about 4:00 p.m. The operator of the polygraph was not located for about two hours, during which time the suspects received food and drink. The questioning started about 8:00 p.m. and an hour and a half later the suspect stated that he might have done it. It was not until after 10:00 p.m. that an effort was made to locate the United States Commissioner and in fact the suspect was not taken before the Commissioner until the following morning. The court in reversing the case stated:

> We can not sanction this extended delay resulting in a confession, without subordinating the general rule of prompt arraignment to the discretion of the arresting officers in finding exceptional circumstances for its disregard.

Here the court did not rely on the free and voluntary rule but reversed the decision because there had been a delay in bringing the accused before the United States Commissioner in violation of the United States Code.

Both the free and voluntary rule and the delay in arraignment rule are now applicable to the states. The free and voluntary rule was made applicable to the states at an early date, the Supreme Court using the Fourteenth Amendment due process clause again as the vehicle for making the amendment apply to the states. It

---

[14] Mallory v. United States, 354 U.S. 449, 1 L.Ed.(2d) 1479, 77 S.Ct. 1356 (1957).

was not, however, until the *Miranda* decision in 1966 that the delay in arraignment restrictions were applied to the states.[15]

The restrictions concerning the use of the confession as evidence were broadened in 1966. The confessions in the case of *Miranda v. Arizona* and each of the three companion cases were declared inadmissible by the Supreme Court because the suspects were not given the required warnings. The Supreme Court held that if the confession is to be admissible, the person who has been taken into custody or otherwise deprived of his freedom of action in any significant way must be warned before questioning that, (1) he has a right to remain silent; (2) if he does make a statement, anything he says can and will be used against him in court; (3) he has a right to have an attorney present or to consult with an attorney; and (4) if he cannot afford an attorney one will be appointed prior to any questioning if he so desires.

Not only must these warnings be given initially, but the opportunity to exercise these rights must be afforded throughout the questioning. If the accused indicates at any stage of the questioning that he does not wish to be interrogated or he wishes to consult an attorney, the questioning must stop.

Due to these restrictions on the use of confessions there are many who claim that the confession can no longer be used as an investigative tool. However, experience has indicated that this is not true. In fact the Supreme Court in the *Miranda* case stated that confessions remain a proper element in law enforcement and that any statement given freely and voluntarily without any compelling influence is admissible in evidence. The court went on to say that there is no requirement for the police to stop a person who enters a police station and states that he wishes to confess to a crime or a person who calls the police to offer a confession or any other statement he desires to make. The court continued by saying voluntary statements of any kind are not barred by the Fifth Amendment and their admissibility is not affected by our holding today.

Confessions continue to be admitted into evidence and the

---

[15] Miranda v. Arizona, 384 U.S. 436, 36 OhioOp.(2d) 237, 16 L.Ed. (2d) 694, 86 S.Ct. 1602 (1966). See case in Part II.

skilled and informed investigator can obtain confessions or statements and comply with the requirements established by the courts. Even if the strict requirements of *Miranda* are not fully guarded, but the confession is still voluntarily given, the evidence may be admitted for impeachment purposes.[15a]

In the *Harris* case the defendant was charged with selling heroin and at the trial took the stand in his own defense. The prosecution did not offer a confession made by the defendant during the prosecutor's case in chief because there was some question as to whether the *Miranda* warnings had been given. The prosecution did, however, offer the confession to impeach the testimony of the defendant after he took the stand. The Supreme Court allowed the admission of the confession even though the *Miranda* warnings had not necessarily been given, explaining that the confession could be used for impeachment purposes if freely and voluntarily made. In so doing the court reasoned that:

> Having voluntarily taken the stand, petitioner was under an obligation to speak truthfully and accurately, and the prosecution did no more than utilize the traditional truth-testing devices of the adversary process.

The discussion concerning the admissibility of confessions would not be complete without mention of the Omnibus Crime Control and Safe Streets Act of 1968. The applicable part of this Act is Section 3501 (c) which reads as follows:

> In any criminal prosecution by the United States or by the District of Columbia, a confession made or given by a person who is a defendant therein, while such person was under arrest or other detention in the custody of any law enforcement officer or law enforcement agency, shall not be inadmissible solely because of delay in bringing such person before a commissioner or other officer empowered to commit persons charged with offenses against the laws of the United States or of the District of Columbia if such confession is found by the trial judge to have been made voluntarily and if the weight to be given the confession is left to the jury and if such confession was made or given by such person within six hours immediately following his arrest or other detention: Provided, That the time limitation con-

---

[15a] Harris v. New York, 401 U.S. 222, 91 S.Ct. 643 (1971).

tained in this subsection shall not apply in any case in which the delay in bringing such person before such commissioner or other officer beyond such six-hour period is found by the trial judge to be reasonable considering the means of transportation and the distance to be traveled to the nearest available such commissioner or other officer.[5b]

This section in effect states that a confession shall not be inadmissible in evidence in a federal court solely because the confession was obtained during a delay in arraignment. It also establishes the maximum time as six hours between the arrest and the making of the confession but gives the judge discretion to admit the confession even if more than six hours have elapsed if the judge finds the delay reasonable. In effect Congress has by legislation attempted to nullify the delay in arraignment rule as established by the *McNabb* and *Mallory* cases.

Another section of the Omnibus Crime Control and Safe Streets Act of 1968 attempts to modify some of the legal requirements as interpreted by the Supreme Court in the *Miranda v. Arizona* case. Section 3501 of the Act which would change the requirements for warning prior to custodial interrogations reads as follows:

> (a) In any criminal prosecution brought by the United States or by the District of Columbia, a confession, as defined in subsection (e) hereof, shall be admissible in evidence if it is voluntarily given. Before such confession is received in evidence, the trial judge shall, out of the presence of the jury, determine any issue as to voluntariness. If the trial judge determines that the confession was voluntarily made, it shall be admitted in evidence and the trial judge shall permit the jury to hear relevant evidence on the issue of voluntariness and shall instruct the jury to give such weight to the confession as the jury feels it deserves under all the circumstances.
>
> (b) The trial judge in determining the issue of voluntariness shall take into consideration all the circumstances surrounding the giving of the confession, including (1) the

---

[5b] Two U.S. Circuit Courts of Appeals (U.S. v. Hathorn, 451 F.(2d) 1337 (1971) and U.S. v. Halbert, 436 F.(2d) 1226 (1970)) have considered the application of this Act. Both Courts hold that more than a six hour delay does not necessarily make the confession inadmissible.

§ 14.5 CRIMINAL EVIDENCE FOR POLICE 280

time elapsing between arrest and arraignment of the defendant making the confession, if it was made after arrest and before arraignment, (2) whether such defendant knew the nature of the offense with which he was charged or of which he was suspected at the time of making the confession, (3) whether or not such defendant was advised or knew that he was not required to make any statement and that any such statement could be used against him, (4) whether or not such defendant had been advised prior to questioning of his right to the assistance of counsel, and (5) whether or not such defendant was without the assistance of counsel when questioned and when giving such confession.

The presence or absence of any of the above-mentioned factors to be taken into consideration by the judge need not be conclusive on the issue of voluntariness of the confession.

Two questions concerning these congressional enactments are apparent. One of these is, will the provisions be declared unconstitutional when considered by the Supreme Court of the United States so as to make the confessions inadmissible even though declared to be admissible by the Congress? The second question is, how do these congressional acts affect the admissibility of confessions in state courts?

There is a good possibility that at least part of this Act will be upheld as constitutional but there will be no certainty until a case is appealed to the Supreme Court.

As to the second question, there is every reason to believe that if the state court authorizes the use of confessions obtained in accordance with the congressional enactment, that the Supreme Court of the United States will uphold the admissibility. The Supreme Court would have difficulty in applying higher standards to state proceedings than those required in federal criminal prosecutions.

It is apparent from this discussion concerning confessions and statements that although the courts have established strict rules concerning their admissibility, confessions and admissions are still admissible and continue to be valuable tools in the investigative process. Generally, statements obtained in accordance with the requirements established by the Supreme Court will be good admissible evidence. There is yet some doubt concerning confession evidence which is obtained in accordance with the statutes but which is obtained by officers who did not comply with the Supreme Court requirements.

§ 14.6 Self-incrimination and related protections

Often evidence is challenged because the officer in obtaining the evidence violated the Fifth Amendment privilege against self-incrimination. The pertinent section of the Constitution concerning self-incrimination provides that, "No person ... shall be compelled in any criminal case to be a witness against himself." This provision, like the Fourth Amendment search and seizure provision, was included as a part of the Bill of Rights and ratified so as to become a part of the Constitution in 1791. The Fifth Amendment restrictions were not made applicable to the states until 1964.[16] The Supreme Court of the United States in the *Malloy* case held:

> We hold today that the Fifth Amendment's exception from compulsory self-incrimination is also protected by the Fourteenth Amendment against abridgment by the states.

This in effect means that the standards to be applied will be at least equal to the standards as determined by the Supreme Court and not the standards which have been developed by the state courts. After many conflicting decisions the Supreme Court in the case of *Schmerber v. California*[17] clearly limited the application of the self-incrimination provisions holding:

> We hold that the privilege protects the accused only from being compelled to testify against himself, or otherwise provide the state with evidence of a testimonial or communicative nature, and that the withdrawal of blood and use of the analysis in question in this case did not involve compulsion to these ends.

Following this interpretation, obtaining fingerprints and photographs, requiring appearance in the lineup, taking blood samples, or taking handwriting specimens does not violate the self-incrimination protection. On the other hand if the accused is forced to take

---

[16] Malloy v. Hogan, 378 U.S. 1, 12 L.Ed.(2d) 653, 84 S.Ct. 1489 (1964).

[17] 384 U.S. 757, 16 L.Ed.(2d) 908, 86 S.Ct. 1826 (1966).

a lie-detector test or in any other way to give evidence of a testimonial or a communicative nature, the self-incrimination provisions are violated and evidence so obtained will be inadmissible.

Recently the court procedures followed in introducing evidence have also been challenged as violating the Fifth Amendment. The procedure in most courts has been for the defendant to take the stand in his own defense before other defense witnesses if he is to take the stand at all. As a matter of fact, most states had either rules or laws which required the defendant take the stand before any other witnesses for the defense. This was challenged in the case of *Brooks v. Tennessee*.[17a] The Supreme Court there held that this requirement that the defendant take the stand before other defense witnesses violates the self-incrimination protection of the Fifth Amendment and the due process protection of the Fourteenth Amendment. The Court said, "This rule requiring the defendant to take the stand first cuts down on the privilege to remain silent by making its assertion costly." Now the Constitution as interpreted requires that the defense attorney be authorized to put the defendant on the stand at any time during the defendant's case in chief, as he sees fit.

§ 14.6a Due process exclusions

Closely related to the self-incrimination protections are the limitations which the due process clause of the Fourteenth Amendment imposes on the conduct of criminal proceedings of the states. If investigators, in obtaining evidence, violate the due process clause, evidence obtained thereby will not be admitted. The reasoning here, as in other instances, is that to allow the admission of such evidence would encourage conduct which is prohibited by the Constitution.

Although the courts have refused to define specifically what is included in the due process protection, some examples help to understand what evidence will be excluded on these grounds. One of these is the case of *Rochin v. California*.[18] In this case deputy sheriffs in Los Angeles, after forcing their way into the accused's

---

[17a] 406 U.S. 605, 92 S.Ct. 891 (1972).

[18] Rochin v. California, 342 U.S. 165, 96 L.Ed. 183, 72 S.Ct. 205 (1952).

room, attempted to extract capsules from the accused's mouth. Failing in this attempt, the accused was taken to a hospital and at the officers' insistence the accused's stomach was pumped and two capsules containing morphine were obtained. These were used in evidence against the accused. The United States Supreme Court reversed the conviction and directed that this evidence not be used aginst the accused, not on the grounds that this violated the self-incrimination protection but that such conduct violated the due process clause of the Fourteenth Amendment. The court said, "To sanction the brutal conduct would be to afford brutality the cloak of law."

Therefore, if evidence is obtained by federal agents in violation of the due process clause of the Fifth Amendment or by state agents in violation of the due process clause of the Fourteenth Amendment, such evidence will be held inadmissible.

§ 14.7 Right to counsel as it relates to the exclusion of evidence

One of the protections of the Bill of Rights which has been very broadly interpreted in recent years is the section of the Sixth Amendment providing that, "In all criminal prosecutions, the accused shall enjoy the right . . . to have the assistance of counsel for his defense." In early decisions this right was made available to the accused only at the trial but more recently it was made applicable during the investigation.[19]

As a means of enforcing the right to counsel provisions, a confession or statement obtained when the counsel protections are not granted will be excluded from evidence. For example, in the *Escobedo* case the defendant moved to suppress the use of incriminating statements taken after he had requested counsel and counsel had been refused. In reversing the state court decision the Supreme Court stated,

> (W)here, as here, the investigation is no longer a general inquiry into an unsolved crime but has begun to focus on a particular suspect, the suspect has been taken into police

---

[19] Escobedo v. Illinois, 378 U.S. 478, 32 OhioOp.(2d) 31, 12 L.Ed.(2d) 977, 84 S.Ct. 1758 (1964).

custody, the police carry out a process of interrogation that lends itself to eliciting incriminating statements, the suspect has requested and has been denied an opportunity to consult with his lawyer and the police have not effectively warned him of his absolute constitutional rights to remain silent, the accused has been denied the "assistance of counsel" in violation of the Sixth Amendment to the Constitution as "made obligatory, upon the States by the Fourteenth Amendment. . . " and no statement elicited by the police during interrogation may be used against him at a criminal trial.

Although in the *Escobedo* case the accused requested counsel the Supreme Court in the *Miranda* case of 1966 stated that such a request was not necessary. Under the *Miranda* ruling the burden is placed upon the police to inform the suspect of his constitutional right and to refrain from asking any further questions unless the accused knowingly waives his right to counsel.

From these and other cases it is obvious that if the accused requests counsel during the interrogation and counsel is not allowed, statements obtained will not be admissible. And under the *Miranda* reasoning if a person is taken into custody or questioned with the view to obtaining incriminating statements, the police must advise him of his right to counsel, either retained or appointed. If this procedure is not followed, a confession obtained will probably not be admissible. There is a possibility that the provisions of the Omnibus Crime Control Act of 1968 might have some effect on this requirement but as yet this has not been decided by the Supreme Court.

Another decision which has had quite a bit of influence on the admissibility of evidence where the right to counsel is an issue is *United States* v. *Wade*.[20] This case concerned the right to counsel during the police lineup. In the *Wade* case the Supreme Court stated that both Wade and his counsel should have been notified of the impending post indictment lineup and that counsel's presence should have been a requisite to conduct of the lineup, absent an intelligent waiver. The best method of enforcing this

---

[20] 388 U.S. 218, 18 L.Ed.(2d) 1149, 87 S.Ct. 1926 (1967).

right to counsel at the lineup is to prohibit the in-court identification by witnesses if the court finds that the pretrial confrontation or lineup tainted the in-court identification. In other words, the Supreme Court reasoned that the post-indictment lineup was a critical stage of the proceedings and counsel should be present unless waived if the identifying witness is to testify in court. In justifying this stand the court stated,

> Since it appears that there is a grave potential for prejudice, intentional or not, in the pretrial lineup, which may not be capable of reconstruction at trial, and since presence of counsel itself can often avert prejudice and assure a meaningful confrontation at trial, there can be little doubt that for Wade the post-indictment lineup was a critical stage of the prosecution.

If the attorney is present or if the accused intelligently waives the right to an attorney, then the witness can be called upon in court to identify the accused. It is not the lineup itself that is prohibited without counsel, and a lineup is appropriate where the witness making the identification will not be called upon to identify the accused at trial. Also, there is some indication that the prosecutor may be authorized to show that the pretrial confrontation for identification did not taint the in-court identification. In such circumstances the in-court identification could be admissible even though counsel was not present at the pre-trial confrontation.

In 1972 the United States Supreme Court placed limitations on the right to counsel at the lineup.[21] After reiterating the opinion that the lineup does not deprive the accused of self-incrimination rights, the Court further explained that counsel is not required at a pre-arrest, pre-indictment identification confrontation. The Court distinguished this from the *Wade* post-indictment confrontation for identification explaining:

> The initiation of judicial criminal proceedings is far from a mere formalism. It is the starting point of our whole system of adversary criminal justice. For it is only then that the government has committed itself to prosecute, and only then that the adverse positions of government and defendant have solidified. . . . It is this point, therefore, that marks the

[21] Kirby v. Illinois, 406 U.S. 682, 92 S.Ct. 1877 (1972).

commencement of the "criminal prosecution" to which alone the explicit guarantees of the Sixth Amendment are applicable.

The modified rule, therefore, is that the post-indictment lineup or confrontation for identification is a critical stage and the right to counsel privilege attaches if the witness is to identify the accused at trial. However, the pre-arrest, pre-indictment confrontation is not a critical stage and identifying evidence may be offered at trial even if counsel were not present at the lineup or showup.

In 1968 Congress, as a part of the Omnibus Crime Control Act, enacted legislation which would in effect allow eyewitness testimony as to the identity of the accused even though counsel was not present at the lineup or at the confrontation. This provision is as follows:

> The testimony of a witness that he saw the accused commit or participate in the commission of the crime for which the accused is being tried shall be admissible in evidence in a criminal prosecution in any trial court ordained and established under Article III of the Constitution of the United States.

This provision has not been tested in the Supreme Court and there is a good possibility that because of the broad coverage it will be held unconstitutional at least in part.

§ 14.8 Summary

Although the traditional common-law doctrine was that evidence would be admissible if relevant even though obtained illegally, much evidence is not admissible if a constitutional provision is violated. Exclusionary rules were developed over a period of years and made applicable both to federal and state courts on a piecemeal basis.

Under the present rules as established by the U.S. Supreme Court and lower courts, evidence obtained by search and seizure in violation of the Constitution is inadmissible in both federal and state courts. The cases must be searched thoroughly to determine what is considered an illegal search.

Although wiretap evidence was at first not considered to be within the constitutional provisions, recent cases have held that wiretapping and eavesdropping are within the protection of the Fourth Amendment. Under the Omnibus Crime Control Act of 1968 certain wiretap and eavesdrop evidence is admissible if the statutory requirements are met. Evidence obtained in violation of the statute will not be admitted into court.

As a means of insuring that confessions will be obtained freely and voluntarily, courts have established rules which prohibit the admissibility of confessions obtained in violation of established standards. Although evidence has been challenged because it was obtained in violation of the self-incrimination protection, this protection is generally limited to evidence of a testimonial or a communicative nature. Evidence which is interpreted to be of a testimonal or communicative nature is inadmissible unless this protection is waived.

Evidence is also excluded if the right to counsel provisions of the Sixth Amendment are violated. Again it is essential that cases be studied carefully to determine the various courts' interpretations as to what is considered a violation of the Sixth Amendment.

Although certain evidence is excluded because constitutional provisions have been violated, the investigator and prosecutor should not take a negative attitude. The investigator who understands the limitations and protects the rights of the individual can generally obtain evidence which will be admitted into court.

Chapter 15

PRACTICAL CONSIDERATIONS IN COLLECTING AND PRESENTING EVIDENCE

Section
15.1 Introduction
15.2 Developing the "evidence sense"
15.3 Steps in evaluating evidence
15.4 Preparing real evidence for trial
15.5 Preparing for the use of testimonial evidence
15.6 Coordinating efforts in preparing for trial
15.7 Convincing the jury beyond a reasonable doubt
15.8 Sources of evidence
15.9 Summary

§ 15.1 Introduction

It can be safely stated that there is some physical evidence of every crime committed. This is not to say that there is enough such evidence to convict for each crime committed. However, many criminals go free because the investigator either is unable to locate and identify the evidence or the evidence that has been located is inadmissible for one reason or another. In almost every criminal case the success of the prosecution depends upon the ability of the investigator to properly collect and prepare the evidence for trial.

The purpose of this chapter is to give the reader some practical suggestions concerning the collection and preservation of evidence in order that the evidence can be used effectively. Emphasis will be placed on the use of evidence from a legal point of view rather than from the technical point of view. However, to know the law is not enough in itself; knowledge of the proper techniques for finding, evaluating, protecting, preserving, preparing, and presenting evidence is equally important.

§ 15.2 Developing the "evidence sense"

The qualified officer, especially the investigator, considers the admissibility of evidence at every stage of the investigation. He cannot wait until the evidence has been obtained and then determine if it will be admissible. It is necessary that he not only read the rules of evidence and study carefully the admissibility requirements but he must understand the reasons behind these rules. He must develop an evidence sense. One way to start in developing this evidence sense is to consider the role of the juror. Each juror has been instructed that he is to determine the facts from the evidence presented in court. The searcher is, therefore, not only concerned with the admissibility of the evidence, but is equally concerned with the effect the evidence will have on the jury or judge who determines the facts in the case.

The investigator and prosecutor may be convinced that there is sufficient evidence to establish guilt but unless that evidence is admissible in court and is presented properly, it cannot be considered by the jury. The officer cannot let the fact that he has worked the case from the very beginning and is convinced of the guilt of the accused cause him to neglect the proper preparation of evidence for the trial. Careful analysis and classification of each piece of evidence will give that piece of evidence the value it deserves as a single piece of evidence and as it relates to other evidence. And just as important, the investigator should be able to articulate to the court and jury his interpretation as to the effect of each piece of evidence and when appropriate, his reasoning upon the effect it has in determining the final questions of fact.

The opponent of the evidence, usually the defendant in a criminal case, will attempt to point out the weaknesses in the evidence itself or the probative value of the evidence. For example, the investigator in a murder case may attempt to prove guilt by showing the weapon used in a homicide was the property of the accused. However, the investigator or the prosecutor can expect that the defendant will attempt to refute the claim that he was the user of the murder weapon. The defense may, and probably will, attempt to show the weapon was stolen from him a month ago or a year ago, thus giving greater emphasis to the hypothesis that someone else was present at the time of the homicide. The investigating agent and the prosecutor must then be prepared to show that the weapon was in fact in the possession of the accused as near to the time of the homicide as possible. To overlook this in the preparation and presentation of the case could cause that doubt which would lead the jury to conclude that the defendant was not "guilty beyond a reasonable doubt." In other words, the trained investigator will anticipate other hypotheses which are available to the opponent as explaining away the force of the evidence.

The investigator who has developed an evidence sense will be aware of the rules of evidence and how they are applied in an actual court situation as he works every case from the very outset.

§ 15.3 Steps in evaluating evidence

According to Mr. Wigmore, there are four steps to be followed in analyzing each piece of evidence to determine its assets and shortcomings.[1] These four steps are:

- *1 State precisely the objective of the evidence and what exactly is its supposed value.*

The investigator should evaluate each piece of evidence and determine what factor of the case is to be proved or disproved by this piece of evidence. Each piece of evidence should help in determining: (a) If the suspect was at or near the scene of the crime or had an opportunity to commit the crime; (b) If the suspect had a motive for committing the crime; (c) Whether the elements of an offense are present; (d) If the accused has any defense.

- *2 State in specific terms precisely what the logical possibilities are for the opponent to explain away the inference.*

After the investigator has determined exactly what inference he expects the trier of facts to draw from a piece of evidence, each piece of evidence can then be scrutinized to see if the opponent can offer evidence to explain away the inference that he hopes to show from this piece of evidence. For example, if the prosecution intends to prove that the homicide was accomplished with a certain type of knife and finds evidence of the fact that the accused has such a weapon, he can be certain that the accused will attempt to show that there are many other weapons of this type or that he did not have the weapon at the time of the homicide.

---

[1] Wigmore, PRINCIPLES OF JUDICIAL PROOF, Little, Brown & Co. (1931).

- *3 Investigate the evidential probabilities for the opponent in dealing with the evidential facts.*

After all of the possibilities as stated in step two have been ascertained, the investigator should determine which of these possibilities has merit and plan to counter any attempt to explain away the inference.

- *4 Analyze the effect of a mass of evidential facts.*

After examining each of the pieces of evidence and determining its value, all of the pieces should be assembled to determine the overall effect of the evidence. If some piece of evidence is missing, it will have to be produced or an explanation found.

If these steps are considered in analyzing the evidence obtained by the prosecution, there is a good possibility that the weaknesses in the case will be determined before trial and in many instances there will be an opportunity to fill in the gaps. Also there will be a better possibility that the evidence will be given the weight it deserves at the trial.

§ 15.4 Preparing real evidence for trial

As was indicated in previous chapters, in many instances real evidence is more persuasive than the testimony of witnesses. Generally the court will admit real evidence to prove the questions and issues. Some examples of real evidence admitted in criminal cases are:

1. Weapons.

2. Other instruments used to commit the crime (such as burglary tools).

3. Evidence to show the identity of the accused (such as fingerprints and footprints).

4. Evidence to show that the accused was at the scene of the crime (such as blood stains, and paint chips or dust found on the clothing).

The investigator cannot assume that this evidence will be admitted merely because it is relevant or because it would help to determine the actual facts of the case. It will not be possible here to discuss all of the details concerning the mechanics of protecting evidence; however, some discussion will help the investigator to avoid the obvious pitfalls which in the past have made evidence inadmissible.[2]

Proof is necessary to establish that the evidence obtained at the scene of the crime is in fact that evidence which is introduced in court.[3] It should therefore be appropriately marked and a complete and accurate record of the chain of possession maintained. That is, the investigator when acting as a witness will be called upon to show that no one tampered with the evidence or substituted a piece of evidence for that which was actually found by the officer.

But this requirement is not carried to an unreasonable extreme. For example, in a recent Virginia rape case the defendant claimed it was error to allow the introduction of bloody underwear as there was no absolute chain of possession. The Virginia Supreme Court, however, upheld the admission explaining:[3a]

> We did not hold that the Commonwealth is required in every case to establish an unbroken chain of possession before an item may be admitted into evidence. Rather, we held that where the results of a chemical or other technical analysis of an item are sought to be introduced into evidence, it must be shown with reasonable certainty that there was no alteration or substitution of the item.

The prosecution will also be required to show that the object introduced is in substantially the same condition as when used in connection with the crime or he must explain the change.

---

[2] For details concerning the techniques of investigation and processing of real evidence for trial, see the following publications:
Vanderbosch, CRIMINAL INVESTIGATION, International Association of Chiefs of Police (1968).
CRIMINAL INVESTIGATION AND PHYSICAL EVIDENCE HANDBOOK, prepared by the State of Wisconsin Crime Laboratory, Document Sales and Distribution, State Office Building, Madison, Wisconsin 53703.
Kirk, CRIMINAL INVESTIGATION, Interscience (1960).
Richardson, SCIENTIFIC EVIDENCE FOR POLICE OFFICERS, The W. H. Anderson Co. (1963).
SUGGESTIONS FOR HANDLING PHYSICAL EVIDENCE, Federal Bureau of Investigation.

[3] Miller v. Pate, 386 U.S. 1, 17 L.Ed.(2d) 690, 87 S.Ct. 785 (1967). Case included in Part II.

[3a] Whaley v. Com., 200 S.E.(2d) 556 (1973).

Although the prosecutor is responsible for the proper introduction of various items of physical or real evidence, in many instances it is the investigator or the officer who assumes responsibility and blame, if any, for the errors in collecting and preserving the items of evidence. Nevertheless, the officer-witness should not be unduly concerned because of the objections or arguments of the defense attorney if he has in fact followed the proper procedures in preparing the evidence for trial.

In testifying concerning the physical evidence the officer-witness should be positive in his identification of the specimen and there should be no guesswork during the investigator's testimony.

If the results of tests, experiments or demonstrations are to be introduced in court, as for example the introduction of evidence to show that the bullet found at the scene came from the same gun as that owned by the defendant, a foundation must be laid by the prosecution. The prosecution may and probably will be required to show, for example, that the tests or experiments have been made under similar conditions as those existing at the time of the offense. Evidence to show that the experiment was honestly and fairly made and that the results have a tendency to prove or disprove some material issue arising out of the occurrence involved will usually be necessary. Obviously, evidence to show that the articles used in the test (for example, the bullet found at the scene of the crime) were in fact the articles used in connection with the crime will be required.

If evidence of this type is to be given the weight it is entitled to receive, the person who conducted the test and who is to testify in court must be competent and have the ability to intelligently articulate the results of the test before the jury.

§ 15.5 Preparing for the use of testimonial evidence

In some criminal cases the only evidence available is of the testimonial variety. As in the case of real evidence proper preparation and planning for the use of testimonial evidence are necessary in order to avoid embarrassment and possibly the loss of a case.

This planning starts even before the crime is committed. Often the beat officer or investigator who first arrives on the scene makes efforts to protect the physical evidence but does not seek out witnesses. All instructions concerning investigation of crimes should include a requirement that the first person on the scene locate and identify witnesses and record all remarks as well as make notes concerning the demeanor of the witnesses at the time. As witnesses often alter their original version of the circumstances and sometimes tend to dramatize the issue, the original comments should be carefully noted so that these witnesses can be reminded at later interviews. Also, victims or witnesses often either consciously or subconsciously forget and if their comments are not recorded at the time by the beat officer, these points will be lost.

The ultimate responsibility for selecting witnesses and psychologically preparing them for the trial is in the hands of the prosecutor. As in many other situations, however, the responsibility sometimes is passed to the investigator. And far too often the witness becomes the forgotten person in the criminal justice system even though his testimony is so important that without it, no case could be made.

Although there is some indication of improvement, still in most cases there are long delays between the incident and the trial. The delays are often requested by the defense attorney for the very purpose of discouraging the witnesses. The continuances and long waiting periods may cause the witnesses to be away from work and in almost every case are financially unprofitable. Because of these frustrations countless numbers of witnesses are reluctant to get involved in reporting crime or testifying as witnesses even when their testimony is crucial. For this reason, it is often necessary to explain to the witness the importance of his testimony in the criminal justice system. It is the responsibility of the court and prosecutor to keep the delays to the minimum, recognizing the importance of the witness testimony.

Some factors to weigh in selecting witnesses and preparing for the case of witness' testimony are:

(1) *A prosecution witness may not be available to testify.*

Especially today, where the cases sometimes are delayed one, two, or three years, there is a good possibility that a witness upon whom the prosecution is relying cannot be available for one reason or another. Where possible, alternate witnesses should be available and every effort should be made to keep up with the addresses of the witnesses in the case.

In some instances witnesses will purposely be unavailable. Recent incidents, especially those relating to organized crime, point up the necessity of keeping the witnesses available to testify.

(2) *Witnesses may be impeached.*

Prosecution witnesses, as well as defense witnesses, may be impeached; that is, evidence may be introduced to show that their testimony should not be given credit. When it has been determined that the prospective witness has a criminal record or for some other reason will be challenged, this fact should immediately be made known to the prosecutor so that he can prepare for the challenge by the defense.

(3) *Often statements made by witnesses at the trial will not be the same as their pretrial statements.*

As the experienced prosecutor knows, too often, for one reason or another, the witness will change his testimony at the trial or refuse to testify at all. The investigator and prosecutor can avoid serious pitfalls by preparing for such contingencies.

(4) *Witnesses often vacillate under stress.*

One purpose of the cross-examination is to bring out the true facts. However, a clever defense attorney can distort this process and so confuse the witness that the jury will have reason to doubt the statements of the witness. Often, creating this apparent uncertainty on the part of the witness will result in doubt concerning one or more elements of the crime and result in a hung jury or acquittal. To some extent, this fluctuation and uncertainty on the part of the witness can be avoided by proper counseling prior to trial. Care must be taken, however, to avoid "coaching" the witness.

In many cases the successful prosecution depends solely on the testimony of witnesses. To insure that this evidence will be presented and given proper weight, the investigator should know each witness, take necessary steps to see that the witness will be at the trial and if possible have substitute or alternate evidence to be used if the witness is not available or refuses to testify.

§ 15.6 Coordinating efforts in preparing for trial

One reason our criminal justice system has not been totally

§ 15.6

successful is that the efforts of the various elements in the system have not been properly coordinated. This is especially true concerning the coordination of the efforts of the investigative agencies and the prosecutors. As a result, guilty persons often go free or the prosecution settles for conviction on a lesser offense with a lesser penalty.

Depending on the type and seriousness of the crime, from two to hundreds of persons take part in the investigation and prosecution. In the most simple case the investigator, or even the patrolman who first arrives at the scene, conducts the investigation at the crime scene, interviews witnesses, obtains and prepares the real evidence, and puts the case in order for trial. In some cases, however, many persons may take part in the investigation and one piece of real evidence may go through many hands. In either situation, the evidence can become so contaminated that it will not be of any value whatsoever.

To insure that the incident is properly investigated and to make certain that all legitimate evidence will be admissible and given proper weight, a well-defined procedure should be initiated. The investigation, to be successful, requires close cooperation between the members of the various divisions in the police department and cooperation between the enforcement agents and the prosecutor's office. It is safe to say that this cooperation is not enjoyed in many jurisdictions.

In the usual case the patrolman is the first to arrive at the scene of the crime. Depending on departmental policy (or lack of policy) the officer who first arrives at the scene either starts the investigation immediately or merely protects the scene until the arrival of the detective. Often the lack of coordination starts here.

The first step in guaranteeing cooperation and resulting efficiency is the preparation of a detailed procedural guide to be followed by members of the department. The procedural guide should explain, in as much detail as possible, the functions of the patrolman who first arrives at the scene, the responsibility of the detective and the procedure to be followed by personnel assigned to the crime laboratory, both at the scene and at the laboratory. The procedure to be followed in protecting the crime scene, photographing the scene, handling the evidence, transporting the evidence, interviewing witnesses and preparing the case for court should be determined in advance, written in detail, and thoroughly discussed in and out of the classroom.

Every department, regardless of its size, should have one person who acts as a liaison officer with the prosecutor's office either on a part-time or full-time basis. This officer will have the responsibility of reviewing all cases to see if they have been properly prepared for trial. He will then work with the prosecutor to insure that the prosecutor understands the case and is familiar with the witnesses who will testify. He will also make sure that all of the evidence that is necessary has been accumulated and prepared.

In some states the practice has been established whereby the prosecutor, the investigating officer, and the police-prosecution liaison officer have a formal pre-trial conference. At this conference the case is discussed in detail and the prosecutor evaluates the case. The prosecutor often requests a further investigation by the department if some additional information is needed.

With proper pre-trial planning, proper instructions, and proper coordination there is a good possibility that the best case possible can be presented at the trial. Certainly it is too late to find at the trial that some piece of evidence is missing.

§ 15.7 Convincing the jury beyond a reasonable doubt

Although the major persuasion in civil cases is by a preponderance of evidence, a greater degree of confidence by the trier of the facts is required in criminal cases. This is justified because the consequences to the life, liberty, and good name of the accused from a conviction of crime may be more serious than the effects of an adverse judgment in a civil case.[4] The requirement that the accused be found guilty "beyond a reasonable doubt" dates back to the Fourth Century when the rule was developed in England. It is now settled and accepted. To the investigator this is an important requirement. Since definitions were given in earlier chapters, no effort will be made here to give sample definitions of the term. The purpose of this section is to remind the investigator of the practical effects of this evidence rule in criminal situations.

---
[4] McCormick, LAW OF EVIDENCE,
§ 321, West Publishing Co. (1954).

To insure that each element of the crime is shown beyond a reasonable doubt, the following suggestions should be considered when conducting the investigation:

1. Be aware of the burden of proof requirements from the very start of the investigation.

2. Determine in advance the elements which must be proved in order to obtain a conviction.

3. Photograph and sketch the crime scene, indicating the relative positions of pieces of evidence and the victim, if any.

4. Record carefully all facts as obtained from witnesses and victims as well as the facts disclosed by a careful inspection of the scene.

5. Carefully secure, protect, and preserve all physical evidence and make a record indicating the description, location and condition of each piece.

6. Reach conclusions only after carefully evaluating all of the facts.

7. Obtain sufficient evidence to convince the jury as well as the investigators that a crime has been committed and that the accused committed the specific crime as charged. Don't be satisfied with the bare necessities.

8. Seek the assistance of all units within the department, including the records section, crime laboratory, and patrol division.

9. Utilize available assistance from other agencies in obtaining evidence, preparing evidence and presenting evidence at the trial.

10. After the investigation has been completed, have someone else evaluate the case to determine if there is sufficient evidence and to insure that evidence is prepared for trial.

11. Evaluate each case after trial to avoid mistakes in future cases.

§ 15.8 Sources of evidence

Recognizing that it is the responsibility of the investigator to obtain evidence in such quantities as will prove each element of the crime beyond a reasonable doubt, it is necessary that all sources of evidence be considered. It will not be possible here to discuss in detail the techniques to be used in obtaining evidence from each of these sources. However, some of the sources will be discussed briefly.

a. Individuals

The primary source of evidence is people. This fact is recognized by all experienced investigators and agencies. This, of course, includes not only witnesses to the crime or victims of the crime but people who are familiar with the victim, who know the neighborhood and can give general information which may lead to the perpetrator or furnish evidence of his guilt. This also includes reputable informants and in some instances and under the right conditions informants who are not too reputable. The investigator who develops the habit of asking the right questions will obtain much evidence of value.

b. The crime scene

The careful search of a properly protected crime scene will usually reveal evidence which is of great value. Crime scene search techniques must therefore be developed and followed.

c. Police records

Police records of the department where the investigation is being conducted as well as records of other departments and of federal agencies often produce valuable evidence. These obviously will give leads to further investigation.

d. Records and documents from other agencies

Records and documents from agencies such as probation and parole offices, boards of education, vital statistics, the Bureau of Immigration and Naturalization, the Bureau of Narcotics, colleges and universities, credit bureaus, and other such agencies are valuable as sources of information.

e. Crime laboratories

More and more crime laboratories are being established throughout the country. The professional people in these laboratories not only can evaluate evidence which has been located but can give the investigator very valuable leads concerning what to look for in conducting an investigation.

f. Publications

City directories and even telephone directories are of real value in conducting investigations. Also directories of public officials, public agencies, industries, businesses, etc., should not be overlooked.

g. Private investigative agencies

With the increasing number of private investigative or security agencies, these should not be overlooked as a source of information. Such agencies as the National Auto Theft Bureau, the National Board of Fire Underwriters, and the local and national private security agencies can often give the investigator information which he could not obtain elsewhere and which will save him many hours of labor.

The investigator who uses ingenuity in locating the sources of information and utilizes the sources effectively will not only be able to conduct an investigation more thoroughly but will be able to conduct the investigation more quickly.

§ 15.9 Summary

The good investigator can develop an evidence sense. To do this, he must be conscious from the very start of the investigation that the ultimate purpose is to obtain evidence which will be legally admissible and which will assist the jury or judge in deciding the facts.

Real evidence is important and often determines whether the guilty person will go free or be convicted. However, in order to obtain the maximum effect from the evidence, it is essential that the prosecution show that the evidence was obtained legally and properly. Also, the manner of protecting and presenting the real evidence has a great bearing on the weight given to it by the triers of fact.

Testimonial evidence, too, is only as good as the witness who presents this evidence. Therefore, prospective witnesses should be investigated and their testimony evaluated prior to trial. One of the best ways to be certain that the case will be presented as effectively as possible is to coordinate the efforts of the people not only within the department but those of other agencies such as the prosecutor's office. Without such cooperation and coordination there is a good possibility and even a probability that weak points will not be discovered until it is too late.

The investigator who takes advantage of all opportunities in obtaining legitimate evidence, is aware of all the sources of evidence. And one who uses ingenuity and imagination in utilizing these sources, will reap the rewards in the form of better prepared cases.

To be successful, the investigator must be familiar with the techniques in obtaining and preparing evidence for trial, but must also be concerned with the legal principles which will determine if the evidence can pass the tests required before it can be considered by the jury or the judge who tries the case.

PART II:

JUDICIAL DECISIONS RELATING TO PART I

(*For Table of Cases, see page 305*)

The judicial decisions in this part of the book have been edited and reprinted in order to make the textual discussion in Part I more meaningful. For maximum benefit, they should be read immediately following the chapters they accompany. Although they are included under designated chapter headings to exemplify points brought out in that chapter, many of the cases cut across chapter lines. For example, *Kirschbaum* v. *United States* which is included under Chapter 3 of Part II, primarily concerns the use of relevant evidence. However, the principle of "present recollection revived" is also discussed. In studying the cases specific points which relate to the particular chapter should be sought, but other legal points should also be noted.

It is not enough to learn the decision or rule of law of a particular case. To fully appreciate the significance of a rule, and to be capable of applying the rule intelligently, the reasoning of the court in reaching the decision must also be considered. Although a court decides only the case before it, the decision rendered often has much more far-reaching effect. Especially in the more important cases the rules serve as guidelines for future cases in which similar factual patterns arise. Therefore, the facts are of vital importance and careful attention must be paid to them in reading the cases.

Cases which follow have been selected as examples and because of their importance as precedents. Therefore, both federal and state cases are included. Due to space limitations, editing has been necessary. However, every effort has been made not to delete those parts of the case which bear directly on the points discussed. For the reader who desires to acquire the full text of these cases or to research the cases cited in Part I, the material including the full text of the case is usually available in law schools or court house libraries.

Because this book is prepared primarily for persons involved in the criminal procedure process, criminal cases have been selected for study. It is obviously impossible to include a case for each point discussed, therefore, other cases that are cited should be studied for a more comprehensive understanding of legal rules.

When this book is used as a text, it is recommended that selected cases be assigned to students and that they be required to report on the cases.

TABLE OF CASES IN PART II

	Page
Austin v. United States, 418 F(2d) 456 (DC Cir 1969)	409
Barnes v. United States, 412 US 837, 93 SCt 2357 (1973)	381
Commonwealth v. Brown, 388 Pa 613, 131 A(2d) 367 (1957)	446
Donnelly v. United States, 228 US 243, 57 LEd 820, 33 SCt 449 (1913)	442
Funk v. United States, 290 US 371, 78 LEd 369, 54 SCt 212 (1933)	307
Gillars v. United States, 182 F(2d) 962 (DC Cir 1950)	334
Hawkins v. United States, 358 US 74, 3 LEd(2d) 125, 79 SCt 136 (1958)	416
Holmes v. State, 112 S(2d) 511 (1959)	318
In re Winship, 397 US 358, ... SCt ... (1970)	342
Kirschbaum v. United States, 407 F(2d) 562 (8th Cir 1969)	325
Klebs v. State, 305 NE(2d) 781 (1974)	481
Long v. State, 274 P(2d) 553 (Okla 1954)	434
Mapp v. Ohio, 367 US 643, 16 OhioOp(2d) 384, 6 LEd(2d) 1081, 81 SCt 1680 (1961)	496
Maxwell v. United States, 368 F(2d) 735 (9th Cir 1966)	479
McNeely v. United States, 353 F(2d) 913 (8th Cir 1965)	474
Michelson v. United States, 335 US 469, 93 LEd 168, 69 SCt 213 (1948)	400
Miller v. Pate, 386 US 1, 17 LEd(2d) 690, 87 SCt 785 (1967)	532
Miranda v. State of Arizona, 384 US 436, 36 OhioOp(2d) 237, 16 LEd(2d) 694, 86 SCt 1062 (1966)	513
Morris v. State, 242 A(2d) 559 (Md 1968)	413
Mullen v. United States, 263 F(2d) 275 (DC Cir 1958)	420
Overton v. United States, 403 F(2d) 444 (1968)	456
People v. Washington, 81 CalRptr 5, 459 P(2d) 259 (1969)	449
People v. Zackowitz, 245 NY 192, 172 NE 466 (1930)	328
Roberts v. State of Florida, 164 S(2d) 817 (Fla 1964)	491
Schmerber v. State of California, 384 US 757, 16 LEd(2d) 908, 86 SCt 1826 (1966)	468
Shanks v. State, 185 Md 437, 45 A(2d) 85 (1945)	485
Smith v. Smith, 454 F(2d) 572 (1971)	349

	Page
Spencer v. Texas, 385 US 554, 17 LEd(2d) 606, 87 SCt 648 (1967)	365
State v. Collins, 294 Pac 957 (Mont 1930)	428
State v. Lawrence, 234 P(2d) 600 (Utah 1951)	374
State v. Ross, 7 Wash.App. 62, 497 P(2d) 1343 (1972)	386
State v. Sauer, 38 Minn 438, 38 NW 355 (1888)	341
State v. Slaughter, 70 Wash(2d) 935, 425 P(2d) 876 (1967)	362
United States v. Alexander, 326 F(2d) 736 (4th Cir 1964)	460
United States v. Durham, 319 F(2d) 590 (4th Cir 1963)	395
United States v. Gipson, 385 F(2d) 341 (7th Cir 1967)	324
United States v. Nelson, 419 F(2d) 1237 (1969)	356
United States v. Robinson, 414 US 218, 66 OhioOp(2d) 202, 94 SCt 467 (1973)	504

Cases relating to **Chapter 1**

HISTORY AND DEVELOPMENT OF RULES OF EVIDENCE

FUNK v. UNITED STATES

290 U.S. 371, 78 L.Ed. 369,
54 S.Ct. 212 (1933)

Mr. Justice SUTHERLAND delivered the opinion of the Court.

The sole inquiry to be made in this case is whether in a federal court the wife of the defendant on trial for a criminal offense is a competent witness in his behalf. Her competency to testify against him is not involved.

The petitioner was twice tried and convicted in a federal District Court upon an indictment for conspiracy to violate the prohibition law. His conviction on the first trial was reversed by the Circuit Court of Appeals upon a ground not material here. 46 F.(2d) 417. Upon the second trial, as upon the first, defendant called his wife to testify in his behalf. At both trials she was excluded upon the ground of incompetency. The Circuit Court of Appeals sustained this ruling upon the first appeal, and also upon the appeal which followed the second trial. 66 F.(2d) 70. We granted certiorari, limited to the question as to what law is applicable to the determination of the competency of the wife of the petitioner as a witness.

Both the petitioner and the government, in presenting the case here, put their chief reliance on prior decisions of this court. The government relies on United States v. Reid, 12 How. 361, 13 L.Ed. 1023; Logan v. United States, 144 U.S. 263, 12 S.Ct. 617, 36 L.Ed. 429; Hendrix v. United States, 219 U.S. 79, 31 S.Ct. 193, 196, 55 L.Ed. 102; and Jin Fuey Moy v. United States, 254 U.S. 189, 41 S.Ct. 98, 65 L.Ed. 214. Petitioner contends that these cases, if not directly contrary to the decisions in Benson v. United States, 146 U.S. 325, 13 S.Ct. 60, 36 L.Ed. 991, and Rosen v. United States, 245 U.S. 467, 38 S.Ct. 148, 150, 62 L.Ed. 406, are so in principle. We shall first briefly review these cases, with the exceptions of the Hendrix Case and the Jin Fuey Moy Case, which we leave for consideration until a later point in this opinion.

In the Reid Case, two persons had been jointly indicted for a murder committed upon the high seas. They were tried separately, and it was held that one of them was not a competent witness in behalf of the other who was first tried. The trial was held in Virginia; and by a statute of that state passed in 1849, if applicable in a federal court, the evidence would have been competent. Section 34 of the Judiciary Act of 1789 (28 USCA § 725) declares that the laws of the several states, except where the Constitution, treaties, or statutes of the United States otherwise provide, shall be regarded as rules of decision in trials at common law in the courts of the United States in cases where they apply; but the court said that this referred only to civil cases, and did not apply in the trial of criminal offenses against the United States. It was conceded that there was no act of Congress prescribing in express words the rule by which the federal courts would be governed in the admission of testimony in criminal cases. "But," the court said (page 363 of 12 How.), "we think it may be found with sufficient certainty, not indeed in direct terms, but by necessary implication, in the acts of 1789 and 1790, establishing the courts of the United States, and providing for the punishment of certain offences."

The court pointed out that the Judiciary Act regulated certain proceedings to be had prior to impaneling the jury, but contained no express provision concerning the mode of conducting the trial after the jury was sworn, and prescribed no rule in respect of the testimony to be taken. Obviously, however, it was said, some certain and established rule upon the subject was necessary to enable the courts to administer the criminal jurisprudence of the United States, and Congress must have intended to refer them to some known and established rule "which was supposed to be so familiar and well understood in the trial by jury that legislation upon the subject would be deemed superfluous. This is necessarily to be implied from what these acts of Congress omit, as well as from what they contain." Page 365 of 12 How. The court concluded that this could not be the common law as it existed at the time of the emigration of the colonists or the rule which then prevailed in England, and [therefore] the only known rule which could be supposed to have been in the mind of Congress was that which was in force in the respective states when the federal courts were established by the Judiciary Act of 1789. Applying this rule, it was decided that the witness was incompetent.

In the Logan Case it was held that the competency of a witness to testify in a federal court sitting in one state was not affected by his conviction and sentence for felony in another state; and that the competency of another witness was not affected by his conviction of felony in a Texas state court, where the witness had since been pardoned. The indictment was for an offense committed in Texas and there tried. The decision was based, not upon any statute of the United States, but upon the ground that the subject "is governed by the common law, which, as has been seen, was the law of Texas * * * at the time of the admission of Texas into the Union as a state." Page 303 of 144 U.S., 12 S.Ct. 617, 630.

We next consider the two cases upon which petitioner relies. In the Benson Case two persons were jointly indicted for murder. On motion of the government there was a severance, and Benson was first tried. His codefendant was called as a witness on behalf of the government. The Reid Case had been cited as practically decisive of the question. But the court, after pointing out what it conceived to be distinguishing features in that case, said (page 335 of 146 U.S., 13 S.Ct. 60, 63): "We do not feel ourselves, therefore, precluded by that case from examining this question in the light of general authority and sound reason." The alleged incompetency of the codefendant was rested upon two reasons, first, that he was interested, and, second, that he was a party to the record, the basis for the exclusion at common law being fear of perjury. "Nor," the court said, "were those named the only grounds of exclusion from the witness stand. Conviction of crime, want of religious belief, and other matters were held sufficient. Indeed, the theory of the common law was to admit to the witness stand only those presumably honest, appreciating the sanctity of an oath, unaffected as a party by the result, and free from any of the temptations of interest. The courts were afraid to trust the intelligence of jurors. But the last 50 years have wrought a great change in these respects, and today the tendency is to enlarge the domain of competency, and to submit to the jury for their consideration as to the credibility of the witness those matters which heretofore were ruled sufficient to justify his exclusion. This change has been wrought partially by legislation and partially by judicial construction." Attention then is called to the fact that Congress in 1864 had enacted that no witness should be excluded from testifying in any civil action, with certain exceptions, because he was a party to or interested in the issue tried; and that in 1878 (c. 37, 20 Stat. 30 [28 USCA § 632]) Congress made the defendant in any criminal case a competent witness at his own request. The opinion then continues (page 337 of 146 U.S., 13 S.Ct. 60, 64):

"Legislation of similar import prevails in most of the states. The spirit of this legislation has controlled the decisions of the courts, and steadily, one by one, the merely technical barriers which excluded witnesses from the stand have been removed, till now it is generally, though perhaps not universally, true that no one is excluded therefrom unless the lips of the originally adverse party are closed by death, or unless some one of those peculiarly confidential relations, like that of husband and wife, forbids the breaking of silence.

"* * * If interest and being party to the record do not exclude a defendant on trial from the witness stand, upon what reasoning can a codefendant, not on trial, be adjudged incompetent?"

That case was decided December 5, 1892. Twenty-five years later this court had before it for consideration the case of Rosen v. United States, supra. Rosen had been tried and convicted in a federal District Court for conspiracy. A person jointly indicted with Rosen, who had been convicted upon his plea of guilty, was called as a witness by the government and allowed to testify over Rosen's objection. This court sustained the competency of the witness. After saying that, while the decision in the Reid Case had not been specifically overruled, its authority was seriously shaken by the decisions in both the Logan and Benson Cases, the court proceeded to dispose of the question, as it had been disposed of in the Benson Case, "in the light of general authority and of sound reason."

"In the almost twenty [twenty-five] years," the court said, "which have elapsed since the decision of the Benson Case, the disposition of courts and of legislative bodies to remove disabilities from witnesses has continued, as that decision shows it had been going forward before, under dominance of the conviction of our time that the truth is more likely to be arrived at by hearing the testimony of all persons of competent understanding who may seem to have knowledge of the facts involved in a case, leaving the credit and weight of such testimony to be determined by the jury or by the court, rather than by rejecting witnesses as incompetent, with the result that this principle has come to be widely, almost universally, accepted in this country and in Great Britain.

"Since the decision in the Benson Case we have significant evidence of the trend of congressional opinion upon this subject in the removal of the disability of witnesses convicted of perjury, Rev. St. § 5392, by the enactment of the federal Criminal Code in 1909 with this provision omitted and section 5392 repealed. This is significant, because the disability to testify, of persons convicted of perjury, survived in some jurisdictions much longer than many of the other common-law disabilities, for the reason that the offense concerns directly the giving of testimony in a court of justice, and conviction of it was accepted as showing a greater disregard for the truth than it was thought should be implied from a conviction of other crime.

"Satisfied as we are that the legislation and the very great weight of judicial authority which have developed in support of this modern rule, especially as applied to the competency of witnesses convicted of crime, proceed upon sound principle, we conclude that the dead hand of the common-law rule of 1789 should no longer be applied to such cases as we have here, and that the ruling of the lower courts on this first claim of error should be approved."

It is well to pause at this point to state a little more concisely what was held in these cases. It will be noted, in the first place, that the decision in the Reid Case was not based upon any express statutory provision. The court found from what the congressional legislation omitted to say, as well as from what it actually said, that in establishing the federal courts in 1789 some definite rule in respect of the testimony to be taken in criminal cases must have been in the mind of Congress; and the rule which the court thought was in the mind of that body was that of the common law as it existed in the thirteen original states in 1789. The Logan Case in part rejected that view, and held that the controlling rule was that of the common law in force at the time of the admission of the state in which the particular trial was held. Taking the two cases together, it is plain enough that the ultimate doctrine announced is that, in the taking of testimony in criminal cases, the federal courts are bound by the rules of the common law as they existed at a definitely specified time in the respective states, unless Congress has otherwise provided.

With the conclusion that the controlling rule is that of the common law, the Benson Case and the Rosen Case do not conflict; but both cases reject the notion, which the two earlier ones seem to accept, that the courts, in the face of greatly changed conditions, are still chained to the ancient formulae and are powerless to declare and enforce modifications deemed to have been wrought in the common law itself by force of these changed conditions. Thus, as we have seen, the court in the Benson Case pointed to the tendency during the preceding years to enlarge the domain of competency, significantly saying that the changes had been wrought not only by legislation but also "partially by judicial construction"; and that it was the *spirit* (not the *letter* be it observed) of this legislation which had controlled the decisions of the courts and steadily removed the merely technical barriers in respect of incompetency, until generally no one was excluded from giving testimony, except under certain peculiar conditions which are set forth. It seems difficult to escape the conclusion that the specific ground upon which the court there rested its determination as to the competency of a codefendant was that, since the defendant had been rendered competent, the competency of the codefendant followed as a natural consequence.

This view of the matter is made more positive by the decision in the Rosen Case. The question of the testimonial competency of a person jointly indicted with the defendant was disposed of, as the question had been in the Benson Case, "in the light of general authority and of sound reason." The conclusion which the court reached was based, not upon any definite act of legislation, but upon the trend of congressional opinion and of legislation (that is to say of legislation generally), and upon the great weight of judicial authority which, since the earlier decisions, had developed in support of a more modern rule. In both cases the court necessarily proceeded upon the theory that the resultant modification which these important considerations had wrought in the rules of the old common law was within the power of the courts to declare and make operative.

That the present case falls within the principles of the Benson and Rosen Cases, and especially of the latter, we think does not reasonably admit of doubt.

The rules of the common law which disqualified as witnesses persons having an interest long since in the main have been abolished both in England and in this country; and what was once regarded as a sufficient ground for excluding the testimony of such persons altogether has come to be uniformly and more sensibly regarded as affecting the credit of the witness only. Whatever was the danger that an interested witness would not speak the truth—and the danger never was as great as claimed—its effect has been minimized almost to the vanishing point by the test of cross-examination, the increased intelligence of jurors, and perhaps other circumstances. The modern rule which has removed the disqualification from persons accused of crime gradually came into force after the middle of the last century, and is today universally accepted. The exclusion of the husband or wife is said by this court to be based upon his or her interest in the event. Jin Fuey Moy v. United States, supra. And whether by this is meant a practical interest in the result of the prosecution or merely a sentimental interest because of the marital relationship makes little difference. In either case, a refusal to permit the wife upon the ground of interest to testify in behalf of her husband, while permitting him, who has the greater interest, to testify for himself, presents a manifest incongruity.

Nor can the exclusion of the wife's testimony, in the face of the broad and liberal extension of the rules in respect of the competency of witnesses generally, be any longer justified, if it ever was justified, on any ground of public policy. It has been said that to admit such testimony is against public policy because it would endanger the harmony and confidence of marital relations, and, moreover, would subject the witness to the temptation to commit perjury. Modern legislation, in making either spouse competent to testify in behalf of the other in criminal cases, has definitely rejected these notions, and in the light of such legislation and of modern thought they seem to be altogether fanciful. The public policy of one generation may not, under changed conditions, be the public policy of another. Patton v. United States, 281 U.S. 276, 306, 50 S.Ct. 253, 74 L.Ed. 854, 70 A.L.R. 263.

The fundamental basis upon which all rules of evidence must rest —if they are to rest upon reason—is their adaptation to the successful development of the truth. And, since experience is of all teachers the most dependable, and since experience also is a continuous process, it follows that a rule of evidence at one time thought necessary to the ascertainment of truth should yield to the experience of a succeeding generation whenever that experience has clearly demonstrated the fallacy or unwisdom of the old rule.

It may be said that the court should continue to enforce the old rule, however contrary to modern experience and thought, and however opposed, in principle, to the general current of legislation and of judicial opinion it may have become, leaving to Congress the responsibility of changing it. Of course, Congress has that power; but, if Congress fails to act, as it has failed in respect of the matter now under review, and the court be called upon to decide the question, is it not the duty of the court, if it possess the power, to decide it in accordance with present-day standards of wisdom and justice rather than in accordance with some outworn and antiquated rule of the past? That this court has the power to do so is necessarily implicit in the opinions delivered in deciding the Benson and Rosen Cases. And that implication, we think, rests upon substantial ground. The rule of the common law which denies the competency of one spouse to testify in behalf of the other in a criminal prosecution has not been modified by congressional legislation; nor has Congress directed the federal courts to follow state law upon that subject, as it has in respect of some other subjects. That this court and the other federal courts, in this situation and by right of their own powers, may decline to enforce the ancient rule of the common law under conditions as they now exist, we think is not fairly open to doubt.

In Hurtado v. California, 110 U.S. 516, 530, 4 S.Ct. 111, 118, 28 L.Ed. 232, this court, after suggesting that it was better not to go too far back into antiquity for the best securities of our liberties, said:

"It is more consonant to the true philosophy of our historical legal institutions to say that the spirit of personal liberty and individual right, which they embodied, was preserved and developed by a progressive growth and wise adaptation to new circumstances and situations of the forms and processes found fit to give, from time to time, new expression and greater effect to modern ideas of self-government.

"This flexibility and capacity for growth and adaptation is the peculiar boast and excellence of the common law. * * * And as it was the characteristic principle of the common law to draw its inspiration from every fountain of justice, we are not to assume that the sources of its supply have been exhausted. On the contrary, we should expect that the new and various experiences of our own situation and system will mould and shape it into new and not less useful forms."

Compare Holden v. Hardy, 169 U.S. 366, 385-387, 18 S.Ct. 383, 42 L.Ed. 780.

To concede this capacity for growth and change in the common law by drawing "its inspiration from every fountain of justice," and at the same time to say that the courts of this country are forever bound to perpetuate such of its rules as, by every reasonable test, are found to be neither wise nor just, because we have once adopted them as suited to our situation and institutions at a particular time, is to deny to the common law in the place of its adoption a "flexibility and capacity for growth and adaptation" which was "the peculiar boast and excellence" of the system in the place of its origin.

The final question to which we are thus brought is not that of the power of the federal courts to amend or repeal any given rule or principle of the common law, for they neither have nor claim that power, but it is the question of the power of these courts, in the complete absence of congressional legislation on the subject, to declare and effectuate, upon common-law principles, what is the present rule upon a given subject in the light of fundamentally altered conditions, without regard to what has previously been declared and practiced. It has been said so often as to have become axiomatic that the common law is not immutable but flexible, and by its own principles adapts itself to varying conditions. In Ketelsen v. Stilz, 184 Ind. 702, 111 N.E. 423, L.R.A. 1918D, 303, Ann. Cas. 1918A, 965, the Supreme Court of that state, after pointing out that the common law of England was based upon usages, customs, and institutions of the English people as declared from time to time by the courts, said (page 707, of 184 Ind., 111 N.E. 423, 425):

"The rules so deduced from this system, however, were continually changing and expanding with the progress of society in the application of this system to more diversified circumstances and under more advanced periods. The common law by its own principles adapted itself to varying conditions and modified its own rules so as to serve the ends of justice as prompted by a course of reasoning which was guided by these generally accepted truths. One of its oldest maxims was that where the reason of a rule ceased the rule also ceased, and it logically followed that when it occurred to the courts that a particular rule had never been founded upon reason, and that no reason existed in support thereof, that rule likewise ceased, and perhaps another sprang up in its place which was based upon reason and justice as then conceived. No rule of the common law could survive the reason on which it was founded. It needed no statute to change it but abrogated itself."

That court then refers to the settled doctrine that an adoption of the common law in general terms does not require, without regard to local circumstances, an unqualified application of all its rules; that the rules, as declared by the English courts at one period or another, have been controlling in this country only so far as they were suited to and in harmony with the genius, spirit, and objects of American institutions; and that the rules of the common law considered proper in the eighteenth century are not necessarily so considered in the twentieth. "Since courts have had an existence in America," that court said (page 708 of 184 Ind., 111 N.E. 423, 425), "they have never hesitated to take upon themselves the responsibility of saying what are the proper rules of the common law."

And the Virginia Supreme Court of Appeals, in Hanriot v. Sherwood, 82 Va. 1, 15, after pointing to the fact that the common law of England is the law of that commonwealth except so far as it has been altered by statute, or so far as its principles are inapplicable to the state of the country, and that the rules of the common law had undergone modification in the courts of England, notes with obvious approval that "the rules of evidence have been in the courts of this country undergoing such modification and changes, according to the circumstances of the country and the manner and genius of the people."

The Supreme Court of Connecticut, in Beardsley v. City of Hartford, 50 Conn. 529, 542, 47 Am. Rep. 677, after quoting the maxim of the common law, cessante ratione legis, cessat ipsa lex, said:

"This means that no law can survive the reasons on which it is founded. It needs no statute to change it; it abrogates itself. If the reasons on which a law rests are overborne by opposing reasons, which in the progress of society gain a controlling force, the old law, though still good as an abstract principle, and good in its application to some circumstances, must cease to apply as a controlling principle to the new circumstances."

The same thought is expressed in People v. Randolph, 2 Parker, Cr. R. (N.Y.) 174, 177:

"Its rules [the rules of the common law] are modified upon its own principles and not in violation of them. Those rules being founded in reason, one of its oldest maxims is, that where the reason of the rule ceases the rule also ceases."

Judgment reversed.

Mr. Justice CARDOZO concurs in the result.

Mr. Justice McREYNOLDS and Mr. Justice BUTLER are of opinion that the judgment of the court below is right and should be affirmed.

Cases relating to **Chapter 3**

RELEVANCY AND MATERIALITY

HOLMES v. STATE

112 S.(2d) 511

Court of Appeals of Alabama.
March 24, 1959.

Rehearing Denied April 7, 1959.

Holmes has appealed from a conviction of involuntary manslaughter carrying a twelve months' jail sentence.

The homicide charged was the killing of Doyle Wayne Wright and his two and a half year old daughter, Donna Faye, in a collision between automobiles driven by Wright and by Holmes.

The wreck occurred about nine o'clock on the night of November 8, 1957, at a point on the Talladega-Sylacauga road somewhat north from the Alpine turn off. Holmes was traveling south going from Talladega toward Sylacauga. Wright was headed north.

There were only two eye witnesses, Holmes and Mr. J. W. Moore, a friend of his, who had followed him in another car all the way from Talladega.

The fact that two deaths resulted from the same transaction does not make the indictment duplicitous. See Nixon v. State, Ala., 105 So.2d 349, a case of Nixon's car simultaneously striking three children.

The State offered the testimony of Robert Elders who was caught with a flat tire on his car at a point "something like a mile" from the point of collision. He saw Holmes' and Moore's cars pass going toward Sylacauga. He was able to observe them for only about an eighth of a mile looking from where his car was stopped toward the point of collision. This appears the result of Elders' being parked on the side of a hill.

As to what he could hear of the cars after they had gone by, Elders testified:

"Well, yeah, I could hear them a pretty good piece, but I couldn't say just how far I could hear them. Something like a quarter of a mile I reckon surely. I couldn't say I could hear them any further. I wasn't paying any attention to that."

After the lapse of some fifteen minutes, Elders came upon the scene of the wreck.

The testimony went:

"Q. What is your opinion as to the speed of the red and black automobile?

"Mr. Stringer: Now, if your Honor please we renew our objection to that on the ground that it calls for irrelevant, immaterial, incompetent and illegal testimony and on the further ground the witness is not shown to be qualified to express an opinion, and on the further ground—express an opinion about the matter inquired about—and on the further ground that the speed of the automobile which the witness says he saw at the place where he saw it sheds no material evidence upon the speed of the automobile at the time the alleged collision took place, sheds no material evidence upon the matters involved in this case.

"The Court: I'll overrule.

"Mr. Stringer: We except.

"A. You wanted me to estimate the speed I thought he was making. I would say he was at least making 75 or 80 miles an hour.

"Q. That is your best judgment? A. Yes, sir.

"Mr. Stringer: We move to exclude that answer.

"The Court: That is your best judgment you said?

"A. Yes, sir.

"The Court: I'll overrule.

"Mr. Stringer: We except."

On his cross-examination, Elders was asked:

"Q. Did you judge the speed by the sound it made when it passed? A. Yes, sir, from the sound when it come in sight until it left out of my hearing."

And again we find:

"Q. How far did it travel before it got out of your sight? A. I couldn't say just exactly how far he traveled before he got out of my sight, something like—

"Q. (interrupting) Well, you were down there, weren't you? A. —something like the distance from here to the post office over there.

"Q. After that he went over a hill out of your sight? A. That's right.

"Q. You don't know what speed he made after he got out of your sight? A. Well, no.

"Q. And that was nearly a mile from the time—in other words, the distance from the place where he got out of your sight to the place where you saw these cars down there in a wrecked condition, that was nearly a mile, wasn't it? A. Something nearly a mile.

"Q. And you don't know whether he slowed up or went faster when he went out of your sight, is that right? A. No, sir, I don't know."

Evidence of speed at a remote point has been admitted "when it relates to a place not so remote as that a *fair* inference *may* be indulged that *substantially* such speed was *probably* maintained to and at the time of the accident." Townsend v. Adair, 223 Ala. 150, 134 So. 637, 639. (Italics added.) The application of this somewhat iffy formula is committed to the sound discretion of the trial judge. Whittaker v. Walker, 223 Ala. 167, 135 So. 185.

The distances in the Alabama cases run: Utility Trailer Works v. Phillips, 249 Ala. 61, 20 So.2d 289 ($\frac{9}{10}$ mile, variation in grade; not error to exclude); Hodges v. Wells, 226 Ala. 558, 147 So. 672 (several miles; error to admit; reversed on other grounds); Bains Motor Co. v. Le Croy, 209 Ala. 345, 96 So. 483 (several hundred feet; not error to admit; reversed on another ground); Davies v. Barnes, 201 Ala. 120, 77 So. 612 (1½ blocks; not error to admit; 4-3 court).

In Lessman v. West, 20 Ala.App. 289, 101 So. 515, the car remained in view from its first being seen until impact.

A prosecution witness (in Bradford v. State, 166 Miss. 296, 146

So. 635) was on the porch of his home about a mile from the collision when he saw appellant drive past going from fifty to fifty-five miles an hour. The cutout never slowed down until the collision. The court held that based upon this continuous perception the testimony had probative value.

In a criminal case, Graham v. State, 25 Ala.App. 44, 140 So. 621, this court, per Sanford, J., held that error, if any, in admitting evidence (among other things) of speed at a point one-fourth mile distant was cured by instructing the jury not to consider "the testimony * * * about meeting a car."

In the opinion in what seems to be the first case involving a motor car, Davies v. Barnes, supra, Judge Somerville was careful to point out that speed at one point does not create even a rebuttable (or disputable) presumption of continuing status. However, where, very shortly after the distant observation (1½ blocks), the vehicle hit a flagman (the plaintiff), the opinion states the speed then was "clearly a fact for the jury to consider, as affording an inference of fact with respect to its probable speed and control" at the time of striking the flagman. Thus, it would seem the court has treated the testimony as circumstantial evidence.

On rehearing (with three very able justices dissenting), after referring to Louisville & N. R. Co. v. Woods, 105 Ala. 561, 17 So. 41, Mr. Justice Somerville went on:

"So far as the prima facie relevancy of the evidence in the instant case is concerned, we think the question is foreclosed by the decision in the Woods case.

"If the subsequent developments in the course of the trial nullified this prima facie relevancy, which we need not determine, a motion should have been made for its exclusion, failing which the trial judge cannot be put in error for its original rightful admission.

"We, of course, do not overlook the difference between a railroad train running on rails, and probably observing the obligations of a schedule time, and an automobile running on the highway at the will of its driver. There is a difference, but the difference is in the strength of the inference, and its probative value, and not in the principle of relevancy and admissibility.

"*With respect to the distance at which previous speed is admissible for this purpose, there must indeed be some limit;* but, as in all similar cases, this will depend upon the facts of each case, and must be left to the sound discretion of the trial court." [201 Ala. 120, 77 So. 613] (Italics added.)

Was Elders' testimony of Holmes' speed relevant to blame for the fatal wreck? Wide latitude is given as to the admission of circumstantial evidence, but there the test is whether a particular fact, in connection with all the others, forms a chain tending to show guilt, Russell v. State, Ala. 38 So. 291. Thus, fact A alone may prove nothing on an issue, but if fact B with fact A gives a logical inference of the existence of C, then A has relevancy as to C. On the other hand, a mirror casts no light of its own, and if its reflection colors or twists the image, then there is distortion.

Here, the testimony was not admitted under an offer to connect it up later; nor, as we read the record, is there anything but conjecture that Holmes continued headlong into the night. Indeed, Moore, the State's witness, said Holmes was travelling at about the legal speed limit when he (Moore) first observed Wright coming into Holmes' side of the road. Moreover, Elders was somewhat confused as to the color of Moore's car. . . .

The following from Barrett v. Shirley, Miss., 95 So.2d 471, 473, seems self explanatory:

"We first consider the assignment dealing with the testimony of C. C. Zimmerman, which was admitted over objection of appellant. Zimmerman testified that he was driving north along Highway 45 just out of Quitman about one-fourth or one-half mile south of the scene of the accident; that a black and white Buick passed him at a speed of 75 or 80 miles per hour; that three or four minutes later he came upon the accident and recognized the Barrett Buick as the one that passed him. He did not say that he saw the accident or that the Buick continued to the place of the accident at the same speed.

* * * * * *

"We recognize that the trial court has some discretion in excluding or admitting such testimony, but the area within which such discretion may be exercised is limited.

"As a general rule where the speed of a vehicle is a factor in determining the proximate cause of a collision the evidence as to speed should be limited to the time of, or immediately before, the collision, and the court should exclude evidence of speed prior to and remote from the collision in question; but evidence of prior speed may be admitted if (1) the evidence shows that the vehicle continued to be operated approximately at the same speed until the collision occurs, or (2) where the circumstances are such, because of the nearness of the prior speed to the collision in point of time and distance or because of other factors, that the prior speed has substantial evidential value as to the speed of the vehicle at the time of, or immediately before, the collision.

"Zimmerman did not testify that he saw the Buick automobile when it approached the curve north of which the accident occurred. In fact, he did not testify to anything other than the speed at some point south of the place of collision and that he came upon the scene of the accident some three or four minutes after the Buick passed him. In our opinion, this does not establish causal connection with the accident. It was not shown that the Buick continued at or about the same speed to the place of collision. Under the circumstances of this case, the speed of the Barrett Buick at the place testified by Zimmerman has no substantial evidential value as to the speed at the time of, or immediately before, the collision. The jury would have had to speculate to draw the inference that Barrett continued to operate at such a high rate of speed around the curve that he had just turned before reaching the place where the accident occurred. This testimony was too remote and was inadmissible."

Certainly, as seems to be universally conceded, the test of relevancy of this sort of evidence must depend upon the facts of each case. Usually the facts of any given case are of such a peculiar composition as to afford little help in going from one case to another. Then, too, for us to say a trial judge has abused the discretion committed to him (particularly where only vague qualitative standards have been given him) comes near to being blind man's bluff. But we perceive a light of connected doctrine in the Alabama cases which leads us to consider that the instant testimony should have been excluded.

In this case, we consider that Elders' testimony was not relevant on the issue of guilt or of any proper subordinate issue presented by the record. Also, we consider its admission was probably prejudicial to Holmes' substantial right, and, therefore, the judgment below is due to be

Reversed and remanded.

UNITED STATES v. GIPSON

385 F.(2d) 341

United States Court of Appeals Seventh Circuit.

October 18, 1967.

PER CURIAM.

This appeal is from a conviction under a provision of the Dyer Act prohibiting the receipt and concealment of a stolen motor vehicle (18 U.S.C. § 2313). The indictment charged that on June 22, 1966, in Evansville, Indiana, defendant received and concealed a 1963 Oldsmobile that had been transported interstate, and that he knew the car had been stolen. The defendant was found guilty after a bench trial.

The evidence showed that this Oldsmobile belonged to Leonard Smith of Griffith, Indiana, and that he immediately reported its Calumet City, Illinois, theft on December 5, 1965. The title to the car was in the name of the owner's father, Emmett Smith.

The District Court received testimony that defendant, using the name of Emmett Smith, had been arrested in Florida in March 1966 for motor vehicle violations, and that he was then driving the stolen Oldsmobile. The court also received in evidence an April 1966 application for an Alabama license tag for this Oldsmobile. This application was signed in the name of Emmett Smith but was not in the handwriting of the owner's father. An Indiana police officer testified that defendant admitted he had obtained the Alabama registration in the name of Emmett Smith.

On June 22, 1966, Allen Goodridge borrowed this Oldsmobile from defendant in Evansville, Indiana. While driving the car three or four hours later, he was arrested for second degree burglary. The car then bore Alabama license plates.

On appeal, although conceding that such evidence would be admissible to show a scheme or plan or identity, defendant asserts that the District Court should not have received evidence concerning the Florida motor vehicle violations. This evidence disclosed his claim to be Emmett Smith, the title-holder of the automobile. Proof of the Florida offenses was properly admitted to show defendant's scheme or plan to conceal his wrongful possession of the car. E.g., United States v. Crowe, 188 F.2d 209, 212 (7th Cir. 1951).

Defendant also asserts that documentary evidence concerning his two Florida arrests and concerning the Alabama license application was improperly received. The Florida documents were received to corroborate the testimony of the two Florida police officers. They certainly would not tend to prejudice the District Court trying this case, for he had already properly received testimony about defendant's Florida arrests. The Alabama application was received to show that this Oldsmobile had been in Alabama and that the same Alabama plates found on the car on June 22, 1966, had been issued for this car. This evidence was relevant to show that defendant had resorted to concealment. It also bore on the interstate transportation of the car. In our view, the Alabama document was of sufficient probative value to justify its admissibility. A trial judge has wide latitude in ruling on relevancy and materiality. We conclude that there was no abuse of discretion in receiving the three documentary exhibits.

The judgment is affirmed.

KIRSCHBAUM v. UNITED STATES

407 F.(2d) 562

United States Court of Appeals Eighth Circuit.

March 6, 1969.

MEHAFFY, Circuit Judge.

Delbert Lester Kirschbaum, Sr., the defendant, was convicted by trial to a jury upon each count of a two-count indictment which charged the interstate transportation of "lewd, lascivious and filthy films" for the purpose of sale and distribution in violation of 18 U.S.C. § 1465, and which charged in the second count a conspiracy to commit the substantive act in violation of 18 U.S.C. § 371. The trial court sentenced defendant upon each count to a term of three years, the sentences to run concurrently, and upon condition that defendant be confined in a jail type or treatment institution for a period of sixty days with the remainder of the sentence suspended and probation allowed for two years and ten months as authorized by 18 U.S.C. § 3651.

The issues here involve the sufficiency of the evidence and evidentiary rulings of the trial court. We affirm the judgment of conviction.

* * *

Defendant next argues that the court erred in failing to strike the testimony of witness Sloan. Sloan's testimony revealed the nature of the conspiracy. He identified Persich and Curtis of Peoria, Illinois as distributors of films. He made a trip to Peoria with Beaver in early 1964 where he contacted both Curtis and Persich. Sloan discussed with defendant the selling of films, and defendant actually engaged Sloan to go to Peoria to pick up films. Defendant furnished money for the films as well as a bus ticket, but Sloan changed his mind, and when he later told defendant that his part of the deal was off Sloan was informed by defendant that he was not needed any more as defendant had been able to obtain Sloan's sales list and also was able to make the purchase contact. His testimony disclosed defendant's intent to buy the films in Peoria from Persich and sell the films in Des Moines. We have held that generally evidence of the conduct of the accused shortly before the offense which is inconsistent with his innocence is relevant and admissible. Cicinto v. United States, 212 F.2d 8, 11 (8th Cir. 1954), *cert. denied*, 348 U.S. 884, 75 S.Ct. 125, 99 L.Ed. 695 (1954). In our view, the evidence of this witness was competent as related to both the substantive and conspiracy charges in the indictment.

Finally, it is contended that the court erred in permitting witness Lynch to testify as to his present recollections because before the trial he had reviewed a prior statement he had made some three years before to the FBI. The defense was furnished a copy of this statement when Lynch took the witness stand, and Lynch did not refresh his memory while on the witness stand. On cross-examination, Lynch testified that his testimony was based on his memory, but he apparently was confused by some of the questions commencing with the query as to whether he had any independent recollection as to what happened on April 20, 1964 other than what he had reviewed in the statement, and his answer was "No, sir." When this confusion arose, the court asked the witness whether after looking at the notes it had caused him to refresh his memory as to the events that occurred back in 1964, and he said that it did. When asked by the court whether his testimony was based solely on what was in the notes, his answer was "No, sir. I had a recollection but I was trying to follow as closely to the statements I made, in my testimony. Therefore, I—so I wouldn't err."

The court observed that the examination of the witness indicated that he was testifying to several matters not contained in the statement he furnished the FBI, and held his testimony admissible. This is not the type of testimony condemned by reason of reading from a statement. As noted, the witness had merely refreshed his memory by reading the statement before commencement of trial. It had been some three years since the events in question and the witness had a perfect right to read the statement at that time and refresh his memory. In Redfearn v. United States, 375 F.2d 767 (5th Cir. 1967), the court stated:

> "We have carefully considered the contention of the appellants that the trial court erred in permitting the principal prosecution witness to testify extensively from a statement made up by him from his original field notes, thereafter destroyed. It is clear from a reading of the transcript of the trial that the witness testified that his recollection was refreshed by the written statement. We, therefore, conclude that the trial court did not err in permitting his testimony to be received in evidence even though on some occasions he stated that without reference to the written statement he could not recall all of the events that had transpired."

Having considered all assignments of error advanced and finding them to be without merit, the judgment of conviction is affirmed.

PEOPLE v. ZACKOWITZ
254 N.Y. 192, 172 N.E. 466
Court of Appeals of New York.

July 8, 1930.

CARDOZO, C. J.

On November 10, 1929, shortly after midnight, the defendant in Kings county shot Frank Coppola and killed him without justification or excuse. A crime is admitted. What is doubtful is the degree only.

Four young men, of whom Coppola was one, were at work repairing an automobile in a Brooklyn street. A woman, the defendant's wife, walked by on the opposite side. One of the men spoke to her insultingly, or so at least she understood him. The defendant, who had dropped behind to buy a newspaper, came up to find his wife in tears. He was told she had been insulted, though she did not then repeat the words. Enraged, he stepped across the street and upbraided the offenders with words of coarse profanity. He informed them, so the survivors testify, that "if they did not get out of there in five minutes, he would come back and bump them all off." Rejoining his wife, he walked with her to their apartment house located close at hand. He was heated with liquor which he had been drinking at a dance. Within the apartment he induced her to tell him what the insulting words had been. A youth had asked her to lie with him, and had offered her $2. With rage aroused again, the defendant went back to the scene of the insult and found the four young men still working at the car. In a statement to the police, he said that he had armed himself at the apartment with a .25-caliber automatic pistol. In his testimony at the trial he said that this pistol had been in his pocket all the evening. Words and blows followed, and then a shot. The defendant kicked Coppola in the stomach. There is evidence that Coppola went for him with a wrench. The pistol came from the pocket, and from the pistol a single shot, which did its deadly work. The defendant walked away and at the corner met his wife who had followed him from the home. The two took a taxicab to Manhattan, where they spent the rest of the night at the dwelling of a friend. On the way the defendant threw his pistol into the river. He was arrested on January 7, 1930, about two months following the crime.

At the trial the vital question was the defendant's state of mind at the moment of the homicide. Did he shoot with a deliberate and premeditated design to kill? Was he so inflamed by drink or by anger or by both combined that, though he knew the nature of his act, he was the prey to sudden impulse, the fury of the fleeting moment? People v. Caruso, 246 N.Y. 437, 446, 159 N.E. 390. If he went forth from his apartment with a preconceived design to kill, how is it that he failed to shoot at once? How reconcile such a design with the drawing of the pistol later in the heat and rage of an affray? These and like questions the jurors were to ask themselves and answer before measuring the defendant's guilt. Answers consistent with guilt in its highest grade can reasonably be made. Even so, the line between impulse and deliberation is too narrow and elusive to make the answers wholly clear. The sphygmograph records with graphic certainty the fluctuations of the pulse. There is no instrument yet invented that records with equal certainty the fluctuations of the mind. At least, if such an instrument exists, it was not working at midnight in the Brooklyn street when Coppola and the defendant came together in a chance affray. With only the rough and ready tests supplied by their experience of life, the jurors were to look into the workings of another's mind, and discover its capacities and disabilities, its urges and inhibitions, in moments of intense excitement. Delicate enough and subtle is the inquiry, even in the most favorable conditions, with every warping influence excluded. There must be no blurring of the issues by evidence illegally admitted and carrying with it in its admission an appeal to prejudice and passion.

Evidence charged with that appeal was, we think, admitted here. Not only was it admitted, and this under objection and exception, but the changes were rung upon it by prosecutor and judge. Almost at the opening of the trial the people began the endeavor to load the defendant down with the burden of an evil character. He was to be put before the jury as a man of murderous disposition. To that end they were allowed to prove that at the time of the encounter and at that of his arrest he had in his apartment, kept there in a radio box, three pistols and a tear-gas gun. There was no claim that he had brought these weapons out at the time of the affray, no claim that with any of them he had discharged the fatal shot. He could not have done so, for they were all of different caliber. The end to be served by laying the weapons before the jury was something very different. The end was to bring persuasion that here was a man of vicious and dangerous propensities, who because of those propensities was more likely to kill with deliberate and premeditated design than a man of irreproachable life and amiable manners. Indeed, this is the very ground on which the introduction of the evidence is now explained and defended. The district attorney tells us in his brief that the possession of the weapons characterized the defendant as "a desperate type of criminal," a "person criminally inclined." The dissenting opinion, if it puts the argument less bluntly, leaves the substance of the thought unchanged. "Defendant was presented to the jury as a man having dangerous weapons in his possession, making a selection therefrom and going forth to put into execution his threats to kill." The weapons were not brought by the defendant to the scene of the encounter. They were left in his apartment where they were incapable of harm. In such circumstances, ownership of the weapons, if it has any relevance at all, has relevance only as indicating a general disposition to make use of them thereafter, and a general disposition to make use of them thereafter is without relevance except as indicating a "desperate type of criminal," a criminal affected with a murderous propensity.

We are asked to extenuate the error by calling it an incident; what was proved may have an air of innocence if it is styled the history of the crime. The virus of the ruling is not so easily extracted. Here was no passing reference to something casually brought out in the narrative of the killing, as if an admission had been proved against the defendant that he had picked one weapon out of several. Here in the forefront of the trial, immediately following the statement of the medical examiner, testimony was admitted that weapons, not the instruments of the killing, had been discovered by the police in the apartment of the killer; and the weapons with great display were laid before the jury, marked as exhibits, and thereafter made the subject of animated argument. Room for doubt there is none that in the thought of the jury, as in that of the district attorney, the tendency of the whole performance was to

People v. Zackowitz

characterize the defendant as a man murderously inclined. The purpose was not disguised. From the opening to the verdict, it was flaunted and avowed.

If a murderous propensity may be proved against a defendant as one of the tokens of his guilt, a rule of criminal evidence, long believed to be of fundamental importance for the protection of the innocent, must be first declared away. Fundamental hitherto has been the rule that character is never an issue in a criminal prosecution unless the defendant chooses to make it one. Wigmore, Evidence, vol. 1, §§ 55, 192. In a very real sense a defendant starts his life afresh when he stands before a jury, a prisoner at the bar. There has been a homicide in a public place. The killer admits the killing, but urges self-defense and sudden impulse. Inflexibly the law has set its face against the endeavor to fasten guilt upon him by proof of character or experience predisposing to an act of crime. Wigmore, Evidence, vol. 1, §§ 57, 192; People v. Molineux, 168 N.Y. 264, 61 N.E. 286, 62 L.R.A. 193. The endeavor has been often made, but always it has failed. At times, when the issue has been self-defense, testimony has been admitted as to the murderous propensity of the deceased, the victim of the homicide (People v. Druse, 103 N.Y. 655, 8 N.E. 733; People v. Rodawald, 177 N.Y. 408, 70 N.E. 1; Wigmore, Evidence, vol. 1, § 63, 246), but never of such a propensity on the part of the killer. The principle back of the exclusion is one, not of logic, but of policy. Wigmore, vol. 1, §§ 57, 194; People v. Richardson, 222 N.Y. 103, 109, 110, 118 N.E. 514. There may be cogency in the argument that a quarrelsome defendant is more likely to start a quarrel than one of milder type, a man of dangerous mode of life more likely than a shy recluse. The law is not blind to this, but equally it is not blind to the peril to the innocent if character is accepted as probative of crime. "The natural and inevitable tendency of the tribunal—whether judge or jury—is to give excessive weight to the vicious record of crime thus exhibited, and either to allow it to bear too strongly on the present charge, or to take the proof of it as justifying a condemnation irrespective of guilt of the present charge." Wigmore, Evidence, vol. 1, § 194, and cases cited. . . .

The endeavor was to generate an atmosphere of professional criminality. It was an endeavor the more unfair in that, apart from the suspicion attaching to the possession of these weapons, there is nothing to mark the defendant as a man of evil life. He was not in crime as a business. He did not shoot as a bandit shoots in the hope of wrongful gain. He was engaged in a decent calling, an optician regularly employed, without criminal record, or criminal associates. If his own testimony be true, he had gathered these weapons together as curios, a collection that interested and amused him. Perhaps his explanation of their ownership is false. There is nothing stronger than mere suspicion to guide us to an answer. Whether the explanation be false or true, he should not have been driven by the people to the necessity of offering it. Brought to answer a specific charge, and to defend himself against it, he was placed in a position where he had to defend himself against another, more general and sweeping. He was made to answer to the charge, pervasive and poisonous even if insidious and covert, that he was a man of murderous heart, of criminal disposition.

The judgment of conviction should be reversed, and a new trial ordered.

POUND, J. (dissenting).

The people may not prove against a defendant crimes not alleged in the indictment committed on other occasions than the crime charged as aiding the proofs that he is guilty of the crime charged unless such proof tends to establish (1) motive; (2) intent; (3) absence of mistake or accident; (4) a common scheme or plan embracing the commission of two or more crimes so related to each other that proof of the one tends to establish the other; (5) the identity of the person charged with the commission of the crime on trial. These exceptions are stated generally and not with categorical precision and may not be all-inclusive. People v. Molineux, 168 N.Y. 264, 61 N.E. 286, 62 L.R.A. 193; People v. Pettanza, 207 N.Y. 560, 101 N.E. 428; People v. Moran, 246 N.Y. 100, 106, 158 N.E. 35. None of them apply here, nor were the weapons offered under an exception to the general rule. They were offered as a part of the transaction itself. The accused was tried only for the crime charged. The real question is whether the matter relied on has such a connection with the crime charged as to be admissible on any ground. If so, the fact that it constitutes another distinct crime does not render it inadmissible. Com. v. Snell, 189 Mass. 12, 21, 75 N.E. 75, 3 L.R.A. (N.S.) 1019. The rule laid down in the Molineux Case has never been applied to prevent the people from proving all the elements of the offense charged, although separate crimes are included in such proof. Thus in this case no question is made as to the separate crime of illegal possession of the weapon with which the killing was done. It was "a part of the history of the case" having a distinct relation to and bearing upon the facts connected with the killing. People v. Governale, 193 N.Y. 581, 86 N.E. 554; People v. Rogers, 192 N.Y. 331, 85 N.E. 135, 15 Ann. Cas. 177; People v. Hill, 198 N.Y. 64, 91 N.E. 272; People v. Rodawald, 177 N.Y. 408, 70 N.E. 1.

* * *

The judgment of conviction should be affirmed.

Cases relating to **Chapter 4**

COMPETENCY

GILLARS v. UNITED STATES
182 F.(2d) 962
United States Court of Appeals
District of Columbia Circuit.
Decided May 19, 1950.

FAHY, Circuit Judge.

Appellant was convicted of treason in a jury trial in the United States District Court for the District of Columbia. Treason alone of crimes is defined in the Constitution, as follows:

"Treason against the United States, shall consist only in levying War against them, or in adhering to their Enemies, giving them Aid and Comfort. * * *" U.S. Const. Art. III, § 3.

The First Congress, in 1790, provided by statute,

"* * * That if any person or persons, owing allegiance to the United States of America, shall levy war against them, or shall adhere to their enemies, giving them aid and comfort within the United States or elsewhere, and shall be thereof convicted, on confession in open court, or on the testimony of two witnesses to the same overt act of the treason whereof he or they shall stand indicted, such person or persons shall be adjudged guilty of treason against the United States, * * *." 1 Stat. 112 (1790).

The indictment alleges that appellant was born in Maine, was a citizen of and owed allegiance to the United States, that within the German Reich, after December 11, 1941, to and including May 8, 1945, in violation of her duty of allegiance she knowingly and intentionally adhered to the enemies of the United States, to wit, the Government of the German Reich, its agents, instrumentalities, representatives and subjects with which the United States was at war, and gave to said enemies aid and comfort within the United States and elsewhere, by participating in the psychological warfare of the German Government against the United States. This participation is alleged to have consisted of radio broadcasts and the making of phonographic recordings with the intent that they would be used in broadcasts to the United States and to American Expeditionary Forces in French North Africa, Italy, France and England. The indictment charges the commission of ten overt acts, each of which is described, and, finally, that following commission of the offense the District of Columbia was the first Federal Judicial District into which appellant was brought.

Eight of the ten alleged overt acts were submitted to the jury. A verdict of guilty was returned, based on the commission of overt act No. 10, which is set forth in the indictment as follows:

"10. That on a day between January 1, 1944 and June 6, 1944, the exact date being to the Grand Jurors unknown, said defendant, at Berlin, Germany, did speak into a microphone in a recording studio of the German Radio Broadcasting Company, and thereby did participate in a phonographic recording and cause to be phonographically recorded a radio drama entitled "Vision of Invasion," said defendant then and there well knowing that said recorded radio drama was to be subsequently broadcast by the German Radio Broadcasting Company to the United States and to its citizens and soldiers at home and abroad as an element of German propaganda and an instrument of psychological warfare."

We now discuss the several matters raised by appellant as grounds for reversal.

I

THE SUFFICIENCY AND WEIGHT OF THE EVIDENCE

Appellant contends the verdict was contrary to the evidence and to the weight of the evidence. The argument runs as follows: The indictment charged that at various times appellant spoke into a microphone and her voice was later sent over the radio; that two of the ten overt acts of this character were withdrawn, leaving eight for jury consideration; that of these she was acquitted of seven; that she admitted speaking into the microphone and sending her views over the radio but denied any intention to betray; and that therefore the jury, having in mind this admission, concluded there was no intent to betray in the case of seven overt acts. From this it is argued that the finding of treasonable intention as to one overt act could not have been made consistently with acquittal of these other overt acts.

If, however, there is sufficient evidence to support the verdict of guilty based on the commission of the tenth overt act alone we may not reverse even were we of opinion that the evidence was equally strong to support a conviction based on other alleged overt acts as to which appellant was acquitted. A jury verdict need not be consistent.

"Consistency in the verdict is not necessary. Each count in an indictment is regarded as if it was a separate indictment. Latham v. The Queen, 5 Best & Smith 635, 642, 643; Selvester v. United States, 170 U.S. 262, 18 S.Ct. 580, 42 L.Ed. 1029. * * *" Dunn v. United States, 1931, 284 U.S. 390, 393, 52 S.Ct. 189, 190, 76 L.Ed. 356, 80 A.L.R. 161.

The evidence was sufficient to support the verdict on the tenth overt act. There was before the jury evidence from which they could find the following: Appellant was a native born citizen of the United States and therefore owed allegiance to the United States; in 1940 she was thirty-nine years of age; she had studied dramatics and had been employed in the United States as an actress; she left the United States in 1933, and took up residence in Berlin in 1934; on May 6, 1940, she was employed there by the German Broadcasting Company as announcer on the European Services; within a few months after this employment she was made mistress of ceremonies of the European Services; in 1941 she took part also in an overseas service program broadcast to the United States; the United States declared war on Germany December 11, 1941; the German Radio Broadcasting Company was a tax-supported agency of the German Government; it consisted of two main branches, the Home Branch and the Foreign Branch; the Foreign Branch in turn consisted of the European Service and the Overseas Service; the purpose of the broadcasts by the Foreign Branch was to disseminate to the Armed Forces and civilians of the United States and her allies propaganda along lines laid down by the German Propaganda Ministry and the Foreign Office to aid Germany and to weaken the war effort of the nations at war with her; daily conferences were held among Goebbels, head of the Ministry of Public Enlightenment and Propaganda of the German Government, and representatives of the Foreign Office to formulate propaganda lines; these were followed by conferences of the Director of the Foreign Branch with the officials of the Overseas Service about the propaganda lines to be pursued; the employees of the Overseas Service followed the propaganda instructions then announced; the lines of propaganda for broadcast to the citizens and Armed Forces of the United States were that Germany was superior in various ways; she was fighting against Communistic domination of the world; the United States was improperly influenced to enter and remain in the war by Jewish interests; German fighting forces were superior; Germany had secret military weapons such as the V-1 and V-2 rockets; an attempted invasion of Germany would be disastrous; the United States should not oppose Germany in its fight to save Christianity and world salvation from the Communists; the President would sell his country to the Russians and was improperly influenced by Jewish advisers; the people of the United States should not follow the policy of the war effort of their Government; the war was a British war.

. . .

In the light of the uncontradicted evidence of her participation in the recording of *Vision of Invasion*, testified to by more than two witnesses, as a part of her employment by an agency of the German Government, and the evidence as to the nature and purpose of this employment, of the intended use of the recordings and programs, the evidence of her citizenship, and the fact of war between the United States and Germany, we hold that the evidence furnished an adequate basis for the jury to find that appellant, while owing allegiance to the United States, adhered to the enemy, giving such enemy aid and comfort, and that this was done knowingly and with the intention of aiding the enemy in the war in which it was then engaged with the United States. Furthermore, we find no necessary inconsistency between the jury's conviction on overt Act No. 10 and their acquittal on others. They might reasonably have distinguished between the nature of *Vision of Invasion* and other recordings.

II

THE QUESTION OF THE COMPETENCY AND CREDIBILITY OF CERTAIN WITNESSES

(A) As a subsidiary to her attack on the sufficiency of the evidence appellant contends that the witness Schnell, who was one of three who testified to her participation in the recording of *Vision of Invasion*, was an incompetent witness because he stated that he did not believe in the God of the Bible. He also testified that he did not believe in rewards or punishments after death. It appears from his full statement, set forth in the margin, that he recognized a right and duty of society to force members to speak the truth. He was permitted to testify on affirmation.

The D.C. Code, Title 14, Section 101, reads as follows:

"All evidence shall be given under oath according to the forms of the common law, except that where a witness has conscientious scruples against taking an oath, he may, in lieu thereof, solemnly, sincerely, and truly declare and affirm; * * *"

The Government contends that Schnell affirmed in accordance with this provision. We read the permission to affirm because of conscientious scruples against taking an oath to apply to one who believes in God but does not believe in oath-taking in court. The witness Schnell was not of that character. He did not believe in the God before whom an oath is taken "according to the forms of the common law," Who is indeed the God of the Bible. United States v. Lee, C.C.D.C. 1834, 26 Fed.Cas. page 908, No. 15,586; United States v. Kennedy, C.C.D.Ill. 1843, 26 Fed.Cas. page 761, No. 15,524; Wakefield v. Ross, C.C.D.R.I. 1827, 28 Fed.Cas. page 1346, No. 17,050; Anonymous, 1839, 1 Fed.Cas. page 999, No. 446. The early common law rule, and therefore the rule which at an earlier period would have prevailed under the Code might well have rendered Schnell incompetent. But the Code must now be read with Rule 26 of the Federal Rules of Criminal Procedure, 18 U.S.C.A., which provides, *inter alia*:

"* * * competency and privileges of witnesses shall be governed, except when an act of Congress or these rules otherwise provide, by the principles of the common law as they may be interpreted by the courts of the United States in the light of reason and experience."

A fair reading together of the Code and the Rule leads to the conclusion that the common law rule in the District of Columbia is to be interpreted now in the light of reason and experience. This brings into the area of competence witnesses who were under disability under the older criteria. For example, in Rosen v. United States, 1917, 245 U.S. 467, 38 S.Ct. 148, 62 L.Ed. 406, the Supreme Court in substance held that the former common law rule disqualifying criminals from being witnesses could no longer be followed; conviction of crime will be considered in testing the credibility of a witness but will not exclude him from the stand. See, also, United States v. Peterson, D.C.E.D.Pa. 1938, 24 F.Supp. 470; United States v. Segelman, D.C.W.D.Pa. 1949, 83 F.Supp. 890. In Gantz v. State, 1916, 18 Ga.App. 154, 88 S.E. 993, 994, a similar rationale was applied where the witness disclaimed any belief in God. The court said:

"* * * The sufficiency of the test as to the competency of a witness is necessarily largely a matter of judicial discretion * * *

"* * * In our view it is not essential to the competency of a witness that he shall know where he will go after death. Although lack of faith on this subject might affect his credit with the jury, it would not disqualify him from being a witness. * * *"

The course of change is traced in Underhill, Criminal Evidence, 4th Ed. Ch. 28. See, also, Wigmore on Evidence, 3rd Ed. Vol. VI, § 1816 et seq. Even therefore if we assume that the Code provision is a test of competency and not merely a prescription of the sanction under which one shall testify, it does not, when read with Rule 26, exclude as incompetent the nonbeliever in the God of the Bible.

We note that the affirmation in this case was not in the words of the Code, "* * * he may, in lieu thereof, solemnly, sincerely, and truly declare and affirm"; but such an affirmation, as we have said, is for one who believes but does not wish to swear. No words are prescribed for the affirmation of such a witness as Schnell. It was for the court to adopt appropriate words. Those used were adequate for an affirmation under pain and penalty of perjury.

(B) Some argument seems to be made that the testimony of the witness von Richter, who like Schnell testified to the participation by appellant in the recording of *Vision of Invasion*, could not be relied upon in support of an overt act of treason because he was a member of the Nazi party and had been seen wearing a Nazi membership button during the war. This argument is without legal significance. Whether or not the witness should be believed was for the jury. It is not clear appellant contends von Richter could not qualify as a witness; we refer to the matter only because counsel has done so though we are not certain his reference was intended to evoke a ruling.

(C) Appellant urges that the witness Haupt should not have been heard in support of proof of an overt act because he testified that his own participation in *Vision of Invasion* was under compulsion and fear of death. The suggested conclusion that this rendered incredible his testimony regarding the participation of the accused does not follow. It is not claimed his testimony regarding her participation was elicited by fear or compulsion and no reason is advanced why it necessarily should have been disregarded by the jury.

We note at this point that no question was raised at the trial as to the competency of von Richter or Haupt. Furthermore, appellant admitted her participation in the recording of *Vision of Invasion*. Nevertheless our above rulings on competency and the admissibility of testimony are not based upon this admission. We do not discuss the question whether her admission dispensed with the need of other testimony as to the commission of overt act No. 10 (see Cramer v. United States, 325 U.S. 1, dissenting opinion at page 63, 65 S.Ct. 918, 89 L.Ed. 1441) because independently of her testimony the constitutional requirement of two witnesses to the same overt act was met.

· · ·

Judgment affirmed.

Cases relating to **Chapter 5**

BURDEN OF PROOF

STATE v. SAUER

38 Minn. 438, 38 N.W. 355

(*Supreme Court of Minnesota.* May 25, 1888.)

MITCHELL, J. The defendant was convicted of the crime of an assault in the second degree. In his charge to the jury, the court, after instructing them that, to entitle the state to a verdict, the guilt of defendant must be proved beyond a reasonable doubt, added: "This does not mean beyond any doubt, but beyond a doubt for which you can give a reason." This is assigned as error. This definition is not without some authority to support it, (see *Com. v. Harman,* 4 Pa. St. 274;) and we are not prepared to say that it contains any error prejudicial to defendant. Like many other definitions of the term which have been given, it does not define, but itself requires definition. The most serious objection to it is that it is liable to be understood as meaning a doubt for which a juror could express or state a reason in words. A juror may, after a consideration and comparison of all the evidence, feel a reasonable doubt as to the guilt of a defendant, and yet find it difficult to state the reason for the doubt. The term "reasonable doubt" is almost incapable of any definition which will add much to what the words themselves imply. In fact it is easier to state what it is not than what it is; and it may be doubted whether any attempt to define it will not be more likely to confuse than to enlighten a jury. A man is the best judge of his own feelings, and he knows for himself whether he doubts better than any one else can tell him. Where any explanation of what is meant by a reasonable doubt is required, it is safer to adopt some definition which has already received the general approval of the authorities, especially those in our own state.

The defendant introduced evidence of his good character in the trait involved in the charge made against him. On this point the court charged the jury that "good character may have its weight in any case to this extent: that if there is a question of doubt, it may determine the matter in his favor." While this language is a little obscure, we think its evident meaning, and the one which the jury would naturally place upon it, is that evidence of good character is not to be considered at all, unless the other evidence in the case, considered by itself, leaves a doubt upon the minds of the jury as to defendant's guilt; in short, that such evidence may be used to solve such a doubt, but not to establish it. Such a rule practically deprives a defendant of all benefit of evidence of his good character; for if, on the other evidence, there is a reasonable doubt, he is entitled to an acquittal without it; and, in a case not otherwise doubtful, where alone he needs the evidence for the purpose of making it doubtful, he is denied the benefit of it. <u>Evidence of good character is admissible to support the original presumption of innocence, and is to go to the jury</u>, and be considered by them in connection with all the other evidence in the case. If they are satisfied of his guilt beyond a reasonable doubt, they must find him guilty, notwithstanding his previous good character; on the other hand, if, after considering all the evidence, (that of good character included,) they have a reasonable doubt, they must acquit. Good character is a fact varying greatly in its value, according to the proofs to which it is opposed. Cases may be made out so strong that no proof of character can make them doubtful; while in others the evidence against a person might be such that evidence of good character would produce a reasonable doubt of his guilt. Good character, when proven, is a fact in the case that may tend, in a greater or lesser degree, to establish innocence; and it is not to be put to one side by the jury, in order, first, to ascertain whether the other evidence, considered by itself, does not establish guilt beyond a reasonable doubt.

For this error in the charge, the verdict is set aside, and a new trial ordered.

IN RE WINSHIP
APPEAL FROM THE COURT OF APPEALS OF NEW YORK
Decided March 31, 1970
397 U.S. 358, 51 OhioOp.(2d) 323, 90 S.Ct. 1068

MR. JUSTICE BRENNAN delivered the opinion of the Court.

Constitutional questions decided by this Court concerning the juvenile process have centered on the adjudicatory stage at "which a determination is made as to whether a juvenile is a 'delinquent' as a result of alleged misconduct on his part, with the consequence that he may be committed to a state institution." *In re Gault*, 387 U.S. 1, 13, 40 OhioOp.(2d) 378, 383 (1967). *Gault* decided that, although the Fourteenth Amendment does not require that the hearing at this stage conform with all the requirements of a criminal trial or even of the usual administrative proceeding, the Due Process Clause does require application during the adjudicatory hearing of "'the essentials of due process and fair treatment.'" *Id.*, at 30. This case presents the single, narrow question whether proof beyond a reasonable doubt is among the "essentials of due process and fair treatment" required during the adjudicatory stage when a juvenile is charged with an act which would constitute a crime if committed by an adult.

Section 712 of the New York Family Court Act defines a juvenile delinquent as "a person over seven and less than sixteen years of age who does any act which, if done by an adult, would constitute a crime." During a 1967 adjudicatory hearing, conducted pursuant to § 742 of the Act, a judge in New York Family Court found that appellant, then a 12-year-old boy, had entered a locker and stolen $112 from a woman's pocketbook. The petition which charged appellant with delinquency alleged that his act, "if done by an adult, would constitute the crime or crimes of Larceny." The judge acknowledged that the proof might not establish guilt beyond a reasonable doubt, but rejected appellant's contention that such proof was required by the Fourteenth Amendment. The judge relied instead on § 744(b) of the New York Family Court Act which provides that "[a]ny determination at the conclusion of [an adjudicatory] hearing that a [juvenile] did an act or acts must be based on a preponderance of the evidence." During a subsequent dispositional hearing, appellant was ordered placed in a training school for an initial period of 18 months, subject to annual extensions of his commitment until his 18th birthday—six years in appellant's case. The Appellate Division of the New York Supreme Court, First Judicial Department, affirmed without opinion, 30 App. Div. 2d 781, 291 N.Y.S. 2d 1005 (1968). The New York Court of Appeals then affirmed by a four-to-three vote, expressly sustaining the constitutionality of § 744(b), 24 N.Y.2d 196, 247 N.E.2d 253 (1969). We noted probable jurisdiction, 396 U.S. 885 (1969). We reverse.

The requirement that guilt of a criminal charge be established by proof beyond a reasonable doubt dates at least from our early years as a Nation. The "demand for a higher degree of persuasion in criminal cases was recurrently expressed from ancient times, [though] its crystallization into the formula 'beyond a reasonable doubt' seems to have occurred as late as 1798. It is now accepted in common law jurisdictions as the measure of persuasion by which the prosecution must convince the trier of all the essential elements of guilt." C. McCormick, Evidence § 321, pp. 681-682 (1954); see also 9 J. Wigmore, Evidence § 2497 (3d ed. 1940). Although virtually unanimous adherence to the reasonable-doubt standard in common-law jurisdictions may not conclusively establish it as a requirement of due process, such adherence does "reflect a profound judgment about the way in which law should be enforced and justice administered." *Duncan* v. *Louisiana,* 391 U.S. 145, 155, 45 OhioOp.(2d) 198, 203 (1968).

Expressions in many opinions of this Court indicate that it has long been assumed that proof of a criminal charge beyond a reasonable doubt is constitutionally required. See, for example, *Miles* v. *United States,* 103 U.S. 304, 312 (1881); *Davis* v. *United States,* 160 U.S. 469, 488 (1895); *Holt* v. *United States,* 218 U.S. 245, 253 (1910); *Wilson* v. *United States,* 232 U.S. 563, 569-570 (1914); *Brinegar* v. *United States,* 338 U.S. 160, 174 (1949); *Leland* v. *Oregon,* 343 U.S. 790, 795 (1952); *Holland* v. *United States,* 348 U.S. 121, 138 (1954); *Speiser* v. *Randall,* 357 U.S. 513, 525-526 (1958). Cf. *Coffin* v. *United States,* 156 U.S. 432 (1895). Mr. Justice Frankfurter stated that "[i]t is the duty of the Government to establish . . . guilt beyond a reasonable doubt. This notion—basic in our law and rightly one of the boasts of a free society—is a requirement and a safeguard of due process of law in the historic, procedural content of 'due process.'" *Leland* v. *Oregon, supra,* at 802-803 (dissenting opinion). In a similar vein, the Court said in *Brinegar* v. *United States, supra,* at 174, that "[g]uilt in a criminal case must be proved beyond a reasonable doubt and by evidence confined to that which long experience in the common-law tradition, to some extent embodied in the Constitution, has crystallized into rules of evidence consistent with that standard. These rules are historically grounded rights of our system, developed to safeguard men from dubious and unjust convictions, with resulting forfeitures of life, liberty and property." *Davis* v. *United States, supra,* at 488, stated that the requirement is implicit in "constitutions . . . [which]

recognize the fundamental principles that are deemed essential for the protection of life and liberty." In *Davis* a murder conviction was reversed because the trial judge instructed the jury that it was their duty to convict when the evidence was equally balanced regarding the sanity of the accused. This Court said: "On the contrary, he is entitled to an acquittal of the specific crime charged if upon all the evidence there is reasonable doubt whether he was capable in law of committing crime. . . . No man should be deprived of his life under the forms of law unless the jurors who try him are able, upon their consciences, to say that the evidence before them . . . is sufficient to show beyond a reasonable doubt the existence of every fact necessary to constitute the crime charged." *Id.*, at 484, 493.

The reasonable-doubt standard plays a vital role in the American scheme of criminal procedure. It is a prime instrument for reducing the risk of convictions resting on factual error. The standard provides concrete substance for the presumption of innocence—that bedrock "axiomatic and elementary" principle whose "enforcement lies at the foundation of the administration of our criminal law." *Coffin v. United States, supra,* at 453. As the dissenters in the New York Court of Appeals observed, and we agree, "a person accused of a crime . . . would be at a severe disadvantage, a disadvantage amounting to a lack of fundamental fairness, if he could be adjudged guilty and imprisoned for years on the strength of the same evidence as would suffice in a civil case." 24 N.Y.2d, at 205, 247 N.E.2d, at 259.

The requirement of proof beyond a reasonable doubt has this vital role in our criminal procedure for cogent reasons. The accused during a criminal prosecution has at stake interests of immense importance, both because of the possibility that he may lose his liberty upon conviction and because of the certainty that he would be stigmatized by the conviction. Accordingly, a society that values the good name and freedom of every individual should not condemn a man for commission of a crime when there is reasonable doubt about his guilt. As we said in *Speiser v. Randall, supra,* at 525-526: "There is always in litigation a margin of error, representing error in factfinding, which both parties must take into account. Where one party has at stake an interest of transcending value—as a criminal defendant his liberty—this margin of error is reduced as to

him by the process of placing on the other party the burden of
... persuading the factfinder at the conclusion of the trial of his
guilt beyond a reasonable doubt. Due process commands that no
man shall lose his liberty unless the Government has borne the
burden of ... convincing the factfinder of his guilt." To this end,
the reasonable-doubt standard is indispensable, for it "impresses
on the trier of fact the necessity of reaching a subjective state of
certitude of the facts in issue." Dorsen & Rezneck, In Re Gault
and the Future of Juvenile Law, 1 Family Law Quarterly, No. 4,
pp. 1, 26 (1967).

Moreover, use of the reasonable-doubt standard is indispensable
to command the respect and confidence of the community in applications of the criminal law. It is critical that the moral force
of the criminal law not be diluted by a standard of proof that leaves
people in doubt whether innocent men are being condemned. It
is also important in our free society that every individual going
about his ordinary affairs have confidence that his government
cannot adjudge him guilty of a criminal offense without convincing
a proper factfinder of his guilt with unmost certainty.

Lest there remain any doubt about the constitutional stature
of the reasonable-doubt standard, we explicitly hold that the Due
Process Clause protects the accused against conviction except
upon proof beyond a reasonable doubt of every fact necessary
to constitute the crime with which he is charged.

We turn to the question whether juveniles, like adults, are
constitutionally entitled to proof beyond a reasonable doubt when
they are charged with violation of a criminal law. The same considerations that demand extreme caution in factfinding to protect the
innocent adult apply as well to the innocent child. We do not
find convincing the contrary arguments of the New York Court
of Appeals. Gault rendered untenable much of the reasoning relied
upon by that court to sustain the constitutionality of § 744(b). The
Court of Appeals indicated that a delinquency adjudication "is not
a 'conviction' (§ 781); that it affects no right or privilege, including
the right to hold public office or to obtain a license (§ 782); and
a cloak of protective confidentiality is thrown around all the proceedings (§§ 783-784)." 24 N.Y.2d, at 200, 247 N.E.2d, at 255-256. The court said further: "The delinquency status is not made
a crime; and the proceedings are not criminal. There is, hence, no

deprivation of due process in the statutory provision [challenged by appellant]. . . ." 24 N.Y.2d, at 203, 247 N.E.2d, at 257. In effect the Court of Appeals distinguished the proceedings in question here from a criminal prosecution by use of what *Gault* called the " 'civil' label-of-convenience which has been attached to juvenile proceedings." 387 U.S., at 50. But *Gault* expressly rejected that distinction as a reason for holding the Due Process Clause inapplicable to a juvenile proceeding. 387 U.S., at 50-51. The Court of Appeals also attempted to justify the preponderance standard on the related ground that juvenile proceedings are designed "not to punish, but to save the child." 24 N.Y.2d, at 197, 247 N.E.2d, at 254. Again, however, *Gault* expressly rejected this justification. 387 U.S., at 27, 40 OhioOp.(2d), at 389. We made clear in that decision that civil labels and good intentions do not themselves obviate the need for criminal due process safeguards in juvenile courts, for "[a] proceeding where the issue is whether the child will be found to be 'delinquent' and subjected to the loss of his liberty for years is comparable in seriousness to a felony prosecution." *Id.*, at 36.

Nor do we perceive any merit in the argument that to afford juveniles the protection of proof beyond a reasonable doubt would risk destruction of beneficial aspects of the juvenile process. Use of the reasonable-doubt standard during the adjudicatory hearing will not disturb New York's policies that a finding that a child has violated a criminal law does not constitute a criminal conviction, that such a finding does not deprive the child of his civil rights, and that juvenile proceedings are confidential. Nor will there be any effect on the informality, flexibility, or speed of the hearing at which the factfinding takes place. And the opportunity during the post-adjudicatory or dispositional hearing for a wide-ranging review of the child's social history and for his individualized treatment will remain unimpaired. Similarly, there will be no effect on the procedures distinctive to juvenile proceedings that are employed prior to the adjudicatory hearing.

The Court of Appeals observed that "a child's best interest is not necessarily, or even probably, promoted if he wins in the particular inquiry which may bring him to the juvenile court." 24 N.Y.2d, at 199, 247 N.E.2d, at 255. It is true, of course, that the juvenile may be engaging in a general course of conduct inimical to his welfare that calls for judicial intervention. But that intervention cannot take the form of subjecting the child to the stigma of a finding that he violated a criminal law and to the possibility of institutional confinement on proof insufficient to convict him were he an adult.

We conclude, as we concluded regarding the essential due process safeguards applied in *Gault*, that the observance of the standard of proof beyond a reasonable doubt "will not compel the States to abandon or displace any of the substantive benefits of the juvenile process." *Gault, supra,* at 21.

Finally, we reject the Court of Appeals' suggestion that there is, in any event, only a "tenuous difference" between the reasonable-doubt and preponderance standards. The suggestion is singularly unpersuasive. In this very case, the trial judge's ability to distinguish between the two standards enabled him to make a finding of guilt that he conceded he might not have made under the standard of proof beyond a reasonable doubt. Indeed, the trial judge's action evidences the accuracy of the observation of commentators that "the preponderance test is susceptible to the misinterpretation that is calls on the trier of fact merely to perform an abstract weighing of the evidence in order to determine which side has produced the greater quantum, without regard to its effect in convincing his mind of the truth of the proposition asserted." Dorsen & Rezneck, *supra,* at 26-27.

In sum, the constitutional safeguard of proof beyond a reasonable doubt is as much required during the adjudicatory stage of a delinquency proceeding as are those constitutional safeguards applied in *Gault*—notice of charges, right to counsel, the rights of confrontation and examination, and the privilege against self-incrimination. We therefore hold, in agreement with Chief Judge Fuld in dissent in the Court of Appeals, "that, where a 12-year-old child is charged with an act of stealing which renders him liable to confinement for as long as six years, then, as a matter of due process . . . the case against him must be proved beyond a reasonable doubt." 24 N.Y.2d, at 207, 247 N.E.2d, at 260.

Reversed.

Concurring and dissenting opinions not included.

JACK HENRY SMITH v. S. LAMONT SMITH
United States Court of Appeals
Fifth Circuit.
December 14, 1971.
Rehearing and Rehearing En Banc Denied
Feb. 1, 1972.
454 F.2d 572

Before THORNBERRY, MORGAN and CLARK, Circuit Judges.
THORNBERRY, Circuit Judge:

This is an appeal from the district court's determination on petition for habeas corpus that the Georgia alibi charge violates due process standards, 321 F.Supp. 482.

On March 12, 1969, petitioner was convicted by a jury of two counts of burglary. During the trial, petitioner asserted the impossibility of his guilt based on alibi. Petitioner, along with three other witnesses, testified that he was in Dallas, Texas at the same time the crime was committed in Atlanta, Georgia. In rebuttal, the State introduced into evidence prior inconsistent statements by both petitioner and his alibi witnesses, along with other facts tending to discredit the witnesses' credibility. The issue of petitioner's presence at the scene of the crime was thus hotly contested at the trial.

The trial judge, in accordance with settled Georgia law, charged the jury as follows:

> He contends and sets up his defense under the law what is known as an alibi and I charge you alibi as a defense involves the impossibility of the accused's presence at the scene of the offense at the time of its commission and the range of the evidence in respect to time and place must be such as reasonably to exclude the possibility of presence. Alibi as a defense must be established to the reasonable satisfaction of the jury and must be such as reasonably to exclude the possibility of the presence of the defendant at the scene of the offense at the time of its commission. When so established to the reasonable satisfaction of the jury, the jury should acquit. Any evidence in the nature of an alibi should be considered by the jury in connection with all other evidence in the case and if in doing so the jury should entertain a reasonable doubt as to the guilt of the accused they should acquit.

The law of alibi consists of two branches. The first is to overcome proof of guilt strong enough to exclude all reasonable doubt, the onus is on the accused to verify his alleged alibi, not beyond reasonable doubt, but to the reasonable satisfaction of the jury. The second is that, nevertheless, any evidence whatever of alibi is to be considered on the general case with the rest of the testimony, and if a reasonable doubt of guilt be raised by the evidence as a whole, the doubt must be given in favor of innocence.

The State contends that the Georgia charge, considered in its entirety, did not shift the burden of proving alibi to the defendant. Moreover, it argues that any possibility of prejudice was cured by the trial court's further instruction that the burden was on the State to prove beyond a reasonable doubt all essential elements of the crime, which necessarily included the element of presence.

Petitioner's due process contention depends primarily upon the application of a number of Eighth Circuit cases dealing with the Iowa alibi charge.

In the first applicable case, Johnson v. Bennett, 8th Cir. 1967, 386 F.2d 677, the Iowa court had charged the jury that the defendant had the burden to prove his alibi defense by a preponderance of the evidence. The trial court, however, had added:

> The evidence upon this point is to be considered by the jury, and if upon the whole case including the evidence of an alibi, there is a reasonable doubt of defendant's guilt, you should acquit him.

386 F.2d at 682.

The Eighth Circuit panel, finding no merit to defendant's due process contention, stated:

> . . . [I]n other instructions the court stressed the presumption of innocence, reasonable doubt and the necessity of the State proving all essential elements of the case beyond a reasonable doubt. It is difficult to say on the basis of the instructions as a whole that the defendant was deprived of any substantial constitutional right.

386 F.2d at 682.

The Supreme Court immediately granted certiorari. Johnson v. Bennett, 390 U.S. 1002, 88 S.Ct. 1247, 20 L.Ed.2d 102 (1968). Before final determination of *Johnson,* however, the Eighth Circuit went en banc to consider Stump v. Bennett, 8th Cir. 1968, 398 F.2d 111, involving the same Iowa charge:

Before you can acquit the defendant by reason of this defense [alibi] you must find that he has established it by a preponderance or greater weight of the evidence bearing upon it.

398 F.2d at 115.

The Eighth Circuit, with the three members of the *Johnson* panel dissenting, found that the Iowa charge, in spite of the added reasonable doubt instruction, tended to burden the defendant with proving that he was not present at the scene of the crime. Such a burden of proof on an essential element of the crime was found to violate due process standards. The Court reasoned:

By shifting the burden of proof to a person who claims to have been elsewhere at the time of the crime, there is created an irrational and arbitrary presumption of guilt. It arises not by reason of a proof of fact from which a fair inference might be drawn but from the mere happening that the defendant offers testimony in an attempt to establish innocence. When this occurs, unless the defendant can succeed in overbalancing the state's evidence, the jury is expressly told he cannot be acquitted by reason of his sole claim to innocence. . . . [T]his presumption would conflict with the overriding presumption of innocence with which the law endows the accused and which extends to every element of the crime. . . . [I]ncriminating presumptions are not to be improvised by the judiciary.

398 F.2d at 116.

Moreover, the Court went on to state:

Beyond violating petitioner's right to have the state assume the burden to prove (beyond a reasonable doubt) his presence at the crime, we think the Iowa instruction and its judicial application is patently offensive in other ways to the defendant's basic constitutional rights. . . . [O]nly when the defendant seeks to produce witnesses to corroborate his non-presence [does] the Iowa rule incongruously penalize him with the burden of persuasion as to his non-presence. . . . Thus an innocent person, whose only refuge of innocence may be proof of his non-presence and non-participation in the crime itself, must risk this greater burden because he tries to bring witnesses forward to substantiate his story. He must choose between the exercise of two constitutionally guaranteed rights. He must surrender either the right to offer corroborative evidence of his innocence or else his traditional

right to have the state assume the burden of proving his guilt beyond a reasonable doubt. Under the Iowa rule he cannot have both. Such a procedure can have no other purpose than to "chill the assertion of constitutional rights by penalizing those who choose to exercise them. . . ." This is an impermissible burden.
398 F.2d at 120. . . .

We note a similar struggle in the decisional process of Georgia courts in dealing with the alibi charge at issue here. Shortly after the Eighth Circuit decisions, the Georgia Appeals Court held the charge involved in the instant case unconstitutional on the basis of *Stump* and *Johnson*. Parham v. State, 120 Ga. App. 723, 171 S.E.2d 911 (1969). The Georgia Supreme Court, however, in Thornton v. State, 226 Ga. 837, 178 S.E.2d 193 (1970), held the Georgia charge to be distinguishable on its face from the Iowa charge and refused to follow *Parham*.

Earlier Georgia cases are often confusing and similarly irreconcilable in their interpretation, application, and assessment of the effect of the alibi charge. The Georgia alibi doctrine was first enunciated in Harrison v. State, 83 Ga. 129, 9 S.E. 542 (1889), wherein the Georgia Supreme Court approved the following charge:

Well, now, the next thing is as to the strength of the evidence of *alibi*,—what that evidence (considering the credibility of the witnesses, and what the witnesses testified to) amounts to. The laws says that it must outweigh the evidence introduced on the part of the state, provided, as I have charged you, if the state's evidence is sufficiently strong, without more, to produce a conviction in your minds of the guilt of the prisoner beyond a reasonable doubt. In order to remove that,—the *alibi,—the testimony sustaining the alibi, in the judgment of the jury, should outweigh or preponderate over the evidence for the state*. (Emphasis added)

9 S.E. at 543. . . .

More recently, in Porter v. State, 200 Ga. 246, 36 S.E.2d 794 (1946), the Georgia Supreme Court has sustained this interpretation of the charge. In *Porter* the court, citing *Harrison* and *Bone*, stated:

The defendant by his statement and witnesses introduced in his behalf sought to establish an alibi. "Alibi, as a defense, involves the impossibility of the accused's presence at the scene of the offense at the time of its commission; and the range of the evidence, in respect to the time and place, must

be such as reasonably to exclude the possibility of presence."
. . . The burden is on the accused to sustain his defense of alibi to the reasonable satisfaction of the jury *in order to overcome proof of his guilt of the crime with which he is charged.*

The jury was authorized to find that the defendant has not established his alibi, they being the judges of the credibility of the witnesses and of the weight to be given the defendant's statement, and that he had *not overcome the prima facie case made by the State under each count of the indictment, and accordingly to return a verdict of guilty as charged in each count.* (Emphasis added)

Periodic criticism of the charge involved here can be found throughout the instruction's stormy history In Bone v. State, *supra*, the court noted:

. . . [I]t would be logical, I think, that the facts of an alibi should come into the case like any other matters of defense, to be considered the same way, and affect the mind of the jury only as they believe the truth to be. Being a part of the evidence, these facts should be considered with the other evidence in the case, and, after due consideration of the evidence as a whole, the defendant should have the benefit of all reasonable doubt as to his guilt. However this may be, the law of this state is settled as above set out, and I follow as it is written.

30 S.E. at 848. . . .

The State contends, as did the Georgia Supreme Court in *Parham*, that the Iowa alibi charge, found to be constitutionally impermissible by the Eighth Circuit, is distinguishable on its face from the Georgia charge in two respects. First, the Iowa charge required a preponderance of the evidence on the alibi issue; whereas the Georgia charge only requires that the jury be "reasonably satisfied." Secondly, the Iowa charge was mandatory, *requiring* the jury to find no alibi in the absence of a preponderance of proof from the defendant; whereas Georgia gives its juries a "choice" between two burdens of proof.

We can see no significant distinction between the two charges. Although it is possible that the Georgia charge does not require a preponderance of the evidence, the fact of which even Georgia courts are not convinced, we find the actual standard utilized to be immaterial. It is enough to say that it is clear that Georgia defendants have *some* burden on their alibi defense. See Bone v. State, *supra*. If this were not so, it would be difficult to discern any reason for the courts' giving the charge in the first place. See Green, Georgia Law of Evidence, § 21, at 75-77. No such burden can be sustained under our Constitution. Evidence of alibi should come into a case like any other evidence and must be submitted to the jury for consideration of whether the evidence as a whole on the issue of presence proves the defendant's guilt beyond a reasonable doubt. See Falgout v. United States, 5th Cir. 1922, 279 F. 513.

We likewise find the Georgia instruction to be no less mandatory than the Iowa charge. Georgia instructs, "Alibi as a defense *must* be established" to the jury's satisfaction; whereas Iowa charged, "Before you can acquit . . . by reason of this defense you *must* find" by a preponderance of the evidence. The difference in the obligation thus imposed is minimal at best, and the effect of the respective charges on the jury is most assuredly identical. We hasten to point out that in both the Iowa and Georgia cases, the jury was further instructed to consider *all* the evidence, including that of alibi, in determining the guilt of defendants beyond a reasonable doubt. In both states, therefore, the jury had a "choice" of applying two conflicting burdens of proof. A jury may not, however, have such an option to ignore the reasonable doubt test on the issue of presence in a criminal prosecution. The Constitution, and more specifically the due process clause of the Fourteenth Amendment, permits of no such "choice."

We have little doubt that the Georgia charge, by affirmatively presenting such an option to the jury, caused confusion in the instant case and created a substantial likelihood of the jury's incorrectly placing the burden of proof on the petitioner much to his prejudice. As noted by the Eighth Circuit in *Stump*, this Court cannot determine with precision where the jury in any particular case placed the burden of proof. This does not prevent this Court from using its collective common sense in the instant case. Accordingly, we must presume that prejudice resulted.

This Court recognizes that a criminal defendant is not entitled to a perfect trial under our Constitution. Lutwak v. United States, 344 U.S. 604, 73 S.Ct. 481, 97 L.Ed. 593 (1953). Habeas corpus will not lie to challenge a jury charge in the absence of a clear denial of due process so as to render the trial fundamentally unfair. Higgins v.

Wainwright, 5th Cir. 1970, 424 F.2d 177; McDonald v. Sheriff of Palm Beach County, Florida, 5th Cir. 1970, 422 F.2d 839. In light of these principles, there is yet no doubt that a shift in the burden of proof of an essential element of the crime does rise to constitutional proportions and renders the trial fundamentally unfair. The presumption of innocence and the harsh burden of proof placed on the State in criminal prosecutions are two of the oldest and most fundamental rights protected by our Constitution. See, e. g., Coffin v. United States, 156 U.S. 432, 15 S.Ct. 394, 39 L.Ed. 481 (1895). They purport to protect all citizens from the threat of punishment by mistake. They are therefore far too important and fundamental to be classified as less than constitutionally protected. See Deutch v. United States, 367 U.S. 456, 81 S.Ct. 1587, 6 L.Ed.2d 963 (1961); Speiser v. Randall, 357 U.S. 513, 78 S.Ct. 1332, 2 L.Ed.2d 1460 (1958); Morrison v. California, 291 U.S. 82, 54 S.Ct. 281, 78 L.Ed. 664 (1934); Cummings v. Missouri, 4 Wall. 277, 18 L.Ed. 356 (1866).

With all due deference to the State of Georgia and the charge used there since 1889, we cannot give constitutional sanction to a doctrine, no matter how ancient, which serves no useful function whatsoever and which creates the clear probability that a defendant may be deprived of one of our most cherished rights.

Accordingly, we affirm.

Cases relating to **Chapter 6**

DIRECT AND CIRCUMSTANTIAL EVIDENCE

UNITED STATES v. ROY ARTHUR NELSON
United States Court of Appeals
Ninth Circuit.
Nov. 20, 1969.
419 F.2d 1237

BROWNING, Circuit Judge:

Roy Arthur Nelson and Frank Brewton were indicted for robbery of a federally-insured institution in violation of 18 U.S.C. § 2113(a) (1964). Brewton was found incompetent to stand trial. Nelson was tried separately and convicted. He has appealed on three grounds, all of which relate to the use of circumstantial evidence to secure his conviction.

The government offered direct evidence of the following facts. Brewton entered a bank and presented a teller with a written demand for money. The teller handed Brewton $627 in currency, including five marked $20 bills. Meanwhile, an unidentified person was observed sitting in a car in an adjacent parking lot, racing the engine. Brewton fled from the bank to the waiting car and entered on the passenger side. The car immediately sped away. Shortly thereafter, a police officer, alerted to these incidents, observed the car, with two male occupants, at an intersection some blocks away. The car fled. The officer pursued at high speed. After a chase the car slowed down, defendant alighted from the driver's side and ran, and was captured. Currency in the amount of $125 was taken from his person. The car, driverless, crashed into a tree. Brewton emerged from the wreck, and was arrested after attempting to conceal $502 in currency, including the marked bills taken from the bank, under an adjacent building. Ten to fifteen minutes elapsed between the robbery of the bank and defendant's flight from the car.

Defendant asserts that since he was charged as a principal in the bank robbery rather than as an accessory after the fact, the government was required to prove that he had actual knowledge that Brewton intended to rob the bank. We assume, arguendo, that proof of precisely that specific knowledge was required.

Defendant contended below, and in this court, that such proof was lacking. He argued that if such knowledge could be inferred at all, the inference must be based upon the prior inference that he was the man waiting in the car while the robbery occurred—and such an "inference upon an inference" was precluded by law. Further, he argued that even if the jury were permitted to infer that he knowingly acted as the "get-away" driver, there was no evidence that he knew Brewton planned to commit a robbery, as distinguished from some other illegal act, or planned to rob the bank, and not one of the several stores and offices in the area, and that circumstantial evidence which does not "exclude every hypothesis but that of guilt" is insufficient as a matter of law.

The court denied a motion for acquittal based on these grounds, and rejected proposed instructions embodying the theories that a conviction could not be based upon inferences drawn from other inferences, or upon circumstances "which while consistent with guilt, are not inconsistent with innocence."

The legal theories upon which defendant relies, although clearly wrong, are repeatedly asserted in the trial courts of this circuit and in fruitless appeals to this court. It would be a boon to both the parties and the courts if they could be laid finally to rest.

For at least a third of a century this court has rejected the notion that it is improper to infer a fact at issue from other facts which have been established by circumstantial evidence. E. K. Wood Lumber Co. v. Anderson, 81 F.2d 161, 166 (9th Cir. 1936); Ross v. United States, 103 F.2d 600, 606 (9th Cir. 1939); Fegles Construction Co. v. McLaughlin Construction Co., 205 F.2d 637, 639-640 (9th Cir. 1953); Toliver v. United States, 224 F.2d 742, 745 (9th Cir. 1955); Medrano v. United States, 315 F.2d 361, 362 (9th Cir. 1963); Devore v. United States, 368 F.2d 396, 399 (9th Cir. 1966). As Professor Wigmore has said, "[t]here is no such orthodox rule; nor can be. If there were, hardly a single trial could be adequately presented." 1 Wigmore, Evidence, § 41, at 435 (3rd ed. 1940).

The error in this discredited doctrine is clearly reflected in the defendant's formulation: it assumes that a fact established by circumstantial evidence is not a "proven fact." But as we have repeatedly said, circumstantial evidence is not inherently less probative than direct evidence. Under some conditions it may even be more reliable, as this case illustrates.

The intermediate fact at issue here was whether defendant was the driver of the car waiting in the parking lot. That fact was established to a moral certainty by circumstances proven by uncontradicted and unquestioned testimony. Unless defendant was Brewton's accomplice waiting in the get-away car, it is all but inconceivable that he would have been driving that car with Brewton as a passenger a few minutes after Brewton ran from the bank to the car and was driven from the scene; that he would have had part of the stolen currency in his possession, and Brewton the rest; and that upon seeing the police officer he would have driven away at high speed, and later fled from the officer on foot.

If none of this circumstantial evidence had been available and the only evidence offered had been a courtroom identification of the defendant by a witness who had a fleeting glimpse of the driver as the car stood in the parking lot, the truth of the fact that defendant was that man would not have been established with equal certainty.

Of course either direct or circumstantial evidence may fail to prove the fact in issue—direct evidence because the credibility of the witness is destroyed; circumstantial evidence for that reason, or because the inference from the proven circumstances to the fact in issue is too speculative, or remote. Whether such a failure has occurred is an appropriate inquiry in any case—be the evidence direct, circumstantial, or both. But since under some conditions circumstantial evidence may be equally or more reliable than direct evidence, it would be wholly irrational to impose an absolute bar upon the use of circumstantial evidence to prove any fact, including a fact from which another fact is to be inferred.

The trial court therefore properly refused to instruct the jury that "one inference may not be based upon another inference to support a conclusion of fact." It would be error for the jury, the trial court, or this court, to apply such an arbitrary formula in the performance of their respective roles in the fact-finding process.

It is also clear that the court properly rejected defendant's proposed instruction embodying a variation on the theme that circumstantial evidence must exclude every hypothesis but that of guilt.

This much, at least, is settled by Holland v. United States, 348 U.S. 121, 75 S.Ct. 127, 99 L.Ed. 150 (1955). What the *Holland* court said is brief, and well worth repeating in full:

"The petitioners assail the refusal of the trial judge to instruct that where the Government's evidence is circumstantial it must be such as to exclude every reasonable hypothesis other than that of guilt. There is some support for this type of instruction in the lower court decisions, Garst v. United States, 4 Cir., 180 F. 339, 343; Anderson v. United States, 5 Cir., 30 F.2d 485-487; Stutz v. United States, 5 Cir., 47 F.2d 1029, 1030; Hanson v. United States, 6 Cir., 208 F.2d 914, 916, but the better rule is that where the jury is properly instructed on the standards for reasonable doubt, such an additional instruction on circumstantial evidence is confusing and incorrect, United States v. Austin-Bagley Corp., 2 Cir., 31 F.2d 229, 234, cert. denied, 279 U.S. 863, 49 S.Ct. 479, 73 L.Ed. 1002; United States v. Becker, 2 Cir., 62 F.2d 1007, 1010; 1 Wigmore, Evidence (3d ed.), §§ 25-26.

Circumstantial evidence in this respect is intrinsically no different from testimonial evidence. Admittedly, circumstantial evidence may in some cases point to a wholly incorrect result. Yet this is equally true of testimonial evidence. In both instances, a jury is asked to weigh the chances that the evidence correctly points to guilt against the possibility of inaccuracy or ambiguous inference. In both, the jury must use its experience with people and events in weighing the probabilities. If the jury is convinced beyond a reasonable doubt, we can require no more." 348 U.S. at 139-140, 75 S.Ct. at 137 (emphasis added).

The Supreme Court did more than reject the particular instruction before it; it clearly stated that *no* instruction is to be given distinguishing the manner in which direct and circumstantial evidence are to be weighed. Since circumstantial and testimonial evidence are indistinguishable so far as the jury's fact-finding function is concerned, all that is to be required of the jury is that it weigh *all* of the evidence, direct or circumstantial, against the standard of reasonable doubt.

Our holdings are in accord with this interpretation of *Holland*. Mull v. United States, 402 F.2d 571, 575 (9th Cir. 1968); Ramirez v. United States, 350 F.2d 306, 307-308 (9th Cir. 1965); Armstrong v. United States, 327 F.2d 189, 194 (9th Cir. 1964); Strangway v. United States, 312 F.2d 283, 285 (9th Cir. 1963). Indeed, this was the rule in this circuit prior to *Holland*. Samuel v. United States, 169 F.2d 787, 791 (9th Cir. 1948); McCoy v. United States, 169 F.2d 776, 784 (9th Cir. 1948); *see also* Penosi v. United States, 206 F.2d 529, 530 (9th Cir. 1953).

Thus the trial court properly instructed the jury that "the law makes no distinction between direct and circumstantial evidence but simply requires that the jury be satisfied of the defendant's guilt beyond a reasonable doubt from all the evidence in the case," including "such reasonable inferences as seem justified, in the light of your own experience." Under *Holland* and the uniform decisions of this court, no additional instruction was required, and none would have been proper. The contrary dictum in Matthews v. United States, 394 F.2d 104, 105 (9th Cir. 1968), must therefore be disregarded. . . .

The second question is that specifically raised by the defendant, namely, whether the court is also to inquire whether the evidence "excludes every hypothesis but that of guilt."

Precisely as put, the test is unquestionably wrong. Although we have frequently stated the rule as defendant does, it has never been held that the evidence must exclude "*every* hypothesis," as distinguished from every reasonable hypothesis, of innocence. Furthermore, in applying the test, the question is not whether the court itself would find that every reasonable hypothesis of innocence had been excluded, but rather whether the jurors could reasonably arrive at that conclusion.

Thus, as first stated in this court in Stoppelli v. United States, 183 F.2d 391, 393 (9th Cir. 1950), the test was as follows:

"The testimony * * * was sufficient to go to the jury if its nature was such that reasonable minds could differ as to whether inferences other than guilt could be drawn from it. It is not for us to say that the evidence was insufficient because we, or any of us, believe that inferences inconsistent with guilt may be drawn from it. To say that would make us triers of the fact. We may say that the evidence is insufficient to sustain the verdict only if we can conclude *as a matter of law* that reasonable minds, as triers of the fact, must be in agreement that reasonable hypotheses other than guilt could be drawn from the evidence."

This formulation, commonly condensed to "whether 'reasonable minds could find the evidence excludes every hypothesis but that of guilt,'" appears frequently in our opinions.

Yet this is precisely the standard which was rejected by the Supreme Court in Holland v. United States, *supra*, 348 U.S. at 139,

75 S.Ct. 127, as a guide for the jury, on the ground that it was "confusing and incorrect." *Id.* at 140, 75 S.Ct. 127. Our opinions demonstrate that it is equally confusing as a guide for the reviewing court. Moreover, if it is "incorrect" as an instruction defining the jury's duty, it must be equally "incorrect" as a test for determining whether the jury has performed its duty within the limits fixed by the instructions. Accordingly, most courts have held that its use as a test of the sufficiency of the evidence on review is inconsistent with *Holland*.

The "reasonable hypothesis" test was formulated for the evaluation of circumstantial evidence; it is often referred to as the "circumstantial evidence test." *See, e. g.*, Comment, Sufficiency of Circumstantial Evidence in a Criminal Case, 55 Colum.L.Rev. 549 (1955). As we have noted, the Supreme Court rejected the test in *Holland* on the premise that there is no essential difference in the mental processes required of the jury in weighing direct and circumstantial evidence. As to both, "the jury must use its experience with people and events in weighing the probabilities. If the jury is convinced beyond a reasonable doubt, we can require no more." *Holland*, 348 U.S. at 140, 75 S.Ct. at 138.

The key word is "probabilities." The jury cannot determine that a proposition is true or false, but only that it is more or less probable. Guilt "is proved beyond a reasonable doubt if it is proved not only to be more probable than its contradictory but to be much more probable than its contradictory." Adler & Michael, The Trial of an Issue of Fact I, 34 Colum.L.Rev. 1224, 1256 (1934). The required degree of probability is reached if the jury is free of "the kind of doubt that would make a person hesitate to act" in the more serious and important affairs of his own life. Holland v. United States, *supra*, 348 U.S. at 140, 75 S.Ct. at 138.

It adds only an illusion of certainty, and is both misleading and wrong, to attempt to describe this broad exercise of practical judgment in abstract generalizations borrowed from the terminology of formal logic.

The "reasonable hypothesis" test does not reflect what juries and reviewing courts in reality do. Juries constantly convict, and the convictions are duly affirmed, on evidence upon which none would hesitate to act but which cannot be said to exclude as a matter of inexorable logic, every reasonable hypothetical consistent with innocence.

Moreover, the impression left by appellate court opinions is that the "reasonable hypothesis" standard may lead to serious departures from the proper appellate role in evaluating the sufficiency of evidence. Courts following the rule exhibit a noticeable tendency to divide the evidence into separate lines of proof, and analyze and test each line of proof independently of others rather than considering the evidence as an interrelated whole. The sufficiency of the evidence is often tested against theoretical and speculative possibilities not fairly raised by the record, and inferences are sometimes considered which, though entirely possible or even probable, are drawn from evidence which the jury may have disbelieved.

We affirm the denial of the motion for acquittal in this case because we are satisfied that the jurors reasonably could decide that they would not hesitate to act in their own serious affairs upon factual assumptions as probable as the conclusion that defendant planned and executed the robbery of the bank as a joint venture with Brewton in which each carried out a prearranged role.

Affirmed.

STATE v. SLAUGHTER

70 Wash.(2d) 935, 425 P.(2d) 876

Supreme Court of Washington.
March 30, 1967.

HALE, Judge.

The injury produced by a weapon may be more telling evidence of a crime than the weapon itself. Defendant doubts this truism and appeals his conviction of assault in the second degree because, although no weapon was found or introduced in evidence, the trial court had the jury answer a special interrogatory asking whether defendant had been armed with a deadly weapon.

Elizabeth Ruiz owned and managed the Miller Apartments at 1520½ Broadway, in Tacoma. Earl McFerrian worked for her around the place part of the time; other times when work was available he did farm labor. Both knew the defendant, Willie Tillman Slaughter, from his visits to the apartment house. Mrs. Ruiz said that Mr. Slaughter had been the cause of confusion and arguments whenever he came there. She had seen him in the apartment house about ten times within a month and a half, and had warned him to stay away or she would call the police.

Seeing him in the hallway again July 13, 1965, she went up to him, told him to leave, and, turning away, returned to her kitchen. Shortly thereafter, she heard a commotion in the hallway and the sound of someone falling. She went to her apartment doorway just in time to see the defendant leaving. She described it this way:

> Q. And when you went to your door there, what did you see? A. I seen a guy lying on the floor. I only thought he hit him but he was lying on the floor and Mr. Slaughter was standing up over him. Q. Did you say anything to Mr. Slaughter? A. Yes. I asked him what was wrong with him, was he losing his mind or was he crazy. Q. What did Mr. Slaughter say? A. He didn't say anything, he turned around and went down the steps.

The man she saw on the floor was Earl McFerrian. She said that defendant and McFerrian were the only two people present in the hallway at the time.

Mr. McFerrian testified that he noticed defendant and Mrs. Ruiz arguing; that he was in the lobby when Mrs. Ruiz walked away, leaving him and Slaughter in the hallway; that he asked Slaughter what was wrong; and that defendant, without warning, suddenly turned and struck him hard, knocking him down. As he went down, he fell against an upholstered armchair. When he got up, he was bleeding. Mrs. Ruiz called the police who, observing the blood and concluding that Mr. McFerrian had been cut on his right side and needed medical attention, had him taken to the hospital.

Dr. Paul Hageman, intern at the hospital, treated Mr. McFerrian on his arrival at the emergency room. He said that McFerrian had two lacerations across the front of his chest, an upper one two inches long just below the right nipple, and the other five inches long located down about the last rib. The cuts, he said, were neat, without jagged edges, resembling those made by a surgical knife or scalpel. He said that he sutured the two wounds. He stated they were not in a line with each other and were located so that two cutting motions would necessarily be required to inflict them—that is, whoever cut Mr. McFerrian had to strike twice. He stated further that, in his opinion, the two wounds were serious enough to cause great pain and suffering and even death.

Defendant, testifying in his own behalf, denied being present in the Miller Apartments that day, or participating in any way in an assault upon McFerrian. No knife or other sharply edged cutting instrument was found at the scene of the affray or shown to be in defendant's possession.

The prosecuting attorney for Pierce County charged the defendant by amended information with assault in the second degree under RCW 9.11.020(4), which, in pertinent part, states:

> Every person who, under circumstances not amounting to assault in the first degree—
>
> * * * * * *
>
> (4) Shall willfully assault another with a weapon or other instrument or thing likely to produce bodily harm * * *

Defendant now appeals the judgment and sentence of conviction entered upon a jury verdict of guilty. He challenges the sufficiency of the evidence to support the verdict because of the state's failure to produce a weapon and assigns error to the court's instruction and special interrogatory concerning a deadly weapon.

As to the first major point, we are unable to agree with defendant that the evidence was insufficient to support a conviction. In addition to the circumstantial evidence, we have the testimony of Mr. McFerrian that defendant struck him, knocked him down, and, although he did not see the weapon which produced them, the blows inflicted the wounds which required suturing and medical care. The sight of a blade in defendant's hand would have added little to the direct evidence that he struck his victim, knocked him down, and in so doing inflicted two cutting wounds. Viewed in the light of the argument between Mrs. Ruiz and defendant, followed immediately with her leaving the two men alone in the hallway, and the complete absence of any other evidence explaining or implying that the wounds could have been inflicted by another person, or by accident, we have proof of circumstances rivaling in persuasiveness direct evidence that the victim saw a weapon in defendant's hand when the blow was struck.

Indeed, the only circumstantial aspect of McFerrian's evidence was the short interval between his seeing and feeling of the blow and his seeing and feeling the wounds. The remainder of McFerrian's testimony gave direct evidence of what he saw, heard and felt with his own senses. Even if he were to accept defendant's view that all of the evidence must be regarded as circumstantial, we are of the opinion that the evidence falls within the rules governing proof of guilt by circumstantial evidence as set forth in State v. Courville, 63 Wash.2d 498, 387 P.2d 938 (1963) and 20 Am.Jur. Evidence § 1217 (1939), which requires that, in a conviction based on circumstantial evidence, such evidence not only must concur to show defendant guilty, and be consistent with a hypothesis of guilt, but also must be inconsistent with any other rational conclusion and exclude every other reasonable theory or hypothesis except that of guilt. It is the jury, under proper instructions, which makes the determination whether the circumstantial evidence excludes every reasonable hypothesis consistent with innocence. State v. Grenz, 26 Wash.2d 764, 175 P.2d 633 (1946). Neither State v. Lillie, 60 Wash. 200, 110 P. 801 (1910), nor State v. Donofrio, 141 Wash. 132, 250 P. 951 (1926), referred to by defendant, seem applicable to the present case although we apprehend those cases to correctly express the law.

Affirmed.

SPENCER v. TEXAS
385 U.S. 554, 17 L.Ed.(2d) 606, 87 S.Ct. 648.

United States Supreme Court.

Decided January 23, 1967.

Mr. Justice HARLAN delivered the opinion of the Court.

Texas, reflecting widely established policies in the criminal law of this country, has long had on its books so-called recidivist or habitual-criminal statutes. Their effect is to enhance the punishment of those found guilty of crime who are also shown to have been convicted of other crimes in the past. The three cases at hand challenge the procedures employed by Texas in the enforcement of such statutes.

Until recently, and at the time of the convictions before us, the essence of those procedures was that, through allegations in the indictment and the introduction of proof respecting a defendant's past convictions, the trial jury in the pending charge was fully informed of such previous derelictions, but was also charged by the court that such matters were not to be taken into account in assessing the defendant's guilt or innocence under the current indictment.

The facts in the cases now here are these. In Spencer (No. 68), the petitioner was indicted for murder, with malice, of his common-law wife. The indictment alleged that the defendant had previously been convicted of murder with malice, a factor which if proved would entitle the jury to sentence the defendant to death or to prison for not less than life under Texas Penal Code, Art. 64, note 1, supra, whereas if the prior conviction was not proved the jury could fix the penalty at death or a prison term of not less than two years, see Texas Penal Code, Art. 1257. Spencer made timely objections to the reading to the jury of that portion of the indictment, and objected as well to the introduction of evidence to show his prior conviction. The jury was charged that if it found that Spencer had maliciously killed the victim, and that he had previously been convicted of murder with malice, the jury was to "assess his punishment at death or confinement in the penitentiary for life." The jury was instructed as well that it should not consider the prior conviction as any evidence of the defendant's guilt on the charge on which he was being tried. Spencer was found guilty and sentenced to death.

In Bell (No. 69), the petitioner was indicted for robbery, and the indictment alleged that he had been previously convicted of bank robbery in the United States District Court for the Southern District of Texas. Bell moved to quash the indictment on the ground, similar to that in Spencer, that the allegation and reading to the jury of a prior offense was prejudicial and would deprive him of a fair trial. Similar objections were made to the offer of documentary evidence to prove the prior conviction. The court's charge to the jury stated that the prior conviction should not be considered in passing upon the issue of guilt or innocence on the primary charge. The sentencing procedure in this non-capital case was somewhat different from that in Spencer. The jury was instructed that if it found the defendant guilty only of the present robbery charge, it could fix his sentence at not less than five years nor more than life. See Texas Penal Code, Art. 1408. But if it found that Bell had also been previously convicted as alleged in the indictment, it should bring in a verdict of guilty of robbery by assault and a further finding that the allegations "charging a final conviction for the offense of bank robbery are true." The jury so found, and the judge fixed punishment, set by law for such a prior offender, at life imprisonment in the penitentiary. See Texas Penal Code, Art. 62, note 1, supra.

The Reed case (No. 70), involving a third-offender prosecution for burglary, see Texas Penal Code, Art. 63, note 1, supra, entailed the same practice as followed in Bell.

The common and sole constitutional claim made in these cases is that Texas' use of prior convictions in the current criminal trial of each petitioner was so egregiously unfair upon the issue of guilt or innocence as to offend the provisions of the Fourteenth Amendment that no state shall "deprive any person of life, liberty, or property, without due process of law * * *." We took these cases for review, 382 U.S. 1022, 1023, 1025, 86 S.Ct. 649, 15 L.Ed.(2d) 537, 538, 539, because the courts of appeals have divided on the issue. For reasons now to follow we affirm the judgments below.

The road to decision, it seems to us, is clearly indicated both by what the petitioners in these cases do not contend and by the course of the authorities in closely related fields. No claim is made here that recidivist statutes are themselves unconstitutional, nor could there be under our cases. Such statutes and other enhanced sentence laws, and procedures designed to implement their underlying policies, have been enacted in all the states, and by the federal government as well. See e.g., 18 U.S.C. Section 2114 (1964 ed.), Fed.Rules Crim. Proc. 32 (c) (2); D.C. Code Section 22-104 (1961 ed.). Such statutes, though not in the precise procedural circumstances here involved, have been sustained in this Court on several occasions against contentions that they violate constitutional strictures dealing with double jeopardy, ex post facto laws, cruel and unusual punishment, due process, equal protection, and privileges and immunities. Moore v. State of Missouri, 159 U.S. 673, 16 S.Ct. 179, 40 L.Ed. 301; McDonald v. Commonwealth of Massachusetts, 180 U.S. 311, 21 S.Ct. 389, 45 L.Ed. 542; Graham v. State of West Virginia, 224 U.S. 616, 32 S.Ct. 583, 56 L.Ed. 917; Gryger v. Burke, 334 U.S. 728, 68 S.Ct. 1256, 92 L.Ed. 1683; Oyler v. Boles, 368 U.S. 448, 82 S.Ct. 501, 7 L.Ed.(2d) 446.

Nor is it contended that it is unconstitutional for the jury to assess the punishment to be meted out to a defendant in a capital or other criminal case, or to make findings as to whether there was or was not a prior conviction even though enhanced punishment is left to be imposed by the judge. The states have always been given wide leeway in dividing responsibility between judge and jury in criminal cases. Hallinger v. Davis, 146 U.S. 314, 13 S.Ct. 105, 36 L.Ed. 986; Maxwell v. Dow, 176 U.S. 581, 20 S.Ct. 448, 44 L.Ed. 597; cf. Chandler v. Fretag, 348 U.S. 3, 75 S.Ct. 1, 99 L.Ed. 4; Giaccio v. State of Pennsylvania, 382 U.S. 399, 405, n. 8, 86 S.Ct. 518, 522, 15 L.Ed.(2d) 447.

Petitioners do not even appear to be arguing that the Constitution is infringed if a jury is told of a defendant's prior crimes. The rules concerning evidence of prior offenses are complex, and vary from jurisdiction to jurisdiction, but they can be summarized broadly. Because such evidence is generally recognized to have potentiality for prejudice, it is usually excluded except when it is particularly probative in showing such things as intent. Nye & Nissen v. **United States, 336 U.S. 613, 69 S.Ct. 766, 93 L.Ed. 919;** Ellisor v. State, 162 Tex.Cr.R. 117, 282 S.W.(2d) 393, an element in the crime, Doyle v. State, 59 Tex.Cr.R. 39, 126 S.W. 1131, identity, Chavira v. State, 167 Tex.Cr.R. 197, 319 S.W.(2d) 115, malice, Moss v. State, Tex.Cr.App., 364 S.W.(2d) 389, motive, Moses v. State, 168 Tex. Cr.R. 409, 328 S.W.(2d) 885, a system of criminal activity, Haley v. State, 87 Tex.Cr.R. 519, 223 S.W. 202, or when the defendant has raised the issue of his character, Michelson v. United States, 335 U.S. 469, 69 S.Ct. 213, 93 L.Ed. 168; Perkins v. State, 152 Tex.Cr.R. 321, 213 S.W.(2d) 681, or when the defendant has testified and the state seeks to impeach his credibility, Giacone v. State, 124 Tex. Cr.R. 141, 62 S.W.(2d) 986.[7]

---

[7] These Texas cases reflect the rules prevailing in nearly all common-law jurisdictions. See generally McCormick on Evidence Sections 157-158 (1954 ed.); 1 Wharton's Criminal Evidence Sections 221-243 (Anderson ed., 1955); 1 Wigmore on Evidence Sections 215-218 (1964 ed.); Note, Other Crimes Evidence at Trial, 70 Yale L.J. 763 (1961). For the English rules, substantially similar, see Cross, Evidence 292-333 (2d ed. 1963). Recent commentators have criticized the rule of general exclusion, and have suggested a broader range of admissibility. Model Code of Evidence, Rule 311; Carter, The Admissibility of Evidence of Similar Facts, 69 L.Q.Rev. 80 (1953), 70 L.Q.Rev. 214 (1954); Note, Procedural Protections of the Criminal Defendant, 78 Harv.L.Rev. 426, 435-451 (1964). For the use of this type of evidence in continental jurisdictions, see Glanville Williams, The Proof of Guilt 181 (2d ed. 1958); 1 Wigmore, Supra, section 193.

Spencer v. Texas

Under Texas law the prior convictions of the defendants in the three cases before the Court today might have been admissible for any one or more of these universally accepted reasons. In all these situations, as under the recidivist statutes, the jury learns of prior crimes committed by the defendant, but the conceded possibility of prejudice is believed to be outweighed by the validity of the state's purpose in permitting introduction of the evidence. The defendants' interests are protected by limiting instructions, see Giacone v. State, supra, and by the discretion residing with the trial judge to limit or forbid the admission of particularly prejudicial evidence even though admissible under an accepted rule of evidence. See Spears v. State, 153 Tex.Cr.R. 14, 216 S.W.(2d) 812; 1 Wigmore on Evidence Section 29a (1940 ed.); Uniform Rule of Evidence 45; Model Code of Evidence, Rule 303.

This general survey sufficiently indicates that the law of evidence, which has been chiefly developed by the states, has evolved a set of rules designed to reconcile the possibility that this type of information will have some prejudicial effect with the admitted usefulness it has as a factor to be considered by the jury for any one of a large number of valid purposes. The evidence itself is usually, and in recidivist cases almost always, of a documentary kind, and in the cases before us there is no claim that its presentation was in any way inflammatory. Compare Marshall v. United States, 360 U.S. 310, 79 S.Ct. 1171, 3 L.Ed.(2d) 1250. To say the United States Constitution is infringed simply because this type of evidence may be prejudicial and limiting instructions inadequate to vitiate prejudicial effects, would make inroads into this entire complex code of state criminal evidentiary law, and would threaten other large areas of trial jurisprudence. For example, all joint trials, whether of several codefendants or of one defendant charged with multiple offenses, furnish inherent opportunities for unfairness when evidence submitted as to one crime (on which there may be an acquittal) may influence the jury as to a totally different charge. See Delli Paoli v. United States, 352 U.S. 232, 77 S.Ct. 294, 1 L.Ed.(2d) 278; cf. Opper v. United States, 348 U.S. 84, 75 S.Ct. 158, 99 L.Ed. 101; Krulewitch v. United States, 336 U.S. 440, 69 S.Ct. 716, 93 L.Ed. 790. This type of prejudicial effect is acknowledged to inhere in criminal practice, but it is justified on the grounds that (1) the jury is expected to follow instructions in limiting this evidence to its proper function, and (2) the convenience of trying different crimes against the same person, and connected crimes against different defendants, in the same trial as a valid governmental interest.

It is fair to say that neither the Jackson case nor any other due process decision of this Court even remotely supports the proposition that the states are not free to enact habitual offender statutes of the type Texas has chosen and to admit evidence during trial tending to prove allegations required under the statutory scheme.

Tolerance for a spectrum of state procedures dealing with a common problem of law enforcement is especially appropriate here. The rate of recidivism is acknowledged to be high, a wide variety of methods of dealing with the problem exists, and experimentation is in progress. The common-law procedure for applying recidivist statutes, used by Texas in the cases before us, which requires allegations and proof of past convictions in the current trial, is, of course, the simplest and best known procedure. Some jurisdictions deal with the recidivist issue in a totally separate proceeding, see e.g., Oyler v. Boles, 368 U.S. 448, 82 S.Ct. 501, 7 L.Ed.(2d) 446, and as already observed (note 2, supra) Texas to some extent has recently changed to that course. In some states such a proceeding can be instituted even after conviction on the new substantive offense, see Ore.Rev. Stat. Section 168.040 (1959 Supp.); Graham v. State of West Virginia, 224 U.S. 616, 32 S.Ct. 583, 56 L.Ed. 917. The method for determining prior convictions varies also between jurisdictions affording a jury trial on this issue, e.g., Fla.Stat.Ann. Section 775.11 (1944 ed.), and those leaving that question to the court, see, e.g., Fed.Rule Crim.Proc. 32 (a); Mo.Rev.Stat. Section 556.280(2) (1966 Supp.). Another procedure, used in Great Britain and Connecticut, see, Coinage Offenses Act, 1861, 24 and 25 Vic., c. 99; State v. Ferrone, 96 Conn. 160, 113 A. 452, requires that the indictment allege both the substantive crime and the prior conviction, that both parts be read to the defendant prior to trial, but that only the allegations relating to the substantive crime be read to the jury. If the defendant is convicted, the prior offense elements are then read to the jury which considers any factual issues raised. Yet another system relies upon the parole authorities to withhold parole in accordance with their findings as to prior convictions. See, e.g., N.J.Stat. Ann. Section 30:4-123.12 (1964 ed.). And within each broad approach described, other variations occur.

A determination of the "best" recidivist trial procedure necessarily involves a consideration of a wide variety of criteria, such as which method provides most adequate notice to the defendant and an opportunity to challenge the accuracy and validity of the alleged prior convictions, which method best meets the particular jurisdiction's allocation of responsibility between court and jury, which method is best accommodated to the state's established trial procedures, and of course which method is apt to be the least prejudicial in terms of the effect of prior-crime evidence on the ultimate issue of guilt or innocence. To say that the two-stage jury trial on the English-Connecticut style is probably the fairest, as some commentators and courts have suggested, and with which we might well agree were the matter before us in a legislative or rule-making context, is a far cry from a constitutional determination that this method of handling the problem is compelled by the Fourteenth Amendment. Two-part jury trials are rare in our jurisprudence; they have never been compelled by this Court as a matter of constitutional law, or even as a matter of federal procedure. With recidivism the major problem that it is, substantial changes in trial procedure in countless local courts around the country will be required were this Court to sustain the contentions made by these petitioners. This we are unwilling to do. To take such a step would be quite beyond the pale of this Court's proper function in our federal system. It would be a wholly unjustifiable encroachment by this Court upon the constitutional power of states to promulgate their own rules of evidence to try their own state-created crimes in their own state courts, so long as their rules are not prohibited by an provision of the United States Constitution, which these rules are not. The judgments in these cases are affirmed.

Affirmed.

• • •

Mr. Chief Justice WARREN, with whom Mr. Justice FORTAS concurs, dissenting in Nos. 68 and 69, and concurring in No. 70.

• • •

It seems to me that the use of prior convictions evidence in these cases is fundamentally at odds with traditional notions of due process, not because this procedure is not the nicest resolution of conflicting but legitimate interests of the state and the accused, but because it needlessly prejudices the accused without advancing any legitimate interest of the state. If I am wrong in thinking that the introduction of prior convictions evidence serves no valid purpose I am not alone, for the Court never states what interest of the state is advanced by this procedure. And this failure, in my view, undermines the logic of the Court's opinion.

There is much said about the valid purpose of enhanced punishment for repeating offenders, with which I agree, and about the variety of occasions in criminal trials in which prior crimes evidence is admitted as having some relevance to the question of guilt or innocence. But I cannot find support for this procedure in either the purposes of recidivist statutes or by analogy to the traditional occasions where prior crimes evidence is admitted. And the Court never faces up to the problem of trying to justify this recidivist procedure on the grounds that the state would not violate due process if it used prior convictions simply as evidenec of guilt because it showed criminal propensity.

Recidivist statutes have never been thought to allow the state to show probability of guilt because of prior convictions. Their justification is only that a defendant's prior crimes should lead to enhanced punishment for any subsequent offenses. Recidivist statutes embody four traditional rationales for imposing penal sanctions.[1] A man's prior crimes are thought to aggravate his guilt for subsequent crimes, and thus greater than usual retribution is warranted. Similarly, the policies of insulating society from persons whose past conduct indicates their propensity to criminal behavior, of providing deterrence from future crime, and of rehabilitating criminals are all theoretically served by enhanced punishment according to recidivist statutes. None of these four traditional justifications for recidivist statutes are related in any way to the burden of proof to which the state is put to prove that a crime has currently been committed by the alleged recidivist. The fact of prior convictions is not

---

[1] See generally, Note, Recidivist Procedures, 40 N.Y.U.L.Rev. 332 (1960).

intended by recidivist statutes to make it any easier for the state to prove the commission of a subsequent crime. The state does not argue in these cases that its statutes are, or constitutionally could be, intended to allow the prosecutor to introduce prior convictions to show the accused's criminal disposition. But the Court's opinion seems to accept, without discussion, that this use of prior crimes evidence would be consistent with due process.

The concurring opinion of Mr. Justice STEWART is not included.

Only part of the dissenting opinion of Mr. Chief Justice WARREN with whom Mr. Justice FORTAS concurred is included.

The dissenting opinion of Mr. Justice BRENNAN with whom Mr. Justice DOUGLAS joined is not included.

Cases relating to **Chapter 7**

SUBSTITUTES FOR EVIDENCE
JUDICIAL NOTICE

STATE v. LAWRENCE
234 P.(2d) 600
Supreme Court of Utah.
July 19, 1951.

CROCKETT, Justice.

This case comes to us on an appeal from a conviction of grand larceny, arising out of the theft of an automobile. Two questions are presented: First, where there is no evidence of value except a description of the property involved, is it prejudicial error for the court to instruct the jury that the value of the property is greater than $50 and that if defendant is guilty at all he is guilty of grand larceny? The necessity of answering the first question in the affirmative gives rise to the second: Where such error has been committed, can the cause be remanded for retrial without violating the constitutional guarantee of the accused not to be placed twice in jeopardy for the same offense? After a consideration of the problems involved touching upon those questions we answer both in the affirmative.

At the conclusion of the evidence, the defendant's counsel moved the court for a directed verdict on the ground that there had been no evidence of value of the stolen car. The State's attorney might properly and with little difficulty have moved to reopen and supply the missing evidence. He did not do so but instead argued that judicial notice could be taken of the value of the car. The court denied defendant's motion and included in its instructions to the jury the following:

"Grand Larceny so far as it might be material in this case is committed when the property taken is of a value exceeding $50.00.

"In this case you will take the value of this property as being in excess of $50.00 and therefore the defendant, if he is guilty at all, is guilty of grand larceny."

It is conceded by the State that there was no direct evidence of value and that the only testimony in the record upon which a finding of value could be based was that of the owner of the automobile describing it saying it was in excellent condition.

This is not a case where the defendant either expressly or impliedly admitted the value, or by conduct or statements of himself or counsel, allowed it to be assumed that the matter was not disputed. His plea of not guilty cast upon the State the burden of proving every essential element of the offense by evidence sufficient to convince the jury beyond a reasonable doubt. In a charge of grand larceny, one of those essentials is that the value be greater than $50. A conviction for that offense cannot stand unless there is satisfactory evidence of the value of the property. State v. Harris, Mo., 267 S.W. 802; People v. Leach, 106 Cal.App. 442, 290 P. 131. Ordinarily, judicial notice will not be taken of the value of personal property, 31 C.J.S., Evidence, § 101, page 701, and as will later appear herein, this is unquestionably so in connection with the instruction given in this case.

We direct our attention to the argument of the prosecution that the court could take judicial notice of the value of the car and so instruct the jury: Judicial notice is the taking cognizance by the court of certain facts without the necessity of proof, 31 C.J.S., Evidence, § 6, page 509. One class of factual material which is the subject of judicial notice is that dealt with by statute. Section 104-46-1, U.C.A. 1943, provides: "Courts take judicial notice of the following facts": and proceeds to list in eight separate categories, such things as English words, whatever is established by law, acts of departments of government, seals of courts, states and the United States, etc. It would be of no value to list them all here because the value of the car in question could not be thought to come under any subdivision of that statute by any stretch of the imagination.

Section 104-54-4, U.C.A. 1943, under the Code of Civil Procedure provides in part: "* * * Whenever the knowledge of the court is by law made evidence of a fact, the court is to declare such knowledge to the jury, who are bound to accept it."

The word "knowledge" in the foregoing section is apparently used advisedly, there being a distinction between "judicial knowledge" of public records, laws, etc. which the court is deemed to notice by virtue of his office and "judicial notice" of things which are commonly known. 31 C.J.S., Evidence, § 6, page 509, 20 Am.Jur. 47. The further discussion in this opinion will show that this statute has no application to the instant case. We are not here concerned with what the result might be if the evidence in question were such that the statute required that the jury be bound to accept it.

Beyond the scope of the statute providing that certain matters will be taken judicial notice of, there is another class of facts which are so well known and accepted that they are judicially noticed without taking the time, trouble and expense necessary to prove them. Under this doctrine the court will consider, without proof of such generally known facts, its knowledge of what is known to all persons of ordinary intelligence. 31 C.J.S., Evidence, § 7, page 510. This court has recognized that class of judicial notice in a great variety of matters, a few examples of which are: Rugg v. Tolman, 39 Utah 295, 117 P. 54, (that assignment or garnishment of wages ordinarily imputes no wrong or misconduct to the debtor); Union Savings & Inv. Co. v. District Court of Salt Lake County, 44 Utah 397, 140 P. 221, (the general purpose and methods of doing business of building and loan associations); Salt Lake City v. Board of Education of Salt Lake City, 52 Utah 540, 175 P. 654 (location of school buildings); Utah State Fair Ass'n v. Green, 68 Utah 251, 249 P. 1016 (that betting follows horse racing); State Tax Commission v. City of Logan, 88 Utah 406, 54 P.2d 1197 (that most consumers of electrical energy are constant users). For numerous cases on judicial notice of many different subjects of common knowledge outside the classes covered by our statute see Pacific Digest, Evidence, [key] 1 to 52, Inc. The taking of judicial notice of this latter class of commonly known evidentiary facts does not establish them so conclusively as to prevent the presentation of contrary evidence or the making of a finding to the contrary. The subject is treated in Wigmore on Evidence, 3d Ed., Sections 2555 et sequi, and he states in Section 2567: "(a) That a matter is judicially noticed means merely that it is taken as true without the offering proof by the party who should ordinarily have done so. This is because the court assumes that the matter is so notorious that it will not be disputed. But the opponent is not prevented from disputing the matter by evidence, if he believes it disputable."

State v. Lawrence

In discussing this further, Wigmore refers to statutes which expressly provide that the judicial notice is the final determination and binding on the jury; and in Subsection b of the above section, continues: "* * * Does it signify that the settlement of the matter rests with the judge and not with the jury, that the jury are to accept the fact from the judge, and that so far as any further investigation is concerned, it is for the judge alone? Such is the view sometimes found, in decisions as well as statutes [citing statutes including Utah]. *Yet it seems rather that the jury are not concluded;* that the process of notice is intended chiefly for expedition of proof; *and remains possible for the jury to negative it.*" (Emphasis added.)

See also 31 C.J.S., Evidence, § 13, page 520, note 62.

Accordingly, if we assume that the value of the car is of that class of facts which is so well known that judicial notice should be taken thereof, that would not necessarily be conclusive upon the jury. It would merely take the place of evidence. Upon that basis the court could have instructed the jury to this effect: If you believe from the evidence beyond a reasonable doubt that the defendant stole the automobile in question and that it was a 1947 Ford Sedan in good condition, then you may take into consideration your knowledge acquired in the every day affairs of life in determining what value you will place upon said automobile.

Suppose any number of thoroughly competent and credible witnesses had testified that the car was worth more than $50, and there had been no evidence to the contrary, no matter how clear and convincing the evidence might have been, in a criminal case it was not the prerogative of the court to tell the jury that they have to believe it and so find. See State v. Estrada, Utah, 1951, 227 P.2d 247, 248, wherein this court reiterated the time-honored rule that it is the sole and exclusive province of the jury to determine the facts in criminal cases, whether the evidence offered by the State is strong or weak; and expressly stated:

"If the trial judge may not find a verdict of guilty, so, likewise he may not find any of the facts which are necessary elements of the crime for which the accused is being tried. * * * The provision of our State Constitution which grants accused persons the right to a trial by jury extends to each and all of the facts which must be found to be present to constitute the crime charged, and *such right may not be invaded by the presiding judge indicating to the jury that any of such facts are established by the evidence."*

(Emphasis added.)

See that case and the case of State v. Green, 78 Utah 580, 6 P. 2d 177, cited therein for the further elaboration on this principle.

It is to be admitted that upon the surface there doesn't appear to be much logic to the thought that a jury would not be bound to find that the car involved here (1947 Ford 2-Door Sedan) is worth more than $50. However, under our jury system, it is traditional that in criminal cases juries can, and sometimes do, make findings which are not based on logic, nor even common sense. No matter how positive the evidence of a man's guilt may be, the jury may find him not guilty and no court has any power to do anything about it. Notwithstanding the occasional incongruous result, this system of submitting all of the facts in criminal cases to the jury and letting them be the exclusive judges thereof has lasted for some little time now and with a fair degree of success. If the result in individual cases at times seems illogical, we can be consoled by the words of Mr. Justice Holmes, that in some areas of the law, "a page of history is worth a volume of logic." We, who live with it, have a fervent devotion to the jury system, in spite of its faults. We would not like to see it destroyed nor whittled away. If a court can take one important element of an offense from the jury and determine the facts for them because such fact seems plain enough to him, then which element cannot be similarly taken away, and where would the process stop?

For the court to instruct the jury as it did in its Instruction No. 4 "* * * you will take the value of this property as being in excess of $50.00" was an invasion of their province as the exclusive triers of the fact and was prejudicial error. This case presents different problems than were considered in State v. Angle, 61 Utah 432, 215 P. 531. No case has been cited which supports the action of the trial court. One case has been found, certain language of which seems to indicate that the court could take judicial notice of the value of the car, State v. Phillips, 106 Kan. 192, 186 P. 743, 744, the court said: "We must not assume to be more ignorant than everybody else, and everybody else knows that such a car is worth more than $20."

But that case did not involve an instruction as to the value the jury must place on the car as in the instant case. In the Phillips case, the judgment was attacked for failure to prove value but the court recited that the defendant himself testified that he and his accomplice had sold the car for $200 (ten times the amount necessary to make grand larceny in that State) and taken $100 each. The evidence of value was sufficient and the conviction was affirmed.

This appeal presents no question relating to the failure of the court to submit the question of the included offense of petty larceny to the jury and the effect of Section 105-34-6, U.C.A. 1943, which provides that the jury may find the defendant guilty of any necessarily included offense. That grand larceny usually includes the offense of petty larceny. See People v. Wilder, 52 Cal.App. 320, 198 P. 841; People v. McElroy, 116 Cal. 583, 48 P. 718; Commander v. State, 28 Ala.App. 42, 178 So. 241.

The major portion of the Attorney General's brief deals with the contention that if the failure to prove value requires a reversal of the case, the defendant is not entitled to go free, but only to a new trial. With this we agree. It is well settled that reversal of a conviction at the instance of the defendant, and subsequent remand of the case for new trial does not constitute the defendant twice in jeopardy to entitle him to go free. 15 Am. Jur. 89, Crim. Law, Sec. 427; People v. Travers, 77 Cal. 176, 19 P. 268; People v. Eppinger, 109 Cal. 294, 41 P. 1037; People v. Stratton, 136 Cal.App. 201, 28 P.2d 695. And see Sec. 105-39-2, U.C.A. 1943, and State v. Kessler, 15 Utah 142, 49 P. 293.

Judgment of the lower court is reversed and the cause remanded for a new trial.

WADE, McDONOUGH, and HENRIOD, JJ., concur.

WOLFE, Chief Justice (dissenting).

I dissent. It is a well known fact of common and general knowledge that a 1947, 2-door Ford sedan in excellent condition was worth more than $50 when it was stolen in March, 1950 There is sufficient notoriety of the value of this model car for the trial court to properly take judicial notice thereof.

• • •

Defendant argued that the jury should be directed to find a verdict of not guilty upon the ground that there was no evidence as to the value of this automobile. The court took judicial notice of the obvious fact that the car was worth more than $50 and so instructed the jury. The doctrine of judicial notice of generally well known facts has been invoked in many criminal cases. Wharton's Criminal Evidence, 10th Ed. Vol. 1, Chapter VI. The rule should be the same in civil cases as in criminal cases, American Law Institute, Model Code of Evidence, Rule 1, 2 and 801. The majority opinion incorrectly assumes that in this state our Constitution forbids the trial court in a criminal case to take judicial notice of any of the facts necessary to proof of the offense. I believe we are carrying the rule of State v. Green too far.

The fact that this car was a 1947 model in excellent condition is itself very good evidence of the fact that it was worth substantially more than $50. This is a chattel with which we are all familiar and no reasonable mind could believe that it was worth less than $50. Thus, the testimony of the owner of the automobile as to its make, model and condition made out a prima facie case as to its value. Instead of presenting evidence to rebut what the value of the car was, defendant seeks a reversal of the conviction contending that the State failed in its burden of proof. But the proof is plainly there. . . . I would therefore affirm the judgment.

PRESUMPTIONS, INFERENCES, AND STIPULATIONS

BARNES v. UNITED STATES
Certiorari to the United States Court of
Appeals for the Ninth Circuit
Decided June 18, 1973
412 U.S. 837, 93 S.Ct. 2357

Mr. Justice Powell delivered the opinion of the Court.

Petitioner Barnes was convicted in United States District Court on two counts of possessing United States Treasury checks stolen from the mails, knowing them to be stolen, two counts of forging the checks, and two counts of uttering the checks, knowing the endorsements to be forged. The trial court instructed the jury that ordinarily it would be justified in inferring from unexplained possession of recently stolen mail that the defendant possessed the mail with knowledge that it was stolen. We granted certiorari to consider whether this instruction comports with due process. 409 U.S. 1037 (1972).

The evidence at petitioner's trial established that on June 2, 1971, he opened a checking account using the pseudonym "Clarence Smith." On July 1, and July 3, 1971, the United States Disbursing Office at San Francisco mailed four Government checks in the amounts of $269.02, $154.70, $184, and $268.80 to Nettie Lewis, Albert Young, Arthur Salazar, and Mary Hernandez, respectively. On July 8, 1971, petitioner deposited these four checks into the "Smith" account. Each check bore the apparent endorsement of the payee and a second endorsement by "Clarence Smith."

At petitioner's trial the four payees testified that they had never received, endorsed, or authorized endorsement of the checks. A Government handwriting expert testified that petitioner had made the "Clarence Smith" endorsement on all four checks and that he had signed the payees' names on the Lewis and Hernandez checks. Although petitioner did not take the stand, a postal inspector testified to certain statements made by petitioner at a post-arrest interview. Petitioner explained to the inspector that he received the checks in question from people who sold furniture for him door to door and that the checks had been signed in the payees' names when he received them. Petitioner further stated that he could not name or identify any of the salespeople. Nor could he substantiate the existence of any furniture orders because the salespeople allegedly wrote their orders on scratch paper that had not been retained. Petitioner admitted that he executed the Clarence Smith endorsements and deposited the checks but denied making the payees' endorsements.

The District Court instructed the jury that "[p]ossession of recently stolen property, if not satisfactorily explained, is ordinarily a circumstance from which you may reasonably draw the inference and find, in the light of the surrounding circumstances shown by the evidence in the case, that the person in possession knew the property had been stolen."

The jury brought in guilty verdicts on all six counts, and the District Court sentenced petitioner to concurrent three-year prison terms. The Court of Appeals for the Ninth Circuit affirmed, finding no lack of "rational connection" between unexplained possession of recently stolen property and knowledge that the property was stolen. 466 F.2d 1361 (1972). Because petitioner received identical concurrent sentences on all six counts, the court declined to consider his challenges to conviction on the forgery and uttering counts. We affirm.

We begin our consideration of the challenged jury instruction with a review of four recent decisions which have considered the validity under the Due Process Clause of criminal law presumptions and inferences. *Turner* v. *United States*, 396 U.S. 398 (1970); *Leary* v. *United States*, 395 U.S. 6 (1969); *United States* v. *Romano*, 382 U.S. 136 (1965); *United States* v. *Gainey*, 380 U.S. 63 (1965).

In *United States* v. *Gainey, supra,* the Court sustained the constitutionality of an instruction tracking a statute which authorized the jury to infer from defendant's unexplained presence at an illegal still that he was carrying on "the business of a distiller or rectifier without having given bond as required by law." Relying on the holding of *Tot* v. *United States*, 319 U.S. 463, 467 (1943), that there must be a "rational connection between the fact proved and the ultimate fact presumed," the Court upheld the inference on the basis of the comprehensive nature of the "carrying on" offense and the common knowledge that illegal stills are secluded, secret operations. The following Term the Court determined, however, that presence at an illegal still could not support the inference that the defendant was in possession, custody, or control of the still, a narrower offense. "Presence is relevant and admissible evidence in a trial on a possession charge; but absent some showing of the defendant's function at the still, its connection with possession is too tenuous to permit a reasonable inference of guilt—'the inference of the one from proof of the other is arbitrary. . . .' *Tot v. United States,* 319 U.S. 463, 467." *United States v. Romano, supra,* at 141.

Three and one-half years after *Romano,* the Court in *Leary v. United States, supra,* considered a challenge to a statutory inference that possession of marihuana, unless satisfactorily explained, was sufficient to prove that the defendant knew that the marihuana had been illegally imported into the United States. The Court concluded that in view of the significant possibility that any given marihuana was domestically grown and the improbability that a marihuana user would know whether his marihuana was of domestic or imported origin, the inference did not meet the standards set by *Tot, Gainey,* and *Romano.* Referring to these three cases, the *Leary* Court stated that an inference is "'irrational' or 'arbitrary,' and hence unconstitutional, unless it can at least be said with substantial assurance that the presumed fact is more likely than not to flow from the proved fact on which it is made to depend." 395 U.S., at 36. In a footnote the Court stated that since the challenged inference failed to satisfy the more-likely-than-not standard, it did not have to "reach the question whether a criminal presumption which passes muster when so judged must also satisfy the criminal 'reasonable doubt' standard if proof of the crime charged or an essential element thereof depends upon its use." *Id.,* at 36 n. 64.

Finally, in *Turner v. United States, supra,* decided the year following *Leary,* the Court considered the constitutionality of instructing the jury that it may infer from possession of heroin and cocaine that the defendant knew these drugs had been illegally imported. The Court noted that *Leary* reserved the question of whether the more-likely-than-not or the reasonable-doubt standard controlled in criminal cases, but it likewise found no need to resolve that question. It held that the inference with regard to heroin was valid judged by either standard. 396 U.S., at 416. With regard to cocaine, the inference failed to satisfy even the more-likely-than-not standard. *Id.,* at 419.

The teaching of the foregoing cases is not altogether clear. To the extent that the "rational connection," "more likely than not," and "reasonable doubt" standards bear ambiguous relationships to one another, the ambiguity is traceable in large part to variations in language and focus rather than to differences of substance. What has been established by the cases, however, is at least this: that if a statutory inference submitted to the jury as sufficient to support conviction satisfies the reasonable-doubt standard (that is, the evidence necessary to invoke the inference is sufficient for a rational juror to find the inferred fact beyond a reasonable doubt) as well as the more-likely-than-not standard, then it clearly accords with due process.

In the present case we deal with a traditional common-law inference deeply rooted in our law. For centuries courts have instructed juries that an inference of guilty knowledge may be drawn from the fact of unexplained possession of stolen goods. James Thayer, writing in his Preliminary Treatise on Evidence (1898), cited this inference as the descendant of a presumption "running through a dozen centuries." *Id.*, at 327. Early American cases consistently upheld instructions permitting conviction upon such an inference, and the courts of appeals on numerous occasions have approved instructions essentially identical to the instruction given in this case. This longstanding and consistent judicial approval of the instruction, reflecting accumulated common experience, provides strong indication that the instruction comports with due process.

This impressive historical basis, however, is not in itself sufficient to establish the instruction's constitutionality. Common-law inferences, like their statutory counterparts, must satisfy due process standards in light of present-day experience. In the present case the challenged instruction only permitted the inference of guilt from *unexplained* possession of recently stolen property. The evidence established that petitioner possessed recently stolen Treasury checks payable to persons he did not know, and it provided no plausible explanation for such possession consistent with innocence. On the basis of this evidence alone common sense and experience tell us that petitioner must have known or been aware of the high probability that the checks were stolen. Cf. *Turner v. United States*, 396 U.S., at 417; *Leary v. United States*, 395 U.S., at 46. Such evidence was clearly sufficient to enable the jury to find beyond a reasonable doubt that petitioner knew the checks were stolen. Since the inference thus satisfies the reasonable-doubt standard, the most stringent standard the Court has applied in judging permissive criminal law inferences, we conclude that it satisfies the requirements of due process. . . .

Since we find that the statute was correctly interpreted and that the trial court's instructions on the inference to be drawn from unexplained possession of stolen property were fully consistent with petitioner's constitutional rights, it is unnecessary to consider petitioner's challenges to his conviction on the forging and uttering counts.

Affirmed.

MR. JUSTICE DOUGLAS, dissenting.

The use of presumptions and inferences to prove an element of the crime is indeed treacherous, for it allows men to go to jail without any evidence on one essential ingredient of the offense. It thus implicates the integrity of the judicial system. We held in *In re Winship*, 397 U.S. 358, 364, 51 OhioOp.(2d) 323, 327, 90 S.Ct. 1068, that the Due Process Clause requires "proof beyond a reasonable doubt of every fact necessary to constitute the crime. . . ." Some evidence of wrongdoing is basic and essential in the judicial system, unless the way of prosecutors be made easy by dispensing with the requirement of presumption of innocence, which is the effect of what the Court does today. In practical effect the use of these presumptions often means that the great barriers to the protection of procedural due process contained in the Bill of Rights are subtly diluted.

May Congress constitutionally enact a law that says juries can convict a defendant without any evidence at all from which an inference of guilt could be drawn?

The step we take today will be applauded by prosecutors, as it makes their way easy. But the Bill of Rights was designed to make the job of the prosecutor difficult. There is a presumption of innocence. Proof beyond a reasonable doubt is necessary. The jury, not the court, is the factfinder. These basic principles make the use of these easy presumptions dangerous. What we do today is, I think, extremely disrespectful of the constitutional regime that controls the dispensation of criminal justice.

MR. JUSTICE BRENNAN, with whom MR. JUSTICE MARSHALL joins, dissenting.

Petitioner was charged in two counts of a six-count indictment with possession of United States Treasury checks stolen from the mails, knowing them to be stolen. The essential elements of such an offense are (1) that the defendant was in possession of the checks, (2) that the checks were stolen from the mails, and (3) that the defendant knew that the checks were stolen. The Government proved that petitioner had been in possession of the checks and that the checks had been stolen from the mails; and, in addition, the Government introduced some evidence intended to show that petitioner knew or should have known that the checks were stolen. But rather than leaving the jury to determine the element of "knowledge" on the basis of that evidence, the trial court instructed it that it was free to infer the essential element of "knowledge" from petitioner's unexplained possession of the checks. In my view, that instruction violated the Due Process Clause of the Fifth Amendment because it permitted the jury to convict even though the actual evidence bearing on "knowledge" may have been insufficient to establish guilt beyond a reasonable doubt. I therefore dissent. . . .

In short, the practical effect of the challenged instruction was to permit the jury to convict petitioner even if it found insufficient or disbelieved all of the Government's evidence bearing directly on the issue of "knowledge." By authorizing the jury to rely exclusively on the inference in determining the element of "knowledge," the instruction relieved the Government of the burden of proving that element beyond a reasonable doubt. The instruction thereby violated the principle of *Winship* that every essential element of the crime must be proved beyond a reasonable doubt.
1.

"IN THE SUPERIOR COURT OF THE STATE OF
WASHINGTON IN AND FOR YAKIMA COUNTY

STATE OF WASHINGTON, Plaintiff, vs. RICHARD E. ROSS Defendant.	FILED MAR 31, 1971 AGNES L. THOMAS, County Clerk By Lucille Tesh, Deputy NO. 16164 STIPULATION

"WHEREAS, RICHARD E. ROSS, in the presence of his attorney, JOHN NICHOLSON, has been advised prior to any questioning or interrogation of his constitutional rights, to-wit: to remain silent; that any disclosures, statement, admission or confession he makes or which lead to other evidence could and will be used against him in a criminal prosecution; to have a lawyer of his own choice, or an attorney appointed by the court if he is without funds or property, present and representing him prior to any questioning or interrogation and prior to giving or making any disclosure, statement, admission or confession; and his right to stop the questioning and exercise any of his above-stated constitutional rights at any time by indicating his wish to do so, as well as his above-stated constitutional rights in reference to his examination by polygraph or lie detector including his right to refuse to take a polygraph test, and by this stipulation, the admissibility into evidence of all applicable and germane questions, answers and results of his polygraph test, whether favorable or unfavorable to him in the event he is criminally charged with SECOND DEGREE ASSAULT.

"WHEREAS, RICHARD E. ROSS having been advised of his above-stated rights, has requested an opportunity to take a polygraph or lie detector examination to verify his statements of not committing the act of second degree assault.

"WHEREAS, having been advised of my constitutional rights above-stated and the evidentary [sic] implications of this stipulation regarding my examination by polygraph, I, RICHARD E. ROSS am aware of and understand my above-stated constitutional rights and have after consultation with my attorney herein, made a conscious decision, without promises, threats, force or coercion by anyone, to forego and waive said rights; now, therefore,

"In consideration of being granted the opportunity to take a polygraph or lie detector test, it is hereby agreed between RICHARD E. ROSS and his attorney herein, JOHN NICHOLSON, and ROBERT N. HACKETT, JR., Deputy Prosecuting Attorney, that said polygraph test will be given on the 18th day of January, 1971, by the Yakima Police Department, and all questions, answers and results of the test applicable and germane to a charge of SECOND DEGREE ASSAULT, whether favorable or unfavorable to RICHARD E. ROSS will be admissible in evidence in any trial.

"By this stipulation, Richard E. Ross and his attorney herein, and the State of Washington, by and through its attorney, Robert N. Hackett, Jr., expressly waive any legal objection whatsoever that either party might have to the admission to evidence of all questions, answers and results of said polygraph test which are applicable and germane to the charge herein of Second Degree Assault—Two counts, whether favorable or unfavorable to the defendant, Richard E. Ross.

"This stipulation has been entered into freely, voluntarily and knowingly by all parties hereto with full awareness and explanation of the possible legal consequences.

"DATED this 18th day of January, 1971.

"/s/ Richard E. Ross
Richard E. Ross
―――――――――――――
Defendant
"/s/ John Nicholson
John Nicholson
―――――――――――――
Attorney for Defendant
"/s/ Robert N. Hackett, Jr.
Robert N. Hackett, Jr.
―――――――――――――
Deputy Prosecuting Attorney

"WITNESSES:
―――――――――――――
―――――――――――――"

STATE of Washington
v.
Richard E. ROSS
Court of Appeals of Washington,
June 7, 1972.
7 Wash. App. 62, 497 P.2d 1343

EVANS, Judge.

Defendant Richard E. Ross was charged by information with two counts of second-degree assault with a knife. The first count charged him with assault upon one Loy Ray Markle, and the second count charged him with assault upon one Josephine Wait. In a trial to the court without a jury Ross was found guilty upon the first count. The second count was dismissed, based upon a finding that Josephine Wait was cut by a knife wielded by the defendant, but that it was not done intentionally. Defendant appeals from judgment and sentence entered on count 1.

Defendant's assignments of error 1, 3 and 4 constitute a factual appeal from the findings entered by the trial court. An examination of the record reveals substantial evidence, supplied by three eye witnesses to the incident and two eye witnesses to the actions and statements of the defendant Ross immediately following the incident, which support the trial court's findings and conclusions.

It is not the function of the appellate court to reevaluate the credibility of witnesses. As disclosed by its memorandum opinion and its findings of fact, the trial court carefully reviewed and evaluated the evidence. Those findings support the court's conclusions of law and will not be disturbed.

Defendant next contends the trial court erred in allowing the prosecuting attorney to attempt to impeach its own witness, Anna Ramirez. We do not agree.

Anna Ramirez had maintained a close personal relationship with the defendant Ross for several years. It was she who made the police call which resulted in his arrest, and she was present with several other witnesses when Ross was pointed out to the police as the "man they were after." However, when called as a state's witness she testified that she, not Ross, accidentally stabbed Markle with a knife which she had previously obtained from the kitchen to protect herself from Ross, and that Ross was not in the kitchen before the stabbing. The prosecuting attorney claimed surprise and asked her if she had not told him before trial that Ross was in the kitchen shortly before the stabbing. Mrs. Ramirez answered that she did not recall. When asked if she had not previously stated that Ross had a shiny object in his hand before the stabbing she denied making such a statement. The state did not offer any impeaching testimony. We find nothing in the record to suggest the trial court's finding that Anna Ramirez committed perjury was based upon the prosecuting attorney's questions. Independent of these questions, there was substantial evidence that the testimony of Anna Ramirez was a fabrication, motivated by a desire to help her boy friend, Ross. Since the trial was to a court and not to a jury we find no reversible error resulting from the questions asked by the prosecuting attorney.

Defendant also assigns error to the admission of results of a polygraph test which was based upon a stipulation that the results, whether favorable or unfavorable, would be admissible in evidence.

Such a stipulation was entered into by the defendant Ross, his attorney, and the prosecuting attorney. Pursuant to that stipulation a test was conducted by Sgt. Nesary of the Yakima City Police Department. In a pretrial conference with the defendant Ross, his attorney, the prosecuting attorney, and Sgt. Nesary present, four questions to be asked of defendant Ross were formulated and agreed upon. When Sgt. Nesary was called to the stand as a witness the following transpired:

> Mr. Nicholson: Your Honor, for the sake of time, the defense will stipulate that Mr. Ross and counsel entered into a stipulation with Mr. Hackett, wherein Ross volunteered to take a polygraph and did take it with Sgt. Nesary.

Without objection, Sgt. Nesary then testified to his training and experience as a polygraph operator and that the test was conducted under proper conditions. The questions which had previously been agreed upon were: (1) Do you know for sure who intentionally cut Markle? (2) Did you intentionally cut Markle? (3) Did you intentionally swing a knife at Josephine Wait? and (4) Before Markle was cut, did you have a knife in your hand? Sgt. Nesary testified that he received a deceptive reaction to questions 1, 2 and 4, which related to the assault involving Markle, and that Ross's answer of "No" to the third question, relating to the assault charge upon Josephine Wait, was not deceptive. In his opinion, Ross was not telling the complete truth in answering questions 1, 2 and 4. Sgt. Nesary was cross-examined at length as to his qualifications and training, the conditions under which the test was administered, and the limitations of and possibility of error in the technique of polygraph interrogation.

The court found that the polygraph machine was in good working order, that Sgt. Nesary was an experienced operator of a polygraph, and that accurate readings of the results of such a test can be obtained in about 90 per cent of all tests.

Our Supreme Court has had occasion to comment on the admissibility of the results of a polygraph test in several cases.

In State v. Rowe, 77 Wash.2d 955, 468 P.2d 1000 (1970) the defendant, unrepresented by counsel, requested a polygraph test. The examination was given and the court points out that there was no stipulation concerning admissibility of the results. The report of the test was inconclusive. Defendant offered evidence of his willingness to take the test in order to show a consciousness of innocence. In holding the trial court was correct in rejecting defendant's offer, the Supreme Court stated, at 958, 468 P.2d at 1003:

> Since it is generally held that polygraph tests are not judicially acceptable, 22A C.J.S. Criminal Law § 645(2) (1961), it is obvious that a defendant should not be permitted to introduce evidence of his professed willingness to take such a test. Commonwealth v. Saunders, 386 Pa. 149, 125 A.2d 442 (1956); State v. Chang, 46 Hawaii 22, 374 P.2d 5 (1962). At best such an offer is a self-serving act or declaration which is made without any possible risk. If the offer is accepted and the test given, the results cannot be used in evidence whether they were favorable or unfavorable. Commonwealth v. Saunders, *supra*; State v. LaRocca, 81 N.J.Super. 40, 194 A.2d 578 (1963). In short, a defendant has everything to gain and nothing to lose by making the offer, so the conduct underlying the so-called inference of innocence can well be feigned, artificial and wholly unreliable.
>
> Thus, even if the defendant was effectively precluded from raising the issue by fear that the test results might be disclosed, the trial court committed no error. The defendant's offer of evidence was patently self-serving and thus inadmissible at the outset.

Seattle Police Officers' Guild v. Seattle, 80 Wash.2d 307, 494 P. 2d 485 (1972) involved a departmental administrative investigation of an alleged pay-off system in the police department. During the course of inquiry the acting chief of police proposed to require certain officers to submit to a polygraph examination under threat of dismissal if they refused to cooperate. This proposal was based upon a police department general order which required the cooperation of officers in internal departmental investigations.

As we read the majority opinion, it attributed some probative value to a polygraph test when it stated, at page 320, 494 P.2d at page 463:

> if, in the exercise of prudent judgment, the investigating authority determines it reasonably necessary to utilize the polygraph examination as an investigatory tool to test the dependability of prior answers of suspected officers to question specifically, narrowly, and directly related to the performance of their official duties, then, such investigating authority may

properly request such officers to submit to a polygraph test under pain of dismissal for refusal.

However, as to the admissibility of the polygraph test in any subsequent criminal proceedings, the court continued, at page 320, 494 P.2d at page 463:

> Bearing in mind that the reasonableness of an investigating authority's request, under varying circumstances, can be subjected to judicial scrutiny and abuses of discretion thereby curbed, coupled with the fact that, in any event, the results of a polygraph test and a subject's willingness or unwillingness to take the test cannot be admitted into evidence in subsequent criminal proceedings, we see no constitutional or legal barrier to the conclusion we have reached.

In State v. Stiltner, 80 Wash.2d 47, 491 P.2d 1043 (1971), as in State v. Rowe, *supra*, the court again indicated that, generally speaking, polygraph tests are not yet judicially acceptable, but at the same time indicated a distinction may be drawn when there is a stipulation that the results of such a test will be admitted. *Stiltner* involved pretrial publicity of lie detector tests given four persons but refused by defendant. The court stated, at page 51, 491 P.2d at page 1046:

> And in publicizing the cooperation of the other four clerks in submitting to the lie detector, the publicity did not disclose that the defendant's refusal to submit was upon advice of counsel, who very properly *refused to agree to the prosecutor's condition that the results of the test would be admitted as evidence in the trial.*

(Italics ours.) Thus, our Supreme Court has made it clear that, absent a stipulation, the results of a polygraph test cannot be admitted into evidence in a criminal proceeding over objection of a defendant, but those decisions do not meet the issue here presented. None of them involves an agreement of all parties that the results may be admitted.

Courts from other jurisdictions have found a valid distinction between the admissibility of polygraph tests taken upon stipulation that the results will be admissible in evidence, and those where there is no such stipulation. State v. Valdez, 91 Ariz. 274, 371 P.2d 894 (1962); State v. Chambers, 104 Ariz. 247, 451 P.2d 27 (1969); State v. Forgan, 104 Ariz. 497, 455 P.2d 975 (1969). *See, also*, State v. McNamara, 252 Iowa 19, 104 N.W.2d 568 (1960); People v. Houser, 85 Cal.App.2d 686, 193 P.2d 937 (1948); Herman v. Eagle

Star Ins. Co., 283 F.Supp. 33 (D.C. Cal.1969).

While all courts are not in complete agreement, we are persuaded that the better rule is that the results of a polygraph test are admissible for the purpose of corroboration under the conditions and limitations set forth in State v. Valdez, *supra*, which we adopt verbatim. They are as follows:

> (1) That the [prosecuting attorney], defendant and his counsel all sign a written stipulation providing for defendant's submission to the test and for the subsequent admission at trial of the graphs and the examiner's opinion thereon on behalf of either defendant or the state.
>
> (2) That notwithstanding the stipulation the admissibility of the test results is subject to the discretion of the trial judge, i.e., if the trial judge is not convinced that the examiner is qualified or that the test was conducted under proper conditions he may refuse to accept such evidence.
>
> (3) That if the graphs and examiner's opinion are offered in evidence the opposing party shall have the right to cross-examine the examiner respecting:
>   a. the examiner's qualifications and training;
>   b. the conditions under which the test was administered;
>   c. the limitations of and possibilities for error in the technique of polygraphic interrogation; and
>   d. at the discretion of the trial judge, any other matter deemed pertinent to the inquiry.
>
> (4) That if such evidence is admitted the trial judge should instruct the jury that the examiner's testimony does not tend to prove or disprove any element of the crime with which a defendant is charged but at most tends only to indicate that at the time of the examination defendant was not telling the truth. Further, the jury members should be instructed that it is for them to determine what corroborative weight and effect such testimony should be given.

All of the above conditions applicable to the present case have been met. As already noted, there was substantial evidence that defendant Ross committed the assault charged against him. The polygraph evidence was merely corroborative, and the trial court treated it as such. Defendant was given the right to cross-examine the examiner regarding his qualifications and training, the conditions under which the test was administered, and the limitations and possibility of error in technique of polygraph interrogation. The court found that the polygraph machine was in good working order, and that Sgt. Nesary was an experienced polygraph operator. Under these circumstances we hold admission into evidence of the results of the polygraph test was within the discretion of the trial judge.

We find no abuse of that discretion.

Judgment affirmed.

Munson, C. J., and Green, J., concur.

Cases relating to Chapter 8

EXAMINATION OF WITNESSES

UNITED STATES v. DURHAM

319 F.(2d) 590

United States Court of Appeals
Fourth Circuit.

Decided June 4, 1963.

BOREMAN, Circuit Judge.

Defendant below, Turner Lee Durham, appeals from his conviction in the United States District Court for the Middle District of North Carolina for violation of 18 U.S.C. § 2312. The conviction will be affirmed.

Durham and one Henry Morris Tolbert were indicted for transporting a 1951 Mercury automobile from Winston-Salem, North Carolina, to Myrtle Beach, South Carolina, on or about July 14, 1962, knowing that the vehicle had been stolen. In a separate count of the same indictment, Thomas Allen Wingo and Larry Wayne Utt were charged with similarly transporting a 1959 Austin Healy automobile from Winston-Salem to Myrtle Beach on or about the same date. Shortly before the jury was impaneled to try the case, Wingo changed his plea from not guilty to guilty. Durham, Tolbert and Utt entered pleas of not guilty. At the close of the Government's evidence, motions for judgments of acquittal were granted as to defendants Utt and Tolbert. Durham did not testify and called no witnesses. The jury found Durham guilty and he was sentenced to a term of imprisonment.

Durham's sole contention on appeal is that the District Court committed reversible error in permitting the United States Attorney to ask Wingo, who testified for the Government, leading questions. In summary the facts, as stated by Wingo in his testimony, are these. Wingo had worked as an offset pressman for the Atlas Supply Company where he had access to some blank checks imprinted with the name of its subsidiary, the Mercury Distributing Company. He became acquainted with defendant Durham in the spring of 1962 and later stole several hundred of the Mercury Distributing Company checks. On July 10, 1962, Durham, Wingo, Tolbert and a man named Brown drove to Charlotte, North Carolina. Either while traveling to Charlotte or after arriving there, Wingo forged one of the stolen checks in the amount of $3,926.34, payable to the order of Jack Johnson (a fictitious name). Wingo then used this check to open a checking account at the Bank of Charlotte in the name of Jack Johnson. Wingo testified that he wrote the forged check in the presence of Durham and that Durham accompanied him to the bank, but he was unable to recall whether the check was written in the car or in the bank and he did not know Durham's exact location in the bank at the time he opened the account. Subsequently, while still in Charlotte, Wingo and Durham attempted to negotiate checks drawn on the account in the name of Jack Johnson.

A day or so later, after their return to Winston-Salem, Durham and Wingo purchased a 1951 Mercury at a used car lot where Durham had formerly worked. Durham made out a check, drawn on the Bank of Charlotte in the amount of $200.00, and Wingo signed the name Jack Johnson as maker. The bill of sale for the Mercury was made out to Durham. Later that afternoon, Durham and Wingo returned to the used car lot and purchased a 1959 Austin Healy Sprite for which Wingo traded in his Plymouth and gave a check in the amount of $750.00, again drawn on the Bank of Charlotte and signed "Jack Johnson." Early the next morning Durham and Tolbert drove the 1951 Mercury and Wingo and Utt drove the Austin Healy from Winston-Salem to Myrtle Beach, South Carolina, where all four were subsequently arrested.

Durham's defense was based on the theory that he did not have knowledge that the automobile was stolen, an essential element of the crime charged. Durham's counsel argued to the jury and here contends that Durham did not know the bogus checks were worthless and that he did not know Wingo's correct name. Durham contends that it was reversible error for the District Court to allow the United States Attorney to ask Wingo the following questions on the ground that they were leading:

> QUESTION ONE: "Didn't you testify he [Durham] was in the bank with you at the time this account was opened?"

QUESTION TWO: "When you [he?] knew your name was Wingo, you were using a false name?"

QUESTION THREE: "You say you all planned this together?"

QUESTION FOUR: "You say you all planned this, and they had asked you to write this check which was deposited in the Bank of Charlotte?"

The essential test of a leading question is whether it so suggests to the witness the specific tenor of the reply desired by counsel that such a reply is likely to be given irrespective of an actual memory. The evil to be avoided is that of supplying a false memory for the witness. 3 Wigmore, Evidence § 769 (3d ed. 1940); see also De Witt v. Skinner, 232 F. 443, 445 (8th Cir. 1916). However, the extent to which the use of leading questions may be indulged or limited is a matter primarily for the discretion of the trial judge and an appellate court will intervene only if there is a clear abuse of discretion. Generally, abuse of discretion is not found in the absence of prejudice or clear injustice to the defendant.

It is Durham's argument that by asking the four questions noted above, the United States Attorney put answers necessary to establish the Government's case in the mouth of a witness who had shown himself to be uncertain about those very facts; since the questions tended to show that Durham had known Wingo's correct name and had knowingly participated in the scheme to obtain money by false pretenses, they tended to rebut his defense of lack of knowledge that the car was stolen. Also, it is argued, since Wingo had plead guilty but had not then been sentenced, his desire to please the United States Attorney can be assumed and should be taken into account. Therefore, Durham contends, the district judge abused his discretion by allowing questions which were leading and resulted in prejudice to Durham. The Government does not make any claim that it was faced with a special situation, such as surprise due to the change of testimony by a witness, the need to refresh the memory of a witness, the hostile attitude of a witness, or the need to make specific points in rebuttal. The Government asserts merely that the questions were not leading and contends that no prejudice to Durham and no abuse of discretion could arise because each of the specific questions of which Durham complains tended merely to corroborate facts previously presented in Wingo's testimony. A review of Wingo's testimony shows that this contention of the Government is well supported by the record.

Prior to Question One, propounded by the United States Attorney on direct examination, Wingo testified that he had opened a checking account with the Bank of Charlotte using the fictitious name of Jack Johnson, and that Durham was with him at the time. Later, on cross-examination by Durham's counsel, the witness repeated this testimony and added that he did not watch Durham while in the bank, but was positive Durham was there. In the light of this testimony, Durham suffered no prejudice from the asking of Question One and there was no abuse of discretion on the part of the trial judge in permitting it.

The remaining three questions of which the defendant complains were asked by the United States Attorney on a brief redirect examination of Wingo following his cross-examination by Durham's counsel. At the outset of the redirect examination, Wingo testified without any objection by defense counsel that he believed Durham knew his name as Wingo, and that before going to Charlotte he and Durham had used the name Jack Johnson to pass forged Mercury Distributing Company checks at many places over the state. Then Question Two was asked in the following exchange:

"Q. You did use Jack Johnson sometimes or did you use Jack Johnson all of the time?

"A. Well, Jack Johnson most of the time; and one or two other times we used another name. It was still a false name.

"Q. [*Question Two*] When you [he ?] knew your name was Wingo, you were using a false name?

"MR. POWELL: [*Counsel for Durham*] Objection.

"THE WITNESS: That's right.

"THE COURT: Objection overruled."

There is a difference of opinion between the attorneys as to whether Question Two was asked using the word "you" or the word "he," as shown in the brackets. However, in either event, no prejudice to Durham resulted from the question. In prior testimony, Wingo had clearly stated *both* that he used a false name to pass the checks and that he believed Durham knew his name was Wingo. Therefore, no new information was elicited by the question and Wingo's answer was merely repetitive.

The examination which included Questions Three and Four followed immediately and clearly related the above testimony to earlier testimony by Wingo on direct and cross-examination that, at the suggestion of Durham and their two companions on the trip to Charlotte, he had written the forged check and opened the account in the Bank of Charlotte:

"Q. (By Mr. Murdock) You say you don't have any idea how many of these checks you and Durham cashed?

"A. No.

"Q. Before you went to Charlotte?

"A. No.

"Q. [*Question Three*] You say you all planned this together?

"A. Yes, sir. Well, I don't quite understand the question.

"MR. POWELL: Objection.

"THE COURT: Objection overruled.

"Q. [*Question Four*] (By Mr. Murdock) You say you all planned this, and they had asked you to write this check which was deposited in the Bank of Charlotte?

"A. Yes.

"MR. POWELL: Objection.

"THE COURT: Objection overruled.

"Q. (By Mr. Murdock) All right.

"A. They wanted me to write larger checks and under false pretenses to get money, and under the plan, they should have been larger checks than what they were because we were to have shared in it. It was just a false pretense to get money."

Again no resulting prejudice is apparent. The United States Attorney merely permitted his witness to restate prior testimony and eliminate an appearance of confusion which may have arisen as a result of certain testimony on cross-examination.

On the facts inquired about in each of the four questions Wingo gave consistent answers and even elaborated on his previous testimony, as in the last answer quoted above. It is clear that no false answers were supplied by these questions, that Durham was not prejudiced, and that the District Court did not abuse its discretion in overruling objections to the questions. The record clearly supports a finding that Durham participated in the transportation of the automobile in interstate commerce with knowledge that it had been stolen.

Affirmed.

MICHELSON v. UNITED STATES
335 U.S. 469, 93 L.Ed. 168, 69 S.Ct. 213
Decided December 20, 1948.

On Writ of Certiorari to the United States Court of Appeals for the Second Circuit.

Solomon Michelson was convicted of bribing a federal revenue agent. Judgment of conviction was affirmed by the Circuit Court of Appeals, 165 F.2d 732, and defendant brings certiorari.

Affirmed.

Mr. Justice JACKSON delivered the opinion of the Court.

In 1947 petitioner Michelson was convicted of bribing a federal revenue agent. The Government proved a large payment by accused to the agent for the purpose of influencing his official action. The defendant, as a witness on his own behalf, admitted passing the money but claimed it was done in response to the agent's demands, threats, solicitations, and inducements that amounted to entrapment. It is enough for our purposes to say that determination of the issue turned on whether the jury should believe the agent or the accused.

On direct examination of defendant, his own counsel brought out that, in 1927, he had been convicted of a misdemeanor having to do with trading in counterfeit watch dials. On cross-examination it appeared that in 1930, in executing an application for a license to deal in second-hand jewelry, he answered "no" to the question whether he had theretofore been arrested or summoned for any offense.

Defendant called five witnesses to prove that he enjoyed a good reputation. Two of them testified that their acquaintance with him extended over a period of about thirty years and the others said they had known him at least half that long. A typical examination in chief was as follows:

"Q. Do you know the defendant Michelson? A. Yes.

"Q. How long do you know Mr. Michelson? A. About 30 years.

"Q. Do you know other people who know him? A. Yes.

"Q. Have you had occasion to discuss his reputation for honesty and truthfulness and for being a law-abiding citizen? A. It is very good.

"Q. You have talked to others? A. Yes.

"Q. And what is his reputation? A. Very good."

These are representative of answers by three witnesses; two others replied, in substance, that they never had heard anything against Michelson.

On cross-examination, four of the witnesses were asked, in substance, this question: "Did you ever hear that Mr. Michelson on March 4, 1927, was convicted of a violation of the trademark law in New York City in regard to watches?" This referred to the twenty-year-old conviction about which defendant himself had testified on direct examination. Two of them had heard of it and two had not.

To four of these witnesses the prosecution also addressed the question the allowance of which, over defendant's objection, is claimed to be reversible error:

"Did you ever hear that on October 11th, 1920, the defendant, Solomon Michelson, was arrested for receiving stolen goods?"

None of the witnesses appears to have heard of this.

The trial court asked counsel for the prosecution, out of presence of the jury, "Is it a fact according to the best information in your possession that Michelson was arrested for receiving stolen goods?" Counsel replied that it was, and to support his good faith exhibited a paper record which defendant's counsel did not challenge.

The judge also on three occasions warned the jury, in terms that are not criticized, of the limited purpose for which this evidence was received.

Defendant-petitioner challenges the right of the prosecution so to cross-examine his character witnesses. The Court of Appeals held that it was permissible. The opinion, however, points out that the practice has been severely criticized and invites us, in one respect, to change the rule. Serious and responsible criticism has been aimed, however, not alone at the detail now questioned by the Court of Appeals but at common-law doctrine on the whole subject of proof of reputation or character. It would not be possible to appraise the usefulness and propriety of this cross-examination without consideration of the unique practice concerning character testimony, of which such cross-examination is a minor part.

Courts that follow the common-law tradition almost unanimously have come to disallow resort by the prosecution to any kind of evidence of a defendant's evil character to establish a probability of his guilt. Not that the law invests the defendant with a presumption of good character, Greer v. United States, 245 U.S. 559, 38 S.Ct. 209, 62 L.Ed. 469, but it simply closes the whole matter of character, disposition and reputation on the prosecution's case-in-chief. The State may not show defendant's prior trouble with the law, specific criminal acts, or ill name among his neighbors, even though such facts might logically be persuasive that he is by propensity a probable perpetrator of the crime. The inquiry is not rejected because character is irrelevant; on the contrary, it is said to weigh too much with the jury and to so overpersuade them as to prejudge one with a bad general record and deny him a fair opportunity to defend against a particular charge. The overriding policy of excluding such evidence, despite its admitted probative value, is the practical experience that its disallowance tends to prevent confusion of issues, unfair surprise and undue prejudice.

But this line of inquiry firmly denied to the State is opened to the defendant because character is relevant in resolving probabilities of guilt. He may introduce affirmative testimony that the general estimate of his character is so favorable that the jury may infer that he would not be likely to commit the offense charged. This privilege is sometimes valuable to a defendant for this Court has held that such testimony alone, in some circumstances, may be enough to raise a reasonable doubt of guilt and that in the federal courts a jury in a proper case should be so instructed. Edgington v. United States, 164 U.S. 361, 17 S.Ct. 72, 41 L.Ed. 467.

When the defendant elects to initiate a character inquiry, another anomalous rule comes into play. Not only is he permitted to call witnesses to testify from hearsay, but indeed such a witness is not allowed to base his testimony on anything but hearsay. What commonly is called "character evidence" is only such when "character" is employed as a synonym for "reputation." The witness may not testify about defendant's specific acts or courses of conduct or his possession of a particular disposition or of benign mental and moral traits; nor can he testify that his own acquaintance, observation, and knowledge of defendant leads to his own independent opinion that defendant possesses a good general or specific character, inconsistent with commission of acts charged. The witness is, however, allowed to summarize what he has heard in the community, although much of it may have been said by persons less qualified to judge than himself. The evidence which the law permits is not as to the personality of defendant but only as to the shadow his daily life has cast in his neighborhood. This has been well described in a different connection as "the slow growth of months and years, the resultant picture of forgotten incidents, passing events, habitual and daily conduct, presumably honest because disinterested, and safer to be trusted because prone to suspect. * * * It is for that reason that such general repute is permitted to be proven. It sums up a multitude of trivial details. It compacts into the brief phrase of a verdict the teaching of many incidents and the conduct of years. It is the average intelligence drawing its conclusion." Finch J., in Badger v. Badger, 88 N.Y. 546, 552, 42 Am.Rep. 263.

While courts have recognized logical grounds for criticism of this type of opinion-based-on-hearsay testimony, it is said to be justified by "overwhelming considerations of practical convenience" in avoiding innumerable collateral issues which, if it were attempted to prove character by direct testimony, would complicate and confuse the trial, distract the minds of jurymen and befog the chief issues in the litigation. People v. Van Gaasbeck, 189 N.Y. 408, 418, 82 N.E. 718, 22 L.R.A., N.S., 650, 12 Ann. Cas. 745.

Another paradox in this branch of the law of evidence is that the delicate and responsible task of compacting reputation hearsay into the "brief phrase of a verdict" is one of the few instances in which conclusions are accepted from a witness on a subject in which he is not an expert. However, the witness must qualify to give an opinion by showing such acquaintance with the defendant, the community in which he has lived and the circles in which he has moved, as to speak with authority of the terms in which generally he is regarded. To require affirmative knowledge of the reputation may seem inconsistent with the latitude given to the witness to testify when all he can say of the reputation is that he has "heard nothing against defendant." This is permitted upon assumption that, if no ill is reported of one, his reputation must be good. But this answer is accepted only from a witness whose knowledge of defendant's habitat and surroundings is intimate enough so that his failure to hear of any relevant ill repute is an assurance that no ugly rumors were about.

Thus the law extends helpful but illogical options to a defendant. Experience taught a necessity that they be counterweighted with equally illogical conditions to keep the advantage from becoming an unfair and unreasonable one. The price a defendant must pay for attempting to prove his good name is to throw open the entire subject which the law has kept closed for his benefit and to make himself vulnerable where the law otherwise shields him. The prosecution may pursue the inquiry with contradictory witnesses to show that damaging rumors, whether or not well-grounded, were afloat— for it is not the man that he is, but the name that he has which is put in issue. Another hazard is that his own witness is subject to cross-examination as to the contents and extent of the hearsay on which he bases his conclusions, and he may be required to disclose rumors and reports that are current even if they do not affect his own conclusion. It may test the sufficiency of his knowledge by asking what stories were circulating concerning events, such as one's arrest, about which people normally comment and speculate. Thus, while the law gives defendant the option to show as a fact that his reputation reflects a life and habit incompatible with commission of the offense charged, it subjects his proof to tests of credibility designed to prevent him from profiting by a mere parade of partisans.

To thus digress from evidence as to the offense to hear a contest as to the standing of the accused, at its best opens a tricky line of inquiry as to a shapeless and elusive subject matter. At its worst it opens a veritable Pandora's box of irresponsible gossip, innuendo and smear. In the frontier phase of our law's development, calling friends to vouch for defendant's good character, and its counterpart—calling the rivals and enemies of a witness to impeach him by testifying that his reputation for veracity was so bad that he was unworthy of belief on his oath—were favorite and frequent ways of converting an individual litigation into a community contest and a trial into a spectacle. Growth of urban conditions, where one may never know or hear the name of his next-door neighbor, have tended to limit the use of these techniques and to deprive them of weight with juries. The popularity of both procedures has subsided, but courts of last resort have sought to overcome danger that the true issues will be obscured and confused by investing the trial court with discretion to limit the number of such witnesses and to control cross-examination. Both propriety and abuse of hearsay reputation testimony, on both sides, depend on numerous and subtle considerations, difficult to detect or appraise from a cold record, and therefore rarely and only on clear showing of prejudicial abuse of discretion will Courts of Appeals disturb rulings of trial courts on this subject.

Wide discretion is accompanied by heavy responsibility on trial courts to protect the practice from any misuse. The trial judge was scrupulous to so guard it in the case before us. He took pains to ascertain, out of presence of the jury, that the target of the question was an actual event, which would probably result in some comment among acquaintances if not injury to defendant's reputation. He satisfied himself that counsel was not merely taking a random shot at a reputation imprudently exposed or asking a groundless question to waft an unwarranted innuendo into the jury box.

The question permitted by the trial court, however, involves several features that may be worthy of comment. Its form invited hearsay; it asked about an arrest, not a conviction, and for an offense not closely similar to the one on trial; and it concerned an occurrence many years past.

Since the whole inquiry, as we have pointed out, is calculated to ascertain the general talk of people about defendant, rather than the witness' own knowledge of him, the form of inquiry, "Have you heard?" has general approval, and "Do you know?" is not allowed.

A character witness may be cross-examined as to an arrest whether or not it culminated in a conviction, according to the overwhelming weight of authority. This rule is sometimes confused with that which prohibits cross-examination to credibility by asking a witness whether he himself has been arrested.

Arrest without more does not, in law any more than in reason, impeach the integrity or impair the credibility of a witness. It happens to the innocent as well as the guilty. Only a conviction, therefore, may be inquired about to undermine the trustworthiness of a witness.

Arrest without more may nevertheless impair or cloud one's reputation. False arrest may do that. Even to be acquitted may damage one's good name if the community receives the verdict with a wink and chooses to remember defendant as one who ought to have been convicted. A conviction, on the other hand, may be accepted as a misfortune or an injustice, and even enhance the standing of one who mends his ways and lives it down. Reputation is the net balance of so many debits and credits that the law does not attach the finality to a conviction when the issue is reputation, that is given to it when the issue is the credibility of the convict.

The inquiry as to an arrest is permissible also because the prosecution has a right to test the qualifications of the witness to bespeak the community opinion. If one never heard the speculations and rumors in which even one's friends indulge upon his arrest, the jury may doubt whether he is capable of giving any very reliable conclusions as to his reputation.

In this case the crime inquired about was receiving stolen goods; the trial was for bribery. The Court of Appeals thought this dissimilarity of offenses too great to sustain the inquiry in logic, though conceding that it is authorized by preponderance of authority. It asks us to substitute the Illinois rule which allows inquiry about arrest, but only for very closely similar if not identical charges, in place of the rule more generally adhered to in this country and in England. We think the facts of this case show the proposal to be inexpedient.

The good character which the defendant had sought to establish was broader than the crime charged and included the traits of "honesty and truthfulness" and "being a law-abiding citizen." Possession of these characteristics would seem as incompatible with offering a bribe to a revenue agent as with receiving stolen goods. The crimes may be unlike, but both alike proceed from the same defects of character which the witnesses said this defendant was reputed not to exhibit. It is not only by comparison with the crime on trial but by comparison with the reputation asserted that a court may judge whether the prior arrest should be made subject of inquiry. By this test the inquiry was permissible. It was proper cross-examination because reports of his arrest for receiving stolen goods, if admitted, would tend to weaken the assertion that he was known as an honest and law-abiding citizen. The cross-examination may take in as much ground as the testimony it is designed to verify. To hold otherwise would give defendant the benefit of testimony that he was honest and law-abiding in reputation when such might not be the fact; the refutation was founded on convictions equally persuasive though not for crimes exactly repeated in the present charge.

The inquiry here concerned an arrest twenty-seven years before the trial. Events a generation old are likely to be lived down and dropped from the present thought and talk of the community and to be absent from the knowledge of younger or more recent acquaintances. The court in its discretion may well exclude inquiry about rumors of an event so remote, unless recent misconduct revived them. But two of these witnesses dated their acquaintance with defendant as commencing thirty years before the trial. Defendant, on direct examination, voluntarily called attention to his conviction twenty years before. While the jury might conclude that a matter so old and indecisive as a 1920 arrest would shed little light on the present reputation and hence propensities of the defendant, we cannot say that, in the context of this evidence and in the absence of objection on this specific ground, its admission was an abuse of discretion.

We do not overlook or minimize the consideration that "the jury almost surely cannot comprehend the Judge's limiting instructions," which disturbed the Court of Appeals. The refinements of the evidentiary rules on this subject are such that even lawyers and judges, after study and reflection, often are confused, and surely jurors in the hurried and unfamiliar movement of a trial must find them almost unintelligible. However, limiting instructions on this subject are no more difficult to comprehend or apply than those upon various other subjects; for example, instructions that admissions of a co-defendant are to be limited to the question of his guilt and are not to be considered as evidence against other defendants, and instructions as to other problems in the trial of conspiracy charges. A defendant in such a case is powerless to prevent his cause from being irretrievably obscured and confused; but, in cases such as the one before us, the law foreclosed this whole confounding line of inquiry, unless defendant thought the net advantage from opening it up would be with him. Given this option, we think defendants in general and this defendant in particular have no valid complaint at the latitude which existing law allows to the prosecution to meet by cross-examination an issue voluntarily tendered by the defense. See Greer v. United States, 245 U.S. 559, 38 S.Ct. 209, 62 L.Ed. 469.

We end, as we began, with the observation that the law regulating the offering and testing of character testimony may merit many criticisms. England, and some states have overhauled the practice by statute. But the task of modernizing the longstanding rules on the subject is one of magnitude and difficulty which even those dedicated to law reform do not lightly undertake.

The law of evidence relating to proof of reputation in criminal cases has developed almost entirely at the hands of state courts of last resort, which have such questions frequently before them. This Court, on the other hand, has contributed little to this or to any phase of the law of evidence, for the reason, among others, that it has had extremely rare occasion to decide such issues, as the paucity of citations in this opinion to our own writings attests. It is obvious that a court which can make only infrequent sallies into the field cannot recast the body of case law on this subject in many, many years, even if it were clear what the rules should be.

We concur in the general opinion of courts, textwriters and the profession that much of this law is archaic, paradoxical and full of compromises and compensations by which an irrational advantage to one side is offset by a poorly reasoned counter-privilege to the other. But somehow it has proved a workable even if clumsy system when moderated by discretionary controls in the hands of a wise and strong trial court. To pull one misshapen stone out of the grotesque structure is more likely simply to upset its present balance between adverse interests than to establish a rational edifice.

The present suggestion is that we adopt for all federal courts a new rule as to cross-examination about prior arrest, adhered to by the courts of only one state and rejected elsewhere. The confusion and error it would engender would seem too heavy a price to pay for an almost imperceptible logical improvement, if any, in a system which is justified, if at all, by accumulated judicial experience rather than abstract logic.

The judgment is

Affirmed.

AUSTIN v. UNITED STATES
418 F.(2d) 456
United States Court of Appeals
District of Columbia Circuit.

Decided March 7, 1969.

SPOTTSWOOD W. ROBINSON, III, Circuit Judge:

The sole question presented on this appeal, from a conviction of robbery, is whether the trial judge erred in barring certain testimony by appellant which was proffered as part of an ongoing effort to impeach a police officer who was a principal witness for the Government. The basis of the attempted impeachment was appellant's claim that prior to the offense on trial a fellow officer had accepted a bribe, and that appellant had implicated the officer-witness in the affair. With this involvement of perhaps the most despicable charge that can be lodged against a public servant—a charge here that has never been proved—we leave the officers nameless in this opinion.

On the night of October 6-7, 1967, two men assaulted the complainant on a street, robbed him of 25 cents and ran away. The scuffle attracted the attention of an off-duty policeman, Officer A, who was then in his car at a nearby intersection awaiting a change of traffic lights. From previous contacts with appellant, Officer A, so he was later to testify, recognized appellant as one of the robbers. The officer then parked the car, and joined other police officers and the complainant in a canvass of the area. Appellant and the man who became his co-defendant were soon spotted, identified as the offenders and placed under arrest. At their trial, appellant and his co-defendant were identified by the complainant and Officer A as the parties who committed the robbery. The jury, discarding their protest that they were innocent and were merely returning to a night club when arrested, found them guilty.

When defense counsel voiced his desire to explore Officer A's possible bias toward appellant, the trial judge held a hearing, out of the jury's presence, at which the officer was quizzed extensively by counsel on both sides, and after which the judge defined the latitude which the proof as to bias would be indulged. The trial resuming before the jury, Officer A on direct examination detailed his observations and activities relative to the robbery, and on cross-examination responded to questions probing his knowledge of the alleged bribery and his relationship with the policeman allegedly bribed, Officer B. The facts elicited in this fashion, never sought to be contradicted by appellant, laid before the jury a picture rather full in both respects.

During several months in the first half of 1967, it developed, Officers A and B were assigned as partners in the operation of a police wagon. One day they stopped a car driven by appellant and discovered that he was unable to produce an operator's license or a registration card for the vehicle. Officer A testified that he was disposed to arrest appellant, who on that occasion intimated a willingness to pay a small sum of money, but that Officer B took charge of the matter and apparently dropped it, and somewhat later was indicted for bribery on appellant's accusation. Officer A was thereafter called before his precinct captain and with him the bribery was discussed, and from this, Officer A admitted, he assumed that appellant had lodged the bribery charge against him as well as Officer B. The latter was suspended from the police force, thus terminating their joint tours of duty and seemingly all other contacts also.

During the presentation of the case for the defense, counsel for appellant proffered the latter's testimony on one aspect of the bias issue. Appellant would state, it was represented, that he did implicate Officer A in the bribery. Concurring in the Government's view that the officer's belief on that score rather than the actual fact was the important criterion, the trial judge denied the request. We hold that, under the circumstances, the judge's ruling was correct, and that the conviction must accordingly be affirmed.

Our decisions reflect great solicitude for an endeavor by the accused to establish bias on the part of a prosecution witness. They establish the propriety of the showing either by cross-examination or by extrinsic evidence, and indicate the broad range over which the inquiry may extend. We have admonished, however, that when the accused has been afforded a reasonable opportunity to make the point, the trial judge has discretionary authority to limit the scope of the proof. And courts have traditionally exercised their inherent power to confine the impeaching effort to evidentiary items possessing a potential for connoting bias.

Here the trial judge permitted defense counsel's cross-examination of Officer A not only in regard to the traffic episode but also in reference to the witness' relationships with Officer B and with appellant himself. Among the topics of interrogation was the degree to which Officer A was alert to the consideration that appellant had implicated him as well as Officer B in the alleged bribery. Officer A admitted that he had assumed that appellant had similarly accused him of the wrongdoing since he had been questioned on the subject by his precinct captain, explaining, in apparent candor, that that was as much as he really knew.

What appellant wanted to say, however, and what the trial judge ruled he would not be permitted to say, was that he actually did inculpate Officer A. The difficulty, however, is that this testimony would not have increased Officer A's awareness, when on direct examination he recounted the details of the robbery, that appellant's accusation also extended to him. Bias is a state of mind, and only those events which can influence the mind at the moment of testifying are relevant to a demonstration of bias. The pertinent factor here was not what appellant did in the way of attributing bribery to Officer A, but what Officer A understood that appellant had done.

The proffered testimony had no tendency to show that Officer A was any more knowledgeable as to the charge than he had already admitted that he was, and the judge was on sound ground in excluding it.

Affirmed.

Cases relating to **Chapter 9**

TESTIMONIAL PRIVILEGES

MORRIS v. STATE

242 A.(2d) 559

Court of Special Appeals of Maryland.

June 3, 1968.

MORTON, Judge.

The Appellant was convicted of obtaining money under false pretenses from the Baltimore City Welfare Department on the basis of testimony which established that while he was receiving Welfare payments under the name of George Chesnut, he failed to notify the Department that he was at the same time receiving income from gainful employment under the name George Morris.

As a part of its proof that the Appellant on occasion had used the name George Morris, the State offered in evidence several statements which were produced by an attorney who had formerly represented the Appellant in a civil matter, which statements bore the signature, George Morris. Also, the attorney's receptionist was permitted to testify, over objection, that the Appellant was known by the name of George Morris and also as George Chesnut and that the office files indicated that he used both names. The Appellant asserted that his real name was George Chesnut and he denied ever having used the name George Morris. He admitted, however, that the attorney who produced the statements had previously represented him in a civil matter.

In this appeal, it is contended that the introduction of statements bearing the signature George Morris and the testimony of the receptionist identifying the Appellant as George Morris and George Chesnut were in violation of the confidential relationship between attorney and client. The statements were offered not for their substance but solely for the purpose of identifying the Appellant as a client who had represented his name to be George Morris. Thus, the question for determination is whether the identity of a client is protected by the privilege which ordinarily attaches to communications arising out of the attorney-client relationship. While the issue appears to be one of the first impression in this State, it has been the subject of decision in a number of jurisdictions throughout the Country.

The principle of the attorney-client privilege is grounded in the common law, and, according to Professor Wigmore, its history goes back at least to the reign of Elizabeth I. See 8 Wigmore, Evidence, Sec. 2290 (McNaughton, rev. 1961). In some States the privilege has been recognized and regulated by statute; but by and large, the common law principle has remained unchanged even in those states which have enacted specific statutes since they have been interpreted as simply reflecting the common law doctrine. Professor Wigmore phrases the principle as follows (supra, Sec. 2292):

> "(1) Where legal advice of kind is sought (2) from a professional legal advisor in his capacity as such, (3) the communications relating to that purpose, (4) made in confidence (5) by the cilent (6) are at his insistence permanently protected (7) from disclosure by himself or by the legal adviser, (8) except the protection be waived."

It is apparent from the foregoing statement that what is sought primarily to be protected are the communications between the client and the attorney, the modern theory being that an individual in a free society should be encouraged to consult with his attorney whose function is to counsel and advise him and he should be free from apprehension of compelled disclosures by his legal adviser. Miller, The Challenge to the Attorney-Client Privilege, 39 Va.L.R. 262, 268 (1963). However, since resort to the privilege obviously tends to stifle the truth, which is what courts are seeking to ascertain, the privilege is not without limitations. See McCormick, Evidence, Sec. 94. Thus, in Colton v. United States, (CCA 2d) 306 F.2d 633, cert. den. 371 U.S. 951, 83 S.Ct. 505, 9 L.Ed.2d 499, Chief Judge Lumbard, after reciting the attorney-client privilege, stated (p. 637):

> "But, although the word 'communications' must be broadly interperted in this context, see 8 Wigmore, Evidence, § 2306 (McNaughton, rev. 1961), the authorities are clear that the privilege extends essentially only to the substance of matters

communicated to an attorney in professional confidence. Thus the identity of a client, or the fact that a given individual has become a client are matters which an attorney normally may not refuse to disclose, even though the fact of having retained counsel may be used as evidence against the client."

It appears, therefore, to be well settled that "the rule making communications between attorney and client privileged from disclosure ordinarily does not apply where the inquiry is confined to the fact of the attorney's employment and the name of the person employing him since the privilege presupposes the relationship of client and attorney and therefore it does not attach to its creation." See collection of cases in Anno.—Disclosure of Clients Name or Business, 114 A.L.R. 1332. See also 3 Wharton's Criminal Evidence, Sec. 809 (Anderson's Edition); Wigmore, supra, Sec. 2313; McCormick, supra, Sec. 94; 97 C.J.S. Witnesses § 283e.

Most of the authorities agree that there may be special circumstances under which the revelation of a client's identity may violate the attorney-client privilege, as for example, where so much of a confidential communication has already been disclosed that revealing the identity of the client would amount to a full disclosure of the confidential communication. NLRB v. Harvey, (CCA 4th) 349 F.2d 900, 16 A.L.R.3d 1035. In the case at bar, however, no special circumstances are present. We think it is clear that the substance of the statements upon which the Appellant's signature appeared was not placed in evidence, the purpose of offering them being solely to identify the Appellant. His objection goes only to the signatures which constituted evidence that the Appellant had previously represented his name to be George Morris and which afforded an opportunity to compare those signatures with those of the endorsements on the Welfare checks and the employer's checks. It is apparent, therefore, that the revelation of the Appellant's identity by the attorney's receptionist and the production of the Appellant's signatures, under the circumstances here existing, did not constitute a violation of the confidential relationship between the Appellant and his previously employed attorney and, accordingly, his objection to their admission is without merit.

Judgment affirmed.

HAWKINS v. UNITED STATES
358 U.S. 74, 3 L.Ed. (2d) 125, 79 S.Ct. 136 (1958)
Decided November 24, 1958.

Mr. Justice BLACK delivered the opinion of the Court.

Petitioner was convicted and sentenced to five years imprisonment by a United States District Court in Oklahoma on a charge that he violated the Man Act, 18 U.S.C. § 2421, by transporting a girl from Arkansas to Oklahoma for immoral purposes. Over petitioner's objection the District Court permitted the Government to use his wife as a witness against him. Relying on Yoder v. United States (Okla.) 80 F.2d 665, the Court of Appeals for the Tenth Circuit held that this was not error. 249 F.2d 735. As other Courts of Appeals have followed a long-standing rule of evidence which bars a husband or wife from testifying against his spouse, we granted certiorari. 355 U.S. 925, 2 L.Ed.2d 356, 78 S.Ct. 383.

The common-law rule, accepted at an early date as controlling in this country, was that husband and wife were incompetent as witnesses for or against each other. The rule rested mainly on a desire to foster peace in the family and on a general unwillingness to use testimony of witnesses tempted by strong self-interest to testify falsely. Since a defendant was barred as a witness in his own behalf because of interest, it was quite natural to bar his spouse in view of the prevailing legal fiction that husband and wife were one person. See 1 Coke, Commentary Upon Littleton (19th ed. 1832) 6b. The rule yielded to exceptions in certain types of cases, however. Thus, this Court in Stein v. Bowman (U.S.) 13 Pet. 209, 10 L.Ed. 129, while recognizing "the general rule that neither a husband nor wife can be a witness for or against the other," noted that the rule does not apply "where the husband commits an offence against the person of his wife." (U.S.) 13 Pet., at 221. But the Court emphasized that no exception left spouses free to testify for or against each other merely because they so desired. (U.S.) 13 Pet., at 223.

Aside from slight variations in application, and despite many critical comments, the rule stated in Stein v. Bowman was followed by this and other federal courts until 1933 when this Court decided

Funk v. United States, 290 U.S. 371, 78 L.Ed. 369, 54 S.Ct. 212, 93 A.L.R. 1136. That case rejected the phase of the common-law rule which excluded testimony by spouses *for* each other. The Court recognized that the basic reason underlying this exclusion of evidence had been the practice of disqualifying witnesses with a personal interest in the outcome of a case. Widespread disqualifications because of interest, however, had long since been abolished both in this country and in England in accordance with the modern trend which permitted interested witnesses to testify and left it for the jury to assess their credibility. Certainly, since defendants were uniformly allowed to testify in their own behalf, there was no longer a good reason to prevent them from using their spouses as witnesses. With the original reason for barring favorable testimony of spouses gone the Court concluded that this aspect of the old rule should go too.

The Funk case, however, did not criticize the phase of the common-law rule which allowed either spouse to exclude adverse testimony by the other, but left this question open to further scrutiny. 290 U.S., at 373; Griffin v. United States, 336 U.S. 704, 714, 715, 93 L.Ed. 993, 998, 999, 69 S.Ct. 814. More recently, Congress has confirmed the authority asserted by this Court in Funk to determine admissibility of evidence under the "principles of the common law as they may be interpreted . . . in the light of reason and experience." Fed. Rules Crim. Proc. 26. The Government does not here suggest that authority, reason or experience require us wholly to reject the old rule forbidding one spouse to testify against the other. It does ask that we modify the rule so that while a huband or wife will not be compelled to testify against the other, either will be free to do so voluntarily. Nothing in this Court's cases supports such a distinction between compelled and voluntary testimony, and it was emphatically rejected in Stein v. Bowman (U.S.) 13 Pet. 209, 10 L.Ed. 129, supra, a leading American statement of the basic principles on which the rule rests. (U.S.) 13 Pet., at 223. Consequently, if we are to modify the rule as the Government urges, we must look to experience and reason, not to authority.

While the rule forbidding testimony of one spouse *for* the other was supported by reasons which time and changing legal practices had undermined, we are not prepared to say the same about the rule barring testimony of one spouse *against* the other. The basic reason the law has refused to pit wife against husband or husband against wife in a trial where life or liberty is at stake was a belief that such a policy is necessary to foster family peace, not only for the benefit of husband, wife and children, but for the benefit of the public as well. Such a belief has never been unreasonable and is not now. Moreover, it is difficult to see how family harmony is less disturbed by a wife's voluntary testimony against her husband than by her compelled testimony. In truth, it seems probable that much more bitterness would be engendered by voluntary testimony than by that which is compelled. But the Government argues that the fact a husband or wife testifies against the other voluntarily is strong indication that the marriage is already gone. Doubtless this is often true. But not all marital flare-ups in which one spouse wants to hurt the other are permanent. The widespread success achieved by courts throughout the country in conciliating family differences is a real indication that some apparently broken homes can be saved provided no unforgivable act is done by either party. Adverse testimony given in criminal proceedings would, we think, be likely to destroy almost any marriage.

Of course, cases can be pointed out in which this exclusionary rule has worked apparent injustice. But Congress or this Court, by decision or under its rule-making power, 18 U.S.C. § 3771, can change or modify the rule where circumstances or further experience dictate. In fact, specific changes have been made from time to time. Over the years the rule has evolved from the common-law absolute disqualification to a rule which bars the testimony of one spouse against the other unless both consent. See Stein v. Bowman (U.S.) supra; Funk v. United States, 290 U.S. 371, 78 L.Ed. 369, 54 S.Ct. 212, 93 A.L.R. 1136, supra; Benson v. United States, 146 U.S. 325, 331-333, 36 L.Ed. 991, 994, 995, 13 S.Ct. 60; United States v. Mitchell (C.A. 2 N.Y.) 137 F.2d 1006, 1008. In 1887 Congress enabled either spouse to testify in prosecutions against the other for bigamy, polygamy or unlawful cohabitation. 24 Stat. 635. See Miles v. United States, 103 U.S. 304, 315, 316, 26 L.Ed. 481, 485. Similarly, in 1917, and again in 1952, Congress made wives and husbands competent to testify against each other in prosecutions for importing aliens for immoral purposes. 39 Stat. 878 (1917), re-enacted as 66 Stat. 230, 8 U.S.C. § 1328 (1952).

Other jurisdictions have been reluctant to do more than modify the rule. English statutes permit spouses to testify against each other in prosecutions for only certain types of crimes. See Evidence of Spouses in Criminal Cases, 99 Sol. J. 551. And most American states retain the rule, though many provide exceptions in some classes of cases. The limited nature of these exceptions shows there is still a widespread belief, grounded on present conditions, that the law should not force or encourage testimony which might alienate husband and wife, or further inflame existing domestic differences. Under these circumstances we are unable to subscribe to the idea that an exclusionary rule based on the persistent instincts of several centuries should now be abandoned. As we have already indicated, however, this decision does not foreclose whatever changes in the rule may eventually be dictated by "reason and experience."

• • •

Reversed.

Mr. Justice STEWART, concurring.

The rule of evidence we are here asked to re-examine has been called a "sentimental relic." It was born of two concepts long since rejected: that a criminal defendant was incompetent to testify in his own case, and that in law husband and wife were one. What thus began as a disqualification of either spouse from testifying at all yielded gradually to the policy of admitting all relevant evidence, until it has now become simply a privilege of the criminal defendant to prevent his spouse from testifying against him. Compare Stein v. Bowman (U.S.) 13 Pet. 209, 10 L.Ed. 129; Wolfle v. United States, 291 U.S. 7, 14, 78 L.Ed. 617, 619, 54 S.Ct. 279; Funk v. United States, 290 U.S. 371, 78 L.Ed. 369, 54 S.Ct. 212, 93 A.L.R. 1136.

Any rule that impedes the discovery of truth in a court of law impedes as well the doing of justice. When such a rule is the product of a conceptualism long ago discarded, is universally criticized by scholars, and has been qualified or abandoned in many jurisdictions, it should receive the most careful scrutiny. Surely "reason and experience" require that we do more than indulge in mere assumptions, perhaps naive assumptions, as to the importance of this ancient rule to the interests of domestic tranquillity.

In the present case, however, the Government does not argue

that this testimonial privilege should be wholly withdrawn. We are asked only to hold that the privilege is that of the witness and not the accused. Under such a rule the defendant in a criminal case could not prevent his wife from testifying against him, but she could not be compelled to do so.

A primary difficulty with the Government's contention is that this is hardly the case in which to advance it. A supplemental record filed subsequent to the oral argument shows that before "Jane Wilson" testified, she had been imprisoned as a material witness and released under $3,000 bond conditioned upon her appearance in court as a witness for the United States. These circumstances are hardly consistent with the theory that her testimony was voluntary. Moreover, they serve to emphasize that the rule advanced by the Government would not, as it argues, "create a standard which has the great advantage of simplicity." On the contrary, such a rule would be difficult to administer and easy to abuse. Seldom would it be a simple matter to determine whether the spouse's testimony were really voluntary, since there would often be ways to compel such testimony more subtle than the simple issuance of a subpoena, but just as cogent. Upon the present record, and as the issues have been presented to us, I therefore concur in the Court's decision.

MULLEN v. UNITED STATES
263 F.(2d) 275

United States Court of Appeals
District of Columbia Circuit.

Decided December 4, 1958.

Before Mr. Justice REED, retired, and EDGERTON and FAHY, Circuit Judges.

EDGERTON, Circuit Judge.

This appeal is from a conviction under D.C.Code (1951) § 22-901, which makes it a crime to "torture, cruelly beat, abuse, or otherwise wilfully maltreat" a child. Appellant's young children were found chained in her house while she was absent. There was evidence that she had chained them, and also that she had done so for their "protection." The District Court rightly charged the jury as a matter of law that appellant did not "torture" the children. But with regard to the statutory words "abuse" and "wilfully maltreat," the court charged the jury to decide whether appellant "was acting reasonably under the circumstances or whether it was unreasonable and dangerous."

It was certainly unreasonable, and probably dangerous, to chain the children. But if appellant chained them for their own protection, she did not "abuse" or "wilfully maltreat" them within the meaning of the Code. That language calls for something worse than good intentions coupled with bad judgment. As we recently held in construing less explicit statutory language, "the common law concept of crime as a combination of an evil state of mind with the doing of an evil act applies to this felony." Levine v. United States, 104 U.S.App.D.C. ——, 261 F.2d 747; Morisette v. United States, 342 U.S. 246, 72 S.Ct. 240, 96 L.Ed. 288. The court's charge omitted the requirement of an evil state of mind and was therefore erroneous.

The jury might well have acquitted appellant but for the erroneous charge. We therefore reverse under F.R. Crim.P.Rule 52(b), 18 U.S.C. Cf. Screws v. United States, 325 U.S. 91, 107, 65 S.Ct. 1031, 89 L.Ed. 1495. We do not consider other alleged errors.

Appellant is a woman of limited understanding. She was indicted more than two years ago and imprisoned more than one year. We commend these facts to the consideration of the United States Attorney.

Reversed.

FAHY, Circuit Judge (concurring).

In concurring I add that another ground for reversal is urged by appellant, namely, the admission in evidence of the testimony of a minister of statements made to the minister by the appellant as a penitent in preparation for receiving communion as a Lutheran communicant. Not desiring to delay the decision, I will file at a later date a statement of my views on the question of the admissibility of this testimony.

Statement by Circuit Judge FAHY, with Whom Circuit Judge

EDGERTON Concurs, and Separate Statement by Circuit Judge EDGERTON, on the Question of the Admissibility of Certain Testimony.

January 29, 1959

FAHY, Circuit Judge, with whom Circuit Judge EDGERTON concurs: When the case was decided December 4, 1958, I concurred and stated that I would later give my views on the question of admissibility of the testimony of a minister as to statements made to him by appellant as a penitent in preparation for receiving communion as a Lutheran communicant. The question is whether these statements were privileged communications, such as those between husband and wife and client and attorney, and, therefore, not admissible in evidence.

The minister had testified briefly as a character witness for appellant. He then appears to have become troubled because of what occurred subsequent to his testimony. Appellant had taken the stand and had denied chaining the children. The minister then asked to see the trial judge and visited him in chambers, where he stated that he felt he had been unable to say all that his conscience impelled him to say. As a result the judge himself recalled the minister as the court's witness to give further evidence. After stating his impressions of the family and the relations between the children and appellant, their mother, the minister testified as follows:

"[A]fter I had seen the defendant in the District Jail, she came to my office. She wanted to know whether she could come to communion. I advised her that as long as there was any suspicion as to her mistreating the children by chaining them I could not admit her to communion; that the Good Book says that if we confess our sins God is faithful and just to forgive us our sins and to cleanse us from all unrighteousness.

"She admitted that she had chained the children with the explanation that she did it for their protection * * *

"I advised her and counselled with her that that was wrong and sinful."

The lack of objection to this testimony does not preclude our ruling upon its admissibility. There was no affirmative consent to its use, and the fact that the judge called the witness tended to restrain objection. In addition, uncertainty as to the applicable rule of evidence goes far to excuse failure to object. But more important, the testimony was so critical that we should exercise our discretion to consider its admissibility even if not required to do so. "'Plain errors * * * affecting substantial rights may be noticed although they were not brought to the attention of the court.' Rule 52(b), Fed.Rules Crim. Proc. 18 U.S.C.A." Pinkard v. United States, 99 U.S.App.D.C. 394, 395, 240 F.2d 632, 633. Appellant had denied chaining the children and there was no direct evidence that she had done so except a reluctant assent drawn from her loyal, six-year-old son after he had been subjected to a lengthy and persistent examination, despite his age, during which he had repeatedly exonerated his mother.

A further preliminary matter. Was the disclosure of appellant to the minister a confidential confession to a spiritual adviser? The answer would be clearer were the relationship of priest and penitent involved, where the priest is known to be bound to silence by the discipline and laws of his church. The present witness appears not to have felt bound in this manner. But I think the privilege if it exists includes a confession by a penitent to a minister in his capacity as such to obtain such spiritual aid as was sought and held out in this instance. The minister definitely indicated that by confessing her sins to him appellant would receive the spiritual benefits she desired. In any event, enough was indicated to cause further inquiry by the court as to the character of the disclosure if doubt remained. In these circumstances I deem it appropriate to reach the question of admissibility, especially as the question might arise again should the case be retried. My view is that such a confession is a privileged communication which is not competent evidence on a trial, at least in the absence of the penitent's consent to its use.

In Totten v. United States, 92 U.S. 105, 107, 23 L.Ed. 605, the Supreme Court said:

> "[S]uits cannot be maintained which would require a disclosure of the confidence of the confessional, or those between husband and wife, or of communications by a client to his counsel for professional advice, or of a patient to his physician for a similar purpose."

This was dictum, since the confessional privilege was not involved. So, too, is Judge Learned Hand's statement in McMann v.

Securities and Exchange Commission, 2 Cir., 1937, 87 F.2d 377, 378, 109 A.L.R. 1445, certiorari denied McMann v. Engle, 301 U.S. 684, 57 S.Ct. 785, 81 L.Ed. 1342, where he included among the traditional privileges that of a penitent. And Judge Holtzoff of our District Court has also said in passing that under the law of the United States privileged communications include that of "clergyman and penitent" as well as those of attorney and client and physician and patient. These statements, though not decisions on the question, indicate the correct position. They assume the existence of the privilege.

It is highly probable that the priest-penitent privilege was part of the common law of England in the centuries preceding the Reformation. See the lengthy study by Nolan, The Law of the Seal of Confession, 13 Catholic Encyc. 649-65. This same study demonstrates, however, that after the Reformation the privilege was by no means generally recognized, and in fact appears to have been abrogated or abandoned. Because of this it is said the claimed privilege was not one at common law and, therefore, if now to be recognized must be enacted into statute, which Congress has not done. However, as we shall see, recognition of the privilege in federal courts does not depend upon finding that it has either existed uniformly at common law or has been approved in terms by act of Congress. Before enlarging upon this it is worth noting that even during the post-Reformation period, when religious and political tensions largely set the pattern in such matters, judicial decisions and legal writings were not uniformly hostile to the privilege.

The resolution of the problem today for federal courts is to be found in a proper application of Rule 26, Fed.R.Crim. P., adopted in 1948 under the authority of Congress. This Rule provides:

"* * * The admissibility of evidence and the competency and privileges of witnesses shall be governed, except when an act of Congress or these rules otherwise provide, by the principles of the common law as they may be interpreted by the courts of the United States in the light of reason and experience."

This was decisional law even before thus formalized in a Rule. See Notes of the Advisory Committee on the Rules, where it is stated that Rule 26 reflects the decisions of the Supreme Court in Funk v.

United States, 290 U.S. 371, 54 S.Ct. 212, 78 L.Ed. 369, and in Wolfle v. United States, 291 U.S. 7, 54 S.Ct. 279, 78 L.Ed. 617. And see Hawkins v. United States, 358 U.S. 74, 79 S.CT. 136, 3 L.Ed.2d 125, decided as recently as November 24, 1958, where, though adhering to the rule disqualifying a wife from testifying in a criminal case against her husband, the Court restated the authority conferred upon the federal courts by Rule 26 "to determine admissibility of evidence under the principles of the common law as they may be interpreted * * * in the light of reason and experience.'"

The developments and governing principles are explained in Lutwak v. United States, 344 U.S. 604, 613-615, 73 S.Ct. 481, 487, 97 L.Ed. 593, as follows:

"The Funk case left the rules of evidence as to the competency of witnesses to be formulated by the federal courts or Congress in accordance with reason and experience. Wolfle v. United States, 291 U.S. 7, 12 [54 S.Ct. 279]. There followed the promulgation by this Court of Rule 26 of the Federal Rules of Criminal Procedure. * * * This rule was a paraphrase of Mr. Justice Stone's statement in Wolfle, 291 U.S. at [page] 12 [54 S.Ct. at page 279].

"Under this rule, the competency of witnessess is to be governed by the principles of the common law as they *may be* interpreted by the courts in the light of reason and experience. The governing principles are not necessarily as they had existed at common law. Congress has not acted, and has specifically authorized this Court to prescribe rules of criminal procedure, but the rules do not specifically answer the problem here. Therefore, it is open to us to say whether we shall go further and abrogate this common-law rule disqualifying one spouse from testifying in criminal cases *against* the other spouse.

* * * * * *

"'It has been said so often as to have become axiomatic that the common law is not immutable but flexible, and by its own principles adapts itself to varying conditions.' Funk v. United States, supra, 290 U.S. at page 383, 54 S.Ct. at page 216."

Funk v. United States, supra, involved the competency of a wife to testify on behalf of her husband on trial for crime in a federal court. In departing from the common law rule which would have rendered her incompetent the Court quoted approvingly from the opinion in Rosen v. United States, 245 U.S. 467, 471, 38 S.Ct. 148, 150, 62 L.Ed. 406, where in a case involving the old rule disqualifying a witness convicted of crime, the Court had concluded "that the dead hand of the common-law rule of 1789 should no longer be applied to such cases * * *."

The decisions to which we have referred, as well as Rule 26, leave the federal courts, with ultimate authority in the Supreme Court, free to resolve our present question without additional legislation. It is true that the trend of decisions has been chiefly in the direction of enlarging rather than restricting the area of admissibility of evidence, but the governing principle is the same. When reason and experience call for recognition of a privilege which has the effect of restricting evidence the dead hand of the common law will not restrain such recognition.

We come then to the final question whether reason and experience do call for present recognition of the confessor-confessant privilege. For the answer we rely heavily upon the lengthy discussion of privileged communications contained in 8 Wigmore, Evidence §§ 2285-2296 (3d ed.). It is there shown that all the conditions of the basic common law applicable to privileged communications apply to the relationship of priest-penitent. The author says "this privilege has adequate grounds for recognition" when tested by the four canons governing privileged communications, namely,

"(1) The communications must originate in a *confidence* that they will not be disclosed;

"(2) This element of *confidentiality must be essential* to the full and satisfactory maintenance of the relation between the parties;

"(3) The *relation* must be one which in the opinion of the community ought to be sedulously *fostered;* and

"(4) The *injury* that would inure to the relation by the disclosure of the communications must be *greater than the benefit* thereby gained for the correct disposal of litigation." [Italics in the original.]

It thus appears that non-recognition of the privilege at certain periods in the development of the common law was inconsistent with the basic principles of the common law itself. It would be no service to the common law to perpetuate in its name a rule of evidence which is inconsistent with the foregoing fundamental guides furnished by that law. And, as we have seen, the denial was never uniform or resolute, so strong were the claims of reason in support of the privilege. See discussion in Wigmore, supra, at §§ 2394-96; People v. Daniel Phillips and Wife, 1 West.L.J. 109 (1813). In our own time, with its climate of religious freedom, there remains no barrier to adoption by the federal courts of a rule of evidence on this subject dictated by sound policy.

Sound policy—reason and experience—concedes to religious liberty a rule of evidence that a clergyman shall not disclose on a trial the secrets of a penitent's confidential confession to him, at least absent the penitent's consent. Knowledge so acquired in the performance of a spiritual function as indicated in this case is not to be transformed into evidence to be given to the whole world. As Wigmore points out, such a confidential communication meets all the requirements that have rendered communications between husband and wife and attorney and client privileged and incompetent. The benefit of preserving these confidences inviolate overbalances the possible benefit of permitting litigation to prosper at the expense of the tranquility of the home, the integrity of the professional relationship, and the spiritual rehabilitation of a penitent. The rules of evidence have always been concerned not only with truth but with the manner of its ascertainment.

EDGERTON, Circuit Judge.

I think a communication made in reasonable confidence that it will not be disclosed, and in such circumstances that disclosure is shocking to the moral sense of the community, should not be disclosed in a judicial proceeding, whether the trusted person is or is not a wife, husband, doctor, lawyer, or minister. As Mr. Justice Holmes said of wire-tapping, "We have to choose, and for my part I think it a less evil that some criminals should escape than that the Government should play an ignoble part." Olmstead v. United States, 277 U.S. 438, 470, 48 S.Ct. 564, 575, 72 L.Ed. 944 (dissenting opinion).

Cases relating to **Chapter 10**

OPINION TESTIMONY

STATE v. COLLINS

294 Pac. 957

Supreme Court of Montana.

December 13, 1930.

CALLAWAY, C. J.

Defendant and one Fishbeck were accused by information "of the crime of assault with intent to commit a felony," in that on or about January 11, 1930, they "did wilfully, unlawfully and feloniously assault, one Dolores Pickett, a female person under the age of eighteen years, to-wit: of the age of sixteen years, and not the wife of either of said defendants, by forcibly and violently seizing the said Dolores Pickett, and forcing her into a bedroom and violently pushing her over and upon a bed, in and upon the premises of the defendant, S. R. Collins, also known as 'Nig' Collins, near Plentywood, Montana, in said county and state, against her will and without her consent, and then and there did struggle with her, the said Dolores Pickett, with the intent in them, the said defendants, to then and there commit a felony upon the person of the said Dolores Pickett, and to have sexual intercourse with her and to rape the said Dolores Pickett: the said defendants, S. R. Collins, otherwise known as 'Nig' Collins, and the said Frank J. Fishbeck, each being a male person over the age of twenty-one years."

1. The accused were arraigned upon February 28, and pleaded not guilty. On March 3, without objection, the cause was assigned for trial upon March 25th, but upon March 12th the accused filed a motion for a continuance upon the ground that a large proportion of the persons qualified for jury duty in the county were affected by bias and prejudice on the merits of the case; and therefore it would be impossible to select a fair and impartial jury for the trial. The motion was supported by many affidavits, and the state filed many affidavits denying the material parts of the affidavits filed by the accused. After consideration the court denied the motion. This is as-

signed as error, but we cannot see any abuse of discretion, and unless it is shown that the court abused its discretion in granting or denying the postponement of a trial, the order will be affirmed.

When the case was called for trial, the defendants, in response to the court's inquiry, said they were ready for trial, but demanded separate trials. The state thereupon elected to try defendant Collins first. A jury was impaneled, apparently without difficulty, and the trial proceeded. The jury found defendant Collins, who will be referred to hereafter simply as the defendant, guilty of assault in the second degree, and the court rendered judgment against him. He moved for a new trial, which was denied. He then appealed from the judgment and from the order denying him a new trial.

2. The transcript tells a sordid story. It appears that defendant owned a place about a mile and a quarter from Plentywood, known as Nig Collins' chicken ranch. The residence upon the place is divided into a small dance hall, four bedrooms, a dining room, and a kitchen. It had borne the reputation of being a house of prostitution, but no one was living there at the time of the alleged crime but defendant himself. Although defendant, forty-four years of age, had lived at the house during 1929, he did not deny that prostitution was carried on there during that year. The most he would say was that he could not swear whether it had been practiced there or not.

From the testimony of the state's witnesses it appears that on January 9, 1930, three high school girls, Dolores Pickett, sixteen years of age, Eugenie Garneau, two days past eighteen, and Lucille Wright, seventeen, were at a table in a café in Plentywood. Frank J. Fishbeck, a married man, thirty-six years of age, came to the table where the girls were seated and engaged in a whispered conversation with Dolores. He whispered, "Do you want to go on a party?" She said she did not know, "who is going along?" He said: "Nig Collins. Get your friend Genie. * * * We might go out to Nig's place." Dolores said she did not know, she would talk to Genie about it, but she did not think they would go unless all went along, meaning to include Lucille. Fishbeck said he would get Stanley Palubicki for Lucille. Dolores said she would see about it. The party was to be on Saturday night. After Fishbeck went away, she talked in whispers with the other girls about the party, but it seems they did not come to any definite conclusion. On Saturday evening the girls met. Doubtless all were inclined to accept Fishbeck's invitation, but they had not decided to go to the chicken ranch. They walked about the streets a bit, eventually passing Kavon's Garage, which was run by Fishbeck and Palubicki, and as they did the three men came out; it was about 8:30 in the evening. Fishbeck said, "Do you want to go on that party?" and, receiving an affirmative answer, he told them to go down by the Farmer-Labor Temple and they (the men) would meet them there. The girls went to the place appointed and found the car in which they were to go in the alley behind the temple. Defendant was driving. The girls protested mildly against going to the chicken ranch, but upon being told no one else would be there, tacitly gave their consent to having the party there. They knew the excursion was not free from peril; when the car stopped they hung back, permitting the men to precede them into the house, and agreed if any one of them should be attacked, "we'll all stick together," and this the sequel shows they attempted to do. The house was warm, ready for their reception.

In the dining room there were a radio, buffet, table, and chairs. They turned on the radio and for a time played cards and checkers or danced. After they had been there about fifteen minutes, Fishbeck said it was about time they had some drinks, and defendant said he would get them, which he did. The drinks consisted mainly of whisky. Three rounds of drinks were served. After the first drink, defendant kissed Dolores and Fishbeck kissed Eugenie. It was not long before there was conversation of a salacious character. While defendant was playing checkers with Lucille, he suggested sexual intercourse to her. Nothing came of this. Fishbeck proposed to Genie in the hearing of all that the two go into a bedroom and have sexual intercourse, and afterwards made the same proposal to Lucille; both girls refused. Shortly after that, defendant and Dolores went into the kitchen to get something to eat, and while there defendant said to Dolores, "Let's go into the bedroom," and when she said, "No," he grabbed her wrists and against her angry protests pulled her down a little hallway and into a bedroom which was dark; there was no light there. He pushed her upon a bed, and when she tried to get up got on the bed with her and threw his left leg over her legs. She said defendant "would pull my dress up and I grabbed his hand. I was lying on the bed on my back and my feet were hanging over the bed. His right arm was around me and his left hand was loose. * * * When he pushed me on the bed, I hollered for Genie and then a few minutes after that I hollered for her again. I was on the bed about ten minutes and all that time I was trying to get up and couldn't because he had one leg over me. He had his leg over me, just over my legs. During that time I was fighting; fought for ten minutes." She kept asking him to let her up and he would not do it; she spoke loudly and in anger. The others were in the dining room, "but the radio was going and you couldn't hear what they said." Her clothing was not disarranged, except that her skirts were lifted above her knees; they were raised five or six inches or possibly a foot above the knees. The bedroom door was not closed. Finally, Dolores said, she heard Genie crying and told defendant there was something wrong in the other room and to let her up. He then released her.

In the meantime Fishbeck had again asked Eugenie to go into the bedroom and she again refused. He then said, "I will take you in there then," and started toward the bedroom, but Lucille got up and stood in front of the door, and he said to Lucille, "I will take you in there then," and attempted to do so, but Eugenie then stood in front of the door. Despite the seriousness of the subject these three seem to have maintained good humor. But when Eugenie heard Dolores call "Genie" and started for the door Fishbeck's humor seemed to change. Eugenie got as far as the hallway when Fishbeck intercepted her, pulled her back into the dining room, and pushed her into a chair; she kicked him and arose to her feet; he hit her in the face and knocked her back onto the chair. She then hit him on the head with a glass which caused the blood to flow and he hit her violently on the nose, upon which she cried out. It was a refined party!

Palubicki, it seems, took no active part in any of these affairs. He simply desisted from interfering. After the defendant and Dolores returned to the dining room and the blood was washed from Fishbeck's head and Genie's nose, all returned to Plentywood.

It is argued that, granting defendant did as Dolores says he did, he is not guilty of an assault with intent to rape, and the court should have granted defendant's motion for a directed verdict. Incidentally, the court could have done no more than to advise the jury to acquit. Section 11995, Rev. Codes 1921. The court did not err in its ruling. With what intent did defendant seize this sixteen year old girl by the wrists, drag her through an unlighted hallway into a bedroom shrouded in darkness, throw her upon the bed, forcibly retain her there, raise her skirt, and hold her prone upon her back while she fought with him for ten minutes? For what purpose was he struggling with her? What was he about in that dark room? Was he reciting the Psalms to her, praying with her, chiding her for drinking whisky in a house of ill repute? On the contrary, the circumstances can leave no doubt in the mind of any one but a simpleton that her consent given—consent which the law did not permit her to give—he would have debauched her. Plainly enough he intended to do so. The sole extenuating circumstances in his favor are that he did not take by force that which otherwise was denied him. He assaulted her by laying violent hands upon her, by throwing her upon the bed, by throwing his body upon her, by his other acts when he had her in her disgraceful position. His intent being plain, the crime charged is proven. People v. Porter, 48 Cal. App. 237, 191 P. 951; People v. Moore, 155 Cal. 237, 100 P. 688; Dickens v. People, 60 Colo. 141, 152 P. 909; Lee v. State, 7 Okl. Cr. 141, 122 P. 111.

The rule laid down in State v. Hennessy, 73 Mont. 20, 234 P. 1094, does not apply in cases of assault with intent to rape when prosecutrix is under the age of consent.

3. Dolores was asked if she knew what the defendant was trying to do, when he had her upon the bed, and she said, "Yes." Then the question was put, "What was he trying to do?" Counsel for defendant objected: "No foundation laid for the question, calling for a conclusion of the witness at the present time." The court having overruled the objection, the witness said, "He was trying to have sexual intercourse with me." Counsel then moved to strike the answer as a "conclusion of the witness and no foundation laid" which was overruled. Error is assigned. It is true that the witness was allowed to state her conclusion. How she could have come to a different conclusion it is difficult to conjecture. To say that this girl, under the circumstances, did not know exactly what defendant's actions meant, is to cast doubt upon her intelligence, and there is no hint in the record that she was not intelligent. "A man's intention, may

be manifested, by his words, or his actions, and when known, may be sworn to with as much certainty, as any other fact. When a witness undertakes to swear to a thing of that kind, the jury, who hear the oath, will value it at what it is worth." Delancy v. Little, 4 Serg. & R. (Pa.) 503, quoted in 1 Wigmore on Evidence (2d Ed.) p. 1066. The difficulty in attempting to distinguish between "opinion" on the one hand and "fact" or "knowledge" on the other, in the multitudinous affairs of everyday life, is discussed by Dean Wigmore in section 1919 of the second edition of his work on Evidence; and see sections 1928 and 1929.

However well justified may be the criticism of the "Opinion" rule, the general rule in this country is that a witness may state facts and not his opinions or conclusions, but there are exceptions to this rule as well settled as is the rule itself. "An ordinary witness may be permitted to testify to his opinion or conclusion where the facts as they appeared to him at the time cannot clearly and adequately be reproduced, described and detailed to the jury." 16 C. J. 747. Or, as was said by this court in State v. Lucey, 24 Mont. 295, 61 P. 994, 997, a witness "may be permitted to state his conclusion upon matters with which he is specially acquainted, but which cannot be specifically described," citing section 460 of Wharton's Criminal Evidence. When the evidence speaks upon such matters of common observation and experience as that the jurors are just as competent to draw inferences therefrom as the witness, there is no necessity for receiving the opinion of the witness thereon. "When the opinion of a nonexpert witness is received, the facts and circumstances upon which he bases his opinion or conclusion should be stated as far as is practicable in order that the jury may have some basis to test the value of his opinion." 16 C. J. 748. In determining whether the conclusions or opinions of either an ordinary or an expert witness are admissible, the court must exercise a large measure of discretion. "In determining what is a statement of fact, as distinguished from an opinion or a conclusion, the courts sometimes disregard," and should disregard "distinctions which are more metaphysical than substantial and hold admissible a statement although it may fall under the head of opinions or conclusions and represents such a simple and rudimentary inference as to be practically a statement of fact. The immediate conclusions of a witness drawn from what he saw and heard are not rejected as opinion evidence." 16 C. J. 749.

While it is true that the question and answer under consideration were perhaps unnecessary for the reason that the jury without the answer had enough before it to determine the fact issue correctly, the answer, based as it was upon the witness' prior testimony, was a compound of fact and conclusion—a "shorthand rendering of the facts" as they were observed and experienced by her, and it was not error to receive it. State v. Lucey, supra. It must be clear to every one that, even if the witness had possessed an unusual faculty of transmitting knowledge by language, facial expression, and gesture, it was impossible for her to portray to the jury with keen accuracy the actions of the defendant, the surrounding conditions considered.

• • •

Judgment affirmed.

LONG v. STATE
274 P.(2d) 553
Criminal Court of Appeals of Oklahoma.
September 22, 1954.

JONES, Judge.

The defendant, Almon Rollins Long, was charged by an information filed in the County Court of Comanche County with the offense of driving an automobile recklessly on a highway; a jury was waived and the case was tried to a special judge who found the defendant guilty and sentenced him to pay a fine of $100 and costs.

The single issue presented on appeal is whether the trial court erred in permitting the highway patrolman to testify over the objection of counsel for the accused to the point of impact or place on the highway where the collision between the automobile being driven by the defendant and the one being driven by one King occurred.

The collision occurred at about 9:30 a. m. The proof of the State showed that one Creed King was driving his automobile in a westerly direction and that he was emerging from an S-curve about 1.6

miles east of Cache when he observed the car of defendant approaching from the west at a speed of about 70 miles an hour; that when defendant's car reached a point about 100 feet from the King automobile, it started at about a 45° angle across the highway and collided with the King automobile on the north side of the center line of the highway.

Lt. C. W. Adams, a highway patrolman, reached the scene of the collision shortly after it occurred. The cars had not been moved. He testified to the relative positions of the automobiles as he observed them upon his arrival at the scene of the collision. He detailed his experience as a patrolman in investigating accidents and the skill he had obtained from such training and experience as a patrolman, and based upon his training and experience he was allowed to state his conclusion as to where the impact occurred based upon his personal observation of the facts, especially relative to skid marks which he saw on the pavement. During the testimony of this witness the record discloses the following occurred:

"Q. Based on your experience as a trooper and as a Lieutenant in the Highway Patrol, did you find from investigating these various collisions that certain physical evidence was always found at the point of impact by vehicles, such as glass or dirt or any other actual objects that marked the point of impact?

"Mr. Smith: Objection, as leading and suggestive; incompetent, irrelevant and immaterial.

"The Court: Overruled. A. Yes, sir.

"Q. When you investigated the collision between the King and Long vehicles, what physical evidence was on the ground, insofar as rubbish, dirt, glass, etc. are concerned?

"Mr. Smith: Objection, as leading and suggestive and incompetent, irrelevant and immaterial.

"The Court: Sustained. Lieutenant, state what, based upon your experience, led you to formulate an opinion as to where the impact occurred. A. Marks left by the tires from both vehicles were plainly visible at the point of impact. The tire marks were left from the point of impact to where they stopped.

"Mr. Smith: Objection to the answer; he is not qualified to testify as to where the impact occurred.

"Mr. Cavanagh: He saw certain skid marks leading from both directions and where these marks met.

"The Court: Objection overruled.

"Mr. Smith: We further object to counsel attempting to put words in the witness' mouth.

"Mr. Cavanagh: We apologize to the Court. I thought that was what he stated.

"The Court: Continue your interrogation.

"Mr. Smith: Note our exception.

"The Court: Allowed.

"Q. Where was the Long vehicle from the point that you believe was the point of impact? A. Across the center line, approximately half and half; a little more to the north side than to the south.

"Q. When we speak of the Long vehicle, we are speaking of the Chrysler. The King vehicle is referred to as the Plymouth. A. Yes, sir.

"Mr. Smith: We object to the question and answer on the grounds that no proper predicate has been laid as to the expression of the witness.

"The Court: Overruled.

"Mr. Cavanagh: I was asking how far was the vehicle from the point of impact.

"Mr. Smith: I withdraw the objection.

"Mr. Cavanagh: My question should have been: How far was Long's vehicle from the point of impact after it came to rest?

"Mr. Smith: May I have a ruling, in the light of developments, as to his misunderstanding. I request a further ruling and clarification as to the objections I made as to the point of impact, to the question previously propounded.

"The Court: I have ruled that, based upon his testimony and his long experience as an investigator and officer, he has laid the proper predicate to opinionate as to the physical objects at the scene.

"Mr. Cavanagh: You are permitting him to testify as to the point of impact?

"The Court: That is correct.

"Mr. Smith: Exception, please.

"The Court: Exception allowed.

"Q. How far was the Long vehicle from the point of impact?

"Mr. Smith: I want to renew my objection to any question relating to or assuming any given point of impact, for the reason that the witness has never laid the proper predicate.

"Mr. Cavanagh: Strike that question. Where was the point of impact with relation to the center line of the highway?

"Mr. Smith: Objection to that question. No proper predicate has been laid. It's incompetent, irrelevant and immaterial. If the Court will give me an exception, and note that it is perpetual, to all of this line of testimony, I'll appreciate it.

"The Court: Overruled and exception allowed. We will treat your objection as perpetual. Answer the question, please. A. The Long vehicle was across the center line and approximately on the center line, with the King vehicle just a little north of the center line. The Long vehicle was astraddle the center line at the point of impact.

"Q. Was the Long vehicle north or south of the center line? A. Right on the center line."

Counsel for the accused in his brief cites the following cases as susstaining his position: Maben v. Lee, Okl., 260 P.2d 1064; Washita Valley Grain Co. v. McElroy, Okl., 262 P.2d 133; Rodgers v. Oklahoma Wheat Pool Terminal Corp., 186 Okl. 171, 96 P.2d 1040; Hadley v. Ross, 195 Okl. 89, 154 P.2d 939.

Counsel for the State in his brief contends that the cases cited by the appellant are not in point because of the difference in the factual situation involved and cites the case of Andrews v. Moery, Okl., 240 P.2d 447, as being more nearly in point.

It is established law that an expert should not be allowed to give opinion testimony where the subject is one of common knowledge as to which facts can be independently described to the jury and understood by them and they can form a reasonable opinion for themselves. 20 Am.Jur. 651. However, it is equally well established that in relation to matters relevant to the issues of a case, when it is not possible or practicable to place before the jury all of the primary facts and circumstances in such way as to enable the jury to form an intelligent conclusion from them, qualified witnesses who have had means of personal observation may state their opinions, conclusions, and impressions formed from such facts and circumstances as come under their observation. 20 Am.Jur. 640.

In the cases cited by counsel for the appellant to sustain his contention, the testimony of the alleged expert was held inadmissible where it was based upon his record of investigation which included hearsay statements given to the officer. In Maben v. Lee, supra, [260 P.2d 1065] which is the principal case relied upon by appellant, the Supreme Court of Oklahoma stated:

> "In a negligence action growing out of automobile accident it was reversible error to admit, over defendant's objections, evidence of highway patrolman who investigated accident in course of his official duties, wherein he expressed his opinions and conclusions, based principally upon hearsay evidence, and purported to fix responsibility for such accident."

The cases cited by appellant supra do not appear to us to be in point with the proposition herein involved but the reasoning of the Supreme Court has been of assistance in deciding the question here presented. Undoubtedly the determining factor in each of those cases was the proof that the conclusion of the expert was based partially upon hearsay statements made to him by third parties concerning certain alleged occurrences at the place of collision. In the instant case no such hearsay evidence was involved. Here the testimony of the highway patrolman was based upon his personal observation of the relative positions of the automobiles at the scene of the collision and skid marks discernible upon the pavement. In Andrews v. Moery, supra, [240 P.2d 449] two officers appeared upon the scene shortly after the collision and made an investigation. In the opinion the Supreme Court stated:

"They both testified as to the width of the pavement at the point of the impact; that the pavement was smooth and dry. They noticed the condition and position of both cars after the accident occurred. They found dirt, glass and other debris on the street where the impact occurred. Plaintiff's car was located about 50 feet beyond the point of impact. They saw skid marks which in their opinion were made by the truck leading from a point where the brakes were apparently applied up to the point of impact. They measured the skid marks and found them to be 120 feet in length. Each of these witnesses testified that from experience gained by him as an officer he was able to give a fairly accurate opinion as to the rate of speed the truck was traveling at the time of the collision based on the length of the skid marks and other physical facts found by him to exist. Each stated that in his opinion the truck at that time was traveling at a speed of about 45 to 50 miles per hour.

"The above evidence was admitted over and against objection of defendants urged on the ground that it called for a conclusion of the witnesses and invaded the province of the jury."

After reviewing various authorities, the Supreme Court held that the trial court did not err in the admission of such evidence. The law of the case as shown in the syllabus is as follows:

"Opinion evidence of expert as to speed of truck involved in accident based upon length of skid marks is admissible.

"A witness who had testified that on arriving at the scene of a collision between an automobile and a truck which happened shortly before, but which he did not see, he observed skid marks leading from the place where the brakes of the truck were applied and leading up to the truck, may properly be asked whether in his opinion the skid marks observed by him were made by the truck."

Under the rule which permits witnesses to testify to conclusions and opinions drawn from facts observed by them and not capable of being adequately reproduced before the court or jury, the opinions of such witnesses are admissible as to the speed of vehicles before the collision, Andrews v. Moery, supra; the location of a spot where a train struck a steer, Fanning v. Long Island Railroad Co.,

2 Thomp. & C., N.Y., 585; as to the relative position of two boats at the time they collided, Patrick v. The J. Q. Adams, 19 Mo. 73; and as to whether the position of a wagon was such that it could have come out of a certain driveway, Nesbit v. Crosby, 74 Conn. 554, 51 A. 550.

A statement of the general rules and the citation of cases seemed to make the question here presented one of which disposition may be easily made, but in the application of those rules, the disposition was not so simple. In every criminal case it is the duty of the court or jury hearing the case to attempt to arrive at the truth. Opinion testimony of experts is only admissible in cases of necessity where to arrive at the truth and a proper understanding of the facts in issue requires some explanation of those facts or some deduction therefrom by persons who have scientific or specialized knowledge or experience. In every criminal case the testimony of witnesses involves in a way a conclusion or opinion of the witness. A statement by a witness as to what he had seen is of course a conclusion of the witness but the fact that the testimony of a witness is a conclusion by the witness or that it pertains to the ultimate fact in issue before the court or jury is not alone the test as to its admissibility. It would appear that the trial court should be vested with a discretion as to the admission of such evidence and whether it would aid in determining the truth or whether it would be an improper invasion of the province of the jury.

In the instant case the trial court in the absence of a jury was particularly concerned as to where the point of impact was located. Before the patrolman finished testifying the following occurred:

> "The Court: I would like to see if I understood your testimony. From your examination of the scene, it is your conclussion, based on the physical facts and your experience as an investigator, that the Long vehicle was across the center line at the time of the impact? A. It was half and half; a little more to the north than to the actual center."

Evidently the court felt that he was unable to definitely determine as a matter within his common knowledge, based upon the testimony as to the skid marks and debris, the point where the collision occurred. King stated the collision occurred on the north side of the center line of the highway and that defendant was driving his automobile at a speed of approximately 70 miles an hour. The defendant was equally emphatic that the collision occurred on the south of the center line of the highway and that he was operating his automobile at a speed not exceeding 40 to 45 miles an hour while King was coming around the curve "at a high rate of speed." Five photographs taken by a newspaper photographer within a few minutes after the collision occurred were admitted in evidence and the trial court in his summation stated that based upon the photographs and the testimony of the highway patrolman as to the point of impact, he found that the defendant was guilty of reckless driving by driving across the center line of the highway at a high rate of speed and striking the automobile of King. The question here presented might be viewed in a different light if the case had been tried to a jury, but where a case is tried to the court in the absence of a jury, it is presumed that the court in arriving at his decision considered only the competent evidence and disregarded any incompetent evidence that might have been admitted and too, here the court himself elicited the disputed testimony because of a desire on his part to arrive at the truth.

No witness testified for the defendant to corroborate his statement that he was blameless for the collision. On the other hand on cross-examination he admitted that he had been twice convicted for driving an automobile on the public highway while in an intoxicated condition, one of which convictions was sustained in Garfield County and another in Oklahoma County.

It is our conclusion that the admission of the testimony of the highway patrolman under the circumstances of this case did not constitute error and that the judgment and sentence of the County Court of Comanche County should be and the same is hereby affirmed.

POWELL, P. J., and BRETT, J., concur.

Cases relating to **Chapter 11**

THE HEARSAY RULE AND EXCEPTIONS

DONNELLY v. UNITED STATES
228 U.S. 243, 57 L.Ed. 820, 33 S.Ct. 449
(1913)

Mr. JUSTICE PITNEY delivered the opinion of the court.

Plaintiff in error was convicted in the Circuit Court of the United States for the Northern District of California, upon an indictment for murder, and, having been sentenced to life imprisonment, sues out this writ of error. The indictment charged him with the murder of one Chickasaw, an Indian, within the limits of an Indian reservation known as the Extension of the Hoopa Valley Reservation, in the County of Humboldt, in the State and Northern District of California. The evidence tended to show that Chickasaw, who was an Indian and a member of the Klamath Tribe, was shot through the body and mortally wounded while he was in or near the edge of the water of the Klamath River, at a place within the exterior limits of the Extension.

The trial proceeded upon the theory that the crime was committed within the river bed and below ordinary highwater mark—a theory favorable to the plaintiff in error, in that it furnishes the basis for one of the principal contentions made in his behalf. The indictment does not allege, nor did the Government undertake to prove, that plaintiff in error was of Indian blood; there was evidence tending to show that he was a white man; and the trial judge instructed the jury in effect that this question was immaterial. It was contended that the Circuit Court was without jurisdiction, first, because the place of the commission of the alleged offense was not within the limits of the Extension of the Hoopa Valley Reservation, but was upon the Klamath River, and therefore outside of those limits; and, secondly, because it did not appear that the defendant was an Indian. These contentions, having been overruled below, are renewed here, and some other jurisdictional questions are raised. In addition, it is contended that the Circuit Court erred in refusing to permit the plaintiff in error to introduce evidence tending to show that one Joe Dick, a deceased Indian, had confessed just before his death that it was he who had shot and killed the Indian Chickasaw.

* * *

The indictment and conviction are based upon § 2145, Rev. Stat., providing that certain general laws of the United States as to the punishment of crimes committed in any place within the sole and exclusive jurisdiction of the United States, except the District of Columbia, "shall extend to the Indian country," and upon § 5339, Rev. Stat., which enacts that any person who commits murder in any place under the exclusive jurisdiction of the United States shall suffer death.

* * *

Hearsay evidence, with a few well recognized exceptions, is excluded by courts that adhere to the principles of the common law. The chief grounds of its exclusion are, that the reported declaration (if in fact made) is made without the sanction of an oath, with no responsibility on the part of the declarant for error or falsification, without opportunity for the court, jury, or parties to observe the demeanor and temperament of the witness, and to search his motives and test his accuracy and veracity by cross-examination, these being most important safeguards of the truth, where a witness testifies in person, and as of his own knowledge; and, moreover, he who swears in court to the extra-judicial declaration does so (especially where the alleged declarant is dead) free from the embarrassment of present contradiction and with little or no danger of successful prosecution for perjury. It is commonly recognized that this double relaxation of the ordinary safeguards must very greatly multiply the probabilities of error, and that hearsay evidence is an unsafe reliance in a court of justice.

One of the exceptions to the rule excluding it is that which permits the reception, under certain circumstances and for limited purposes, of declarations of third parties made contrary to their own interest; but it is almost universally held that this must be an interest of a pecuniary character; and the fact that the declaration, alleged to have been thus extra-judicially made, would probably subject the declarant to a criminal liability is held not to be sufficient to constitute it an exception to the rule against hearsay evidence. So it was held in two notable cases in the House of Lords—*Berkeley Peerage Case* (1811), 4 Camp. 401; *Sussex Peerage Case* (1844), 11 Cl. & Fin. 85, 103, 109; 8 Eng. Reprint, 1034, 1042—recognized as of controlling authority in the courts of England.

In this country there is a great and practically unanimous weight of authority in the state courts against admitting evidence of confessions of third parties made out of court and tending to exonerate the accused. Some of the cases . . . (*West* v. *State*, 76 Alabama 98; *Davis* v. *Commonwealth*, 95 Kentucky 19; and *People* v. *Hall*, 94 California 595, 599) are precisely in point with the present case, in that the alleged declarant was shown to be deceased at the time of the trial. In *West* v. *State* the defendant offered to prove by a witness that he heard one Jones say on his death bed that he had killed Wilson, the deceased. The Supreme Court sustained the ruling of the trial judge excluding the evidence. In *Davis* v. *Commonwealth*, the offer excluded was to prove by a witness that one Pearl confessed to him on his death bed that he had killed the person for whose murder Davis was on trial. The Court of Appeals of Kentucky affirmed the conviction. In *People* v. *Hall* it appeared that defendant and one Kingsberry were arrested together for an alleged burglary, attempted to escape, were fired upon and wounded by one of the captors; that a physician was sent for to treat them, and that Kingsberry died from the effects of his wound before any complaint was filed against either of the parties. "In his own behalf the defendant offered to prove that after a careful examination the physician was satisfied that Kingsberry's wounds were necessarily fatal, and that he so informed him at the time; that Kingsberry admitted to the physician that he fully realized that he was mortally wounded and was on the point of death, and had given up all hope of ever getting well; that he was conscious of death, and that thus having a sense of impending death, and without hope of reward, he made a full, free, and complete confession to said physician in relation to this alleged crime, stating that he himself had planned the entire scheme, and that Hall had nothing to do with it and was not connected with the guilt, and was in all respects innocent of any criminal act or intent in the matter." This evidence was excluded, and the Supreme Court of California sustained the ruling, saying: "The rule is settled beyond controversy that in a prosecution for crime the declaration of another person that he committed the crime is not admissible. Proof of such declarations is mere hearsay evidence, and is always excluded, whether the person making it be dead or not" (citing cases that are among those included in the note).

We do not consider it necessary to further review the authorities, for we deem it settled by repeated decisions of this court, commencing at an early period, that declarations of this character are to be excluded as hearsay.

Mima Queen and Child v. *Hepburn* (1813), 7 Cranch 290, 295, 296, 297, was a suit in which the petitioners claimed freedom, and certain depositions were rejected by the trial court as hearsay. This court, speaking through Chief Justice Marshall, said: "These several opinions of the court (meaning the trial court) depend on one general principle. The decision of which determines them all. It is this: that hearsay evidence is incompetent to establish any specific fact, which fact is in its nature susceptible of being proved by witnesses who speak from their own knowledge. . . . It was very justly observed by a great judge that 'all questions upon the rules of evidence are of vast importance to all orders and degrees of men; our lives, our liberty, and our property are all concerned in the support of these rules, which have been matured by the wisdom of ages, and are now revered from their antiquity and the good sense in which they are founded.' One of these rules is that 'hearsay' evidence is in its own nature inadmissible. That this species of testimony supposes some better testimony which might be adduced in the particular case, is not the sole ground of its exclusion. Its intrinsic weakness, its incompetency to satisfy the mind of the existence of the fact, and the frauds which might be practiced under its cover combine to support the rule that hearsay evidence is totally inadmissible. . . . The danger of admitting hearsay evidence is sufficient to admonish courts of justice against lightly yielding to the introduction of fresh exceptions to an old and well-established rule; the value of which is felt and acknowledged by all. If the circumstance that the eye witnesses of any fact be dead should justify the introduction of testimony to establish that fact from hearsay, no man could feel safe in any property, a claim to which might be supported by proof so easily obtained. . . . This court is not inclined to extend the exceptions further than they have already been carried."

This decision was adhered to in *Davis* v. *Wood* (1816), 1 Wheat. 6, 8; *Lessee of Scott* v. *Ratliffe* (1831), 5 Pet. 81, 86; *Ellicott* v. *Pearl* (1836), 10 Pet. 412, 436, 437; *Wilson* v. *Simpson* (1850), 9 How. 109, 121; *Hopt* v. *Utah* (1883), 110 U.S. 574, 581. And see *United States* v. *Mulholland*, 50 Fed. Rep. 413, 419.

The evidence of the Dick confession was properly excluded.

No error appearing in the record, the judgment is

Affirmed.

COMMONWEALTH v. BROWN
388 Pa. 613, 131 A.(2d) 367
Supreme Court of Pennsylvania.
April 26, 1957.

BELL, Justice.

A narrow but very important question is raised in this case: Was it reversible error to charge the jury that a dying declaration in a homicide case has the same effect as if it were made under oath?

Mary E. Brown was indicted for murder but was convicted of voluntary manslaugter. Defendant and Vivian Gay apparently in a fit of jealousy, attacked Dorothy Francis, the decedent, on the street. Dorothy Francis was killed by a knife wound in the breast. Who stabbed her was the crucial factual question, Vivian Gay blaming Mary Brown and Mary Brown blaming Vivian Gay. Two eyewitnesses testified that defendant, Mary Brown, attacked Dorothy Francis with a knife, while Vivian Gay beat her with a golf club. Defendant denied that she had a knife or that she stabbed Dorothy Francis, and testified that Vivian Gay was the one who had the knife and inflicted the mortal wound. Vivian Gay testified that she saw Mary Brown, the defendant, stab Dorothy Francis, and that while they were both in jail, defendant admitted to her that she had stabbed Dorothy Francis. Moreover, Dorothy Francis, just before her death and at a time when she knew she was about to die, made a dying declaration that Mary Brown, the defendant, stabbed her.

The Judge's charge to the jury was lengthy and very able with the one possible exception which is here alleged for error, namely, that if the jury were satisfied beyond a reasonable doubt that Dorothy Francis believed she was about to die and had no hope of recovery when she stated that Mary Brown stabbed her "you can give that statement the same effect as though it were made under oath." Because of the conflict of evidence, the Court's charge on this point was important.

The subject of dying declarations and the restrictions and limitations on their admissibility were analyzed and reviewed by this Court in Commonwealth v. Knable, 369 Pa. 171, 175-176, 85 A.2d 114, 116. In that case the Court pertinently said:

"Dying declarations of the deceased concerning the circumstances of his injuries are admissible in the trial of a person accused of killing him. To validate a dying declaration it is not necessary that the wounded man expressly say that he knows that he is dying; it suffices, if at the time the declaration is made, the declarant believed he was in fact dying and that death was imminent, and death did actually ensue. ° ° ° In passing upon the admissibility of an alleged dying declaration all the attendant circumstances should be considered, including the weapon which wounded him, the nature and extent of his injuries, his physical condition, his conduct, and what was said to and by him: Commonwealth v. Lockett, 291 Pa. 319, 139 A. 836; Commonwealth v. Puntario, 271 Pa. 511, 115 A. 831; Commonwealth v. Peyton, 360 Pa. 441, 62 A.2d 37; Commonwealth v. Plubell, 367 Pa. 452, 80 A.2d 825; Wigmore on Evidence, Third Edition, Vol. 5, Sec. 1442. Whether the attendant facts and circumstances of the case warrant the admission of a statement as a dying declaration is in the first instance for the court, but, when admitted, the declarant's state of mind *and the credibility, interpretation and weight to be given his statement are for the jury* under proper instructions [citing cases]."

However, that case did not answer the exact question here involved, and there are relatively few cases and text authorities directly on the point.

Dying declarations in homicide cases have from ancient times been admitted in evidence either (1) because of solemnity—the solemnity of the occasion and the fear of punishment in the hereafter if one tells a lie just before death, or (2) because of necessity—since the victim of the homicide cannot testify its admission is necessary to protect the public against homicidal criminals and prevent a miscarriage of justice. However, a number of authorities point out that while it is a substitute for an oath and its credibility and weight is for the jury, it is merely heresay and is not the equivalent of nor does it have the same value or weight as the testimony of a witness given under oath in open Court which, of course, is subject to cross-examination. In our judgment, both grounds justify the admissibility of dying declarations; the value and weight of such declarations (if the trial Court admits them), all authorities agree, are for the jury.

If a dying declaration is not the equivalent of sworn testimony under oath, what weight is the jury to give it if they believe it, and how can a trial Judge express to them the difference in value and weight of dying declarations as contrasted with sworn testimony? Would not any such attempt merely serve to confuse the jury?

Some authorities which limit the value and weight to be given to dying declarations, point out that the declarant may be influenced by hatred or revenge or similar unworthy motives, but this is equally applicable to any despicable character who takes the witness stand. " 'When every hope of this world is gone, when every motive to falsehood is silenced, and the mind is induced by the most powerful considerations to speak the truth, a situation so solemn and aweful is considered by the law as creating the most impressive of sanctions.' 1 Wharton's Criminal Law, § 669; 3 Russell by Greaves 250; 1 Greenleaf, §§ 156, 162, 346; 1 Taylor on Evidence 616." Brown v. Commonwealth, 73 Pa. 321, at page 327.

Expressed in other words, when a person is faced with death which he knows is impending and he is about to see his Maker face to face, is he not more likely to tell the truth than is a witness in Court who knows that if he lies he will have a locus penitentiae, an opportunity to repent, confess and be absolved of his sin? For all these reasons, we believe, weighing all the pros and cons, that it is in the best interests of the public that a dying declaration should be considered as the equivalent of testimony given under oath in open Court. However, from a realistic point of view, it would seem advisable for a trial Judge to omit, in his charge to the jury, any comparison and merely say that the question whether the declarant believed he was dying at the time he made the declaration, and the credibility, interpretation and weight to be given his statement under the attendant facts and circumstances of the case, are for the jury.

Appellant relies upon Commonwealth v. Gardner, 282 Pa. 458, 128 A. 87, and Commonwealth v. Lockett, 291 Pa. 319, 139 A. 836. In Commonwealth v. Gardner, 282 Pa. 458, 128 A. 87, 92, supra, the declarant, during the period when she was dying, made several conflicting statements and consequently her credibility was considerably shaken. Perhaps for this reason, the Court said: "Dying declarations" are admissible under certain circumstances, but if they are admissible they "are not to be considered as though given under the sanctity of an oath." In Commonwealth v. Lockett, 291 Pa. 319, 139 A. 836, supra, a dying declaration which was made in the form of an affidavit was admitted in evidence. Nevertheless, the Court said, 291 Pa. at pages 322-323, 139 A. at page 838: "* * * This grave situation *supplies* the place of an oath taken in open Court, although the statement so given is not considered the equivalent of sworn testimony, as the declarant is not brought face to face with the accused and the opportunity to cross-examine is lacking * * *."

A dying declaration should in our judgment be given the same value and weight as sworn testimony, and any statement to the contrary in prior cases will not be followed by us.

Judgment affirmed.

PEOPLE v. WASHINGTON
81 Cal.Rptr. 5, 459 P.(2d) 259
Supreme Court of California.
October 3, 1969.

TRAYNOR, Chief Justice.

By indictment Mrs. Leiala Spencer, Kenneth Davis, and defendant Ernest Washington, were jointly charged with the robbery and murder of Benjamin Kay. The trial court granted defendant's motion for severance, and thereafter a jury found him guilty of first degree murder (Pen. Code, § 187) and first degree robbery (Pen. Code, § 211) and fixed the penalty for the murder at death. The trial court denied motions for a new trial and to reduce the penalty and entered judgment on the verdict. It stayed execution of sentence for both crimes pending this automatic appeal. (Pen.Code, § 1239, subd. (b).)

Mr. Kay owned a department store in San Diego. He made many credit sales to welfare recipients and other people who had low incomes. He personally collected from his credit customers by calling on them at their homes at the beginning and middle of each month when welfare recipients receive their checks. He carried as much as $1,000 in cash so that he could cash his customers' checks on such visits. On November 1, 1967, he was fatally beaten and robbed just after he had called at the home of Mrs. Spencer to make a collection.

The crime took place about 9 p. m. behind Mrs. Spencer's house. The area was very dark, for someone had tampered with the lights at the back of the house next door that otherwise would have illuminated the area. A witness saw Mr. Kay walk toward the back of Mrs. Spencer's house and heard him knock at the back door. Shortly thereafter he was found still alive but badly beaten. He died in a hospital the next morning.

A web of evidence implicated defendant in the crime. About ten days before it occurred, when defendant was visiting a witness at her house in the neighborhood, he looked out a window and said: "That's Ben Kay. He carries about five or six hundred dollars around with him every day * * * and all you have to do is knock him in the head." He also mentioned that Kay came around on the first and sixteenth of every month.

On the afternoon of the day of the crime, Mr. Kay's son saw Mrs. Spencer and defendant together across the street from the Kay store gesturing in its direction. Defendant was then living at Mrs. Spencer's house, and he made a long distance telephone call from there about 7:05 p. m on November 1.

Before November 1, defendant was unemployed and ineligible

for relief. His car had been repossessed and he had unsuccessfully sought to borrow money from a friend. Between 7:30 and 8 on the evening of November 1, however, he telephoned another friend, Elvernon White, asked if he could use White's car, and said that he might have some money with which to get his own car back. At 8:30 the next morning he went to the dealer who had repossessed his car, paid him $100 and retrieved his car. Witnesses who saw him on the following days testified that he had many $20 bills and spent money freely. About 9 on the evening of the murder he checked into a motel some six minutes walking distance from Mrs. Spencer's house. He stayed for three days and paid the motel rent in cash.

Between 9:45 and 11 on the morning of November 2, defendant, Mrs. Spencer, and Davis were in the apartment of the witness, Rodney Pitts. Pitts testified that the three spent some time in his kitchen whispering, that Mrs. Spencer had quite a few bills and many money orders that she had apparently purchased, and that she gave some of the money and money orders to Davis. When defendant left Pitts' apartment about 11 a. m., he met his friend Elvernon White on the street and told him, "I'm hot. I think I have killed a man," or "I have killed a man."

Defendant was arrested on November 4 as he was preparing to leave San Diego. He made several statements to police officers in which he gave differing accounts of the crime and the parts he, Davis, and Mrs. Spencer played in it. He was repeatedly warned of his constitutional rights, and he does not contend that any of his statements were inadmissible. Although defendant never admitted to the officers that he attacked Mr. Kay, he told them that he was present when Mrs. Spencer planned to have Davis rob Mr. Kay after Mr. Kay left her house; he admitted that he and Davis went behind Mrs. Spencer's house when Mr. Kay approached and stated that Davis hit him with a pipe, and that when Mr. Kay yelled, Davis hit him twice more. Defendant claimed that he got scared, walked away, and shortly therafter checked into a motel. In a later statement defendant revised his account of the crime and stated that Mrs. Spencer "hit the old man; that she followed him out of the house and hit him with the pipe from the rear, from the back." He further stated that Mrs. Spencer had removed the light fixture from the back of the house next door.

The prosecution also introduced evidence that while defendant was in jail awaiting trial, he wrote two letters requesting friends to testify that he was at their houses from 5 to 8:30 on the evening of November 1.

Defendant testified in his own defense. He denied any involvement in the robbery and murder and stated that from 7:30 until 10 on the evening of November 1, he was in downtown San Diego looking for his wife. He denied having made many of the admissions attributed to him and testified that other admissions that he made were false.

• • •

Defendant contends that the trial court erred in admitting into evidence statements made by Mr. Kay to a nurse shortly after he was taken to a hospital. The trial court admitted the statements over objection under the spontaneous statement exception to the hearsay rule. (Evid.Code, § 1240). Mr. Kay was unconscious when he arrived at the hospital about 45 minutes after the crime was committed. An officer asked the emergency room nurse to ask Mr. Kay what happened to him. He did not respond to her initial inquiries, but in about 20 minutes he regained consciousness for three or four minutes. The nurse again asked him what happened to him, and he said either "I was beaten" or "I was robbed." She then asked him if he knew who had done it and he replied "no." She then asked, "Was there more than one person involved?" and he said, "There was more than one." "Was there two involved?" she inquired, and he replied, "Maybe two or three." There was a pause of about 30 seconds between each question and the reply.

Section 1240 of the Evidence Code provides: "Evidence of a statement is not made inadmissible by the hearsay rule if the statement: (a) Purports to narrate, describe, or explain an act, condition, or event perceived by the declarant; and (b) Was made spontaneously while the declarant was under the stress of excitement caused by such perception." The section codified an existing exception to the hearsay rule (Law Revision Commission Comment to § 1240), which was carefully restated in Showalter v. Western Pacific R. R. Co. (1940) 16 Cal.2d 460, 468, 106 P.2d 895, 900. To be admissible, "(1) there must be some occurrence startling enough to produce * * * nervous excitement and render the utterance spontaneous and unreflecting; (2) the utterance must have been before there has been time to contrive and misrepresent, i. e., while the nervous excitement may be supposed still to dominate and the reflective powers to be yet in abeyance; and (3) the utterance must relate to the circumstance of the occurrence preceding it." (Wigmore on Evidence, [2d ed.], sec. 1750.)

Neither lapse of time between the event and the declarations nor the fact that the declarations were elicited by questioning deprives the statements of spontaneity if it nevertheless appears that they were made under the stress of excitement and while the reflective powers were still in abeyance. (Lane v. Pacific Greyhound Lines (1945) 26 Cal.2d 575, 583, 160 P.2d 21; People v. Costa (1953) 40 Cal.2d 160, 168, 252 P.2d 1; Showalter v. Western Pacific R. R. Co., supra, 16 Cal.2d 460, 467, 106 P.2d 895; Wiley v. Easter (1962) 203 Cal.App.2d 845, 854, 21 Cal.Rptr. 905.) In the present case Mr. Kay was unconscious for most of the time between the beating and the nurse's questions. (See People v. Costa, supra.) He had suffered brain damage and was having difficulty breathing. The evidence supports the trial court's findings that Mr. Kay did not have power to reflect on his answers and that the slowness of his responses resulted, not from reflection, but from his critical physical condition. Accordingly, the trial court did not err in ruling that the statements were admissible under section 1240. (See Showalter v. Western Pacific R. R. Co., supra, 16 Cal.2d 460, 468-469, 106 P.2d 895; Ungefug v. D'Ambrosia (1967) 250 Cal.App.2d 61, 67, 58 Cal.Rptr. 223; People v. Fain (1959) 174 Cal.App.2d 856, 861, 345 P.2d 305; 6 Wigmore, Evidence (3d ed. 1940) § 1750, p. 154; Witkin, Evidence (2d ed. 1966) § 547, p. 520.) Moreover, that decision was for the trial court alone to make, and it therefore did not err in failing to instruct the jury to disregard the statements if the jury found them not to have been spontaneous within the meaning of section 1240. (Evid.Code, § 405; People v. Cruz (1968) 264 Cal.App.2d 350, 360, fn. 11, 70 Cal.Rptr. 603; cf. People v. Bazaure (1965) 235 Cal.App. 2d 21, 38, 44 Cal.Rptr. 831, stating rule applicable before the adoption of the Evidence Code.)

Defendant contends that seven prospective jurors were excused for cause in violation of Witherspoon v. Illinois (1968) 391 U.S. 510,

88 S.Ct. 1770, 20 L.Ed.2d 776. We need not canvass the entire group cited by defendant, for it is clear that at least one venireman was excused in violation of the standards set forth in that case. (See People v. Bradford (1969) 70 A.C. 347, 358-359, 74 Cal.Rptr. 726, 450 P.2d 46.)

Venireman Norbert Elsner twice indicated on the first day of *voir dire* that he could vote for the death penalty, though he would be loath to do so on circumstantial evidence alone unless that evidence were "very strong." On the second day the following colloquy took place between Mr. Elsner and the bench.

"PROSPECTIVE JUROR ELSNER: Your Honor, I have certain reservations where I can't vote for taking a man's life.

"THE COURT: Do you feel your responses to the Court yesterday were not—

"PROSPECTIVE JUROR ELSNER: They were in truth yesterday. Its just that I have given it more thought. I had never thought about it as being a personal responsibility in this case. I seem to be going the other way today. Up to this point I had never thought I was against capital punishment, but for some reason I tend to be drifting that way. The answers I gave the prosecuting attorney yesterday I think were—

"THE COURT: Are you satisfied at this time in your own mind that you entertain a conscientious opinion with reference to the death penalty?

"PROSPECTIVE JUROR ELSNER: I feel I would be hesitant to vote for a death penalty.

"THE COURT: All right. You may be excused, Mr. Elsner."

Witherspoon held that "a sentence of death cannot be carried out if the jury that imposed or recommended it was chosen by excluding venirement for cause simply because they voiced general objections to the death penalty or expressed conscientious or religious scruples against its infliction." (391 U.S. at p. 522, 88 S.Ct. at p. 1777.) In the instant case Elsner did not even indicate that he objected to the death penalty, but only that he was "drifting that way." His feeling that he would be "hesitant" to impose the death penalty is one undoubtedly shared by many who would nevertheless impose it in some cases. (See e. g., Witherspoon v. Illinois, supra, 391 U.S. 510, 515, fn. 8, 88 S.Ct. 1770; People v. Bradford, supra, 70 A.C. 347, 359, 74 Cal.Rptr. 726, 450 P.2d 46.) Elsner's statements did not make it "unmistakably clear (1) that [he] would *automatically* vote against the imposition of capital punishment without regard to any evidence that might be developed at the trial ° ° ° or (2) that [his] attitude toward the death penalty would prevent [him] from making an impartial decision as to the defendant's guilt." (391 U.S. at p. 522, fn. 21, 88 S.Ct. at p. 1777.)

The judgment is reversed insofar as it relates to the penalty on the conviction for murder. In all other respects the judgment is affirmed.

PETERS, TOBRINER, MOSK, BURKE and SULLIVAN, JJ., concur.

McCOMB, J., would affirm the judgment in its entirety.

OVERTON v. UNITED STATES
403 F.2d 444 (1968)
WILLIAM A. McRAE, Jr., District Judge:

This is an appeal by James T. Overton from a conviction on the second count of a two count indictment charging a conspiracy to intimidate a witness in a federal prosecution, and the substantive offense of intimidating the witness. The statute involved is 18 U.S.C. § 1503.

Richard Hinton was under investigation by the FBI in connection with a bank robbery. He told the agents he had participated in the robbery with Charles Ray Overton, brother of appellant.

Before the date set for the trial of Charles Ray Overton, appellant commenced a series of personal contacts with Mrs. Betty Hinton, wife of the witness Richard Hinton. During this period Hinton was at all times in the Travis County Jail, Austin.

On April 20, 1967, appellant telephoned Mrs. Hinton at her home in Austin, and said "Betty, this isn't a threat. But somebody up there is doing some talking, and tell Richard to tell whoever it is to shut up." Mrs. Hinton promptly delivered that message to her husband in the jail.

Shortly aftewward, appellant and his wife went to the Hinton home and had a conversation with Mrs. Hinton. Appellant asked Mrs. Hinton if Richard Hinton was going to take the stand and testify against Charles Ray Overton. Appellant told Mrs. Hinton that he had seen a statement which had been made by Richard Hinton. He also told her that he would hate to see his brother get more time to serve in the penitentiary. Appellant then commented that he did not know what was wrong with Richard, and that Richard should know that he wouldn't be able to live in Austin and "walk the streets." Mrs. Hinton likewise conveyed this statement to Richard Hinton.

A little later appellant again returned to the Hinton house and asked Mrs. Hinton if Richard was going to take the stand against appellant's brother.

On May 14, 1967, the day before the trial of Charles Ray Overton, Richard Hinton advised the prosecutor and the FBI agent assigned to the case that he was going to refuse to testify because he was afraid for himself and his family. He stated that his fears were based upon the various reports made to him by his wife after the telephone call and the visits by appellant to the Hinton house.

After reflection, Hinton decided to resume his cooperation with the authorities, and he did in fact testify at the trial of Charles Ray Overton and others.

Appellant's first contention is that the evidence is not sufficient to sustain a conviction under count two of the indictment, which charges that appellant did corruptly and by threats endeavor to influence, intimidate and impede the witness Richard Hinton in violation of 18 U.S.C. § 1503. This contention is manifestly without merit.

It was incumbent upon the prosecution to prove beyond a reasonable doubt that appellant acted either corruptly or by threats in an endeavor either to influence, intimidate or impede the witness Hinton. Smith v. United States, 234 F.2d 385 (5th Cir. 1956), Samples v. United States, 121 F.2d 263 (5th Cir. 1941). Even "experimental approaches" to the corruption of a juror in the discharge of his duty is, without regard to success or failure, a violation of the law. United States v. Russell, 255 U.S. 138, 41 S.Ct. 260, 65 L.Ed. 553 (1921). The prosecution fully met the burden imposed by law.

Appellant urges that the trial court erred in denying his pretrial motion for bill of particulars, in which he requested that the government be ordered to tell him exactly what he was alleged to have said to Mrs. Hinton on the occasions as set forth in the indictment. The granting of a motion for bill of particulars lies within the sound discretion of the trial court. It is not the function of a bill of particulars to provide a detailed disclosure of the government's evidence in advance of trial. Wong Tai v. United States, 273 U.S. 77, 47 S.Ct. 300, 71 L.Ed. 545 (1927), Johnson v. United States, 207 F.2d 314 (5th Cir. 1953). There is no contention that failure to have a bill of particulars resulted in any surprise during the trial. The indictment itself contained ample allegations to put appellant on notice as to the time, place and persons involved in each conversation. There was clearly no abuse of discretion by the trial judge in denying the motion.

Appellant's timely motion for change of venue was based on the assertion that radio, television and newspaper coverage of his past conduct prejudiced his right to a fair and impartial trial. The motion was supported by two affidavits which were executed approximately one year before the trial. In pressing his argument, appellant pointed out that the district judge, during another criminal proceeding against him about four months before the trial in the present case, said "it is a matter of common knowledge hereabout, that no case has ever been given any more publicity than the Overton cases. ° ° ° I don't know whether there is any truth in what they say about him or not or about his brothers, but I know that that kind of atmosphere and that kind of condition is not conducive to a fair trial as a matter of presumption." The district judge denied appellant's motion, with the reservation that if an impartial jury could not be selected venue would be changed. The judge was of the opinion that conditions had changed sufficiently to remove any presumption that appellant could not receive a fair trial. As the government pointed out, no question of prejudice was made to appear on the part of any juror during the voir dire and no juror was challenged for cause by either side. Considering the record as a whole, there was no abuse of discretion by the trial judge in denying the motion for change of venue. Greenhill v. United States, 298 F.2d 405 (5th Cir. 1962). See Estes v. United States, 335 F.2d 609 (5th Cir. 1964).

Mrs. Hinton testified as to the content of the conversations she had with appellant Overton. She also testified that she communicated the substance of these conversations to her husband who was in jail. Hinton himself then took the stand and testified, over the timely objection of Overton's attorney, that his wife had reported to him that she had had the conversations with Overton. In his testimony Hinton related the substance of what his wife reported to him as having been said to her by Overton. Appellant strongly urges that his testimony of Hinton was a violation of the hearsay rule and was accordingly inadmissible. The government responds that Hinton's testimony has nothing to do with the hearsay rule, but was admissible as evidence of a "verbal act."

The verbal act doctrine is technically not an exception to the hearsay rule. The words offered in evidence were not offered for the purpose of proving the truth of the assertions they contained, but merely for the purpose of establishing the fact that the statements which Mrs. Hinton testified that she had made to her husband were in fact made to him by her. This was plainly pointed out when counsel for the government stated that the messages delivered to Richard Hinton by his wife were "for the purpose of showing that the conversations took place in fact, rather than for the purpose of proving the truth of the assertions contained in the remarks made by Mrs. Hinton to her husband. * * *" The conversations were admissible as "verbal acts." They were not offered to show the truth of the assertions. Ward v. United States, 296 F.2d 898 (5th Cir. 1961).

It was essential that appellant should have Mrs. Hinton make contact with the witness Richard Hinton and tell him what appellant had said regarding Richard Hinton's decision to testify against appellant's brother. Mrs. Hinton may be regarded as appellant's agent, or the conduit through which appellant communicated with the witness. Hicks v. United States, 173 F.2d 570 (4th Cir. 1949). See also Phillips v. United States, 356 F.2d 297 (9th Cir. 1965).

The rule is well stated by Wigmore who points out that "[w]herever an utterance is offered to evidence the *state of mind* which ensued *in another person* in consequence of the utterance, it is obvious that no assertive or testimonial use is sought to be made of it, and the utterance is therefore admissible, so far as the Hearsay rule is concerned." VI Wigmore, Evidence, 235 (3rd ed.)

In any event, the admission of the conversations was not prejudicial in view of Mrs. Hinton's prior testimony reciting the details of her conversations with appellant and her statement that the messages were in fact delivered to the witness Richard Hinton. Bedell v. United States, 78 F.2d 358 (8th Cir. 1935).

The judgment of conviction is
Affirmed.

Cases relating to Chapter 12

DOCUMENTARY EVIDENCE

UNITED STATES v. ALEXANDER

326 F.(2d) 736

United States Court of Appeals

Fourth Circuit.

Decided Jan. 17, 1964.

BOREMAN, Circuit Judge.

Appellant, Ernest Franklin Alexander, and one Robinson were charged in a two-count indictment with violations of the laws relating to the postal service. The first count charged that Alexander and Robinson had taken from an authorized depository for mail matter a letter addressed to Sammie W. Woodall, 205 North Franklin Road, Greenville, South Carolina, containing a United States Treasury check made payable to the addressee. The second count charged the possession of the particular Treasury check which was the "contents" of the letter addressed to Sammie W. Woodall, with knowledge that the same had been stolen, taken or abstracted from an authorized depository for mail matter. Alexander entered a plea of not guilty as to both counts and alone was tried before a jury. Upon his motion, the first count was dismissed as to him and the jury returned a verdict of guilty as charged in the second count. Defendant did not testify in his own defense. The admission, over objection, of certain evidence is challenged on appeal. We think that the defendant is entitled to a new trial.

It is uncontroverted that on the fourth day of February, 1963, two Greenville County Sheriff's deputies, in response to a telephoned tip from an undisclosed source, proceeded to a point on Furman Road in Greenville County, South Carolina, where they spotted Alexander and his co-indictee, Robinson, walking along the roadway. Robinson undertook to run away from the officers but was apprehended within a short distance and a check, not here involved, was taken from his person. Alexander offered no resistance and, at the officer's request, took a seat in the rear of the sheriff's car. Mc-

Call, one of the deputies, testified that while the other deputy was struggling with Robinson he saw Alexander, who was then seated in the sheriff's car, drop or throw a check out of the car. McCall stated that he retrieved the check and subsequently turned it over to McClure, a government postal inspector who was called in after Alexander and Robinson were taken to the sheriff's office.

There was no direct proof of the material allegations of the indictment. The Government relied entirely upon circumstantial evidence to prove that the check which Alexander had in his possession had been contained in a letter which was taken from an authorized depository for mail matter. A substantial part of that evidence was the testimony of Mrs. Sammie W. Woodall, a widow lady who lived approximately three-quarters of a mile from the spot where Alexander and Robinson were apprehended. She testified that she received each month from the United States a Social Security check made payable to her in the amount of $106.20; that the check came to her by United States mail and was delivered to the mailbox at her residence on the third day of each month, but when the third fell on Sunday the check was always delivered on Monday, the fourth; that on Monday, the fourth day of February, 1963, she left her home in the morning and upon her return in the afternoon the check which she was expecting to receive that day was not in the mailbox; that a check payable to her in the amount of $106.20 was subsequently delivered to her and she cashed it at a store; that she had never given *any* check to the defendant, Alexander. There was no direct evidence to show that the check, or a letter in which it was contained, had been stolen or taken from Mrs. Woodall's mailbox. Over timely objection by the defense, several government witnesses were permitted to testify as to the terms of the check and a copy of the check was admitted in evidence.

The first witness presented by the Government was C. V. McCall, Special Deputy Sheriff for Greenville County. In addition to his account of the circumstances of the arrest, McCall testified that when shown the check which he, McCall, had given the postal inspector, Alexander admitted having had it in his possession and throwing it from the car. Officer McCall described the check as follows: "It was to Sammie W. Woodall, 205 North Franklin Road, Greenville, South Carolina."

The postal inspector, Earl W. McClure, was the second government witness. He testified that after the defendant's arrest he went to the sheriff's office where he obtained from the arresting officers the check which Officer McCall had retrieved; that he showed the check, which he described as addressed to Sammie W. Woodall in the amount of $106.20, to Alexander who admitted having dropped the check out of the police car; that he subsequently caused the check to be delivered to the payee, Mrs. Sammie W. Woodall, with instructions to cash it; that while the check was in his possession he, McClure, attempted to have a copy made of it with a thermofax machine; that the machine did not reproduce the name and address of the payee and he typed those terms on the copy. The copy prepared by the postal inspector was admitted in evidence and the terms were read to the jury by the inspector.

The next witness called by the Government was Officer Shirley of the Greenville County Sheriff's office. After refreshing his memory from notations which he had made, he testified that, in his presence, the defendant admitted to Postal Inspector McClure that he had had in his possession a check which the witness described as payable "to Sammie W. Woodall, 205 North Franklin Road, Greenville, S. C., in the amount of $106.20."

The envelope from which the check was allegedly taken was not produced and apparently was not found. The check itself, although described in detail in the indictment, was not offered in evidence. The record indicates that the check was delivered to the alleged payee and, pursuant to instructions given by the postal inspector, was cashed by her. In the normal course of banking operations the check would have reached the drawee in Birmingham, Alabama. There is nothing in the testimony to show that the check could not have been produced at the trial.

It is the defendant's contention that the admission of the copy and the parol evidence to show the terms of the check, without the production of the check itself or a reasonable explanation of the Government's failure to produce it, violated the "best evidence rule" and constituted prejudicial error. The Government concedes that there was no sufficient foundation laid for the introduction of secondary evidence; it argues, however, that the evidence objected to was introduced to show the *identity* of a specific physical object, namely, the check, and hence its admission was not violative of the best evidence rule.

It has often been stated as a universal rule of evidence that the best evidence that is obtainable in the circumstances of the case must be adduced to prove any disputed fact. Although the rule apparently enjoyed a broader application at one time, it is now generally recognized that the "best evidence" phrase denotes only the rule of evidence which requires that the contents of an available written document be proved by introduction of the document itself. So limited, there is no question as to the meaning of the rule. As stated in 20 Am.Jur., Evidence § 406 (1958):

> "Where proof is to be made of some fact which is recorded in a writing, the best evidence of the contents of the writing consists in the actual production of the document itself. Any proof of a lower degree is secondary evidence which will be received as proof only where nonproduction of the writing is properly accounted for. The contents of a written instrument may not, as a general rule, be proved by parol, unless the failure to produce the paper itself is accounted for. The principle is controlling in every case wherein it is sought to prove the contents of written instruments of any kind whatsoever. * * *"

As defined by McCormick, the rule is that "in proving the terms of a writing, where such terms are material, the original writing must be produced, unless it is shown to be unavailable for some reason other than the serious fault of the proponent." McCormick, Evidence § 196 (1954).

It would seem that this case, involving as it does secondary evidence of a writing, without any explanation of the failure to produce the writing itself, is within the mandate of the best evidence rule. The Government argues, however, that the rule is not applicable here because the purpose of the Government in offering the evidence was only to *identify* the check found in Alexander's possession. With this contention we cannot agree. It is true, as the Government urges, that the best evidence rule is aimed only at excluding evidence which concerns the contents of a writing; and testimony as to other facts about a writing, such as its existence or identity, may be admissible. As stated in IV Wigmore, Evidence § 1242 (3d ed. 1940):

"[T]he rule applies only to the *terms of the document*, and not to any *other facts about* the document. In other words, the rule applies to exclude testimony designed to establish the *terms* of the document, and requires the document's production instead, but does not apply to exclude testimony which concerns the document without aiming to establish its terms: * * *."

Here, however, the very purpose of the evidence objected to was to establish the terms of the check. The identity of the check could be established only by proof of its terms; the check was not described merely in general terms as a physical object, such as "a check" or "a Government check," but instead its terms were set forth with particularity; indeed the copy purported to include its every characteristic. It is clear that the Government's primary purpose was to prove the terms of the check in accordance with the indictment which set forth those terms in detail, including the serial number, symbol, amount and the name and address of the payee. Moreover, the terms of the check, if properly proved, would tend to establish that the check which Alexander had in his possession was the same check which Mrs. Woodall should have received and which should have been delivered to her mailbox. Without proof of its terms, there was virtually nothing in the record to connect the check with the mails or its possession with the offense charged. The terms of the check were vitally material to the Government's case.

A careful examination of certain cases cited by the Government convinces us that they do not support the Government's position.

• • •

Another case cited by the Government, United States v. Calamaro, 137 F.Supp. 816 (E.D.Pa.1956), is of similar import. There the defendant, a pickup man in a numbers operation, was indicted and convicted of failing to pay the special gambler's tax imposed by the Internal Revenue Code. He moved for a judgment of acquittal and alternatively for a new trial, assigning as error, *inter alia*, the admission of testimony of police officers pertaining to the numbers slips taken from his possession, without the production of the slips themselves. The arresting officers had testified that they had taken from the possession of defendant 48 sheets of paper which were three inches wide and seven inches long, and that there were 1800 notations of three-digit numbers followed by dashes and other numbers on the papers. The officers characterized the sheets as "banker slips." The District Court found no error in the admission of the testimony. Significantly, however, the court emphasized that

> "* * * The government was required to prove only that the slips had existed, that they were numbers slips, and that the defendant had been carrying them. *The government had no burden and made no attempt to prove the specific contents of the slips.* Consequently, the best evidence rule has no application to the problem presented by the failure to produce the numbers slips in the present case. * * *" 137 F.Supp. at 818-819. (Emphasis supplied.)

On appeal the District Court's decision in the Calamaro case was reversed but on other grounds.

Of the other cases cited by the Government, only one, Banovitch v. Commonwealth, 196 Va. 210, 83 S.E.2d 369 (1954), involved testimony concerning the terms of a written instrument. There the terms were not in issue and the court stated only that the testimony was not secondary evidence.

It is correct, as the Government asserts, that the cases cited support the proposition that oral testimony may be allowed to establish the *existence* or *identity* of a written document. But it is significant that each of those cases indicates that the testimony may not go so far as to include the terms of the writing. Such a conclusion is strengthened by a consideration of the purpose of the best evidence rule.

The real purpose of, and reasons for, the best evidence rule are well stated by Dean Wigmore:

> "These reasons are simple and obvious enough, as dictated by common sense and long experience. They may be summed up in this way: "(1) As between a supposed literal copy and the original, the copy is always liable to errors on the part of the copyist, whether by wilfulness or by inadvertence; this contingency wholly disappears when the original is produced. Moreover, the original may contain, and the copy will lack, such features of handwriting, paper, and the like, as may afford the opponent valuable means of learning legitimate objections to the significance of the document. (2)

As between oral testimony, based on recollection, and the original, the added risk, almost the certainty, exists, of errors of recollection due to the difficulty of carrying in the memory literally the tenor of the document." IV Wigmore, Evidence § 1179 (3d ed. 1940).

Little reflection upon the reasons for the rule is required to note its applicability in the present case. Here the indictment alleged the terms of the check with particularity and the Government undertook to prove those terms as circumstantial evidence of the unlawful possession of the check as charged in the second count of the indictment. Any error in such proof could easily have been of significant legal consequence. Consider, for example, the effect of a witness' failure to notice, or a reproducing machine's failure to copy, an indorsement on the back of the check. We are convinced that it was for the purpose of avoiding the possibility of such errors as might have occurred here that the best evidence rule was formulated.

As pointed out by Wigmore, "where a document is referred to as *identical* with or the same as another document, or as helping to identify some transaction or some other physical object, the question is a difficult one; and the ruling will depend upon whether in the case in hand greater emphasis and importance is to be given to the detailed marks of peculiarity, or to the document as a whole regarded as an ordinary describable thing." Here the emphasis was clearly and of necessity on the "detailed marks of peculiarity" which the check bore. The Government could not have sustained its burden by merely showing that the defendant had a Government check in his possession; proof was required to establish that the check which the defendant possessed was, to his knowledge, contained in a letter which had been stolen, taken or abstracted from the mail. The prosecution was obviously aware of the fact that in the absence of proof of the specific terms and contents of the check its case must fail. We believe the evidence went beyond that which is permissible for the purpose of identifying a physical object. As between a written instrument and a copy or parol description thereof, the rule operates to accept the former and exclude the latter. As to its contents, the writing is certain; any oral description thereof necessarily involves the frailties of human recollection and any copy, the hazards of faulty duplication. In addition, there exists the possibility of prejudice or interest influencing either the testimony of a witness or the accuracy of the copy. Given a choice between the two, the law accepts the certain and rejects the uncertain. The defendant is entitled to a new trial.

Alexander assigns as error the suggestions of the District Court as to calling certain witnesses and the participation by the court in the examination of such witnesses. Having noted error in admitting secondary evidence of the contents of the check, we need not consider this contention except to point out that the participation by the court was limited to an effort to establish a proper foundation for the introduction of secondary evidence of the check's contents. Since it is conceded here that a sufficient foundation was not laid, any error in this respect would not be prejudicial.

Reversed and remanded.

Cases relating to Chapter 13

REAL EVIDENCE
GENERAL
SCHMERBER v. STATE OF CALIFORNIA
384 U.S. 757, 16 L.Ed. (2d) 908,
86 S.Ct. 1826 (1966)
Decided June 20, 1966.

Mr. Justice BRENNAN delivered the opinion of the Court.

Petitioner was convicted in Los Angeles Municipal Court of the criminal offense of driving an automobile while under the influence of intoxicating liquor. He had been arrested at a hospital while receiving treatment for injuries suffered in an accident involving the automobile that he had apparently been driving. At the direction of a police officer, a blood sample was then withdrawn from petitioner's body by a physician at the hospital. The chemical analysis of this sample revealed a percent by weight of alcohol in his blood at the time of the offense which indicated intoxication, and the report of this analysis was admitted in evidence at the trial. Petitioner objected to receipt of this evidence of the analysis on the ground that the blood had been withdrawn despite his refusal, on the advice of his counsel, to consent to the test. He contended that in that circumstance the withdrawal of the blood and the admission of the analysis in evidence denied him due process of law under the Fourteenth Amendment, as well as specific guarantees of the Bill of Rights secured against the States by that Amendment: his privilege against self-incrimination under the Fifth Amendment; his right to counsel under the Sixth Amendment; and his right not to be subjected to unreasonable searches and seizures in violation of the Fourth Amendment. The Appellate Department of the California Superior Court rejected these contentions and affirmed the conviction. In view of constitutional decisions since we last considered these issues in Breithaupt v. Abram, 352 U.S. 432, 77 S.Ct. 408, 1 L.Ed.2d 448—see Escobedo v. State of Illinois, 378 U.S. 478, 84 S.Ct. 1758, 12 L.Ed.2d 977; Malloy v. Hogan, 378 U.S. 1, 84 S.Ct. 1489, 12 L.Ed. 2d 653, and Mapp v. State of Ohio, 367 U.S. 643, 81 S.Ct.

1684, 6 L.Ed.2d 1081—we granted certiorari. 382 U.S. 971, 86 S.Ct. 542, 15 L.Ed.2d 464. We affirm.

I.

THE DUE PROCESS CLAUSE CLAIM

Breithaupt was also a case in which police officers caused blood to be withdrawn from the driver of an automobile involved in an accident, and in which there was ample justification for the officer's conclusion that the driver was under the influence of alcohol. There, as here, the extraction was made by a physician in a simple, medically acceptable manner in a hospital environment. There, however, the driver was unconscious at the time the blood was withdrawn and hence had no opportunity to object to the procedure. We affirmed the conviction there resulting from the use of the test in evidence, holding that under such circumstances the withdrawal did not offend "that 'sense of justice' of which we spoke in Rochin v. (people of) California, 1952, 342 U.S. 165 [96 L.Ed. 183, 72 S.Ct. 205, 25 ALR 2d 1396]." 352 U.S. at 435, 77 S.Ct. at 410. *Breithaupt* thus requires the rejection of petitioner's due process argument, and nothing in the circumstances of this case or in supervening events persuades us that this aspect of *Breithaupt* should be overruled.

II.

THE PRIVILEGE AGAINST SELF-INCRIMINATION CLAIM

Breithaupt summarily rejected an argument that the withdrawal of blood and the admission of the analysis report involved in that state case violated the Fifth Amendment privilege of any person not to "be compelled in any criminal case to be a witness against himself," citing Twining v. State of New Jersey, 211 U.S. 78, 29 S.Ct. 14, 53 L.Ed. 97. But that case, holding that the protections of the Fourteenth Amendment do not embrace this Fifth Amendment privilege, has been succeeded by Malloy v. Hogan, 378 U.S. 1, 8, 84 S.Ct. 1489, 1493, 12 L.Ed.2d 653. We there held that "(t)he Fourteenth Amendment secures against state invasion the same privilege that the Fifth Amendment guarantees against federal infringement—the right of a person to remain silent unless he chooses to speak in the unfettered exercise of his own will and to suffer no penalty °°° for such silence." We therefore must now decide whether the withdrawal of the blood and admission in evidence of the analysis involved in this case violated petitioner's privilege. We hold that the privilege protects an accused only from being compelled to testify against himself, or otherwise provide the State with evidence of a testimonial or communicative nature, and that the withdrawal of blood and use of the analysis in question in this case did not involve compulsion to these ends.

It could not be denied that in requiring petitioner to submit to the withdrawal and chemical analysis of his blood the State compelled him to submit to an attempt to discover evidence that might be used to prosecute him for a criminal offense. He submitted only after the police officer rejected his objection and directed the physician to proceed. The officer's direction to the physician to administer the test over petitioner's objection constituted compulsion for the purposes of the privilege. The critical question, then, is whether petitioner was thus compelled "to be a witness against himself."

If the scope of the privilege coincided with the complex of values it helps to protect, we might be obliged to conclude that the privilege was violated. In Miranda v. Arizona, 384 U.S., p. 22, 86 S.Ct. 1620, 16 L.Ed.2d, the Court said of the interests protected by the privilege: "All these policies point to one overriding thought; the constitutional foundation underlying the privilege is the respect a government—state or federal—must accord to the dignity and integrity of its citizens. To maintain a 'fair state-individual balance,' to require the government 'to shoulder the entire load,' °°° to respect the inviolability of the human personality, our accusatory system of criminal justice demands that the government seeking to punish an individual produce the evidence against him by its own independent labors, rather than by the cruel, simple expedient of compelling it from his own mouth." The withdrawal of blood necessarily involves puncturing the skin for extraction, and the percent by weight of alcohol in that blood, as established by chemical analysis, is evidence of criminal guilt. Compelled submission fails on one view to respect the "inviolability of the human personality." Moreover, since it enables the State to rely on evidence forced from the accused, the compulsion violates at least one meaning of the requirement that the State procure the evidence against an accused "by its own independent labors."

As the passage in Miranda implicitly recognizes, however, the privilege has never been given the full scope which the values it helps to protect suggest. History and a long line of authorities in lower courts have consistently limited its protection to situations in which the State seeks to submerge those values by obtaining the evidence against an accused through "the cruel, simple expedient of compelling it from his own mouth. °°° In sum, the privilege is fulfilled only when the person is guaranteed the right 'to remain silent unless he chooses to speak in the unfettered exercise of his own will.'" Ibid. The leading case in this Court is Holt v. United States, 218 U.S. 245, 31 S.Ct. 2, 54 L.Ed. 1021.

There the question was whether evidence was admissible that the accused, prior to trial and over his protest, put on a blouse that fitted him. It was contended that compelling the accused to submit to the demand that he model the blouse violated the privilege. Mr. Justice Holmes, speaking for the Court, rejected the argument as "based upon an extravagant extension of the 5th Amendment," and went on to say: "(T)he prohibition of compelling a man in a criminal court to be a witness against himself is a prohibition of the use of physical or moral compulsion to extort communications from him, not an exclusion of his body as evidence when it may be material. The objection in principle would forbid a jury to look at a prisoner and compare his features with a photograph in proof." 218 U.S., at 252-253, 31 S.Ct., at 6.

It is clear that the protection of the privilege reaches an accused's communications, whatever form they might take, and the compulsion of responses which are also communications, for example, compliance with a subpoena to produce one's papers. Boyd v. United States, 116 U.S. 616, 6 S.Ct. 524, 29 L.Ed. 746. On the other hand, both federal and state courts have usually held that it offers no protection against compulsion to submit to fingerprinting, photographing, or measurements, to write or speak for identification, to appear in court, to stand, to assume a stance, to walk, or to make a particular gesture. The distinction which has emerged often expressed in different ways, is that the privilege is a bar against compelling "communications" or "testimony," but that compulsion which makes a suspect or accused the source of "real or physical evidence" does not violate it.

Although we agree that this distinction is a helpful framework for analysis, we are not to be understood to agree with past applications in all instances. There will be many cases in which such a distinction is not readily drawn. Some tests seemingly directed to obtain "physical evidence," for example, lie detector tests measuring changes in body function during interrogation, may actually be directed to eliciting responses which are essentially testimonial. To compel a person to submit to testing in which an effort will be made to determine his guilt or innocence on the basis of physiological responses, whether willed or not, is to evoke the spirit and history of the Fifth Amendment. Such situations call to mind the principle that the protection of the privilege "is as broad as the mischief against which it seeks to guard." Counselman v. Hitchcock, 142 U.S. 547, 562, 12 S.Ct. 195, 198.

In the present case, however, no such problem of application is presented. Not even a shadow of testimonial compulsion upon or enforced communication by the accused was involved either in the extraction or in the chemical analysis. Petitioner's testimonial capacities were in no way implicated; indeed, his participation except as a donor, was irrelevant to the results of the test which depend on chemical analysis and on that alone. Since the blood test evidence, although an incriminating product of compulsion, was neither petitioner's testimony nor evidence relating to some communicative act or writing by the petitioner, it was not inadmissible on privilege grounds.

Note: Parts of case relating to the right to counsel and search and seizure are not included. This case should be read in full for a more complete understanding of the rules concerning admissibility of the real evidence.

Affirmed.

Mr. Justice HARLAN, whom Mr. Justice STEWART joins, concurring.

In joining the Court's opinion I desire to add the following comment. While agreeing with the Court that the taking of this blood test involved no testimonial compulsion, I would go further and hold that apart from this consideration the case in no way implicates the Fifth Amendment. Of my dissenting opinion and that of Mr. Justice White in Miranda v. Arizona, 384 U.S., 86 S.Ct. 1643, 16 L.Ed. 2d.

Mr. Chief Justice WARREN dissenting.

While there are other important constitutional issues in this case, I believe it is sufficient for me to reiterate my dissenting opinion in Briethaupt v. Abram, 352 U.S. 432, 440, 77 S.Ct. 408, 412, as the basis on which to reverse this conviction.

Mr. Justice Black with whom Mr. Justice Douglas joins, dissenting.

I would reverse petitioner's conviction. I agree with the Court that the Fourteenth Amendment made applicable to the States the Fifth Amendment's provision that "No person * * * shall be compelled in any criminal case to be a witness against himself." But I disagree with the Court's holding that California did not violate petitioner's constitutional right against self-incrimination when it compelled him, against his will, to allow a doctor to puncture his blood vessels in order to extract a sample of blood and analyze it for alcoholic content, and then used that analysis as evidence to convict petitioner of a crime.

* * *

Mr. Justice DOUGLAS, dissenting.

I adhere to the views of the Chief Justice in his dissent in Breithaupt v. Abram, 352 U.S. 432, 440, 77 S.Ct. 408, 412, 1 L.Ed.2d 448, and to the views I stated in my dissent in that case (id., 442, 77 S. Ct. 413) and add only a word.

We are dealing with the right of privacy which, since the Breithaupt case, we have held to be within the penumbra of some specific guarantees of the Bill of Rights. Griswold v. State of Connecticut, 381 U.S. 479, 85 S.Ct. 1678, 14 L.Ed.2d 510. Thus the Fifth Amendment marks "a zone of privacy" which the Government may not force a person to surrender. Id., 484, 85 S.Ct. 1681. Likewise the Fourth Amendment recognizes that right of the people to be secure "in their persons." Ibid. No clearer invasion of this right of privacy can be imagined than forcible bloodletting of the kind involved here.

Mr. Justice FORTAS, dissenting.

I would reverse. In my view, petitioner's privilege against self-incrimination applies. I would add that, under the Due Process Clause, the State, in its role as prosecutor, has no right to extract blood from an accused or anyone else, over his protest. As prosecutor, the State has no right to commit any kind of violence upon the person, or to utilize the results of such a tort, and the extraction of blood, over protest, is an act of violence. Cf. Chief Justice Warren's dissenting opinion in Breithaupt v. Abram, 352 U.S. 432, 440, 77 S.Ct. 408, 412, 1 L.Ed.2d 448.

McNEELY v. UNITED STATES
353 F.(2d) 913
United States Court of Appeals
Eighth Circuit.
Dec. 28, 1965.

GIBSON, Circuit Judge.

These are appeals from the United States District Court for the Eastern District of Missouri in which appellants were jointly tried before a jury and convicted of violating Title 18, U.S.C.A. § 2115, burglary of a United States Post Office.

Sometime during the night of July 26 or early morning of July 27, 1964, a branch Post Office in Maplewood, Missouri, was forceably entered and an unsuccessful attempt was made to break into the safe. This burglary was unbeknown to Patrolman Walton of the neighboring suburb of Brentwood when he observed two men in an automobile parked with its motor running in a closed filling station. The time was 12:45 a.m. July 27, 1964. Patrolman Walton pulled his unmarked police car into the service station and the parked car sped away in the opposite direction. Patrolman Walton pursued the suspicious car and with his spotlight signaled it to stop. The signal was not heeded, and the car continued at speeds exceeding the posted limit of 30 m. p. h. by at least 15 miles per hour. As the car was making a right-hand turn directly in front of Patrolman Walton, he observed the passenger in the front seat push a large canvas bag from the front window. As the bag hit the pavement he saw "pieces of metal" come out of the bag, one of which he specifically recognized as a sledge hammer. He heard the sound of metal striking the pavement, and was forced to swerve his automobile to avoid running into the scattered contents of the bag. A short time later the fleeing car turned into a dead end street; Patrolman Walton blocked the entrance of the street and arrested the occupants on the stated charge of littering. The driver of the car was identified as defendant McNeely and the passenger was defendant Johnson. Upon returning the few blocks to where the bag was thrown from the car, Patrolman Walton and an assisting officer discovered some heavy duty gloves and tools of the type commonly used to commit burglaries. Appellants were promptly arrested for the Missouri felony of illegal possession of burglary tools. While they were in custody of the Brentwood police, appellants' clothes were separately taken from them and sent in separate packages to a United States Government laboratory for examination. Appellants were subsequently transferred to Federal authorities and tried for burglary of the Maplewood Post Office.

The bag, tools, and gloves found on the street were introduced at the trial. The tools were connected with the scene of the crime by comparisons of these tools to other evidence found at the scene. Markings or striations from the face of the sledge hammer were matched with markings found on the handle of the safe. A broken punch recovered from the safe dial was compared with the broken end of a punch found with the tools. Finally, bits of paint and debris found on these tools and the gloves were compared with samples of debris gathered from the scene of the burglary. The jury was allowed to make visual comparisons between the evidence gathered from the street and the evidence from the Post Office and its safe. In addition, a government witness testified as an expert that the above exhibits compared positively with each other.

From the clothes of McNeely and Johnson were lifted certain paint chips and minute debris. These chips and debris were likewise compared with the chips and debris found on the tools and gloves and with debris samples gathered from the Post Office. The jury was allowed to make a visual comparison through a microscope, and the government's expert witness testified that the debris on appellants' clothing was identical to the debris from the scene of the burglary and likewise was identical to debris found on the tools and gloves.

Appellants argue that the admission into evidence of the tools and gloves found in the street was erroneous because the connection between these tools, the appellants, and the crime in question requires piling one inference upon another. For instance appellants say that it is only an inference that these tools were in the bag thrown from the car. To connect appellants to the crime, the jury must base this inference on the additional inference that these tools were used in the commission of the crime. This is not permissible as a matter of law, say appellants.

They also point out that the evidence found on the clothing of McNeely is admissible only against McNeely and the evidence on Johnson's clothing is admissible only against Johnson; and, contend it was error not to caution or instruct the jury to this effect, even though appellants made no such request of the Court.

Finally, appellant McNeely complains that his arrest was illegal in that the stated grounds for arrest was littering, when in fact he admittedly was not observed throwing anything from the car. Therefore, the resultant search and seizure of his clothing was illegal and the evidence seized therefrom was inadmissible.

It is the opinion of this Court that none of the objections are meritorious and that the trial court's judgments should be affirmed.

As to the appellant's first contention, we agree that it is improper for a court to allow a jury to draw inferences based solely upon another inference. However, that well-known rule of evidence has no application to the facts of this case. The jury was not asked to infer that the tools in question were in the possession of appellants and then infer that the tools were used in the burglary. There is direct positive evidence on this issue. Furthermore, there was positive, direct, and circumstantial evidence that the tools in question were in the possession of appellants and thrown from their fleeing car.

First, there is no doubt that these tools were positively identified as the tools used in the burglary. The impressions made by a hammer on the safe door matched the impressions found upon the sledge hammer that was recovered from the street. The broken punch found in the safe dial was identified as the remaining half to the piece of punch found with the tools. In addition small particles of paint and dust which were removed from the scene of the crime identically matched particles which were removed from the tools.

Second, from the web of circumstantial and direct evidence there can be little doubt that these tools were in the possession of appellants and were thrown from their car. While in close pursuit of the car occupied by appellants, Officer Walton directly observed defendant Johnson throw the identified bag from the car. When the bag hit the street, in addition to hearing the sound of metal striking the pavement, he was able to testify that he saw "pieces of metal" fly from the bag, and identify one of the pieces as a sledge hammer. Patrolman Walton testified that the street was clear prior to the bag being jettisoned, that he had to swerve to keep from running over the discharged objects, and that upon his return within a few minutes to the spot where the bag was thrown he found the bag containing some tools, gloves and various other tools scattered near the bag. All of this took place in the early morning hours on a residential street that Patrolman Walton observed to be completely deserted except for himself and appellants. The tools, bag, and gloves found in the street were identified by Patrolman Walton and admitted into evidence.

In addition, small particles of paint and dust were removed from the clothing of McNeely and Johnson. Identical particles were removed both from the tools and from the scene of the crime. This evidence connects the tools to the appellants and places all of them at the scene of the burglary. Since the tools can be further identified as the ones actually used in the attempt to crack the safe, the web of evidence strongly implicates appellants as the perpetrators of the burglary. The involvement of appellants in the burglary was completed with no impermissible use of evidence.

The direct evidence of appellants attempting to rid themselves of burglary tools while fleeing from the law points an accusatory finger at them; the circumstantial evidence matching these tools to the scene of the crime by striations on the tools and the broken matching punch, together with their clothes containing debris and paint chips from the scene of the offense, irrefragably marks appellants as the perpetrators of the Post Office burglary. The direct evidence is clear. The circumstantial evidence is consistent with the guilt of appellants and is inconsistent with every reasonable hypothesis of their innocence. From this evidence the jury could conclude guilt beyond a reasonable doubt. Strauss v. United States, 311 F.2d 926 (5 Cir. 1963).

Our position on this issue is fortified by a prior decision of ours in Smith v. United States, 331 F.2d 265 (8 Cir. 1964). That case dealt with the same evidentiary issue and presented a factual situation quite similar, though not as strong, as the facts in the case at bar. In Smith a police officer was pursuing a fleeing car on a highway at speeds in the vicinity of 100 miles per hour. At a distance of about 300 feet the officer observed, "an object moving across the highway ° ° ° He also saw numerous objects appearing to be paper fluttering in the air, but concededly *he did not see the bag or other objects thrown from the moving car.* ° ° °" (Emphasis supplied). In allowing introduction of testimony concerning burglary tools, checks, and currency which allegedly came from the speeding car, this Court at page 279 echoed what continues to be our sentiment in this case, "We do not view this testimony as allowing the jury to pile inference on inference and thus arrive at a verdict of guilty based upon mere suspicion and conjecture."

As to appellants' second argument, again no one would seriously challenge the proposition that evidence taken from one defendant, under circumstances presented here, should not be considered against a co-defendant, and when requested the Court should caution or so instruct the jury. This principle, however, has no application in this case because appellants made no effort to inform the trial court of their desire to have the jury so instructed.

° ° °

Appellants assert that the jury was required to be instructed that the paint and debris coming from McNeely's clothes be considered only against McNeely and the paint and debris coming from Johnson's clothes be considered only against Johnson. The paint chips and dust found on McNeely's clothes, however, were of essentially the same type and quality as the debris recovered from Johnson's clothing. On the clothing of McNeely and on the clothing of Johnson was debris which matched samples gathered from the scene of the burglary. The debris from each of the defendants likewise matched the debris found on some of the burglary tools. Therefore, this is not a case where evidence admissible against one defendant is of a different quality and nature than the evidence admissible against a co-defendant. Due to the identical quality of the evidence found on both defendants, we do not feel that the lack of instruction on its proper use substantially prejudices either of the appellants.

In addition, when the jury was allowed to view the evidence from each of the defendants' clothes through the microscope, evidence seized from McNeely was clearly designated as such, and evidence from Johnson was clearly designated as coming from Johnson. The evidence against each was persuasive and did not require any additional probative evidence on the issue of placing the clothes at the scene of the offense.

Finally, this was not the only evidence linking appellants to the crime. It was clear from other evidence that the tools were used in the burglary, and it was demonstrated that the appellants threw these tools out of their car while being pursued by Patrolman Walton.

Judgments affirmed.

MAXWELL v. UNITED STATES

368 F.(2d) 735

United States Court of Appeals
Ninth Circuit.

Nov. 7, 1966.

HAMLEY, Circuit Judge.

John Henry Maxwell was indicted for first degree murder committed in Indian country, in violation of 18 U.S.C. §§ 1111 and 1152 (1964). He pleaded not guilty. At his trial the jury returned a verdict of guilty of murder in the first degree "without capital punishment." A judgment of conviction and sentence to imprisonment for life was entered, from which Maxwell takes this appeal.

The essential facts pertaining to the killing may be briefly stated. About four o'clock on the afternoon of March 9, 1964, Maxwell entered a bar in Parker, Arizona, located within the boundaries of the Colorado Indian Reservation. For some hours prior to that time he had had very little to eat and had consumed a pint of intoxicating liquor. From four to seven thirty p. m. Maxwell continued to drink at the bar. He quarreled with the bar maid when she refused to serve him because he had been using foul language.

About seven p. m., Donald Short, a stranger to Maxwell, entered the bar. He verbally intervened in the quarrel between Maxwell and the bar maid. A short time later, while the two men were standing six or seven feet apart, Maxwell shot Short in the abdomen, causing Short's death.

• • •

Maxwell next contends that the trial court erred in admitting in evidence, over his objection, a photograph of the body of the deceased. The photograph was introduced in evidence during the testimony of Dr. Thomas B. Jarvis, who testified for the Government concerning an autopsy he had performed on the body of the deceased. Dr. Jarvis testified that the body shown in the photograph was the one on which he had performed the autopsy, and that, having known that person during his lifetime he knew the body was that of Donald Short.

Maxwell's attorney objected to reception of the photograph on the ground that it was not needed for purposes of identification and that any relevance that it may have was outweighed by the bias and prejudice it would engender against Maxwell. The Government took the position that the photograph was relevant in proving that Short's life had been taken. The trial court overruled the objection, holding that the picture was not sufficiently inflammatory to be prejudicial. Before the photograph was shown to the jury, and to minimize any prejudice which might be caused by the photograph, the trial court excised the lower part of the photograph which showed the wound in the abdomen.

The admission or rejection of photographs lies largely in the sound discretion of the trial court, and in the absence of a showing of abuse of discretion, the trial court's ruling will not be disturbed on appeal. See Rivers v. United States, 9 Cir., 270 F.2d 435, 438, quoting to this effect, State v. Griffith, 52 Wash.2d 721, 727, 328 P.2d 897, 900. In *Rivers* we also approved as a valid statement of the considerations which should guide a trial court in exercising this discretion, the following language in People v. Chavez, 50 Cal.2d 778, 792, 329 P.2d 907, 916:

> "Such photographs should be excluded where their principal effect would be to inflame the jurors against the defendant because of the horror of the crime; on the other hand, if they have a probative value with respect to a fact in issue that outweighs the danger of prejudice to the defendant, they are admissible, and the resolution of this question is primarily for the trial court in the exercise of its discretion."

The photograph in question was relevant and material evidence tending to prove the crime charged. The Government might have been able to prove the charge without producing the photograph. It was not required to take that chance, however, unless the picture was of such a gruesome and horrifying nature that its probative value was outweighed by the danger of inflaming the jury against Maxwell. We have examined the photograph and find it to be relatively innocuous. The trial court did not abuse its discretion in receiving the photograph in evidence and in permitting the jury to see a part of it.

• • •

Judgment affirmed.

RESULTS OF EXAMINATIONS AND TESTS
KLEBS v. STATE
305 N.E. 2d 781 (1974)

ROBERTSON, Presiding Judge.

The defendant-appellant (Klebs) was convicted in a bench trial of causing death while driving under the influence of liquor, IC 9-4-1-54, Ind.Ann.Stat. § 47-2001 (Burns 1973). Klebs was sentenced from one to two years and fined $500. The three issues in his overruled motion to correct errors are:

1. Was the proper foundation laid for admission of the breathalyzer test results;

2. Was it error to admit a copy of the test results rather than the original document; and
3. Was the evidence sufficient to support the verdict?

When viewed most favorably to the State, the evidence discloses that during the late afternoon and early evening hours of May 5, 1972, Klebs visited the House of Stewart's Restaurant and Lounge in Hammond, Indiana. While there he consumed a steak dinner and between eight to ten bourbon and waters over a three and a half hour period. After Klebs departed he was involved in a head-on collision with another automobile a short distance from the restaurant. The driver of the other car died as a result of the accident. Eyewitnesses testified that Kleb's auto had weaved across the center line of the road several times and that he had difficulty in negotiating a turn on to another street before the fatal collision. Following the accident police officers took Klebs to the Hammond Police Station where Lieutenant Awe administered the breathalyzer test pursuant to IC 9-4-4.5-1 and 9-4-4.5-3, Ind.Ann.Stat. § 47-2003c and § 47-2003e (Burns 1973). The test results indicated .19% by weight of alcohol in Klebs' blood.

The Indiana legislature has provided that evidence of the alchohol content of a defendant's blood, as shown by a chemical analysis of his breath, is admissible as evidence. Evidence of .10% or more, by weight of alcohol in the defendant's blood, is prima facie evidence that he was under the influence of intoxicating liquor sufficiently to lessen his driving ability to such an extent as to endanger other persons using the public highways. IC 9-4-1-56, Ind.Ann.Stat. § 47-2003 (Burns 1973). Another statute sets forth certain requirements that must be met prior to the test results being accepted as evidence. That statute reads:

"The director of the state department of toxicology of the Indiana University school of medicine is hereby authorized and empowered to adopt the necessary rules and. regulations to set standards for the selection, training, certification and recertification of chemical test' operators and to provide for the periodic inspection of chemical devices. *No chemical test for intoxication shall be considered as evidence for the purpose of this chapter [9-4-4.5-1—9-4-4.5-6] if it is not performed by a person certified as a valid operator by the state department of toxicology of the Indiana University school of medicine, and no equipment shall be used for such chemical tests which has not been inspected and approved under the rules and regulations* adopted by such department. . . ." (Emphasis added.) IC 9-4-4.5-6, Ind.Ann.Stat. § 47-2003h (Burns Code ed. 1973)

The department of toxicology's rules and regulations filed pursuant to the foregoing statute provide in pertinent part:

"C. Certification and recertification of chemical test operators.

1. All persons who have successfully completed an approved course in the theory and operation of chemical test devices shall be certified as chemical test operators by the director of the department of toxicology.

2. Certification shall be valid for two [2] years from the date of certification. A certification card shall be issued to the certified operator and such card shall bear an expiration date.

3. Recertification procedure shall be determined by the director of the department of toxicology.

4. Those seeking recertification must attain a score of 70% or more on a written examination similar in content to the final examination given at the completion of the school for training chemical test operators and successfully completing actual breath tests using a chemical test device and a known water-alcohol solution in a breath test simulator.

. . ." Ind.Admin.Rules and Regulations Rule (47-2003h)-1 (Burns 1973).

The final statutory provision of concern to the instant case reads:

"(d) The term 'chemical test' for the purposes of this chapter means an analysis by such *persons using such techniques* and equipment *as shall have been approved by the department of toxicology* of the Indiana University school of medicine of the breath, blood, urine or other bodily substance for the determination of the presence of alcohol or drugs, or a combination of alcohol and drugs in such quantities as to constitute intoxication or 'under the influence' as that term may be defined by statute." (Emphasis added.) IC 9-4-4.5-2, Ind.Ann.Stat. § 47-2003d (Burns Code ed. 1973).

From the foregoing statutes Klebs has extracted three requirements for a proper foundation for the admission of the test results. Those three requirements are:

1. The test was administered by an operator certified by the department of toxicology;

2. The equipment used in the test was inspected and approved by the department of toxicology, and
3. The operator used techniques approved by the department of toxicology.

It is the State's contention that these requirements were fulfilled.

We cannot conclude, as a matter of law, that the State sustained its burden in establishing a foundation for admission of the results of the breathalyzer test. There was a fatal evidentiary absence germane to each of the three requirements. There was no evidence to show the operator was certified within the two years prior to administering the test in the instant case as required by the rules prescribed by the department of toxicology. The operator's testimony said by the State to establish the machine's inspection and approval was as follows:

"Q. Did you know of your own knowledge of its inspection and operating efficiency?
A. Yes.
Q. Would you state to the Court the degree of operating efficiency of the machine that you used and of which you are testifying about. Or perhaps instead of efficiency I should say accuracy.
A. Plus or minus. I can't answer that."

We are of the opinion that this testimony falls short of establishing that the machine used to test Klebs had been properly inspected by the department of toxicology. Lieutenant Awe described the technique used to administer the test in response to a preliminary voir dire by Klebs' counsel, however, the record is devoid of any evidence to establish that the procedure described resembled the procedure approved by the department of toxicology.

It is axiomatic that error also existed in admitting a copy of the results of the breathalyzer test irrespective of Klebs' position that the Exhibit violated the Best Evidence rule.

Although we have determined that error exists, it is our conclusion that such error is not reversible because of other proof establishing Klebs' guilt. Independent testimony regarding the amount of intoxicants consumed and the erratic driving culminating in the death of another was sufficient to prove the essential elements of the offense charged.

Klebs points out that none of the State's witnesses were of the opinion that he was intoxicated before or after the collision and that the presence of strong paint fumes in his vehicle and the lack of sleep prior to the incident could account for the manner in which Klebs drove. Where two logical, but opposing, inferences are presented it is beyond the province of this court to determine which should be accepted by the trier of fact. Young v. State (1971), Ind., 273 N.E.2d 285. It is the trier of fact's province to decide which to believe. Fisher v. State (1973), Ind., 291 N.E.2d 76; Cravens v. State (1971), Ind., 275 N.E.2d 4. In determining whether the evidence was sufficient we will not weigh the evidence nor pass upon the credibility of witnesses, but will consider only that evidence together with the reasonable inferences that may be drawn therefrom which supports the verdict of the trial court. Sanchez v. State (1971), 256 Ind. 140, 267 N.E.2d 374; Glover v. State (1970), 253 Ind. 536, 255 N.E.2d 657. Nor will we disturb the judgment of the trial court if there is substantial evidence of probative value to establish every material element of the crime charged beyond a reasonable doubt. Phillips v. State (1973), Ind., 295 N.E.2d 592; Dunn v. State (1973), Ind., 293 N.E.2d 32.

Having found no reversible error the judgment of the trial court is affirmed.

Lowdermilk and Lybrook, JJ., concur.

SHANKS v. STATE
185 Md. 437, 45 A.(2d) 85
Court of Appeals of Maryland.
Dec. 18, 1945.

MARBURY, Chief Judge.

Appellant was indicted in Baltimore City for the crime of rape, tried before the court sitting without a jury, found guilty, and sentenced to be hanged. From the judgment and sentence of the Criminal Court of Baltimore City this appeal is taken.

During the course of the trial, evidence was offered of the result of various blood tests, taken by Dr. Freimuth, a toxicologist attached to the office of the Chief Medical Examiner of the State and former toxicologist and serologist of the Federal Bureau of Investigation in Washington. No objection was made to the qualification of Dr.

Freimuth, but the admission in evidence of the result of these tests was objected to, and constitutes the basis for this appeal.

Scientific tests of human blood are now almost universally used in appropriate cases and the results are accepted as evidence where they are found to be admissible for the purpose offered in a particular legal proceeding. The possibilities were first brought to the attention of the medical world when Dr. Karl Landsteiner, afterwards a Nobel prize winner, announced in 1900 the result of his experiments showing that all persons, without regard to race, sex or health, could be divided into three blood groups (later increased to four). Other discoveries were made later, and the blood tests now given are generally known as the Landsteiner-Wiener, Landsteiner-Levine or Landsteiner-Bernstein tests. These tests have been recognized by the courts in Europe since 1924, their chief use being in paternity cases. Up to 1929, the tests were said to be used in over 1,500 court cases in Vienna. In Germany, they had been used in over 5,000 cases by 1929. In Great Britain, they were used in two murder cases as early as 1930 and 1931. The first case in this country seems to have been in 1931. In the early cases evidence of the tests was not admitted, because the courts here were not convinced of their general acceptance and reliability. See State v. Damm, 62 S.D. 123, 252 N.W. 7, 104 A.L.R. 430; Beuschel v. Manowitz, 241 App.Div. 888, 272 N.Y. S. 165. Blood tests are now accepted everywhere, scientifically, as accurate, and the courts and legislatures have generally followed the same view. The trial courts in this state have so accepted them for a number of years, and the Legislature in 1941, by Chapter 307 of the Acts of that year, specifically provided that such tests could be used in bastardy proceedings. 1943 Supplement, Flack's Annotated Code, art. 12, § 17. The act provides that the result of the test shall be received in evidence "but only in case definite exclusion is established." Discussions of the general subject may be found in an article by Dr. Flacks, Volume 23, American Bar Association Journal, p. 472, in Wigmore on Evidence, 3dEd., Vol. 1, pars. 165A and 165B, beginning page 616, in article by Milton J. Vogelhut of the Baltimore City Bar, Daily Record, November 18, 1935. See also Journal of Criminal Law and Criminology, Vol. 25, p. 198; Yale Law Journal, Vol. 43, p. 651; Oregon Law Review, Vol. 17, p. 177.

Almost all of the reported cases have to do with paternity tests, which are an extension of the ordinary blood tests. The testimony of

Dr. Freimuth, in this case, explains the blood grouping in the following words, "There are in the main four major blood groups in the international system of grouping, and they are

"Group O, in which you will find approximately 45% of the population;

"Group A, in which you will find approximately 42% of the population, and

"Group B, in which you will find approximately 10% of the population, and

"Group AB, in which you will find the remaining 3%."

The paternity tests are based upon further scientific discoveries, that the child of two people having the same blood group cannot be in one of the other blood groups, but if the two parents have different blood grouping, then a different situation arises. The statutes, including the Maryland statute above referred to, generally provide, and the cases generally hold, that blood tests in paternity cases are only evidence in case definite exclusion is established. That means that if the child has blood O, and both the mother and the putative father have blood O, that is no evidence that the putative father is really the father, because 45% of the population have that same blood. But if the child has blood A and both the mother and the putative father have blood O, then it is evidence to exclude the father, because a combination of two persons both with blood O cannot produce a child with group A.

• • •

In the case before us, the prosecuting witness, while going home about 2 o'clock in the morning on December 31, 1944, was seized by someone, beaten, carried into a vacant yard, kept there for some time, was criminally assaulted twice, and then was permitted to leave. The appellant was arrested on the morning of the same day at his home in Baltimore County, police having discovered that he had been in the neighborhood of the crime. At the time of his arrest, an overcoat with blood stains on it was found in his room behind a wardrobe. When asked how he got these blood stains he told the officer that he was in a fight with a colored girl in front of 1603 Edmonston Avenue, and that was how the blood got on his overcoat.

The girl was identified as Elizabeth Moore. She was sent for by the police and asked in appellant's presence if she had been in a fight with him. She said she had been beaten up by him and that her nose was bleeding as a result, but denied that she had put certain scratches on his face. Appellant did not say whether the blood came from the scratches on his face, or from the colored girl. The prosecuting witness identified appellant as the man who had assaulted her. The motorman of the street car which took the appellant to Govanson the morning of December 31st noticed that his face was scratched and that he had blood on his overcoat, and there were other witnesses who testified against the appellant and whose testimony tended to show that he was the criminal. The clothes of the prosecuting witness had blood on them which she testified had not been there before the attack, and the doctor at Franklin Square Hospital, who examined her at 4:45 on the morning of the attack, testified that she was bleeding then. A police sergeant found blood on the snow in the yard and also saw the prosecuting witness with blood running into her eyes. The bloody coat of the accused was offered in evidence. Dr. Freimuth made five separate blood tests which showed as follows:

Blood from coat of accused, type O.

Blood from Elizabeth Moore, the colored girl, with whom the accused had a fight, type A.

Blood from the prosecuting witness, type O.

Blood from clothes of prosecuting witness, type O.

Blood from the snow found in the yard, type O.

It is urgently pressed upon us by appellant that the testimony of Dr. Freimuth with respect to the blood found upon the coat of appellant should have been excluded because it was in violation of the constitutional right of the appellant to refuse to testify against himself. It is difficult to say how this contention can be sustained. Clothing is admissible in evidence if it is so connected with a crime as to throw light upon a material inquiry in the case. Ford v. State, 181 Md. 303, 29 A.2d 833. In the case of Allen v. State recently decided by this Court, 183 Md. 603, 39 A.2d 820, 823, the constitutional guarantee attempted to be invoked in this case was discussed at considerable length, and cases from many jurisdictions cited. That was a case where an accused, on a witness stand, was required to try on a hat found at the scene of the crime. This court speaking through Judge Melvin said, "In passing upon these border-line cases, of which the one at bar is a striking illustration, the test is who furnished or produced the evidence?" In his opinion Judge Melvin also quotes from the case of Ward v. State, 27 Okl.Cr. 362, 228 P. 498, the following passage, which shows the distinction between experiments made by the accused in court and experiments made outside of court and testified to by other witnesses: "The difference is this, * * * that when such comparisons and experiments are made outside of court, the evidence thereto falls from the lips of witnesses other than the defendant. The production of such evidence, therefore, and the testimony thereto, is not that of the defendant but of other witnesses; while, on the other hand, if the defendant is required against his objection in open court, in the presence of the jury, to make such experiments and comparisons, no extraneous evidence is required, and the constitutional prohibition is thereby violated." In the case at bar the appellant did not testify. The blood was taken from his coat, and the evidence as to it was produced by another witness. We can find no justification for his contention that his constitutional rights were violated in this respect.

. . .

Here the State's case against the accused rests upon his identification by the prosecuting witness as the man who assaulted her, plus an accumulation of circumstances tending to corroborate her testimony. These circumstances were: (1) That he boarded a street car near the scene of the crime, a short time after the assault was committed, (2) that he had blood on his **coat** when on the car, (3) that the blood on his **coat** was of a type different from that of Elizabeth Moore, with whom he said he had a fight, (4) that the blood **was of the same type as that of the prosecuting witness, (5) that the prosecuting witness was bleeding, with blood running into her eyes, and on her clothing, shortly after she was assaulted, and (6) that blood of that same type was found on the snow at the alleged scene of the assault. None of these circumstances, standing alone, would prove conclusively that appellant was the guilty man, but taken together they constitute a chain of circumstantial evidence tending to corroborate the testimony of the prosecuting witness, and to support the inference that the accused was the person who committed the crime.**

• • •

In Underhill, Criminal Evidence, 4th Ed., § 15, p. 16, it is said: "In a prosecution built on circumstantial evidence, all circumstances that might serve to clarify the issues or assist in arriving at the truth are admissible, although remote."

This Court said in the case of Wilson v. State, 181 Md. 1, 7, 26 A.2d 770, 774: "It has been held by this Court that the opinions of medical experts are admissible as to the cause which produced, or probably produced, or might have produced, a certain physical condition. The opinion of an expert as to the probability, or even the possibility, of the cause of a certain condition may frequently be of aid to the jury."

• • •

In the case of Goldstein v. State, 179 Md. 697, 22 A.2d 471, 472, approved in Purviance v. State, Md., 44 A.2d 474, Chief Judge Bond said, "probability is the only requirement, however, and here the probability amounts to little short of certainty. And if there was any room for doubt, the decision was one on the weight of the evidence, not on any question of admissibility."

We see no valid objection in the idea that the jury (or the Court in this case) might attach too much importance to the scientific evidence, and might regard it as positive proof. Recently, during World War II, blood banks, as they were called, were accumulated from millions of people for use directly or as blood plasma in transfusions in hospitals and on the battle fields. There could be few people in the country who failed to know of this, and who did not also understand that when a transfusion was made, it had to be of blood of the same type as that of the patient. Blood types, therefore, are now matters of common or ordinary knowledge. Even were they not, if the jury or judge is told that 45% of the population have "O" blood, we cannot assume that this statement would be disregarded and not given its proper weight in determining the evidentiary value of the testimony. Judges and juries must be presumed to have average intelligence at least, and no assumption to the contrary can be made for the purpose of excluding otherwise admissible testimony.

If it be suggested that there is an analogy to bastardy cases where blood tests are used only to disprove paternity and where the statute permits testimony as to the result of the test "only in case definite exclusion is established," it must be borne in mind that the courts and the legislatures are there dealing with a situation where self-incrimination is involved, and where the nonscientific evidence is often quite unreliable and scientific evidence may be conclusive as to nonpaternity. The blood of the accused must be taken to make such a test, and the statute limits the evidence thus given by him to that in his favor. The Maryland statute does not purport to establish a universal rule of evidence, and has no application whatever in other classes of cases. In this way the statute encourages voluntary facts which may be conclusive.

Finding no error, we will affirm the judgment and sentence appealed from.

Judgment affirmed with costs.

ROBERTS v. STATE OF FLORIDA
164 S.(2d) 817
Supreme Court of Florida.
March 6, 1964.

THORNAL, Justice.

John Henry Roberts and John Alfred Adderley seek reversal of verdicts and judgments convicting them of first degree murder without recommendation of mercy.

We have for consideration numerous alleged errors in the trial proceeding.

At approximately 11:30 A.M., Friday, May 12, 1961, Benjamin Franklin Campbell, Jr., was shot while tending his grocery store. A customer, standing across the store, heard one shot and also heard a voice announce "You shot me." The customer ran to an adjoining kitchen area where Mrs. Campbell was preparing her husband's dinner. Mrs. Campbell also heard a statement, "I am shot." Upon entering the store proper, she found her husband lying on the floor mortally wounded. The drawer of the cash register was open and she noted that certain ten and twenty dollar bills which were previously in the drawer had disappeared. Before entering the store from the kitchen Mrs. Campbell dialed the telephone operator to call for an ambulance and the police. While on the phone she saw the heads of two people as they were leaving the front of the store. At about 6:00 P.M., May 12, 1961, John Henry Roberts was taken into custody. He was arrested initially for "investigation of the homicide." At about 11:30 P.M., May 12, 1961, John Alfred Adderley was similarly arrested. From about 6:30 P.M. until about 1:30 A.M., Roberts was interrogated by law enforcement officers. He denied any connection with the crime. Shortly after midnight May 13, and within approximately one hour after his arrest, Adderley made a full confession of his participation in the robbery and murder. He implicated Roberts. At about 11:45 A.M., May 13, 1961, Adderley was brought face to face with Roberts. Adderley stated "It was a terrible thing we did. They have caught us * * * the only thing * * * to do * * * (is) * * * to tell the truth." Thereupon, around noon on Saturday, May 13, Roberts likewise gave a full confession, the essential aspects of which were factually corroborative of the confession made by Adderley. At the trial the defendants repudiated their confessions and undertook to establish alibis. They were found guilty of first degree murder by separate verdicts. There were no mercy recommendations. The death sentences ensued. The appellants have filed separate briefs. They seek reversal on numerous grounds which we shall discuss.

* * *

The state placed in evidence a .25 caliber pistol which was shown to have belonged to Roberts. Also in evidence was a shell case found at the scene of the crime and a slug removed from the body of the victim. The state then called Ed Bigler, a ballistics expert, who testified that he had test-fired the pistol and had compared the markings on the test bullet with those from the evidence bullet removed from the victim. This he did under a comparison microscope. On the basis of this experiment he submitted the opinion that the bullet which resulted in Campbell's death had been fired from the gun belonging to Roberts. The test bullet was not placed in evidence. Both Adderley and Roberts contend that the test bullet should also have been filed in evidence so that the jury could compare it with the evidence bullet which had caused the death. It is clear that the markings on the bullets could not be identified with the naked eye. Additionally, they could be interpreted only by one trained in the science or experience of ballistics.

Thompson v. Freeman, 111 Fla. 433, 149 So. 740, cited by appellants, does not support their position. It involved the authenticity of a document and was governed by a statute. We have no such situation in the instant case.

It is now well established that a witness, who qualifies as an expert in the science of ballistics, may identify a gun from which a particular bullet was fired by comparing the markings on that bullet with those on a test bullet fired by the witness through the suspect gun. An expert will be permitted to submit his opinion based on such an experiment conducted by him. The details of the experiment should be described to the jury. Riner v. State, 128 Fla. 848, 176 So. 38, Rehearing Denied, 131 Fla. 243, 179 So. 404; State v. Vuckovich, 61 Mont. 480, 203 P. 491; Edwards v. State, 198 Md. 132, 81 A.2d 631, 83 A.2d 578, 26 A.L.R.2d 874.

In McKenna v. People, 124 Colo. 112, 235 P.2d 351, it was held that the opinion of an expert based on the test firing of a gun could be offered in evidence without the necessity of submitting a corroborating microphotograph for inspection by the jurors. In McKenna the expert relied upon a comparison of the test bullet with the evidence bullet under a comparison microscope. This was the identical procedure followed in the case at bar. In State v. Wojculewicz, 140 Conn. 487, 101 A.2d 495, the Court held that it was unnecessary to place the test bullet in evidence to sustain the admissibility of the expert's opinion based upon an experiment in which the test bullet was fired.

In cases such as these the opinion of the witness is allowed under the rules which govern other forms of expert testimony. He will be permitted to submit his conclusions where it is shown that by training and experience he is qualified to give an expert opinion on the basis of the ballistic tests which he himself conducted. It is not necessary that the test be conducted in the presence of the jury nor is it required that the expert submit to the jury the actual test materials. It was not error to refuse to compel the state to produce the test bullet.

When the jury was being qualified on voir dire the trial judge explained to them that it would be their function to determine the facts on the basis of the evidence. He told them that it was his duty to explain the law and their duty to apply the law to the facts. He informed them that even though they disagree with him on some statement of law, nevertheless, it was their responsibility to accept the law as he announced it. In the course of these remarks the judge stated, "If the court is mistaken as to what the law is it is not the duty of the jury to correct him, but there is a way that it can be corrected through appellate procedure." Both appellants contend that this statement constituted reversible error. They base their contention on Pait v. State, Fla. 112 So.2d 380 and Blackwell v. State, 76 Fla. 124, 79 So. 731, 1 A.L.R. 502. In the cited cases the state attorney argued to the jury that if they committed any error it could be corrected in the Supreme Court. We held that in effect these remarks merely suggest to the jury that they need not be too greatly concerned about the results of their deliberations because there would be an appellate court to review them. Such was not the effect of the statement of the trial judge in the instant case. He impressed the jurors with the importance of their responsibility regarding factual determinations. He correctly informed them that they had no responsibility in deciding the law of the case. The power of an appellate court to review his decisions on the law did not in any particular relieve the jurors of any aspect of their vital responsibility in settling the facts. Overstreet v. State, 143 Fla. 794, 197 So. 516.

The state produced a witness, Boswell, who testified that on Monday, May 8, 1961, he accompanied Roberts to the establishment of one Livingston for the purpose of pawning Roberts' pistol. Boswell handled the negotiations with Livingston. Other testimony revealed that Roberts had redeemed his pistol from Livingston on the morning of the homicide. This was the pistol which was identified as the murder weapon. Cross-examination of Boswell indicated that he too had been taken into custody on the day the murder was committed. He was then asked "Were you a suspect?" The state's objection to the question was sustained. The defendants then made a proffer to show that if they were permitted to continue this line of questioning they could prove that Boswell had spent some five hours in jail under "suspicion" for the same crime and that "by virtue of being accused of this crime himself that he was likely to have given evidence in favor of the City [Sic] in order to get himself off the hook ° ° °." The judge refused the proffer.

A defendant is permitted wide latitude in the cross-examination of a state witness to show the motive of the witness in giving testimony for the state. It is permissible to interrogate the witness on the subject of any agreement to grant him leniency or immunity from prosecution in exchange for his testimony. Henderson v. State, 135 Fla. 548, 185 So. 625, 120 A.L.R. 742; Spaeth v. United States, 6 Cir., 232 F.2d 776, 62 A.L.R.2d 606.

The proffer in the instant case did not include a showing that the witness was still suspected of the crime nor did it include a tender of proof that the state had made any concessions to him in exchange for his testimony. The proffer merely submitted a conclusion that the witness "was likely to have given evidence" in favor of the state's position. Moreover, if Boswell had been completely discredited, there was other reliable testimony regarding the pawning of the pistol. In fact, Roberts himself testified to the pawning of the pistol on May 8 and its redemption on May 12. There was no question but that the gun belonged to Roberts, that he pawned it on May 8 and retrieved it on May 12. The ruling of the trial judge on the attempted cross-examination of Boswell was not reversible error.

• • •

In addition to the contentions made by the appellants, we have reviewed the evidence in detail as required by Section 924.32, Florida Statutes, F.S.A. On the basis of this examination we fail to find that the interests of justice require a new trial.

The judgments are affirmed.

It is so ordered.

Cases relating to **Chapter 14**

EVIDENCE UNCONSTITUTIONALLY OBTAINED

MAPP v. OHIO

367 U.S. 643, 16 Ohio Op.(2d) 384, 6 L.Ed.(2d)
1081, 81 S.Ct. 1680

Appeal from the Supreme Court of Ohio.

Decided June 19, 1961.

Mr. Justice Clark delivered the opinion of the Court.

Appellant stands convicted of knowingly having had in her possession and under her control certain lewd and lascivious books, pictures, and photographs in violation of § 2905.34 of Ohio's Revised Code. As officially stated in the syllabus to its opinion, the Supreme Court of Ohio found that her conviction was valid though "based primarily upon the introduction in evidence of lewd and lascivious books and pictures unlawfully seized during an unlawful search of defendant's home . . . ." 170 Ohio St. 427-428, 11 Ohio Op.(2d) 169, 166 N.E.(2d) 387, 388.

On May 23, 1957, three Cleveland police officers arrived at appellant's residence in that city pursuant to information that "a person [was] hiding out in the home, who was wanted for questioning in connection with a recent bombing, and that there was a large amount of policy paraphernalia being hidden in the home." Miss Mapp and her daughter by a former marriage lived on the top floor of the two-family dwelling. Upon their arrival at that house, the officers knocked on the door and demanded entrance but appellant, after telephoning her attorney, refused to admit them without a search warrant. They advised their headquarters of the situation and undertook a surveillance of the house.

The officers again sought entrance some three hours later when four or more additional officers arrived on the scene. When Miss Mapp did not come to the door immediately, at least one of the several doors to the house was forcibly opened and the policemen gained admittance. Meanwhile Miss Mapp's attorney arrived, but the officers, having secured their own entry, and continuing in their defiance of the law, would permit him neither to see Miss Mapp nor to enter the house. It appears that Miss Mapp was halfway down the stairs from the upper floor to the front door when the officers, in this highhanded manner, broke into the hall. She demanded to see the search warrant. A paper, claimed to be a warrant, was held up by one of the officers. She grabbed the "warrant" and placed it in her bosom. A struggle ensued in which the officers recovered the piece of paper and as a result of which they handcuffed appellant because she had been "belligerent" in resisting their official rescue of the "warrant" from her person. Running roughshod over appellant, a policeman "grabbed" her, "twisted [her] hand," and she "yelled [and] pleaded with him" because "it was hurting." Appellant, in handcuffs, was then forcibly taken upstairs to her bedroom where the officers searched a dresser, a chest of drawers, a closet and some suitcases. They also looked into a photo album and through personal papers belonging to the appellant. The search spread to the rest of the second floor including the child's bedroom, the living room, the kitchen and a dinette. The basement of the building and a trunk found therein were also searched. The obscene materials for possession of which she was ultimately convicted were discovered in the course of that widespread search.

At the trial no search warrant was produced by the prosecution, nor was the failure to produce one explained or accounted for. At best, "There is, in the record, considerable doubt as to whether there ever was any warrant for the search of defendant's home." 170 Ohio St., at 430, 11 OhioOp.(2d), at 170, 166 N.E.(2d), at 389. The Ohio Supreme Court believed a "reasonable argument" could be made that the conviction should be reversed "because the 'methods' employed to obtain the [evidence] . . . were such as to 'offend "a sense of justice,"'" but the court found determinative the fact that the evidence had not been taken "from defendant's person by the use of brutal or offensive physical force against defendant." 170 Ohio St., at 431, 166 N.E.(2d), at 389-390.

The State says that even if the search were made without authority, or otherwise unreasonably, it is not prevented from using the unconstitutionally seized evidence at trial, citing *Wolf* v. *Colorado,* 338 U.S. 25 (1949), in which this Court did indeed hold "that in a prosecution in a State court for a State crime the Fourteenth Amendment does not forbid the admission of evidence obtained by an unreasonable search and seizure." At p. 33. On this appeal, of which we have noted probable jurisdiction, 364 U.S. 868, it is urged once again that we review that holding.

I.

Seventy-five years ago, in *Boyd v. United States*, 116 U.S. 616, 630 (1886), considering the Fourth and Fifth Amendments as running "almost into each other" on the facts before it, this Court held that the doctrines of those Amendments

> "apply to all invasions on the part of the government and its employés of the sanctity of a man's home and the privacies of life. It is not the breaking of his doors, and the rummaging of his drawers, that constitutes the essence of the offence; but it is the invasion of his indefeasible right of personal security, personal liberty and private property . . . . Breaking into a house and opening boxes and drawers are circumstances of aggravation; but any forcible and compulsory extortion of a man's own testimony or of his private papers to be used as evidence to convict him of crime or to forfeit his goods, is within the condemnation . . . [of those Amendments]."

The Court noted that

> "constitutional provisions for the security of person and property should be liberally construed. . . . It is the duty of courts to be watchful for the constitutional rights of the citizen, and against any stealthy encroachments thereon." At p. 635.

In this jealous regard for maintaining the integrity of individual rights, the Court gave life to Madison's prediction that "independent tribunals of justice . . . will be naturally led to resist every encroachment upon rights expressly stipulated for in the Constitution by the declaration of rights." I Annals of Cong. 439 (1789). Concluding, the Court specifically referred to the use of the evidence there seized as "unconstitutional." At p. 638.

Less than 30 years after *Boyd*, this Court, in *Weeks v. United States*, 232 U.S. 383 (1914), stated that "the Fourth Amendment . . . put the courts of the United States and Federal officials, in the exercise of their power and authority, under limitations and restraints [and] . . . forever secure[d] the people, their persons, houses, papers and effects against all unreasonable searches and seizures under the guise of law . . . and the duty of giving to it force and effect is obligatory upon all entrusted under our Federal system with the enforcement of the laws." At pp. 391-392.

Specifically dealing with the use of the evidence unconstitutionally seized, the Court concluded:

"If letters and private documents can thus be seized and held and used in evidence against a citizen accused of an offense, the protection of the Fourth Amendment declaring his right to be secure against such searches and seizures is of no value, and, so far as those thus placed are concerned, might as well be stricken from the Constitution. The efforts of the courts and their officials to bring the guilty to punishment, praiseworthy as they are, are not to be aided by the sacrifice of those great principles established by years of endeavor and suffering which have resulted in their embodiment in the fundamental law of the land." At p. 393.

Finally, the Court in that case clearly stated that use of the seized evidence involved "a denial of the constitutional rights of the accused." At p. 398. Thus, in the year 1914, in the *Weeks* case, this Court "for the first time" held that "in a federal prosecution the Fourth Amendment barred the use of evidence secured through an illegal search and seizure." *Wolf v. Colorado, supra,* at 28. This Court has ever since required of federal law officers a strict adherence to that command which this Court has held to be a clear, specific, and constitutionally required—even if judicially implied—deterrent safeguard without insistence upon which the Fourth Amendment would have been reduced to "a form of words." Holmes, J., *Silverthorne Lumber Co. v. United States,* 251 U.S. 385, 392 (1920). It meant, quite simply, that "conviction by means of unlawful seizures and enforced confessions . . . should find no sanction in the judgments of the courts . . . ," *Weeks v. United States, supra,* at 392, and that such evidence "shall not be used at all." *Silverthorne Lumber Co. v. United States, supra,* at 392.

Likewise, time has set its face against what *Wolf* called the "weighty testimony" of *People v. Defore*, 242 N.Y. 13, 150 N.E. 585 (1926). There Justice (then Judge) Cardozo, rejecting adoption of the *Weeks* exclusionary rule in New York, had said that "[t]he Federal rule as it stands is either too strict or too lax." 242 N.Y., at 22, 150 N.E., at 588. However, the force of that reasoning has been largely vitiated by later decision of this Court. These include the recent discarding of the "silver platter" doctrine which allowed federal judicial use of evidence seized in violation of the Constitution by state agents, *Elkins v. United States, supra;* the relaxation of the formerly strict requirements as to standing to challenge the use of evidence thus seized, so that now the procedure of exclusion, "ultimately referable to constitutional safeguards," is available to anyone even "legitimately on [the] premises" unlawfully searched, *Jones v. United States*, 362 U.S. 257, 266-267 (1960); and, finally, the formulation of a method to prevent state use of evidence unconstitutionally seized by federal agents, *Rea v. United States*, 350 U.S. 214 (1956). Because there can be no fixed formula, we are admittedly met with "recurring questions of the reasonableness of searches," but less is not to be expected when dealing with a Constitution, and, at any rate, "[r]easonableness is in the first instance for the [trial court] . . . to determine." *United States v. Rabinowitz*, 339 U.S. 56, 63 (1950).

It, therefore, plainly appears that the factual considerations supporting the failure of the *Wolf* Court to include the *Weeks* exclusionary rule when it recognized the enforceability of the right to privacy against the States in 1949, while not basically relevant to the constitutional consideration, could not, in any analysis, now be deemed controlling.

* * * *

The ignoble shortcut to conviction left open to the State tends to destroy the entire system of constitutional restraints on which the liberties of the people rest. Having once recognized that the right to privacy embodied in the Fourth Amendment is enforceable against the States, and that the right to be secure against rude invasions of privacy by state officers is, therefore, constitutional in origin, we can no longer permit that right to remain an empty promise. Because it is enforceable in the same manner and to like effect as other basic rights secured by the Due Process Clause, we can no longer permit it to be revocable at the whim of any police officer who, in the name of law enforcement itself, chooses to suspend its enjoyment. Our decision, founded on reason and truth, gives to the individual no more than that which the Constitution guarantees him, to the police officer no less than that to which honest law enforcement is entitled, and, to the courts, that judicial integrity so necessary in the true administration of justice.

The judgment of the Supreme Court of Ohio is reversed and the cause remanded for further proceedings not inconsistent with this opinion.

Reversed and remanded.

[*Note. The concurring opinions of* MR. JUSTICE BLACK *and* MR. JUSTICE DOUGLAS *have been omitted.*]

MR. JUSTICE HARLAN, *whom* MR. JUSTICE FRANKFURTER *and* MR. JUSTICE WHITTAKER join, dissenting.

In overruling the *Wolf* case the Court, in my opinion, has forgotten the sense of judicial restraint which, with due regard for *stare decisis,* is one element that should enter into deciding whether a past decision of this Court should be overruled. Apart from that I also believe that the *Wolf* rule represents sounder Constitutional doctrine than the new rule which now replaces it.

I.

From the Court's statement of the case one would gather that the central, if not controlling, issue on this appeal is whether illegally state-seized evidence is Constitutionally admissible in a state prosecution, an issue which would of course face us with the need for re-examining *Wolf.* However, such is not the situation. For, although that question was indeed raised here and below among appellant's subordinate points, the new and pivotal issue brought to the Court by this appeal is whether § 2905.34 of the Ohio Revised Code making criminal the *mere* knowing possession or control of obscene material, and under which appellant has been convicted, is consistent with the rights of free thought and expression assured against state action by the Fourteenth Amendment. That was the pal issue which was decided by the Ohio Supreme Court, which was tendered by appellant's Jurisdictional Statement, and which was briefed and argued in this Court.

In this posture of things, I think it fair to say that five members of this Court have simply "reached out" to overrule *Wolf*. With all respect for the views of the majority, and recognizing that *stare decisis* carries different weight in Constitutional adjudication than it does in nonconstitutional decision, I can perceive no justification for regarding this case as an appropriate occasion for re-examining *Wolf*.

The action of the Court finds no support in the rule that decision of Constitutional issues should be avoided wherever possible. For in overruling *Wolf* the Court, instead of passing upon the validity of Ohio's § 2905.34, has simply chosen between two Constitutional questions. Moreover, I submit that it has chosen the more difficult and less appropriate of the two questions. The Ohio statute which, as construed by the State Supreme Court, punishes knowing possession or control of obscene material, irrespective of the purposes of such possession or control (with exceptions not here applicable) and irrespective of whether the accused had any reasonable opportunity to rid himself of the material after discovering that it was obscene, surely presents a Constitutional question which is both simpler and less far-reaching than the question which the Court decides today. It seems to me that justice might well have been done in this case without overturning a decision on which the administration of criminal law in many of the States has long justifiably relied.

Since the demands of the case before us do not require us to reach the question of the validity of *Wolf*, I think this case furnishes a singularly inappropriate occasion for reconsideration of that decision, if reconsideration is indeed warranted. Even the most cursory examination will reveal that the doctrine of the *Wolf* case has been of continuing importance in the administration of state criminal law. Indeed, certainly as regards its "non-exclusionary" aspect, *Wolf* did no more than articulate the then existing assumption among the States that the federal cases enforcing the exclusionary rule "do not bind [the States], for they construe provisions of the Federal Constitution, the Fourth and Fifth Amendments, not applicable to the States." *People v. Defore*, 242 N.Y. 13, 20, 150 N.E. 585, 587. Though, of course, not reflecting the full measure of this continuing reliance, I find that during the last three Terms, for instance, the issue of the inadmissibility of illegally state-obtained evidence appears on an average of about fifteen times per Term just in the *informa pauperis* cases summarily disposed of by us. This would indicate both that the issue which is now being decided may well have untoward practical ramifications respecting state cases long since disposed of in reliance on *Wolf*, and that were we determined to re-examine that doctrine we would not lack future opportunity.

The occasion which the Court has taken here is in the context of a case where the question was briefed not at all and argued only extremely tangentially. The unwisdom of overruling *Wolf* without full-dress argument is aggravated by the circumstance that that decision is a comparatively recent one (1949) to which three members of the present majority have at one time or other expressly subscribed, one to be sure with explicit misgivings. I would think that our obligation to the States, on whom we impose this new rule, as well as the obligation of orderly adherence to our own processes would demand that we seek that aid which adequate briefing and argument lends to the determination of an important issue. It certainly has never been a postulate of judicial power that mere altered disposition, or subsequent membership on the Court, is sufficient warrant for overturning a deliberately decided rule of Constitutional law.

Thus, if the Court were bent on reconsidering *Wolf*, I think that there would soon have presented itself an appropriate opportunity in which we could have had the benefit of full briefing and argument. In any event, at the very least, the present case should have been set down for reargument, in view of the inadequate briefing and argument we have received on the *Wolf* point. To all intents and purposes the Court's present action amounts to a summary reversal of *Wolf*, without argument.

I am bound to say that what has been done is not likely to promote respect either for the Court's adjudicatory process or for the stability of its decisions. Having been unable, however, to persuade any of the majority to a different procedural course, I now turn to the merits of the present decision.

[*NOTE: Part II of the dissenting openers is omitted.*]

UNITED STATES v. WILLIE ROBINSON, JR.
414 U.S. 218, 66 OhioOp.(2d) 202, 94 S.Ct. 467
[December 11, 1973]

MR. JUSTICE REHNQUIST delivered the opinion of the Court.

Respondent Robinson was convicted in United States District Court for the District of Columbia of the possession and facilitation of concealment of heroin in violation of 26 U.S.C. § 4704(a) (1964 ed.), and 21 U.S.C. § 174 (1964 ed.). He was sentenced to concurrent terms of imprisonment for these offenses. On his appeal to the Court of Appeals for the District of Columbia Circuit, that court first remanded the case to the District Court for evidentiary hearing concerning the scope of the search of respondent's person which had occurred at the time of his arrest. *United States v. Robinson*, — App. D.C. —, 447 F.2d 1215 (1971). The District Court made findings of fact and conclusions of law adverse to respondent, and he again appealed. This time the Court of Appeals *en banc* reversed the judgment of conviction, holding that the heroin introduced in evidence against respondent had been obtained as a result of a search which violated the Fourth Amendment to the United States Constitution. *United States v. Robinson*, — App. D.C. —, 471 F. 2d 1082 (1972). We granted certiorari, 410 U.S. 982 (1973), and set the case for argument together with *Gustafson v. Florida*, No. 71-1669, 414 U.S. 260, 66 OhioOp.(2d) 275 (1973), also decided today.

On April 23, 1968, at approximately 11 o'clock p.m., Officer Richard Jenks, a 15-year veteran of the District of Columbia Metropolitan Police Department, observed the respondent driving a 1965 Cadillac near the intersection of 8th and C Streets, Southeast, in the District of Columbia. Jenks, as a result of previous investigation following a check of respondent's operator's permit four days earlier, determined there was reason to believe that respondent was operating a motor vehicle after the revocation of his operator's permit. This is an offense defined by statute in the District of Columbia which carries a mandatory minimum jail term, a mandatory minimum fine, or both. 40 D.C. Code § 302(d).

Jenks signaled respondent to stop the automobile, which respondent did, and all three of the occupants emerged from the car. At that point Jenks informed respondent that he was under arrest for "operating after revocation and obtaining a permit by misrepresentation." It was assumed by the majority of the Court of Appeals and is conceded by the respondent here that Jenks had probable cause to arrest respondent, and that he effected a full custody arrest.

In accordance with procedures prescribed in Police Department instructions, Jenks then began to search respondent. He explained at a subsequent hearing that he was "face to face" with the respondent, and "placed [his] hands on [the respondent], my right hand to his left breast like this (demonstrating) and proceeded to pat him down thus (with the right hand)." During this patdown, Jenks felt an object in the left breast pocket of the heavy coat respondent was wearing, but testified that he "couldn't tell what it was" and also that he "couldn't actually tell the size of it." Jenks then reached into the pocket and pulled out the object, which turned out to be a "crumpled up cigarette package." Jenks testified that at this point he still did not know what was in the package:

"As I felt the package I could feel objects in the package but I couldn't tell what they were. . . . I knew they weren't cigarettes."

The officer then opened the cigarette pack and found 14 gelatin capsules of white powder which he thought to be, and which later analysis proved to be, heroin. Jenks then continued his search of respondent to completion, feeling around his waist and trouser legs, and examining the remaining pockets. The heroin seized from the respondent was admitted into evidence at the trial which resulted in his conviction in the District Court.

The opinion for the plurality judges of the Court of Appeals, written by Judge Wright, the concurring opinion of Chief Judge Bazelon, and the opinion for the dissenting judges, written by Judge Wilkey, gave careful and comprehensive treatment to the authority of a police officer to search the person of one who has been validly arrested and taken into custody. We conclude that the search conducted by Jenks in this case did not offend the limits imposed by the Fourth Amendment, and we therefore reverse the judgment of the Court of Appeals.

I

It is well settled that a search incident to a lawful arrest is a traditional exception to the warrant requirement of the Fourth Amendment. This general exception has historically been formulated into two distinct propositions. The first is that a search may be made of the *person* of the arrestee by virtue of the lawful arrest. The second is that a search may be made of the area within the control of the arrestee.

Examination of this Court's decisions in the area show that these two propositions have been treated quite differently. The validity of the search of a person incident to a lawful arrest has been regarded as settled from its first enunciation, and has remained virtually unchallenged until the present case. The validity of the second proposition, while likewise conceded in principle, has been subject to differing interpretations as to the extent of the area which may be searched.

Because of the rule requiring exclusion of evidence obtained in violation of the Fourth Amendment was first enunciated in *Weeks v. United States,* 232 U.S. 383 (1914), it is understandable that virtually all of this Court's search and seizure law has been developed since that time. In *Weeks,* the Court made clear its recognition of the validity of a search incident to a lawful arrest:

> "What then is the present case? Before answering that inquiry specifically, it may be well by a process of exclusion to state what it is not. It is not an assertion of the right of the government, always recognized under English and American law, to search the person of the accused when legally arrested to discover and seize the fruits or evidences of crime. This right has been uniformly maintained in many cases. I Bishop on Criminal Procedure, § 211; Wharton, Criminal Plead. and Practice, 8th ed., § 60; *Dillion v. O'Brien and Davis,* 16 Cox C. C. 245." 232 U. S., at 392.

Agnello v. United States, 269 U.S. 20 (1925), decided 11 years after *Weeks,* repeats the categorical recognition of the validity of a search incident to lawful arrest:

> "The right without a search warrant contemporaneously to search persons lawfully arrested while committing crime and to search the place where the arrest is made in order to find and seize things connected with the crime as well as weapons and other things to effect an escape from custody, is not to be doubted." *Id.,* at 30.

Throughout the series of cases in which the Court has addressed the second proposition relating to a search incident to a lawful arrest—the permissible area beyond the person of the arrestee which such a search may cover—no doubt has been expressed as to the unqualified authority of the arresting authority to search the person of the arrestee. E. g., *Carroll* v. *United States,* 267 U.S. 132 (1925); *Marron* v. *United States,* 275 U.S. 192 (1927); *Go-Bart Co.* v. *United States,* 282 U.S. 344 (1931); *United States* v. *Lefkowitz,* 285 U.S. 452 (1932); *Harris* v. *United States,* 331 U.S. 145 (1947); *Trupiano* v. *United States,* 334 U.S. 699 (1948); *United States* v. *Rabinowitz,* 339 U.S. 56 (1950); *Preston* v. *United States,* 376 U.S. 364 (1964); *Chimel* v. *California,* 395 U.S. 752 (1969). In *Chimel,* where the Court overruled *Rabinowitz* and *Harris* as to the area of permissible search incident to a lawful arrest, full recognition was again given to the authority to search the *person* of the arrestee:

> "When an arrest is made, it is reasonable for the arresting officer to search the person arrested in order to remove any weapons that the latter might seek to use in order to resist arrest or effect his escape. Otherwise, the officer's safety might well be endangered, and the arrest itself frustrated. In addition, it is entirely reasonable for the arresting officer to search for and seize *any evidence* on the arrestee's person in order to prevent its concealment or destruction." 395 U.S., at 762-763.

Three years after the decision in *Chimel, supra,* we upheld the validity of a search in which heroin had been taken from the person of the defendant after his arrest on a weapons charge, in *Adams* v. *Williams,* 407 U.S. 143 (1972), saying:

> "Under the circumstances surrounding Williams' possession of the gun seized by Sergeant Connolly, the arrest on the weapons charge was supported by probable cause, and the search of his person and of the car incident to that arrest was lawful." *Id.,* at 149.

Last Term in *Cupp* v. *Murphy,* 412 U.S. 291, 295 (1973), we again reaffirmed the traditional statement of the authority to search incident to a valid arrest.

Thus the broadly stated rule, and the reasons for it, have been repeatedly affirmed in the decisions of this Court since *Weeks* v. *United States* nearly 60 years ago. Since the statements in the cases speak not simply in terms of an exception to the warrant requirement, but in terms of an affirmative authority to search, they clearly imply that such searches also meet the Fourth Amendment's requirement of reasonableness.

II

In its decision of this case, the majority of the Court of Appeals decided that even after a police officer lawfully places a suspect under arrest for the purpose of taking him into custody, he may not ordinarily proceed to fully search the prisoner. He must instead conduct a *limited* frisk of the outer clothing and remove such weapons that he may, as a result of that limited frisk, reasonably believe the suspect has in his possession. While recognizing that *Terry* v. *Ohio,* 392 U.S. 1, 44 OhioOp.(2d) 383 (1968), dealt with a permissible "frisk" incident to an investigative stop based on less than probable cause to arrest, the Court of Appeals felt that the principles of that case should be carried over to this probable cause arrest for driving while one's license is revoked. Since there would be no further evidence of such a crime to be obtained in a search of the arrestee, the Court held that only a search for weapons could be justified.

Terry v. *Ohio, supra,* did not involve an arrest for probable cause, and it made quite clear that the "protective frisk" for weapons which it approved might be conducted without probable cause. 392 U.S., at 21-22, 24-25, 44 OhioOp.(2d), at 393-395. The Court's opinion explicitly recognized that there is a "distinction in purpose, character, and extent between a search incident to an arrest and a limited search for weapons":

"The former, although justified in part by the acknowledged necessity to protect the arresting officer from assault with a concealed weapon, *Preston* v. *United States,* 376 U.S. 364, 367 (1964), is also justified on other grounds, *ibid.,* and can therefore involve a relatively extensive exploration of the person. A search for weapons in the absence of probable cause to arrest, however, must, like any other search, be strictly circumscribed by the exigencies which justify its initiation. *Warden* v. *Hayden,* 387 U.S. 294, 310 (1967) (MR. JUSTICE FORTAS, concurring). Thus it must be limited to that which is necessary for the discovery of weapons which might be used to harm the officer or others nearby, and may realistically be characterized as something less than a 'full' search even though it remains a serious intrusion.

". . . An arrest is a wholly different type of intrusion upon the individual freedom from a limited search for weapons, and the interests each is designed to serve are likewise quite different. An arrest is the initial stage of a criminal prosecution. It is intended to vindicate society's interest in having its laws obeyed, and it is inevitably accompanied by future interference with the individual's freedom of movement, whether or not trial or conviction ultimately follows. The protective search for weapons, on the other hand, constitutes a brief, though far from inconsiderable, intrusion upon the sanctity of the person." 392 U.S., at 25-26 (footnote omitted).

Terry, therefore, affords no basis to carry over to a probable cause arrest the limitations this Court placed on a stop-and-frisk search permissible without probable cause.

The Court of Appeals also relied on language in *Peters* v. *New York*, 392 U.S., at 66, a companion case to *Terry*. There the Court held that the police officer had authority to search Peters because he had probable cause to arrest him, and went on to say:

". . . the incident search was obviously justified 'by the need to seize weapons and other things which might be used to assault an officer or effect an escape, as well as by the need to prevent the destruction of evidence of the crime.' *Preston* v. *United States*, 376 U.S. 364, 367 (1964). Moreover, it was reasonably limited in scope by these purposes. Officer Laskey did not engage in an unrestrained and thoroughgoing examination of Peters and his personal effects." 392 U.S., at 67.

It is of course possible to read the second sentence from this quotation as imposing a novel limitation on the established doctrine set forth in the first sentence. It is also possible to read it as did Mr. Justice Harlan in his concurring opinion:

"The second possible source of confusion is the Court's statement that Officer Laskey did not engage in an unrestrained and thorough-going examination of Peters and his personal effects. *Ante*, at 67. Since the Court found probable cause to arrest Peters, and since an officer arresting on probable cause is entitled to make a very full incident search, I assume that this is merely a factual observation. As a factual matter, I agree with it." 392 U.S., at 77 (footnote omitted).

We do not believe that the Court in *Peters* intended in one unexplained and unelaborated sentence to impose a novel and far reaching limitation on the authority to search the person of an arrestee incident to his lawful arrest. While the language from

Peters was quoted with approval in *Chimel* v. *California, supra,* 395 U.S., at 764, it is preceded by a full exposition of the traditional and unqualified authority of the arresting officer to search the arrestee's person. 395 U.S., at 763. We do not believe that either *Terry* or *Peters,* when considered in the light of the previously discussed statements of this Court, justified the sort of limitation upon that authority which the Court of Appeals fashioned in this case.

While these earlier authorities are sketchy, they tend to support the broad statement of the authority to search incident to arrest found in the successive decisions of this Court, rather than the restrictive one which was applied by the Court of Appeals in this case. The scarcity of case law before *Weeks* is doubtless due in part to the fact that the exclusionary rule there enunciated had been first adopted only 11 years earlier in Iowa; but it would seem to be also due in part to the fact that the issue was regarded as well-settled.

The Court of Appeals in effect determined that the *only* reason supporting the authority for a *full* search incident to lawful arrest was the possibility of discovery of evidence or fruits. Concluding that there could be no evidence or fruits in the case of an offense such as that with which respondent was charged, it held that any protective search would have to be limited by the conditions laid down in *Terry* for a search upon less than probable cause to arrest. Quite apart from the fact that *Terry* clearly recognized the distinction between the two types of searches, and that a different rule governed one than governed the other, we find additional reason to disagree with the Court of Appeals.

The justification or reason for the authority to search incident to a lawful arrest rests quite as much on the need to disarm the suspect in order to take him into custody as it does on the need to preserve evidence on his person for later use at trial. *Agnello* v. *United States, supra; Abel* v. *United States,* 362 U.S. 217 (1960). The standards traditionally governing a search incident to lawful arrest are not, therefore, commuted to the stricter *Terry* standards by the absence of probable fruits or further evidence of the particular crime for which the arrest is made.

Nor are we inclined, on the basis of what seems to us to be a rather speculative judgment, to qualify the breadth of the general authority to search incident to a lawful custodial arrest on an assumption that persons arrested for the offense of driving while their license has been revoked are less likely to be possessed of dangerous weapons than are those arrested for other crimes. It is scarcely open to doubt that the danger to an officer is far greater in the case of the extended exposure which follows the taking of a suspect into custody and transporting him to the police station than in the case of the relatively fleeting contact resulting from the typical *Terry*-type stop. This is an adequate basis for treating *all* custodial arrests alike for purposes of search justification.

But quite apart from these distinctions, our more fundamental disagreement with the Court of Appeals arises from its suggestion that there must be litigated in each case the issue of whether or not there was present one of the reasons supporting the authority for a search of the person incident to a lawful arrest. We do not think the long line of authorities of this Court dating back to *Weeks*, nor what we can glean from the history of practice in this country and in England, requires such a case by case adjudication. A police officer's determination as to how and where to search the person of a suspect whom he has arrested is necessarily a quick *ad hoc* judgment which the Fourth Amendment does not require to be broken down in each instance into an analysis of each step in the search. The authority to search the person incident to a lawful custodial arrest, while based upon the need to disarm and to discover evidence, does not depend on what a court may later decide was the probability in a particular arrest situation that weapons or evidence would in fact be found upon the person of the suspect. A custodial arrest of a suspect based on probable cause is a reasonable intrusion under the Fourth Amendment; that intrusion being lawful, a search incident to the arrest requires no additional justification. It is the fact of the lawful arrest which establishes the authority to search, and we hold that in the case of a lawful custodial arrest a *full* search of the person is not only an exception to the warrant requirement of the Fourth Amendment, but is also a "reasonable" search under that Amendment.

IV

The search of respondent's person conducted by Officer Jenks in this case and the seizure from him of the heroin, were permissible under established Fourth Amendment law. While thorough, the search partook of none of the extreme or patently abusive characteristics which were held to violate the Due Process Clause of the Fourteenth Amendment in *Rochin v. California,* 342 U.S. 165 (1952). Since it is the fact of custodial arrest which gives rise to the authority to search, it is of no moment that Jenks did not indicate any subjective fear of the respondent or that he did not himself suspect that respondent was armed. Having in the course of a lawful search come upon the crumpled package of cigarettes, he was entitled to inspect it; and when his inspection revealed the heroin capsules, he was entitled to seize them as "fruits, instrumentalities, or contraband" probative of criminal conduct. *Harris v. United States, supra,* 331 U.S., at 154-155; *Warden v. Hayden,* 387 U.S. 294, 299, 307 (1967); *Adams v. Williams, supra,* 407 U.S., at 149. The judgment of the Court of Appeals holding otherwise is

Reversed.

MR. JUSTICE MARSHALL, with whom MR. JUSTICE DOUGLAS and MR. JUSTICE BRENNAN join, dissenting.

Certain fundamental principles have characterized this Court's Fourth Amendment jurisprudence over the years. Perhaps the most basic of these was expressed by Mr. Justice Butler, speaking for a unanimous Court in *Go-Bart Co. v. United States,* 282 U.S. 344 (1931): "There is no formula for the determination of reasonableness. Each case is to be decided on its own facts and circumstances." 282 U.S., at 357. As we recently held, "The constitutional validity of a warrantless search is preeminently the sort of question which can only be decided in the concrete factual context of the individual case." *Sibron v. New York,* 392 U.S. 40, 59, 44 OhioOp.(2d) 402, 410-411 (1968). And the intensive, at times painstaking, case by case analysis characteristic of our Fourth Amendment decisions bespeaks our "jealous regard for maintaining the integrity of individual rights." *Mapp v. Ohio,* 367 U.S. 643, 647, 16 OhioOp.(2d) 384, 386 (1961). See also *Weeks v. United States,* 232 U.S. 383, 393 (1914).

In the present case, however, the majority turns its back on these principles, holding that "the fact of the lawful arrest" always establishes the authority to conduct a full search of the arrestee's person, regardless of whether in a particular case "there was present one of the reasons supporting the authority for a search of the person incident to a lawful arrest." *Ante,* at ----------. The majority's approach represents a clear and marked departure from our long tradition of case-by-case adjudication of the reasonableness of searches and seizures under the Fourth Amendment. I continue to believe that "[t]he scheme of the Fourth Amendment becomes meaningful only when it is assured that at some point the conduct of those charged with enforcing the laws can be subjected to the more detached, neutral scrutiny of a judge who must evaluate the reasonableness of a particular search or seizure in light of the particular circumstances." *Terry* v. *Ohio,* 392 U.S. 1, 21, 44 OhioOp. (2d) 383, 393 (1968). Because I find the majority's reasoning to be at odds with these fundamental principles, I must respectfully dissent.

MIRANDA v. STATE OF ARIZONA
384 U.S. 436, 36 OhioOp.(2d) 237, 16 L.Ed.(2d) 694, 86 S.Ct. 1062
Decided June 13, 1966.

Mr. Chief Justice WARREN delivered the opinion of the Court.

The cases before us raise questions which go to the roots of our concepts of American criminal jurisprudence: the restraints society must observe consistent with the Federal Constitution in prosecuting individuals for crime. More specifically, we deal with the admissibility of statements obtained from an individual who is subjected to custodial police interrogation and the necessity for procedures which assure that the individual is accorded his privilege under the Fifth Amendment to the Constitution not to be compelled to incriminate himself.

We dealt with certain phases of this problem recently in *Escobedo* v. *State of Illinois,* 378 U.S. 478, 32 O.O.(2d) 31, 84 S.Ct. 1758, 12 L.Ed.(2d) 977 (1964). There, as in the four cases before us, the law enforcement officials took the defendant into custody and interrogated him in a police station for the purpose of obtaining a confession. The police did not effectively advise him of his right to remain silent or of his right to consult with his attorney. Rather, they confronted him with an alleged accomplice who accused him of having perpetrated a murder. When the defendant denied the accusation and said "I didn't shoot Manuel, you did it," they handcuffed him and took him to an interrogation room. There, while handcuffed and standing, he was questioned for four hours until he confessed. During this interrogation, the police denied his request to speak to his attorney, and they prevented his retained attorney, who had come to the police station, from consulting with him. At his trial, the State, over his objection, introduced the confession against him. We held that the statements thus made were constitutionally inadmissible.

This case has been the subject of judicial interpretation and spirited legal debate since it was decided two years ago. Both state and federal courts, in assessing its implications, have arrived at varying conclusions. A wealth of scholarly material has been written tracing its ramifications and underpinnings. Police and prosecutor have speculated on its range and desirability. We granted certiorari in these cases, 382 U.S. 924, 925, 937, 86 S.Ct. 318, 320, 395, 15 L.Ed. (2d) 338, 339, 348, in order further to explore some facets of the problems, thus exposed, of applying the privilege against self-incrimination to in-custody interrogation, and to give concrete constitutional guidelines for law enforcement agencies and courts to follow.

We start here, as we did in *Escobedo*, with the premise that our holding is not an innovation in our jurisprudence, but is an application of principles long recognized and applied in other settings. We have undertaken a thorough re-examination of the *Escobedo* decision and the principles it announced, and we reaffirm it. That case was but an explication of basic rights that are enshrined in our Constitution—that "No person * * * shall be compelled in any criminal case to be a witness against himself," and that "the accused shall * * * have the Assistance of Counsel"—rights which were put in jeopardy in that case through official overbearing. These precious rights were fixed in our Constitution only after centuries of persecution and struggle. And in the words of Chief Justice Marshall, they were secured "for ages to come and * * * designed to approach immortality as nearly as human institutions can approach it," *Cohens v. Commonwealth of Virginia*, 6 Wheat. 264, 387, 5 L.Ed. 257 (1821).

Over 70 years ago, our predecessors on this Court eloquently stated:

"The maxim 'Nemo tenetur seipsum accusare,' had its origin in a protest against the inquisitorial and manifestly unjust methods of interrogating accused persons, which has long obtained in the continental system, and, until the expulsion of the Stuarts from the British throne in 1688, and the erection of additional barriers for the protection of the people against the exercise of arbitrary power, was not uncommon even in England. While the admissions or confessions of the prisoner, when voluntarily and freely made, have always ranked high in the scale of incriminating evidence, if an accused person be asked to explain his apparent connection with a crime under investigation, the ease with which the questions put to him may assume an inquisitorial character, the temptation to press the witness unduly, to browbeat him if he be timid or reluctant, to push him into a corner, and to entrap him into fatal contradictions, which is so painfully evidenced in many of these earlier state trials, notably in those of Sir Nicholas Throckmorton, and Udal, the Puritan minister, made the system so odious as to give rise to a demand for its total abolition. The change in the English criminal procedure in that particular seems to be founded upon no statute and no judicial opinion, but upon a general and silent acquiescence of the courts in a popular demand. But, however adopted, it has become firmly embedded in English, as well as in American jurisprudence. So deeply did the inequities of the ancient system impress themselves upon the minds of the American colonists that the states, with one accord, made a denial of the right to question an accused person a part of their fundamental law, so that a maxim, which in England was a mere rule of evidence, became clothed in this country with the impregnability of a constitutional enactment." *Brown v. Walker,* 161 U.S. 591, 596-597, 16 S.Ct. 644, 646, 40 L.Ed. 819 (1896).

In stating the obligation of the judiciary to apply these constitutional rights, this Court declared in *Weems v. United States,* 217 U.S. 349, 373, 30 S.Ct. 544, 551, 54 L.Ed. 793 (1910):

"* * * our contemplation cannot be only what has been, but of what may be. Under any other rule a constitution would indeed be as easy of application as it would be deficient in efficacy and power. Its general principles would have little value, and be converted by precedent into impotent and lifeless formulas. Rights declared in words might be lost in reality. And this has been recognized. The meaning and vitality of the Constitution have developed against narrow and restrictive construction."

This was the spirit in which we delineated, in meaningful language, the manner in which the constitutional rights of the individual could be enforced against overzealous police practices. It was necessary in *Escobedo*, as here, to insure that what was proclaimed in the Constitution had not become but a "form of words," *Silverthorne Lumber Co. v. United States*, 251 U.S. 385, 392, 40 S.Ct. 182, 64 L.Ed. 319 (1920), in the hands of government officials. And it is in this spirit, consistent with our role as judges, that we adhere to the principles of *Escobedo* today.

Our holding will be spelled out with some specificity in the pages which follow but briefly stated it is this: the prosecution may not use statements, whether exculpatory or inculpatory, stemming from custodial interrogation of the defendant unless it demonstrates the use of procedural safeguards effective to secure the privilege against self-incrimination. By custodial interrogation, we mean questioning initiated by law enforcement officers after a person has been taken into custody or otherwise deprived of his freedom of action in any significant way. As for the procedural safeguards to be employed, unless other fully effective means are devised to inform accused persons of their right of silence and to assure a continuous opportunity to exercise it, the following measures are required. Prior to any questioning, the person must be warned that he has a right to remain silent, that any statement he does make may be used as evidence against him, and that he has a right to the presence of an attorney, either retained or appointed. The defendant may waive effectuation of these rights, provided the waiver is made voluntarily, knowingly and intelligently. If, however, he indicates in any manner and at any stage of the process that he wishes to consult with an attorney before speaking there can be no questioning. Likewise, if the individual is alone and indicates in any manner that he does not wish to be interrogated, the police may not question him. The mere fact that he may have answered some questions or volunteered some statements on his own does not deprive him of the right to refrain from answering any further inquiries until he has consulted with an attorney and thereafter consents to be questioned.

Miranda v. State of Arizona

I.

The constitutional issue we decide in each of these cases is the admissibility of statements obtained from a defendant questioned while in custody and deprived of his fredeom of action. In each, the defendant was questioned by police officers, detectives, or a prosecuting attorney in a room in which he was cut off from the outside world. In none of these cases was the defendant given a full and effective warning of his rights at the outset of the interrogation process. In all the cases, the questioning elicited oral admissions, and in three of them, signed statements as well which were admitted at their trials. They all thus share salient features—incommunicado interrogation of individuals in a police-dominated atmosphere, resulting in self-incriminating statements without full warnings of constitutional rights.

• • •

Because of the adoption by Congress of Rule 5(a) of the Federal Rules of Criminal Procedure, and the Court's effectuation of that Rule in *McNabb* v. *United States*, 318 U.S. 332, 63 S.Ct. 608, 87 L.Ed. 819 (1943), and *Mallory* v. *United States*, 354 U.S. 449, 77 S.Ct. 1356, 1 L.Ed.(2d) 1479 (1957), we have had little occasion in the past quarter century to reach the constitutional issues in dealing with federal interrogations. These supervisory rules, requiring production of an arrested person before a commissioner "without unnecessary delay" and excluding evidence obtained in default of that statutory obligation, were nonetheless responsive to the same considerations of Fifth Amendment policy that unavoidably face us now as to the States. In *McNabb*, 318 U.S., at 343-344, 63 S.Ct., at 614, and in *Mallory*, 354 U.S., at 455-456, 77 S.Ct., at 1359-1360, we recognized both the dangers of interrogation and the appropriateness of prophylaxis stemming from the very fact of interrogation itself.

Our decision in *Malloy* v. *Hogan*, 378 U.S. 1, 84 S.Ct. 1489, 12 L.Ed.(2d) 653 (1964), necessitates an examination of the scope of the privilege in state cases as well. In *Malloy*, we squarely held the privilege applicable to the States, and held that the substantive standards underlying the privilege applied with full force to state court proceedings.

It was in this manner that *Escobedo* explicated another facet of the pre-trial privilege, noted in many of the Court's prior decisions: the protection of rights at trial. That counsel is present when statements are taken from an individual during interrogation obviously enhances the integrity of the fact-finding processes in court. The presence of an attorney, and the warnings delivered to the individual, enable the defendant under otherwise compelling circumstances to tell his story without fear, effectively, and in a way that eliminates the evils in the interrogation process. Without the protections flowing from adequate warning and the rights of counsel, "all the careful safeguards erected around the giving of testimony, whether by an accused or any other witness, would become empty formalities in a procedure where the most compelling possible evidence of guilt, a confession, would have already been obtained at the unsupervised pleasure of the police." *Mapp* v. *Ohio*, 367 U.S. 643, 685, 16 O.O.(2d) 384, 404, 81 S.Ct. 1684, 1707, 6 L.Ed. (2d) 1081 (1961) (Harlan, J., dissenting). Cf. *Pointer* v. *State of Texas*, 380 U.S. 400, 85 S.Ct. 1065, 13 L.Ed.(2d) 923 (1965).

III.

Today, then, there can be no doubt that the Fifth Amendment privilege is available outside of criminal court proceedings and serves to protect persons in all settings in which their freedom of action is curtailed from being compelled to incriminate themselves. We have concluded that without proper safeguards the process of in-custody interrogation of persons suspected or accused of crime contains inherently compelling pressures which work to undermine the individual's will to resist and to compel him to speak where he would not otherwise do so freely. In order to combat these pressures and to permit a full opportunity to exercise the privilege against self-incrimination, the accused must be adequately and effectively apprised of his rights and the exercise of those rights must be fully honored.

It is impossible for us to foresee the potential alternatives for protecting the privilege which might be devised by Congress or the States in the exercise of their creative rule-making capacities. Therefore we cannot say that the Constitution necessarily requires adherence to any particular solution for the inherent compulsions of the interrogation process as it is presently conducted. Our decision in no way creates a constitutional strait-jacket which will handicap sound efforts at reform, nor is it intended to have this effect. We encourage Congress and the States to continue their laudable search for increasingly effective ways of protecting the rights of the individual while promoting efficient enforcement of our criminal laws. However, unless we are shown other procedures which are at least as effective in apprising accused persons of their right of silence and in assuring a continuous opportunity to exercise it, the following safeguards must be observed.

At the outset, if a person in custody is to be subjected to interrogation, he must first be informed in clear and unequivocal terms that he has the right to remain silent. For those unaware of the privilege, the warning is needed simply to make them aware of it— the threshold requirement for an intelligent decision as to its exercise. More important, such a warning is an absolute prerequisite in overcoming the inherent pressures of the interrogation atmosphere. It is not just the subnormal or woefully ignorant who succumb to an interrogator's imprecations, whether implied or expressly stated, that the interrogation will continue until a confession is obtained or that silence in the face of accusation is itself damning and will bode ill when presented to a jury. Further, the warning will show the individual that his interrogators are prepared to recognize his privilege should he choose to exercise it.

The Fifth Amendment privilege is so fundamental to our system of constitutional rule and the expedient of giving an adequate warning as to the availability of the privilege so simple, we will not pause to inquire in individual cases whether the defendant was aware of his rights without a warning being given. Assessments of the knowledge the defendant possessed, based on information as to his age, education, intelligence, or prior contact with authorities, can never be more than speculative; a warning is a clearcut fact. More important, whatever the background of the person interrogated, a warning at the time of the interrogation is indispensable to overcome its pressures and to insure that the individual knows he is free to exercise the privilege at that point in time.

The warning of the right to remain silent must be accompanied by the explanation that anything said can and will be used against the individual in court. This warning is needed in order to make him aware not only of the privilege, but also of the consequences of forgoing it. It is only through an awareness of these consequences that there can be any assurance of real understanding and intelligent exercise of the privilege. Moreover, this warning may serve to make the individual more acutely aware that he is faced with a phase of the adversary system—that he is not in the presence of persons acting solely in his interest.

• • •

Accordingly we hold that an individual held for interrogation must be clearly informed that he has the right to consult with a lawyer and to have the lawyer with him during interrogation under the system for protecting the privilege we delineate today. As with the warnings of the right to remain silent and that anything stated can be used in evidence against him, this warning is an absolute prerequisite to interrogation. No amount of circumstantial evidence that the person may have been aware of this right will suffice to stand in its stead. Only through such a warning is there ascertainable assurance that the accused was aware of this right.

If an individual indicates that he wishes the assistance of counsel before any interrogation occurs, the authorities cannot rationally ignore or deny his request on the basis that the individual does not have or cannot afford a retained attorney. The financial ability of the individual has no relationship to the scope of the rights involved here. The privilege against self-incrimination secured by the Constitution applies to all individuals. The need for counsel in order to protect the privilege exists for the indigent as well as the affluent. In fact, were we to limit these constitutional rights to those who can retain an attorney, our decisions today would be of little significance. The cases before us as well as the vast majority of confession cases with which we have dealt in the past involve those unable to retain counsel. While authorities are not required to relieve the accused of his poverty, they have the obligation not to take advantage of indigence in the administration of justice. Denial of counsel to the indigent at the time of interrogation while allowing an attorney to those who can afford one would be no more supportable by reason or logic than the similar situation at trial and on appeal struck down in *Gideon* v. *Wainwright,* 372 U.S. 335, 23 O.O.(2d) 258, 83 S.Ct. 792, 9 L.Ed.(2d) 799 (1963), and *Douglas* v. *People of State of California,* 372 U.S. 353, 83 S.Ct. 814, 9 L.Ed.(2d) 811 (1963).

In order fully to apprise a person interrogated of the extent of his rights under this system then, it is necessary to warn him not only that he has the right to consult with an attorney, but also that if he is indigent a lawyer will be appointed to represent him. Without this additional warning, the admonition of the right to consult with counsel would often be understood as meaning only that he can consult with a lawyer if he has one or has the funds to obtain one. The warning of a right to counsel would be hollow if not couched in terms that would convey to the indigent—the person most often subjected to interrogation—the knowledge that he too has a right to have counsel present. As with the warnings of the right to remain silent and of the general right to counsel, only by effective and express explanation to the indigent of this right can there be assurance that he was truly in a position to exercise it.

Once warnings have been given, the subsequent procedure is clear. If the individual indicates in any manner, at any time prior to or during questioning, that he wishes to remain silent, the interrogation must cease. At this point he has shown that he intends to exercise his Fifth Amendment privilege; any statement taken after the person invokes his privilege cannot be other than the product of compulsion, subtle or otherwise. Without the right to cut off questioning, the setting of in-custody interrogation operates on the individual to overcome free choice in producing a statement after the privilege has been once invoked. If the individual states that he wants an attorney, the interrogation must cease until an attorney is present. At that time, the individual must have an opportunity to confer with the attorney and to have him present during any subsequent questioning. If the individual cannot obtain an attorney and he indicates that he wants one before speaking to police, they must respect his decision to remain silent.

This does not mean, as some have suggested, that each police station must have a "station house lawyer" present at all times to advise prisoners. It does mean, however, that if police propose to interrogate a person they must make known to him that he is entitled to a lawyer and that if he cannot afford one, a lawyer will be provided for him prior to any interrogation. If authorities conclude that they will not provide counsel during a reasonable period of time in which investigation in the field is carried out, they may do so without violating the person's Fifth Amendment privilege so long as they do not question him during that time.

If the interrogation continues without the presence of an attorney and a statement is taken, a heavy burden rests on the Government to demonstrate that the defendant knowingly and intelligently waived his privilege against self-incrimination and his right to retained or appointed counsel. *Escobedo v. State of Illinois*, 378 U.S. 478, 490 n. 14, 32 O.O.(2d) 31, 36, 84 S.Ct. 1758, 1764, 12 L.Ed.(2d) 977. This Court has always set high standards of proof for the waiver of constitutional rights, *Johnson v. Zerbst*, 304 U.S. 458, 58 S.Ct. 1019, 82 L.Ed. 1461 (1938), and we reassert these standards as applied to in-custody interrogation. Since the State is responsible for establishing the isolated circumstances under which the interrogation takes place and has the only means of making available corroborated evidence of warnings given during incommunicado interrogation, the burden is rightly on its shoulders.

An express statement that the individual is willing to make a statement and does not want an attorney followed closely by a statement could constitute a waiver. But a valid waiver will not be presumed simply from the silence of the accused after warnings are given or simply from the fact that a confession was in fact eventually obtained. A statement we made in *Carnley v. Cochran*, 369 U.S. 506, 516, 82 S.Ct. 884, 890, 8 L.Ed.(2d) 70 (1962), is applicable here:

"Presuming waiver from a silent record is impermissible. The record must show, or there must be an allegation and evidence which show, that an accused was offered counsel but intelligently and understandingly rejected the offer. Anything less is not waiver."

See also *Glasser v. United States*, 315 U.S. 60, 62 S.Ct. 457, 86 L.Ed. 680 (1942). Moreover, where in-custody interrogation is involved, there is no room for the contention that the privilege is waived if the individual answers some questions or gives some information on his own prior to invoking his right to remain silent when interrogated.

• • •

Our decision is not intended to hamper the traditional function of police officers in investigating crime. See *Escobedo v. State of Illinois*, 378 U.S. 478, 492, 32 O.O.(2d) 31, 37, 84 S.Ct. 1758, 1765.

When an individual is in custody on probable cause, the police may, of course, seek out evidence in the field to be used at trial against him. Such investigation may include inquiry of persons not under restraint. General on-the-scene questioning as to facts surrounding a crime or other general questioning of citizens in the fact-finding process is not affected by our holding. It is an act of responsible citizenship for individuals to give whatever information they may have to aid in law enforcement. In such situations the compelling atmosphere inherent in the process of in-custody interrogation is not necessarily present.

In dealing with statements obtained through interrogation, we do not purport to find all confessions inadmissible. Confessions remain a proper element in law enforcement. Any statement given freely and voluntarily without any compelling influences is, of course, admissible in evidence. The fundamental import of the privilege while an individual is in custody is not whether he is allowed to talk to the police without the benefit of warnings and counsel, but whether he can be interrogated. There is no requirement that police stop a person who enters a police station and states that he wishes to confess to a crime, or a person who calls the police to offer a confession or any other statement he desires to make. Volunteered statements of any kind are not barred by the Fifth Amendment and their admissibility is not affected by our holding today.

To summarize, we hold that when an individual is taken into custody or otherwise deprived of his freedom by the authorities and is subjected to questioning, the privilege against self-incrimination is jeopardized. Procedural safeguards must be employed to protect the privilege, and unless other fully effective means are adopted to notify the person of his right of silence and to assure that the exercise of the right will be scrupulously honored, the following measures are required. He must be warned prior to any questioning that he has the right to remain silent, that anything he says can be used against him in a court of law, that he has the right to the presence of an attorney, and that if he cannot afford an attorney one will be appointed for him prior to any questioning if he so desires. Opportunity to exercise these rights must be afforded to him throughout the interrogation. After such warnings have been given, and such opportunity afforded him, the individual may knowingly and intelligently waive these rights and agree to answer questions or make a statement. But unless and until such warnings and waiver are demonstrated by the prosecution at trial, no evidence obtained as a result of interrogation can be used against him.

• • •

V.

Because of the nature of the problem and because of its recurrent significance in numerous cases, we have to this point discussed the relationship of the Fifth Amendment privilege to police interrogation without specific concentration on the facts of the cases before us. We turn now to these facts to consider the application to these cases of the constitutional principles discussed above. In each instance, we have concluded that statements were obtained from the defendant under circumstances that did not meet constitutional standards for protection of the privilege.

No. 759. *Miranda v. Arizona.*

On March 13, 1963, petitioner, Ernesto Miranda, was arrested at his home and taken in custody to a Phoenix police station. He was there identified by the complaining witness. The police then took him to "Interrogation Room No. 2" of the detective bureau. There he was questioned by two police officers. The officers admitted at trial that Miranda was not advised that he had a right to have an attorney present. Two hours later, the officers emerged from the interrogation room with a written confession signed by Miranda. At the top of the statement was a typed paragraph stating that the confession was made voluntarily, without threats or promises of immunity and "with full knowledge of my legal rights, understanding any statement I make may be used against me."

At his trial before a jury, the written confession was admitted into evidence over the objection of defense counsel, and the officers testified to the prior oral confession made by Miranda during the interrogation. Miranda was found guilty of kidnapping and rape. He was sentenced to 20 to 30 years' imprisonment on each count, the sentences to run concurrently. On appeal, the Supreme Court of Arizona held that Miranda's constitutional rights were not violated in obtaining the confession and affirmed the conviction. 98 Ariz. 18, 401 P.(2d) 721. In reaching its decision, the court emphasized heavily the fact that Miranda did not specifically request counsel.

We reverse. From the testimony of the officers and by the admission of respondent, it is clear that Miranda was not in any way apprised of his right to consult with an attorney and to have one present during the interrogation, nor was his right not to be compelled to incriminate himself effectively protected in any other manner. Without these warnings the statements were inadmissible. The mere fact that he signed a statement which contained a typed-in clause stating that he had "full knowledge" of his "legal rights" does not approach the knowing and intelligent waiver required to relinquish constitutional rights. Cf. *Haynes v. State of Washington,* 373 U.S. 503, 512-513, 83 S.Ct. 1336, 1342, 10 L.Ed.(2d) 513 (1963); *Haley.v. State of Ohio,* 332 U.S. 596, 601, 36 O.O. 530, 68 S.Ct. 302, 304, 92 L.Ed. 224 (1948) (opinion of Mr. Justice Douglas).

No. 760. *Vignera v. New York.*

Petitioner, Michael Vignera, was picked up by New York police on October 14, 1960, in connection with the robbery three days earlier of a Brooklyn dress shop. They took him to the 17th Detective Squad headquarters in Manhattan. Sometime thereafter he was taken to the 66th Detective Squad. There a detective questioned Vignera with respect to the robbery. Vignera orally admitted the robbery to the detective. The detective was asked on cross-examination at trial by defense counsel whether Vignera was warned of his right to counsel before being interrogated. The prosecution objected to the question and the trial judge sustained the objection. Thus, the defense was precluded from making any showing that warnings had not been given. While at the 66th Detective Squad, Vignera was identified by the store owner and a saleslady as the man who robbed the dress shop. At about 3:00 p.m. he was formally arrested. The police then transported him to still another station, the 70th Precinct in Brooklyn, "for detention." At 11:00 p. m. Vignera was questioned by an assistant district attorney in the presence of a hearing reporter who transcribed the questions and Vignera's answers. This verbatim account of these proceedings contains no statement of any warnings given by the assistant district attorney. At Vignera's trial on a charge of first degree robbery, the detective testified as to the oral confession. The transcription of the statement taken was also introduced in evidence. At the conclusion of the testimony, the trial judge charged the jury in part as follows:

"The law doesn't say that the confession is void or invalidated because the police officer didn't advise the defendant as to his rights. Did you hear what I said? I am telling you what the law of the State of New York is."

Vignera was found guilty of first degree robbery. He was subsequently adjudged a third-felony offender and sentenced to 30 to 60 years' imprisonment. The conviction was affirmed without opinion by the Appellate Division, Second Department, 21 A.D.(2d) 752, 252 N.Y.S.(2d) 19, and by the Court of Appeals, also without opinion, 15 N.Y.(2d) 970, 259 N.Y.S.(2d) 857, 207 N.E.(2d) 527, remittitur amended, 16 N.Y.(2d) 614, 261 N.Y.S.(2d) 65, 209 N.E.(2d) 110. In argument to the Court of Appeals, the State contended that Vignera had no constitutional right to be advised of his right to counsel or his privilege against self-incrimination.

We reverse. The foregoing indicates that Vignera was not warned of any of his rights before the questioning by the detective and by the assistant district attorney. No other steps were taken to protect these rights. Thus he was not effectively apprised of his Fifth Amendment privilege or of his right to have counsel present and his statements are inadmissible.

No. 761. *Westover v. United States.*

At approximately 9:45 p.m. on March 20, 1963, petitioner, Carl Calvin Westover, was arrested by local police in Kansas City as a suspect in two Kansas City robberies. A report was also received from the FBI that he was wanted on a felony charge in California. The local authorities took him to a police station and placed him in a line-up on the local charges, and at about 11:45 p.m. he was booked. Kansas City police interrogated Westover on the night of his arrest. He denied any knowledge of criminal activities. The next day local officers interrogated him again throughout the morning. Shortly before noon they informed the FBI that they were through interrogating Westover and that the FBI could proceed to interrogate him. There is nothing in the record to indicate that Westover was ever given any warning as to his rights by local police. At noon, three special agents of the FBI continued the interrogation in a private interview room of the Kansas City Police Department, this time with respect to the robbery of a savings and loan association and a bank in Sacramento, California. After two or two and one-half hours, Westover signed separate confessions to each of these two robberies which had been prepared by one of the agents during the interrogation. At trial one of the agents testified, and a paragraph on each of the statements states, that the agents advised Westover that he did not have to make a statement, that any statement he made could be used against him, and that he had the right to see an attorney.

Westover was tried by a jury in federal court and convicted of the California robberies. His statements were introduced at trial. He was sentenced to 15 years' imprisonment on each count, the sentences to run consecutively. On appeal, the conviction was affirmed by the Court of Appeals for the Ninth Circuit. 342 F.(2d) 684.

We reverse. On the facts of this case we cannot find that Westover knowingly and intelligently waived his right to remain silent and his right to consult with counsel prior to the time he made the statement. At the time the FBI agents began questioning Westover, he had been in custody for over 14 hours and had been interrogated at length during that period. The FBI interrogation began immediately upon the conclusion of the interrogation by Kansas City police and was conducted in local police headquarters. Although the two law enforcement authorities are legally distinct and the crimes for which they interrogated Westover were different, the impact on him was that of a continuous period of questioning. There is no evidence of any warning given prior to the FBI interrogation nor is there any evidence of an articulated waiver of rights after the FBI commenced their interrogation. The record simply shows that the defendant did in fact confess a short time after being turned over to the FBI following interrogation by local police. Despite the fact that the FBI agents gave warnings at the outset of their interview, from Westover's point of view the warnings came at the end of the interrogation process. In these circumstances an intelligent waiver of constitutional rights cannot be assumed.

We do not suggest that law enforcement authorities are precluded from questioning any individual who has been held for a period of time by other authorities and interrogated by them without appropriate warnings. A different case would be presented if an accused were taken into custody by the second authority, removed both in time and place from his original surroundings, and then adequately advised of his rights and given an opportunity to exercise them. But here the FBI interrogation was conducted immediately following the state interrogation in the same police station— in the same compelling surroundings. Thus, in obtaining a confession from Westover the federal authorities were the beneficiaries of the pressure applied by the local in-custody interrogation. In these circumstances the giving of warnings alone was not sufficient to protect the privilege.

No. 584. *California v. Stewart.*

In the course of investigating a series of purse-snatch robberies in which one of the victims had died of injuries inflicted by her assailant, respondent, Roy Allen Stewart, was pointed out to Los Angeles police as the endorser of dividend checks taken in one of the robberies. At about 7:15 p.m., January 31, 1963, police officers went to Stewart's house and arrested him. One of the officers asked Stewart if they could search the house to which he replied "go ahead." The search turned up various items taken from the five robbery victims. At the time of Stewart's arrest, police also arrested Stewart's wife and three other persons who were visiting him. These four were jailed along with Stewart and were interrogated. Stewart was taken to the University Station of the Los Angeles Police Department where he was placed in a cell. During the next five days, police interrogated Stewart on nine different occasions. Except during the first interrogation session, when he was confronted with an accusing witness, Stewart was isolated with his interrogators.

During the ninth interrogation session, Stewart admitted that he had robbed the deceased and stated that he had not meant to hurt her. Police then brought Stewart before a magistrate for the first time. Since there was no evidence to connect them with any crime, the police then released the other four persons arrested with him.

Nothing in the record specifically indicates whether Stewart was or was not advised of his right to remain silent or his right to counsel. In a number of instances, however, the interrogating officers were asked to recount everything that was said during the interrogations. None indicated that Stewart was ever advised of his rights.

Stewart was charged with kidnapping to commit robbery, rape, and murder. At his trial, transcripts of the first interrogation and the confession at the last interrogation were introduced in evidence. The jury found Stewart guilty of robbery and first degree murder and fixed the penalty as death. On appeal, the Supreme Court of California reversed. 62 Cal.(2d) 571, 43 Cal.Rptr. 201, 400 P.(2d) 97. It held that under this Court's decision in *Escobedo*, Stewart should have been advised of his right to remain silent and of his right to counsel and that it would not presume in the face of a silent record that the police advised Stewart of his rights.

We affirm. In dealing with custodial interrogation, we will not presume that a defendant has been effectively appraised of his rights and that his privilege against self-incrimination has been adequately safeguarded on a record that does not show that any warnings have been given or that any effective alternative has been employed. Nor can a knowing and intelligent waiver of these rights be assumed on a silent record. Furthermore, Stewart's steadfast denial of the alleged offenses through eight of the nine interrogations over a period of five days is subject to no other construction than that he was compelled by persistent interrogation to forego his Fifth Amendment privilege.

Therefore, in accordance with the foregoing, the judgments of the Supreme Court of Arizona in No. 759, of the New York Court of Appeals in No. 760, and of the Court of Appeals for the Ninth Circuit in No. 761 are reversed. The judgment of the Supreme Court of California in No. 584 is affirmed. It is so ordered.

Judgments of Supreme Court of Arizona in No. 759, of New York Court of Appeals in No. 760, and of the Court of Appeals for the Ninth Circuit in No. 761 reversed.

Judgment of Supreme Court of California in No. 584 affirmed.

Mr. Justice CLARK, dissenting in Nos. 759, 760, and 761 and concurring in result in No. 584.

It is with regret that I find it necessary to write in these cases. However, I am unable to join the majority because its opinion goes too far on too little, while my dissenting brethren do not go quite far enough. Nor can I join in the Court's criticism of the present practices of police and investigatory agencies as to custodial interrogation. The materials it refers to as "police manuals" are, as I read them, merely writings in this field by professors and some police officers. Not one is shown by the record here to be the official manual of any police department, much less in universal use in crime detection. Moreover the examples of police brutality mentioned by the Court are rare exceptions to the thousands of cases that appear every year on the law reports. The police agencies—all the way from municipal and state forces to the federal bureaus—are responsible for law enforcement and public safety in this country. I am proud of their efforts, which in my view are not fairly characterized by the Court's opinion.

Mr. Justice HARLAN, whom Mr. Justice STEWART and Mr. Justice WHITE join, dissenting.

I believe the decision of the Court represents poor constitutional law and entails harmful consequences for the country at large. How serious these consequences may prove to be only time can tell. But the basic flaws in the Court's justification seem to me readily apparent now once all sides of the problem are considered.

IV. Conclusions.

All four of the cases involved here present express claims that confessions were inadmissible, not because of coercion in the traditional due process sense, but solely because of lack of counsel or lack of warnings concerning counsel and silence. For the reasons stated in this opinion, I would adhere to the due process test and reject the new requirements inaugurated by the Court. On this premise my disposition of each of these cases can be stated briefly.

In two of the three cases coming from state courts, *Miranda v. Arizona* (No. 759) and *Vignera v. New York* (No. 760), the confessions were held inadmissible and no other errors worth comment are alleged by petitioners. I would affirm in these two cases. The other state case is *California v. Stewart* (No. 584), where the state supreme court held the confession inadmissible and reversed the conviction. In that case I would dismiss the writ of certiorari on the ground that no final judgment is before us, 28 United States Code Section 1257 (1964 ed.); putting aside the new trial open to the State in any event, the confession itself has not even been finally excluded since the California Supreme Court left the State free to show proof of a waiver. If the merits of the decision in *Stewart* be reached, then I believe it should be reversed and the case remanded so the state supreme court may pass on the other claims available to respondent.

In the federal case, *Westover* v. *United States* (No. 761), a number of issues are raised by petitioner apart from the one already dealt with in this dissent. None of these other claims appears to me tenable, nor in this context to warrant extended discussion. It is urged that the confession was also inadmissible because not voluntary even measured by due process standards and because federal state cooperation brought the McNabb-Mallory rule into play under *Anderson* v. *United States,* 318 U.S. 350, 63 S.Ct. 599, 87 L.Ed. 829. However, the facts alleged fall well short of coercion in my view, and I believe the involvement of federal agents in petitioner's arrest and detention by the State too slight to invoke *Anderson.* I agree with the Government that the admission of the evidence now protested by petitioner was at most harmless error, and two final contentions— one involving weight of the evidence and another improper prosecutor comment—seem to me without merit. I would therefore affirm Westover's conviction.

In conclusion: Nothing in the letter or the spirit of the Constitution or in the precedents squares with the heavy handed and one-sided action that is so precipitously taken by the Court in the name of fulfilling its constitutional responsibilities. The foray which the Court takes today brings to mind the wise and farsighted words of Mr. Justice Jackson in *Douglas* v. *City of Jeannette,* 319 U.S. 157, 181, 63 S.Ct. 877, 889, 87 L.Ed. 1324 (separate opinion): "This Court is forever adding new stories to the temples of constitutional law, and the temples have a way of collapsing when one story too many is added."

Cases relating to Chapter 15

PRACTICAL CONSIDERATIONS IN COLLECTING AND PRESENTING EVIDENCE

MILLER v. PATE
386 U.S. 1, 17 L.Ed.(2d) 690, 87 S.Ct. 785
Decided Feb. 13, 1967.

Mr. Justice STEWART delivered the opinion of the Court.

On November 26, 1955, in Canton, Illinois, an eight-year-old girl died as the result of a brutal sexual attack. The petitioner was charged with her murder.

Prior to his trial in an Illinois court, his counsel filed a motion for an order permitting a scientific inspection of the physical evidence the prosecution intended to introduce. The motion was resisted by the prosecution and denied by the court. The jury trial ended in a verdict of guilty and a sentence of death. On appeal the judgment was affirmed by the Supreme Court of Illinois. On the basis of leads developed at a subsequent unsuccessful state clemency hearing, the petitioner applied to a federal district court for a writ of habeas corpus. After a hearing, the court granted the writ and ordered the petitioner's release or prompt retrial. The Court of Appeals reversed, and we granted certiorari to consider whether the trial that led to the petitioner's conviction was constitutionally valid. We have concluded that it was not.

There was no eyewitnesses to the brutal crime which the petitioner was charged with perpetrating. A vital component of the case against him was a pair of men's underwear shorts covered with large, dark, reddish-brown stains—People's Exhibit 3 in the trial record. These shorts had been found by a Canton policeman in a place known as the Van Buren Flats three days after the murder. The Van Buren Flats were about a mile from the scene of the crime. It was the prosecution's theory that the petitioner had been wearing these shorts when he committed the murder, and that he had afterwards removed and discarded them at the Van Buren Flats.

During the presentation of the prosecution's case, People's Exhibit 3 was variously described by witnesses in such terms as the "bloody shorts" and "a pair of jockey shorts stained with blood." Early in the trial the victim's mother testified that her daughter "had type 'A' positive blood." Evidence was later introduced to show that the petitioner's blood "was of group 'O'."

Against this background the jury heard the testimony of a chemist for the State Bureau of Crime Identification. The prosecution established his qualifications as an expert, whose "duties include blood identification, grouping and typing both dry and fresh stains," and who had "made approximately one thousand blood typing analyses while at the State Bureau." His crucial testimony was as follows:

> "I examined and tested 'People's Exhibit 3' to determine the nature of the staining material upon it. The result of the first test was that this material upon the shorts is blood. I made a second examination which disclosed that the blood is of human origin. I made a further examination which disclosed that the blood is of group 'A'."

The petitioner, testifying in his own behalf, denied that he had ever owned or worn the shorts in evidence as People's Exhibit 3. He himself referred to the shorts as having "dried blood on them."

In argument to the jury the prosecutor made the most of People's Exhibit 3:

> "Those shorts were found in the Van Buren Flats, with blood. What type blood? Not 'O' blood as the defendant has, but 'A'—type 'A'."

And later in his argument he said to the jury:

> "And, if you will recall, it has never been contradicted the blood type of Janice May was blood type 'A' positive. Blood type 'A.' Blood type 'A' on these shorts. It wasn't 'O' type as the defendant has. It is 'A' type, what the little girl had."

Such was the state of the evidence with respect to People's Exhibit 3 as the case went to the jury. And such was the state of the record as the judgment of conviction was reviewed by the Supreme Court of Illinois. The "blood stained shorts" clearly played a vital part in the case for the prosecution. They were an important link in the chain of circumstantial evidence against the petitioner, and, in the context of the revolting crime with which he was charged, their gruesomely emotional impact upon the jury was incalculable.

So matters stood with respect to People's Exhibit 3, until the present habeas corpus proceeding in the Federal District Court. In this proceeding the State was ordered to produce the stained shorts, and they were admitted in evidence. It was established that their appearance was the same as when they had been introduced at the trial as People's Exhibit 3. The petitioner was permitted to have the shorts examined by a chemical microanalyst. What the microanalyst found cast an extraordinary new light on People's Exhibit 3. The reddish-brown stains on the shorts were not blood, but paint.

The witness said that he had tested threads from each of the 10 reddish-brown stained areas on the shorts, and that he had found that all of them were encrusted with mineral pigments "* * * which one commonly uses in the preparation of paints." He found "no traces of human blood." The State did not dispute this testimony, its counsel contenting himself with prevailing upon the witness to concede on cross-examination that he could not swear that there had never been any blood on the shorts.

It was further established that counsel for the prosecution had known at the time of the trial that the shorts were stained with paint. The prosecutor even admitted that the Canton police had prepared a memorandum attempting to explain "how this exhibit contains all the paint on it."

In argument at the close of the habeas corpus hearing counsel for the State contended that "[e]verybody" at the trial had known that the shorts were stained with paint. That contention is totally belied by the record. The microanalyst correctly described the appearance of the shorts when he said, "I assumed I was dealing * * * with a pair of shorts which was heavily stained with blood. * * * [I]t would appear to a layman * * * that what I see before me is a garment heavily stained with blood." The record of the petitioner's trial reflects the prosecution's consistent and repeated misrepresentation that People's Exhibit 3 was, indeed, "a garment heavily stained with blood." The prosecution's whole theory with respect to the exhibit depended upon that misrepresentation. For the theory was that the victim's assailant had discarded the shorts *because* they were stained with blood. A pair of paint-stained shorts, found in an abandoned building a mile away from the scene of the crime, was virtually valueless as evidence against the petitioner. The prosecution deliberately misrepresented the truth.

More than 30 years ago this Court held that the Fourteenth Amendment cannot tolerate a state criminal conviction obtained by the knowing use of false evidence. Mooney v. Holohan, 294 U.S. 103, 55 S.Ct. 340, 79 L.Ed. 791. There has been no deviation from that established principle. Napue v. People of State of Illinois, 360 U.S. 264, 79 S.Ct. 1173, 3 L.Ed.2d 1217; Pyle v. State of Kansas, 317 U.S. 213, 63 S.Ct. 177, 87 L.Ed. 214; cf. Alcorta v. State of Texas, 355 U.S. 28, 78 S.Ct. 103, 2 L.Ed2d 9. There can be no retreat from that principle here.

The judgment of the Court of Appeals is reversed and the case is remanded for further proceedings consistent with this opinion. It is so ordered.

Reversed and remanded.

RULES OF EVIDENCE FOR UNITED STATES COURTS AND MAGISTRATES

(Effective July 1, 1975)

ARTICLE I. GENERAL PROVISIONS

Rule 101. Scope

These rules govern proceedings in the courts of the United States and before United States magistrates, to the extent and with the exceptions stated in rule 1101.

Rule 102. Purpose and Construction

These rules shall be construed to secure fairness in administration, elimination of unjustifiable expense and delay, and promotion of growth and development of the law of evidence to the end that the truth may be ascertained and proceedings justly determined.

Rule 103. Rulings on Evidence

(a) Effect of erroneous ruling.--Error may not be predicated upon a ruling which admits or excludes evidence unless a substantial right of the party is affected, and
    (1) Objection.--In case the ruling is one admitting evidence, a timely objection or motion to strike appears of record, stating the specific ground of objection, if the specific ground was not apparent from the context; or
    (2) Offer of proof.--In case the ruling is one excluding evidence, the substance of the evidence was made known to the court by offer or was apparent from the context within which questions were asked.
(b) Record of offer and ruling.--The court may add any other or further statement which shows the character of the evidence, the form in which it was offered, the objection made, and the ruling thereon. It may direct the making of an offer in question and answer form.
(c) Hearing of jury.--In jury cases, proceedings shall be conducted, to the extent practicable, so as to prevent inadmissible evidence from being suggested to the jury by any means, such as making statements or offers of proof or asking questions in the hearing of the jury.
(d) Plain error.--Nothing in this rule precludes taking notice of plain errors affecting substantial rights although they were not brought to the attention of the court.

Rule 104. Preliminary Questions

(a) Questions of admissibility generally.--Preliminary questions concerning the qualification of a person to be a witness, the existence of a privilege, or the admissibility of evidence shall be determined by the court, subject to the provisions of subdivision (b). In making its determination it is not bound by the rules of evidence except those with respect to privileges.

(b) Relevancy conditioned on fact.--When the relevancy of evidence depends upon the fulfillment of a condition of fact, the court shall admit it upon, or subject to, the introduction of evidence sufficient to support a finding of the fulfillment of the condition.

(c) Hearing of jury.--Hearings on the admissibility of confessions shall in all cases be conducted out of the hearing of the jury. Hearings on other preliminary matters shall be so conducted when the interests of justice require or, when an accused is a witness, if he so requests.

(d) Testimony by accused.--The accused does not, by testifying upon a preliminary matter, subject himself to cross-examination as to other issues in the case.

(e) Weight and credibility.--This rule does not limit the right of a party to introduce before the jury evidence relevant to weight or credibility.

Rule 105. Limited Admissibility

When evidence which is admissible as to one party or for one purpose but not admissible as to another party or for another purpose is admitted, the court, upon request, shall restrict the evidence to its proper scope and instruct the jury accordingly.

Rule 106. Remainder of or Related Writings or Recorded Statements

When a writing or recorded statement or part thereof is introduced by a party, an adverse party may require him at that time to introduce any other part or any other writing or recorded statement which ought in fairness to be considered contemporaneously with it.

ARTICLE II. JUDICIAL NOTICE

Rule 201. Judicial Notice of Adjudicative Facts

(a) Scope of rule.--This rule governs only judicial notice of adjudicative facts.

(b) Kinds of facts.--A judicially noticed fact must be one not subject to reasonable dispute in that it is either (1) generally known within the territorial jurisdiction of the trial court or (2) capable of accurate and ready determination by resort to sources whose accuracy cannot reasonably be questioned.

(c) When discretionary.--A court may take judicial notice, whether requested or not.

(d) When mandatory.--A court shall take judicial notice if requested by a party and supplied with the necessary information.

(e) Opportunity to be heard.--A party is entitled upon timely request to an opportunity to be heard as to the propriety of taking judicial notice and the tenor of the matter noticed. In the absence of prior notification, the request may be made after judicial notice has been taken.

(f) Time of taking notice.--Judicial notice may be taken at any stage of the proceeding.

(g) Instructing jury.--In a civil action or proceeding, the court shall instruct the jury to accept as conclusive any fact judicially noticed. In a criminal case, the court shall instruct the jury that it may, but is not required to, accept as conclusive any fact judicially noticed.

ARTICLE III. PRESUMPTIONS IN CIVIL ACTIONS AND PROCEEDINGS

Rule 301. Presumptions in General in Civil Actions and Proceedings

In all civil actions and proceedings not otherwise provided for by Act of Congress or by these rules, a presumption imposes on the party against whom it is directed the burden of going forward with evidence to rebut or meet the presumption, but does not shift to such party the burden of proof in the sense of the risk of nonpersuasion, which remains throughout the trial upon the party on whom it was originally cast.

Rule 302. Applicability of State Law in Civil Actions and Proceedings

In civil actions and proceedings, the effect of a presumption respecting a fact which is an element of a claim or defense as to which State law supplies the rule of decision is determined in accordance with State law.

ARTICLE IV. RELEVANCY AND ITS LIMITS

Rule 401. Definition of "Relevant Evidence"

"Relevant evidence" means evidence having any tendency to make the existence of any fact that is of consequence to the determination of the action more probable or less probable than it would be without the evidence.

Rule 402. Relevant Evidence Generally Admissible; Irrelevant Evidence Inadmissible

All relevant evidence is admissible, except as otherwise provided by the Constitution of the United States, by Act of

Congress, by these rules, or by other rules prescribed by the Supreme Court pursuant to statutory authority. Evidence which is not relevant is not admissible.

Rule 403. Exclusion of Relevant Evidence on Grounds of Prejudice, Confusion, or Waste of Time

Although relevant, evidence may be excluded if its probative value is substantially outweighed by the danger of unfair prejudice, confusion of the issues, or misleading the jury, or by considerations of undue delay, waste of time, or needless presentation of cumulative evidence.

Rule 404. Character Evidence Not Admissible To Prove Conduct; Exceptions; Other Crimes

(a) Character evidence generally.--Evidence of a person's character or a trait of his character is not admissible for the purpose of proving that he acted in conformity therewith on a particular occasion, except:

  (1) Character of accused.--Evidence of a pertinent trait of his character offered by an accused, or by the prosecution to rebut the same;
  (2) Character of victim.--Evidence of a pertinent trait of character of the victim of the crime offered by an accused, or by the prosecution to rebut the same, or evidence of a character trait of peacefulness of the victim offered by the prosecution in a homicide case to rebut evidence that the victim was the first aggressor;
  (3) Character of witness.--Evidence of the character of a witness, as provided in rules 607, 608 and 609.

(b) Other crimes, wrongs, or acts.--Evidence of other crimes, wrongs, or acts is not admissible to prove the character of a person in order to show that he acted in conformity therewith. It may, however, be admissible for other purposes, such as proof of motive, opportunity, intent, preparation, plan, knowledge, identity, or absence of mistake or accident.

Rule 405. Methods of Proving Character

(a) Reputation or opinion.--In all cases in which evidence of character or a trait of character of a person is admissible, proof may be made by testimony as to reputation or by testimony in the form of an opinion. On cross-examination, inquiry is allowable into relevant specific instances of conduct.

(b) Specific instances of conduct.--In cases in which character or a trait of character of a person is an essential element of a charge, claim, or defense, proof may also be made of specific instances of his conduct.

Rule 406. Habit; Routine Practice

Evidence of the habit of a person or of the routine practice of an organization, whether corroborated or not and regardless of the presence of eyewitnesses, is relevant to prove that the conduct of the person or organization on a particular occasion was in conformity with the habit or routine practice.

Rule 407. Subsequent Remedial Measures

When, after an event, measures are taken which, if taken previously, would have made the event less likely to occur, evidence of the subsequent measures is not admissible to prove negligence or culpable conduct in connection with the event. This rule does not require the exclusion of evidence of subsequent measures when offered for another purpose, such as proving ownership, control, or feasibility of precautionary measures, if controverted, or impeachment.

Rule 408. Compromise and Offers to Compromise

Evidence of (1) furnishing or offering or promising to furnish, or (2) accepting or offering or promising to accept, a valuable consideration in compromising or attempting to compromise a claim which was disputed as to either validity or amount, is not admissible to prove liability for or invalidity of the claim or its amount. Evidence of conduct or statements made in compromise negotiations is likewise not admissible. This rule does not require the exclusion of any evidence otherwise discoverable merely because it is presented in the course of compromise negotiations. This rule also does not require exclusion when the evidence is offered for another purpose, such as proving bias or prejudice of a witness, negativing a contention of undue delay, or proving an effort to obstruct a criminal investigation or prosecution.

Rule 409. Payment of Medical and Similar expenses

Evidence of furnishing or offering or promising to pay medical, hospital, or similar expenses occasioned by an injury is not admissible to prove liability for the injury.

Rule 410. Offer To Plead Guilty; Nolo Contendere; Withdrawn Plea of Guilty

Except as otherwise provided by Act of Congress, evidence of a plea of guilty, later withdrawn, or a plea of nolo contendere, or of an offer to plead guilty or nolo contendere to the crime charged or any other crime, or of statements made in connection with any of the foregoing pleas or offers, is not admissible in any civil or criminal action, case, or proceeding against the person who made the plea or offer. This rule shall not apply to the introduction of voluntary and reliable statements made in court on the record in connection with any of the foregoing pleas or offers where offered for impeachment purposes or in a subsequent prosecution of the declarant for perjury or false statement.

This rule shall not take effect until August 1, 1975, and shall be superseded by any amendment to the Federal Rules of Criminal Procedure which is inconsistent with this rule, and which takes effect after the date of the enactment of the Act establishing these Federal Rules of Evidence.

Rule 411. Liability Insurance

Evidence that a person was or was not insured against liability is not admissible upon the issue whether he acted negligently or otherwise wrongfully. This rule does not require the exclusion of evidence of insurance against liability when offered for another purpose, such as proof of agency, ownership, or control, or bias or prejudice of a witness.

ARTICLE V. PRIVILEGES

Rule 501. General Rule

Except as otherwise required by the Constitution of the United States or provided by Act of Congress or in rules prescribed by the Supreme Court pursuant to statutory authority, the privilege of a witness, person, government, State, or political subdivision thereof shall be governed by the principles of the common law as they may be interpreted by the courts of the United States in the light of reason and experience. However, in civil actions and proceedings, with respect to an element of a claim or defense as to which State law supplies the rule of decision, the privilege of a witness, person, government, State, or political subdivision thereof shall be determined in accordance with State law.

ARTICLE VI. WITNESSES

Rule 601. General Rule of Competency

Every person is competent to be a witness except as otherwise provided in these rules. However, in civil actions and proceedings, with respect to an element of a claim or defense as to which State law supplies the rule of decision, the competency of a witness shall be determined in accordance with State law.

Rule 602. Lack of Personal Knowledge

A witness may not testify to a matter unless evidence is introduced sufficient to support a finding that he has personal knowledge of the matter. Evidence to prove personal knowledge may, but need not, consist of the testimony of the witness himself. This rule is subject to the provisions of rule 703, relating to opinion testimony by expert witnesses.

Rule 603. Oath or Affirmation

Before testifying, every witness shall be required to declare that he will testify truthfully, by oath or affirmation administered in a form calculated to awaken his conscience and impress his mind with his duty to do so.

Rule 604. Interpreters

An interpreter is subject to the provisions of these rules relating to qualification as an expert and the administration of an oath or affirmation that he will make a true translation.

Rule 605. Competency of Judge as Witness

The judge presiding at the trial may not testify in that trial as a witness. No objection need be made in order to preserve the point.

Rule 606. Competency of Juror as Witness

(a) At the trial.--A member of the jury may not testify as a witness before that jury in the trial of the case in which he is sitting as a juror. If he is called so to testify, the opposing party shall be afforded an opportunity to object out of the presence of the jury.

(b) Inquiry into validity of verdict or indictment.--Upon an inquiry into the validity of a verdict or indictment, a juror may not testify as to any matter or statement occurring during the course of the jury's deliberations or to the effect of anything upon his or any other juror's mind or emotions as influencing him to assent to or dissent from the verdict or indictment or concerning his mental processes in connection therewith, except that a juror may testify on the question whether extraneous prejudicial information was improperly brought to the jury's attention or whether any outside influence was improperly brought to bear upon any juror. Nor may his affidavit or evidence of any statement by him concerning a matter about what he would be precluded from testifying be received for these purposes.

Rule 607. Who May Impeach

The credibility of a witness may be attacked by any party, including the party calling him.

Rule 608. Evidence of Character and Conduct of Witness

(a) Opinion and reputation evidence of character.--The credibility of a witness may be attacked or supported by evidence in the form of opinion or reputation, but subject to these limitations: (1) the evidence may refer only to character for truthfulness or untruthfulness, and (2) evidence of truthful character is admissible only after the character of the witness for truthfulness has been attacked by opinion or reputation evidence or otherwise.

(b) Specific instances of conduct.--Specific instances of the conduct of a witness, for the purpose of attacking or supporting his credibility, other than conviction of crime as provided in rule 609, may not be proved by extrinsic evidence. They may, however, in the discretion of the court, if probative of truthfulness or untruthfulness, be inquired into on cross-examination of the witness (1) concerning his character for truthfulness or untruthfulness, or (2) concerning the character for truthfulness or untruthfulness of another witness as to which character the witness being cross-examined has testified.

The giving of testimony, whether by an accused or by any other witness, does not operate as a waiver of his privilege against self-incrimination when examined with respect to matters which relate only to credibility.

Rule 609. Impeachment by Evidence of Conviction of Crime

(a) General rule.--For the purpose of attacking the credibility of a witness, evidence that he has been convicted of a crime shall be admitted if elicited from him or established by public record during cross-examination but only if the crime (1) was punishable by death or imprisonment in excess of one year under the law under which he was convicted, and the court determines that the probative value of admitting this evidence outweighs its prejudicial effect to the defendant, or (2) involved dishonesty or false statement, regardless of the punishment.

(b) Time limit.--Evidence of a conviction under this rule is not admissible if a period of more than ten years has elapsed since the date of the conviction or of the release of the witness from the confinement imposed for that conviction, whichever is the later date, unless the court determines, in the interests of justice, that the probative value of the conviction supported by specific facts and circumstances substantially outweighs its prejudicial effect. However, evidence of a conviction more than 10 years old as calculated herein, is not admissible unless the proponent gives to the adverse party sufficient advance written notice of intent to use such evidence to provide the adverse party with a fair opportunity to contest the use of such evidence.

(c) Effect of pardon, annulment, or certificate of rehabilitation.--Evidence of a conviction is not admissible under this rule if (1) the conviction has been the subject of a pardon, annulment, certificate of rehabilitation, or other equivalent procedure based on a finding of the rehabilitation of the person convicted, and that person has not been convicted of a subsequent crime which was punishable by death or imprisonment in excess of one year, or (2) the conviction has been the subject of a pardon, annulment, or other equivalent procedure based on a finding of innocence.

(d) Juvenile adjudications.--Evidence of juvenile adjudications is generally not admissible under this rule. The court may, however, in a criminal case allow evidence of a juvenile adjudication of a witness other than the accused if conviction of the offense would be admissible to attack the credibility of an adult and the court is satisfied that admission in evidence is necessary for a fair determination of the issue of guilt or innocence.

(e) Pendency of appeal.--The pendency of an appeal therefrom does not render evidence of a conviction inadmissible. Evidence of the pendency of an appeal is admissible.

Rule 610. Religious Beliefs or Opinions

Evidence of the beliefs or opinions of a witness on matters of religion is not admissible for the purpose of showing that by reason of their nature his credibility is impaired or enhanced.

Rule 611. Mode and Order of Interrogation and Presentation

(a) Control by court.--The court shall exercise reasonable control over the mode and order of interrogating witnesses and presenting evidence so as to (1) make the interrogation and presentation effective for the ascertainment of the truth, (2) avoid needless consumption of time, and (3) protect witnesses from harassment or undue embarrassment.

(b) Scope of cross-examination.--Cross-examination should be limited to the subject matter of the direct examination and matters affecting the credibility of the witness. The court may, in the exercise of discretion, permit inquiry into additional matters as if on direct examination.

(c) Leading questions.--Leading questions should not be used on the direct examination of a witness except as may be necessary to develop his testimony. Ordinarily leading questions should be permitted on cross-examination. When a party calls a hostile witness, an adverse party, or a witness identified with an adverse party, interrogation may be by leading questions.

Rule 612. Writing Used To Refresh Memory

Except as otherwise provided in criminal proceedings by section 3500 of title 18, United States Code, if a witness

uses a writing to refresh his memory for the purpose of testifying, either--
  (1) while testifying, or
  (2) before testifying, if the court in its discretion determines it is necessary in the interests of justice, an adverse party is entitled to have the writing produced at the hearing, to inspect it, to cross-examine the witness thereon, and to introduce in evidence those portions which relate to the testimony of the witness. If it is claimed that the writing contains matters not related to the subject matter of the testimony the court shall examine the writing in camera, excise any portions not so related, and order delivery of the remainder to the party entitled thereto. Any portion withheld over objections shall be preserved and made available to the appellate court in the event of an appeal. If a writing is not produced or delivered pursuant to order under this rule, the court shall make any order justice requires, except that in criminal cases when the prosecution elects not to comply, the order shall be one striking the testimony or, if the court in its discretion determines that the interests of justice so require, declaring a mistrial.

Rule 613. Prior Statements of Witnesses

(a) Examining witness concerning prior statement.--In examining a witness concerning a prior statement made by him, whether written or not, the statement need not be shown nor its contents disclosed to him at that time, but on request the same shall be shown or disclosed to opposing counsel.

(b) Extrinsic evidence of prior inconsistent statement of witness.--Extrinsic evidence of a prior inconsistent statement by a witness is not admissible unless the witness is afforded an opportunity to explain or deny the same and the opposite party is afforded an opportunity to interrogate him thereon, or the interests of justice otherwise require. This provision does not apply to admissions of a party-opponent as defined in rule 801(d)(2).

Rule 614. Calling and Interrogation of Witnesses by Court

(a) Calling by court.--The court may, on its own motion or at the suggestion of a party, call witnesses, and all parties are entitled to cross-examine witnesses thus called.

(b) Interrogation by court.--The court may interrogate witnesses, whether called by itself or by a party.

(c) Objections.--Objections to the calling of witnesses by the court or to interrogation by it may be made at the time or at the next available opportunity when the jury is not present.

Rule 615. Exclusion of Witnesses

At the request of a party the court shall order witnesses excluded so that they cannot hear the testimony of other witnesses, and it may make the order of its own motion.

This rule does not authorize exclusion of (1) a party who is a natural person, or (2) an officer or employee of a party which is not a natural person designated as its representative by its attorney, or (3) a person whose presence is shown by a party to be essential to the presentation of his cause.

ARTICLE VII. OPINIONS AND EXPERT TESTIMONY

Rule 701. Opinion Testimony by Lay Witnesses

If the witness is not testifying as an expert, his testimony in the form of opinions or inferences is limited to those opinions or inferences which are (a) rationally based on the perception of the witness and (b) helpful to a clear understanding of his testimony or the determination of a fact in issue.

Rule 702. Testimony by Experts

If scientific, technical, or other specialized knowledge will assist the trier of fact to understand the evidence or to determine a fact in issue, a witness qualified as an expert by knowledge, skill, experience, training, or education, may testify thereto in the form of an opinion or otherwise.

Rule 703. Bases of Opinion Testimony by Experts

The facts or data in the particular case upon which an expert bases an opinion or inference may be those perceived by or made known to him at or before the hearing. If of a type reasonably relied upon by experts in the particular field in forming opinions or inferences upon the subject, the facts or data need not be admissible in evidence.

Rule 704. Opinion on Ultimate Issue

Testimony in the form of an opinion or inference otherwise admissible is not objectionable because it embraces an ultimate issue to be decided by the trier of fact.

Rule 705. Disclosure of Facts or Data Underlying Expert Opinion

The expert may testify in terms of opinion or inference and give his reasons therefor without prior disclosure of the underlying facts or data, unless the court requires otherwise. The expert may in any event be required to disclose the underlying facts or data on cross-examination.

Rule 706. Court Appointed Experts

(a) Appointment.--The court may on its own motion or on the motion of any party enter an order to show cause why expert witnesses should not be appointed, and may request the parties to submit nominations. The court may appoint any expert witnesses agreed upon by the parties, and may appoint expert witnesses of its own selection. An expert witness shall not be appointed by the court unless he consents to act. A witness so appointed shall advise the parties of his findings, if any; his deposition may be taken by any party; and he may be called to testify by the court or any party. He shall be subject to cross-examination by each party, including a party calling him as a witness.

(b) Compensation.--Expert witnesses so appointed are entitled to reasonable compensation in whatever sum the court may allow. The compensation thus fixed is payable from funds which may be provided by law in criminal cases and civil actions and proceedings involving just compensation under the fifth amendment. In other civil actions and proceedings the compensation shall be paid by the parties in such proportion and at such time as the court directs, and thereafter charged in like manner as other costs.

(c) Disclosure of appointment.--In the exercise of its discretion, the court may authorize disclosure to the jury of the fact that the court appointed the expert witness.

(d) Parties' experts of own selection.--Nothing in this rule limits the parties in calling expert witnesses of their own selection.

ARTICLE VIII. HEARSAY

Rule 801. Definitions

The following definitions apply under this article:
(a) Statement.--A "statement" is (1) an oral or written assertion or (2) nonverbal conduct of a person, if it is intended by him as an assertion.
(b) Declarant.--A "declarant" is a person who makes a statement.
(c) Hearsay.--"Hearsay" is a statement, other than one made by the declarant while testifying at the trial or hearing, offered in evidence to prove the truth of the matter asserted.
(d) Statements which are not hearsay.--A statement is not hearsay if--
(1) Prior statement by witness.--The declarant testifies at the trial or hearing and is subject to cross-examination concerning the statement, and the statement is (A) inconsistent with his testimony, and was given under oath subject to the penalty of perjury at a trial, hearing, or other proceeding, or in a deposition, or (B) consistent with his testimony and is offered to rebut an express or implied charge against him of recent fabrication or improper influence or motive, or
(2) Admission by party-opponent.--The statement is offered against a party and is (A) his own statement, in either his individual or a representative capacity or (B) a statement of which he has manifested his adoption or belief in its truth, or (C) a statement by a person

authorized by him to make a statement concerning the subject, or (D) a statement by his agent or servant concerning a matter within the scope of his agency or employment, made during the existence of the relationship, or (E) a statement by a coconspirator of a party during the course and in furtherance of the conspiracy.

Rule 802. Hearsay Rule

Hearsay is not admissible except as provided by these rules or by other rules prescribed by the Supreme Court pursuant to statutory authority or by Act of Congress.

Rule 803. Hearsay Exceptions; Availability of Declarant Immaterial

The following are not excluded by the hearsay rule, even though the declarant is available as a witness:

(1) Present sense impression.--A statement describing or explaining an event or condition made while the declarant was perceiving the event or condition, or immediately thereafter.

(2) Excited utterance.--A statement relating to a startling event or condition made while the declarant was under the stress of excitement caused by the event or condition.

(3) Then existing mental, emotional, or physical condition.--A statement of the declarant's then existing state of mind, emotion, sensation, or physical condition (such as intent, plan, motive, design, mental feeling, pain, and bodily health), but not including a statement of memory or belief to prove the fact remembered or believed unless it relates to the execution, revocation, identification, or terms of declarant's will.

(4) Statements for purposes of medical diagnosis or treatment.--Statements made for purposes of medical diagnosis or treatment and describing medical history, or past or present symptoms, pain, or sensations, or the inception or general character of the cause or external source thereof insofar as reasonably pertinent to diagnosis or treatment.

(5) Recorded recollection.--A memorandum or record concerning a matter about which a witness once had knowledge but now has insufficient recollection to enable him to testify fully and accurately, shown to have been made or adopted by the witness when the matter was fresh in his memory and to reflect that knowledge correctly. If admitted, the memorandum or record may be read into evidence but may not itself be received as an exhibit unless offered by an adverse party.

(6) Records of regularly conducted activity.--A memorandum, report, record, or data compilation, in any form, of acts, events, conditions, opinions, or diagnoses, made at or near the time by, or from information transmitted by, a person with knowledge, if kept in the course of a regularly conducted business activity, and

if it was the regular practice of that business activity to make the memorandum, report, record, or data compilation, all as shown by the testimony of the custodian or other qualified witness, unless the source of information or the method or circumstances of preparation indicate lack of trustworthiness. The term "business" as used in this paragraph includes business, institution, association, profession, occupation, and calling of every kind, whether or not conducted for profit.

(7) Absence of entry in records kept in accordance with the provisions of paragraph (6).--Evidence that a matter is not included in the memoranda reports, records, or data compilations, in any form, kept in accordance with the provisions of paragraph (6), to prove the nonoccurrence or nonexistence of the matter, if the matter was of a kind of which a memorandum, report, record, or data compilation was regularly made and preserved, unless the sources of information or other circumstances indicate lack of trustworthiness.

(8) Public records and reports.--Records, reports, statements, or data compilations, in any form, of public offices or agencies, setting forth (A) the activities of the office or agency, or (B) matters observed pursuant to duty imposed by law as to which matters there was a duty to report, excluding, however, in criminal cases matters observed by police officers and other law enforcement personnel, or (C) in civil actions and proceedings and against the Government in criminal cases, factual findings resulting from an investigation made pursuant to authority granted by law, unless the sources of information or other circumstances indicate lack of trustworthiness.

(9) Records of vital statistics.--Records or data compilations, in any form, of births, fetal deaths, deaths, or marriages, if the report thereof was made to a public office pursuant to requirements of law.

(10) Absence of public record or entry.--To prove the absence of a record, report, statement, or data compilation, in any form, or the nonoccurrence or nonexistence of a matter of which a record, report, statement, or data compilation, in any form, was regularly made and preserved by a public office or agency, evidence in the form of a certification in accordance with rule 902, or testimony, that diligent search failed to disclose the record, report, statement, or data compilation, or entry.

(11) Records of religious organizations.--Statements of births, marriages, divorces, deaths, legitimacy, ancestry, relationship by blood or marriage, or other similar facts of personal or family history, contained in a regularly kept record of a religious organization.

(12) Marriage, baptismal, and similar certificates.--Statements of fact contained in a certificate that the maker performed a marriage or other ceremony or administered a sacrament, made by a clergyman, public official, or other person authorized by the rules or practices of a religious organization or by law to perform the act certified, and purporting to have been issued at the

time of the act or within a reasonable time thereafter.

(13) Family records.--Statements of fact concerning personal or family history contained in family Bibles, genealogies, charts, engravings on rings, inscriptions on family portraits, engravings on urns, crypts, or tombstones, or the like.

(14) Records of documents affecting an interest in property.--The record of a document purporting to establish or affect an interest in property, as proof of the content of the original recorded document and its execution and delivery by each person by whom it purports to have been executed, if the record is a record of a public office and an applicable statute authorizes the recording of documents of that kind in that office.

(15) Statements in documents affecting an interest in property.--A statement contained in a document purporting to establish or affect an interest in property if the matter stated was relevant to the purpose of the document, unless dealings with the property since the document was made have been inconsistent with the truth of the statement or the purport of the document.

(16) Statements in ancient documents.--Statements in a document in existence twenty years or more the authenticity of which is established.

(17) Market reports, commercial publications.--Market quotations, tabulations, lists, directories, or other published compilations, generally used and relied upon by the public or by persons in particular occupations.

(18) Learned treatises.--To the extent called to the attention of an expert witness upon cross-examination or relied upon by him in direct examination, statements contained in published treatises, periodicals, or pamphlets on a subject of history, medicine, or other science or art, established as a reliable authority by the testimony or admission of the witness or by other expert testimony or by judicial notice. If admitted, the statements may be read into evidence but may not be received as exhibits.

(19) Reputation concerning personal or family history.--Reputation among members of his family by blood, adoption, or marriage, or among his associates, or in the community, concerning a person's birth, adoption, marriage, divorce, death, legitimacy, relationship by blood, adoption, or marriage, ancestry, or other similar fact of his personal or family history.

(20) Reputation concerning boundaries or general history.--Reputation in a community, arising before the controversy, as to boundaries of or customs affecting lands in the community, and reputation as to events of general history important to the community or State or nation in which located.

(21) Reputation as to character.--Reputation of a person's character among his associates or in the community.

(22) Judgment of previous conviction.--Evidence of a final judgment, entered after a trial or upon a plea of guilty (but not upon a plea of nolo contendere), adjudg-

ing a person guilty of a crime punishable by death or imprisonment in excess of one year, to prove any fact essential to sustain the judgment, but not including, when offered by the Government in a criminal prosecution for purposes other than impeachment, judgments against persons other than the accused. The pendency of an appeal may be shown but does not affect admissibility.

(23) Judgment as to personal, family or general history, or boundaries.--Judgments as proof of matters of personal, family or general history, or boundaries, essential to the judgment, if the same would be provable by evidence of reputation.

(24) Other exceptions.--A statement not specifically covered by any of the foregoing exceptions but having equivalent circumstantial guarantees of trustworthiness, if the court determines that (A) the statement is offered as evidence of a material fact; (B) the statement is more probative on the point for which it is offered than any other evidence which the proponent can procure through reasonable efforts; and (C) the general purposes of these rules and the interests of justice will best be served by admission of the statement into evidence. However, a statement may not be admitted under this exception unless the proponent of it makes known to the adverse party sufficiently in advance of the trial or hearing to provide the adverse party with a fair opportunity to prepare to meet it, his intention to offer the statement and the particulars of it, including the name and address of the declarant.

Rule 804. Hearsay Exceptions: Declarant Unavailable

(a) Definition of unavailability.--"Unavailability as a witness" includes situations in which the declarant--

(1) is exempted by ruling of the court on the ground of privilege from testifying concerning the subject matter of his statement; or

(2) persists in refusing to testify concerning the subject matter of his statement despite an order of the court to do so; or

(3) testifies to a lack of memory of the subject matter of his statement; or

(4) is unable to be present or to testify at the hearing because of death or then existing physical or mental illness or infirmity; or

(5) is absent from the hearing and the proponent of his statement has been unable to procure his attendance (or in the case of a hearsay exception under subdivision (b) (2), (3), or (4), his attendance or testimony) by process or other reasonable means.

A declarant is not unavailable as a witness if his exemption, refusal, claim of lack of memory, inability, or absence is due to the procurement or wrongdoing of the proponent of his statement for the purpose of preventing the witness from attending or testifying.

(b) Hearsay exceptions.--The following are not excluded by the hearsay rule if the declarant is unavailable as a witness:

(1) Former testimony.--Testimony given as a witness at another hearing of the same or a different proceeding, or in a deposition taken in compliance with law in the course of the same or another proceeding, if the party against whom the testimony is now offered, or, in a civil action or proceeding, a predecessor in interest, had an opportunity and similar motive to develop the testimony by direct, cross, or redirect examination.

(2) Statement under belief of impending death.--In a prosecution for homicide or in a civil action or proceeding, a statement made by a declarant while believing that his death was imminent, concerning the cause or circumstances of what he believed to be his impending death.

(3) Statement against interest.--A statement which was at the time of its making so far contrary to the declarant's pecuniary or proprietary interest, or so far tended to subject him to civil or criminal liability, or to render invalid a claim by him against another, that a reasonable man in his position would not have made the statement unless he believed it to be true. A statement tending to expose the declarant to criminal liability and offered to exculpate the accused is not admissible unless corroborating circumstances clearly indicate the trustworthiness of the statement.

(4) Statement of personal or family history.--(A) A statement concerning the declarant's own birth, adoption, marriage, divorce, legitimacy, relationship by blood, adoption, or marriage, ancestry, or other similar fact of personal or family history, even though declarant had no means of acquiring personal knowledge of the matter stated; or (B) a statement concerning the foregoing matters, and death also, of another person, if the declarant was related to the other by blood, adoption, or marriage or was so intimately associated with the other's family as to be likely to have accurate information concerning the matter declared.

(5) Other exceptions.--A statement not specifically covered by any of the foregoing exceptions but having equivalent circumstantial guarantees of trustworthiness, if the court determines that (A) the statement is offered as evidence of a material fact; (B) the statement is more probative on the point for which it is offered than any other evidence which the proponent can procure through reasonable efforts; and (C) the general purposes of these rules and the interests of justice will best be served by admission of the statement into evidence. However, a statement may not be admitted under this exception unless the proponent of it makes known to the adverse party sufficiently in advance of the trial or hearing to provide the adverse party with a fair opportunity to prepare to meet it, his intention to offer the statement and the particulars of it, including the name and address of the declarant.

Rule 805. Hearsay Within Hearsay

Hearsay included within hearsay is not excluded under

the hearsay rule if each part of the combined statements conforms with an exception to the hearsay rule provided in these rules.

Rule 806. Attacking and Supporting Credibility of Declarant

When a hearsay statement, or a statement defined in Rule 801(d)(2), (C), (D), or (E), has been admitted in evidence, the credibility of the declarant may be attacked, and if attacked may be supported, by any evidence which would be admissible for those purposes if declarant had testified as a witness. Evidence of a statement or conduct by the declarant at any time, inconsistent with his hearsay statement, is not subject to any requirement that he may have been afforded an opportunity to deny or explain. If the party against whom a hearsay statement has been admitted calls the declarant as a witness, the party is entitled to examine him on the statement as if under cross-examination.

ARTICLE IX. AUTHENTICATION AND IDENTIFICATION

Rule 901. Requirement of Authentication or Identification

(a) General provision.--The requirement of authentication or identification as a condition precedent to admissibility is satisfied by evidence sufficient to support a finding that the matter in question is what its proponent claims.

(b) Illustrations.--By way of illustration only, and not by way of limitation, the following are examples of authentication or identification conforming with the requirements of this rule:

(1) Testimony of witness with knowledge.--Testimony that a matter is what it is claimed to be.

(2) Nonexpert opinion on handwriting.--Nonexpert opinion as to the genuineness of handwriting, based upon familiarity not acquired for purposes of the litigation.

(3) Comparison by trier or expert witness.--Comparison by the trier of fact or by expert witnesses with specimens which have been authenticated.

(4) Distinctive characteristics and the like.--Appearance, contents, substance, internal patterns, or other distinctive characteristics, taken in conjunction with circumstances.

(5) Voice identification.--Identification of a voice, whether heard firsthand or through mechanical or electronic transmission or recording, by opinion based upon hearing the voice at any time under circumstances connecting it with the alleged speaker.

(6) Telephone conversations.--Telephone conversations, by evidence that a call was made to the number assigned at the time by the telephone company to a particular person or business, if (A) in the case of a person, circumstances, including self-identification, show the person answering to be the one called, or (B) in the case of a business, the call was made to a place

of business and the conversation related to business reasonably transacted over the telephone.

(7) Public records or reports.--Evidence that a writing authorized by law to be recorded or filed and in fact recorded or filed in a public office, or a purported public record, report, statement, or data compilation, in any form, is from the public office where items of this nature are kept.

(8) Ancient documents or data compilation.--Evidence that a document or data compilation, in any form, (A) is in such condition as to create no suspicion concerning its authenticity, (B) was in a place where it, if authentic, would likely be, and (C) has been in existence 20 years or more at the time it is offered.

(9) Process or system.--Evidence describing a process or system used to produce a result and showing that the process or system produces an accurate result.

(10) Methods provided by statute or rule.--Any method of authentication or identification provided by Act of Congress or by other rules prescribed by the Supreme Court pursuant to statutory authority.

Rule 902. Self-authentication

Extrinsic evidence of authenticity as a condition precedent to admissibility is not required with respect to the following:

(1) Domestic public documents under seal.--A document bearing a seal purporting to be that of the United States, or of any State, district, Commonwealth, territory, or insular possession thereof, or the Panama Canal Zone, or the Trust Territory of the Pacific Islands, or of a political subdivision, department, officer, or agency thereof, and a signature purporting to be an attestation or execution.

(2) Domestic public documents not under seal.--A document purporting to bear the signature in his official capacity of an officer or employee of any entity included in paragraph (1) hereof, having no seal, if a public officer having a seal and having official duties in the district or political subdivision of the officer or employee certifies under seal that the signer has the official capacity and that the signature is genuine.

(3) Foreign public documents.--A document purporting to be executed or attested in his official capacity by a person authorized by the laws of a foreign country to make the execution or attestation, and accompanied by a final certification as to the genuineness of the signature and official position (A) of the executing or attesting person, or (B) of any foreign official whose certificate of genuineness of signature and official position relates to the execution or attestation or is in a chain of certificates of genuineness of signature and official position relating to the execution or attestation. A final certification may be made by a secretary of embassy or legation, consul general, consul, vice consul, or consular agent of the United States, or a diplomatic or consular official of the foreign country

assigned or accredited to the United States. If reasonable opportunity has been given to all parties to investigate the authenticity and accuracy of official documents, the court may, for good cause shown, order that they be treated as presumptively authentic without final certification or permit them to be evidenced by an attested summary with or without final certification.

(4) Certified copies of public records.--A copy of an official record or report or entry therein, or of a document authorized by law to be recorded or filed and actually recorded or filed in a public office, including data compilations in any form, certified as correct by the custodian or other person authorized to make the certification, by certificate complying with paragraph (1), (2), or (3) of this rule or complying with any Act of Congress or rule prescribed by the Supreme Court pursuant to statutory authority.

(5) Official publications.--Books, pamphlets, or other publications purporting to be issued by public authority.

(6) Newspapers and periodicals.--Printed materials purporting to be newspapers or periodicals.

(7) Trade inscriptions and the like.--Inscriptions, signs, tags, or labels purporting to have been affixed in the course of business and indicating ownership, control, or origin.

(8) Acknowledged documents.--Documents accompanied by a certificate of acknowledgment executed in the manner provided by law by a notary public or other officer authorized by law to take acknowledgments.

(9) Commercial paper and related documents.-- Commercial paper, signatures thereon, and documents relating thereto to the extent provided by general commercial law.

(10) Presumptions under Acts of Congress.--Any signature, document, or other matter declared by Act of Congress to be presumptively or prima facie genuine or authentic.

Rule 903. Subscribing Witness' Testimony Unnecessary

The testimony of a subscribing witness is not necessary to authenticate a writing unless required by the laws of the jurisdiction whose laws govern the validity of the writing.

ARTICLE X.   CONTENTS OF WRITINGS, RECORDINGS, AND PHOTOGRAPHS

Rule 1001. Definitions

For purposes of this article the following definitions are applicable:

(1) Writings and recordings.--"Writings" and "recordings" consist of letters, words, or numbers, or their equivalent, set down by handwriting, typewriting, printing, photostating, photographing, magnetic impulse, mechanical or electronic recording, or other form of

data compilation.

(2) Photographs.--"Photographs" include still photographs, X-ray films, video tapes, and motion pictures.

(3) Original.--An "original" of a writing or recording is the writing or recording itself or any counterpart intended to have the same effect by a person executing or issuing it. An "original" of a photograph includes the negative or any print therefrom. If data are stored in a computer or similar device, any printout or other output readable by sight, shown to reflect the data accurately, is an "original."

(4) Duplicate.--A "duplicate" is a counterpart produced by the same impression as the original, or from the same matrix, or by means of photography, including enlargements and miniatures, or by mechanical or electronic re-recording, or by chemical reproduction, or by other equivalent techniques which accurately reproduces the original.

Rule 1002. Requirement of Original

To prove the content of a writing, recording, or photograph, the original writing, recording, or photograph is required, except as otherwise provided in these rules or by Act of Congress.

Rule 1003. Admissibility of Duplicates

A duplicate is admissible to the same extent as an original unless (1) a genuine question is raised as to the authenticity of the original or (2) in the circumstances it would be unfair to admit the duplicate in lieu of the original.

Rule 1004. Admissibility of Other Evidence of Contents

The original is not required, and other evidence of the contents of a writing, recording, or photograph is admissible if--

(1) Originals lost or destroyed.--All originals are lost or have been destroyed, unless the proponent lost or destroyed them in bad faith; or

(2) Original not obtainable.--No original can be obtained by any available judicial process or procedure; or

(3) Original in possession of opponent.--At a time when an original was under the control of the party against whom offered, he was put on notice, by the pleadings or otherwise, that the contents would be a subject of proof at the hearing, and he does not produce the original at the hearing; or

(4) Collateral matters.--The writing, recording, or photograph is not closely related to a controlling issue.

Rule 1005   Public Records

The contents of an official record, or of a document authorized to be recorded or filed and actually recorded or filed, including data compilations in any form, if otherwise admissible, may be proved by copy, certified as correct in accordance with rule 902 or testified to be correct by a witness who has compared it with the original. If a copy which complies with the foregoing cannot be obtained by the exercise of reasonable diligence, then other evidence of the contents may be given.

Rule 1006. Summaries

The contents of voluminous writings, recordings, or photographs which cannot conveniently be examined in court may be presented in the form of a chart, summary, or calculation. The originals, or duplicates, shall be made available for examination or copying, or both, by other parties at reasonable time and place. The court may order that they be produced in court.

Rule 1007. Testimony or Written Admission of Party

Contents of writings, recordings, or photographs may be proved by the testimony or deposition of the party against whom offered or by his written admission, without accounting for the nonproduction of the original.

Rule 1008. Functions of Court and Jury

When the admissibility of other evidence of contents of writings, recordings, or photographs under these rules depends upon the fulfillment of a condition of fact, the question whether the condition has been fulfilled is ordinarily for the court to determine in accordance with the provisions of rule 104. However, when an issue is raised (a) whether the asserted writing ever existed, or (b) whether another writing, recording, or photograph produced at the trial is the original, or (c) whether other evidence of contents correctly reflects the contents, the issue is for the trier of fact to determine as in the case of other issues of fact.

ARTICLE XI. MISCELLANEOUS RULES

Rule 1101. Applicability of Rules

(a) Courts and magistrates.--These rules apply to the United States district courts, the District Court of Guam, the District Court of the Virgin Islands, the District Court for the District of the Canal Zone, the United States courts of appeals, the Court of Claims, and to United States magistrates, in the actions, cases, and proceedings and to the extent hereinafter set forth. The terms "judge" and "court" in these rules include United States magistrates, referees in bankruptcy, and commissioners of the Court of Claims.

(b) Proceedings generally.--These rules apply generally to civil actions and proceedings, including admiralty and maritime cases, to criminal cases and proceedings, to contempt proceedings except those in which the court may act summarily, and to proceedings and cases under the Bankruptcy Act.

(c) Rule of privilege.--The rule with respect to privileges applies at all stages of all actions, cases, and proceedings.

(d) Rules inapplicable.--The rules (other than with respect to privileges) do not apply in the following situations:

  (1) Preliminary questions of fact.--The determination of questions of fact preliminary to admissibility of evidence when the issue is to be determined by the court under rule 104.
  (2) Grand jury.--Proceedings before grand juries.
  (3) Miscellaneous proceedings.--Proceedings for extradition or rendition; preliminary examinations in criminal cases; sentencing, or granting or revoking probation; issuance of warrants for arrest, criminal summonses, and search warrants; and proceedings with respect to release on bail or otherwise.

(e) Rules applicable in part.--In the following proceedings these rules apply to the extent that matters of evidence are not provided for in the statutes which govern procedure therein or in other rules prescribed by the Supreme Court pursuant to statutory authority: the trial of minor and petty offenses by United States magistrates; review of agency actions when the facts are subject to trial de novo under section 706(2)(F) of title 5, United States Code; review of orders of the Secretary of Agriculture under section 2 of the Act entitled "An Act to authorize association of producers of agricultural products" approved February 18, 1922 (7 U.S.C. 292), and under sections 6 and 7(c) of the Perishable Agricultural Commodities Act, 1930 (7 U.S.C. 499f, 499g(c)); naturalization and revocation of naturalization under sections 310-318 of the Immigration and Nationality Act (8 U.S.C. 1421-1429); prize proceedings in admiralty under sections 7651-7681 of title 10, United States Code; review of orders of the Secretary of the Interior under section 2 of the Act entitled "An Act authorizing associations of producers of aquatic products" approved June 25, 1934 (15 U.S.C. 522); review of orders of petroleum control boards under section 5 of the Act entitled "An Act to regulate interstate and foreign commerce in petroleum and its products by prohibiting the shipment in such commerce of petroleum and its products produced in violation of State law, and for other purposes," approved February 22, 1935 (15 U.S.C. 715d); actions for fines, penalties, or forfeitures under part V of title IV of the Tariff Act of 1930 (19 U.S.C. 1581-1624), or under the Anti-Smuggling Act (19 U.S.C. 1701-1711); criminal libel for condemnation, exclusion of imports, or other proceedings under the Federal Food, Drug, and Cosmetic Act (21 U.S.C. 301-392); disputes between seamen under sections 4079, 4080, and 4081 of the Revised Statutes (22 U.S.C. 256-258); habeas corpus under sections 2241-2254 of title 28, United States Code; motions to vacate, set aside or correct sentence under section 2255 of title 28, United States Code; actions for penalties for refusal to transport destitute seamen under section 4578 of the Revised Statutes (46 U.S.C. 679);

actions against the United States under the Act entitled "An Act authorizing suits against the United States in admiralty for damage caused by and salvage service rendered to public vessels belonging to the United States, and for other purposes," approved March 3, 1925 (46 U.S.C. 781-790), as implemented by section 7730 of title 10, United States Code.

Rule 1102. Amendments

Amendments to the Federal Rules of Evidence may be made as provided in section 2076 of title 28 of the United States Code.

Rule 1103. Title

These rules may be known and cited as the Federal Rules of Evidence.

Sec. 2. (a) Title 28 of the United States Code is amended--

(1) by inserting immediately after section 2075 the following new section:

"§2076. Rules of evidence

"The Supreme Court of the United States shall have the power to prescribe amendments to the Federal Rules of Evidence. Such amendments shall not take effect until they have been reported to Congress by the Chief Justice at or after the beginning of a regular session of Congress but not later than the first day of May, and until the expiration of one hundred and eighty days after they have been so reported; but if either House of Congress within that time shall by resolution disapprove any amendment so reported it shall not take effect. The effective date of any amendment so reported may be deferred by either House of Congress to a later date or until approved by Act of Congress. Any rule whether proposed or in force may be amended by Act of Congress. Any provision of law in force at the expiration of such time and in conflict with any such amendment not disapproved shall be of no further force or effect after such amendment has taken effect. Any such amendment creating, abolishing, or modifying a privilege shall have no force or effect unless it shall be approved by act of Congress"; and

(2) by adding at the end of the table of sections of chapter 131 the following new item:

"2076. Rules of evidence."

(b) Section 1732 of title 28 of the United States Code is amended by striking out subsection (a), and by striking out "(b)."

(c) Section 1733 of title 28 of the United States Code is amended by adding at the end thereof the following new subsection:

"(c) This section does not apply to cases, actions, and proceedings to which the Federal Rules of Evidence apply."

INDEX

References are to sections

ABORTION, 8.20, 11.6

ACCIDENT REPORTS
Auto, 8.9, 11.9
Railroad, 9.2, 11.9

ADMISSIONS
(See Prior Activities; Self-Incrimination)

ADULTERY, 9.20b

AFFIRMATIVE DEFENSES, 2.6b, 5.8 to 5.11
Alibi, 5.10
Duress, 5.9
Excuse, 5.8
Insanity, 5.8, 5.9, 5.11
Intoxication, 5.9
Mitigation, 5.8
Self-defense, 5.9

AGE, 10.2

ALCOHOL
(See Intoxication; Liquor)

ALCOMETER, 13.12b

ALIBI
Defense, as, 5.10

ALIEN
Deportation hearing, 5.8
Importing for immoral purposes, 4.10

ANTIRACKETEERING ACT, 6.3, 8.8

ARRAIGNMENT
Delay in, 14.5

ARRESTS
Record of, 8.18

ASSAULT, 2.4, 4.10, 13.13

ATTORNEY
(See Counsel)

ATTORNEY/CLIENT
(See Privileged Communications)

AUTHENTICATION, 2.7
Documents, 12.2, 13.16

AUTOPSY REPORTS, 12.6

BALLISTICS, 13.17, 15.4
   Breech-face markings, 13.17
   Defined, 10.9g
   Experiments outside court, 13.10
   Firing-pin mark, 13.17
   Gunpowder burns, 13.17
   Relevancy, 3.10

BALLISTICS TESTS
   Competency and admissibility, 4.3

BEST EVIDENCE RULE, 4.1, 12.8, 12.9

BEYOND A REASONABLE DOUBT
   (See Burden of Proof)

BIAS
   Witness, 8.17

BIGAMY, 4.10, 9.20b

BLACK MUSLIMS
   Judicial notice, 7.3

BLOOD
   Bloodstains, 13.3d, 15.4
   Examine accused for traces, 13.11

BLOODHOUNDS
   Tracking with, 4.5

BLOODSTAINS, 13.3d, 15.4

BLOOD TESTS
   Assault, 13.13
   Competency and admissibility, 4.3
   Implied consent, 13.12d
   Intoxication, 7.7, 13.12a, 13.12d
   Lab technician may test, 10.9c
   Non-support, 13.13
   Paternity, 7.7, 10.5, 13.13
   Rape, 13.13
   Relevancy, 3.10
   Search and seizure, 13.12a
   Self-incrimination, 9.7, 13.12a, 14.6

BOMB, 13.3a

BRAKES
   (See Motor Vehicles)

BREATHALIZER, 13.12b

BREATH TESTS
   (See Intoxication)

BREECH-FACE MARKINGS, 13.17

BRIBERY, 6.9, 8.20

BULLETS
  (See Ballistics)

BURDEN OF PROOF, 5.1 to 5.13
  (See also Affirmative Defenses)
  Beyond a reasonable doubt, 5.1, 5.5, 5.6, 5.7, 15.7
  Civil cases compared, 2.4
  Clear and convincing evidence, 5.4
  Defined, 5.2
  Every element of crime, 5.7
  On accused, when, 5.8
  Preponderance of the evidence, 5.3

BURGLARY, 6.1, 13.3b, 13.3e

BUSINESS RECORDS, 11.9, 12.9

CAPACITY TO COMMIT CRIME
  (See also Insanity)
  Intoxication, 3.8b
  Rape, 3.8b

CARBON COPIES
  Use as evidence, 12.9

CENSUS DATA, 9.2

CHALLENGING EVIDENCE, 2.7, 8.1

CHARACTER, 3.9, 6.5, 6.6, 8.13
  Defined, 6.5
  Witnesses, 8.13, 8.18

CHECK
  Passing fraudulent, 6.11
  Possession of stolen, 12.8

CHILD WITNESS
  Competency, 4.6, 4.9
  Leading questions, 8.7d

CIRCUMSTANCES PRECEDING THE CRIME, 3.6

CIRCUMSTANTIAL EVIDENCE, 6.1 to 6.15
  (See also Character; Identification of Persons or Things; Judicial Notice; see also other crime headings)
  Bloodhounds, tracking with, 4.5
  Case based solely on, 5.6
  Defined, 2.1d, 6.2
  Direct evidence distinguished, 6.2
  Flight by accused, 6.2
  Habit or custom, 6.8
  Inferences, 6.3
  Intent, motive, or knowledge, 6.11
  Reputation of victim of crime, 6.7
  Similar or related acts or circumstances, 6.9
  Sufficiency of, 6.4
  Suspicion, 6.3
  Telephone calls, 4.4
  Weight of, 5.6, 6.1, 6.4

CIVIL AVIATION BOARD
    Accident reports, 9.2

CIVIL EVIDENCE
    Distinguished, 2.4

CLEAR AND CONVINCING EVIDENCE, 5.4

CLERGYMEN
    (See Priest-Penitent Privilege)

CLOTHING
    Identification of accused, 3.5, 13.3b, 13.3c, 13.3e
    Modeled by accused, 9.7, 13.11
    Scientific analysis, 10.9g
    Self-incrimination, 9.7, 13.3c, 13.11

COERCION
    Confession, 2.3c
    Relevancy, 3.8

COMMON KNOWLEDGE, 7.4

COMPETENCY OF EVIDENCE
    (See also Witnesses)
    "Bloodhound" evidence, 4.4
    Defined, 4.1, 4.2
    Evidence and witness, generally, 4.13
    Negative evidence, 4.6
    Religious belief, 4.12
    Telephone conversations, 4.5
    Tests, 4.3
    Witness convicted of crime, 4.11
    Witness, of, 4.7
        Grounds for challenging, 4.8 *et seq.*

CONCEALMENT OF ACCUSED, 3.7

CONDITION OF EXHIBIT, 13.3e

CONFESSIONS
    (See Self-Incrimination)

CONSPIRACY, 3.3, 3.9

CONSTITUTIONAL RULES, 4.1
    (See also Blood Tests; Search and Seizure; Self-incrimination)
    Address of witness, 8.12
    Counsel, right to, 2.3d, 14.5, 14.7
    Cross-examination, 8.10, 8.12
    Insanity as an affirmative defense, 5.8
    Name of witness, 8.12
    Photographs, identification of accused by, 3.4
    Presumptions—
        Gun, possession of, 7.25
        Guns, interstate shipment, 7.25
        Narcotics imported, 7.25
        Statutory, 7.24, 7.25
        Still, accused at, 7.25

CONSTITUTIONAL RULES—*Continued*
    Statutory presumptions, 7.29
    Stipulations, 7.26
    View of the scene, 13.4
    Violation of, in obtaining evidence, 14.1

CONVERSION
    Criminal, 6.8

CONVICTION OF CRIME
    (See Cross Examination at Other crimes)

COORDINATING EFFORTS FOR TRIAL, 15.6

CORPUS DELICTI, 5.7

CORROBORATING EVIDENCE
    Defined, 2.1k

COUNSEL
    Right to, exclusion of evidence, 14.7

COUNTERFEITING, 8.19

COURT
    Accused appearing for identification, 13.1, 13.2, 13.11

COURT RECORDS, 7.16

CRIME LABORATORY
    Expert testimony, 10.9a

CRIMES
    Previous *(See Other Crimes)*

CRIMINAL RECORD
    (See Cross Examination at Other crimes)

CROSS-EXAMINATION
    Address of witness, 8.12
    Bias of witness, 8.17
    By defense, 2.6a, 2.6c
    By prosecution, 2.6b
    Character witnesses, 8.13, 8.18
    Constitutional requirements, 8.10, 8.12
    Conviction of crime, 8.18
    Employment, 8.12
    Expert witness, 10.8, 13.14
    Identification of accused by photograph, 3.4
    Impeachment of witness, 8.15
    Indictments, 8.18
    Juvenile record, 8.18
    Leading questions, 8.7e
    Name of witness, 8.12
    Other crimes, 8.18
    Photographs, 3.4
    Polygraph operator, 13.14
    Practical considerations, 15.5
    Prior inconsistent statements, 8.16, 8.19, 8.20
    Recross examination, 8.14

CROSS-EXAMINATION—*Continued*
    Redirect examination, 8.14
    Rehabilitation of witness after, 8.20
    Scope and extent, 8.11, 8.12
    Scope, rule, 8.11
    Self-incrimination, 9.8
    Summaries of records, 12.10

CUMULATIVE EVIDENCE
    Defined, 2.1j

CUSTODY OF EXHIBIT
    Police, by, 13.3e

DEATH CERTIFICATE, 12.6

DECLARATIONS AGAINST INTEREST, 11.5

DEEDS, 12.2

DEFENSES
    (*See also Affirmative Defenses*)
    Alibi, 5.10

DEFINITIONS
    Ballistics, 10.9g
    Burden of proof, 5.2
    Character, 6.5
    Circumstantial evidence, 2.1d, 6.2
    Competency, 4.1, 4.2
    Corpus delicti, 5.7
    Corroborating evidence, 2.1k
    Cumulative evidence, 2.1j
    Direct evidence, 2.1c, 6.2
    Document, 12.1
    Documentary evidence, 2.1f
    Evidence, 2.1a, 2.1e
    Expert witness, 10.2, 10.6
    Hearsay evidence, 2.1m
    Impeachment, 8.15
    Inference, 7.17
    Judicial notice, 7.1, 7.2
    Legal evidence, 2.1b
    Materiality, 2.8b, 3.2b
    Opinion testimony, 10.1a
    Presumptions and inferences distinguished, 7.19
    Prima facie evidence, 2.1h
    Privileged communication, 9.1, 9.2
    Proof, 2.1i
    Real evidence, 2.1g, 13.2
    Refreshing memory, 8.8, 8.9
    Relevant evidence, 2.1l
    Testimony, 2.1e

DEGREE OF PROOF, 2.4

DIRECT EVIDENCE
    (*See also Identification of Persons or Things; Witnesses*)
    Defined, 2.1c, 6.2

DIRECT EXAMINATION, 8.1
(See Witnesses)

DISORDERLY CONDUCT, 6.9

DOCUMENTS, 12.1 to 12.2
(See also Treatise; Judicial Notice; Public Records)
Ancient, 11.12, 12.3, 12.4
Authentication, 12.2, 13.16
Autopsy report, 12.6
Best evidence rule, 4.1, 12.8, 12.9
Death certificate, 12.6
Deeds, 12.2
Defined, 12.1
Definition of documentary evidence, 2.1f
Duplicate originals, 12.8
Newspapers, 12.4
Refreshing memory, 8.8
Summaries of records, 10.9d, 12.10
Witnesses, need for, 2.5

DOGS
Admissibility of "bloodhound evidence," 4.4

DRUNKENNESS
(See Intoxication)

DRUNKOMETER, 13.12b

DUPLICATE ORIGINAL DOCUMENTS, 12.8

DURESS
Burden of proof as excuse for the crime, 5.9
Obtaining evidence by, 2.3c, 14.5, 14.6

DYER ACT, 6.3, 6.9, 6.11

DYING DECLARATIONS, 2.4, 11.6

EAVESDROPPING, 13.8, 14.4

ELECTRONIC SURVEILLANCE, 13.8

EMBEZZLEMENT, 6.11, 8.13, 11.5

EMPLOYMENT
Place of, 8.12

EQUAL EMPLOYMENT OPPORTUNITY PROCEEDING, 9.2

EVALUATING EVIDENCE, 15.3

EVIDENCE
Admissibility under Rules, 2.7
Competency *(See Competency of Evidence)*
Defined, 2.1
Degree of proof, 2.4
Direct and circumstantial distinguished, 6.2
    Suspicion, 6.3
Flight doctrine, 3.7
Negative, 4.6

EVIDENCE—*Continued*
    Relevancy and materiality, rules for, 3.11
    Substitutions for *(See Judicial Notice; Presumptions, Inferences and Stipulations)*
    Weight —
        Incriminating circumstances, 3.7

EVIDENCE IN CHIEF, 2.6

EXAMINATION OF WITNESSES
    (See Expert Witnesses; Leading Questions; Testimony; Witnesses)

EXAMINE BODY OF ACCUSED
    (See Search and Seizure)

EXCEPTIONS TO RULINGS OF JUDGE, 2.7

EXCLUDING EVIDENCE
    Avoid undue prejudice, 2.3b
    Constitutional, 2.3d
    Prohibit unreliable items, 2.3c
    Protect interests and relationships, 2.3a

EXCLUSIONARY RULE, 14.2

EXPERIMENTAL AND SCIENTIFIC EVIDENCE, 13.10, 15.4
    (See also Ballistics; Blood Tests; Intoxication; Motor Vehicles)
    Clothing, 10.9g
    Hair, 10.5, 10.9g
    Judicial notice, 7.7
    Laboratory results, 10.9g
    Photographs, 13.5
    Relevancy, 3.10
    See, ability to, 13.10
    Spectrogram voice identification, 13.19
    Speed detection devices, 13.18

EXPERT WITNESSES, 10.4
    (See also Blood Tests)
    Accountant, 10.9d
    Airplane crashes, 10.9b
    Auto accidents, 10.9a
    Ballistics analyst, 13.17
    Breath tests for intoxication, 13.12b
    Cross-examination, 10.8, 13.14
    Defined, 10.1, 10.6
    Examination, 10.7
    Fingerprints, 10.9f, 13.16
    Handwriting, 10.9e, 12.7
    Insanity, 4.3, 7.19
    Laboratory technicians, 10.9c, 10.9g
    Medical testimony, 10.9c
    Photographs, use of, 10.9a
    Polygraph operator, 7.26, 13.14
    Possibility, 10.5
    Probability, 10.5
    Qualifications of, 11.5, 11.7, 11.11

FALSE NAME, 3.7

FAMILY HISTORY, 11.11

FEDERAL RULES
(See Rules)

FEES
Attorney, 9.11

FIFTH AMENDMENT
Proof of fact, 7.29

FINGERPRINT CARD, 13.16
Signing, 9.7

FINGERPRINTS, 13.16, 15.4
Expert witness needed for identity, 11.10j, 13.16
Footprints, 13.13, 13.16, 15.4
Judicial notice, 13.16
Palmprints, 13.13, 13.16
Photographs, 11.10j, 13.16
Self-incrimination, 9.7, 13.1, 13.11, 13.16, 14.6

FIREARMS
(See Guns)

FIRING-PIN MARK, 13.17

FIRST AMENDMENT
Newspaper, privileged communications, 9.23

FLIGHT
By accused, 3.3, 3.7, 6.2

FOOTPRINTS, 13.13, 13.16, 15.4

FORCE OR DURESS
To get evidence, 2.3c, 14.5, 14.6

FORGERY, 6.13
(See Handwriting)

FORMER TESTIMONY, 11.4

FORM OF QUESTIONS, 2.8a
Argumentative, 2.8a
Confusing or misleading, 2.8a
Leading, 2.8a

FOURTEENTH AMENDMENT
Proof of facts, 7.29

FRAUD
Marriage ceremony performed to preclude spousal testimony, 4.10

FUGITIVE FROM JUSTICE
Presumption of death, 7.23

GAMBLING, 11.3

GENEALOGY, 11.11

GEOGRAPHIC FACTS, 7.6

GESTURES
(See Self-Incrimination)

GLASS, 10.9g

GLOVES, 13.3b

GOVERNMENT SECRETS, 9.24

GRAND JURY
Rules procedure re pretrial flow of evidence, 2.42
Witnesses, 9.5

GUNPOWDER BURNS, 13.17
(See Ballistics)

GUNS
(See also Ballistics; Weapons)
Possession of, 7.25
Presumption of interstate shipment, 7.25
Relevancy, 3.3

HANDWRITING, 13.16
Expert opinion, 11.10e
Lay opinion, 10.3e
Photos of, 13.5e
Self-incrimination, 9.7, 11.10e, 13.1, 13.11, 14.6

HEARSAY, 2.3c, 11.1 to 11.12
(See also Judicial Notice; Public Records)
Accident reports, 11.9
Ancient documents, 11.12, 12.3, 12.4
Business records—
    Federal rule, 11.9
Character witnesses, 6.6, 8.13, 8.18
Declarations against interest, 11.5
Defined, 11.2
Documents generally, 8.9, 12.1
Dying declarations, 2.4, 11.6
Family history, 11.11
Former testimony, 11.4
Hospital records, 11.9
Learned treatises, 11.12
Non-testimonial utterances, 11.11a
Physical or mental condition, 11.7
Prior inconsistent statements, 8.16, 8.19, 8.20
Radar speed meter, 13.18
Spontaneous utterances, 11.8
State of mind, 11.7, 11.10
Surveys, public opinion, 11.10
Verbal acts, 11.3

HEARSAY RULE, 11.1
Exceptions to, 11.12

HISTORICAL FACTS, 7.5

HISTORY
Evidence of, 1.1 to 1.6
Jury, of, 1.2, 1.3

HOMICIDE
(See also Guns; Weapons)
Ballistics, 13.17
Bloodstains, 13.3d
Character evidence, 6.6
Counsel, advice of, 9.12
Death certificate, 12.6
Dying declarations, 11.6
Examination of victim, 13.11
Habit or custom, 6.8
Intoxication as a defense, 3.8b
Motor vehicle, use of, 3.3
Other crimes, 6.10, 6.11
Other crimes committed at same time, 3.3
Photographs, 13.5b, 13.5d
Prior inconsistent statements, 8.19
Reputation of victim, 6.7
Self-defense, 6.7
Sound recordings, 13.8
Spontaneous utterances, 11.8
Truth serum, 13.15

HOSPITAL RECORDS, 11.9

HOSTILE WITNESSES, 8.7b

HOUSEBREAKING, 11.8

HUSBAND AND WIFE
Testimony by or for each other, 4.10

HYPOTHETICAL QUESTIONS, 10.7

IDENTIFICATION OF PERSONS OR THINGS
Generally, 3.4, 3.5

IMMUNITY FROM PROSECUTION, 9.9

IMPEACHMENT
Witness of —
Rule, 8.16 *et seq.*

IMPLIED CONSENT, 13.12d

IN-CUSTODY INTERROGATION
(See Self-Incrimination)

INDICTMENTS
Record of, 8.18

INFERENCE, 6.3, 6.4
Defined, 7.17

INFORMANT
Confidential, 9.23

INNOCENCE
Presumption of, 7.20

INSANITY
Admissibility of testimony, 4.8
Alcoholism, 7.19
Burden of proof, 5.8, 5.9, 5.11
Irresistible impulse, 3.8a
Negative evidence, 4.3
Opinion of expert, 4.3, 7.19
Opinion of laymen, 4.3, 7.19, 10.2, 10.3a, 10.3c
Presumption of sanity, 5.11, 7.19
Relevancy, 3.8
Standards for, 3.8a
Trial procedure, 2.6c, 2.6e
Witness, of, 4.8

INSTRUMENTS USED IN THE CRIME
(See Weapons)

INTENT
Intoxication affecting, 3.8b
Other crimes, 6.11
Proof of, 6.3
State of mind, 11.7, 11.10

INTERPRETERS, 8.6

INTIMIDATING A WITNESS, 11.3

INTOXICATION
Alcometer, 13.12b
Blood tests, 7.7, 13.12a, 13.12d
Breathalizer, 13.12b
Breath analysis checklist, 8.9
Breath tests, 13.12b
Burden of proof, 5.9
Chemical tests, 13.10
Defense, as a, 3.8b
Drunkometer, 13.12b
Implied consent to test, 13.12d
Opinion as to, 10.3b
Rape, physical incapability, 3.8b
Relevancy, 3.8
Smell of alcohol, 10.3d
Urine tests, 13.12c

IRRESISTIBLE IMPULSE, 3.8a
Johnson v. Louisiana, 2.4

JUDGE
Authority under Rules, 2.5
Charge to jury, 2.5
Control of testimony, 8.3, 8.12
Determination of witness's competency, 4.7, 4.8, 4.9
Discretion of, 3.3, 3.10, 8.3, 8.7, 8.11, 8.13, 8.15, 8.18
Duties generally, 2.5, 6.10, 8.3, 8.8

JUDICIAL NOTICE, 7.3
    Black Muslims, 7.3
    Common knowledge, 7.4
    Court records, 7.16
    Defined, 7.1, 7.2
    Fingerprinting, 13.16
    Geographical facts, 7.6
    Historical facts, 7.5
    Jurisdiction of courts, 7.15
    Laws and regulations, 7.9 to 7.15
    Rule discussion, 7.3
    Scientific facts, 7.7
    Speed detection devices, 13.18
    Words and phrases, 7.8

JURISDICTION OF COURTS, 7.15

JURY
    Duties, 2.5
    History, 1.2, 1.3
        Inclination to reject weak evidence, 2.4
    Reasonable doubt, instruction (federal requirement), 6.3
    State statute provides 9 of 12 may find defendant guilty, 2.4

JUVENILE COURT, 8.18

KIDNAPPING, 6.11

KNOWLEDGE
    Other crimes to show, 6.11

LARCENY, 3.9, 11.2

LEADING QUESTIONS, 8.7
    Children, 8.7d
    Cross-examination, 8.7e
    Erroneous statements, 8.7c
    Hostile witnesses, 8.7b
    Introductory matters, 8.7a
    Language, difficulty with, 8.7d
    Memoranda to refresh memory, 8.7f, 8.8

LEGAL EVIDENCE
    Defined, 2.1b

LICENSE, 12.8

LIE DETECTOR, 13.14

LINEUP, 13.11, 14.6, 14.7

LIQUOR
    Identification of, 10.3d
    License, 12.8
    Possession, 12.8
    Sales observed, 13.9
    Similar acts in violation of liquor laws, 6.9
    Stills, 7.25

MAIL
Receipt, presumption of, 7.25

MAIL FRAUD, 7.19, 12.10

MANN ACT
Airplane tickets, 11.9
Other crimes, 6.11
Spouse's testimony, 4.10, 9.20b

MAPS, 13.9

MARKING ITEMS FOR IDENTIFICATION, 13.3e

MARKS
Examining accused for, 13.11

MATERIALITY
Defined, 2.8b, 3.2b
Identity of persons, 3.4
Relevancy distinguished, 3.2c

MENTAL INCOMPETENCE
Witness, preclusion of testimony on ground of, Rule, 8.2

MITIGATION, 5.8

MODUS OPERANDI, 3.9, 6.12, 13.3a

MOTIVE, 3.9, 6.11

MOTOR VEHICLES
(See also Accident Reports; Intoxication)
Brake experiments, 13.10
Certificate of title, 12.5
Dyer Act, 6.3, 6.9, 6.11
Expert opinions, 10.9a
Headlight experiments, 13.10
Impact, point of, 10.9a
Negligence, inference of, 6.3
Owner presumed to be the operator, 7.25
Photographs, use of, 10.9a, 13.5c
Speed, 3.10, 10.3f, 10.9a
Speed detection devices, 7.7, 13.18
Speed experiments, 13.10
Spontaneous utterances, 11.8
Theft of, 6.9, 6.10, 11.9

NAME OF WITNESS, 8.12

NARCOTICS
Hearsay, 11.5
Importation, presumption of, 7.25
Name of witness or informer, 8.12, 9.23
Other crimes, 6.11
Photographs, 13.5c
Police custody of the exhibit, 13.3e
Prior activities, relevancy, 3.6
Search and seizure, 14.3, 14.6

NARCOTICS—*Continued*
    Telephone calls, 4.4
    Use by witness, 4.7

NEGATIVE EVIDENCE, 4.3, 6.6, 6.8

NEGLECT OF FAMILY, 4.10

NEWSPAPER
    Privileged communications, 9.23

NEWS PUBLICITY, 3.4

NON-SUPPORT, 13.13

OATH OF WITNESSES, 8.5

OBJECTIONS, 2.7, 2.8, 3.1

OFFICIAL ACTS
    (See Public Records)

ONE ISSUE
    Admissibility on, 3.3

OPINION EVIDENCE
    (See also Expert Witnesses)
    Age of subject, 10.2
    Appearance, 10.3a
    Character of accused, 6.6
    Crime laboratory expert, 10.92
    Distinguished, 10.1a
    Expert testimony, 10.12
    Habit or custom, 6.8
    Handwriting, 10.3e, 12.7
    Identification of accused, 10.3d
    Insanity, 4.3, 7.19, 10.2, 10.3a, 10.3c
    Intoxication, 10.3b
    Nonexpert, federal rule, 10.2
    Speed, 10.3f

ORDER OF PRESENTENCING EVIDENCE, 2.6

PALMPRINTS, 13.16

PARKING AUTOS, 7.25

PAST RECOLLECTION RECORDED, 8.8, 8.9

PATERNITY
    Blood tests, 7.7, 10.5, 13.13
    Physical comparison, 13.2

PERJURY
    (See Witnesses)

PHOTOGRAPHS, 13.5
    Aerial photos, 13.5e
    Auto accident, 10.9a, 13.5c
    Biasing eyewitness with, 3.4
    Business records, 12.9

PHOTOGRAPHS—*Continued*
    Cross-examination, 3.4
    Constitutional rules, 3.4
    Colored prints, 13.5d
    Documents, of, 12.9
    Enlargements, 13.5e
    Expert witness, use by, 10.9a
    Fingerprints, 10.9f, 13.16
    Foundation, 13.5, 13.6
    Gruesome, 13.5b
    Handwriting, 13.5c
    Identifying persons, 3.4
    Inflammatory, 13.5b, 13.5d
    Laboratory, 13.5
    Movies, 13.6
    Posed, 3.4, 13.5a
    Prejudicial, 2.3b
    Self-incrimination, 13.1, 13.11, 14.6
    Time of taking, 13.5c
    Verification, 13.5, 13.6
    X-rays, 13.7

PHYSICAL EXAMINATION
    Of accused, generally, 13.11

PHYSICIAN-PATIENT PRIVILEGE, 9.2, 9.14 to 9.18

POISON, 10.9c

POLICEMAN
    Arrest by, requirements for evidence under rules of procedure, 2.4a

POLICE REPORTS
    (See Accident Reports)

POLYGRAPH, 13.14
    Agreement of parties to admission, 7.26
    Judicial notice, 7.7
    Self-incrimination, 13.14, 14.6
    Stipulations re admissibility of results, 7.32

PORNOGRAPHY, 3.6
    Stipulations vs. admissibility of results, 7.32

POSSESSING STOLEN PROPERTY, 6.3

POWDER BURNS, 13.17

PREJUDICIAL ITEMS
    Excluded generally, 3.3, 3.10, 4.2

PREPARATION FOR TRIAL, 15.6

PREPONDERANCE OF THE EVIDENCE, 5.3

PRESUMED DECEDENTS LAW, 7.23

PRESUMPTIONS, INFERENCES AND STIPULATIONS
    Accused, flight or concealment by, 7.27

PRESUMPTIONS, INFERENCES AND STIPULATIONS—*Continued*
    Classifications—
        Rebuttable; conclusive, 7.33
    Concealment, 7.27
    Death, 7.21
    Defined, 7.19
    Flight, 7.27
    Innocence, 7.20
    Mail, receipt presumed, 7.25
    Official acts, 7.24
    Presumed decedents law, 1.23
    Sanity, 7.21
    Statutory, 7.28
        Constitutionality, 7.29
    Stolen property, possession, 7.26
    Suicide, 7.22

PRETRIAL
    Federal rules, 2.4a

PRIEST-PENITENT PRIVILEGE, 2.3a, 9.2, 9.22

PRIMA FACIE CASE, 5.2

PRIMA FACIE EVIDENCE
    Death certificates, 12.6
    Defined, 2.1h
    Guilt, of, 7.24, 7.25

PRIOR ACTIVITIES, 3.6
    (See Relevancy)

PRIVILEGED COMMUNICATIONS
    Attorney/client, 9.8
        Exceptions, 9.9, 9.10
        Waiver, 9.11
    Clergymen, 9.20
    Confidential informant, 9.21
    Federal rules, 9.1
    Government secrets, 9.22
    Husband/wife, 9.17
        Duration, 9.19
        Exceptions, 9.18
        Third party, 9.18
    Physician/patient, 9.12, 9.14, 9.16
        Exception, 9.13, 9.14
        Waiver, 9.15

PROBABILITY, 10.5

PROCEDURAL RULES
    (See Rules of Evidence)

PROOF
    Defined, 2.1i

PROSECUTION
    Rebuttal by, 2.6

PUBLIC OFFICIAL
Presumption of regularity supports official acts, 7.24

PUBLIC RECORDS, 12.2, 12.5
Accident reports, 11.9
Authentication, 12.2, 13.16
Autopsy reports, 12.6
Civil Aviation Board reports, 9.2
Death certificate, 12.6
Fingerprint cards, 13.16
Prima facie evidence, 2.1h, 12.5
Regularity of official acts presumed, 7.22

QUESTIONING BY POLICE
(See Self-Incrimination)

QUESTIONS
Argumentative, 2.8a
Form, 2.8a
Leading, 2.8a
Substance, 2.8b

RADAR SPEED METER, 7.7, 13.18

RAILROAD ACCIDENT REPORTS, 9.2, 11.9

RAPE
Blood tests, 13.13
Body scrapings, 13.11
Character evidence, 6.6
Child witnesses, 4.9
Exhibit victim, 13.2
Hair comparisons, 10.5
Intoxication as a defense, 3.8b
Other offenses, 3.9
Reputation of victim, 6.7
Self-incrimination, 14.5
Spontaneous utterance, 11.8

REAL EVIDENCE, 13.1 to 13.20
(See also Ballistics; Blood Tests; Clothing; Experimental and Scientific Evidence; Fingerprints; Motor Vehicles; Photographs; Search and Seizure; Self-Incrimination; Weapons)
Authentication, 2.7, 12.2
Ballistics, 13.17
Blackboard, 13.9
Blood grouping tests, 13.13
Bloodstains, 13.3d, 15.4
Bomb, 13.3a
Chemical explosives, 13.19a
    Admissibility, 13.20
Condition of item, 13.3e
Custody of item by police, 13.3e
Defined, 2.1g, 13.2
Diagrams, maps, and models, 13.9
Dust, 13.3e, 15.4
Electronic surveillance, 13.8
Fingerprint, 13.16

REAL EVIDENCE—*Continued*
    Glass, 10.9g
    Identity of item, 13.3e
    Instruments used in the crime, 13.3b
    Intoxication tests, 13.12
    Items connected with the crime, 13.3
    Lie detector, 13.14
    Maps, 13.9
    Models, 13.9
    Motion pictures, 13.6
    Paint chips, 13.3e, 15.4
    Physical examination, 13.11
    Polygraph, 13.14
    Presentation procedure, 2.7
    RADAR, speed detection, 13.18
    Sound recordings, 13.8
    Spectrogram voice identification, 13.19
    Speed detection devices, 13.18
    Tests—
        Chemical (neutron activation), 13.19a
        Examination of the person, 13.11b
            Alcohol, 13.12
            Blood grouping, 13.13
        Polygraph, 13.14
    Truth serum, 13.15
    View of the scene, 13.4
    Voice identification, 13.19
    Witnesses, need for, 2.5
    X-rays, 13.7

REASONABLE DOUBT
    (*See also Burden of Proof*)
    Federal requirement, 6.3

REBUTTAL, 2.6c

RECEIVING STOLEN PROPERTY, 6.3

RECORDS
    (*See also Accident Reports; Public Records*)
    Ancient, 11.12, 12.3, 12.4
    Business, 11.9, 12.9
    Carbon copies as evidence, 12.9
    Computer sheets, 11.9
    Hospital, 11.9
    Summaries, 12.10

RECROSS-EXAMINATION, 8.14

REDIRECT EXAMINATION, 8.14

REFRESHING MEMORY, 8.7f, 8.8, 8.16

REGULATIONS, GOVERNMENT, 7.14

REHABILITATION OF WITNESSES, 8.20

REJOINDER, 2.6d

RELEVANCY, 3.1 to 3.11
  Alibi, 3.8
  Ballistics, 3.10
  Blood tests, 3.10
  Character of accused, 3.9
  Circumstances preceding the crime, 3.6, 3.8b
  Circumstances subsequent to the crime, 3.7
  Character of accused, 3.9
  Clothing, 13.3c
  Coercion, 3.8
  Concealment, 3.7
  Conspiracy, 3.9
  Defined, 2.8b, 3.2a
  Elements of offense, 3.2d
  Experimental and scientific evidence, 3.10
  False name, 3.7
  Flight by accused, 3.7
  Guns, 3.3
  Identity of persons, 3.2d, 3.4
  Identity of things, 3.5
  Insanity, 3.8
  Intoxication, 3.8
  Materiality distinguished, 3.2c
  Motive, 3.2d
  Motor vehicle speed, 3.10
  Other crimes, 3.9, 6.9
  Resisting arrest, 3.7
  Self defense, 3.8
  Suicide attempted by accused, 3.7
  Weapons, 3.10

RELIGIOUS BELIEF OF WITNESSES, 4.6, 4.9, 4.12

REPORTS
  Gunshot wound, 9.15
  Medical examiner's, 13.11

REPUTATION
  Defendant, 6.6
  Defined, 6.5
  Victim, 6.7

RESISTING ARREST, 3.7

RIOT, 5.7

ROBBERY
  Clothing, 13.3c
  Fingerprint cards, 13.16
  Impeachment of witness, 8.15
  Modus operandi, 6.12
  Motive, 6.11
  Photographs, 13.5
  Rehabilitation of witness, 8.20
  State of mind, 10.3a
  Weapons, 3.3, 13.3a

RULES OF EVIDENCE
   Admissibility, 2.7, 3.3
   Character and reputation, 3.9, nn 32, 33
   Character trait, admissibility, 6.4, 6.5
      Habit or custom of person, 6.7
   Clergymen, 9.20
   Cross-examination, 8.11
   Hearsay evidence defined, 2.1m
      Business records, 11.9
   Hearsay statement—
      Against interest, 11.5
   Judge limiting punishment, 2.5
   Judicial control of testimony, 8.3
   Judicial notice, 7.3
   Opinion testimony, 10.2, 10.4
   Physician/patient privileged communication, 9.12
   Presumption, effect, 7.30
   Pretrial flow of evidence, 2.4a
   Privileged communications, 9.1
   Relevant evidence defined, 2.11
   Secondary evidence, 12.9
   Similar or related circumstances, 6.8
   Witness, impeaching, 8.16 et seq.
   Witness' testimony precluded on grounds of incompetency, 8.2
   Witnesses—
      Character evidence, 8.3
      Impeaching, 8.16 et seq.

SANITY
   (See also Insanity)
   Presumption of, 7.21

SCIENTIFIC EVIDENCE
   (See Experimental and Scientific Evidence)

SEARCH AND SEIZURE
   Admissible evidence, 14.3
   Blood, examine accused for traces, 13.11
   Blood tests, 13.12a
   Body samples from accused, 13.11
   Eavesdropping, 13.8, 14.4
   Fingerprinting, 13.16
   Force or duress to obtain items, 2.3c
   Sound recordings, 13.8
   Wiretaps, 1.4, 13.8, 14.4

SEARCH WARRANT, 9.23, 14.3

SECRETS
   Government, 9.24

SEE, ABILITY TO, 13.10

SELF-DEFENSE
   Burden of proof, 5.9
   Relevancy, 3.8
   Reputation of victim, 6.7

SELF-INCRIMINATION, 2.6
(See also Blood Tests)
Arraignment, delay in, 14.5
Breath tests, 13.12b
Clothing modeled by accused, 9.7, 13.3c, 13.11
Coercion, 2.3c
Comment by prosecutor, 9.8
Counsel, right to, 14.5, 14.7
Court, appearing for identification in, 13.1, 13.2, 13.11
Cross-examination, 9.8
Documents held by accused, 5.8
Eavesdropping, 13.8, 14.4
Examine accused's body, 13.11
Fingerprinting, 9.7, 13.1, 13.11, 13.16, 14.6
Force or duress, 2.3c
Gestures, 13.1, 13.11
Grand jury witness, 9.5
Handwriting exemplars, 9.7, 10.9e, 13.1, 13.11, 14.6
Immunity from prosecution, 9.9
Implied consent to alcohol test, 13.12d
In-custody interrogation, 9.6, 8.19, 14.5 to 14.8
Lineup, 13.11, 14.6, 14.7
Marks, examine accused for, 13.11
Measurements of accused, 13.1, 13.11
Photograph of accused, 13.1, 13.11, 14.6
Physical examination of accused, 13.11
Polygraph, 13.14, 14.6
Real evidence generally, 13.1
Speaking for identification, 13.1, 13.11
Standing for identification, 9.7, 13.1, 13.11
Truth serum, 13.15
Waiver, 9.6
Walking, 13.1, 13.11

SEPARATION OF WITNESSES, 8.4

SEX CRIMES
(See Rape)

SEXUALLY DANGEROUS PERSONS, 1.4

SHOPHOOKS, 11.9

SHOPLIFTING, 6.8

SIMILAR ACTS, 6.9

SMELLS, 10.3d, 13.2

SOURCES OF EVIDENCE, 15.8

SPEAKING
For identification, 13.1, 13.11, 13.19
Voice, identification of, 4.4, 10.3d

SPECTROGRAM, 13.19

SPEED
(See Motor Vehicles)

SPEED DETECTION DEVICES, 13.18

SPONTANEOUS UTTERANCES, 11.8

STANDING
  For identification, 9.7, 13.1, 13.11

STATE OF MIND, 11.7, 11.10

STATUTE OF LIMITATIONS, 5.7

STILLS, 7.25

STIPULATIONS, 7.31
  Polygraph tests, 7.32

STOLEN PROPERTY
  Unexplained possession, presumption, 7.26

STOMACH PUMPING, 14.6

SUICIDE
  Attempted by accused, 3.7
  Death certificate, 12.6
  Presumption against, 7.22
  State of mind, 11.7

SUMMARIES OF RECORDS, 11.10d, 12.10

SURPRISE ITEMS
  Excluded, 3.3

SURPRISE WITNESSES, 8.16

SURVEYS
  Public opinion, 11.10

TAMPERING WITH EVIDENCE, 13.3e, 15.4

TAMPERING WITH WITNESSES, 13.8

TAPE RECORDER
  Surveillance, 13.8

TAX FRAUD, 12.10

TELEPHONE CONVERSATIONS
  Competency and admissibility, 4.5

TESTIMONY
  (See also Character; Cross-Examination; Expert Witnesses; Hearsay; Leading Questions; Opinion Evidence; Physician-Patient Privilege; Priest-Penitent Privilege; Privileged Communications; Relevancy; Self-Incrimination; Witnesses)
  Challenge to a question, 2.7
  Defined, 2.1e
  Dying declarations, 2.4, 11.6
  Means of presenting, 2.7
  Objections, 2.7, 2.8, 3.1
  Practical considerations, 15.5
  Privileged communications, 9.1 et seq.

TESTIMONY—*Continued*
    Self-incriminating—
        Immunity from criminal prosecution, 9.7
    Stipulated, 7.31
        Polygraph, 7.32

TESTIMONIAL PRIVILEGES
(See Privileged Communications)

THEFT, 11.2, 11.9

THREATENING TELEPHONE CALLS, 11.3

TIME
    Undue use of, at trial, 3.3

TREATISE, 7.2, 10.8, 11.12, 12.11
(See Books)

TRIAL
    Order of presenting evidence, 2.6

TRUTH SERUM, 13.15

TYPEWRITER PRINTS, 11.10f

URINE TESTS, 13.12c

VALUATION OF PROPERTY, 10.7

VASCAR, 13.18

VENUE OF CRIME, 5.7

VERBAL ACTS, 11.3

VICTIM
    Character trait, admissibility under rules, 6.4

VIEW OF THE SCENE, 13.4

VOICE
    (See also Speaking)
    Identification by, 4.4, 10.3d
    Spectrogram, 13.19

WALKING FOR IDENTIFICATION, 13.1, 13.11

WEAPONS, 13.3a, 13.3e, 15.2 to 15.4
    Dusting and cleaning, 13.3e
    Interstate shipment, 7.25
    Presumption from possession of, 7.25
    Relevancy, 3.10

WIRETAPS, 1.4, 13.8, 14.4

WITNESSES, 8.1 to 8.22
    (See also Cross-Examination; Leading Questions; Privileged Communications; Questions; Self-Incrimination)
    Accused as, 1.4, 2.6b
    Address of witness, 8.12

WITNESSES —*Continued*
    Authenticating real evidence, 2.7
    Bias or prejudice, 8.17
    Character, 6.5, 6.6, 8.13, 8.18
    Children, 4.6, 4.9, 8.7d
    Collateral, irrelevant, or immaterial matters, 8.10, 8.11
    Competency, 4.7 et seq.
        Convicted of crime, 4.11
    Credibility, federal rule limitations—
        Impeachment, 8.16 et seq
    Documents, 2.5
    Essential qualities and characteristics, 8.2
    Expert testimony, 10.1a
        Crime laboratory, 10.9a
    Grand jury, 9.5
    Impeaching, 8.16
        Crime, conviction of, 8.18
    Insane, 4.6 to 4.8
    Interpreters, 8.6
    Judicial control of testimony, 8.3
    Memory, 8.8, 8.19a
    Name of witnesses, 8.12
    Narcotics, use of, 4.7
    Oath, 8.5
    Past recollection recorded, 8.8, 8.9
    Pecuniary interest in the suit, 4.6
    Perjury, prior conviction of, 4.6, 4.11
    Prior inconsistent statements, 8.16, 8.19, 8.20
    Procedure at trial, 2.7
    Recross-examination, 8.14
    Redirect examination, 8.14
    Refreshing memory, 8.7f, 8.8, 8.16
    Rehabilitation, 8.20
    Relationship to a party, 4.6
    Religious belief, 4.6, 4.9, 4.12
    Role in trial, 2.5
    Separation of, 8.4
    Stipulated testimony, 7.26
    Suprise witness, 8.16
    Tampering with, 13.8
    Testimony—
        First hand knowledge, 8.5a
    Unavailable for trial, 11.4

WORDS AND PHRASES, 7.8